Civil War Era Federal Income Taxpayers
Jackson County, Missouri
1862-1866

Volume 1

David W. Jackson

The Orderly Pack Rat
2022

Jackson, David W., and James A. Tharp. *Civil War Era Federal Income Taxpayers: Jackson County, Missouri, 1862-1866.* Two Volumes. (Kansas City, Mo.: The Orderly Pack Rat, 2022).

Jackson, David W. (1969-) and Tharp, James Alan (1946-)
    Civil War Era Federal Income Taxpayers: Jackson County, Missouri, 1862-1866. Volume One. (Kansas City, Mo.: The Orderly Pack Rat, 2022).
319 p.   cm.
  Includes bibliographical references, illustrations, and index.

ISBN-13:   979-8-9861924-1-3   (The Orderly Pack Rat)

1. Income Tax. 2. Taxation. 3. Taxation—Lists—Missouri—Jackson County. 4. Kansas City (Mo.)—History—Indexes. 5. Jackson County (Mo.)—History—Indexes. 6. Jackson County (Mo.)—Genealogy. 7. Missouri—History—Civil War, 1861-1865. I. Jackson, David W. 1969-. II. Tharp, James Alan 1946-. III. Title.

Cover and book design by David W. Jackson, The Orderly Pack Rat.

Published by:
The Orderly Pack Rat
david.jackson@orderlypackrat.com
orderlypackrat.com

Introduction

The Civil War Sesquicentennial in Missouri, commemorated between 2011-2015, inspired the creation of this index to a rarely used Civil War-era record series that documents the first Federal income tax paid by Missouri residents. I am indebted to my longtime friend and colleague, James A. Tharp, for identifying this little-known resource, devoting significant time abstracting all information from the Jackson County, Missouri, portion of the tax assessment rolls, and then constructing robust data files for each taxpayer.

The Internal Revenue Act of July 1, 1862 (12 Stat. 432) intended "to provide internal revenue to support the government and to pay interest on public dept." The Internal Revenue Assessment Lists represent a "progressive" tax *initially* levied a 3% tax on annual incomes over $600 and 5% on income over $10,000. Annual, monthly, and special lists comprise this series that date roughly from 1862-1865. The income tax was a small part of a complicated system of Federal duties, stamp taxes, and fees the government collected from individuals and businesses.

These little-known records are a valuable source of information for biographical, genealogical, and local history research. Local business history and information about professionals and trades people is also evident in these assessment lists. According to Cynthia G. Fox, Chief of the Military and Civil Records Unit at the National Archives and Records Administration, *"They can also be used in conjunction with census records, later tax records, and state and local records to document the growth of industries, shifting patterns of wealth, migration patterns, and even the incidence of women in the work force."*

Records from 34 states and territories are currently available on microfilm. This study of Jackson County, Missouri's representation in this record group may inspire other states and Missouri counties to access this important, but infrequently cited record group.

Jackson County's Tax rolls are extant for 1862-1863. There were 271 residents taxed by the federal government in the years in which the Civil War raged along the Missouri-Kansas border. Four were female.

The rolls for 1864 through April 1865 (the end of the Civil War) do not appear to have survived. The tax rolls resume the month after the War ended in May 1865, and conclude in December 1866. While post-Civil War Jackson Countians are listed in the comprehensive index, they have not been tabulated or otherwise or interpreted as part of this Civil War-centric study.

For original tax assessments copied from microfilm plus individual taxpayers' files consult James A. Tharp's collection *Civil War Era Federal Income Taxpayers of Jackson County, Missouri,* archived at the Missouri Valley Special Collections, Kansas City Public Library, Kansas City, Missouri.

Tharp also compiled data files for *Jackson County Early Germans.* There were 66 taxpayers from that collection, archived separately in the Missouri Valley Special Collections.

Civil War Era Federal Income Taxpayers

Each Civil War taxpayer's individual data file is encapsulated here in a collection of published Family Group Sheets. The paper files oftentimes trace genealogies for second- and sometimes third-generation descendants (and in some cases, sheets for taxpayers' ancestors), all derived from documentation from these sources:

Archived photographic collections
Biographies (published)
Birth records
Cemetery tombstone inscription indexes (published)
Church records
Circuit Court case files, Jackson County, Missouri, 1828-1899
City directories
Civil War draft cards
County histories
Death certificates, Missouri, 1910-1960s
Death records, Kansas City, 1898-
Gazetteers, Missouri (published)
Genealogies (published)
Marriage records
Military records (see note about pensions below)
     Draft records; Compiled service records; Pension file index;
     Missouri State Archives database; Provost Marshal's records
Newspapers (microfilm and digitized, including *America's Genealogy Bank*)
Obituaries in local newspapers
Periodicals
U.S. Census, Population Schedules, 1850-1920
U.S. Census, Non-Population Schedules
     Agricultural Schedules, 1850-1900
     Industrial-Manufactures Schedules, 1850-1860
     Mortality Schedules, 1850-1885
     Slave Schedules, 1850-1860
Website databases (*ancestry.com; familysearch.org; findagrave.com*, etc.)

One additional research source consulted for this compilation were Civil War pension files, which are indexed but are not yet (and may never be) microfilmed or digitized. Through a Brownlee Grant of the State Historical Society of Missouri in Columbia, Missouri, a researcher in Washington, D.C., was contracted to photograph the files of ten Civil War taxpayers who later received (directly, or by their widow) a federal pension for their military service to the Union. Since Federal pension files are not microfilmed or digitized, the independent researcher pulled original case files of identified pensioners and photographed pertinent pages.

                                        ~ David W. Jackson

Contents

Volume 1

Volume 2

1

Civil War Taxpayers by Profession

(Followed by the governing chapter of the Internal Revenue Act)

For the first five categories, Apothecaries through Brewers, abbreviated biographies of each taxpayer was constructed from comprehensive Family Group Sheets. These biographies were prepared as an example of what might be created by interested researchers of Jackson County's Civil War-era residents.

Apothecaries

Beginning in August 1862, Congress required all apothecaries whose annual gross receipts or sales exceeded one-thousand dollars to pay ten dollars annually for a license. For the purpose of licensing, apothecaries were "every person who keeps a shop or building where medicines are compounded or prepared according to prescriptions of physicians, and sold." Licensed apothecaries who sold alcohol were not required to be licensed additionally as retail liquor dealers. *(Stats. at Large of USA* 12 (1863): 459, 714-715, and 13 (1864): 255, 257-258.)

Ten apothecaries were licensed in Jackson County, Missouri, during the Civil War—one in Westport, three in Independence, and six in Kansas City. Eight of those apothecaries were native born and two were born in Germany. Three of them ten were also licensed as physicians.

John C. Adkins (1836-1866)
> John C. Adkins, who had settled in Kansas City by 1859, was licensed as Apothecary in September 1862. He was also licensed in September 1866 as Retail Liquor Dealer. City directories 1859 to 1865 describe Adkins's business as "drugs" and "wholesale and retail drugs and medicines."

John C. Agnew (1825/6-ca. 1883)
> John C. Agnew, who had settled in Independence in 1848, was licensed in as Apothecary in September 1862. By 1865 Agnew had moved to Kansas City, where he was a grocer, and later express agent and deputy county marshal.

James C. Beckham (1808-1892)
> James C. Beckham, Independence, who had settled in Jackson County before 1840, was licensed as Apothecary in September 1862. He was also licensed as Retail Liquor Dealer in August 1865 and August 1866. An 1860 directory describes Beckham as "wholesale and retail dealer in drugs, medicines, patent dealer in drugs, medicines, patent medicines, window glass, perfumery, fancy toilet articles, fine brandies and wines, school books, stationery and fancy notions in general."

Joseph Oliver Boggs (1808-1889)

Joseph Oliver Boggs, who had settled in Independence before 1840, was licensed as Apothecary in Westport in May 1866. He was also licensed as Physician in December 1863 and May 1866. An 1860 directory describes Boggs's business as "drugs and medicines, and Insurance agent." By 1870, Dr. Boggs and his wife had emigrated to California, where they both died.

William Webber Ford (1824-1890)

William Webber Ford, who had settled in Kansas City in 1856, was licensed as Apothecary in September 1862. He was also licensed as Builder and as Manufacturer in May 1866. Between March and June 1866, he paid tax on the manufacture of sash and blinds valued at $2049. City directories 1859 to 1865 describe Ford as a carpenter and builder, never as apothecary.

Robert Stockton Hale (1835-1922)

Robert Stockton Hale, who had settled in Kansas City by 1859, was licensed as Apothecary in September 1862. Directories for 1859 and 1860 describe Hale as "wholesale and retail dealer in drugs and medicines." Hale appears to have left Jackson County by 1865; in 1870 he was in Helena, Montana Territory, where he died in 1922.

William Holmes (?-?)

William Holmes, was licensed as Apothecary in Kansas City in September 1862. It is unknown whether this William Holmes was a different person or was actually the William Holmes (1814-1888), who was licensed as Lawyer in April 1863 and May 1866, or the William C. Holmes (1838/39-?), who was licensed as Hotel Keeper in September 1862.

William D. McClanahan (1830/1-?)

William D. McClanahan, who had settled in Independence by 1860, was licensed as Apothecary in September 1862. An 1860 directory described him as "druggist and bookseller."

Dr. Leopold C. Saalborn (1819-1892)

Leopold C. Saalborn, who had emigrated from Germany in 1846 and had settled in Kansas City in 1862, was licensed as Apothecary in June 1865. He was also licensed as Physician in September 1862, June 1865, and May 1866. On the latter date he was also licensed as Retail Liquor Dealer. By 1876 Saalborn had moved to Westport, where he died in 1893.

Dr. Louis A. Schoen (1831-1881)

Louis A. Schoen, who had emigrated from Germany in 1853 and had settled in Kansas City in 1857, was licensed as Apothecary in September 1862. He was also licensed as Physician in September 1862 and May 1866. Directories from 1859 to 1872 listed Schoen as "physician" or "physician and druggist"; after 1872 he was consistently described as "druggist."

Apothecaries in the Internal Revenue Act

Chapter CXIX.—An Act to provide Internal Revenue to support the Government and to pay Interest on the Public Debt. Approved July 1, 1862.

LICENSES.

"Sec. 64. *And be it further enacted,* That on and after the first day of August, eighteen hundred and sixty-two, for each license granted the sum herewith stated shall be respectively and annually paid. Any number of persons carrying on such business in copartnership may transact such business at such place under such license, and not otherwise." (Page 455)

"28. Apothecaries shall pay ten dollars for each license. Every person who keeps a shop or building where medicines are compounded or prepared according to prescriptions of physicians, and sold, shall be regarded an apothecary under this act. But wholesale and retail dealers, who have taken out a license therefore, shall not be required to take out a license as apothecary, anything in this act to the contrary notwithstanding. (Page 458)

"Sec. 65. *And be it further enacted,* That where the annual gross receipts or sales of any apothecaries, confectioners, eating-houses, tobacconists, or retail dealers, shall not exceed the sum of one thousand dollars, such apothecaries, confectioners, eating-houses, and retail dealers shall not be required to take out or pay for license, anything in this act to the contrary notwithstanding; the amount or estimated amount of such annual sales to be ascertained or estimated in such manner as the Commissioner of Internal Revenue shall prescribe, and so of all other annual sales or receipts, where the rate of the license is graduated by the amount of sales or receipts." (Page 459)

"Sec. 66. *And be it further enacted,* That nothing contained in the preceding sections of this act, laying duties on licenses, shall be construed to require a license for the sale of goods, wares, and merchandise made or produced and sold by the manufacturer or producer at the manufactory or place where the same is made or produced; to vintners who sell, at the place where the same is made, wine of their own growth; nor to apothecaries, as to wines or spirituous liquors which they use exclusively in the preparation or making up of medicines for sick, lame, or diseased persons; nor shall the provisions of paragraph number twenty-seven extend to physicians who keep on hand medicines solely for the purpose of making up their own prescriptions for their own patients." (Page 459)

Chapter LXXIV.—An Act to amend an Act entitled "An Act to provide Internal Revenue to support the Government and to pay Interest on the Public Debt," approved July first, eighteen hundred and sixty-two, and for other Purposes. Approved March 3, 1863.

"*Be it enacted by the Senate and House of Representatives of the United States of America in Congress assembled,* That 'An act to provide internal revenue to support the Government and pay interest on the public debt,' approved July first, eighteen hundred and sixty-two, be, and the same hereby is, amend[ed] as hereinafter set forth, namely:—

" . . . That section sixty-four be, and hereby is, so amended . . .by adding to paragraph number twenty-eight the following words: 'Nor shall apothecaries who have taken out a license as such be required to take out a license as retail dealers in liquors in consequence of selling alcohol;' . . ." (Page 714)

"That section sixty-four be, and hereby is, further amended by adding, at the end thereof, the following paragraphs: . . .

"Forty. Retail dealers shall pay ten dollars for each license. Every person whose business or occupation it is to sell or offer for sale any goods, wares, or merchandise of foreign or domestic production, not including wines, spiritous [sic] or malt liquors, but not excluding drugs, medicines, cigars, snuff, or tobacco, and whose annual sales exceed one thousand, and do not exceed twenty-five thousand dollars, shall be regarded as a retail dealer under this act." (Page 715)

Chap. CLXXIII.—*An Act to provide Internal Revenue to support the Government, to pay Interest on the Public Debt, and for other Purposes.* June 30, 1864. . . .

"Sec. 79. *And be it further enacted,* That there shall be paid annually for each license granted, the sum herein stated, respectively. Any number of persons, except lawyers, conveyancers, claim agents, physicians, surgeons, dentists, cattle brokers, horse-dealers, and peddlers, carrying on such business in copartnership, may transact such business at the place specified in their license, and not otherwise, that is to say:— . . .

"Thirty-three. Apothecaries shall pay ten dollars for each license. Every person who keeps a shop or building where medicines are compounded or prepared according to prescriptions of physicians, or where medicines are sold, shall be regarded an apothecary under this act. But wholesale and retail dealers, who have taken out a license therefore, shall not be required to take out a license as apothecary, anything in this act to the contrary notwithstanding; nor shall apothecaries, who have taken out a license as such, be required to take out a license as retail dealers in liquor in consequence of selling alcohol." (Page 255)

"Sec. 80. *And be it further enacted,* That where the annual gross receipts or sales of any apothecaries, confectioners, eating-houses, tobacconists, or retail dealers, except retail dealers in spirituous and malt liquors, shall not exceed the sum of one thousand dollars, such apothecaries, confectioners, eating-houses, tobacconists, and retail dealers shall not be required to take out or pay for license, anything in this act to the contrary notwithstanding; the amount or estimated amount of such annual sales to be ascertained or estimated in such manner as the commissioner of internal revenue shall prescribe, and so of all other annual sales or receipts, where the rate of the license is graduated by the amount of sales or receipts; and where the amount of the license or the rate has been increased, or is liable to be increased, by law above the amount of any existing license to any person, firm, or company, or has been understated or under-estimated, such person, firm, or company shall be again assessed and pay the amount of such increase, which shall be indorsed on the original license, which shall thereafter be held good and sufficient. (Pages 257-258)

"Sec. 81. *And be it further enacted,* That nothing contained in the preceding sections of this act, requiring licenses, shall be construed to require an additional license as a dealer for the sale of goods, wares, and merchandise made or produced and sold by the manufacturer or producer at the manufactory or place where the same is made or produced, or at the principal office or place of business, as provided in section *seventy-three* [seventy-four] of this act; [nor] to *vinters* [vintners] who sell, at the place where the same is made, wine of their own growth; nor to apothecaries, as to wines or spirituous liquors which they use exclusively in the preparation of making up of medicines; nor shall any provisions be construed to prohibit physicians from keeping on hand medicines solely for the purpose of making up their own prescriptions for their own patients." (Page 258)

Auctioneers

Beginning in August 1862, Congress required that auctioneers pay twenty dollars annually for a license, as well as a .5% duty on the gross amount of their auction sales. After 30 June 1864, auctioneers whose annual sales did not exceed $10,000 paid only ten dollars for their annual license, those whose sales exceeded $10,000 still paid $20, and the duty on all annual gross auction sales was reduced to .25%. For purposes of taxation, auctioneers were "every person . . . whose occupation it is to offer property for sale to the highest or best bidder." *(Stats. at Large of USA* 12 (1863): 455, 466-467, 727, and 13 (1864): 255, 273.)

Six persons were licensed as auctioneers in Jackson County, Missouri, during the Civil War—one in Westport and five in Kansas City. Five of those auctioneers were native born and one was born in Canada. One of them was also licensed as Commercial Broker.

James W. Cook (1821-1886)

James W. Cook, who settled in Kansas City in 1856, was licensed as Auctioneer in September 1862 and September 1865. In September/December 1862 he also paid duty on $706.70 in auctions sales and in May 1866 he paid tax on $506 income. City directories between 1860 and 1870 describe Cook as merchant, dairyman, and auctioneer. In later years he was a real estate developer.

John Thornton Frazier (1819-1900)

John Thornton Frazier, who lived in Independence from 1848 to 1854 and in Westport from 1854 to 1900, was licensed in May 1865 as Auctioneer with less than $10,000 annual sales. In September 1862 he had been licensed for one Billiard Table and as Retail Liquor Dealer. In censuses from 1850 to 1880 his occupation was photographer, painter, and artist.

James C. Kevill (1832-1902)

James C. Kevill, who was in Kansas City by 1859, was licensed as Auctioneer in partnership with James P. Turner in April 1863 and May 1865. Kevill and Turner paid duty on $300 auction sales in July 1863 and on $2500 in August and September 1863. That partnership was also licensed as Retail Dealer in September 1862 and as Manufacturer in January and May 1866. The partnership also paid duty on value of mattresses manufactured as follows: $157 in February 1866, $425 in March 1866, $285 in April 1866, $356 in May 1866, and $184 in June 1866. James C. Kevill, as an individual, paid tax in May 1866 on one watch and income of $143. Kevill and Turner's partnership survived until August 1878. After 1865, city directories describe Kevill & Turner as furniture manufacturers and dealers. James C. Kevill died in near poverty in 1902.

[—?—] Payne (?-?)

[—?—] Payne, Kansas City, was licensed as Auctioneer and Retail Dealer, in partnership with George W. Toler, in September 1862. Payne & Toler paid duty on auction sales from July 1863 through May 1865. The Payne and Toler partnership was dissolved in July 1865 upon Payne's retirement. Nothing more is known of Mr. Payne.

George W. Toler (1816-1866)

George W. Toler, who came to Kansas City 1855, was licensed as Auctioneer and Retail Dealer, in partnership with [—?—] Payne, in September 1862. Payne & Toler paid duty on auction sales from July 1863 through May 1865. In July 1865 Toler, in partnership with J. H. Gordon of Saint Louis, was licensed as Commercial Broker and this partnership paid duty on auction sales and broker sales July through September 1865. In May 1866, G. W. Toler and Son was licensed as Auctioneer and Commercial Broker. That partnership paid duty on auction and broker sales from November 1865 through August 1866.

James P. Turner (1835-1879)

James P. Turner, who was in Kansas City by 1859, was licensed as Auctioneer in partnership with James C. Kevill in April 1863 and May 1865. Kevill and Turner paid duty on $300 auction sales in July 1863 and on $2500 in August and September 1863. That partnership was also licensed as Retail Dealer in September 1862 and as Manufacturer in January and May 1866. Kevill & Turner also paid duty on value of mattresses manufactured as follows: $157 in February 1866, $425 in March 1866, $285 in April 1866, $356 in May 1866, and $184 in June 1866. James P. Turner, as an individual, paid tax in May 1866 on one watch and income of $143. After 1865, city directories describe Kevill & Turner as furniture manufacturers and dealers. Their partnership survived until August 1878; Turner, already ill, died the following year of pulmonary tuberculosis.

Auctioneers in the Internal Revenue Act

Chapter CXIX.—An Act to provide Internal Revenue to support the Government and to pay Interest on the Public Debt. Approved July 1, 1862.

LICENSES.

"Sec. 64. *And be it further enacted,* That on and after the first day of August, eighteen hundred and sixty-two, for each license granted the sum herewith stated shall be respectively and annually paid. Any number of persons carrying on such business in copartnership may transact such business at such place under such license, and not otherwise." (Page 455)

"21. Auctioneers shall pay twenty dollars for each license. Every person shall be deemed an auctioneer within the meaning of this act whose occupation it is to offer property for sale to the highest or best bidder.". (Page 455)

AUCTION SALES.

"Sec. 76. *And be it further enacted,* That on and after the first day of August, eighteen hundred and sixty-two, there shall be levied, collected, and paid on all sales of real estate, goods, wares, merchandise, articles, or things, at auction, including all sales of stocks, bonds, and other securities, a duty of one-tenth of one per centum on the gross amount of such sales, and every auctioneer making such sales, as aforesaid, shall at the end of each and every month, or within ten days thereafter, make a list or return to the assistant assessor of the district of the gross amount of such sales, made as aforesaid, with the amount of duty which has accrued, or should accrue threron, which list shall have annexed thereto a declaration under oath or affirmation, in form and manner as may be prescribed by the Commissioner of Internal Revenue, that the same is true and correct, and shall at the same time, as aforesaid, pay to the collector of deputy collector the amount of duty or tax thereupon, as aforesaid, and in default thereof shall be subject ot and pay a penalty of five hundred dollars. In all cases of delinquency in making said list or payment the assessment and collection shall be made in the manner prescribed in the general provisions of this act: *Provided,* That no duty shall be levied under the provisions of this section upon any sales by judicial or executive officers making auction sales by virtue of a judgment or decree of any court, nor to public sales made by executors or administrators." (Pages 466 and 467)

Chapter LXXIV.—An Act to amend an Act entitled "An Act to provide Internal Revenue to support the Government and to pay Interest on the Public Debt," approved July first, eighteen hundred and sixty-two, and for other Purposes. Approved March 3, 1863.

"Sec. 25. *And be it further enacted,* That no auctioneer shall be authorized, by virtue of his license as such auctioneer, to sell any goods or other property in any other district than that in which the license shall have been granted, but lawyers, physicians, surgeons, or dentists, having taken out al license as such, shall not be required to take out any additional license in consequence of practicing their profession within or beyond the limits of the district where licensed." (Page 727)

Chap. CLXXIII.—*An Act to provide Internal Revenue to support the Government, to pay Interest on the Public Debt, and for other Purposes.* June 30, 1864. . . .

"Sec. 79. *And be it further enacted,* That there shall be paid annually for each license granted, the sum herein stated, respectively. Any number of persons, except lawyers, conveyancers, claim agents, physicians, surgeons, dentists, cattle brokers, horse-dealers, and peddlers, carrying on such business in copartnership, may transact such business at the place specified in their license, and not otherwise, that is to say:— . . .

"Thirty. Auctioneers, whose annual sales do not exceed ten thousand dollars, shall pay ten dollars for each license; auctioneers, whose annual sales exceed ten thousand dollars, shall pay twenty dollars for each license. Every person shall be deemed an auctioneer within the meaning of this act, whose business it is to offer property for sale to the highest or best bidder." (Page 255)

AUCTION SALES.
"Sec. 98. *And be it further enacted,* That there shall be levied, collected, and paid, on all sales of real estate, goods, wares, merchandise, articles, or things at auction, including all sales of stocks, bonds, and other securities, a duty of one fourth of one per centum on the gross amount of such sales . . . " (Page 273)

Bankers

Beginning in August 1862, Congress required that bankers pay one-hundred dollars annually for a license. After 30 June 1864, bankers employing a capital not exceeding $50,000 still paid one-hundred for their annual license; if employing a capital exceeding $50,000, they paid $100 plus $2.00 for every thousand dollars of capital employed exceeding $50,000. For purposes of taxation, bankers were "every person . . . who keeps a place of business where credits are opened in favor of any person, firm, or corporation, by the deposit or collection of money or currency, and the same, or any part thereof, shall be paid out or remitted upon the draft, check, or order of such creditor . . . " *(Stats. at Large of USA* 12 (1863): 455, and 13 (1864): 251.)

Only two persons were licensed as bankers in Jackson County, Missouri, during the Civil War.

William R. Bernard (1823-1906)

William R. Bernard, who had settled in Westport in 1847, was licensed as Banker and Wholesale Dealer in April 1863. As member of the Kansas City partnership Bernard & Mastin, he was again licensed as Banker in December 1865 and May 1866. Between July and December 1866, Bernard & Mastin paid duty monthly on bank capital of $15,000 and deposits averaging about $112,000. Bernard was probably best known as an overland freighter.

Hiram Milton Northrup (1818-1893)

Hiram Milton Northrup, who had settled in Jackson County in 1844, was licensed as Banker in Kansas City in September 1862. A short time later, Northrup moved his family to New York City, where he engaged in banking until the Panic of 1873, when the family moved to Wyandotte County, Kansas. His wife, Margaret (Clark) Northrup was a native American of the Wyandotte tribe and Northrup was an adopted member of that tribe, who for many years safeguarded their tribal interests.

Bankers in the Internal Revenue Act

Chapter CXIX.—An Act to provide Internal Revenue to support the Government and to pay Interest on the Public Debt. Approved July 1, 1862.
LICENSES.
"Sec. 64. *And be it further enacted,* That on and after the first day of August, eighteen hundred and sixty-two, for each license granted the sum herewith stated shall be respectively and annually paid. Any number of persons carrying on such business in copartnership may transact such business at such place under such license, and not otherwise." (Page 455)
"1. Bankers shall pay one hundred dollars for each license. Every person shall be deemed a banker within the meaning of this act who keeps a place of business where credits are opened in favor of any person, firm, or corporation, by the deposit or collection of money or currency, and the same, or any part thereof, shall be paid out or remitted upon the draft, check, or order of such creditor, but not to include incorporated banks or other banks legally authorized to issue notes as circulation, nor agents for the sale of merchandise for account of producers or manufacturers. (Page 455)

Chap. CLXXIII.—*An Act to provide Internal Revenue to support the Government, to pay Interest on the Public Debt, and for other Purposes.* June 30, 1864. . . .
"Sec. 79. *And be it further enacted,* That there shall be paid annually for each license granted, the sum herein stated, respectively. Any number of persons, except lawyers, conveyancers, claim agents, physicians, surgeons, dentists, cattle brokers, horse-dealers, and

peddlers, carrying on such business in copartnership, may transact such business at the place specified in their license, and not otherwise, that is to say:—

"One. Bankers, using or employing a capital not exceeding the sum of fifty thousand dollars, shall pay one hundred dollars for each license; when using or employing a capital exceeding fifty thousand dollars, for every additional thousand dollars in excess of fifty thousand dollars, two dollars. Every person, firm, or company, and every incorporated or other bank, having a place of business where credits are opened by the deposit or collection of money or currency, subject to be paid or remitted upon draft, check, or order, or where money is advanced or loaned on stocks, bonds, bullion, bills of exchange, or promissory notes, or where stocks, bonds, bullion, bills of exchange, or promissory notes are received for discount or sale, shall be regarded a banker under this act: *Provided,* That any saving-bank having no capital stock, and whose business is confined to receiving deposits and loaning the same for the benefit of its depositors, and which does not other business of banking, shall not be liable to pay for a license as a banker." (Page 251)

Billiard Rooms

Beginning in August 1862, Congress required that billiard room keepers pay a licensing fee of five dollars for every billiard table in their establishment. After 30 June 1864, the cost of their license increased to ten dollars per table. For purposes of taxation, "every place or building where . . . billiards [are] played, and open to the public with or without price, shall be regarded as a . . . billiard-room . . . " *(Stats. at Large of USA* 12 (1863): 457, and 13 (1864): 256.)

Eleven billiard rooms were licensed in Jackson County, Missouri, during the Civil War— three in Westport and eight in Kansas City. All eleven holders of billiard room licenses were also licensed for other occupations; eight of them as Retail Liquor Dealers. Six of those licensees were native born and five were born in Germany.

John Thornton Frazier (1819-1900)
John Thornton Frazier, who had lived in Independence from 1848 to 1854 and in Westport from 1854 to 1900, was licensed in September 1862 for one Billiard Table and as Retail Liquor Dealer. In May 1865 he was licensed as Auctioneer with less than $10,000 annual sales. In censuses from 1850 to 1880 Frazier's occupation was photographer, painter, and artist.

Alexander L. Harris (1820-1898)
Alexander L. Harris, who had settled in Kansas City in 1857, was licensed in September 1862 for one Billiard Table and as Retail Liquor Dealer. In May 1866 he was taxed on income of $900, a gold watch worth $100 or less, and a pianoforte valued over $400. Harris served two terms as mayor of Kansas City and was also a city councilman and justice of the county court of Jackson County. By 1879 he had moved to Colorado, where he died in 1898 while serving his second term of Durango.

Meredith B. Hedges (1814/5-?)

Meredith B. Hedges, who had settled in Kansas City by 1853, when he served as city marshal, was taxed in May 1865 on income of $488. In June 1866 Hedges was licensed as Retail Liquor Dealer and for two Billiard Tables; in August 1866 he was licensed for one Billiard Table. He served as city councilman in 1857. Censuses and city directories describe Hedges as inn-keeper, livery stable keeper, and railroad contractor.

Harrison R. Kelso (1813/4-?)

Harrison R. Kelso, had settled in Westport by September 1862, when he was licensed for one Billiard Table and as Retail Liquor Dealer. He and his family had lived previously as a farmer at Warrensburg, Missouri, and Fort Scott, Kansas. By 1865 Kelso had moved from Westport to Kansas City, where he was a carpenter and policeman. In the late 1870s he returned to Fort Scott, where he worked as a carpenter and lived with his daughter.

Wendel/Wendelin Loesch (1818-1865)

Wendel/Wendelin Loesch, who had emigrated from Bavaria by 1852, settled in Kansas City before September 1862, when he was licensed for one Billiard Table and as a Retail Liquor Dealer. Directories indicate that Loesch kept a boarding house and saloon. He was in Col. Robert Thompson Van Horn's Battalion, and a Civil War pensioner.

John Long (1846-1908)

John Long, who had emigrated from Bavaria to Saint Louis with his parents in 1848, had settled in Kansas City in 1853. He was licensed in September 1862 for one Billiard Table and as Retail Liquor Dealer. In May 1866 Long was taxed on one gold watch valued at $100 or less. Later, John Long and his brother Adam became quite wealthy from their wholesale grocery business. Today Long is remembered for endowing the $40,000 limestone chapel in Mount Washington Cemetery in Independence, a memorial to his wife. Ironically, John Long's own funeral service was the first to be held there.

William S. Reed (1837/8-?)

William S. Reed, who had settled in Kansas City by 1860, was licensed in September 1862 for one Billiard Table and as Retail Liquor Dealer. Reed was born in Ohio, worked as a saloon keeper in Kansas City at least from 1860 to 1863, served from 22 September to 2 December 1862 as Private in Company C, 77th Regiment Enrolled Missouri Militia, and in October 1863 was unmarried.

Philip Setzler (1834-1923)

Philip Setzler, who had emigrated from Bavaria to Ohio in 1854 and had settled in Kansas City in 1862, was licensed (Setzler & Company) for three Billiard Tables in February 1866 and for six Billiard Tables in May 1866. In September 1862 he had been licensed as Retail and Wholesale Liquor Dealer in partnership with Gustavus Wolf. In August 1865, Philip Setzler was licensed, in partnership with his brother John, as Rectifier. Philip Setzler was also licensed as Insurance Agent in November 1865 and October 1866, and as Retail Liquor Dealer in May 1866. In later years Setzler was a noted Kansas City vintner, wine dealer, and wine garden proprietor.

William R. Sitzler (1835-1887)

William R. Sitzler, an immigrant from Germany, had settled in Kansas City by September 1862, when he was licensed for one Billiard Table. In November 1863 he was also licensed as Retail Liquor Dealer. Censuses and city directories consistently described Sitzler as a saloon keeper.

Addison Snell (1832/3-?)

Addison Snell had settled in Kansas City by September 1862, when he was licensed for one Billiard Table and as Retail Liquor Dealer. In May 1866 he was again licensed as Retail Liquor Dealer and for two billiard tables. City directories describe Snell as a saloon keeper; his occupation recorded in the 1870 census was [live]stock dealer.

Christian Wiedenmann (1835-1909)

Christian Wiedenmann, who had emigrated from Germany ca. 1853, settled in Westport in 1854. He was licensed in September 1862 for one billiard table and as Retail Liquor Dealer. In May 1865 and in August 1866 Wiedenmann was again licensed as Retail Liquor Dealer. His occupation, according to the 1860 census, was carpenter, in the censuses of 1870 and 1880, saloon keeper.

Billiard Rooms in the Internal Revenue Act

Chapter CXIX.—An Act to provide Internal Revenue to support the Government and to pay Interest on the Public Debt. Approved July 1, 1862.

LICENSES.

"Sec. 64. *And be it further enacted,* That on and after the first day of August, eighteen hundred and sixty-two, for each license granted the sum herewith stated shall be respectively and annually paid. Any number of persons carrying on such business in copartnership may transact such business at such place under such license, and not otherwise." (Page 455)

"20. Bowling-alleys and billiard-rooms shall pay according to the number of alleys or tables belonging to or used in the building or place to be licensed. When not exceeding one alley or table, five dollars for each license; and when exceeding one alley or table, five dollars for each additional alley or table. Every place or building where bowls are thrown or billiards played, and open to the public with or without price, shall be regarded as a bowling-alley or billiard-room, respectively, under this act." (Page 457)

Chap. CLXXIII.—*An Act to provide Internal Revenue to support the Government, to pay Interest on the Public Debt, and for other Purposes.* June 30, 1864. . . .

"Sec. 79. *And be it further enacted,* That there shall be paid annually for each license granted, the sum herein stated, respectively. Any number of persons, except lawyers, conveyancers, claim agents, physicians, surgeons, dentists, cattle brokers, horse-dealers, and peddlers, carrying on such business in copartnership, may transact such business at the place specified in their license, and not otherwise, that is to say:— . . .

"Forty. Bowling-alleys and billiard-rooms shall pay ten dollars for every alley or table in the building or place to be licensed. Every place or building where bowls are thrown or billiards played, and open to the public with or without price, shall be regarded as a bowling-alley or billiard-room, respectively, under this act." (Page 256)

Brewers

Beginning in August 1862, Congress required that brewers of less than five-hundred barrels of beer annually pay twenty-five dollars for a license and that brewers of five hundred or more barrels annually pay fifty dollars for a license. Additionally, a duty of one dollar was to be paid for every barrel containing not more than thirty-one gallons (fractional parts to be pro-rated) brewed or manufactured and sold or removed for consumption. For purposes of taxation, brewers were "every person who manufactures fermented liquors of any name or description, for sale, from malt, wholly or in part." *(Stats. at Large of USA* 12 (1863): 450, 453, 455-456, 723, and 13 (1864): 246, 248, 253.)

Six persons, all of them emigrants from Germany, were licensed as brewers in Jackson County, Missouri, during the Civil War—one in Westport and five in Kansas City.

Henry Helfrich (1827/8-?)

Henry Helfrich had settled in Kansas City by August 1862, when he enrolled and entered active service in Company B, 77th Regiment, Enrolled Missouri Militia. The following month he was licensed as Brewer of less than 500 barrels of beer annually. Helfrich & Company, a partnership between Helfrich and Michael Muehlschuster, paid duty through December 1863 on beer brewed ranging from forty barrels per month to only nine and a half barrels. Henry "Hillfrich" appeared on a November 1863 draft registration list as a white German-born laborer aged 35 years and a resident of Kaw Township in Jackson County.

Henry/Heinrich William/Wilhelm Helmreich (1811-1889)

Henry/Heinrich William/Wilhelm Helmreich, who had emigrated from Germany to Saint Louis in 1854 and had settled in Kansas City in 1856, was licensed in September 1862, in partnership with George G. Messerschmidt, as Brewer of less than five hundred barrels of beer annually. Their partnership was dissolved in July 1863 and Helmreich continued as sole proprietor. Helmreich's business grew and in May 1866 he was licensed as Brewer of more than five-hundred barrels of beer annually. He paid tax on 109 barrels of beer produced in just the month of March 1866. However, by September 1866 production had dropped to only six barrels. In September 1870 Helmreich's brewery was sold on the courthouse steps to the highest bidder under a deed of trust. From that time, directories indicate that Helmreich was a saloon keeper.

George G. Messerschmidt (1825-1868)

George G. Messerschmidt, an emigrant from Germany who had settled in Kansas City by 1860, was licensed as Brewer of less than five-hundred barrels of beer annually in September 1862, as partner of Henry Helmreich. Messerschmidt left that partnership in July 1863 and became a grocer and baker. In May 1866 he was licensed as a Retail Liquor Dealer and was taxed on $200 annual income.

Michael Muehlschuster (1813-1870)

Michael Muehlschuster, who had emigrated from Germany to Milwaukee in 1850 and later lived in Cincinnati, settled in Kansas City in 1860. As partner of Henry Hilfrich, he was licensed in September 1862 as Brewer of less than five-hundred barrels of beer annually. In 1864 Muehlschuster became sole proprietor and was licensed in May 1866 as Brewer of more than five-hundred barrels of beer annually, although in the preceding twelve months he paid duty on only 463 barrels or beer.

Peter Schwitzgebel (1821-1882)

Peter Schwitzgebel, who had emigrated from Germany to Saint Louis in 1853, settled in Kansas City in 1855. In September 1862, and again in May 1866 and August 1866, he was licensed as Brewer of more than five-hundred barrels of beer annually. During 1863 Schwitzgebel paid tax on 878.5 barrels of beer brewed and during the year from November 1865 to October 1866, 1246 barrels. By 1870 output had grown to 5400 barrels. In May 1866 Schwitzgebel paid tax on four-hundred dollars income. He is said to have suffered deeply in the Panic of 1873, after which he appears in city directories as a saloon keeper.

Ferdinand "Fred" Wedelich (1823/4-?)

Ferdinand "Fred" Wedelich, an emigrant from Germany, had settled in Westport by December 1858, when he married there. He was licensed in September 1862, and again in May and August 1866, as Brewer of less than five-hundred barrels of beer annually. The average monthly production of Wedelich's brewery was less than ten barrels. In May 1866 he paid tax on $320 income.

Brewers in the Internal Revenue Act

Chapter CXIX.—An Act to provide Internal Revenue to support the Government and to pay Interest on the Public Debt. Approved July 1, 1862.

SPIRITS, BEER, ALE, AND PORTER

"Sec. 50. *And be it further enacted,* That on and after the first day of August, eighteen hundred and sixty-two, there shall be paid on all beer, lager beer, ale, porter, and other similar fermented liquors, by whatever name such liquors may be called, a duty of one dollar for each and every barrel containing not more than thirty-one gallons, and at a like rate for any other quantity or for fractional parts of a barrel, which shall be brewed or manufactured and sold or removed for consumption or sale within the United States or the territories thereof, or within the District of Columbia, after that day; which duty shall be paid by the owner agent, or superintendent of the brewery or premises in which such fermented liquors shall be made, and shall be paid at the time of rendering the accounts of such fermented liquors so chargeable with duty, as required to be rendered by the following section of this act: *Provided,* That fractional parts of a barrel shall be halves, quarters, eights, and sixteenths, and any fractional part containing less than one-sixteenth shall be accounted one-sixteenth; more than one-sixteenth, and not more than one-eight, shall be accounted one-eighth; more than one-eighth, and not more than one-quarter, shall be accounted one-quarter; more than one quarter, and not more than one-half, shall be accounted one-half; more than one-half shall be accounted one barrel." (Page 450)

"Sec. 56. *And be it further enacted,* That every person licensed as aforesaid to distil spirituous liquors, or licensed as a brewer, shall, once in each month, upon the request of the assessor or assistant assessor for the district in which his business as a distiller or brewer may be carried on, respectively, furnish the said assessor or assistant assessor with an abstract of the entries upon his books, herein provided to be made, showing the amount of spirituous liquor distilled and sold, or removed for consumption or sale, or of beer, lager beer, ale, porter, or other fermented liquor made and sold, or removed for consumption or sale, during the preceding month, respectively; the truth and correctness of which abstract shall be verified by the oath of the party so furnishing the same. And the said assessor or assistant assessor shall have the right to examine the books of such person for the purpose of ascertaining the correctness of such abstract. And for any neglect to furnish such abstract when requested, or refusal to furnish an examination of the books as aforesaid, the person so neglecting shall forfeit the sum of five hundred dollars." (Page 453)

LICENSES.
"Sec. 64. *And be it further enacted,* That on and after the first day of August, eighteen hundred and sixty-two, for each license granted the sum herewith stated shall be respectively and annually paid. Any number of persons carrying on such business in copartnership may transact such business at such place under such license, and not otherwise." (Page 455)
"10. Brewers shall pay fifty dollars for each license. Every person who manufactures fermented liquors of any name or description, for sale, from malt, wholly or in part, shall be deemed a brewer under this act; *Provided,* That any person who manufactures less than five hundred barrels per year shall pay the sum of twenty-five dollars for a license. (Page 456)

Chapter LXXIV.—An Act to amend an Act entitled "An Act to provide Internal Revenue to support the Government and to pay Interest on the Public Debt," approved July first, eighteen hundred and sixty-two, and for other Purposes. Approved March 3, 1863.
"Sec. 11. *And be it further enacted . . . Provided,* That, in addition to the fractional parts of a barrel allowed in section fifty of the act to which this act is an amendment, fractional parts of a barrel may be thirds and sixths when the quantity therein contained is not greater than such fractional part represents [sic]; *Provided, further,* That from and after the passage of this act, and until the first day of April, eighteen hundred and sixty-four, there shall be paid on all beer, lager beer, ale, porter, and other similar fermented liquors, by whatever name such liquors may be called, a duty only of sixty cents for each and every barrel containing not more than thirty-one gallons, and at a like rate for any other quantity or for fractional parts of a barrel . . . " (Page 723)

Chap. CLXXIII.—*An Act to provide Internal Revenue to support the Government, to pay Interest on the Public Debt, and for other Purposes.* June 30, 1864. . . .
"Sec. 64. *And be it further enacted,* That there shall be paid on all beer, lager beer, ale, porter, and other similar fermented liquors, by whatever name such liquors may be called, a duty of one dollar for each and every barrel containing not more than thirty-one gallons, and at a like rate for any other quantity, or for fractional parts of a barrel, which shall be brewed or manufactured and sold, or removed for consumption or sale, within the United States or the territories thereof, or within the District of Columbia; which duty shall be paid by the owner, agent, or superintendent of the brewery or premises in which such fermented liquors shall be made, and shall be paid at the time of rendering the accounts of such fermented liquors so chargeable with duty, as hereinafter required: *Provided,* That fractional parts of a barrel shall be halves, thirds, quarters, sixths, eights, and sixteenths; and any fractional part containing less than one sixteenth shall be accounted one sixteenth; more than one sixteenth, and not more than one eighth, shall be accounted one eighth; more than one eighth, and not more than one sixth, shall

be accounted one sixth; more that one sixth, and not more than one quarter, shall be accounted one quarter; more than one quarter, and not more than one third, shall be accounted one third; more than one third, and not more than one half, shall be accounted one half; more than one half shall be accounted one barrel: *Provided, further,* That beer, lager beer, ale, porter, and other fermented liquors in bottles, shall be assessed, according to the quantity contained therein, at the rate of one dollar for thirty-one gallons, when the duty has not been previously paid on the liquors contained therein. (Page 246)

"Sec. 69. *And be it further enacted,* That in all cases in which the duties aforesaid, payable on spirits distilled and sold, or removed for consumption or sale, or beer, lager beer, ale, porter, and other similar fermented liquors, shall not be paid at the time of rendering the account of the same, or at the time when they shall have become payable, as herein required, to the collector or deputy collector of the district, the person or persons chargeable therewith shall pay, in addition, ten per centum on the amount thereof . . . " (Page 248)

"Sec. 79. *And be it further enacted,* That there shall be paid annually for each license granted, the sum herein stated, respectively. Any number of persons, except lawyers, conveyancers, claim agents, physicians, surgeons, dentists, cattle brokers, horse-dealers, and peddlers, carrying on such business in copartnership, may transact such business at the place specified in their license, and not otherwise, that is to say:— . . .

"Seventeen. Brewers shall pay fifty dollars for each license. Every person, firm, or corporation, who manufactures fermented liquors of any name or description, for sale, from malt, wholly or in part, or from any substitute therefore, shall be deemed a brewer under this act: *Provided,* That any person, firm, or corporation who manufactures less than five hundred barrels per year shall pay the sum of twenty-five dollars for a license." (Page 253)

Builders

Beginning 3 March 1863, Congress required that all builders and contractors whose contracts exceed $25,000 annually pay twenty-five dollars for a license. After 30 June 1864, they paid twenty-five dollars if yearly contracts were between $2500 and $25,000; if contracts did exceed the latter amount, they paid an additional one dollar for every excess thousand dollars in contracts. For purposes of taxation, builders and contractors were "every person whose business it is to construct buildings, or ships, or bridges, or canals, or railroads by contract."

Only two persons were licensed as builders in Jackson County, Missouri, during the Civil War.

William Webber Ford (1824-1890) (also licensed Apothecary)
Salathiel S. Smith (1831-?) (also licensed Manufacturer)

(See *Statutes at Large of the United States of America* 12 (1863) 715; and 13 (1864) 257.

Builders in the Internal Revenue Act

Chapter LXXIV.—An Act to amend an Act entitled "An Act to provide Internal Revenue to support the Government and to pay Interest on the Public Debt," approved July first, eighteen hundred and sixty-two, and for other Purposes. Approved March 3, 1863.

"That section sixty-four be, and hereby is, further amended by adding, at the end thereof, the following paragraphs: . . .

"Thirty-five. Builders and contractors shall pay twenty-five dollars for each license. Every person whose business it is to construct buildings, or ships, or bridges, or canals, or railroads by contract, shall be regarded as a builder and contractor under this act: *Provided,* That no license shall be required from any person whose building contracts do not exceed two thousand five hundred dollars in any one year." (Page 715)

Chap. CLXXIII.—*An Act to provide Internal Revenue to support the Government, to pay Interest on the Public Debt, and for other Purposes.* June 30, 1864. . . .

"Sec. 79. *And be it further enacted,* That there shall be paid annually for each license granted, the sum herein stated, respectively. Any number of persons, except lawyers, conveyancers, claim agents, physicians, surgeons, dentists, cattle brokers, horse-dealers, and peddlers, carrying on such business in copartnership, may transact such business at the place specified in their license, and not otherwise, that is to say:— . . .

"Forty-six. Builders and contractors shall pay twenty-five dollars for each license; and if his said contracts in any one year exceed in amount twenty-five thousand dollars, he shall pay one dollar on every additional thousand dollars in excess thereof. Every person whose business it is to construct buildings, or ships, or bridges, or canals, or railroads by contract, shall be regarded as a builder and contractor under this act; *Provided,* That no license shall be required from any person whose building contracts do not exceed two thousand five hundred dollars in any one year." (Page 257)

Butchers

Beginning in March 1863, Congress required that butchers whose annual sales exceeded one-thousand dollars pay ten dollars annually for a license. Licensed butchers did not require additional licensing as retail dealers, even if they sold others items than meat. For purposes of taxation, butchers were "every person whose business it is to sell butchers' meat at retail." Butchers who sold meat at retail from a cart or wagon exclusively paid only five dollars annually for a license and were exempt from additional licensing as peddlers.

Beginning in March 1862 Congress taxed animals slaughtered for sale at the following rates: Thirty cents per head on all cattle slaughtered exceeding eighteen months old; five cents per head on all cattle less than eighteen months old; ten cents per head on all swine over six months old when the number slaughtered exceeded twenty in one year; and five cents per head of all sheep slaughtered. Animals slaughtered for personal consumption were exempted.

In March 1863 those rates were reduced as follows: Twenty cents per head on horned cattle slaughtered; three cents per head on sheep and lambs slaughtered; and six cents per head on hogs slaughtered exceeding one hundred pounds in weight.

In June 1864 the rates changed again: Five cents per head on all cattle and calves slaughtered under three months old; forty cents per head on all cattle and calves slaughtered exceeding three months old; ten cents per head on all swine slaughtered; and five cents per head on all sheep and lambs slaughtered (if slaughtered for pelts, only two cents per head). Further, exemption from tax on animals slaughtered for ones own use were limited to five cattle and twenty calves, swine, sheep, or lambs.

Seventeen Jackson County residents paid for butcher's licenses or paid tax on animals slaughtered for sale during the Civil War—one at an unidentified location, two in Independence, and fourteen in Kansas City.

Henry Ackerman (1830-1865), Kansas City
James H. Bartlett (1835-1926), Bartlett & Frank, Kansas City
Joseph Johann Bittel/Beitel (1831/32-1867), Kansas City (early German immigrant)
James M. Bryant (1826-1905), Independence
Joseph Butcher (1819/20-?), Kansas City
Gilbert G. Crandall (1834/5-?), Kansas City
James Denison (1818-1899), Kansas City
Michael Diveley (1828-1901), Kansas City
Robert Roland Dunbar (1824-1907), Kansas City
Henry Karl Frank (ca. 1827-?), Kansas City (early German immigrant)
Hadley A. Head (ca. 1805-1872), Independence
William Henry Harrison Hockensmith (1813-1884), Jackson County
William Dodson Oldham (1833-1897), Kansas City
Alexander "Alex" Street (1821-1877), Kansas City
James A. Walker (1831-1900), Kansas City
James M. Ward (1831-?), Kansas City
Robert Wyland (1837/38-?), Bartlett & Wyland, Kansas City (early German immigrant)

(See *Statutes at Large of the United States* 12 (1863) 467-468, 715, 718; and 13 (1864) 255-256, 274-275.)

Butchers in the Internal Revenue Act

Chapter LXXIV.—An Act to amend an Act entitled "An Act to provide Internal Revenue to support the Government and to pay Interest on the Public Debt," approved July first, eighteen hundred and sixty-two, and for other Purposes. Approved March 3, 1863.

"That section sixty-four be, and hereby is, further amended by adding, at the end thereof, the following paragraphs: . . .

"Thirty-nine. Butchers shall pay ten dollars for each license. Every person whose business it is to sell butchers' meat at retail shall be regarded as a butcher under this act: *Provided,* That no butcher having taken out a license, and paid ten dollars therefore, shall be required to take out a license as retail dealer on account of selling other articles at the same store, stall, or premises: *Provided, further,* That butchers who retail butchers' meat exclusively from a cart or wagon, by themselves or agents, shall be required to pay five dollars only for each license, any existing law to the contrary notwithstanding, and having taken out a license therefore shall not be required to take out a license as a peddler for retailing butchers' meat, as aforesaid: *And provided further,* That no license shall be required of a butcher whose annual sales do not exceed one thousand dollars." (Page 715)

Chap. CLXXIII.—*An Act to provide Internal Revenue to support the Government, to pay Interest on the Public Debt, and for other Purposes.* June 30, 1864. . . .
"Sec. 79. *And be it further enacted,* That there shall be paid annually for each license granted, the sum herein stated, respectively. Any number of persons, except lawyers, conveyancers, claim agents, physicians, surgeons, dentists, cattle brokers, horse-dealers, and peddlers, carrying on such business in copartnership, may transact such business at the place specified in their license, and not otherwise, that is to say:— . . .
"Thirty-six. Butchers shall pay ten dollars for each license. Every person whose business it is to sell butchers' meat at retail shall be regarded as a butcher under this act: *Provided,* That no butcher having taken out a license, and paid ten dollars therefore, shall be required to take out a license as retail dealer on account of selling other articles at the same store, stall, or premises: *Provided, further,* That butchers whose annual sales do not exceed one thousand dollars, and butchers who retail butchers' meat exclusively by themselves or agents, and persons who sell shell or other fish, or both, traveling from place to place, and not from any shop or stand, shall be required to pay five dollars only for each license, any existing law to the contrary notwithstanding; and having taken out a license therefore, shall not be required to take out a license as a peddler for retailing butchers' meat or fish, as aforesaid. And no license shall be required of persons who sell shell or other fish from handcarts or wheelbarrows exclusively." (Pages 255-256)

Chapter CXIX.—An Act to provide Internal Revenue to support the Government and to pay Interest on the Public Debt. Approved July 1, 1862.
SLAUGHTERED CATTLE, HOGS, AND SHEEP.
"Sec. 78. *And be it further enacted,* That on and after the first day of August, eighteen hundred and sixty-two, there shall be levied, collected, and paid by any person or persons, firms, companies, or agents or employees, thereof, the following duties or taxes, that is to say:
"On all horned cattle exceeding eighteen months old, slaughtered for sale, thirty cents per head;
"On all calves and cattle under eighteen months old, slaughtered for sale, five cents per head;
"On all hogs, exceeding six months old, slaughtered for sale, when the number thus slaughtered exceeds twenty in any one year, ten cents per head;
"On all sheep, slaughtered for sale, five cents per head: *Provided,* That all cattle, hogs, and sheep, slaughtered by any person for his or her own consumption, shall be exempt from duty." (Pages 467-468)

Chapter LXXIV.—An Act to amend an Act entitled "An Act to provide Internal Revenue to support the Government and to pay Interest on the Public Debt," approved July first, eighteen hundred and sixty-two, and for other Purposes. Approved March 3, 1863.
"That section sixty-four be, and hereby is, further amended by adding, at the end thereof, the following paragraphs: . . .
"That section seventy-eight be, and hereby is, amended, by reducing the duty so that on horned cattle, slaughtered, the duty shall be twenty cents per head, on sheep and lambs,

slaughtered, the duty shall be three cents per head, and on hogs, slaughtered, exceeding one hundred pounds in weight, without regard to age, six cents each, and no duty shall be charged on hogs slaughtered of less weight; and the cattle, hogs, and sheep slaughtered by any person for his or her own consumption, not exceeding six of each, shall be exempt from duty." (Page 718)

Chap. CLXXIII.—*An Act to provide Internal Revenue to support the Government, to pay Interest on the Public Debt, and for other Purposes.* June 30, 1864. . . .
SLAUGHTERED CATTLE, SWINE, AND SHEEP.
"Sec. 101. *And be it further enacted,* That there shall be paid by any person, firm, company, or agent or employee thereof, the following duties or taxes, that is to say:—
"On all cattle and calves exceeding three months old, slaughtered, except when slaughtered for the hides and tallow exclusively, forty cents per head.
"On all cattle and calves under three months old, slaughtered, five cents per head.
"On all swine slaughtered, ten cents per head.
"On all sheep and lambs slaughtered, five cents per head.
"Provided, That cattle, not exceeding five in number, and calves, swine, sheep, and lambs, not exceeding in all twenty in number, slaughtered by any person for his or her own consumption, in any one year, shall be exempt from duty; and all sheep slaughtered for the pelts shall pay two cents only per head." (Pages 274-275)

Cattle Brokers

Beginning in August 1862, Congress required that cattle brokers pay ten dollars annually for a license. For purposes of taxation, cattle brokers were "any person whose business it is to buy and sell and deal in cattle, hogs, or sheep."

From June 1863, cattle brokers whose annual sales did not exceed $10,000 paid ten dollars for their license; those whose sales did exceed $10,000 paid one dollar for each additional thousand dollars in sales. There were seven taxed:

Jacob Axline (1813-1864), Hickman's Mills
Columbus G. Carmichael (1832-1881), Blue Township
Aaron Lane Hardage Crenshaw (1805-1890), Sniabar Township
John W. Farrow/Farrar (1825/26-?), Jackson County
Johannes Louis/Ludwig "Lud" Kramer (ca. 1826-1897), Jackson County
    (early German immigrant)
Jedediah E. McKenzie (1824-1892), Kansas City
Robert Covington White (1827-1915), Kansas City (also licensed Horse Dealer)

(See *Statutes at Large of the United States of America* 12 (1863) 458; and 18 (1864) 252.)

Cattle Brokers in the Internal Revenue Act

Chapter CXIX.—An Act to provide Internal Revenue to support the Government and to pay Interest on the Public Debt. Approved July 1, 1862.
LICENSES.
"Sec. 64. *And be it further enacted,* That on and after the first day of August, eighteen hundred and sixty-two, for each license granted the sum herewith stated shall be respectively and annually paid. Any number of persons carrying on such business in copartnership may transact such business at such place under such license, and not otherwise." (Page 455)
"24. Cattle brokers shall pay for each license the sum of ten dollars. Any person whose business it is to buy and sell and deal in cattle, hogs, or sheep, shall be considered as a cattle broker. (Page 458)

Chap. CLXXIII.—*An Act to provide Internal Revenue to support the Government, to pay Interest on the Public Debt, and for other Purposes.* June 30, 1864. . . .
"Sec. 79. *And be it further enacted,* That there shall be paid annually for each license granted, the sum herein stated, respectively. Any number of persons, except lawyers, conveyancers, claim agents, physicians, surgeons, dentists, cattle brokers, horse-dealers, and peddlers, carrying on such business in copartnership, may transact such business at the place specified in their license, and not otherwise, that is to say:— . . .
"Twelve. Cattle brokers, whose annual sales do not exceed ten thousand dollars, shall pay for each license the sum of ten dollars; and if exceeding the sum of ten thousand dollars, one dollar for each additional thousand dollars. Any person whose business it is to buy, or sell, or deal in cattle, hogs, or sheep, shall be considered as a cattle broker." (Page 252)

Claim Agents

Beginning in August 1862, Congress required that claim agents pay ten dollars annually for a license. For purposes of taxation, claim agents were "every person whose business it is to prosecute claims in any of the executive departments of the federal government."
Three persons were licensed as claim agents in Jackson County, Missouri, during the Civil War.

Philip Shelley Brown (1833-1921), Kansas City
John Cutter Gage (1835-1915), Kansas City
Louis Hammerslough (1835-1903), Kansas City (early German immigrant)
(See *Statutes at Large of the United States* 12 (1863) 459; and 13 (1864) 254.)

Claim Agents in the Internal Revenue Act

Chapter CXIX.—An Act to provide Internal Revenue to support the Government and to pay Interest on the Public Debt. Approved July 1, 1862.

LICENSES.

"Sec. 64. *And be it further enacted,* That on and after the first day of August, eighteen hundred and sixty-two, for each license granted the sum herewith stated shall be respectively and annually paid. Any number of persons carrying on such business in copartnership may transact such business at such place under such license, and not otherwise." (Page 455)

"33. Claim agents and agents for procuring patents shall pay ten dollars for each license. Every person whose business it is to prosecute claims in any of the executive departments of the federal government, or procure patents, shall be deemed a claim or patent agent, as the case may be, under this act. (Page 459)

Chap. CLXXIII.—*An Act to provide Internal Revenue to support the Government, to pay Interest on the Public Debt, and for other Purposes.* June 30, 1864. . . .

"Sec. 79. *And be it further enacted,* That there shall be paid annually for each license granted, the sum herein stated, respectively. Any number of persons, except lawyers, conveyancers, claim agents, physicians, surgeons, dentists, cattle brokers, horse-dealers, and peddlers, carrying on such business in copartnership, may transact such business at the place specified in their license, and not otherwise, that is to say:— . . .

"Twenty-three. Claim-agents and agents for procuring patents shall pay ten dollars for each license. Every person whose business it is to prosecute claims in any of the executive departments of the federal government, or procure patents, shall be deemed a claim or patent agent, as the case may be, under this act." (Page 254)

Commercial Brokers

Beginning in August 1862, Congress required that commercial brokers pay fifty dollars annually for a license. The cost of a commercial broker's license was reduced 30 June 1864 to twenty dollars annually. For purposes of taxation, commercial brokers were "any person or firm, except one holding a license as wholesale dealer or banker, whose business it is, as the agent of others, to purchase or sell goods, or seek orders therefore, in original or unbroken packages or produce, or to manage business matters for the owners of vessels, or for the shippers or consignors of freight carried by vessels, or whose business it is to purchase, rent, or sell real estate for others."

Four persons were licensed as commercial brokers in Jackson County, Missouri, during the Civil War.

Washington Henry Chick (1826-1918), Kansas City
George W. Toler (1816-1866), Kansas City
Maj. Samuel D. Vaughan (1817/18-1874), Kansas City
        (also licensed Real Estate Agent/Conveyancer)
David Virdin Whiting (1827-1888), Kansas City

(See *Statutes at Large of the United States* 12 (1863) 457; and 13 (1864) 253.)

Commercial Brokers in the Internal Revenue Act

Chapter CXIX.—An Act to provide Internal Revenue to support the Government and to pay Interest on the Public Debt. Approved July 1, 1862.
LICENSES.
"Sec. 64. *And be it further enacted,* That on and after the first day of August, eighteen hundred and sixty-two, for each license granted the sum herewith stated shall be respectively and annually paid. Any number of persons carrying on such business in copartnership may transact such business at such place under such license, and not otherwise." (Page 455)
"14. Commercial brokers shall pay fifty dollars for each license. Any person or firm, except one holding a license as wholesale dealer or banker, whose business it is, as the agent of others, to purchase or sell goods, or seek orders therefore, in original or unbroken packages or produce, or to manage business matters for the owners of vessels, or for the shippers or consignors of freight carried by vessels, or whose business it is to purchase, rent, or sell real estate for others, shall be regarded a commercial broker under this act. (Page 457)

Chap. CLXXIII.—*An Act to provide Internal Revenue to support the Government, to pay Interest on the Public Debt, and for other Purposes.* June 30, 1864. . . .
"Sec. 79. *And be it further enacted,* That there shall be paid annually for each license granted, the sum herein stated, respectively. Any number of persons, except lawyers, conveyancers, claim agents, physicians, surgeons, dentists, cattle brokers, horse-dealers, and peddlers, carrying on such business in copartnership, may transact such business at the place specified in their license, and not otherwise, that is to say:— . . .
"Fourteen. Commercial brokers shall pay twenty dollars for each license. Any person or firm, whose business it is, as a broker, to negotiate sales or purchases or goods, wares, produce, or merchandise, not otherwise provided for in this act, or seek orders therefore, in original or unbroken packages, or to negotiate freights and other business for the owners of vessels, or for the shippers or consignors or consignees of freight carried by vessels, shall be regarded a commercial broker under this act." (Page 253)

Confectioners

Beginning in August 1862, Congress required that confectioners whose annual gross sales exceed one thousand dollars pay ten dollars annually for a license. For purposes of taxation, confectioners were "any person who sells at retail confectionery, sweetmeats, comfits, or other confects, in any building."
In March 1863 Congress added a duty on confectionery—two cents per pound if valued at fourteen cents per pound of less; three cents per pound if valued at more than fourteen cents and less than forty cents per pound; and five cents per pound if valued at more forty cents or more per pound or if sold otherwise than by the pound.
In June 1864 Congress revised the duty on confectionery as follows: two cents per pound of confectionery valued at twenty cents or less per pound; four cents per pound if valued at more than twenty and less than forty cents per pound; or at the rate of ten percent if valued at more than forty cents per pound of if sold otherwise than by the pound.

Five persons were licensed as confectioners in Jackson County, Missouri, during the Civil War.

Joseph Anderson (?-?), Kansas City
Adolph Beyga (1830/31-?), Kansas City (early German immigrant)
Louis Daenzer (1828-1910), Kansas City (early German immigrant)
William/Wilhelm M. Long (1830-1897), Kansas City (early German immigrant)
Frederick/Friedrich Christian "Fritz" Welland (1837-?), Kansas City (early German immigrant)
Theobald Werry (1826-1879), Westport [early German immigrant;
        his widow was a Civil War pensioner]

(See *Statutes at Large of the United States* 12 (1863) 457-459, 717; and 13 (1864) 254, 257-258, 266.)

Confectioners in the Internal Revenue Act

Chapter CXIX.—An Act to provide Internal Revenue to support the Government and to pay Interest on the Public Debt. Approved July 1, 1862.
        LICENSES.
        "Sec. 64. *And be it further enacted,* That on and after the first day of August, eighteen hundred and sixty-two, for each license granted the sum herewith stated shall be respectively and annually paid. Any number of persons carrying on such business in copartnership may transact such business at such place under such license, and not otherwise." (Page 455)
        "20. Confectioners shall pay ten dollars for each license. Any person who sells at retail confectionery, sweetmeats, comfits, or other confects, in any building, shall be regarded as a confectioner under this act. But wholesale and retail dealers having taken out a license therefore, shall not be required to take out a license as confectioner, anything in this act to the contrary notwithstanding. (Pages 457-458)
        "Sec. 65. *And be it further enacted,* That where the annual gross receipts or sales of any apothecaries, confectioners, eating-houses, tobacconists, or retail dealers, shall not exceed the sum of one thousand dollars, such apothecaries, confectioners, eating-houses, and retail dealers shall not be required to take out or pay for license, anything in this act to the contrary notwithstanding; the amount or estimated amount of such annual sales to be ascertained or estimated in such manner as the Commissioner of Internal Revenue shall prescribe, and so of all other annual sales or receipts, where the rate of the license is graduated by the amount of sales or receipts." (Page 459)

Chapter LXXIV.—An Act to amend an Act entitled "An Act to provide Internal Revenue to support the Government and to pay Interest on the Public Debt," approved July first, eighteen hundred and sixty-two, and for other Purposes. Approved March 3, 1863.
        "That section sixty-four be, and hereby is, further amended by adding, at the end thereof, the following paragraphs: . . .
        "On sugar-candy and all confectionary [sic] made wholly or in part of sugar, valued at fourteen cents per pound or less, two cents per pound; when valued at exceeding fourteen cents and not exceeding forty cents per pound, three cents per pound; when valued at exceeding forty

cents per pound, or when sold otherwise than by the pound, five per centum ad valorem." (Page 717)

Chap. CLXXIII.—*An Act to provide Internal Revenue to support the Government, to pay Interest on the Public Debt, and for other Purposes.* June 30, 1864. . . .

"Sec. 79. *And be it further enacted,* That there shall be paid annually for each license granted, the sum herein stated, respectively. Any number of persons, except lawyers, conveyancers, claim agents, physicians, surgeons, dentists, cattle brokers, horse-dealers, and peddlers, carrying on such business in copartnership, may transact such business at the place specified in their license, and not otherwise, that is to say:— . . .

"Twenty-two. Confectioners shall pay ten dollars for each license. Every person who sells at retail confectionery, sweetmeats, comfits, or other confects, in any building, shall be regarded as a confectioner under this act. But wholesale and retail dealers, having taken out a license therefore, shall not be required to take out a license as confectioner, anything in this act to the contrary notwithstanding." (Page 254)

"Sec. 80. *And be it further enacted,* That where the annual gross receipts or sales of any apothecaries, confectioners, eating-houses, tobacconists, or retail dealers, except retail dealers in spirituous and malt liquors, shall not exceed the sum of one thousand dollars, such apothecaries, confectioners, eating-houses, tobacconists, and retail dealers shall not be required to take out or pay for license, anything in this act to the contrary notwithstanding; the amount or estimated amount of such annual sales to be ascertained or estimated in such manner as the commissioner of internal revenue shall prescribe, and so of all other annual sales or receipts, where the rate of the license is graduated by the amount of sales or receipts; and where the amount of the license or the rate has been increased, or is liable to be increased, by law above the amount of any existing license to any person, firm, or company, or has been understated or under-estimated, such person, firm, or company shall be again assessed and pay the amount of such increase, which shall be indorsed on the original license, which shall thereafter be held good and sufficient. (Pages 257-258)

MANUFACTURES, ARTICLES, AND PRODUCTS.
SPECIFIC AND AD VALOREM DUTY.

"On sugar-candy and all confectionery made wholly or in part of sugar, valued at not exceeding twenty cents per pound, a duty of two cents per pound; exceeding twenty and not exceeding forty cents per pound, a duty of four cents per pound; when exceeding forty cents per pound, or sold by the box, package, or otherwise than by the pound, a duty of ten per centum ad valorem." (Page 266)

Dentists

Beginning in August 1862, Congress required that physicians, surgeons, and dentists pay ten dollars annually for a license to practice. For purposes of taxation, physicians, surgeons, and dentists, as the case may be, were defined as "every person (except apothecaries) whose business it is, for fee and reward, to prescribe remedies or perform surgical operations for the cure of any bodily disease or ailing." Physicians practicing together in partnership required only a single license and licensed physicians were allowed to practice both inside and outside the tax assessment district of their license.

Only three persons were licensed as dentists in Jackson County, Missouri, during the Civil War. [For a comprehensive roster of graduates from Kansas City's various 19th century colleges of science, consult James A. Tharp's compilation, *Colleges of Medicine, Dentistry & Pharmacy, Kansas City, Missouri: Names of 3400 Graduates, 1871-1905.* (Kansas City, Mo.: The Orderly Pack Rat, 2013).]

John W. Evans (ca. 1842-1863), Kansas City
George William Tindall (1832-1908), Kansas City
James Newton Wiley (1838/39 or 21 Nov 1843-1899), Kansas City

(See *Statutes at Large of the United States of America* 12 (1863) 459, 727; and 13 (1864) 257.)

Dentists in the Internal Revenue Act

Chapter CXIX.—An Act to provide Internal Revenue to support the Government and to pay Interest on the Public Debt. Approved July 1, 1862.
LICENSES.
"Sec. 64. *And be it further enacted,* That on and after the first day of August, eighteen hundred and sixty-two, for each license granted the sum herewith stated shall be respectively and annually paid. Any number of persons carrying on such business in copartnership may transact such business at such place under such license, and not otherwise." (Page 455)
"32. Physicians, surgeons, and dentists shall pay ten dollars for each license. Every person (except apothecaries) whose business it is, for fee and reward, to prescribe remedies or perform surgical operations for the cure of any bodily disease or ailing, shall be deemed a physician, surgeon, or dentist, as the case may be, within the meaning of this act. (Page 459)
"Sec. 66. *And be it further enacted,* That nothing contained in the preceding sections of this act, laying duties on licenses, shall be construed to require a license for the sale of goods, wares, and merchandise made or produced and sold by the manufacturer or producer at the manufactory or place where the same is made or produced; to vintners who sell, at the place where the same is made, wine of their own growth; nor to apothecaries, as to wines or spirituous liquors which they use exclusively in the preparation or making up of medicines for sick, lame, or diseased persons; nor shall the provisions of paragraph number twenty-seven extend to physicians who keep on hand medicines solely for the purpose of making up their own prescriptions for their own patients." (Page 459)

Chapter LXXIV.—An Act to amend an Act entitled "An Act to provide Internal Revenue to support the Government and to pay Interest on the Public Debt," approved July first, eighteen hundred and sixty-two, and for other Purposes. Approved March 3, 1863.
"Sec. 25. *And be it further enacted,* That no auctioneer shall be authorized, by virtue of his license as such auctioneer, to sell any goods or other property in any other district than that in which the license shall have been granted, but lawyers, physicians, surgeons, or dentists, having taken out a license as such, shall not be required to take out any additional license in

consequence of practicing their profession within or beyond the limits of the district where licensed." (Page 727)

Chap. CLXXIII.—*An Act to provide Internal Revenue to support the Government, to pay Interest on the Public Debt, and for other Purposes.* June 30, 1864. . . .

"Sec. 79. *And be it further enacted,* That there shall be paid annually for each license granted, the sum herein stated, respectively. Any number of persons, except lawyers, conveyancers, claim agents, physicians, surgeons, dentists, cattle brokers, horse-dealers, and peddlers, carrying on such business in copartnership, may transact such business at the place specified in their license, and not otherwise, that is to say:— . . .

"Forty-four. Physicians, surgeons, and dentists shall pay ten dollars for each license. Every person (except apothecaries) whose business it is, for fee and reward, to prescribe remedies or perform surgical operations for the cure of any bodily disease or ailing, shall be deemed a physician, surgeon, or dentist, as the case may be, within the meaning of this act." (Page 257)

Ferry Boats

John Snoddy Campbell (1814-1865), Kansas City
Capt. James McGargill (1799/1800 or 1806-1870), Independence
Col. Richard Henry Nelson (1812-1884), Kansas City

Ferry Boats in the Internal Revenue Act

Chapter CXIX.—An Act to provide Internal Revenue to support the Government and to pay Interest on the Public Debt. Approved July 1, 1862.
RAILROADS, STEAMBOATS, AND FERRY-BOATS.
"Sec. 80. *And be it further enacted,* That on the first day of August, eighteen hundred and sixty-two, any persons, firms, companies, or corporations... owning, possessing, or having the care or management of any ferry-boat, or vessel used as a verry-boat, propelled by steam or horse power, shall be subject to and pay a duty of one and a half per centum upon the gross receipts of such . . . ferry-boat . . . for the transportation of passengers over and upon said . . . ferry-boats..." (Page 468)

Chapter LXXIV.—An Act to amend an Act entitled "An Act to provide Internal Revenue to support the Government and to pay Interest on the Public Debt," approved July first, eighteen hundred and sixty-two, and for other Purposes. Approved March 3, 1863.
"Sec. 9. *And be it further enacted,* That any person or persons, firms, companies, or corporations, owning or possessing, or having the care of management of any ferry-boat, or vessel used as a ferry-boat, propelled by steam or horse power, in lieu of the duties now imposed by law, shall be subject to pay a duty of one and one half of one per centum upon the gross receipts of such ferry-boat; and the return and payment thereof shall be made in the manner prescribed in the act to which this act is an amendment." (Page 722)

Chap. CLXXIII.—An Act to provide Internal Revenue to support the Government, to pay Interest on the Public Debt, and for other Purposes. June 30, 1864. . . .
    RAILROADS, STEAMBOATS, FERRY-BOATS, AND BRIDGES.
    "Sec. 103. *And be it further enacted,* That every person, firm, company, or corporation owning or possessing, or having the care or management of, any railroad, canal, steamboat, ship, barge, canal-boat, or other vessel, or any stage-coach or other vehicle engaged or employed in the business of transporting passengers or property for hire, or in transporting the mails of the United States, or any canal, the water of which is used for mining purposes, shall be subject to and pay a duty of two and one half per centum upon the gross receipts of such railroad, canal, steamboat, ship, barge, canal-boat, or other vessel, or such stage-coach or other vehicle: *Provided,* That the duty hereby imposed shall not be charged upon receipts for the transportation of persons or property, or mails, between the United States and any foreign port; and any person or persons, firms, companies, or corporations, owning, possessing, or having the care or management of any toll-road, ferry, or bridge, authorized by law to receive toll for the transit of passengers, beasts, carriages, teams, and freight of any description, over such toll-road, ferry, or bridge, shall be subject to and pay a duty of three per centum on the gross amount of all their receipts of every description. But when the gross receipts of any such bridge or toll-road shall not exceed the amount necessarily expended to keep such bridge or road in repair, no tax shall be imposed on such receipts . . . " (Pages 275-276)

Horse Dealers

Jedediah E. McKenzie (1824-1892), Kansas City (also Cattle Dealers)
Robert Covington White (1827-1915), Kansas City (also Cattle Dealers)

Horse Dealers in the Internal Revenue Act

Chapter CXIX.—An Act to provide Internal Revenue to support the Government and to pay Interest on the Public Debt. Approved July 1, 1862.
    LICENSES.
    "Sec. 64. *And be it further enacted,* That on and after the first day of August, eighteen hundred and sixty-two, for each license granted the sum herewith stated shall be respectively and annually paid. Any number of persons carrying on such business in copartnership may transact such business at such place under such license, and not otherwise." (Page 455)
    "22. Horse-dealers shall pay for each license the sum of ten dollars. Any person whose business it is to buy and sell horses or mules shall be regarded a horse-dealer under this act: *Provided,* That if such horse-dealer shall have taken out a license as a livery-stable keeper no new license shall be required. (Page 458)

Chap. CLXXIII.—An Act to provide Internal Revenue to support the Government, to pay Interest on the Public Debt, and for other Purposes. June 30, 1864. . . .
    "Sec. 79. *And be it further enacted,* That there shall be paid annually for each license granted, the sum herein stated, respectively. Any number of persons, except lawyers, conveyancers, claim agents, physicians, surgeons, dentists, cattle brokers, horse-dealers, and

peddlers, carrying on such business in copartnership, may transact such business at the place specified in their license, and not otherwise, that is to say:— . . .

"Seven. Horse-dealers shall pay for each license the sum of ten dollars. Any person whose business it is to buy or sell horses or mules shall be regarded a horse-dealer under this act: *Provided,* That one license having been paid, no additional license shall be required of any horse-dealer who keeps a livery-stable, nor of any livery-stable keeper who may also be a horse-dealer." (Page 252)

Hotels

Emory B. Chadwick (1823/24-1893), Kansas City (Pacific House)
William C. Holmes (1814-1888), Smith & Holms [sic.],
    Kansas City & Westport (Smith Hotel & Commercial House)
Charles Grandison Hopkins (1820-1896), Kansas City (Gilliss House)
Mrs. David McKee (Jane K. Hutchison) (1803/04-1882), Westport
George C./G. Nicholson (1836/37-?), Kansas City
John W. Perry (1815-1887), Independence (also Livery Stable Keeper)
Peter H. Smith (1821/22-?), Smith & Holms [sic.], Kansas City & Westport
    (Smith Hotel & Commercial House)
John W. Wilson (1805-1879), Independence (also Retail Dealer [General Store],
    Wholesale Dealer [unidentified merchandise])

Hotel, Inns, and Taverns in the Internal Revenue Act

Chapter CXIX.—An Act to provide Internal Revenue to support the Government and to pay Interest on the Public Debt. Approved July 1, 1862.
    LICENSES.
    "Sec. 64. *And be it further enacted,* That on and after the first day of August, eighteen hundred and sixty-two, for each license granted the sum herewith stated shall be respectively and annually paid. Any number of persons carrying on such business in copartnership may transact such business at such place under such license, and not otherwise." (Page 455)
    "11. Hotels, inns, and taverns shall be classified and rated according to the yearly rental, or, if not rented, according to the estimated yearly rental of the house and property intended to be occupied for said purposes, as follows, to wit: All cases where the rent or the valuation of the yearly rental of said house and property shall be ten thousand dollars or more shall constitute the first class, and shall pay two hundred dollars for each license; where the rent or the valuation of the yearly rental shall be five thousand dollars and less than ten thousand dollars, the second class, and shall pay one hundred dollars for each license; where the rent or the valuation of the yearly rental shall be twenty-five hundred dollars and less than five thousand dollars, the third class, and shall pay seventy-five dollars for each license; where the rent or the valuation of the yearly rental shall be one thousand dollars and less than twenty-five hundred dollars, the fourth class, and shall pay fifty dollars for each license; where the rent or the valuation of the yearly rental shall be five hundred dollars and less than one thousand dollars, the fifth class, and shall pay twenty-five dollars for each license; where the rent or the valuation of the yearly rental shall

be three hundred dollars and less than five hundred dollars, the sixth class, and shall pay fifteen dollars for each license; where the rent or the valuation of the yearly rental shall be one hundred dollars and less than three hundred dollars, the seventh class, and shall pay ten dollars for each license; where the rent or the valuation of the yearly rental shall be less than one hundred dollars, the eighth class, and shall pay five dollars for each license. Every place where food and lodging are provided for and furnished to travelers and sojourners, in view of payment therefore, shall be regarded as a hotel, inn, or tavern under this act. All steamers and vessels upon waters of the United States, on board of which passengers or travelers are provided with food or lodging, shall be required to take out a license of the fifth class, as aforesaid, under this act. The rental or estimated rental shall be fixed and established by the assessor of the proper district at its proper value, but at not less than the actual rent agreed on by the parties: *Provided,* That if there be any fraud or collusion in the return of actual rent to the assessor, there shall be a penalty equal to double the amount of licenses required by this section, to be collected as other penalties under this act are collected. . (Pages 456-457)

Chapter LXXIV.—An Act to amend an Act entitled "An Act to provide Internal Revenue to support the Government and to pay Interest on the Public Debt," approved July first, eighteen hundred and sixty-two, and for other Purposes. Approved March 3, 1863.

"That section sixty-four be, and hereby is, further amended by adding, at the end thereof, the following paragraphs: . . .

"Forty-three. Retail dealers in liquors shall pay twenty dollars for each license. Every person other than a distiller or brewer, who shall sell or offer for sale any distilled spirits, fermented liquors, or wine of any description, in quantities of three gallons or less, and whose annual sales do not exceed twenty-five thousand dollars, shall be regarded as a retail dealer in liquors under this law; but nothing herein contained shall authorize the sale of any spirits, liquors, wines or malt liquors to be drank on the premises: *Provided,* That no person licensed to keep a hotel, inn, or tavern, shall be allowed to sell any liquors to be taken off the premises, and no person licensed to keep an eating-house shall be allowed to sell spiritous [sic] or vinous liquors. And no person who has taken out a license to keep a hotel, inn, tavern, or eating-house shall be required to take out a license as a tobacconist because of any tobacco or cigars furnished in the usual course of business as a keeper of a hotel, inn, tavern, or eating-house." (Page 716)

Chap. CLXXIII.—*An Act to provide Internal Revenue to support the Government, to pay Interest on the Public Debt, and for other Purposes.* June 30, 1864. . . .

"Sec. 79. *And be it further enacted,* That there shall be paid annually for each license granted, the sum herein stated, respectively. Any number of persons, except lawyers, conveyancers, claim agents, physicians, surgeons, dentists, cattle brokers, horse-dealers, and peddlers, carrying on such business in copartnership, may transact such business at the place specified in their license, and not otherwise, that is to say:— . . .

"Twenty. Hotels, inns, and taverns shall be classified and rated according to the yearly rental, or, if not rented, according to the estimated yearly rental, of the house and property intended to be occupied for said purposes, as follows, to wit: All cases where the rent or valuation of the yearly rental of said house and property shall be two hundred dollars, or less, shall pay ten dollars. And if exceeding two hundred dollars, for any additional one hundred dollars or fractional part thereof in excess of two hundred dollars, five dollars. Every place where food and lodging are provided for and furnished to travelers and sojourners, in view of payment therefore, shall be regarded as a hotel, inn, or tavern under this act: *Provided,* That nothing herein contained shall be construed to exempt keepers of hotels, taverns, and eating-houses in which liquors are sold by retail, to be drank upon the premises, from taking out a license for such sale, for which license they shall pay a tax of twenty-five dollars. The yearly rental shall be fixed and established by the assessor of the proper district at its proper value, but if rented, at not less than the actual rent agreed on by the parties. All steamers and vessels, upon waters of the United States, on board of which passengers or travelers are provided with food or lodgings, shall be subject to, and required to pay, twenty-five dollars for each license: *Provided,* That if there be any fraud or collusion in the return of actual rent to the assessor, there shall be a penalty equal to double the amount of licenses required by this section, to be collected as other penalties under this act are collected." (Page 253-254)

Insurance Agents

Peter Hinters/Hinterschitt (1827-1877), Independence (also Physician)
    (early German immigrant)
Philip Setzler (1834-1923), Kansas City (also Rectifier)
    (early German immigrant)

Insurance Agents in the Internal Revenue Act

Chapter LXXIV.—An Act to amend an Act entitled "An Act to provide Internal Revenue to support the Government and to pay Interest on the Public Debt," approved July first, eighteen hundred and sixty-two, and for other Purposes. Approved March 3, 1863.

"That section sixty-four be, and hereby is, further amended by adding, at the end thereof, the following paragraphs: . . .

"Thirty-eight. Insurance agents shall pay ten dollars for each license. Any person who shall act as agent for any fire, marine, life, mutual, or other insurance company, or companies, shall be regarded as an insurance agent under this act: *Provided,* That no license shall be required of any insurance agent or broker whose receipts, as such agent, are less than the sum of six hundred dollars in any one year." (Page 715)

Chap. CLXXIII.—*An Act to provide Internal Revenue to support the Government, to pay Interest on the Public Debt, and for other Purposes.* June 30, 1864. . . .

"Sec. 79. *And be it further enacted,* That there shall be paid annually for each license granted, the sum herein stated, respectively. Any number of persons, except lawyers, conveyancers, claim agents, physicians, surgeons, dentists, cattle brokers, horse-dealers, and peddlers, carrying on such business in copartnership, may transact such business at the place specified in their license, and not otherwise, that is to say:— . . .

"Twenty-eight. Insurance agents shall pay ten dollars for each license. Any person who shall act as agent of any fire, marine, life, mutual, or other insurance company or companies, shall be regarded as an insurance agent under this act: *Provided,* That no license shall be required of any insurance agent or broker whose receipts, as such agent, are less than the sum of three hundred dollars in any one year." (Page 254)

Lawyers

Beginning in August 1862, Congress required that lawyers pay ten dollars annually for a license to practice. For purposes of taxation, lawyers were defined as "every person whose business it is, for fee or reward, to prosecute or defend causes in any court of record or other judicial tribunal of the United States or of any of the States, or give advice in relation to causes or matter ending therein." Lawyers practicing together in partnership required only a single license and licensed lawyers were allowed to practice both inside and outside the tax assessment district of their license.

Sixteen lawyers were licensed in Jackson County, Missouri, during the Civil War—one in Westport, five in Independence, and ten in Kansas City.

William Leonidas "Lee" Bone (1820-1885), Independence
Henry Butler Bouton (1815-1868), Kansas City
Phillip Shelley Brown (1833-1921), Kansas City (also licensed Claim Agent)
George Washington Buchanan (1814-1901), Independence
William Chrisman (1822-1897), Independence
Abram Comingo (1820-1889), Independence (also licensed Real Estate Agent)
John Cutter Gage (1835-1915), Kansas City (also licensed Claim Agent)
Thomas J. Goforth (1804-1882), Westport
John Ward Henry (1825-1902), Kansas City
William C. Holmes (1814-1888), Kansas City
Judge Jacob Brown "John" Hovey (1818-1874), Kansas City
Robert William Quarles (1847-1920), Kansas City
Lewis Albert Ramage (1814/15-1879), Kansas City
William Stevens (1812-1896), Kansas City
John Henry Taylor (1837-1902), Independence
Marston David Trefren (1822-1916), Kansas City

(See *Statutes at Large of the United States of America* 12 (1863) 459 727; and 13 (1864) 256-257.)

Lawyers in the Internal Revenue Act

Chapter CXIX.—An Act to provide Internal Revenue to support the Government and to pay Interest on the Public Debt. Approved July 1, 1862.
LICENSES.
"Sec. 64. *And be it further enacted,* That on and after the first day of August, eighteen hundred and sixty-two, for each license granted the sum herewith stated shall be respectively and annually paid. Any number of persons carrying on such business in copartnership may transact such business at such place under such license, and not otherwise." (Page 455)
"31. Lawyers shall pay ten dollars for each license. Every person whose business it is, for fee or reward, to prosecute or defend causes in any court of record or other judicial tribunal of the United States or of any of the States, or give advice in relation to causes or matters ending therein, shall be deemed to be a lawyer within the meaning of this act." (Page 459.)

Chapter LXXIV.—An Act to amend an Act entitled "An Act to provide Internal Revenue to support the Government and to pay Interest on the Public Debt," approved July first, eighteen hundred and sixty-two, and for other Purposes. Approved March 3, 1863.

"Sec. 25. *And be it further enacted,* That no auctioneer shall be authorized, by virtue of his license as such auctioneer, to sell any goods or other property in any other district than that in which the license shall have been granted, but lawyers, physicians, surgeons, or dentists, having taken out al license as such, shall not be required to take out any additional license in consequence of practicing their profession within or beyond the limits of the district where licensed." (Page 727)

Chap. CLXXIII.—*An Act to provide Internal Revenue to support the Government, to pay Interest on the Public Debt, and for other Purposes.* June 30, 1864. . . .

"Sec. 79. *And be it further enacted,* That there shall be paid annually for each license granted, the sum herein stated, respectively. Any number of persons, except lawyers, conveyancers, claim agents, physicians, surgeons, dentists, cattle brokers, horse-dealers, and peddlers, carrying on such business in copartnership, may transact such business at the place specified in their license, and not otherwise, that is to say:— . . .

"Forty-three. Lawyers shall pay ten dollars for each license. Every person who, for fee or reward, shall prosecute or defend causes in any court of record or other judicial tribunal of the United States, or of any of the states, or give legal advice in relation to any cause or matter whatever, shall be deemed to be a lawyer within the meaning of this act." (Pages 256-257)

Livery Stable Keepers

Edward Cassidy (1824-1906), Westport & Kansas City
Patrick Cassidy (1827-1870), Westport & Kansas City
Oscar H. Cogswell (1820-1881), Independence (also Retail Dealer [Dry Goods])
James R. Ham (1833-1909), Kansas City
Leonard D. Mettee (1839-1881), Kansas City
    (also Retail Dealer [unidentified merchandise])
John W. Perry (1815-1887), Independence (also Hotel Keeper)
John T. Quarles (1815/16-?), Kansas City
Robert Wyland (1837/38-?), Kansas City (also Butcher) (early German immigrant)

Livery Stable Keepers in the Internal Revenue Act

Chapter CXIX.—An Act to provide Internal Revenue to support the Government and to pay Interest on the Public Debt. Approved July 1, 1862.
    LICENSES.
    "Sec. 64. *And be it further enacted,* That on and after the first day of August, eighteen hundred and sixty-two, for each license granted the sum herewith stated shall be respectively and annually paid. Any number of persons carrying on such business in copartnership may transact such business at such place under such license, and not otherwise." (Page 455)

"23. Livery-stable keepers shall pay ten dollars for each license. Any person whose occupation or business is to keep horses for hire or to let shall be regarded as a livery-stable keeper under this act. (Page 458)

Chap. CLXXIII.—*An Act to provide Internal Revenue to support the Government, to pay Interest on the Public Debt, and for other Purposes.* June 30, 1864. . . .

"Sec. 79. *And be it further enacted,* That there shall be paid annually for each license granted, the sum herein stated, respectively. Any number of persons, except lawyers, conveyancers, claim agents, physicians, surgeons, dentists, cattle brokers, horse-dealers, and peddlers, carrying on such business in copartnership, may transact such business at the place specified in their license, and not otherwise, that is to say:— . . .

"Eight. Livery-stable keepers shall pay ten dollars for each license. Any person whose business it is to keep horses for hire, or to let, or to keep, feed, or board horses for others, shall be regarded as a livery-stable keeper under this act." (Page 252)

Manufacturers and Manufactures—Barrels

Reinhold Frey (1831-1904), Kansas City (early German immigrant)
John/Johann Michael Scherzer (1827/28-1902), Kansas City
    [early German immigrant; was a Civil War pensioner]

Manufacturers and Manufactures—Boots and Shoes

Johannes Phillip/Philipp Becker (1832-1913), Westport
    (early German immigrant; also Retail Dealer [Boots and Shoes])
Henry/Heinrich Borgstede (1835-1888), Kansas City (early German immigrant)
Joseph Anton Fritz (1828/9-1881) (early German immigrant;
    also Retail Liquor Dealer)
William Gabel (1835-1919), Kansas City (early German immigrant;
    also Retail Dealer [Boots and Shoes])
Frank/Franz Langsenkamp (1830-1866), Kansas City (early German immigrant;
    also Retail Dealer [Boots and Shoes])
Christian Rahlf (1826/27-1873), Kansas City (early German immigrant)
Henry Schoepf (1824/25-1883/4), Westport (early German immigrant;
    also Retail Dealer [Boots and Shoes])

Manufacturers and Manufactures—Cigars

Joseph Smith Chick (1828-1908), Kansas City (also Wholesale Dealer)
Christian August Frederick/Friedrich Eckert (1833-1910), Kansas City
    (early German immigrant)

Charles B. Eckhart (ca. 1838-?), Kansas City (early German immigrant)
Wendel/Wendelin Loesch (1818-1865), Kansas City (early German immigrant;
        also Billiard Room Keeper; [was a Civil War pensioner])
Caspar/Kaspar H. Mohr (1825-1898), Kansas City (early German immigrant;
        also Retail Dealer [Cigars]) [was a Civil War pensioner])
Frederick/Friedrich Christian "Fritz" Welland (1837-?), Kansas City
        (early German immigrant; also Confectioner)

Manufacturers and Manufactures—Furniture

Henry Carl Sager (1815-1886), Westport (early German immigrant;
        also Retail Dealer [Furniture])
Edward Stine (1833-1917), Kansas City (also Retail Dealer [Furniture])

Manufacturers and Manufactures—Mattresses

James C. Kevill (1832-1902), Kansas City (early German immigrant;
        also Auctioneers)
James P. Turner (1835-1879), Kansas City (early German immigrant)

Manufacturers and Manufactures—Miscellaneous Manufactures

Joseph (?-?) Anderson, Kansas City (unidentified manufacture;
        also Confectioners)
Thomas Forbes (1822/23-?), Kansas City (lime & bricks) (also Peddler)
William Webber Ford (1824-1890), Kansas City (sash & blinds)
        (also Confectioners)
Louis Hammerslough (1835-1903), Kansas City (clothing) (early German
        immigrant; also Claim Agent, Wholesale Dealer [Clothing])
Franklin Hubbard "Frank" Kump (1834-1923) (soda water;
        early German immigrant)

Manufacturers and Manufactures—Saddlery

Jacob R. Gerhart (1840-1903), Westport (also Retail Dealer [Saddlery])
        (early German immigrant)
Charles W. Kline (1833/34-?), Kansas City

William/Wilhelm M. Long (1830-1897), Kansas City (also Confectioner)
    (early German immigrant)
Isaac W. McDonald (1823-1901), Kansas City (also Retail Dealer [Saddlery])
John W. Modie (1827-1895), Independence
Richard D. Smith (1835-1921), Kansas City (also Retail Dealer [Saddlery])
Salathiel S. Smith (1831-?), Kansas City (also Builder, Retail Dealer [Saddlery])

Manufacturers and Manufactures—Tinware and Stoves

David Gilbert Blair (1821-1911), Kansas City (also Retail Dealer
    [Tinware and Stoves])
Jacob Robert Erkel (1830/31-1870/71), Kansas City (early German immigrant)
Chauncey Wilmont Fairman (1832-1892), Kansas City
    (also Retail Dealer [Tinware and Stoves])
William P. Morrison (1817-1894), Kansas City
Lucien Whitman Pollard (1823-1890), Kansas City
    (also Retail Dealer [Tinware and Stoves])
Phillip Dodridge Pollard (1821-?), Independence
Charles Thomas (1832-1883), Kansas City (early German immigrant)
John Wesley Thompson (1828-1867), Kansas City
    (also Retail Dealer [Tinware and Stoves])

Manufacturers and Manufactures—Wagons

Christian "Chris" Glunz (1833/34-1866), Westport
Frederick "Fred/Fritz Klaber (1830-1866), Westport (also Retail Liquor Dealer)
    (early German immigrant)
John Squire/Squires (?-1863), Westport (wagons)
Mrs. John Squire/Squires (Mary J.) (?-?), Westport (wagons)
Joseph Stegmiller (1821-1886), Westport (wagons) (early German immigrant)
Robert T. Weston (1816-1899), Independence (plows & wagons)

Manufacturers and Manufactures in the Internal Revenue Act

Chapter CXIX.—An Act to provide Internal Revenue to support the Government and to pay Interest on the Public Debt. Approved July 1, 1862.
    LICENSES.
    "Sec. 64. *And be it further enacted,* That on and after the first day of August, eighteen hundred and sixty-two, for each license granted the sum herewith stated shall be respectively and annually paid. Any number of persons carrying on such business in copartnership may transact such business at such place under such license, and not otherwise." (Page 455)

"29. Manufacturers shall pay ten dollars for each license. Any person or persons, firms, companies, or corporations, who shall manufacture by hand or machinery, and offer for sale any goods, wares, or merchandise, exceeding annually the sum of one thousand dollars, shall be regarded a manufacturer under this act. (Page 458)

"Sec. 66. *And be it further enacted,* That nothing contained in the preceding sections of this act, laying duties on licenses, shall be construed to require a license for the sale of goods, wares, and merchandise made or produced and sold by the manufacturer or producer at the manufactory or place where the same is made or produced; to vintners who sell, at the place where the same is made, wine of their own growth; nor to apothecaries, as to wines or spirituous liquors which they use exclusively in the preparation or making up of medicines for sick, lame, or diseased persons; nor shall the provisions of paragraph number twenty-seven extend to physicians who keep on hand medicines solely for the purpose of making up their own prescriptions for their own patients." (Page 459)

Chap. CLXXIII.—*An Act to provide Internal Revenue to support the Government, to pay Interest on the Public Debt, and for other Purposes.* June 30, 1864. . . .

"Sec. 79. *And be it further enacted,* That there shall be paid annually for each license granted, the sum herein stated, respectively. Any number of persons, except lawyers, conveyancers, claim agents, physicians, surgeons, dentists, cattle brokers, horse-dealers, and peddlers, carrying on such business in copartnership, may transact such business at the place specified in their license, and not otherwise, that is to say:— . . .

"Thirty-one. Manufacturers shall pay ten dollars for each license. Any person, firm, or corporation, who shall manufacture by hand or machinery any goods, wares, or merchandise, exceeding annually the sum of one thousand dollars, shall be regarded a manufacturer under this act." (Page 255)

"Sec. 81. *And be it further enacted,* That nothing contained in the preceding sections of this act, requiring licenses, shall be construed to require an additional license as a dealer for the sale of goods, wares, and merchandise made or produced and sold by the manufacturer or producer at the manufactory or place where the same is made or produced, or at the principal office or place of business, as provided in section *seventy-three* [seventy-four] of this act; [nor] to *vinters* [vintners] who sell, at the place where the same is made, wine of their own growth; nor to apothecaries, as to wines or spirituous liquors which they use exclusively in the preparation of making up of medicines; nor shall any provisions be construed to prohibit physicians from keeping on hand medicines solely for the purpose of making up their own prescriptions for their own patients." (Page 258)

Chapter LXXIV.—An Act to amend an Act entitled "An Act to provide Internal Revenue to support the Government and to pay Interest on the Public Debt," approved July first, eighteen hundred and sixty-two, and for other Purposes. Approved March 3, 1863.

"That section sixty-four be, and hereby is, further amended by adding, at the end thereof, the following paragraphs: . . .

"Tailors, boot and shoemakers, milliners and dressmakers, making clothing or articles of dress for men's women's, or children's wear, to order as custom-work, and not for sale generally, shall, to the amount of one thousand dollars, be exempt from duty, and for any excess beyond the amount of one thousand dollars shall pay a duty of one percentum ad valorem." (Page 717)

Chap. CLXXIII.—*An Act to provide Internal Revenue to support the Government, to pay Interest on the Public Debt, and for other Purposes.* June 30, 1864. . . .

MANUFACTURES, ARTICLES, AND PRODUCTS.
SPECIFIC AND AD VALOREM DUTY.

"On ready-made clothing, boots and shoes, gloves, mittens, and moccasins, caps, hats, and bonnets, or other articles of dress for the wear of men, women, or children, five per centum ad valorem: *Provided,* That any tailor, boot or shoe maker, hat, cap, or bonnet maker, milliner or dressmaker, exclusively engaged in manufacturing any of the foregoing articles to order as custom work, and not for sale generally, who shall make affidavit to the assessor or assistant assessor, that the entire amount of such manufactures so made does not exceed the sum of six hundred dollars per annum, shall be exempt from duty; when exceeding six hundred dollars per annum, a duty of three per centum ad valorem on the excess above six hundred dollars." (Pages 269-270)

Chapter CXIX.—An Act to provide Internal Revenue to support the Government and to pay Interest on the Public Debt. Approved July 1, 1862.

MANUFACTURES, ARTICLES, AND PRODUCTS.
SPECIFIC AND AD VALOREM DUTY.

"Sec. 75. *And be it further enacted,* That from and after the said first day of August, eighteen hundred and sixty-two, upon the articles, goods, wares, and merchandise, hereinafter mentioned, which shall thereafter be produced and sold, or be manufactured or made and sold, or removed for consumption, or for delivery to others than agents of the manufacturer or producer within the United States or Territories thereof, there shall be levied, collected, and paid the following duties, to be paid by the producer or manufacturer thereof, that is to say: . . . "(Page 462)

"On cigars, valued at not over five dollars per thousand, one dollar and fifty cents per thousand;

"On cigars, valued at over five and not over ten dollars per thousand, two dollars per thousand;

"On cigars valued at over ten and not over twenty dollars per thousand, two dollars and fifty cents per thousand; "On cigars, valued at over twenty dollars per thousand, three dollars and fifty cents per thousand" (Page 464)

Chap. CLXXIII.—*An Act to provide Internal Revenue to support the Government, to pay Interest on the Public Debt, and for other Purposes.* June 30, 1864. . . .

MANUFACTURES, ARTICLES, AND PRODUCTS.
SPECIFIC AND AD VALOREM DUTY.

"On cigars, valued at over five dollars and not over fifteen dollars per thousand, eight dollars per thousand.

"On cigars, valued at over fifteen dollars and not over thirty dollars per thousand, fifteen dollars per thousand, fifteen dollars per pound.

"On cigars valued at over thirty dollars per thousand and not over forty-five dollars, twenty-five dollars per thousand.

"On cigars, at over forty-five dollars per thousand, forty dollars per thousand, and the valuation of cigars herein mentioned shall in all cases be the value of the cigars exclusive of the tax." (Page 270)

Chap. CLXXIII.—*An Act to provide Internal Revenue to support the Government, to pay Interest on the Public Debt, and for other Purposes.* June 30, 1864. . . .
MANUFACTURES, ARTICLES, AND PRODUCTS.
SPECIFIC AND AD VALOREM DUTY.
"On all furniture, or other articles made of wood, sold in the rough or unfinished, a duty of five per centum ad valorem: *Provided,* That all furniture, or other articles made of wood, previously assessed, and a duty paid thereon, shall be assessed a duty of five per centum ad valorem upon the increased value only thereof when sold in a finished condition." (Page 267)

Chap. CLXXIII.—*An Act to provide Internal Revenue to support the Government, to pay Interest on the Public Debt, and for other Purposes.* June 30, 1864. . . .
MANUFACTURES, ARTICLES, AND PRODUCTS.
SPECIFIC AND AD VALOREM DUTY.
"On brick, draining tiles, and earthern [sic] and stone water-pipes, a duty of three per centum ad valorem." (Page 267)

Chap. CLXXIII.—*An Act to provide Internal Revenue to support the Government, to pay Interest on the Public Debt, and for other Purposes.* June 30, 1864. . . .
MANUFACTURES, ARTICLES, AND PRODUCTS.
SPECIFIC AND AD VALOREM DUTY.
"On artificial mineral waters, soda waters, sarsaparilla water, and all beverages used for like purposes, sold in bottles, or from fountains, or otherwise, and not otherwise provided for, a duty of five per centum ad valorem." (Page 267)

Chap. CLXXIII.—*An Act to provide Internal Revenue to support the Government, to pay Interest on the Public Debt, and for other Purposes.* June 30, 1864. . . .
MANUFACTURES, ARTICLES, AND PRODUCTS.
SPECIFIC AND AD VALOREM DUTY.
"On stoves and hollow-ware and casting of iron exceeding ten pounds in weight for each casting, not otherwise provided for, a duty of three dollars per ton." (Page 268)

Miscellaneous: Eating House

Asa Booher (1810-1866), Kansas City (also Retail Liquor Dealer)

Eating Houses in the Internal Revenue Act

Chapter CXIX.—An Act to provide Internal Revenue to support the Government and to pay Interest on the Public Debt. Approved July 1, 1862.
LICENSES.

"Sec. 64. *And be it further enacted,* That on and after the first day of August, eighteen hundred and sixty-two, for each license granted the sum herewith stated shall be respectively and annually paid. Any number of persons carrying on such business in copartnership may transact such business at such place under such license, and not otherwise." (Page 455)

"12. Eating-houses shall pay ten dollars for each license. Every place where food or refreshments of any kind are provided for casual visitors and sold for consumption therein, shall be regarded as an eating-house under this act. But the keeper of any eating-house having taken out a license therefor shall not be required to take out a license as a confectioner, anything in this act to the contrary notwithstanding. (Page 457)

"Sec. 65. *And be it further enacted,* That where the annual gross receipts or sales of any apothecaries, confectioners, eating-houses, tobacconists, or retail dealers, shall not exceed the sum of one thousand dollars, such apothecaries, confectioners, eating-houses, and retail dealers shall not be required to take out or pay for license, anything in this act to the contrary notwithstanding; the amount or estimated amount of such annual sales to be ascertained or estimated in such manner as the Commissioner of Internal Revenue shall prescribe, and so of all other annual sales or receipts, where the rate of the license is graduated by the amount of sales or receipts." (Page 459)

Chapter LXXIV.—An Act to amend an Act entitled "An Act to provide Internal Revenue to support the Government and to pay Interest on the Public Debt," approved July first, eighteen hundred and sixty-two, and for other Purposes. Approved March 3, 1863.

"That section sixty-four be, and hereby is, further amended by adding, at the end thereof, the following paragraphs: . . .

"Forty-three. Retail dealers in liquors shall pay twenty dollars for each license. Every person other than a distiller or brewer, who shall sell or offer for sale any distilled spirits, fermented liquors, or wine of any description, in quantities of three gallons or less, and whose annual sales do not exceed twenty-five thousand dollars, shall be regarded as a retail dealer in liquors under this law; but nothing herein contained shall authorize the sale of any spirits, liquors, wines or malt liquors to be drank on the premises: *Provided,* That no person licensed to keep a hotel, inn, or tavern, shall be allowed to sell any liquors to be taken off the premises, and no person licensed to keep an eating-house shall be allowed to sell spiritous [sic] or vinous liquors. And no person who has taken out a license to keep a hotel, inn, tavern, or eating-house shall be required to take out a license as a tobacconist because of any tobacco or cigars furnished in the usual course of business as a keeper of a hotel, inn, tavern, or eating-house." (Page 716)

Chap. CLXXIII.—*An Act to provide Internal Revenue to support the Government, to pay Interest on the Public Debt, and for other Purposes.* June 30, 1864. . . .

"Sec. 79. *And be it further enacted,* That there shall be paid annually for each license granted, the sum herein stated, respectively. Any number of persons, except lawyers, conveyancers, claim agents, physicians, surgeons, dentists, cattle brokers, horse-dealers, and peddlers, carrying on such business in copartnership, may transact such business at the place specified in their license, and not otherwise, that is to say:— . . .

"Twenty-one. Eating-houses shall pay ten dollars for each license. Every place where food or refreshments of any kind, not including spirits, wines, ale, beer, or other malt liquors, are provided for casual visitors and sold for consumption therein, shall be regarded as an eating-house under this act. But the keeper of an eating-house, having taken out a license therefore, shall not be required to take out a license as a confectioner, anything in this act to the contra[r]y notwithstanding." (Page 254)

"Sec. 80. *And be it further enacted,* That where the annual gross receipts or sales of any apothecaries, confectioners, eating-houses, tobacconists, or retail dealers, except retail dealers in spirituous and malt liquors, shall not exceed the sum of one thousand dollars, such apothecaries, confectioners, eating-houses, tobacconists, and retail dealers shall not be required to take out or pay for license, anything in this act to the contrary notwithstanding; the amount or estimated amount of such annual sales to be ascertained or estimated in such manner as the commissioner of internal revenue shall prescribe, and so of all other annual sales or receipts, where the rate of the license is graduated by the amount of sales or receipts; and where the amount of the license or the rate has been increased, or is liable to be increased, by law above the amount of any existing license to any person, firm, or company, or has been understated or under-estimated, such person, firm, or company shall be again assessed and pay the amount of such increase, which shall be indorsed on the original license, which shall thereafter be held good and sufficient. (Pages 257-258)

Miscellaneous: Mail Contractor

Capt. Preston Roberts (1825-1898), Independence

Miscellaneous: Stone Cutter

Robert Turner Wilson (1813-1898), Kansas City

Miscellaneous: Tanner

John McDonald (1830-?), Kansas City

Tanner in the Internal Revenue Act

Chap. CLXXIII.—*An Act to provide Internal Revenue to support the Government, to pay Interest on the Public Debt, and for other Purposes.* June 30, 1864. . . .
MANUFACTURES, ARTICLES, AND PRODUCTS.
SPECIFIC AND AD VALOREM DUTY.
"On goat, calf, kid, sheep, horse, hog, and dog skins, curried or finished, a duty of five per centum ad valorem . . .
"On leather of all descriptions, tanned or partially tanned, in the rough, a duty of five per centum ad valorem.

"On leather of all descriptions, tanned or partially tanned, in the rough, a duty of five per centum ad valorem." (Page 269)

Peddlers

Thomas Forbes (1822/23-?), Kansas City (also Manufacturer (Lime and Bricks)
James Johnson (?-?), Kaw Township

Peddlers in the Internal Revenue Act

Chapter CXIX.—An Act to provide Internal Revenue to support the Government and to pay Interest on the Public Debt. Approved July 1, 1862.
    LICENSES.
    "Sec. 64. *And be it further enacted,* That on and after the first day of August, eighteen hundred and sixty-two, for each license granted the sum herewith stated shall be respectively and annually paid. Any number of persons carrying on such business in copartnership may transact such business at such place under such license, and not otherwise." (Page 455)
    "27. Peddlers shall be classified and rated as follows, to wit: when traveling with more than two horses, the first class, and shall pay twenty dollars for each license; when traveling with two horses, the second class, and shall pay fifteen dollars for each license; when traveling with one horse, the third class, and shall pay ten dollars for each license; when traveling on foot, the fourth class, and shall pay five dollars for each license. Any person, except persons peddling newspapers, bibles, or religious tracts, who sells or offers to sell, at retail, goods, wares, or other commodities, traveling from place to place, in the street, or through different parts of the country, shall be regarded a peddler under this act: *Provided,* That any peddler who sells, or offers to sell, dry goods, foreign and domestic, by one or more original packages or pieces, at one time, to the same person or persons, as aforesaid, shall pay fifty dollars for each license. And any person who peddles jewelry shall pay twenty-five dollars for each license: *Provided,* That manufacturers and producers of agricultural tools and implements, garden seeds, stoves, and hollow ware, brooms, wooden ware, and powder, delivering and selling at wholesale any of said articles, by themselves or their authorized agents at places other than the place of manufacture, shall not be required, for any sale thus made, to take out any additional license therefore. (Page 458)

Chap. CLXXIII.—*An Act to provide Internal Revenue to support the Government, to pay Interest on the Public Debt, and for other Purposes.* June 30, 1864. . . .
    "Sec. 79. *And be it further enacted,* That there shall be paid annually for each license granted, the sum herein stated, respectively. Any number of persons, except lawyers, conveyancers, claim agents, physicians, surgeons, dentists, cattle brokers, horse-dealers, and peddlers, carrying on such business in copartnership, may transact such business at the place specified in their license, and not otherwise, that is to say:— . . .
    "Thirty-two. Peddlers shall be classified and rated as follows, to wit: when traveling with more than two horses, or mules, the first class, and shall pay fifty dollars for each license; when traveling with two horses, or mules, the second class, and shall pay twenty-five dollars for each

license; when traveling with one horse, or mule, the third class, and shall pay fifteen dollars for each license; when traveling on foot, the fourth class, and shall pay ten dollars for each license. Any person, except persons peddling only newspapers, Bibles, or religious tracts, who sells or offers to sell, at retail, goods, wares, or other commodities, traveling from place to place, in the street, or through different parts of the country, shall be regarded a peddler under this act: *Provided,* That any peddler who sells, or offers to sell, dry goods, foreign and domestic, by one or more original packages or pieces, at one time, to the same person or persons, shall pay fifty dollars for each license. And any person who peddles jewelry shall pay fifty dollars for each license: *Provided, further,* That manufacturers and producers of agricultural tools and implements, garden-seeds, stoves, and hollow ware, brooms, wooden ware, and powder, delivering and selling at wholesale any of said articles, by themselves or their authorized agents, at places other than the place of manufacture, shall not be required, for any sale thus made, to take out any additional license therefore: *Provided, further,* That nothing contained in this paragraph shall authorize the sale of wine, spirits, or malt liquors." (Page 255)

Photographers

Joseph P. Babbitt (ca. 1831-1888/1900), Kansas City
Solomon Madison Eby (1810/11-1886), Kansas City
Egbert Freeland Russell (1826-1871), Kansas City

[For a comprehensive directory of the various 19th century photographers in and around Kansas City, consult James A. Tharp's forthcoming compilation tentatively titled, *Photographers of the Kansas City, Missouri, Region, 1859-1920.* (Kansas City, Mo.: The Orderly Pack Rat, 2024).]

Photographers in the Internal Revenue Act

Chapter CXIX.—An Act to provide Internal Revenue to support the Government and to pay Interest on the Public Debt. Approved July 1, 1862.
    LICENSES.
    "Sec. 64. *And be it further enacted,* That on and after the first day of August, eighteen hundred and sixty-two, for each license granted the sum herewith stated shall be respectively and annually paid. Any number of persons carrying on such business in copartnership may transact such business at such place under such license, and not otherwise." (Page 455)
    "30. Photographers shall pay ten dollars for each license when the receipts do not exceed five hundred dollars; when over five hundred dollars and under one thousand dollars, fifteen dollars; when over one .thousand dollars, twenty-five dollars. Any person or persons who make for sale photographs, ambrotypes, daguerreotypes, or pictures on glass, metal, or paper, by the actionof light, shall be regarded a photographer under this act. (Pages 458-259)

Chap. CLXXIII.—*An Act to provide Internal Revenue to support the Government, to pay Interest on the Public Debt, and for other Purposes.* June 30, 1864. . . .
    "Sec. 79. *And be it further enacted,* That there shall be paid annually for each license granted, the sum herein stated, respectively. Any number of persons, except lawyers,

conveyancers, claim agents, physicians, surgeons, dentists, cattle brokers, horse-dealers, and peddlers, carrying on such business in copartnership, may transact such business at the place specified in their license, and not otherwise, that is to say:— . . .

"Thirty-four. Photographers shall pay ten dollars for each license when the receipts do not exceed five hundred dollars; when over five hundred dollars and under one thousand dollars, fifteen dollars; when over one thousand dollars, twenty-five dollars. Any person or persons who make for sale photographs, ambrotypes, daguerreotypes, or pictures, by the action of light, shall be regarded a photographer under this act." (Page 255)

Physicians, Surgeons, and Dentists

Beginning in August 1862, Congress required that physicians, surgeons, and dentists pay ten dollars annually for a license to practice. For purposes of taxation, physicians, surgeons, and dentists, as the case may be, were defined as "every person (except apothecaries) whose business it is, for fee and reward, to prescribe remedies or perform surgical operations for the cure of any bodily disease or ailing." Physicians practicing together in partnership required only a single license and licensed physicians were allowed to practice both inside and outside the tax assessment district of their license.

Twenty-nine physicians were licensed in Jackson County, Missouri, during the Civil War—one at an unspecified location in the county, one in Hickman's Mills, two in Sibley, three in Westport, four in Independence, and eighteen in Kansas City.

John J. Armstrong (1795-1869), Independence
Peter Arnoldia (1818-1876), Kansas City
Joseph Oliver Boggs (1808-1889), Westport (also licensed Apothecary)
James Terrell Brown (1827-1887), Sibley & Independence
David A. Bryant (1828-1914), Hickman's Mills
John W. Bryant (1816-1902), Kansas City & Independence
David Y. Chalfant (1830/31-1883), Kansas City
 [His widow was a Civil War pensioner]
Joseph William Chew (1812-1883), Kansas City
Asa Farrar (1809/10-1890), Independence
Joseph Ganghofer (ca. 1817-?), Kansas City (also licensed Retail Liquor Dealer)
 (early German immigrant)
John E. Goodson (1819-1892), Jackson County
Henry Foote Hereford (1827-1900), Westport
Peter Hinters/Hinterschitt (1827-1877), Independence
 (also licensed Insurance Agent, Manufacturer, and Retail Dealer)
 (early German immigrant)
Benjamin Marlin Jewett (1810-1879), Kansas City
Thomas Bryan Lester (1824-1888), Kansas City
 (also licensed Retail Liquor Dealer and Wholesale Liquor Dealer)
Johnston Lykins (1800-1876), Kansas City
Charles Edward Miner (1823-1873), Kansas City

Joel T. Morris (1822-1872), Kansas City (also licensed Retail Liquor Dealer)
George Washington Neville (1821-1904), Kansas City
James Wilson "John" Parker (1822-1907), Westport
Micajah G. Pendleton (1799-1876), Kansas City
Andrew J. Pierce (1832-1896), Kansas City
Erasmus Darwin Ralph (1832-?), Kansas City
Leopold C. "Leo" Saalborn (1819-1892), Kansas City
     (also licensed Retail Liquor Dealer) (early German immigrant)
William Julius Schaerff (1812/13-1881), Kansas City (early German immigrant)
Louis A. Schoen (1831-1881), Kansas City
Nathan M. Smith (1825-1898), Sibley
Leo Twyman (1799-1872), Independence
Joseph Madison Wood (1810-1888), Kansas City

[For a comprehensive roster of graduates from Kansas City's various 19th century colleges of health sciences, consult James A. Tharp's compilation, *Colleges of Medicine, Dentistry & Pharmacy, Kansas City, Missouri: Names of 3400 Graduates, 1871-1905.* (Kansas City, Mo.: The Orderly Pack Rat, 2013).]

(See *Statutes at Large of the United States of America* 12 (1863) 459, 727; and 13 (1864) 257.)

Physicians, Surgeons, and Dentists in the Internal Revenue Act

Chapter CXIX.—An Act to provide Internal Revenue to support the Government and to pay Interest on the Public Debt. Approved July 1, 1862.

LICENSES.

"Sec. 64. *And be it further enacted,* That on and after the first day of August, eighteen hundred and sixty-two, for each license granted the sum herewith stated shall be respectively and annually paid. Any number of persons carrying on such business in copartnership may transact such business at such place under such license, and not otherwise." (Page 455)

"32. Physicians, surgeons, and dentists shall pay ten dollars for each license. Every person (except apothecaries) whose business it is, for fee and reward, to prescribe remedies or perform surgical operations for the cure of any bodily disease or ailing, shall be deemed a physician, surgeon, or dentist, as the case may be, within the meaning of this act. (Page 459)

"Sec. 66. *And be it further enacted,* That nothing contained in the preceding sections of this act, laying duties on licenses, shall be construed to require a license for the sale of goods, wares, and merchandise made or produced and sold by the manufacturer or producer at the manufactory or place where the same is made or produced; to vintners who sell, at the place where the same is made, wine of their own growth; nor to apothecaries, as to wines or spirituous liquors which they use exclusively in the preparation or making up of medicines for sick, lame, or diseased persons; nor shall the provisions of paragraph number twenty-seven extend to physicians who keep on hand medicines solely for the purpose of making up their own prescriptions for their own patients." (Page 459)

Chapter LXXIV.—An Act to amend an Act entitled "An Act to provide Internal Revenue to support the Government and to pay Interest on the Public Debt," approved July first, eighteen hundred and sixty-two, and for other Purposes. Approved March 3, 1863.

"Sec. 25. *And be it further enacted,* That no auctioneer shall be authorized, by virtue of his license as such auctioneer, to sell any goods or other property in any other district than that in which the license shall have been granted, but lawyers, physicians, surgeons, or dentists, having taken out al license as such, shall not be required to take out any additional license in consequence of practicing their profession within or beyond the limits of the district where licensed." (Page 727)

Chap. CLXXIII.—*An Act to provide Internal Revenue to support the Government, to pay Interest on the Public Debt, and for other Purposes.* June 30, 1864. . . .

"Sec. 79. *And be it further enacted,* That there shall be paid annually for each license granted, the sum herein stated, respectively. Any number of persons, except lawyers, conveyancers, claim agents, physicians, surgeons, dentists, cattle brokers, horse-dealers, and peddlers, carrying on such business in copartnership, may transact such business at the place specified in their license, and not otherwise, that is to say:— . . .

"Forty-four. Physicians, surgeons, and dentists shall pay ten dollars for each license. Every person (except apothecaries) whose business it is, for fee and reward, to prescribe remedies or perform surgical operations for the cure of any bodily disease or ailing, shall be deemed a physician, surgeon, or dentist, as the case may be, within the meaning of this act." (Page 257) (Statutes at Large of the United States of America 13 (1864) 257.)

Real Estate Agents/Conveyancers

John Reed Balis (1834-1914), Kansas City
    (also Retail Dealer: Books, Stationery, Fancy Goods)
Abram Comingo (1820-1889), Independence (also Lawyer)
Maj. Samuel D. Vaughan (1817/18-1874), Kansas City (also Commercial Broker)

Real Estate Agents/Conveyancers in the Internal Revenue Act

Chap. CLXXIII.—*An Act to provide Internal Revenue to support the Government, to pay Interest on the Public Debt, and for other Purposes.* June 30, 1864. . . .

"Sec. 79. *And be it further enacted,* That there shall be paid annually for each license granted, the sum herein stated, respectively. Any number of persons, except lawyers, conveyancers, claim agents, physicians, surgeons, dentists, cattle brokers, horse-dealers, and peddlers, carrying on such business in copartnership, may transact such business at the place specified in their license, and not otherwise, that is to say:— . . .

"Twenty-five. Real-estate agents shall pay ten dollars for each license. Every person whose business it is to sell, or offer for sale, real estate for others, or to rent houses, stores, or other buildings or real estate, or to collect rent for others, shall be regarded as a real-estate agent under this act." (Page 254)

Chap. CLXXIII.—*An Act to provide Internal Revenue to support the Government, to pay Interest on the Public Debt, and for other Purposes.* June 30, 1864. . . .

"Sec. 79. *And be it further enacted,* That there shall be paid annually for each license granted, the sum herein stated, respectively. Any number of persons, except lawyers, conveyancers, claim agents, physicians, surgeons, dentists, cattle brokers, horse-dealers, and peddlers, carrying on such business in copartnership, may transact such business at the place specified in their license, and not otherwise, that is to say:— . . .

"Twenty-six. Conveyancers shall pay ten dollars for each license. Every person, other than one holding a license as a lawyer or claim-agent, whose business it is to draw deeds, bonds, mortgages, wills, writs, or other legal papers, or to examine titles to real estate, shall be regarded a conveyancer under this act." (Page 254)

Rectifiers

John A. Aeuer (1827/28-1882), Kansas City (also Manufacturer (Cigars),
     Retail Liquor Dealer, Wholesale Liquor Dealer) (early German immigrant)
Peter William Ditsch (1821-1891), Kansas City (also Retail Liquor Dealer,
     Wholesale Liquor Dealer) (early German immigrant)
Philip Setzler (1834-1923), Kansas City (also Insurance Agent,
     Billiard Room Keeper, Retail Liquor Dealer, Wholesale Liquor Dealer)
     (early German immigrant)

Rectifiers in the Internal Revenue Act

Chapter CXIX.—An Act to provide Internal Revenue to support the Government and to pay Interest on the Public Debt. Approved July 1, 1862.
LICENSES.
"Sec. 64. *And be it further enacted,* That on and after the first day of August, eighteen hundred and sixty-two, for each license granted the sum herewith stated shall be respectively and annually paid. Any number of persons carrying on such business in copartnership may transact such business at such place under such license, and not otherwise." (Page 455)

"8. Rectifiers shall pay twenty five dollars for each license to rectify any quantity of spirituous liquors, not exceeding five hundred barrels or casks, containing not more than forty gallons to each barrel or cask of liquor so rectified; and twenty-five dollars additional for each additional five hundred such barrels, or any fractional part thereof. Every person who rectifies, purifies, or refines spirituous liquors or wines by any process, or mixes distilled spirits, whiskey, brandy, gin, or wine, with any other materials for sale under the name of whiskey, rum, brandy, gin, wine, or any other name or names, shall be regarded as a rectifier under this act. (Page 456)

Chap. CLXXIII.—*An Act to provide Internal Revenue to support the Government, to pay Interest on the Public Debt, and for other Purposes.* June 30, 1864. . . .

"Sec. 79. *And be it further enacted,* That there shall be paid annually for each license granted, the sum herein stated, respectively. Any number of persons, except lawyers, conveyancers, claim agents, physicians, surgeons, dentists, cattle brokers, horse-dealers, and

peddlers, carrying on such business in copartnership, may transact such business at the place specified in their license, and not otherwise, that is to say:— . . .

"Eighteen. Rectifiers shall pay twenty-five dollars for each license to rectify any quantity of spirituous liquors, not exceeding five hundred barrels, packages, or casks, containing not more than forty gallons to each barrel, package, or cask of liquor so rectified; and twenty-five dollars additional for each additional five hundred such barrels, packages, or casks, or any fractional part thereof. Every person, firm, or corporation, who rectifies, purifies, or refines spirituous liquors or wines by any process, or mixes distilled spirits, whiskey, brandy, gin, or wine, with any materials for sale under the name of whiskey, rum, brandy, gin, wine, or any other name, shall be regarded as a rectifier under this act." (Page 253)

Retail Dealer: Books and Stationery

John Reed Balis (1834-1914), Kansas City (also Real Estate Agent)
Matthew "Matt" Foster (1832-1893), Kansas City
John M. Hicks (1836/37-?), Kansas City

Retail Dealer: Boots and Shoes

Johannes Phillip/Philipp Becker (1832-1913), Westport (also Manufacturers:
        Boots and Shoes) (early German immigrant)
William Gabel (1835-1919), Kansas City (early German immigrant)
Frank/Franz Langsenkamp (1830-1866), Kansas City [boots & shoes]
        (early German immigrant)
Henry Schoepf (1824/25-1883/84), Westport [boots & shoes]
        (early German immigrant)

Retail Dealer: Cigars

Peter Hinters/Hinterschitt (1827-1877), Independence (also Physician)
        (early German immigrant)
Caspar/Kaspar H. Mohr (1825-1898), Kansas City (also Manufacturer: Cigars)
        (early German immigrant)
Wendell/Wendelin Loesch (1818-1865), Kansas City (also Billiard Room Keeper)
        (early German immigrant) [His widow was a Civil War pensioner]

Retail Dealer: Clothing

Herman/Hermann Ganz (1833-1920), Kansas City
Emil Reis (1829- post 1910 Pennsylvania), Kansas City

Retail Dealer: Dry Goods

Oscar H. Cogswell (1820-1881), Independence (also Livery Stable Keeper)
Morris J. Friedsam (ca. 1841-1923), Kansas City (also Retail Liquor Dealer)
Dr. James Griffith (1801-1884), Kansas City
William French Bayliss Grigsby (1834-1922), Kansas City & Westport
Clinton H. Moore (1831/32-?) and Company, Kansas City
Carey H. Nall (1835-1875) and Company, Kansas City
James A. Walker (1831-1900), Kansas City (also Butcher)

Retail Dealer: Flour

Perry G. Brock (1831-1900), Independence
William Dodson Oldham (1833-1897), Kansas City (also Butcher)

Retail Dealer: Furniture

Jacob Hartel/Haertel (1822-1882), Kansas City (early German immigrant)
James C. Kevill (1832-1902), Kansas City (also Auctioneers)
Henry Carl Sager (1815-1886), Westport (also Manufacturers: Furniture)
     (early German immigrant)
Edward Stine (1833-1917), Kansas City (also Manufacturers: Furniture)
James P. Turner (1835-1879), Kansas City (also Auctioneers)
Reuben Wallace (1810-1888), Independence (also Wholesale Dealer: Furniture)

Retail Dealer: General Merchandise

Rev. Joab Mitchell Bernard (1800-1879), Westport
George Davis Fogelsong (1823-1891), Westport
John McCoy (1816-1904), Independence
William McCoy (1813-1900), Independence
John W. Wilson (1805-1879), Independence (also Hotel Keeper)

Retail Dealer: Groceries

Henry Beatty Conwell (1831/32-1890), Kansas City
    (also Wholesale Dealers: Groceries)
Charles Dwyer (1826/27-1890), Kansas City (also Retail Liquor Dealers)
Daniel Ensign (1826/27-1898), Kansas City (also Retail Liquor Dealers)
Charles/Karl Jacob Frank (1835-?), Kansas City (also Retail Liquor Dealers)
    (early German immigrant)
James S. Giles (1834/35-?), Kansas City (also Wholesale Dealers: Groceries)
John Tinsley Pendleton (1829-1885), Independence
    (also Wholesale Dealers: Groceries)
Henry Rieke (1830/31-1898), Kansas City (also Retail Liquor Dealers)
    (early German Immigrant) [was a Civil War pensioner]
Dr. Nicolas Joseph Schoen (1828-1910), Westport (early German immigrant)
G. A. Henry Wagner (1831-?), Long and Wagoner [sic.], Kansas City
    (early German immigrant)
Isaiah P. Walker (1826-1886) and Company, Kansas City
    (also Wholesale Liquor Dealer)

Retail Dealer: Hardware

Hiram W. Cooper (1834-1900), Kansas City (also Wholesale Dealers: Hardware)
Frederick Peet Flagler (1832-1906) and Company, Kansas City
    (also Wholesale Dealers: Hardware)
William Henry Gregg (1831-1916), Cooper and Gregg, Kansas City

Retail Dealer: Jewelry and Watches

Albert L. Beatty (1812-1886), Independence
Frederick William Esslinger (1818-1898), Kansas City (early German immigrant)
John Fischell (1824/25-1865), Independence (early German immigrant)
Henry/Heinrich Reinhard Seeger (1824-1897), Kansas City
    (early German immigrant)

Retail Dealer: Leather and Hides

James Denison/Dennison (1818-1899), Kansas City (also Butcher)
Anthony/Anton Philip Sauer (1826-1879), Kansas City (early German immigrant)

Retail Dealer: Lumber

Asa Beebe Cross (1826-1894), Kansas City (Kansas City's first architect)
John S. Duncan (1834-1873), Kansas City
Asa Maddox (1838-1897), Kansas City (also Wholesale Dealer (Lumber))

Retail Dealer: Meat

James M. Bryant (1826-1905), Independence (also Butchers)
Joseph Butcher (1819/20-?), Kansas City (also Butchers)
Gilbert G. Crandall (1834/35-?), Kansas City (also Butchers)
Hadley A. Head (ca. 1805-1872), Independence (also Butchers)
Alexander "Alex" Street (1821-1877), Kansas City (also Butchers)

Retail Dealer: Miscellaneous

William Carroll (1813-1874), Kansas City [china & glass]
Mrs. James P. Linderman (Sarah Ann Yelton) (1829-1889), Kansas City
        [millinery & fancy goods]

Retail Dealer: Outfitting Merchandise

[--?--]Gloom (?-?), Independence
Joseph Chambers "Uncle Joe" Irwin (1818-1900), Independence

Retail Dealer: Saddlery

Jacob R. Gerhart (1840-1903), Westport (also Manufacturer (Saddlery))
        (early German immigrant)
William/Wilhelm M. Long (1830-1897), Kansas City (also Confectioner)
        (early German immigrant)
Isaac W. McDonald (1823-1901), Kansas City (also Manufacturer (Saddlery))
Richard D. Smith (1835-1921), Kansas City (also Manufacturer (Saddlery))
Salathiel S. Smith (1831-?), Kansas City (also Manufacturer (Saddlery))

Retail Dealer: Tinware and Stoves

David Gilbert Blair (1821-1911), Kansas City
    (also Manufacturer (Tinware and Stoves)
Chauncey Wilmont Fairman (1832-1892), Kansas City
    (also Manufacturer (Tinware and Stoves)
Lucien Whitman Pollard (1823-1890), Kansas City
    (also Manufacturer (Tinware and Stoves)
John Wesley Thompson (1828-1867), Kansas City
    (also Manufacturer (Tinware and Stoves)

Retail Dealer: Unidentified Merchandise

John T. Bartleson (1834-1896), Kansas City
John O. Buchanan (1811-1875), Independence
James Blake Hassett (1811/12-?), Sibley
Henry L. Huer/Hugher (1834/35-?), Kansas City [unidentified merchandise]
    (also Wholesale Liquor Dealer) (early German immigrant)
Jacob Keller (1785/86-1867), Independence [unidentified merchandise]
    (also Retail Liquor Dealers) (early German immigrant)
Daniel/David Kennedy (1831/32-?), Kansas City [unidentified merchandise]
    (also Retail Liquor Dealers)
Jedediah E. McKenzie (1824-1892), Kansas City [unidentified merchandise]
    (also Cattle Broker)
James H. Meador (1817-1891), Independence
Leonard Mettee (1839-1881), Kansas City [unidentified merchandise]
    (also Livery Stable Keeper)
John C. Morris (1816-1879), Westport
[--?--]Payne (?-?), Kansas City [unidentified merchandise] (also Auctioneer)
J. H. Rumberg (?-?), Independence
Moses Sampson (1812-1895), Independence [unidentified merchandise]
    (also Retail Liquor Dealers) (early German immigrant)
Isaac Shoenbrun (?-?), Kansas City
George W. Toler (1816-1866), Kansas City [unidentified merchandise]
    (also Commercial Broker)

Retail Dealers in the Internal Revenue Act

Chapter CXIX.—An Act to provide Internal Revenue to support the Government and to pay Interest on the Public Debt. Approved July 1, 1862.
    LICENSES.
    "Sec. 64. *And be it further enacted,* That on and after the first day of August, eighteen hundred and sixty-two, for each license granted the sum herewith stated shall be respectively and

annually paid. Any number of persons carrying on such business in copartnership may transact such business at such place under such license, and not otherwise." (Page 455)

"5. Retail dealers shall pay ten dollars for each license. Every person whose business or occupation is to sell or offer to sell groceries, or any goods, wares, or merchandise, or foreign or domestic production, in less quantities than a whole original piece or package at one time, to the same person, (not including wines, spirituous or malt liquors, but not excluding drugs, medicines, cigars, snuff or tobacco,) shall be regarded as a retail dealer under this act." (Page 455)

"Sec. 65. *And be it further enacted,* That where the annual gross receipts or sales of any apothecaries, confectioners, eating-houses, tobacconists, or retail dealers, shall not exceed the sum of one thousand dollars, such apothecaries, confectioners, eating-houses, and retail dealers shall not be required to take out or pay for license, anything in this act to the contrary notwithstanding; the amount or estimated amount of such annual sales to be ascertained or estimated in such manner as the Commissioner of Internal Revenue shall prescribe, and so of all other annual sales or receipts, where the rate of the license is graduated by the amount of sales or receipts." (Page 459)

Chapter LXXIV.—An Act to amend an Act entitled "An Act to provide Internal Revenue to support the Government and to pay Interest on the Public Debt," approved July first, eighteen hundred and sixty-two, and for other Purposes. Approved March 3, 1863.

"That section sixty-four be, and hereby is, further amended by adding, at the end thereof, the following paragraphs: . . .

"Forty. Retail dealers shall pay ten dollars for each license. Every person whose business or occupation it is to sell or offer for sale any goods, wares, or merchandise of foreign or domestic production, not including wines, spiritous [sic] or malt liquors, but not excluding drugs, medicines, cigars, snuff, or tobacco, and whose annual sales exceed one thousand, and do not exceed twenty-five thousand dollars, shall be regarded as a retail dealer under this act." (Page 715)

Chap. CLXXIII.—*An Act to provide Internal Revenue to support the Government, to pay Interest on the Public Debt, and for other Purposes.* June 30, 1864. . . .

"Sec. 79. *And be it further enacted,* That there shall be paid annually for each license granted, the sum herein stated, respectively. Any number of persons, except lawyers, conveyancers, claim agents, physicians, surgeons, dentists, cattle brokers, horse-dealers, and peddlers, carrying on such business in copartnership, may transact such business at the place specified in their license, and not otherwise, that is to say:— . . .

"Three. Retail dealers shall pay ten dollars for each license. Every person whose business or occupation it is to sell or offer for sale any goods, wares, or merchandise of foreign or domestic production, not including spirits, wines, ale, beer, or other malt liquors, and whose annual sales exceed one thousand, and do not exceed twenty-five thousand dollars, shall be regarded as a retail dealer under this act." (Page 251)

"Sec. 80. *And be it further enacted,* That where the annual gross receipts or sales of any apothecaries, confectioners, eating-houses, tobacconists, or retail dealers, except retail dealers in spirituous and malt liquors, shall not exceed the sum of one thousand dollars, such apothecaries, confectioners, eating-houses, tobacconists, and retail dealers shall not be required to take out or pay for license, anything in this act to the contrary notwithstanding; the amount or estimated amount of such annual sales to be ascertained or estimated in such manner as the commissioner of internal revenue shall prescribe, and so of all other annual sales or receipts, where the rate of the license is graduated by the amount of sales or receipts; and where the amount of the license or the rate has been increased, or is liable to be increased, by law above the amount of any existing license to any person, firm, or company, or has been understated or under-estimated, such person, firm, or company shall be again assessed and pay the amount of such increase, which shall be indorsed on the original license, which shall thereafter be held good and sufficient. (Pages 257-258)

Chap. CLXXIII.—*An Act to provide Internal Revenue to support the Government, to pay Interest on the Public Debt, and for other Purposes.* June 30, 1864. . . .
MANUFACTURES, ARTICLES, AND PRODUCTS.
SPECIFIC AND AD VALOREM DUTY.
"On goat, calf, kid, sheep, horse, hog, and dog skins, curried or finished, a duty of five per centum ad valorem . . .
"On leather of all descriptions, tanned or partially tanned, in the rough, a duty of five per centum ad valorem.
"On leather of all descriptions, tanned or partially tanned, in the rough, a duty of five per centum ad valorem." (Page 269)

Retail Liquor Dealers

John C. Adkins (1836-1866), Kansas City (also Apothecaries)
John A. Aeuer (1827/28-1882), Kansas City (also Rectifiers)
   (early German immigrant)
James C. Beckham (1808-1892), Independence (also Apothecaries)
Asa Booher (1810-1866), Kansas City
   (also Miscellaneous—Eating House Keeper)
Henry Harrison Camp (1838-1914), Kansas City
Phillip Conboy (1833-1905), Westport
Peter William Ditsch (1821-1891), Kansas City (also Rectifiers)
   (early German immigrant)
Michael Diveley (1828-1901, Kansas City (also Wholesale Liquor Dealers)
George Dougherty (1833/34-?), Kansas City
Charles Dwyer (1826/7-1890), Kansas City (also Retail Dealer: Groceries)
Jacob H. Early/Earley (1816-1885), Westport
Daniel Ensign (1826/27-1898), Kansas City (also Retail Dealer: Groceries)
Charles/Karl Jacob Frank (1835-?), Kansas City (also Retail Dealer: Groceries)
   (early German immigrant)
John Thornton Frazier (1819-1900), Westport (also Auctioneer)
Morris J. Friedsam (ca. 1841-1923), Kansas City (also Retail Dealer: Dry Goods)
Joseph Anton Fritz (1828/29-1881) (also Manufacturer: Boots and Shoes)
   (early German immigrant)

Civil War Era Federal Income Taxpayers

Dr. Joseph Ganghofer (ca. 1817-?), Kansas City (also Physicians)
	(early German immigrant)
Thomas H. Green (1837-1916), Kansas City (also Wholesale Liquor Dealers)
Alexander L. Harris (1820-1898), Kansas City (also Billiard Room Keeper)
Meredith B. Hedges (1815-1902), Kansas City (also Billiard Room Keeper)
Andrew Christian Heinzelmann (1836/37-?), Kansas City   (early German immigrant)
Frederick "Fred/Fritz" Hollingshausen (1830-1905), Kansas City
	(early German immigrant) [was a Civil War pensioner]
[--?--] Hough (?-?), Ross and Hough, Westport
Henry L. Huer/Hugher (1834/35-?), Kansas City (also Wholesale Liquor Dealers)
	(early German immigrant)
Philip Jacob (1826/27-?), Kansas City
	(early German immigrant)
Mrs. C. Jacob Jaiser (Augusta Keck) (1818-1893), Kansas City
	(early German immigrant)
Charles Esmond Kearney (1820-1898), Kansas City
	(also Wholesale Liquor Dealers)
Jacob Keller (1785/86-1867), Independence
	(also Retail Dealer [unidentified merchandise])
	(early German immigrant)
Harrison Ray Kelso (1813/14-?), Westport (also Billiard Room Keeper)
Daniel/David Kennedy (1831/32-?), Kansas City
	(also Retail Dealer [unidentified merchandise])
Benjamin "Ben" Kerr (?-?), Kansas City
Frederick "Fred/Fritz" Klaber (1830-1866), Westport
	(also Manufacturer (Wagons and Ox Yokes))
	(early German immigrant)
Bernard/Bernhardt Knapp (1831-1900), Kansas City
	(early German immigrant)
Thomas Bryan Lester (1824-1888), Kansas City (also Physicians)
Wendel/Wendelin Loesch (1818-1865), Kansas City (also Billiard Room Keeper)
	(early German immigrant) [was a Civil War pensioner]
Adam Long (1836-1910), Kansas City (also Wholesale Liquor Dealers)
John/Johannes Long (1846-1908), Kansas City (also Billiard Room Keeper)
	(early German immigrant)
George G. Messerschmidt (1825-1868), Kansas City (also Brewer)
	(early German immigrant)
Joel T. Morris (1822-1872), Kansas City (also Physicians)
William D. Oldham (1833-1897), Kansas City (also Butcher)
Gaudenzio/Gaudenzie Soldani Raffaletti (1819/20-1866), Kansas City
	(early German immigrant)
Bartholomew Reardon (?-1868), Kansas City
	[His widow was a Civil War pensioner]
William S. Reed (1837/38-?), Kansas City (also Billiard Room Keeper)
Henry Rieke (1830/31-ca. 1898), Kansas City (also Retail Dealer: Groceries)
	(early German immigrant) [was a Civil War pensioner]

John A. Rooney (1829/30-ca. 1879), Kansas City
[--?--] Ross (?-?), Ross and Hough, Westport
Dr. Leopold C. "Leo" Saalborn (1819-1893), Kansas City (also Physicians)
    (early German immigrant)
Moses Sampson (1812-1895), Independence
    (also Retail Dealer [unidentified merchandise]) (early German immigrant)
Dr. Nicolas Joseph Schoen (1828-1910), Westport (also Retail Dealer: Groceries)
    (early German immigrant)
William Scully (1826-1892), Kansas City
Philip Setzler (1834-1923), Kansas City (also Rectifiers)
    (early German immigrant)
William R. Sitzler (1835-1887), Kansas City (also Rectifiers)
    (early German immigrant)
Addison Snell (1832/33-?), Kansas City (also Billiard Room Keeper)
Joseph Sprink (ca. 1831-?), Kansas City
    (early German immigrant)
George Sweeney (1820-1889), Kansas City (also Wholesale Liquor Dealers)
    [His widow was a Civil War pensioner]
John Joseph Thoes (1818-1890), Westport
    (early German immigrant)
G. A. Henry Wagner (1831-?), Kansas City (also Retail Dealer: Groceries)
    (early German immigrant)
Theobald Werry (1826-1879), Westport (also Confectioner)
    (early German immigrant) [His widow was a Civil War pensioner]
Christian "Christ" Wiedenmann (1835-1909), Westport (also Billiard Room Keeper)
    (early German immigrant)
Gustavus Adolphus Wolf (1842-1928), Kansas City (also Wholesale Liquor Dealers)
    (early German immigrant)
Augustus Wolter (?-?), Kansas City (early German immigrant)
George Zentner (1820-1888), Kansas City [was a Civil War pensioner]
    (early German immigrant)

Retail Dealers in Liquors in the Internal Revenue Act

Chapter CXIX.—An Act to provide Internal Revenue to support the Government and to pay Interest on the Public Debt. Approved July 1, 1862.
    LICENSES.
    "Sec. 64. *And be it further enacted,* That on and after the first day of August, eighteen hundred and sixty-two, for each license granted the sum herewith stated shall be respectively and annually paid. Any number of persons carrying on such business in copartnership may transact such business at such place under such license, and not otherwise." (Page 455)
    "4. Retail dealers in liquors, including distilled spirits, fermented liquors, and wines of every description, shall pay twenty dollars for each license. Every person who shall sell or offer for sale such liquors in less quantities than three gallons at one time, to the same purchaser, shall be regarded as a retail dealer in liquors under this act. But this shall not authorize any spirits, liquors, wines, or malt liquors, to be drank on the premises. (Page 455)

Chapter LXXIV.—An Act to amend an Act entitled "An Act to provide Internal Revenue to support the Government and to pay Interest on the Public Debt," approved July first, eighteen hundred and sixty-two, and for other Purposes. Approved March 3, 1863.

"That section sixty-four be, and hereby is, further amended by adding, at the end thereof, the following paragraphs: . . .

"Forty-three. Retail dealers in liquors shall pay twenty dollars for each license. Every person other than a distiller or brewer, who shall sell or offer for sale any distilled spirits, fermented liquors, or wine of any description, in quantities of three gallons or less, and whose annual sales do not exceed twenty-five thousand dollars, shall be regarded as a retail dealer in liquors under this law; but nothing herein contained shall authorize the sale of any spirits, liquors, wines or malt liquors to be drank on the premises: *Provided,* That no person licensed to keep a hotel, inn, or tavern, shall be allowed to sell any liquors to be taken off the premises, and no person licensed to keep an eating-house shall be allowed to sell spiritous [sic] or vinous liquors. And no person who has taken out a license to keep a hotel, inn, tavern, or eating-house shall be required to take out a license as a tobacconist because of any tobacco or cigars furnished in the usual course of business as a keeper of a hotel, inn, tavern, or eating-house." (Page 716)

Chap. CLXXIII.—*An Act to provide Internal Revenue to support the Government, to pay Interest on the Public Debt, and for other Purposes.* June 30, 1864. . . .

"Sec. 79. *And be it further enacted,* That there shall be paid annually for each license granted, the sum herein stated, respectively. Any number of persons, except lawyers, conveyancers, claim agents, physicians, surgeons, dentists, cattle brokers, horse-dealers, and peddlers, carrying on such business in copartnership, may transact such business at the place specified in their license, and not otherwise, that is to say:— . . .

"Five. Retail dealers in liquors shall pay twenty-five dollars for each license. Every person who shall sell or offer for sale foreign or domestic spirits, wines, ale, beer, or other malt liquors in quantities of three gallons or less, or whose annual sales, including all sales of other merchandise, do not exceed twenty-five thousand dollars, shall be regarded as a retail dealer in liquors under this act. But nothing herein contained shall authorize the sale of any spirits, wines, or malt liquors to be drank on the premises." (Page 252)

Stage Coach Lines

Mahlon Cottrill (1797-1864), Kansas City
George Harlan Vickroy (1834—1882), Kansas City

Stage Coach Lines in the Internal Revenue Act

Chap. CLXXIII.—*An Act to provide Internal Revenue to support the Government, to pay Interest on the Public Debt, and for other Purposes.* June 30, 1864. . . .
RAILROADS, STEAMBOATS, FERRY-BOATS, AND BRIDGES.

"Sec. 103. *And be it further enacted,* That every person, firm, company, or corporation owning or possessing, or having the care or management of, any railroad, canal, steamboat, ship, barge, canal-boat, or other vessel, or any stage-coach or other vehicle engaged or employed in the business of transporting passengers or property for hire, or in transporting the mails of the United States, or any canal, the water of which is used for mining purposes, shall be subject to and pay a duty of two and one half per centum upon the gross receipts of such railroad, canal, steamboat, ship, barge, canal-boat, or other vessel, or such stage-coach or other vehicle: *Provided,* That the duty hereby imposed shall not be charged upon receipts for the transportation of persons or property, or mails, between the United States and any foreign port; and any person or persons, firms, companies, or corporations, owning, possessing, or having the care or management of any toll-road, ferry, or bridge, authorized by law to receive toll for the transit of passengers, beasts, carriages, teams, and freight of any description, over such toll-road, ferry, or bridge, shall be subject to and pay a duty of three per centum on the gross amount of all their receipts of every description. But when the gross receipts of any such bridge or toll-road shall not exceed the amount necessarily expended to keep such bridge or road in repair, no tax shall be imposed on such receipts . . . " (Pages 275-276)

Tobacconists

Peter Hinters/Hinterschitt (1827-1877), Independence (also Physician)
    (early German immigrant)
John A. Aeuer (1827/28-1882), Kansas City (also Rectifier)
    (early German immigrant)

Tobacconists in the Internal Revenue Act

Chapter CXIX.—An Act to provide Internal Revenue to support the Government and to pay Interest on the Public Debt. Approved July 1, 1862.
    LICENSES.
    "Sec. 64. *And be it further enacted,* That on and after the first day of August, eighteen hundred and sixty-two, for each license granted the sum herewith stated shall be respectively and annually paid. Any number of persons carrying on such business in copartnership may transact such business at such place under such license, and not otherwise." (Page 455)
    "16. Tobacconists shall pay ten dollars for each license. Any person whose business it is to sell, at retail, cigars, snuff, or tobacco in any form, shall be regarded a tobacconist under this act. But wholesale and retail dealers, and keepers of hotels, inns, taverns, having taken out a license therefore, shall not be required to take out a license as tobacconists, anything in this act to the contrary notwithstanding. (Page 457)
    "Sec. 65. *And be it further enacted,* That where the annual gross receipts or sales of any apothecaries, confectioners, eating-houses, tobacconists, or retail dealers, shall not exceed the sum of one thousand dollars, such apothecaries, confectioners, eating-houses, and retail dealers shall not be required to take out or pay for license, anything in this act to the contrary notwithstanding; the amount or estimated amount of such annual sales to be ascertained or estimated in such manner as the Commissioner of Internal Revenue shall prescribe, and so of all

other annual sales or receipts, where the rate of the license is graduated by the amount of sales or receipts." (Page 459)

Chapter LXXIV.—An Act to amend an Act entitled "An Act to provide Internal Revenue to support the Government and to pay Interest on the Public Debt," approved July first, eighteen hundred and sixty-two, and for other Purposes. Approved March 3, 1863.

"That section sixty-four be, and hereby is, further amended by adding, at the end thereof, the following paragraphs: . . .

"Forty. Retail dealers shall pay ten dollars for each license. Every person whose business or occupation it is to sell or offer for sale any goods, wares, or merchandise of foreign or domestic production, not including wines, spiritous [sic] or malt liquors, but not excluding drugs, medicines, cigars, snuff, or tobacco, and whose annual sales exceed one thousand, and do not exceed twenty-five thousand dollars, shall be regarded as a retail dealer under this act." (Page 715)

Chap. CLXXIII.—*An Act to provide Internal Revenue to support the Government, to pay Interest on the Public Debt, and for other Purposes.* June 30, 1864. . . .

"Sec. 79. *And be it further enacted,* That there shall be paid annually for each license granted, the sum herein stated, respectively. Any number of persons, except lawyers, conveyancers, claim agents, physicians, surgeons, dentists, cattle brokers, horse-dealers, and peddlers, carrying on such business in copartnership, may transact such business at the place specified in their license, and not otherwise, that is to say:— . . .

"Thirty-five. Tobacconists shall pay ten dollars for each license. Any person, firm, or corporation whose business it is to sell, at retail, cigars, snuff, or tobacco in any form, shall be regarded a tobacconist under this act. But wholesale and retail dealers, and keepers of hotels, inns, taverns, and eating-houses, having taken out a license therefore, shall not be required to take out a license as tobacconists, anything in this act to the contrary notwithstanding." (Page 255)

"Sec. 80. *And be it further enacted,* That where the annual gross receipts or sales of any apothecaries, confectioners, eating-houses, tobacconists, or retail dealers, except retail dealers in spirituous and malt liquors, shall not exceed the sum of one thousand dollars, such apothecaries, confectioners, eating-houses, tobacconists, and retail dealers shall not be required to take out or pay for license, anything in this act to the contrary notwithstanding; the amount or estimated amount of such annual sales to be ascertained or estimated in such manner as the commissioner of internal revenue shall prescribe, and so of all other annual sales or receipts, where the rate of the license is graduated by the amount of sales or receipts; and where the amount of the license or the rate has been increased, or is liable to be increased, by law above the amount of any existing license to any person, firm, or company, or has been understated or under-estimated, such person, firm, or company shall be again assessed and pay the amount of such increase, which shall be indorsed on the original license, which shall thereafter be held good and sufficient. (Pages 257-258)

Wholesale Dealer: Dry Goods

John Shannon (1825-1865), Kansas City
Philip Shannon (1829-1866), Kansas City
James A. Walker (1831-1900), Kansas City (also Butcher)

Wholesale Dealer: Flour

William Dodson Oldham (1833-1897), Kansas City (also Butcher)
Presley Gray Wilhite (1833-1880), Kansas City

Wholesale Dealer: Groceries

Henry Beatty Conwell (1831/32-1890), Kansas City
        (also Retail Dealer: Groceries)
John Bragg Drinkard (1831-1869), Kansas City
James S. Giles (1834/35-?), Kansas City (also Retail Dealer: Groceries)
Thomas H. Green (1837-1916), Kansas City (Groceries)
        (also Wholesale Liquor Dealers)
Adam Long (1836-1910), Kansas City (Groceries)
        (also Wholesale Liquor Dealers) (early German immigrant)
John Tinsley Pendleton (1829-1885), Independence
        (also Retail Dealer: Groceries)
George Sweeney (1820-1889), Kansas City (Groceries)
        (also Wholesale Liquor Dealers) [was a Civil War pensioner]
James A. Walker (1831-1900), Kansas City (also Butcher)

Wholesale Dealer: Hardware

William B. Cockrell (1833/34-1871), Kansas City (also Wholesale Liquor Dealer)
Hiram W. Cooper, (1834-1900), Kansas City (also Retail Dealer [Hardware])
Frederick Peet Flagler (1832-1906), Kansas City (also Retail Dealer [Hardware])
Albert Jewett (?-?), Kansas City
Henry Sylvester Ward (?-?), Kansas City

Wholesale Dealer: Miscellaneous

Louis Hammerslough (1835-1903), Kansas City (Clothing)
(also Manufacturer: Clothing) (early German immigrant)
Asa Maddox (1838-1897), Kansas City (lumber) (also Retail Dealer: Lumber)
Reuben Wallace (1810-1888), Independence (furniture)
        (also Retail Dealer [Furniture])

Wholesale Dealer: Unidentified Merchandise

Joseph Smith Chick (1828-1908), Kansas City (also Manufacturer: Cigars)
J. S. Coates (?-?), Giles & Coates, Kansas City
Edward Richard Dennison/Denizen (1841-1884), Kansas City
        (also Retail Dealer: Unidentified Merchandise)
Michael Diveley (1828-1901), Kansas City (also Wholesale Liquor Dealer)
James W. Souneso (?-?), Kansas City
John W. Wilson (1805-1879), Independence (also Hotel Keeper)

Wholesale Dealers in the Internal Revenue Act

Chapter CXIX.—An Act to provide Internal Revenue to support the Government and to pay Interest on the Public Debt. Approved July 1, 1862.
        LICENSES.
        "Sec. 64. *And be it further enacted,* That on and after the first day of August, eighteen hundred and sixty-two, for each license granted the sum herewith stated shall be respectively and annually paid. Any number of persons carrying on such business in copartnership may transact such business at such place under such license, and not otherwise." (Page 455)
        "6. Wholesale dealers shall pay fifty dollars for each license. Every person whose business or occupation is to sell, or offer to sell, groceries, or any goods, wares, or merchandise of foreign or domestic production, by one or more original package or piece at one time, to the same purchaser, not including wines, spirituous or malt liquors, shall be deemed a wholesale dealer under this act; but having taken out a license as a wholesale dealer, such person may also sell, as aforesaid, as a retailer. (Page 455)

Chapter LXXIV.—An Act to amend an Act entitled "An Act to provide Internal Revenue to support the Government and to pay Interest on the Public Debt," approved July first, eighteen hundred and sixty-two, and for other Purposes. Approved March 3, 1863.
        "That section sixty-four be, and hereby is, further amended by adding, at the end thereof, the following paragraphs: . . .
        "Forty-one." Wholesale dealers, whose annual sales do not exceed fifty thousand dollars, shall pay twenty-five dollars for each license; if exceeding fifty thousand, and not exceeding one hundred thousand dollars, shall pay fifty dollars for each license; exceeding one hundred thousand and not exceeding two hundred and fifty thousand dollars, shall pay one hundred dollars for each license; exceeding two hundred and fifty thousand and not exceeding five

hundred thousand dollars, shall pay two hundred dollars for each license; exceeding five hundred thousand and not exceeding one million dollars, shall pay three hundred dollars for each license; exceeding one million and not exceeding two million dollars, shall pay five hundred dollars for each license; exceeding two millions of dollars, shall pay two hundred and fifty dollars for every million dollars in excess of two millions of dollars, in addition to the five hundred dollars. Every person shall be regarded as a wholesale dealer under this act whose business or occupation it is to sell or offer to sell any goods, wares, or merchandise of foreign or domestic production, not including distilled spirits, fermented liquors or wines, but not excluding drugs, medicines, cigars, snuff, or tobacco, whose annual sales exceed twenty-five thousand dollars; and the license required by any wholesale dealer shall not be for a less amount than his sales for the previous year, unless he has made or proposes to make some change in his business that will obviously reduce the amount of his annual sales; nor shall any license as wholesale dealer allow any such person to act as a commercial broker: *Provided,* That any license understated may be again assessed." (Pages 715-716)

Chap. CLXXIII.—*An Act to provide Internal Revenue to support the Government, to pay Interest on the Public Debt, and for other Purposes.* June 30, 1864. . . .

"Sec. 79. *And be it further enacted,* That there shall be paid annually for each license granted, the sum herein stated, respectively. Any number of persons, except lawyers, conveyancers, claim agents, physicians, surgeons, dentists, cattle brokers, horse-dealers, and peddlers, carrying on such business in copartnership, may transact such business at the place specified in their license, and not otherwise, that is to say:— . . .

"Two. Wholesale dealers, whose annual sales do not exceed fifty thousand dollars, shall pay fifty dollars for each license; and if exceeding fifty thousand dollars, for every additional thousand dollars in excess of fifty thousand dollars, one dollar. Every person shall be regarded as a wholesale dealer under this act whose business it is to sell, or offer to sell, any goods, wares, or merchandise of foreign or domestic production, not including wines, spirits, or malt liquors, whose annual sales exceed twenty-five thousand dollars. And the license required by any wholesale dealer shall not be for a less amount than his sales for the previous year, unless he has made or proposes to make some change in his business that will, in the judgment of the assessor or assistant assessor, reduce the amount of his annual sales; nor shall any license as a wholesale dealer allow any such person to act as a commercial broker: *Provided,* That any license understated may and shall be again assessed, and that no person holding a license as a wholesale dealer in liquors shall be required to take an additional license on account of the sale of other goods, wares, or merchandise on the same premises." (Page 251)

Wholesale Liquor Dealers

John A. Aeuer (1827/28-1882), Kansas City (also Rectifiers)
    (early German immigrant)
Washington Henry Chick (1826-1918), Kansas City (also Commercial Broker)
William B. Cockrell (1833/34-1871), Kansas City
    (also Wholesale Dealer: Hardware)
Peter William Ditsch (1821-1891), Kansas City (also Rectifiers)

(early German immigrant)
Michael Diveley (1828-1901), Kansas City (also Wholesale Dealer:
    Unidentified Merchandise, Retail Liquor Dealer)
Thomas H. Green (1837-1916), Kansas City
    (also Wholesale Dealer: Groceries, Retail Liquor Dealer)
Henry L. Huer/Hugher (1834/35-?), Kansas City
    (also Retail Liquor Dealer, Retail Dealer: Unidentified Merchandise)
    (early German immigrant)
Charles Esmond Kearney (1820-1898), Kansas City (also Retail Liquor Dealer)
Dr. Thomas Bryan Lester (1824-1888), Kansas City (also Physician)
Adam Long (1836-1910), Kansas City
    (also Retail Liquor Dealer, Wholesale Dealer: Groceries)
    (early German immigrant)
William Dodson Oldham (1833-1897), Kansas City (also Butcher)
Benjamin L. Riggins (1822/23-?), Riggins & Ham, Kansas City
Phillip Setzler (1834-1923), Kansas City (also Rectifiers)
    (early German immigrant)
George Sweeney (1820-1889), Kansas City (also Retail Liquor Dealer,
    Wholesale Dealer: Groceries) [His widow was a Civil War pensioner]
Isaiah P. Walker (1826-1886), Kansas City (also Retail Dealer [Groceries])
Gustavus Adolphus Wolf (1842-1928), Kansas City (also Retail Liquor Dealer)

Wholesale Dealers in Liquors in the Internal Revenue Act

Chapter CXIX.—An Act to provide Internal Revenue to support the Government and to pay Interest on the Public Debt. Approved July 1, 1862.
    LICENSES.
    "Sec. 64. *And be it further enacted,* That on and after the first day of August, eighteen hundred and sixty-two, for each license granted the sum herewith stated shall be respectively and annually paid. Any number of persons carrying on such business in copartnership may transact such business at such place under such license, and not otherwise." (Page 455)
    "3. Wholesale dealers in liquors of any and every description, including distilled spirits, fermented liquors, and wines of all kinds, shall pay one hundred dollars for each license. Every person, other than the distiller, or brewer, who shall sell, or offer for sale, any such liquors or wines in quantities of more than three gallons at one time, to the same purchaser, shall be regarded as a wholesale dealer in liquors within the meaning of this act. (Page 455)

Chapter LXXIV.—An Act to amend an Act entitled "An Act to provide Internal Revenue to support the Government and to pay Interest on the Public Debt," approved July first, eighteen hundred and sixty-two, and for other Purposes. Approved March 3, 1863.
    "That section sixty-four be, and hereby is, further amended by adding, at the end thereof, the following paragraphs: . . .
    "Forty-two. Wholesale dealers in liquors shall pay for each license the amount required in this act for license to wholesale dealers. Every person other than the distiller or brewer, who shall sell or offer for sale any distilled spirits, fermented liquors, and wines of all kinds, in

quantities of more than three gallons at one time, or whose annual sales shall exceed twenty-five thousand dollars, shall take out a license as a wholesale dealer in liquors." (Page 716)

Chap. CLXXIII.—*An Act to provide Internal Revenue to support the Government, to pay Interest on the Public Debt, and for other Purposes.* June 30, 1864. . . .

"Sec. 79. *And be it further enacted,* That there shall be paid annually for each license granted, the sum herein stated, respectively. Any number of persons, except lawyers, conveyancers, claim agents, physicians, surgeons, dentists, cattle brokers, horse-dealers, and peddlers, carrying on such business in copartnership, may transact such business at the place specified in their license, and not otherwise, that is to say:— . . .

"Four. Wholesale dealers in liquors, whose annual sales do not exceed fifty thousand dollars, shall pay fifty dollars for each license; and if exceeding fifty thousand dollars, for every additional one thousand dollars in excess of fifty thousand dollars, one dollar. Every person who shall sell, or offer for sale, any distilled spirits, fermented liquors, or wines of any kind, in quantities of more than three gallons at one time to the same purchaser, or whose annual sales, including sales of other merchandise, shall exceed twenty-five thousand dollars, shall be regarded a wholesale dealer in liquors." (Pages 251-252)

HARRIS HOUSE,

CORNER OF MAIN AND MAIN CROSS STS.,

WESTPORT, MO.

JOHN HARRIS, PROPRIETOR.

THIS HOUSE IS LARGE, COMMODIOUS AND supplied with everything necessary to the comfort and convenience of Travelers and Boarders.

HACKS run regularly between this House and the river, and Stages here connect for all parts of the State and Kansas Territory. oct 15-1y

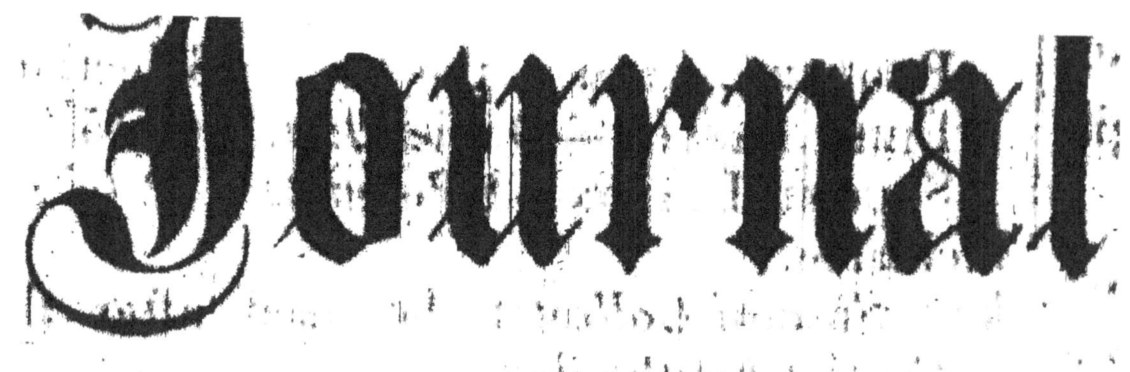

GROCERIES.

COCKRELL & BRO

Wholesale and Retail

GROCERS,

McGee's Addition to Kansas City. Metropolitan Block, No. 9 and 10.

DEALER IN Coffee, Sugar, Molasses, Bacon, Flour, Lard, Rice, Salt, Butter, Cheese, Tobacco, Whisky and all other articles of Family and Plantation supplies. Also, Brandies, Wines, Cigars, Teas, Oils, Nuts, Fruits, Cordials, Preserves, Spices, Extracts, Wooden Ware, Brooms, buckets, Tubs, Baskets, Wrapping Paper, Playing Cards, Nails, and all other goods appertaining to a general Grocery Business, and any articles or brands not in store will always be purchased at lowest prices to fill orders.			COCKRELL & BRO.

August 2d, 1860.—dtf

2

Federal Income Tax Roll
Transcripts, 1862-1863

This chapter transcribes Jackson County taxpayers from "Tax Assessment Lists for Collection Districts in the State of Missouri, 1862-1865." Microfilm publication M776. 22 rolls. Washington: National Archives and Records Administration, 1988.

For original tax assessments copied from microfilm plus individual taxpayers' files consult James A. Tharp's collection *Civil War Era Federal Income Taxpayers of Jackson County, Missouri,* archived at the Kansas City Public Library Missouri Valley Special Collections.

Only extant years during the Civil War (1862-1863) were transcribed to provide the researcher with a *sample* of the exact data collected by the Internal Revenue Service when taxing Civil War-era ancestors. However, all taxpayers from this series of the record group are listed in the comprehensive index at the end of Volume 2.

Roll 15: Division One of Collection District 2 of Missouri

1862	September	8	pages	1863	July	2	pages
	September-December	2	pages		August	2	pages
1863	January	1	page		September	2	pages
	April	2	pages		October	2	pages
	May	2	pages		November	2	pages
	June	1	page		December	2	pages

Roll 20: Division One of Collection District 6 of Missouri

Following Target 4:

1865	May	3	pages

Following Target 5:

1865	July	1	page
	August	2	pages
	May	3	pages
	June	5	pages
	July	4	pages
	August	6	pages
	September	5	pages
	October	5	pages

Roll 21: Division One of Collection District 6 of Missouri

1865	November	6	pages (Following Target 1)

	December	5	pages	
1866	January	4	pages	(Following Target 2)
	February	5	pages	
	March	5	pages	
	April	4	pages	
1866	May	36	pages	(Following Target 3)

Roll 22: Division One of Collection District 6 of Missouri

1866	May	5	pages
	June	6	pages
	July	6	pages
	August	5	pages
	September	4	pages
	October	5	pages
	November	5	pages
	December	5	pages

Supplementary—Final pages, Division 11
District 6, December 1866   2   pages

Annual List
September 1862

    List of Persons residing in Division No. <u>One</u> of Collection District No. <u>Two</u> of the <u>Counties</u> of <u>Jackson, Cass & Bates</u>, liable to a tax under the laws of the United States, and the amount thereof, as assed by <u>Robert Sallsbury</u>, Assistant Assessor.

[Name / Residence / License / Amount of Tax for License / Total Amount Due]

September 1862
Anderson Joseph / Kansas City / Confectioner / $10.00 / $10.00.
Adkins John C / Kansas City / Retail Liquor / $20.00 / /.
Adkins John C / Kansas City / Apothecary / $10.00 / $30.00.
Agnew John C. / Independence / Apothecary / $10.00 / $10.00.
Arnoldi Peter A / Kansas City / Physician / $10.00 / $10.00.
Armstrong John J / Independence / Physician / $10.00 / $10.00.
Butcher Joseph / Kansas City / Retail Dealer $10.00 / $10.00.
Becker Phillip / Westport / Manufacturer / $10.00 / $10.00.
Bryant Ja[me]s M / Independence / Retail Dealer / $10.00 / $10.00.
Bernard Joel / Westport / Retail Dealer / $10.00 / $10.00.
Bartleson John P / K[ansas] City / Retail Dealer / $10.00 / $10.00.
Baileys & Hicks / K[ansas] City / Retail Dealer / $10.00 / $10.00.
Begga Adolph / K[ansas] City / Confectioner / $10.00 / $10.00.
Brown Phillip S / K[ansas] City / Lawyer / $10.00 / $10.00.
Brown Phillip S / K[ansas] City / Claim Agent / $10.00 / $10.00.
Bryant John / K[ansas] City / Physician / $10.00 / $10.00.
Boone W[illia]m L / Independence / Lawyer / $10.00 / $10.00.
Beckham J [P?] / Independence / Apothecary / $10.00 / $10.00.
Buchanan Geo[rge] W / Independence / Lawyer / $10.00 / $10.00.
Blaue D. D / K[ansas] City / Retail Dealer / $10.00 / $10.00.
Beatty Albert / Independ[ence] / Retail Dealer / $10.00 / $10.00.
Bouton Henry B / K[ansas] City / Lawyer / $10.00 / $10.00.
Babbett Ja[me]s P / K[ansas] City / Photographer / $10.00 / $10.00.
Brown Ja[mc]s T / Sibley / Physician / $10.00 / $10.00.
Bryant David A / Jackson County / Physician / $10.00 / $10.00.
Beatty Thomas / Cass County / Physician / $10.00 / $10.00.
Cook James W / K[ansas] City / Auctioneer / $20.00 / $20.00.
Clabour Fred / Westport / Manufacturer / $10.00 / $10.00.
Carroll W[illia]m / K[ansas] City / Retail Dealer / $10.00 / $10.00.
Christian John / Harrisonville / Retail Dealer / $10.00 / $10.00.
Chew Joseph / K[ansas] City / Physician / $10.00 / $10.00.
Chalfant D G / K[ansas] City / Physician / $10.00 / $10.00.
Conv___ Phillip / Westport / Retail Liquor / $20.00 / $20.00.
Chadwick E. B / K[ansas] City / 5th Class Hotel Keeper / $25.00 / $25.00.
Comingo Abraham / K[ansas] City / Lawyer / $10.00 / $10.00.

[Annual List, September 1862, page 2]
Cockrell & Ward / Kansas City / Wholesale Dealer / $50.00 / $50.00.
Crass [sic] Assa [sic] B. / Kansas City / Retail Dealer / $10.00 / $10.00.
Cogswell A H / Independence / Retail Dealer / $10.00 / $10.00.
Chick W H & Co / K[ansas] City / Commercial Broker / $50.00 / $50.00.
Cassady E & P / Westport / Livery Stable Keeper / $10.00 / 5 articles: 2 Hacks,
    2 Buggies, 1 Omnibus, valuation $525.000, tax $8.00/Total due $18.00.

Civil War Era Federal Income Taxpayers

Chick A. S & Co[mpany] / K[ansas] City / Wholesale Dealer / $50.00 / $50.00.
Crenshaw A. L. H / Sn[i]abartown [sic] / Cattle Broker / $10.00 / $10.00.
Crissman W[illia]m / Indep[endence] / Lawyer / $10.00 / $10.00.
Camp H. H. / K[ansas] City / Retail Liqour / $20.00 / $20.00.
Cramer Lewis / Jackson C[ou]n[t]y / Cattle Broker / $10.00 / $10.00.
Denger [sic] Lewis / K[ansas] City / Confectioner / $10.00 / $10.00.
Dwyer Cha[rle]s / K[ansas] City / Retail Dealer / $10.00 / $10.00.
Dwyer Cha[rle]s / K[ansas] City / Retail Liquor / $20.00 / $20.00.
Dively Mike / K[ansas] City / Wholesale Dealer / $50.00 / $50.00.
Dively Mike / K[ansas] City / Wholesale Liquor Dealer / $100.00 / $100.00.
Dively Mike / K[ansas] City / Retail Liquor Dealer / $20.00 / $20.00.
Dietch & Auer / K[ansas] City / Wholesale Liquor Dealer / $100.00 / $100.00.
Dietch & Auer / K[ansas] City / Retail Liquor Dealer / $20.00 / $20.00.
Dietch & Auer / K[ansas] City / Rectifier / $25.00 / $25.00.
Dietch & Auer / K[ansas] City / Tobacconist / $10.00 / $10.00.
Denizen Rich[ar]d / K[ansas] City / Wholesale Dealer / $50.00 / $50.00.
Daugherty Geo[rge] / K[ansas] City / Retail Liquor / $20.00 / $20.00.
Duncan J. S / K[ansas] City / Retail Dealer / $10.00 / $10.00.
Dinker & Conwell / K[ansas] City / Wholesale Dealer / $50.00 / $50.00.
Erkel Jacob R / K[ansas] City / Manufacturer / $10.00 / $10.00.
Eslinger [sic] Fred / K[ansas] City / Retail Dealer / $10.00 / $10.00.
Ebby Sol[omon] M / K[ansas] City / Photographer / $15.00 / $15.00.
Evans J. W / K[ansas] City / Dentist / $10.00 / $10.00.
Early J. H / Westport / Retail Liquor / $20.00 / $20.00.
Fritz Ja[me]s / Westport / Manufacturer / $10.00 / $10.00.
Frazier John / Westport / Billiard Table / $5.00 / $5.00.
Frazier John / Westport / Retail Liquor / $20.00 / $20.00.
Ford W[illia]m W / Kansas City / Apothecary / $10.00 / $10.00.

[Annual List, September 1862, page 3]
Foster Mathew / K[ansas] City / Retail Dealer / $10.00 / $10.00.
Farrer Assa [sic] / Indep[endence] / Physician / $10.00 / $10.00.
Frank Cha[rle]s J. / K[ansas] City / Retail Dealer / $10.00 / $10.00.
Frank Cha[rle]s J. / K[ansas] City / Retail Liquor Dealer / $20.00 / $20.00.
Flaler [sic] F P. & Co[mpany] / K[ansas] City / Retail Liquor Dealer / $10.00/ $10.00.
Foglesang [sic] George B / Westport / Retail Liquor Dealer / $10.00 / $10.00.
Fischell John / Indep[endence] / Retail Liquor Dealer / $10.00 / $10.00.
Fentner George / K[ansas] City / Retail Liquor Dealer / $20.00 / $20.00.
Friedsam M. J / K[ansas] City / Retail Liquor Dealer / $10.00 / $10.00.
Gerhart J. R / Westport / Manufacturer / $10.00 / $10.00.
Garbel [sic] & Rolf [sic] / K[ansas] City / Manufacturer / $10.00 / $10.00.
Garbel [sic] & Rolf [sic] / K[ansas] City / Retail Dealer / $10.00 / $10.00.
Ganghafer [sic] Jos[eph] / K[ansas] City / Physician / $10.00 / $10.00.
Ganghafer [sic] Jos[eph] / K[ansas] City / Apothecary / $10.00 / $10.00.
Griffith Ja[me]s / K[ansas] City / Retail Dealer / $10.00 / $10.00.
Green & Long / K[ansas] City / Wholesale Liquor / $100.00 / $100.00.
Green & Long / K[ansas] City / Retail Liquor / $20.00 / $20.00.
Green & Long / K[ansas] City / Wholesale Dealer / $50.00 / $50.00.
Gregsly W. T. B / K[ansas] City / Retail Dealer / $10.00 / $10.00.
Gague John C / K[ansas] City / Lawyer / $10.00 / $10.00.
Gague John C / K[ansas] City / Claim Agt / $10.00 / $10.00.
Goforth Tho[ma]s J / Westport / Lawyer / $10.00 / $10.00.
Ganz & Reis / K[ansas] City / Retail Dealer / $10.00 / $10.00.
Garbot W[illia]m / Harrisonville / Retail Dealer / $10.00 / $10.00.
Garbot W[illia]m / Harrisonville / Retail Liquor Dealer / $20.00 / $20.00.
Giles Ja[me]s / K[ansas] City / Retail Dealer / $10.00 / $10.00.

Giles & Coats / K[ansas] City / Wholesale Dealer / $50.00 / $50.00.
Helmreich & Co[mpany] / K[ansas] City / Brewers / $25.00 / $25.00.
Harris Alex / K[ansas] City / Billiard Table / $5.00 / $5.00.
Harris Alex / K[ansas] City / Retail Liquor / $20.00 / $20.00.
Hapkins [sic] Cha[rle]s / K[ansas] City / 5[th] Class Hotel Keeper / $25.00 / $25.00.
Hinton [sic] Peter / Indep[endence] / Physician / $10.00 / $10.00.
Hale Robert / K[ansas] City / Apothecary / $10.00 / $10.00.
Hassett J. B / Sibley / Retail Dealer / $10.00 / $10.00.

[Annual List, September 1862, page 4]
Hamelslaugh [sic] & Bro[ther] / Kansas City / Wholesale Dealer / $50.00 / $50.00.
Hamelslaugh [sic] & Bro[ther] / Kansas City / Caim Ag[en]ts / $10.00 / $10.00.
Herriford H. T / Westport / Physician / $10.00 / $10.00.
Huer [sic] He[n]ry L / K[ansas] City / Wholesale Liquor / $100.00 / $100.00.
Huer [sic] He[n]ry L / K[ansas] City / Retail Liquor / $20.00 / $20.00.
Huer [sic] He[n]ry L / K[ansas] City / Retail Dealer / $10.00 / $10.00.
Holms W[illia]m / K[ansas] City / Apothecary / $10.00 / $10.00.
Hovey & He[n]ry / K[ansas] City / Lawyers / $10.00 / $10.00.
Henzling C / K[ansas] City / Retail Liquor / $20.00 / $20.00.
Hollinghausen F / K[ansas] City / Retail Liquor / $20.00 / $20.00.
Hodges M B / K[ansas] City / Livery Stable Keeper / $10.00 /
        1 article: 2[-]Horse Carriage, valuation $100.00, rate 2%, tax $2.00 /
        Total amount due $12.00.
Hartel Jacob / K[ansas] City / Retail Dealer / $10.00 / $10.00.
Hough & Maupin / Harrisonville / Retail Dealer / $10.00 / $10.00.
Hanly & Head / Indep[endence] / Retail Dealer / $10.00 / $10.00.
Helfrich & Co[mpany] / K[ansas] City / Brewer / $25.00 / $25.00.
Irwin Gloom & Co[mpany] / Indep[endence] / Retail Dealer / $10.00 / $10.00.
Jacob Phillip / K[ansas] City / Retail Liquor / $20.00 / $20.00.
Jewitt Albert / K[ansas] City / Wholesale Dealer / $50.00 / $50.00.
Jewitt B M / K[ansas] City / Physician / $10.00 / $10.00.
Jasier [Jaiser] August / K[ansas] City / Retail Liquor / $20.00 / $20.00.
Kearny Cha[rle]s / K[ansas] City / Wholesale Dealer / $50.00 / $50.00.
Kearny Cha[rle]s / K[ansas] City / Wholesale Liquor Dealer / $100.00 / $100.00.
Kearny Cha[rle]s / K[ansas] City / Retail Liquor Dealer / $20.00 / $20.00.
Knapp Bern[ar]d / K[ansas] City / Retail Liquor Dealer / $20.00 / $20.00.
Kievel & Turner / K[ansas] City / Retail Dealer / $10.00 / $10.00.
Keller Jacob / Indep[endence] / Retail Dealer / $10.00 / $10.00.
Kenally D. / K[ansas] City / Retail Liquor Dealer / $20.00 / $20.00.
Kellso H R / Westport / Retail Liquor Dealer / $20.00 / $20.00.
Kerr Ben / K[ansas] City / Retail Liquor Dealer / $20.00 / $20.00.
Kelso H R / Westport / Billiard Table / $5.00 / $5.00.
Long William / K[ansas] City / Manufacturer / $10.00 / $10.00.
Langsenkamp & Co[mpany] / K[ansas] City / Manufacturer / $10.00 / $10.00.

[Annual List, September 1862, page 5]
Loech [sic] Wendall / Kansas City / Retail Liquor / $20.00 / $20.00.
Loech Wendall / Kansas City / Billiard Table / $5.00 / $5.00.
Lykins J / Kansas City / Physician / $10.00 / $10.00.
Long & Wagoner / Kansas Ctiy / Retail Liquor / $20.00 / $20.00.
Long & Wagoner / Kansas City / Retail Dealer / $10.00 / $10.00.
Lester Tho[ma]s B / Kansas City / Physician / $10.00 / $10.00.
Long John / Kansas City / Retail Liquor D[ealer] / $20.00 / $20.00.
Long John / Kansas City / Billiard Table / $5.00 / $5.00.
Linderman S. A / Kansas City / Retail Dealer / $10.00 / $10.00.
Langsenkamp & Co[mpany]. / Kansas City / Retail Dealer / $10.00 / $10.00.

Civil War Era Federal Income Taxpayers

McDonald & Klein / Kansas City / Manufacturer / $10.00 / $10.00.
Modies John W / Indep[endence] / Manufacturer / $10.00 / $10.00.
Morrison W[illia]m / Indep[endence] / Manufacturer / $10.00 / $10.00.
Medow Ja[me]s H / Indep[endence] / Retail Dealer / $10.00 / $10.00.
Maddox Assa [sic] / K[ansas] City / Retail Dealer / $10.00 / $10.00
Melle Leonard / K[ansas] City / Livery Stable keeper / $10.00 /
       2 articles: 1 Buggy, 1 Carriage, valuation $180, rate $1%, tax $2.00 /
       Total amount due $12.00.
Moon C. H & Co[mpany] / K[ansas] City / Retail Dealer / $10.00 / $10.00.
Mohr Casper / K[ansas] City / Tobacconist / $10.00 / $10.00.
McDonald & Kl[e]in / K[ansas] City / Retail Dealer / $10.00 / $10.00.
McClanahan W[illia]m D / Indep[endence] Retail Dealer / $10.00 / $10.00.
McCoy Jno [John] & W[illia]m / Indep[endence] Apothecary / $10.00 / $10.00.
Morris Joel P / K[ansas] City / Physician / $10.00 / $10.00.
Minor Cha[rle]s E / K[ansas] City / Physician / $10.00 / $10.00.
Nall C. H. & Co[mpany] / K[ansas] City / Retail Dealer / $10.00 / $10.00.
Nicholson Geo[rge] G. / K[ansas] City / 5th Class Hotel Keeper / $25.00 / $25.00.
Northrop & Co[mpany] / K[ansas] City / Bankers / $100.00 / $100.00.
Nevill J / K[ansas] City / Physician / $10.00 / $10.00.
Oldham W[illia]m D / K[ansas] City / Retail Liquor / $20.00 / $20.00.
Oldham W[illia]m D / K[ansas] City / Retail Dealer / $10.00 / $10.00.
Pollard & Farmer [sic] / K[ansas] City / Manufacturer / $10.00 / $10.00.
Pollard P. D / Indep[endence] / Manufacturer / $10.00 / $10.00.
Pendleton M / K[ansas] City / Physician / $10.00 / $10.00.

[Annual List, September 1862, page 6]
Perry John W. / Independence / 8th Class Hotel Keeper / $5.00 / $5.00.
Pollard & Farmer [sic] / Kansas City / Retail Dealer / $10.00 / $10.00.
Pierce Andrew / Kansas City / Physician / $10.00 / $10.00.
Payne & Toler / Kansas City / Retail Dealer / $10.00 / $10.00.
Payne & Toler / Kansas City / Auctioneer / $20.00 / $20.00.
[illegible] Ja[me]s W / Westport / Physician / $10.00 / $10.00.
Quarrels [sic] William / K[ansas] City / Lawyer / $10.00 / $10.00.
Quarrels [sic] John / K[ansas] City / Livery Stable Keeper / $10.00 /
       2 articles: 2 2[-]Horse Carriages, valuation $250.00, rate 2%, tax $4.00 /
       Total amount due $14.00.
Ramage Lewis / K[ansas] City / Lawyer / $10.00 / $10.00.
Rolf E. D. / K[ansas] City / Physician / $10.00 / $10.00.
Rooney John / K[ansas] City / Retail Liquor / $20.00 / $20.00.
Rumberg J H. / Indep[endence] / Retail Dealer / $10.00 / $10.00.
Raffalette G. S. & Co[mpany] / K[ansas] City / Retail Liquor Dealer / $20.00 / $20.00.
Riek Hen[r]y / K[ansas] City / Retail Dealer / $10.00 / $10.00.
Riorden B / K[ansas] City / Retail Liquor Dealer / $20.00 / $20.00.
Ross & Hough / W[e]stport / Retail Liquor Dealer / $20.00 / $20.00.
Reed W[illia]m S. / K[ansas] City / Retail Liquor Dealer / $20.00 / $20.00.
Reed W[illia]m S. / K[ansas] City / Billiard Table / $5.00 / $5.00.
Riggins & Ham / K[ansas] City / Livery Stable Keeper / $10.00 /
       3 articles: 2 Buggies & 1 Hack, valuation $340.00, rate 2%, tax $4.00 /
       Total amount due $14.00.
Swietzgabel [sic] & Co[mpany] / K[ansas] City / Brewers / $50.00 / $50.00.
Stegmiller Joseph / Westport / Manufacturer / $10.00 / $10.00.
Squires John / Westport / Manufacturer / $10.00 / $10.00.
Schoff Hen[r]y / Westport / Manufacturer / $10.00 / $10.00.
Steine Edward / K[ansas] City / Retail Dealer / $10.00 / $10.00.
Soger [sic] Hen[r]y / Westport / Manufacturer / $10.00 / $10.00.
Street & Co[mpany] / K[ansas] City / Retail Dealer / $10.00 / $10.00.

Schoen Joseph / Westport / Retail Liquor / $20.00 / $20.00.
Schoen Joseph / Westport / Retail Dealer / $10.00 / $10.00.
Sampson Moses / Indep[endence] / Retail Dealer / $10.00 / $10.00.
Stevens W[illia]m / K[ansas] City / Lawyer / $10.00 / $10.00.
Smith & Holms / K[ansas]City / 5th Class Hotel Keeper / $25.00 / $25.00.
Smith & Holms / K[ansas]City / Retail Liquor / $20.00 / $20.00.
Shoenbrun Isaac / K[ansas] City / Retail Deal[er] / $10.00 / $10.00.

[Annual List, September 1862, page 7]
Snell Addison / Kansas City / Billiard Table / $5.00 / $5.00.
Snell Addison / Kansas City / Retail Liquor / $20.00 / $20.00.
Shoen Lewis A / Kansas City / Apothecary / $10.00 / $10.00.
Shoen Lewis A /Kansas City / Physician / $10.00 / $10.00.
Schaeff W[illia]m J / Kansas City / Physician / $10.00 / $10.00.
Sprunk Joseph / Kansas City / Retail Liquor D[ealer] / $20.00 / $20.00.
Scully W[illia]m / Kansas City / Retail Liquor D[ealer] / $20.00 / $20.00.
Souneso [sic] Ja[me]s W. / Kansas City / Wholesale Dealer / $50.00 / $50.00.
Saur [sic] Anton / Kansas City / Retail Dealer / $10.00 / $10.00.
Schorff [sic] Hen[r]y / Westport / Retail Dealer / $10.00 / $10.00.
Soger Hen[r]y R / K[ansas] City / Retail Dealer / $10.00 / $10.00.
Shannun [sic] J & P / K[ansas] City / Wholesale Dealer / $50.00 / $50.00.
Setzler W[illia]m / K[ansas] City / Billiard Table / $5.00 / $5.00.
Setzler W[illia]m / K[ansas] City / Retail Liquor D[ealer] / $20.00 / $20.00.
Setzler & Wolf / K[ansas] City / Wholesale Liquor D[ealer] / $100.00 / $100.00.
Setzler & Wolf / K[ansas] City / Retail Liquor D[ealer] / $20.00 / $20.00.
Sweeny George / K[ansas] City / Wholesale D[ealer] / $50.00 / $50.00.
Sweeny George / K[ansas] City / Wholesale Liquor D[ealer] / $100.00 / $100.00.
Sweeny George / K[ansas] City / Retail Liquor D[ealer] / $20.00 / $20.00.
Saulbery [sic] L C. / K[ansas] City / Physician / $10.00 / $10.00.
Smith N. M / Sibley / Physician / $10.00 / $10.00.
Thompson J. W / K[ansas] City / Manufacturer / $10.00 / $10.00.
Thompson J. W / K[ansas] City / Wholesale Dealer / $50.00 / $50.00.
Tindall Geo[rge] W / K[ansas] City / Dentist / $10.00 / $10.00.
Thoes John / Westport / Retail Liquor / $20.00 / $20.00.
Twymann [sic] Geo[rge] / Indep[endence] / Physician / $10.00 / $10.00.
Twymann [sic] Geo[rge] / Indep[endence] / 8[th] Class Hotel Keeper / $5.00 / $5.00.
Treffran M D / K[ansas] City / Lawyer / $10.00 / $10.00.
Taylor John H / Indep[endence] / Lawyer / $10.00 / $10.00.
Vaughn Sam[ue]l D / K[ansas] City / Commercial Broker / $50.00 / $50.00.
Ward Ja[me]s M / K[ansas] City / Retail Dealer / $10.00 / $10.00.
Weston Robert / Indep[endence] / Manufacturer / $10.00 / $10.00.
Wederlich Fred / Westport / Brewer / $25.00 / $25.00.

[Annual List, September 1862, page 8]
Wilson & Pendleton / Independence / Retail Dealer / $10.00 / $10.00.
Wilhite P. G / Kansas City / Wholesale Dealer / $50.00 / $50.00.
Walker Is[ai]ah & Co[mpany] / Kansas City / Retail Dealer / $10.00 / $10.00.
Walker Is[ai]ah & Co[mpany] / Kansas City / Retail Liquor Dealer / $20.00 / $20.00.
Wily Ja[me]s M / Kansas City / Dentist / $10.00 / $10.00.
Welland Fred K / Kansas City / Tobacconist / $10.00 / $10.00.
Wolter Augustus / Kansas City / Retail Liquor Dealer / $20.00 / $20.00.
Whiting D. V. / Kansas City / Commercial Broker / $50.00 / $50.00.
Walker Ja[me]s A / Kansas City / Retail Dealer / $10.00 / $10.00.
Wallace Reub[en] / Indep[endence] / Retail Dealer / $10.00 / $10.00.
Widenmann [sic] C. / Westport / Retail Liquor Dealer / $5.00 / $5.00.
Widenmann C. / Westport / Billiard Table / $10.00 / $10.00.

Civil War Era Federal Income Taxpayers

Wood Joseph / K[ansas] City / Physician / $10.00 / $10.00.
White & McKinzie / K[ansas] City / Cattle Broker / $10.00 / $10.00.
White & McKinzie / K[ansas] City / Horse Dealer / $10.00 / $10.00.
Werry Theobold / Westport / Confectioner / $10.00 / $10.00.
Werry Theobold / Westport / Retail Liquor Dealer / $20.00 / $20.00.

Monthly List
September-December 1862

Alphabetical List of Persons in Division No. <u>One</u> of Collection District No. <u>Two</u> of the <u>Counties</u> of <u>Jackson Cass & Bates</u>, liable to a tax under the Excise laws of the United States, and the amount thereof, as assessed by <u>Robert Salesbury, Asst</u> Assessor, and by him returned to the <u>Assessor</u> of said District, for the month of <u>Sept. Oct. Nov. & Decr., 1862</u>.

Assessors must be particular to fill all the blanks in this form, as far as practicable, and to classify and number all articles and occupations upon which taxes are assessed to correspond with the entry in the Abstract.

[Column headings followed by codes (in bold) used in the transcription]
No. of Line.
186<u>2</u>.

Date. **[a.]**
Name. **[b.]**
Location. **[c.]**
Description.
Quantity. **[d.]**
Article or Occupation. **[e.]**
Rate. **[f.]**
Valuation. **[g.]**
Rate of Tax. **[h.]**
Class A, B, or C. **[i.]**
Number in Abstract as Classified. **[j.]**
Amount of Tax.
Class A. Ad Valorem Duty. **[k.]**
Class B. Licenses. **[L.]**
Class C. Enumerated Articles. **[m.]**
Total Amount of Tax Due. **[n.]**

1. a. Sept[ember] 1 to 31st Dec[emb]er / b. **Butcher Joseph** / c. Kansas City / d. 40 / e. Horned Cattle 18 Months Old / h. 30¢ / m. $12.00.
2. a. Sept[ember] 1 to 31st Dec[emb]er / b. Butcher Joseph / c. Kansas City / d. 14 / e. Hogs / h. 10¢ ,/ $1.40
3. a. Sept[ember] 1 to 31st Dec[emb]er / b. Butcher Joseph / c. Kansas City / d. 16 / e. Sheep / h. 5¢ / m. $.80 / n. $14.20
4. a. Sept[ember] to Jan[uar]y / b. **Becker Phillip** / c. Westport / e. Boots & Shoes Manufac[ture]d / g. $416.75 / h. 3¢ / k. $12.50 / n. $12.50
5. [blank]
6. a. Sept[ember] to Jan[uar]y / b. **Campbell Nelson & Co** / c. Kansas City / e. Gross Recpts Fer[r]y Boat / g. 1591.40 / h. 1½ / k. 23.87 / n. 23.87
7. a. Nov[ember] to 31st Dec[embe]r / b. **Cook James W.** / c. Kansas City / e. Auction Sales / g. 706.70 / h. 1/10 / k. .70 / n. .70
8. a. Sept[ember] to 31st Dec[embe]r / b. **Claber Frederick** / c. Westport / e. Wagons & Ox Yokes Manuf[acture]d / g. 90.00 / h. 5 / k. 2.70 / n. 2.70
9. [blank]
10. a. Sept[ember] to 31st Dec[embe]r / b. **Erkel Jacob R** / c. Kansas City / e. Tin Work Manufactured / g. 100.00 / h. 3¢ / k. 3.00 / n. 3.00
11. [blank]

12. a. Sept[ember] to 31ˢᵗ Dec[embe]r / b. **Fortz Joseph A** / c. Westport / e. Boots & Shoes Manufactured / g. 106.00 / h. 3¢ / k. 3.18 / n. 3.18
13. [blank]
14. a. Sept[ember] to 31ˢᵗ Dec[embe]r / b. **Gerhart Jacob R** / c. Westport / e. Harness Manufactured / g. 400.00 / h. 3¢ / k. 12.00 / n. 12.00
15. a. Sept[ember] to 31ˢᵗ Dec[embe]r / b. **Gabel & Ralph** / c. Kansas City / e. Boots & Shoes Manufactured / g. 394.00 / h. 3¢ / k. 11.82 / n. 11.82
16. [blank]
17. a. Sept[ember] to 31ˢᵗ Dec[embe]r / b. **Helmroch [Helmreich] & Messerschmidt** / c. Kansas City / d. 72 1/8 / e. Barrels Beer Brewed / h. 1$ / m. 72.12 / n. 72.12
18. a. Sept[ember] to 31ˢᵗ Dec[embe]r / **Helfrich & Milschuster** / c. Kansas City / d. 40 / e. Barrels Beer Brewed / h. 1$ / m. 40.00 / n. 40.00
19. a. Sept[ember] to 31ˢᵗ Dec[embe]r / b. **Hockensmith, W[illia]m H.** / c. Jackson County / d. 53 / e. Hogs Slaught[ered] for Sale / h. 10¢ / m. 5.30 / n. 5.30
20. a. Sept[ember] to 31ˢᵗ Dec[embe]r / b. **Long William** / Jackson County / e. Harness & Sad[d]lery Manuf[actured] / g. $350.00 / h. 3¢ / k. 10.50 / n. 10.50
21. a. Sept[ember] to 31ˢᵗ Dec[embe]r / b. **Langsenkamp & Co[mpany]** / c. Jackson County / e. Boots & Shoes Manuf[actured] / g. 810.20 / h. 3¢ / k. 24.32 / n. 24.32
22. [blank]
23. a. Sept[ember] to 31ˢᵗ Dec[embe]r / b. **McDonald & Klein** / c. Jackson County / e. Harness & Sad[d]lery Manuf[actured] / g. 248.00 / h. 3¢ / k. 7.44 / n. 7.44
24. a. Sept[ember] to 31ˢᵗ Dec[embe]r / b. **Modies John W** / c. Independence / e. Harness & Sad[d]lery / g. 225.00 / h. 3¢ / k. 6.75 / n. 6.75
25. a. Sept[ember] to 31ˢᵗ Dec[embe]r / **Morrison W[illia]m** / c. Kansas City / e. Sheet Iron Work / g. 657.00 / h. 3¢ / k. 19.71 / n. 19.71
26. a. Sept[ember] to 31ˢᵗ Dec[embe]r / **McGargell James** / c. Independence / e. [Ferry?] Receipts / g. 55.70 / h. 1 1/10 / k. .83 / n. .83
27. [blank]
28. a. Sept[ember] to 31ˢᵗ Dec[embe]r / **Pollard & Farman** / c. Kansas City / e. Tin & S[heet] Iron Manufactured / g. 450.00 / h. 3¢ / k. 13.50 / n. 13.50
29. [blank]
30. a. Sept[ember] to 31ˢᵗ Dec[embe]r / b. **Switzgabel & Co[mpany]** / c. Kansas City / d. 228 1/8 / e. Bar[rels] Beer Brewed / h. 1$ / m. 228.12 / n. 228.12
31. a. Sept[ember] to 31ˢᵗ Dec[embe]r / b. **Street A** / c. Kansas City / d. 33 / e. Hogs Slaughter[e]d for Sale / 10¢ / m. 3.30 / n. 3.30
32. a. Sept[ember] to 31ˢᵗ Dec[embe]r / **Stegmiller Joseph** / c. Westport / e. Wagons Manufactured / g. 75.00 / h. 3¢ / k. 2.25 / n. 2.25
33. a. Sept[ember] to 31ˢᵗ Dec[embe]r / **Squire John** / c. Westport / e. Wagons Manufactured / g. 3200.00 / h. 3¢ / k. 96.00 / n. 96.00
34. a. Sept[ember] to 31ˢᵗ Dec[embe]r / **Shoeff Henry** / c. Westport / e. Boots & Shoes Manufactured / g. 1200.00 / h. 3¢/ k. 36.00 / n. 36.00
35. a. Sept[ember] to 31ˢᵗ Dec[embe]r / **Stein Edward** / c. Kansas City / e. Furniture Manufactured / g. 420.00 / h. 3¢ / k. 12.60 / n. 12.[60]
36. [blank]
37. a. Sept[ember] to 31ˢᵗ Dec[embe]r / b. **Thompson [John] W.** / c. Kansas City / e. Tin & Sheet Iron Work Manufactured / g. 300.00 / h. 3¢ / k. 9.00 / n. [page torn]
38. a. Sept[ember] to 31ˢᵗ Dec[embe]r / b. **Walker Ja[me]s A** / c. Kansas City / d. 100 / e. Horned Cattle 18 Months Old / h. 30¢ / m. 30.00 / n. [page torn]
39. a. Sept[ember] to 31ˢᵗ Dec[embe]r / b. Walker Ja[me]s A / c. Kansas City / d. 100 / e. Hogs Slaught[ered] for Sale / h. 10¢ / m. 10.00 / n. [page torn]
40. a. Sept[ember] to 31ˢᵗ Dec[embe]r / b. Walker Ja[me]s A / c. Kansas City / d. 40 / e. Sheep Slaught[ered] for Sale / h. 5¢ / m. 2.00 / n. [page torn]

[Monthly List, September-December 1862, page 2]
1. a. Sept[ember] to 31ˢᵗ Dec[embe]r / b. **Weston Robert**/ c. Independence / e. Wagons Manufactured / h. 3¢ / k. 2.25 / n. 2.25

Civil War Era Federal Income Taxpayers

2. a. Sept[ember] to 31ˢᵗ Dec[embe]r / b. **Wedelich Ferdinand** / c. Westport / d. 40 / e. Barrels Beer Brewed / h. 1$ / m. 40.00 / n. 40.00

Monthly List
January 1863

Alphabetical List of Persons in Division No. <u>One</u> of Collection District No. <u>Two</u> of the <u>Counties</u> of <u>Jackson Cass & Bates</u>, liable to a tax under the Excise laws of the United States, and the amount thereof, as assessed by <u>Robert Salesbury, Asst</u> Assessor, and by him returned to the <u>Assessor</u> of said District, for the month of <u>January</u>, 1863.

Assessors must be particular to fill all the blanks in this form, as far as practicable, and to classify and number all articles and occupations upon which taxes are assessed to correspond with the entry in the Abstract.

1. a. Jan[uar]y / b. **Becker Phillip** / c. Westport / e. Boots & Shoes Manufactured / g. 50.00 / h. 3¢ / k. 1.50 / n. 1.50
2. a. Jan[uar]y / b. **Butcher Joseph** / c. Kansas City / d. 13 / e. Cattle exceeding 18 Months Old / h. 30¢ / m. 3.90
3. a. Jan[uar[y / b. Butcher Joseph / c. Kansas City / d. 34 / e. Hogs / h. 10 / m. 3.40 / n. 7.30
4. a. Jan[uar]y / b. **Bryant Ja[me]s M** / c. Independence / d. 15 / e. Cattle exceeding 18 Months Old / h. 30¢ / m. 4.50 /
5. a. Jan[uar]y / b. Bryant Ja]me]s M / c. Independence / d. 14 / e. Cattle Under 18 Months Old / h. 5¢ / m. .70 / n. 5.20
6. [blank]
7. a. Jan[uar]y / b. **Fortz Joseph A** / c. Westport / e. Boots & Shoes Manufactured / g. 3.50 / h. 3¢ / k.10½ / n.10½
8. [blank]
9. a. Jan[uar]y / b. **Gabel & Ralph** / c. Kansas City / e. Boots & Shoes Manufactured / g. 90.00 / h. 3¢ / k. 2.70 / n. 2.70
10. a. Jan[uar]y / b. **Gerhart J. R** / c. Kansas City / e. Harness Manufactured / g. 36.00 / h. 3¢ / k. 1.08 45/100 / n. 1.08 45/100
11. [blank]
12. a. Jan[uar]y / b. **Helmroch & Messerschmit** / c. Kansas City / d. 22 / e. Barrels Beer Brewed / h. 1$ / m. 22.00 / n. 22.00
13. a. Jan[uar]y / b. **Helfrich Henry & Co** / c. Kansas City / d. 22 / e. Barrels Beer Brewed / h. 1$ / m 22.00 / n. 22.00
14. [blank]
15. a. Jan[uar]y / b. **Long William** / c. Kansas City / e. Tinware Manufactured / g. 35.00 / h. 3¢ / k. 1.05 / n. 1.05
16. a. Jan[uar]y / b. **Langsenkamp & Co[mpany]** / e. Boots & Shoes Manufactured / g. 214.00 / h. 3¢ / k. 6.42 / n. 6.42
17. [blank]
18. a. Jan[uar]y / b. **Morrison William** / c. Kansas City / e. Tinware Manufactured / g. 13.85 / h. 3¢ / k. 41.55 / n. 41.55
19. a. Jan[uar]y / b. **McDonald & Klein** / c. Kansas City / e. Harness & Sad[d]lery Manufactured / g. 107.00 / h. 3¢ / k. 3.21 / n. 3.21
20. a. Jan[uar]y / b. **Modie John W** / c. Independence / e. Harness & Sad[d]lery Manufactured / g. 140.00 / h. 3¢ / k. 4.20 / n. 4.20
21. [blank]
22. a. Jan[uar]y / b. **Nelson Campbell & Co[mpany]** / c. Kansas City / e. Ferry Gross Receipts / g. 215.70 / h. 1½ / k. 3.23 55/100 / 3.23 55/100
23. [blank]
24. Jan[uar]y / b. **Pollard & Farmer** / c. Kansas City / e. Tinware Manufactured / g. 212.45 / h. 3¢ / k. 6.37 35/100 / n. 6.37 35/100
25. Jan[uar]y / b. **Pallard Phillip D** / c. Independence / e. Tinware Manufactured / g. 187.00 / h. 3¢ / k. 5.61 / n. 5.61
26. [blank]
27. a. Jan[uar]y / b. **Switzgabel P. & Co[mpany]** / c. Kansas City / d. 40 1/8 / d. Barrels Beer Brewed / h. 1$ / m. 40.12 5/100 / n. 40.12 5/100
28. a. Jan[uar]y / b. **Squiers John** / c. Westport / e. Wagons Manufactured / g. 200.80 / h. 3¢ / k. 6.32 4/100 / n. 6.32 4/100
29. a. Jan[uar]y / b. **Shoeff Henry** / c. Westport / e. Boots & Shoes Manufactured / g. 155.00 / h. 3¢ / k. 4.65 / n. 4.65
30. a. Jan[uar]y / b. **Steine Edward** / c. Kansas City / e. Furniture Manufactured / g. 111.00 / h. 3¢ / k. 3.33 / n. 3.33
31. a. Jan[uar]y / b. **Seger Henry** / c. Westport / e. Furniture Manufactured / g. 62.75 / h. 3¢ / k. 1.88 25/100 / n. 1.88 25/100
32. [blank]
33. a. Jan[uar]y / b. **Thompson J. W.** / c. Kansas City / e. Tinware Manufactured / g. 16.15 / h. 3¢ / k. .48 45/100 / n. .48 45/100
34. [blank]
35. a. Jan[uar[y / b. **Wedelich Ferdinand** / c. Westport / d. 6 3/8 / e. Barrels Beer Brewed / h. 1$ / m. 6.37 50/100 /

n. 6.37 50/100 [Annotation: "Error corrected in April March]

36. a. Jan[uar]y / b. **Ward James M** / c. Kansas City / d. 31 / e. Cattle exceeding 18 Months Old / h. 30¢ / m. 9.30

37. a. Jan[uar]y / b. Ward James M / c. Kansas City / 92 / e. Hogs exceeding 6 Months Old / h. 10 / m. 9.20 / n. 18.50

38. [blank]

39. [blank]

40. [blank]

Monthly List
April 1863

Alphabetical List of Persons in Division No. <u>One</u> of Collection District No. <u>Two</u> of the <u>State</u> of <u>Missouri</u>, liable to a tax under the Excise laws of the United States, and the amount thereof, as assessed by <u>Robert Salisbury</u>, <u>Asst</u> Assessor, and by him returned to the <u>Assessor</u> of said District, for the month of <u>April</u>, 1863.

Assessors must be particular to fill all the blanks in this form, as far as practicable, and to classify and number all articles and occupations upon which taxes are assessed to correspond with the entry in the Abstract.

1. a. Jan[uar]y 1 [18]63 / b. **Allen Andrew** / c. Pleasant Hill / e. Retail Dealer / i. B / j. 56 / L. 10.00 / n. 10.00

2. [blank]

3. a. Sept[ember] 1 [18]62 / b. **Bernard W R** / c. Westport / e. Banker / i. B / j. 4 / L. 100.00

4. a. Sept[ember] 1 [18]62 / b. Bernard W R / c. Westport / e. Wholesale Dealer / i. B / j. 64 / L. 50.00 / n. 150.00

5. a. Febr[uary 18]63 / b. **Becker Philip** / c. Westport / e. Boots & Shoes Manuf[acture]d / g. 58.50 / h. 3% / i. A / j. 42 / k. 1.75

6. a. March / b. Becker Philip / c. Westport / e. Boots & Shoes Manuf[acture]d / g. 33.25 / h. 3% / i. A / j. 42 / k. 1.00 / n. 2.75

7. a. Febr[uary] / b. **Butcher Joseph** / c. Kansas City / d. 15 / e cattle exc[eeding] 18 M[onths] / h. 30 / i. C / j. 12 / m. 4.50

8. a. Feb[ruary] / b. Butcher Joseph / c. Kansas City / d. 2 / e. cattle under 18 M[onths] / h. 5 / i. C / j. 13 / m.. .10 / n. 4.60

9. a. M[ar]ch & Ap[ril] / b. **Butcher & Ackermann** / c. Kansas City / d. 29 / e. cattle exc[eeding] 18 months / h. 20 / i. C / j. 12 / m. 5.80

10. a. M[ar]ch & Ap[ril] / b. Butcher & Ackermann / c. Kansas City / d. 8 / e. hogs exc[eeding] 100 lbs / h. 6 / i. C / j. 14 / m. .48

11. a. M[ar]ch & Ap[ril] / b. Butcher & Ackermann / c. Kansas City / d. 5 / e. sheep / h. 3 / i. C / j. 15 / m. .15 / n. 6.43

12. a. M[ar]ch & Ap[ril] / b. **Bryant Ja[me]s M** / c. Independence / d. 10 / e. cattle exc[eeding] 18 m[onths] / h. 20 / i. C / j. 12 / m. 2.00 / n. 2.00

13. a. March 1 / b. **Bartlett & Frank** / c. Independence / e. Retail Dealers / i. B / j. 56 / L. 10.00 / n. 10.00

14. a. Sept[ember] 1 [18]62 / b. **Cottull Vic Kroy & Co[mpany]** / c. Kansas City / d. 8 / e. 2 horse carriages / i. C / j. 8 / m. 16.00 / n. 16.00

15. a. Apr[il] 1 [18]63 / b. **Carmichael C. G** / c. Blue Township / e. Cattle Broker / i. B. / j. 12 / L. 10.00 / n. 10.00

16. a. Sept[ember 18]62 / b. **Cogswell O H** / c. Independence / d. 2 / e. 1 Horse carriages / i. C / j. 7 / m. 2.00

17. a. Sept[ember 18]62 / b. Cogswell O H / c. Independence / d. 2 / e. 2 Horse carriages / i. C / j. 8 / m. 4.00

18. a. March [18]63 / b. Cogswell O H / c. Independence / e. Livery stable Keeper / i. B / j. 40 / L. 10.00 / n. 16.00

19. [blank]

20. a. April 1 [18]63 / b. **Ensign Daniel** / c. Kansas City / e. Retail Dealer / i. B / j. 56 / L. 10.00

21. a. April 1 [18]63 / b. Ensign Daniel / c. Kansas City / e. Retail Liquor Dealer / i. B / j. 57 / L. 20.00 / n. 30.00

22. a. Febr[uar]y [18]63 / b. **Fritz Joseph** / c. Westport / e. Boots & Shoes / g. 23.50 / h. 3% / i. S / j. 53 / k. .70 / n. .70

23. a. Apr[il] 1 [18]63 / b. **Farral, John** / c. Jackson Co[unty] / e. Cattle Broker / i. B /j. 12 / L. 10.00 / n. 10.00

24. a. M[ar]ch 1 [18]63 / b. **Forbs Thomas** / c. Kansas [City] / e. Peddlar / i. B / j. 47 / L. 10.00 / n. 10.00

25. [blank]

26. a. Sept[ember] 1 / b. **Goodson John E** / c. Jackson Co[unty] / e. Physician / i. B / j. 54 / L. 10.00 / n. 10.00

27. a. Febr[uary] / b. **Gable & Ralph** / c. Kansas City / e. Boots & shoes / g. 86.00 / h. 3% i. A / j. 42 / k. 2.58

28. a. M[ar]ch & Apr[il] / b. Gable & Ralph / c. Kanss City / e. Boots & shoes / g. 266.00 / h. 3% / i. A / j. 42 / k. 7.98 / n. 10.56

29. a. Febr[uary] / b. **Garhard, Jacob R** / c. Westport / e. Saddlery / g. 79.25 / h. 3% / i. a / j. 42 / k. 2.37

30. a. M[ar]ch & Apr[il] / b. Garhard, Jacob R / c. Westport / e. Saddlery / g. 387.85 / h. 3% / i. A / j. 42 / k. 11.63 /

81

n. 14.00
31. [blank]
32. a. Febr[uary] / b. **Helmreich Henry & Co[mpany]** / c. Kansas City / d. 23½ / e. Bbls [Barrels] Beer / h. $1 / i. C / j. 2 / m. 23.50
33. a. M[ar]ch & Ap[ril] / b. Helmreich Henry & Co[mpany] / c. Kansas City / d. 128¼ / e. Bbls [Barrels] Beer / h. 60 / i. C / j. 2 / m. 76.95 / n. 100.45
34. a. Febr[uary] / b. **Helfrich Henry & Co[mpany]** / c. Kansas City / d. 20½ / e. Bbls [Barrels] Beer / h. $1 / i. C / j. 2 / m. 20.50
35. a. M[ar]ch & Ap[ril] / b. Helfrich Henry & Co[mpany] / c. Kansas City / d. 56 / e. Bbls [Barrels] Beer / h. 60 / i. C / j. 2 / m. 33.60 / n. 54.15
36. [blank]
37. a. M[ar]ch 1 [18]63 / b. **Holmes, William** / c. Kansas City / e. Lawyer / i. B / j. 39 / L. 10.00 / n. 10.00
38. a. Febr[uary] / b. **Kleber, Fred.** / c. Westport / e. Wagons manufa[cture]d / g. 90.00 / h. 3% / i. A / j. 75 / k. 2.70 / n. 2.70
39. a. M[ar]ch 1 / b. **Keevil & Turner** / c. Kansas City / e. Auctioneers / i. B / j. 3 / L. 20.00 / n. 20.00
40. a. M[ar]ch 1 / b. **Johnson, James** / c. Kaw Township / e. Peddlar / i. B / j. 47 / L. 10.00 / n. 10.00

[Monthly List, April 1863, page 2]
1. [blank]
2. a. Febr[uary] / b. **Long, William** / c. Kansas City / e. Saddlery / g. 45.00 / h. 3% / i. A / j. 42 / k. 1.35
3. a. M[ar]ch & Ap[ril] / b. Long, William / c. Kansas City / e. Saddlery / g. 551.35 / h. 3% / i. A / j. 42 / k. 16.54 / n. 17.89
4. a. Febr[uary] / b. **Lang[s]enkamp F & Co[mpany]** / c. Kansas City / e. Boots & Shoes / g. 161.75 / h. 3% / i. A / j. 42 / k. 4.85
5. a. March & Apr[il] / b. Lang[s]enkamp F & Co[mpany] / c. Kansas City / e. Boots & Shoes / g. 515.25 / h. 3% / i. A / j. 42 / k. 15.45 / n. 20.30
6. a. Febr[uary] to Ap[ril] / b. **McGaigil James** / c. Independence / e. Ferry Boat Receipts / g. 264.00 / h. 1½% / i. A / j. 20 / k. 3.96 / n. 3.96
7. a. Febr[uary] / b. **Moody J[ohn] M** / c. Independence / e. Saddlery / g. 165.10 / h. 3% / i. A / j. 42 / k. 4.95
8. a. M[ar]ch & Apr[il] / b. Moody J[ohn] M / c. Independence / e. Saddlery / g. 718.50 / h. 3% / i. A / j. 42 / k. 21.55 / n. 26.50
9. a. Febr[uary] / b. **Morrison Wm P & Co[mpany]** / c. Kansas City / e. Tinware / g. 75.00 / h. 3% / i. A / j. 72 / k. 2.25
10. a. M[ar]ch & Ap[ril] / b. Morrison Wm P & Co[mpany] / c. Kansas City / e. Tinware / g. 663.44 / h. 3% / i. A / j. 72 / k. 19.90 / n. 22.15
11. Febr[uary] to Apr. / b. **McDonald & Kline** / c. Kansas City / e. Saddlery / g. 1266.25 / h. 3% / i. A / j. 42 / k. 37.98 / n. 37.98
12. a. April 1 [18]63 / b. **McKee Jane** / c. Westport / e. Hotel Keeper 8th cl[ass] / i. B / j. 36 / L. 5.00 / n. 5.00
13. a. Febr[uary] / **Nelson, Campbell & Co[mpany]** / c. Kansas [City] / e. Gross Ferry Receipts / g. 169.10 / h. 1½% i. A / j. 20 / k. 2.53
14. a. M[ar]ch & Apr[il] / b. Nelson, Campbell & Co[mpany] / c. Kansas [City] / e. Gross Ferry Receipts / g. 1205.00 / h. 1½% / i. A / j. 20 / k. 18.07 / n. 20.60
15. a. Febr[uary] / b. **Pollarad & Fairman** / Kansas [City] / e. Tinware / g. 118.00 / h. 3% / i. A / j. 72 / k. 3.54
16. a. M[ar]ch & Ap[ril] / b. Pollard & Fairman / Kansas [City] / e. Tinware / g. 898.00 / h. 3% / i. A / j. 72 / k. 26.94 / n. 30.48
17. a. Sept[ember] 1 [18]62 / b. **Roberts Preston & Co[mpany]** / c. Independence / d. 5 / e. 2 Horse Carriages / h. $2 / i. C / j. 8 / m. 10.00 / n. 10.00
18. a. March 1 [18]63 / b. **Russell E** / c. Kansas City / e. Photographer / i. B / j. 51 / L. 10.00 / n. 10.00
19. a. Febr[uary] / b. **Switzgable & Co[mpany]** / c. Kansas City / d. 39¼ / e. Barrels Beer / h. $1 / i. C / j. 2 / m. 39.25
20. a. M[ar]ch & Apr[il] / b. Switzgable & Co[mpany] / c. Kansas City / d. 214½ / e. Barrels Beer / h. 60 / i. C / j. 2 / m. 128.70 / n. 167.95
21. a. Febr[uary] / b. **Schoepf, Henry** / c. Westport / e. Boots & Shoes / g. 85.00 / h. 3% / i. A / j. 42 / k. 2.55
22. a. M[ar]ch & Ap[ril] / b. Schoepf, Henry / c. Westport / e. 321.00 / g. 321.00 / h. 3$ / i. A / j. 42 / k. 9.63 / n. 12.18
23. a. Febr[uary] / b. **Stein, Edward** / c. Kansas City / e. Furniture / g. 101.50 / h. 3% / i. A / j. 75 / k. 3.04
24. a. M[ar]ch & Ap[ril] / b. Stein, Edward / c. Kansas City / e. Furniture / g. 205.00 / h. 3% / i. A / j. 75 / k. 6.15 / n. 9.19

25. a. Febr[uary] to Ap[ril] / b. **Squire John** / c. Westport / e. Wagons manufac[ture]d / g. 1530.00 / h. 3% / i. A / j. 75 / k. 45.90 / n. 45.90
26. a. Febr[uary] to Ap[ril] / b. **Sager, Henry** / c. Westport / e. Furniture / g. 245.65 / h. 3% / i. A / j. 75 / k. 7.36 / n. 7.36
27. [blank]
28. a. Febr[uary] / b. **Thompson J[ohn] W.** / c. Kansas City / e. Tinware / g. 18.00 / h. 3% / i. A / j. 72 / k. 54
29. a. M[ar]ch & Apr[il] / b. Thompson J[ohn] W. / c. Kansas City / e. Tinware / g. 888.65 / h. 3% / i. A / j. 72 / k. 26.65 / n. 27.19
30. [blank]
31. a. Febr[uary] / b. **Ward, James W** / c. Kansas City / d. 33 / e. Cattle exc[eeding] 18 m[onths] / h. 30¢ / i. C / j. 12 / m. 9.90
32. a. M[ar]ch & Apr[il] / b. Ward, James W / c. Kansas City / d. 65 / e. Cattle exceed[ing] 18 [months] / h. 20 / i. C / j. 12 / m. 13.00
33. a. M[ar]ch & Apr[il] / b. Ward, James W / c. Kansas City / d. 130 / e. Hogs / h. 6 / i. C / j. 14 / m. 7.80 / n. 30.70
34. a. Febr[uary] / b. **Wedlich, F** / c. Kansas City / d. 5½ / e. Bbls [Barrels] Beer / h. $1 / i. C / j. 2 / m. 5.50
35. a. M[ar]ch & Apr[il] / b. Wedlich, F / c. Kansas City / d. 12 / e. Bbls [Barrels] Beer / h. 60 / i. C / j. 2 / m. 7.20
36. a. M[ar]ch & Apr[il] / b. Wedlich, F / c. Kansas City / d. Error in Jan[uar]y Assessment / m .13 / n. 12.83
37. a. April / b. **Weston, Robert** / e. Wagons / g. 96.00 / h. 3% / i. A / j. 75 / k. 2.88 / n. 2.88
38. [blank]
39. [blank]
40. [blank]

**Monthly List
May 1863**

Alphabetical List of Persons in Division No. <u>One</u> of Collection District No. <u>Two</u> of the <u>State</u> of <u>Missouri</u>, liable to a tax under the Excise laws of the United States, and the amount thereof, as assessed by <u>Robert Salisbury</u>, <u>Asst</u> Assessor, and by him returned to the <u>Assessor</u> of said District, for the month of <u>May</u>, 1863.

Assessors must be particular to fill all the blanks in this form, as far as practicable, and to classify and number all articles and occupations upon which taxes are assessed to correspond with the entry in the Abstract.

1   a. [illegible] / b. **[Bartlett] & Frank** / c. Kansas [City] / d. 14 / e. cattle exc[eeding] 18 months / h. 20 / i. C / j. 12 / m. 2.80
2   a. [illegible] / b. [Bartlett] & Frank / c. Kansas [City] / d. 8 / e. cattle under 18 months / h. 5 / i. C / j. 13 / m. .40
3   a. [illegible] / b, [Bartlett] & Frank / c. Kansas [City] / d. 5 / e. Hogs / h. 6 / i. C / j. 14 / m. .30
4   a. [illegible] / b. [Bartlett] & Frank / c. Kansas [City] / c. 4 / e. sheep / h. 3 / i. C / j. 15 / m. .12 / n. 3.62
5   a. [illegible] / b. **[Butc]her & Ackermann** / c. Kansas [City] / d. 16 / e. cattle exc[eeding] 18 m[onths] / h. 20 / i. C / j. 12 / m. 3.20
6   a. [illegible] / b. [Butc]her & Ackermann / c. Kansas [City] / d. 10 / e. cattle under 18 m[onths] / h. 5 / i. C / j. 13 / m. .50
7   a. [illegible] / b. [Butc]her & Ackermann / c. Kansas [City] / d. 4 / e. Hogs / h. 6 / i. C / j. 14 / m. .24
8   a. [illegible] / b. [Butc]her & Ackermann / c. Kansas [City] / d. 5 / e. sheep / h. 3 / i. C / j. 15 / m. .15 / n. 4.09
9   [blank]
10   a. [illegible] / b. **[Camp]bel Nelson & Co[mpany]** / c. Kansas [City] / e. Gross receipts of Ferry / g. 565.00 / h. 1½ / i. A / j. 20 / k. 8.48 / n. 8.48
11   [blank]
12   a. [illegible] / b. _____**ison James** / c. Kansas [City] / c. 12 / e. Cattle exc[eeding] 18 months / h. 20 / i. C / j. 12 / m. 2.40
13   a. [illegible] / b, _____ison James / c. Kansas [City] / c. 5 / e. Cattle under 18 months / h. 5 / i. C / j. 13 / m. .25
14   a. [illegible] / b. _____ison James / c. Kansas [City] / c. 4 / e. sheep / h. 3 / i. C / j. 15 / m. .12 / n. 2.77
15   [blank]
16   a. [illegible] / b. **[Gabe]l & Ralf** / c. Kansas [City] / e. Boots & shoes / g. 140.00 / h. 3% / i. A / j. 42 / k. 4.20 / n. 4.20
17   a. [illegible] / b. **[Garh]ard Jacob R** / c. Westport / e. Saddlery / g. 393.00 / h. 3% / i. A / j. 42 / k. 11.79 / n. 11.79
18   [blank]
19   a. [illegible] / b. **[Helm]erich & Co[mpany]** / c. Kansas City / d. 47½ Bbls [Barrels] Beer / h. 60¢ / i. C / j. 2 /

83

m. 28.50 / n. 28.50

20 a. [illegible] / b. **[Helf]rich & Co[mpany]** / c. Kansas City / d. 27 Bbls [Barrels] Beer / h. 60 / i. C / j. 2 / m. 16.20 / n. 16.20

21 [blank]

22 a. [illegible] / b. **[Kum]p Frank & Co[mpany]** / c. Kansas City / e. Soda Water / g. 1010.00 / h. 3% / i. A / j. 50 / k. 30.30 / 30.30

23 a. [illegible] / b. **[Kli]ne C. W** / c. Kansas City / e. Saddlery / g. 744.90 / h. 3% / i. A / j. 42 / k. 22.34 / n. 22.34 / [Paid?] in Jan[uary] 1ˢᵗ [18]64

24 a. [illegible] / b. **[Kla]ber Fred** / c. Westport / e. Wagons / g. 2340.85 / h. 3% / i. A / j. 75 / k. 70.23 / n. 70.23

25 [blank]

26 a. [illegible] / b. **[Lang]senkamp & C[ompany]** / c. Kansas City / e. Boots & Shoes / g. 313.25 / h. 3% / i. A / j. 42 / k. 9.40 / n. 9.40

27 a. [illegible] / b. **[Lon]g William** / c. Kansas City / e. Saddlery / g. 215.50 / h. 3% / i. A / j. 42 / k. 6.47 / n. 6.47

28 [blank]

29 a. [illegible] / b. **[Mo]hr Casper** / c. Kansas City / d. 7000 / e. Cigars / h. $.0025 / i. C / j. 20 / m. 17.50 / n. 17.50

30 a. [illegible] / b. **[Morr]ison W[illia]m** / c. Kansas City / e. Tinware / g. 917.50 / h. 3% / i. A / j. 72 / k. 27.53 / n. 27.53

31 a. [illegible] / b. **[Moo]die John** / c. Independence / e. Saddlery / g. 405.85 / h. 3% / i. [A?] / j. 42 / k. 12.18 / n. 12.18

32 a. [illegible] / b. **[Mc]Donald John** / c. Kansas [City] / d. 1200 lbs / e. Upper leather / h. 1¢ / i. C / j. 63 / m. 12.00

33 a. [illegible] / b. [Mc]Donald John / c. Kansas [City] / d. 12 doz / sheep skins / g. 42.00 / h. 4% / i. A / j. 65 / k. 1.68

34 a. [illegible] / b. [Mc]Donald John / c. Kansas [City] / d. 75 / e. Calf Skins / h. 6¢ / i. C / j. 68 / m. 4.50 / n. 18.18

35 [blank]

36 a. [illegible] / b. **[Polla]rd & Fairman** / c. Kansas City / e. Tinware / g. 575.15 / h. 3% / i. A / j. 72 / k. 17.25 / n. 17.25

37 [blank]

38 a. [illegible] / b. **[Stin]e Edward** / c. Kansas City / e. Furniture / e. 108.50 / i. A / j. 75 / k. 3.26 / n. 3.26

39 a. [illegible] / b. **[Swi]tzgable & Co[mpany]** / c. Kansas City / d. 73 1/8 / e. Barrels Beer / h. 60¢ / i. C / j. 2 / m. 43.88 / n. 43.88

40 a. [illegible] / b. **[Sag]er Henry** / c. Westport / e. Furniture / g. 91.50 / h. 3% / i. A / j. 75 / k. 2.75 / n. 2.75

[Monthly List, May 1863, page 2]

1 [blank]

2 a. May / b. **Shoepf, H** / c. Westport / e. Boots & Shoes / g. 105.00 / h. 3% / i. A / j. 42 / k. 3.15 / [n. 3.15]

3 a. May / b. **Stegmiller Joseph** / c. Westport / e. Wagons / g. 1285.00 / h. 3% / i. A / j. 75 / k. 38.55 / [n. 38.55]

4 a. May / b. **Squire John** / c. Westport / e. Wagons / g. 3370.00 / h. 3% / i. A / j. 75 / k. 101.10 / [n. 101.10]

5 [blank]

6 a. May / b. **Thompson John W** / c. Kansas [City] / e. Tinware / g. 238.00 / h. 3% / i. A / j. 72 / k. 7.14 / [n. 7.14]

7 [blank]

8 a. May / b. **Ward, James M** / c. [blank] / d. 23 / e. cattle exc[eeding] 18 months / h. 20 / i. C / j. 12 / m. 4.60 / [n. 4.60]

9 a. May / b. **Welland, Fred.** / c. [blank] / d. 14500 / e. Cigars / h. $.0025 / i. C / j. 20 / m. 36.25 / [n. 36.25]

Monthly List
June 1863

Alphabetical List of Persons in Division No. <u>One</u> of Collection District No. <u>Two</u> of the <u>State</u> of <u>Missouri</u>, liable to a tax under the Excise laws of the United States, and the amount thereof, as assessed by <u>Rob[er]t Salisbury</u>, <u>Asst</u> Assessor, and by him returned to the <u>Assessor</u> of said District, for the month of <u>June</u>, 1863.

Assessors must be particular to fill all the blanks in this form, as far as practicable, and to classify and number all articles and occupations upon which taxes are assessed to correspond with the entry in the Abstract.

1. a. June / b. **Butcher & Ackermann** / c. Kansas City / d. 19 / e. Cattle exc[eeding] 18 m[onths] / h. 20 / i. C / j. 12 / m.3.80

2. a. June / b. Butcher & Ackermann / c. Kansas City / d. 9 / e. Cattle under 18 m[onths] / h. 5 / i. C / j. 13 / m .45

3. a. June / b. Butcher & Ackermann / c. Kansas City / d. 4 / e. Hogs / h. 6 / i. C / j. 14 / m. .24

4. a. June / b. Butcher & Ackermann / c. Kansas City / d. 19 / e. Sheep / h. 3 / i. C / j. 15 / m. .57 / n. 5.06
5. a. June / b. **Bartlett & Frank** / c. Kansas City / d. 12 / e. Cattle exc[eeding] 18 m[onths] / h. 20 / i. C / j. 12 / n. 2.40
6. a. June / b. Bartlett & Frank / c. Kansas City / d. 7 / e. Cattle under 18 m[onths] / h. 5 / i. C / j. 13 / n. .35
7. a. June / b. Bartlett & Frank / c. Kansas City / d. 4 / e. Hogs / h. 6 / i. C / j. 14 / n. .24
8. a. June / b. **Bartlett & Frank** / c. Kansas City / d. 11 / e. sheep / h. 3 / i. C / j. 15 / m. .33 / n. 3.32
9. [blank]
10. a. June / b. **Gabel & Rahlf** / c. Kansas City / e. Boots & Shoes / g. 85.00 / h. 3% / i. A / j. 42 / k. 2.55 / n. 2.55
11. a. June / b. **Garhard, Jacob R** / c. Westport / e. Saddlery [sic] / g. 181.30 / h. 3% / i. A / j. 42 / k. 5.44 / n. 5.44
12. [blank]
13. a. June / b. **Helmerich [sic] H & C[ompany]** / c. Kansas City / d. 32½ / e. Bbls [Barrels] Beer / h. 60¢ / i. C / j. 2 / m. 19.50 / n. 19.50
14. a. June / b. **Helfrich H & C[ompany]** / c. Kansas City / d. 27 / e. Bbls [Barrels] Beer / h. 60¢ / i. C / j. 2 / m. 16.20 / n. 16.20
15. [blank]
16. a. June / b. **Kline C W** / c. Kansas City / e. Saddlery / g. 360.00 / h. 3% / i. A / j. 42 / k. 10.80 / n. 10.80
17. a. June / b. **Kump, Frank & C[ompany]** / c. Kansas City / e. Soda Water / g. 683.00 / h. 3% / i. A / j. 50 / k. 20.49 / n. 20.49
18. a. June / b. **Klaber, Fred** / c. Westport / e. Wagons / g. 720.00 / h. 3% / i. A / j. 75 / k. 21.60 / n. 21.60
19. [blank]
20. a. June / b. **Long, William** / c. Kansas City / e. Saddlery / g. 145.00 / h. 3% / i. A / j. 42 / k. 4.35 / n. 4.35
21. a. June / b. **Lang[s]encamp F & C[ompany]** / c. Kansas City / e. Boots & Shoes / g. 287.75 / h. 3% / j. A / j. 42 / k. 8.63 / n. 8.63
22. [blank]
23. a. June / b. **Moodie John W** / c. Independence / e. Saddlery / g. 478.35 / h. 3% / i. A / j. 42 / k. 14.35 / n. 14.35
24. a. June / b. **Morrison W[illia]m** / c. Kansas City / e. Tin Ware / g. 661.15 / h. 3% / i. A / j. 72 / k. 19.83 / n. 19.83
25. a. June / b. **McGargle James** / c. Jackson Co[unty] / e. Gross Receipts of Ferry / g. 118.00 / h. 1½ / i. A / j. 20 / k. 1.77 / n. 1.77
26. [blank]
27. a. June / b. **Nelson, Campbell & Co[mpany]** / c. Kansas City / e. Gross Receipts of Ferry / g. 365.00 / h. 1½ / i. A / j. 20 / k. 5.48 / n. 5.48
28. [blank]
29. a. June / b. **Pollard & Fairman** / c. Kansas City / e. Tinware / g. 420.20 / h. 3 / j. A / j. 72 / k. 12.61 / n. 12.61
30. [blank]
31. a. June / b. **Switzgable Peter & Co[mpany]** / c. Kansas City / d. 72½ / e. Barrels Beer / h. 60 / i. C / j. 2 / m. 43.50 / n. 43.50
32. a. June / b. **Stine Edward** / c. Kansas City / e. Furniture / g. 185.00 / h. 3% / i. A / j. 75 / k. 5.55 / n. 5.55
33. a. June / b. **Squire John** / c. Westport / e. Wagons / g. 405.00 / h. 3% / i. A / j. 75 / k. 12.15 / n. 12.15
34. a. June / b. **Sager Henry** / c. Westport / e. Furniture / g. 115.95 / h. 3% / i. A / j. 75 / k. 3.48 / n. 3.48
35. a. June / b. **Shoeph Henry** / c. Westport / e. Boots & shoes / g. 250.00 / h. 3% / i. A / j. 42 / k. 7.50 / n. 7.50
36. [blank]
37. a. June / b. **Thompson, James W** / c. Kansas City / e. Tinware / g. 234.70 / h. 3% / i. A / j. 72 / k.7.04 / n. 7.04
38. [blank]
39. a. June / b. **Ward, James M** / c. Kansas City / d. 45 / e. cattle exc[eeding] 18 m[onths] h. 2 / i. C / j. 12 / m. 9.00 / n. 9.00
40. a. June / b. **Weidlich, Ferd** / c. Westport / d. 4½ / e. Bbls [Barrels] Beer / h. 60 / i. C / j. 2 / m. 2.70 / n. 2.70

Monthly List
July 1863

Alphabetical List of Persons in Division No. <u>One</u> of Collection District No. <u>Two</u> of the <u>State</u> of <u>Missouri</u>, liable to a tax under the Excise laws of the United States, and the amount thereof, as assessed by <u>Robert Salisbury, Asst</u> Assessor, and by him returned to the <u>Assessor</u> of said District, for the month of <u>July</u>, 1863.

Assessors must be particular to fill all the blanks in this form, as far as practicable, and to classify and number all articles and occupations upon which taxes are assessed to correspond with the entry in the Abstract.

Civil War Era Federal Income Taxpayers

1 a. July / b. **Bartlett & Frank** / c. Kansas City / d. 12 / e. Cattle exc[eeding] 18 months / h. 20¢ / i. C / j. 12 / m. [2.40]

2 a. July / b. Bartlett & Frank / c. Kansas City / d. 6 / e. Cattle under 18 months / h. 5 / i. C / j. 13 / m. [.30]

3 a. July / b. Bartlett & Frank / c. Kansas City / d. 5 / e. Hogs / h. 6 / i. C / j. 14 / m. .18

4 a. July / b. Bartlett & Frank / c. Kansas City / d. 3 / e. sheep / h. 3 / i. C / j. 15 / m. .09 / n. 2.97

5 a. July / b. **Butcher & Ackermann** / c. Kansas City / d. 16 / e. cattle exc[eeding] 18 m[onths] / h. 20¢ / i. C / j. 15 / m. 3.20

6 a. July / b. Butcher & Ackermann / c. Kansas City / d. 10 / e. cattle under 18 m[onths] / h. 5¢ / i. C / j. 13 / m. .50

7 a. July / b. Butcher & Ackermann / c. Kansas City / d. 10 / e. Hogs / h. 6¢ / i. C / j. 14 / m. .60

8 a. July / b. Butcher & Ackermann / c. Kansas City / d. 25 / e. sheep / h. 3¢ / i. C / j. 15 / m. .75 / n. 5.05

9 a. July / b. **Bryant James M** / c. Independence / d. 6 / e. Cattle over 18 m[onths] / h. 20 / i. C / j. 12 / m. 1.20

10 a. July / b. Bryant James M / c. Independence / d. 2 / e. Cattle under 18 m[onths] / h. 5 / i. C / j. 13 / m. .10

11 a. July / b. Bryant James M / c. Independence / d. 12 / e. sheep / h. 3 / i. C / j. 15 / m. .36 / n. 1.66

12 a. July / b. **Borgstada Henry** / c. Kansas City / e. Boots & shoes made to Order / g. 108.00 / h. 1 / i. A / j. 13 / k. 1.08 / n. 1.08

13 [blank]

14 a. July / b. **Fry Reynold** / c. Kansas City / e. Barrels Manufac[ture]d / g. 132.00 / h. 3¢ / i. A / j. 75 / k. 3.96 / n. 3.96

15 [blank]

16 a. July / b. **Gabel & Rahlf** / c. Kansas City / e. Boots & Shoes / g. 112.00 / h. 3 / i. A / j. 42 / k. 3.36 / n. 3.36

17 a. July / b. **Garhard Jacob R** / c. Westport / e. Saddlery / g. 160.00 / h. 3¢ / i. A / j. 42 / k. 4.80 / n. 4.80

18 [blank]

19 a. July / b. **Helfrich H & Co[mpany]** / c. Kansas City / d. 29 ½ / e. Bbls [Barrels] Beer / h. 60 / i. C / j. 2 / m. 17.70 / n. 17.70

20 a. July / b. **Helmerick [sic] & Co[mpany]** / c. Kansas City / d. 51 1/8 / e. Bbls [Barrels] Beer / h. 60 / i. C / j. 2 / m. 30.68 / n. 30.68

21 [blank]

22 a. July / b. **Keevil & Turner** / c. Kansas City / e. Auction Sales / g. 3000.00 / h. 1/10 / i. A / j. 1 / k. 3.00 / n. 3.00

23 a. July / b. **Kline C W.** / c. Kansas City / e. Saddlery / g. 304.00 / h. 5¢ / i. A / j. 42 / k. 9.12 / n. 9.12

24 a. July / b. **Kump F H & Co** / c. Kansas City / e. Soda Water / g. 585.00 / h. 3% / i. A / j. 50 / k. 17.55 / n. 17.55

25 a. July / b. **Klaber, F** / c. Westport / e. Wagons manufac[ture]d / g. 600.00 / h. 3% / i. A / j. 75 / k. 18.00 / n. 18.00

26 [blank]

27 a. July / b. **Lang[s]encamp F & C[ompany]** / c. Kansas City / e. Boots & Shoes / g. 454.35 / h. 3% / i. A / j. 42 / k. 13.63 / n. 13.63

28 a. July / b. **Long, W[illia]m** / c. Kansas City / e. Saddlery / g. 989.00 / h. 3% / i. A / j. 42 / k. 29.67 / n. 29.67

29 [blank]

30 a. July / b. **Morrison, W[illia]m** / c. Kansas City / e. Tinware / g. 684.00 / h. 3 / i. A / j. 72 / k. 20.54 / n. 20.54

31 a. July / b. **Moodie John W** / c. Independence / e. Saddlery / g. 488.00 / h. 3 / i. A / j. 42 / k. 14.64 / n. 14.65

32 a. July / b. **Mohr Casper** / c. Kansas City / d. 1500 / e. Cigars / h. $.0025 / i. C / j. 20 / m. 3.75 / n. 3.75

33 [blank]

34 a. July / b. **Nelson, Campbell & Co[mpany]** / c. Kansas City / e. Receipts of Ferry / g. 484.00 / h. 1½¢ / i. A / j. 20 / k. 7.26 / n. 7.2[6]

35 [blank]

36 a. July / b. **Pollard & Fairman** / c. Kansas City / e. Tinware / g. 701.15 / h. 3¢ / i. A / j. 72 / k. 21.03 / n. 21.0[3]

37 a. July / b. **Payne & Toler** / c. Kansas City / e. Auction Sales / g. 467.60 / h. 1/10 / i. A / j. 1 / k. .47 / n. .4[7]

38 [blank]

39 [blank]

40 a. July / b. **Squire, John** / c. Westport / e. Tinware / g. 100.00 / h. 3 / i. A / j. 75 / k. 3.00 / n. 3.00

[Monthly List, July 1863, page 2]

1 [blank]

2 a. July / b. **Schwitzgabe[l] P & C[ompany]** / c. Kansas City / d. 67½ / e. Barrels Beer / h. 60¢ / i. C / j. 2 / m. 40.50 / n. 40.50

3 a. July / b. **Stine, Edward** / c. Kansas City / e. Furniture / g. 93.00 / h. 3% / i. A / j. 75 / k. 2.79 / n. 2.79

4 a. July / b. **Sager, Henry** / c. Westport / e. Furniture / g. 93.00 / h. 3% / i. A / j. 75 / k. 2.79 / n. 2.79

5 a. July / b. **Schoeff Henry** / c. Westport / e. Boots & Shoes / g. 250.00 / h. 3% / i. A / j. 42 / k. 7.50 / n. 7.50

6   a. July / b. **Smith, Richard** / c. Kansas City / e. Saddlery / g. 200.00 / h. 3% / i. A / j. 42 / k. 6.00 / n. 6.00
7   a. July / b. **Schwarzer [Scherzer], Michael** / c. Kansas City / e. Coopering / g. 210.00 / h. 3% / i. A / j. 75 / k. 6.30 /
    n. 6.30
8   [blank]
9   a. July / b. **Thompson, John W.** / c. Kansas City / e. Tinware / g. 500.00 / h. 3% / i. A / j. 42 / k. 15.00 / n. 15.00
10 [blank]
11 a. July / b. **Welland, C. F.** / c. Kansas City / d. 4000 / e. Cigars / h. $.0025 / i. C / j. 20 / m. 10.00 / n. 10.00
12 a. July / b. **Ward, James M** / c. Kansas City / d. 64 / e. Cattle exc[eeding] 18 m[onths] / h. 20¢ / i. C / j. 12 /
    m. 12.80
13 a. July / b. Ward, James M / c. Kansas City / d. 12 / e. Cattle under 18 m[onths] / h. 5 / i. C / j. 13 / m. .60 / n. 13.40
14 a. July / b. **Wilson, Robert** / c. Kansas City / e. Stone cutting / g. 157.00 / h. 3% / i. A / j. 50 / k. 4.71 / n. 4.71

Monthly List
August 1863

Alphabetical List of Persons in Division No. <u>One</u> of Collection District No. <u>Two</u> of the <u>State</u> of <u>Missouri</u>,
liable to a tax under the Excise laws of the United States, and the amount thereof, as assessed by <u>Robert Salisbury,</u>
<u>Asst</u> Assessor, and by him returned to the <u>Assessor</u> of said District, for the month of <u>August</u>, 1863.

Assessors must be particular to fill all the blanks in this form, as far as practicable, and to classify and
number all articles and occupations upon which taxes are assessed to correspond with the entry in the Abstract.

1   a. August / b. **Bartlett & Wyland** / c. Kansas City / d. 11 / e. Cattle exc[eeding] 18 months / h. 20 / i. C / j. 12 /
    m. 2.20
2   a. August / b. Bartlett & Wyland / c. Kansas City / d. 7 / e. Cattle Under 18 Months / h. 5 / i. C / j. 13 / m. .35
3   a. August / b. Bartlett & Wyland / c. Kansas City / d. 8 / e. Hogs / h. 6 / i. C / j. 14 / m. .48
4   a. August / b. Bartlett & Wyland / c. Kansas City / d. 10 / e. Sheep / h. 3 / i. C / j. 15 / m. .30 / n. 3.33
5   a. August / b. **Butcher & Ackermann** / c. Kansas City / d. 23 / e. Cattle exc[eeding] 18 Months / h. 20 / i. C / j. 12 /
    m. 4.60
6   a. August / b. Butcher & Ackermann / c. Kansas City / d. 8 / e. Cattle under 18 Months / h. 5 / i. C / j. 13 / m. .40
7   a. August / b. Butcher & Ackermann / c. Kansas City / d. 10 / e. Hogs / h. 6 / i. C / j. 14 / m. .60
8   a. August / b. Butcher & Ackermann / c. Kansas City / d. 25 / e. Sheep / h. 3 / i. C / j. 15 / m. .75 / n. 6.35
9   [blank]
10 a. August / b. **Campbell Nelson & Co[mpany]** / c. Kansas City / e. Gross Ferry Receipts / g. 464.00 / h. 1½ / i. A /
    j. 20 / k. 6.96 / n. 6.96
11 a. August / b. **Catrell M & Co[mpany]** / c. Kansas City / e. Gross Express Receipts / g. 1900.00 / h. 2 / i. A / j. 19 /
    k. 39.00 / n. 39.00
12 a. August / b.**Chick J S & Co[mpany]** / c. Kansas City / d. 408 lbs / e. Tobacco / h. 15¢ / i. C / j. 108 / m. 61.20 /
    n.61.20
13 [blank]
14 a. August / b. **Eckhart Ch[arle]s B** / c. Kansas City / d. 2500 / e. Cigars / h. $.0025 / i. C / j. 20 / m. 62.5 / n. 6.25
15 [blank]
16 a. August / b. **Frank & Beddle** / c. Kansas City / d. 15 / e. Cattle exc[eeding] 18 Months / h. 20 / i. C / j. 12 /
    m. 3.00
17 a. August / b. Frank & Beddle / c. Kansas City / d. 7 / e. Cattle under 18 Months / h. 5 / i. C / j. 13 / m. .35
18 a. August / b. Frank & Beddle / c. Kansas City / d. 4 / e. Hogs / h. 6 / i. C / j. 14 / m. .24
19 a. August / b. Frank & Beddle / c. Kansas City / d. 5 / e. Sheep / h. 3 / i. C / j. 15 / m. .18 / n. 3.77
20 [blank]
21 a. August / b. **Gerhart Joseph P** / c. Westport / e. Sad[d]lery / g. 135.80 / h. 3¢ / i. A / j. 42 / k. 4.07 / n. 4.07
22 a. August / b. **Gabel & Ralph** / c. Kansas City / e. Boots & Shoes / g. 145.00 / h. 3¢ / i. A / j. 42 / k. 4.35
23 [blank]
24 a. August / b. **Helfrich H & Co[mpany]** / c. Kansas City / d. 21 / e. Barrels Beer / h. 60¢ / i. C / j. 20 / m. 12.60 /
    n. 12.60
25 a. August / b. **Helmrich & Co[mpany]** / c. Kansas City / d. 8 1/8 / e. Barrels Beer / h. 60¢ / i. C / j. 20 / m. 4.88 /
    n. 4.88
26 [blank]
27 a. August / b. **Kline C. W.** / c. Kansas City / e. Sad[d]lery / g. 205.00 / h. 3¢ / i. A / j. 42 / k. 6.15 / n. 6.15

28 a. August / b.**Kump F. H. & Co** / c. Kansas City / e. Soda Water / g. 340.00 / h. 3¢ / i. A / j. 50 / k. 10.20 / n. 10.20
29 a. August / b. **Klaber F** / c. Westport / e. Wagons / g. 750.00 / h. 3¢ / i. A / j. 75 / k. 22.50 / n. 22.50
30 [blank]
31 a. August / b. **Lang[s]encamp & Co[mpany]** / c. Kansas City / e. Boots & Shoes / g. 349.75 / h. 3¢ / i. A / j. 42 / k. 10.50 / n. 10530
32 a. August / b. **Long William** / c. Kansas City / e. Saddlery / g. 345.80 / h. 3¢ / i. A / j. 42 / k. 10.37 / n. 10.37
33 [blank]
34 a. August / b. **McDonald John** / c. Kansas City / d. 312 lbs / e. Upper Leather / h. 1¢ / i. C / j. 63 / m. 3.12
35 a. August / b. McDonald John / c. Kansas City / d. 8 / e. Calf Skins / h. 6¢ / i. C / j. 68 / m. .48
36 a. August / b. McDonald John / c. Kansas City / d. 8 / e. Sheep Skins / g. 34.00 / h. 4¢ / i. A / j. 65 / k. 1.36 / n. 4.96
37 a. August / b. **Morrison William** / c. Kansas City / e. Tinware / g. 487.64 / h. 3¢ / i. A / j. 72 / k. 14.63 / n. 14.63
38 a. August / b. **Moodies John W** / c. Independence / e. Saddlery / g. 426.00 / h. 3¢ / i. A / j. 42 / k. 12.78 / n. 12.78
39 [blank]
40 a. August / b. **Pollard & Fairman** / c. Kansas City / e. Tinware / g. 284.25 / h. 3¢ / i. A / j. 72 / k. 8.53 / n. 8.53

[Monthly List, August 1863, page 2]
1 [blank]
2 a. Aug[ust] / b. **Stein August** / c. Kansas City / e. Furniture / g. 137.75 / h. 3% / i. A / j. 75 / k. 4.13 / n. 4.13
3 a. Aug[ust] / b. **Switzgable P & Co[mpany]** / c. Kansas City / d. 73¼ / e. Bbls [Barrels] Beer / h. 60¢ / i. C / j. 2 / m. 43.95 / n. 43.95
4 a. Aug[ust] / b. **Smith R** / c. Kansas City / e. Saddlery / g. 60.00 / h. 3¢ / i. A / j. 42 / k. 1.80 / n. 1.80
5 a. Aug[ust] / b. **Stegmiller Joseph** / c. Westport / e. Waggons [sic] / g. 300.00 / h. 3¢ / i. A / j. 75 / k. 9.00 / n. 9.00
6 a. Aug[ust] / b. **Squire John** / c. Westport / e. Waggons [sic] / g. 585.00 / h. 3¢ / i. A / j. 75 / k. 17.55 / n. 17.55
7 a. Aug[ust] / b. **Schoepf Henry** / c. Westport / e. Boots & Shoes / g. 185.50 / h. 3¢ / i. A / j. 42 / k. 5.57 / n. 5.57
8 [blank]
9 a. Aug[ust] / b. **Thompson J. W.** / c. Kansas City / e. Tinware / g. 113.00 / h. 3¢ / i. A / j. 72 / k. 3.39 / n. 3.39
10 [blank]
11 a. Aug[ust] / b. **Welland, C. F** / c. Kansas City / d. 2500 / e. Cigars / h. $.0025 / i. C / j. 20 / m. 6.25 / n. 6.25
12 a. Aug[ust] / b. **Ward James M** / c. Kansas City / d. 85 / e. Cattle exc[eeding] 18 Months / h. 20¢ / i. C / j. 12 / m. 17.00
13 a. Aug[ust] / b. Ward James M / c. Kansas City / d. 12 / e. Cattle Under 18 Months / h. 5¢ / i. C / j. 13 / m. .60
14 a. Aug[ust] / b. Ward James M / c. Kansas City / d. 4 / e. Hogs / h. 6 / i. C / j. 14 / m. .24 / n. 17.84
15 a. Aug[ust] / b. **Weston Robert** / c. Independence / e. Waggons Manuf[acture]d / g. 87.00 / h. 3¢ / i. A / j. 75 / k. 2.61 / n. 2.61

Monthly List
September 1863

Alphabetical List of Persons in Division No. <u>One</u> of Collection District No. <u>Two</u> of the <u>State</u> of <u>Missouri</u>, liable to a tax under the Excise laws of the United States, and the amount thereof, as assessed by <u>Robert Salisbury, Asst</u> Assessor, and by him returned to the <u>Assessor</u> of said District, for the month of <u>September</u>, 1863.

Assessors must be particular to fill all the blanks in this form, as far as practicable, and to classify and number all articles and occupations upon which taxes are assessed to correspond with the entry in the Abstract.

1 a. Sept[em]b[e]r / b. **Bartlett & Wyland** / c. Kansas [City] / d. 18 / e. Cattle exceeding 18 months / h. 20¢ / i. C / j. 12 / m. 3.60
2 a. Sept[em]b[e]r / b. Bartlett & Wyland / c. Kansas [City] / d. 9 / e. Cattle under 18 months / h. 5¢ / i. C / j. 13 / m. .45
3 a. Sept[em]b[e]r / b.Bartlett & Wyland / c. Kansas [City] / d. 18 / e. Hogs over 100 lbs / h. 6¢ / i. C / j. 14 / m. 1.08
4 a. Sept[em]b[e]r / b. Bartlett & Wyland / c. Kansas [City] / d. 13 / e. sheep / h. 3¢ / i. C / j. 15 / m. .39 / n. 5.52
5 a. Sept[em]b[e]r / b. **Butcher & Ackermann** / c. Kansas [City] / d. 14 / e. Cattle exceeding 18 months / h. 20¢ / i. C / j. 12 / m. 2.80
6 a. Sept[em]b[e]r / b. Butcher & Ackermann / c. Kansas [City] / d. 16 / e. Cattle under 18 months / h. 5¢ / i. C / j. 13 / m. .80
7 a. Sept[em]b[e]r / b. / Butcher & Ackermann / c. Kansas [City] / d. 22 / e. Hogs / h. 6¢ / i. C / j. 14 / m. 1.32
8 a. Sept[em]b[e]r / b. / Butcher & Ackermann / c. Kansas [City] / d. 22 / e. sheep / h. 5¢ / i. C / j. 15 / m. .66 / n. 5.58

9 a. Sept[em]b[e]r / b.**Beekey, William** / c. Westport / e. Boots & shoes / g. 61.00 / h. 3% / i. A / j. 42 / k. 1.83 / n. 1.83

10 [blank]

11 a. Sept[em]b[e]r / b. **Campbell Nelson & Co[mpany]** / c. Kansas City / e. Gross Receipts of Ferry / g. 568.00 / h. 1 ½ / i. A / j. 20 / k. 8.52 / n. 8.52

12 [blank]

13 a. Sept[em]b[e]r / b. **Eckert, Fr.** / c. Kansas City / d. 1000 / e. Cigars at $20 per mill / i. C / j. 20 / m. 2.50 / n. 2.50

14 [blank]

15 a. Sept[em]b[e]r / b. **Frank Henry & Co[mpany]** / c. Kansas City / d. 20 / e. Cattle exceeding 18 m[onths] / h. 20¢ / i. C / j. 12 / m. 4.00

16 a. Sept[em]b[e]r / b. Frank Henry & Co[mpany] / c. Kansas City / d. 3 / e. Cattle under 18 m[onths] / h. 5¢ / i. C / j. 13 / m. .15

17 a. Sept[em]b[e]r / b. Frank Henry & Co[mpany] / c. Kansas City / d. 13 / e. Hogs / h. 6¢ / i. C / j. 14 / m. .78

18 a. Sept[em]b[e]r / b. Frank Henry & Co[mpany] / c. Kansas City / d. 11 / e. Sheep / h. 3¢ / i. C / j. 15 / m. .33 / n. 5.26

19 a. Sept[em]b[e]r / b. **Gable & Rahlf** / c. Kansas City / e. Boots & shoes / g. 80.00 / h. 3% / i. A / j. 42 / k. 2.40 / n. 2.40

20 a. Sept[em]b[e]r / b. **Helmerich, Henry** / c. Kansas City / d. 39 ½ / e. Barrels Beer / h. 60 / i. C / j. 2 / m. 23.70 / n. 23.70

21 a. Sept[em]b[e]r / b. **Kump, F. H. & Co[mpany]** / c. Kansas City / e. Soda Water / g. 275.00 / h. 3% / i. A / j. 50 / k. 8.25 / n. 8.25

22 a. Aug[ust] & Sept[ember] / b. **Kivill & Turner** / c. Kansas City / e. Auction Sales / g. 2500.00 / h. 1/10 / i. A / j. 1 / k. 2.50 / n. 2.50

23 a. Sept[em]b[e]r / b. **Kline, C W.** / c. Kansas City / e. Saddlery / g. 185.00 / h. 3% / i. A / j. 42 / k. 5.55 / n. 5.55 "coll. J. M. M."

24 a. Sept[ember] / b. **Klaber Frederick** / c. Westport / e. Wagons Manufac[ture]d / g. 1475.00 / h. 3% / i. A / j. 75 / k. 44.25 / n. 44.25

25 a. Sept[ember] / b. **Langsenkamp & C. F. [Langsenkamp, F., and Company]** / c. Kansas City / e. Boots & shoes Manufac[ture]d / g. 394.00 / h. 3% / i. A / j. 42 / k. 11.82 / n. 11.82

26 a. Sept[ember] / b. **Long, William** / c. Kansas City / e. Saddlery / g. 330.00 / h. 3% / i. A / j. 42 / k. 9.90 / n. 9.90

27 [blank]

28 [blank]

29 A. Aug[ust] & Sep[tember] / b/ **Mohr, Casper** / c. Kansas City / d. 1000 / e. Cigars manufac[ture]d / h. $.0025 / i. C / j. 20 / m. 2.50 / n. 2.50

30 a. Sept[ember] / b. **Morrison, W[illia]m** / c. Kansas City / e. Tin ware / g. 332.00 / h. 3% / i. A / j. 72 / k. 13.53 / n. 13.53

31 . Sept[ember] / b. **Moodie, John H** / c. Kansas City / e. Saddlery / g. 330.00 / h. 3% / i. A / j. 42 / k. 11.46 / n. 11.46

32 [blank]

33 a. Aug[ust] & Sept[ember] / b. **Payne & Toler** / c. Kansas City / e. Auction Sales / g. 3170.00 / h. 1/10 / i. A / j. 1 / k. 3.17 / n. 3.17

34 a. Sep[tember] / b. **Pollard & Fairman** / c. Kansas City / e. Tin Ware / g. 463.00 / h. 3% / i. A / j. 72 / k. 13.89 / n. 13.89

35 a. Sep[tember] / b. **Schoepf, Henry** / c. Westport / e. Boots & Shoes / g. 545.00 / h. 3% / i. A / j. 42 / k. 16.35 / n. 16.35

36 a. Sep[tember] / b. **Switzgabel, Peter** / c. Kansas City / d. 81½ / e. Barrels Beer / h. 60¢ / i. C / j. 2 / m. 48.90 / n. 48.90

37 a. Sep[tember] / b. **Smith, Richard** / c. Kansas City / e. Saddlery / g. 148.00 / h. 3% / i. A / j. 42 / k. 4.44 / n. 4.44

38 a. Sep[tember] / b. **Squire, John** / c. Westport / e. Wagons manufac[ture]d / g. 1895.00 / h. 3% / i. A / j. [blank] / k. 56.85 / n. 56.85

39 a. Sep[tember] / b. **Sager Henry** / c. Westport / e. Furniture / g. 151.00 / h. 3% / i. A / j. 42 / k. 4.53 / n. 4.53

40 a. Sep[tember] / b. **Stine Edward** / c. Kansas City / e. Furniture / g. 70.00 / n. 3% / i. A / j. 42 / k. 2.10 / n. 2.10

[Monthly List, September 1863, page 2]

1 [blank]

2 a. Sept[ember] / b. **Thompson J W.** / c. Kansas City / e. Tinware manufac[ture]d / g. 473.00 / h. 3% / i. A / j. 72 / k. 14.19 / n. 14.19

3   a. Sept[ember] / b. **Thomas, Charles** / c. Kansas City / e. Tinware manufac[ture]d / g. 55.00 / h. 3% / i. A / j. 72 / k. 1.65 / n. 1.65

4   [blank]

5   [blank]

6   a. Sept[ember] / b. **Willand, C. F.** / c. Kansas City / d. 6600 / e. Cigars / f. $.0025 / i. C / j. 20 / m. 16.50 / n. 16.50

7   a. Sept[ember] / b. **Ward, James M** / c. Kansas City / d. 90 / e. Cattle exceed[ing] 18 m[onths] h. 20 / i. C / j. 12 / m. 18.00

8   a. Sept[ember] / b. Ward James M / c. Kansas City / d. 10 / e. Cattle under 18 m[onths] / h. 5 / i. C / j. 13 / m. .50 / n. 18.50

Monthly List
October 1863

Alphabetical List of Persons in Division No. <u>One</u> of Collection District No. <u>Two</u> of the <u>State</u> of <u>Missouri</u>, liable to a tax under the Excise laws of the United States, and the amount thereof, as assessed by <u>Robert Salisbury</u>, <u>Asst</u> Assessor, and by him returned to the <u>Assessor</u> of said District, for the month of <u>October</u>, 1863.

Assessors must be particular to fill all the blanks in this form, as far as practicable, and to classify and number all articles and occupations upon which taxes are assessed to correspond with the entry in the Abstract.

1   a. Oct[o]b[e]r / b. **Butcher & Ackermann** / c. Kansas City / d. 17 / e. Cattle exceeding 18 m[onths] / h. 20¢ / i. C / j. 12 / m. 3.40

2   a. Oct[o]b[e]r / b. Butcher & Ackermann / c. Kansas City / d. 9 / e. Cattle under 18 m[onths] / h. 5 / i. C / j. 13 / m. .45

3   a. Oct[o]b[e]r / b. Butcher & Ackermann / c. Kansas City / d. 26 / e. Hogs / h. 6¢ / i. C / j. 14 / m. 1.56

4   a. Oct[o]b[e]r / b. Butcher & Ackermann / c. Kansas City / d. 18 / e. Sheep / h. 3 / i. C / j. 15 / m. .54 / n. 5.95

5   a. Oct[o]b[e]r / b. **[Brya]nt, James M** / c. Independence / d. 12 / e. Cattle exceed[ing] 18 m[onth] / h. 20¢ / i. C / j. 12 / m. 2.40

6   a. Oct[o]b[e]r / b. [Brya]nt, James M / c. Independence / d. 12 / e. Cattle under 18 m[onths] / h. 5¢ / i. C / j. 13 / m. .60

7   a. Oct[o]b[e]r / b. [Brya]nt, James M / c. Independence / d. 22 / e. sheep / h. 3 / i. C / j. 15 / m. .66 / n. 3.66

8   a. Oct[o]b[e]r / b. **[Bar]tlett & Wyland** / c. Kansas City / d. 19 / e. Cattle exceeding 18 m[onths] / h. 20¢ / i. C / j. 12 / m. 3.80

9   a. Oct[o]b[e]r / b. [Bar]tlett & Wyland / c. Kansas City / d. 3 / e. Cattle under 18 m[onths] / h. 5¢ / i. C / j. 13 / m. .15

10   a. Oct[o]b[e]r / b. [Bar]tlett & Wyland / c. Kansas City / d. 23 / e. Hogs / h. 6¢ / i. C / j. 14 / m. 1.35

11   a. Oct[o]b[e]r / b. [Bar]tlett & Wyland / c. Kansas City / d. 16 / e. sheep / h. 3¢ / i. C / j. 15 / m. .48 / n. 5.81

12   [blank]

13   a. Oct[o]b[e]r / b. **Campbell Nelson & Co[mpany]** / c. Kansas City / e. Gross Receipts of Ferry / g. 689.00 / h. 1½ / i. A / j. 20 / k. 10.34 / n. 10.34

14   a. July & [illegible] / b. **Catrell M & Co[mpany]** / c. Kansas City / e. Gross Receipts of Express / g. 2100.00 / h. 2% / i. A / j. 19 / k. 42.00 / n. 42.00

15   [blank]

16   a. Oct[o]b[e]r / b. **Eckert Frederick** / c. Kansas City / d. 500 / e. Cigars at $20 per m[ill] / h. $.0025 / i. A / j. 20 / m. 1.25 / n. 1.25

17   [blank]

18   a. Oct[o]b[e]r / b. **Fry & Reynolds** / c. Kansas City / e. Barrels manufact[ure]d / g. 77.00 / h. 3% / i. A / j. 75 / k. 2.31 / n. 2.31

19   a. Oct[o]b[e]r / b. **Frank & Dunbar** / c. Kansas City / d. 15 / e. Cattle exceeding 18 months / h. 20¢ / i. C / j. 12 / m. 3.00

20   a. Oct[o]b[e]r / b. **Frank & Dunbar** / c. Kansas City / d. 4 / e. Cattle under 18 months / h. 5¢ / i. C / j. 13 / m. .20

21   a. Oct[o]b[e]r / b. Frank & Dunbar / c. Kansas City / d. 18 / e. Hogs / h. 6¢ / i. C / j. 14 / m. 1.08

22   a. Oct[o]b[e]r / b. Frank & Dunbar / c. Kansas City / d. 3 / e. Sheep / h. 3¢ / i. C / j. 15 / m. .09 / n. 4.37

23   [blank]

24   a. Oct[o]b[e]r / b. **Gabel & Rahlf** / c. Kansas City / e. Boots & shoes / g. 100.00 / h. 3% / i. A / j. 2 / k. 3.00 / n. 3.00

25   a. Oct[o]b[e]r / b. **Gleinz, Christ.** / c. Westport / e. Waggons [sic] etc. / g. 320.00 / h. 3% / i. A / j. 75 / k. 9.60 / n. 9.60

26 a. Oct[o]b[e]r / b. **Gerhart, J R** / c. Kansas City / e. Saddlery & Harness / g. 363.00 / h. 3% / i. A / j. 42 / k. 10.89 / n. 10.89

27 [blank]

28 a. Oct[o]b[e]r / b. **Helmreich, Henry** / c. Kansas City / d. 13 / e. Bbls [Barrels] Beer / h. 60¢ / i. C / j. 2 / m. 7.80 / n. 7.80

29 [blank]

30 a. Oct[o]b[e]r / b. **Long, William** / c. Kansas City / e. Saddlery / g. 275.00 / h. 3% / i. A / j. 42 / k. 82.5 / n. 8.25

31 a. Oct[o]b[e]r / b. **Langsenkamp, F & Co[mpany]** / c. Kansas City / e. Boots & Shoes / g. 440.00 / h. 3% / i. A / j. 42 / k. 13.20 / n. 13.20

32 [blank]

33 a. Oct[o]b[e]r / b. **Mohr, C** / c. Kansas City / d. 500 / e. Cigars at $20 / i. C / j. [blank] / m. 1.25 / n. 1.25

34 a. Oct[o]b[e]r / b. **Morrison W[illia]m** / c. Kansas City / e. Tin Ware / g. 405.00 / h. 3% / i. A / j. 72 / k. 12.15 / n. 12.15

35 a. Oct[o]b[e]r / b. **Moodie, John W** / c. Independence / e. Saddlery / g. 169.00 / h. 3% / i. A / j. 72 / k. 5.07 / n. 5.07

36 [blank]

37 a. Oct[o]b[e]r / b. **Pollard & Fairman** / c. Kansas City / e. Tin Ware etc / g. 357.00 / h. 3% / i. A / j. 72 / k. 10.71 / n. 10.71

38 [blank]

39 a. Oct[o]b[e]r / b. **Squire, John** / c. Westport / e. Wagons etc / g. 1080.00 / h. 3% / i. A / j. [blank] / k. 32.40 / n. 32.50

40 a. Oct[o]b[e]r / b. **Stine, Edward** / c. Kansas City / e. Furniture / g. 75.00 / h. 3% / i. A / j. [blank] / k. 2.25 / n. 2.25

[Monthly List, October 1863, page 2]

1 [blank]

2 a. Oct[ober] / b. **Smith, S. S.** / c. Kansas City / e. Saddlery / g. 337.00 / h. 3% / i. A / j. 42 / k. 10.11 / n. 10.11

3 a. Oct[ober] / b. **Sager, Henry** / c. Westport / e. Furniture / g. 71.00 / h. 3% / i. A / j. 75 / k. 2.13 / n. 2.13

4 a. Oct[ober] / b. **Scwitzgable, Peter** / c. Kansas City / d. 84 1/8 / e. Bb.s [Barrels] of Beer / h. 60 / i. C / j. 2 / m. 50.48 / n. 50.48

5 a. Oct[ober] / b. **Smith, Richard** / c. Kansas City / e. Saddlery / g. 85.00 / h. 3% / i. A / j. 42 / k. 2.55 / n. 2.55

6 a. Oct[ober] / b. **Scherzer, Michael** / c. Kansas City / e. Barrels manufactured / g. 87.00 / h. 3% / i. A / j. 75 / k. 2.61 / n. 2.61

7 [blank]

8 a. Oct[ober] / b. **Thompson, J. W.** / c. Kansas City / e. Tinware manufactured / g. 80.00 / h. 3% / i. A / j. 72 / k. 2.40 / n. 2.40

9 a. Oct[ober] / b. **Thomas Charles** / c. Kansas City / e. Tinware manufactured / g. 65.00 / h. 3% / i. A / j. 72 / k. 1.95 / n. 1.95

10 [blank]

11 a. Oct[ober] / b. **Ward, James M** / c. Kansas City / d. 60 / e. Cattle exceedp[ing] 18 m[onths] / h. 20 / i. C / j. 12 / m. 12.00

12 a. Oct[ober] / b. Ward James M / c. Kansas City / d. 25 / e. Hogs / h. 6 / i. C / j. 14 / m. 1.50 / n. 13.50

13 a. Oct[ober] / b. **Welland, C. F.** / c. Kansas City / d. 5400 / e. Cigars / h. $.0025 / i. C / j. [blank] / m. 13.50 / n. 13.50

Monthly List
November 1863

Alphabetical List of Persons in Division No. <u>One</u> of Collection District No. <u>Two</u> of the <u>State</u> of <u>Missouri</u>, liable to a tax under the Excise laws of the United States, and the amount thereof, as assessed by <u>Robert Salisbury</u>, <u>Asst</u> Assessor, and by him returned to the <u>Assessor</u> of said District, for the month of <u>November</u>, 1863.

1 a. Nov[em]]b[e]r / b. **Becker, Philip** / c. Westport / e. Boots & shoes manufactured / g. 157.00 / h. 3% / i. A / j. 42 / k. 4.71

2 a. Sept[em]]b[e]r / b. Becker, Philip / c. Westport / e. Manufacturer / i. B / j. 42 / L. 6.67 / n. 11.38

3 a. Nov[em]]b[e]r / b. **Bartlett & Wyland** / c. Kansas City / d. 9 / e. Cattle exceedp[ing] 18 m[onths] / h. 20¢ / i. C / j. 12 / m. 1.80

4   a. Nov[em]]b[e]r / b. Bartlett & Wyland / c. Kansas City / d. 1 / e. Cattle under 18 m[onths] / h. 5¢ / i. C / j. 13 / m. .05

5   a. Nov[em]]b[e]r / b. Bartlett & Wyland / c. Kansas City / d. 11 / e. Hogs / h. 6¢ / i. C / j. 14 / m. .66

6   a. Nov[em]]b[e]r / b. Bartlett & Wyland / c. Kansas City / d. 7 / e. Sheep / h. 3¢ / i. C / j. 15 / m. .21 / n. 2.72

7   a. Nov[em]]b[e]r / b. **Butcher & Ackermann** / c. Kansas City / d. 15 / e. Cattle exc[eeding] 18 m[onths] / h. 20¢ / i. C / j. 12 / m. 3.00

8   a. Nov[em]]b[e]r / b. Butcher & Ackermann / c. Kansas City / d. 8 / e. Cattle under 18 m[onths] / h. 5¢ / i. C / j. 13 / m. .40

9   a. Nov[em]]b[e]r / b. Butcher & Ackermann / c. Kansas City / d. 22 / e. Hogs / h. 6¢ / i. C / j. 14 / m. 1.32

10   a. Nov[em]]b[e]r / b. Butcher & Ackermann / c. Kansas City / d. 8 / e. sheep / h. 3¢ / i. C / j. 15 / m. .24 / n. 4.96

11   [blank]

12   [blank]

13   a. Sept[em]b[e]r / b. **Cooper & Gregg** / c. Kansas City / e. Retail Dealers / i. B / j. 56 / L. 6.67 / n. 6.67

14   a. Nov[em]b[e]r / b. **Campbel[l] Nelson & Co[mpany]** / c. Kansas City / e. Gross receipts of Ferry / g. 527.00 / h. 1½% i. A / j. 20 / k. 7.91 / n. 7.91

15   [blank]

16   [blank]

17   a. Nov[em]b[e]r / b. **Dunbar, Robert** / c. Kansas City / e. Butcher / i. B / j. 14 / L. 5.00

18   a. Nov[em]b[e]r / b. Dunbar, Robert / c. Kansas City / d. 12 / e. Cattle exceeding 18 m[onths] / h. 20 / i. C / j. 12 / m. 2.40

19   a. Nov[em]b[e]r / b. Dunbar, Robert / c. Kansas City / d. 12 / e. Hogs / h. 6 / i. C / j. 14 / m. .72

20   a. Nov[em]b[e]r / b. Dunbar, Robert / c. Kansas City / d. 3 / e. sheep / h. 3 / i. C / j. 15 / m. .09 / n. 8.21

21   [blank]

22   [blank]

23   a. Nov[em]b[e]r / b. **Eckert, F.** / c. Kansas City / d. 1800 / e. Cigars / h. $.0025 / i. C / j. 20 / m. 4.50 / n. 4.50

24   [blank]

25   [blank]

26   a. Nov[em]b[e]r / b. **Gerhart, J. R** / c. Kansas City / e. Saddlery / g. 140.00 / h. 3% / i. A / j. 42 / k. 4.20 / n. 4.20

27   a. Nov[em]b[e]r / b. **Gabel & Rahlf** / c. Kansas City / e. Boots & Shoes / g. 200.00 / h. 3% / i. A / j. 42 / k. 6.00 / n. 6.00

28   [blank]

29   [blank]

30   a. Nov[em]b[e]r / b. **Helmreich, Henry** / c. Kansas City / d. 27¼ / e. Bbls [Barrels] Beer / i. C / j. 2 / m. 16.35 / n. 16.35

31   a. Nov[em]b[e]r / b. **Helfreich, Henry** / c. Kansas City / d. 18½ / e. Bbls [Barrels] Beer / i. C / j. 2 / m. 11.10 / n. 11.10

32   [blank]

33   [blank]

34   a. Nov[em]b[e]r / b. **Klaber, Frederick** / c. Westport / e. Waggons [sic] manufact[ure]d / g. 430.00 / h. 3% / i. A / j. 75 / k. 12.90 / n. 12.90

35   [blank]

36   [blank]

37   a. Nov[em]b[e]r / b. **Long, William** / c. Kansas City / e. Saddlery / g. 305.00 / h. 3% / i. A / j. 42 / k. 9.15 / n. 9.15

38   a. Nov[em]b[e]r / b. **Langsenkamp F & Co[mpany]** / c. Kansas City / e. Boots & Shoes / g. 206.00 / h. 3% / i. A / j. 42 / k. 6.18 / n. 6.18

39   [blank]

40   [blank]

[Monthly List, November 1863, page 2]

1   [blank]

2   a. Nov[em]b[e]r / b. **Moodie, John W.** / c. Independence / e. Saddlery / g. 378.00 / h. 3% / i. A / j. 42 / k. 11.34 / n. 11.34

3   a. Nov[em]b[e]r / b. **Morrison, William** / c. Kansas City / e. Tinware / g. 295.00 / h. 3% / i. A / j. 72 / k. 8.85 / n. 8.85

4   a. Nov[em]b[e]r / b. **Mohr, Casper** / c. Kansas City / d. 800 / e. Cigars / h. $.0025 / i. C / j. 20 / m. 2.00 / n. 2.00

5   [blank]

6   [blank]

7   a. Nov[em]b[e]r / b. **Pollard & Fairman** / c. Kansas City / e. Tinware / g. 783.00 / h. 3% / i. A / j. 72 / k. 23.49 / n. 23.49

8   [blank]

9   [blank]

10 a. May / b. **Roberts, Preston** / c. Independence / d. 8 / e. Horse Carriages / h. $2 / i. C / j. 8 / m. 16.00 / n. 16.00

11 [blank]

12 [blank]

13 a. Dec[em]b[e]r 1ˢᵗ / b. **Setzler, William** / c. Kansas City / e. Retail Liquor Dealer / i. B / j. 57 / L. 8.33 / n. 8.33

14 a. Nov[em]b[e]r / b. **Sager, Henry** / c. Westport / e. Furniture / g. 200.00 / h. 3% / i. A / j. 75 / k. 6.00 / n. 6.00

15 a. Nov[em]b[e]r / b. **Stine, Edward** / c. Kansas City / e. Furniture / g. 61.00 / h. 3% / i. A / j. 75 / k. 1.83 / n. 1.83

16 a. Nov[em]b[e]r / b. **Schwitzgabel, Peter** / c. Kansas City / d. 74 1/8 / e. Bbls [Barrels] Beer / h. 60¢ / i. C / j. 2 / m. 44.48 / n. 44.48

17 a. Nov[em]b[e]r / b. **Squire, John** / c. Westport / e. Waggons [sic] manufact[ure]d / g. 542.00 / h. 3% / i. A / j. 75 / k. 16.26 / n. 16.26

18 a. Nov[em]b[e]r / b. **Smith, Richard** / c. Kansas City / e. Saddlery / g. 100.00 / h. 3% / i. A / j. 42 / k. 3.00 / n. 3.00

19 a. Oct[ober] / b. **Shoepf, Henry** / c. Westport / e. Boots & Shoes / g. 350.00 / h. 3% / i. A / j. 42 / k. 10.50

20 a. Nov[em]b[e]r / b. Shoepf, Henry / c. Westport / e. Boots & Shoes / g. 280.00 / h. 3% / i. a / j. 42 / k. 8.40 / n. 18.90

21 a. Nov[em]b[e]r / b. **Stegmiller, Joseph** / c. Westport / e. Waggons [sic] manufact[ure]d / g. 300.00 / h. 3% / i. A / j. 75 / k. 9.00 / n. 9.00

22 a. Nov[em]b[e]r / b. **Smith, S.** / c. Kansas City / e. Saddlery / g. 361.00 / h. 3% / i. A / j. 42 / k. 10.83 / n. 10.83

23 [blank]

24 [blank[

25 a. Nov[em]b[e]r / b. **Ward, James M** / c. Kansas City / d. 70 / e. Cattle exceed[ing] 18 months / h. 20¢ / i. C / j. 12 / m. 14.00

26 a. Nov[em]b[e]r / b. Ward, James M / c. Kansas City / d. 150 / e. Hogs / h. 6¢ / i. C / j. 14 / m. 9.00 / n. 23.00

27 a. Nov[em]b[e]r / b. **Widelich, Ferdinand** / c. Westport / d. 3 1/8 / e. Bbls [Barrels] Beer / h. 60 / i. C / j. 2 / m. 1.88 / n. 1.88

28 a. Nov[em]b[e]r / b. **Welland, C. F.** / c. Kansas City / d. 8000 / e. Cigars / h. $.0025 / i. C / j. 20 / m. 20.00 / n. 20.00

Monthly List
December 1863

      Alphabctical List of Persons in Division No. <u>One</u> of Collection District No. Two of the <u>State</u> of <u>Missouri</u>, liable to a tax under the Excise laws of the United States, and the amount thereof, as assessed by <u>Robert Salisbury</u>, <u>Asst</u> Assessor, and by him returned to the Assessor of said District, for the month of <u>December</u>, 1863.

1   a. Jan[uar]y [18]63 / b. **Axline, Jacob** / c. Hickman's Mills / e. Cattle Broker / i. B / j. 12 / L. 3.33 / n. 3.33

2   a. Dec[ember] [18]63 / b. **Booker, Asa** / c. Kansas City / e. Retail Liquor Dealer / i. B / j. 51 / L. 8.33 / n. 8.33

3   a. Sept[ember] / b. **Brock, Perry** / c. Independence / e. Retail Dealer / i. B / j. 56 / L. 6.67 / n. 6.67

4   a. Sept[ember] / b. **Buchanan John O** / c. Independence / e. Retail Dealer / i. B / j. 56 / L. 6.67 / n. 6.67

5   a. Sept[ember] / b. **Boggs, Joseph O** / c. Westport / e. Physician / i. B / j. 54 / L. 6.67 / n. 6.67

6   a. Sept[ember] / b. **Bryant, David A.** / c. Hickman's Mills / e. Physician / i. B / j. 54 / L. 6.67 / n. 6.67

7   a. December / b. **Butcher & Ackermann** / c. Kansas City / d. 14 / e. Cattle exceed[ing] 18 m[onths] / h. 20 / i. C / j. 12 / m. 2.80

8   a. December / b. Butcher & Ackermann / c. Kansas City / d. 1 / e. Calf / h. 5 / i. C / j. 13 / m. .05

9   a. December / b. Butcher & Ackermann / c. Kansas City / d. 25 / e. hogs / h. 6 / i. C / j. 14 / m. 1.50

10 a. December / b. Butcher & Ackermann / c. Kansas City / d. 4 / e. sheep / h. 3 / i. C / j. 15 / m. .12 / n. 4.47

11 a. December / b. **Bartlett & Wyland** / c. Kansas City / d. 14 / e. Cattle exc[eeding] 18 m[onths] / h. 20 / i. C / j. 12 / m. 2.80

12 a. December / b. Bartlett & Wyland / c. Kansas City / d. 20 / e. Hogs / h. 6 / i. C / j. 14 / m. 1.20

13 a. December / b. Bartlett & Wyland / c. Kansas City / d. 8 / e. sheep / h. 3 / i. C / j. 15 / m. .24 / n. 4.24

14 a. December / b. **Becker Philip** / c. Westport / e. Boots & shoes / g. 75.00 / h. 3% / i. A / j. 42 / k. 2.25 / n. 2.25

93

Civil War Era Federal Income Taxpayers

15 a. Nov[ember] & Dec[ember] / b. **Diveley, Crandall & Co[mpany]** / c. Kansas City / d. 2380 / e. Hogs / h. 6 / i. C / j. 14 / m. 142.80 / n. 142.80
16 a. December / b. **Dunbar R R** / c. Kansas City / d. 8 / e. Cattle exceed[ing] 18 m[onths] / h. 20 / i. C / j. 12 / m. 1.60
17 a. December / b. Dunbar R R / c. Kansas City / d. 7 / e. Hogs / h. 6 / i. C / j. 14 / m. .42
18 a. December / b. Dunbar R R / c. Kansas City / d. 4 / e. sheep / h. 3 / i. C / j. 15 / m. .12 / n. 2.14
19 a. Sept[ember] 1 / b. **Esslinger Frederick** / c. Kansas City / e. Retail Dealer / i. B / j. 56 / L. 6.67 / n. 6.67
20 a. December / b. **Eckert F** / c. Kansas City / d. 500 / e. Cigars / h. $.0025 / i. C / j. 20 / m. 1.25 / n. 1.25
21 a. December / b. **Fry, Reynold** / c. Kansas City / e. Cooperage / g. 66.00 / h. 3% / i. A / j. 75 / k. 1.98 / n. 1.98
22 a. Nov[ember] & Dec[ember] / b. **Frank, C. J.** / c. Kansas City / d. 106 / e. Hogs / h. 6 / i. C / j. 14 / m. 6.36 / n. 6.36
23 a. December / b. **Gluntz, Christian** / c. Westport / e. Waggons [sic] & transfer / g. 312.00 / h. 3% / i. A / j. 75 / k. 9.36 / n. 9.36
24 a. December / b. **Gerhart, Jacob R** / c. Kansas City / e. Saddlery / g. 116.00 / h. 3% / i. A / j. 42 / k. 3.48 / n. 3.48
25 a. December / b. **Gabel & Rahlf** / c. Kansas City / e. Boots & Shoes / g. 192.00 / h.. 3% / i. A / j. 42 / k. 5.76 / n. 5.76
26 a. December / b. **Helferich Henry & Co[mpany]** / c. Kansas City / d. 9½ / e. Bbls [Barrels] Beer / h. 60 / i. C / j. 2 / m. 5.70 / n. 5.70
27 a. December / b. **Helmreich Henry** / c. Kansas City / d. 34 / e. Bbs. [Barrels] Beer / h. 60 / i. C / j. 2 / m. 20.40 / n. 20.40
28 a. December / b. **Langsenkamp & Co[mpany]** / c. Kansas City / e. Boots & Shoes / g. 311.00 / h. 3% / i. A / j. 42 / k. 9.33 / n. 9.33
29 a. December / b. **Long, William** / c. Kansas City / e. Saddlery / g. 240.00 / h. 3% / i. A / j. 42 / k. 7.20 / n.7.20
30 a. December / b. **Morrison, William** / c. Kansas City / e. Tinware / g. 883.00 / h. 3% / i. A / j. 72 / k.26.46 / n. 26.46
31 a. Novo[ember] 1 [18]63 / b. **Morris, John E** / c. Westport / e. Retail Dealer / i. B / j. 56 / L. 5.00 / n. 5.00
32 a. December / b. **Mohr, Casper** / c. Kansas City / d. 800 / e. Cigars / h. $.0025 / i. C / j. 20 / m. 2.00 / n. 2.00
33 a. December / b. **Moodie, John W.** / c. Independence / e. Saddlery / g. 369.00 / h. 3% / i. A / j. 42 / k. 11.07 / n. 11.07
34 a. December / b. **McDonald, John** / c. Kansas City / d. 300 / e. lbs Upper Leather / h. 1¢ / i. C / j. 63 / m. 3.00
35 a. December / b. McDonald, John / c. Kansas City / d. 12 / e. Calf Skins / h. 6¢ / i. C / j. 68 / m. .72
36 a. December / b. McDonald, John / c. Kansas City / e. Sheep skins / g. 48.00 / h. 4% / i. A / j. 65 / k. 1.92
37 a. December / b. **Pollard & Fairman** / c. Kansas City / e. Tinware / g. 1500.00 / h. 3% / i. A / j. 72 / k. 45.00 / n. [45.00]
38 a. December / b. **Sager, Henry** / c. Westport / e. Furniture / g. 65.00 / h. 3% / i. A / j. 75 / k. 1.95 / n. [1.95]
39 a. December / b. **Schroepf [sic], Henry** / c. Westport / e. Boots & Shoes / g. 132.00 / h. 3% / i. A / j. 42 / k. 3.96 / n. [3.96]
40 a. December / b. **Smith, S.** / c. Kansas City / e. Saddler etc / g. 322.00 / h. 3% / i. A / j. [42] / k. 9.60 / n. [9.60]

[Monthly List, December 1863, page 2]
1 [blank]
2 a. Dec[em]b[e]r / b. **Stine, Edward** / c. Kansas City / e. Furniture / g. 98.00 / h. 3% / i. A / j. 75 / L. 2.94 / n. 2.94
3 a. Dec[em]b[e]r / b. **Schwitzgabel Peter** / c. Kansas City / d. 58½ / e. Bbls [Barrels] Beer / h. 60¢ / i. C / j. 2 / m. 35.10 / n. 35.10
4 a. Dec[em]b[e]r / b. **Squires Mary J Adm[inistratri]x** / c. Westport / e. Waggons [sic] etc / g. 190.00 / h. 3% / h. A / j. 75 / k. 5.70 / n. 5.70
5 a. Dec[em]b[e]r / b. **Thomas Charles** / c. Kansas City / e. Tinware / g. 184.00 / h. 3% / i. A / j. 72 / k. 5.52 / n. 5.52
6 a. Dec[em]b[e]r / b. **Welland C F** / c. Kansas City / d. 3200 / e. Cigars / h. $.0025 / i. C / j. 20 / m. 8.00 / n. 8.00
7 a. Dec[em]b[e]r / b. **Ward, James M** / c. Kansas City / d. 50 / e. Cattle exceed[ing] 18 m[onths] / h. 20¢ / i. C / j. 12 / m. 10.00
8 a. Dec[em]b[e]r / b. Ward, James M / c. Kansas City / d. 350 / e. Hogs / h. 6¢ / i. C / j. 14 / m. 21.00 / n. 31.00
9 a. Dec[em]b[e]r / b.**Wedelich Ferdinand** / c. Kansas City / d. 3½ / e. Barrels Beer / h. 60 / i. C / j. 2 / m. 2.10 / n. 2.10

There were no tax lists for 1864 through the end of the Civil War (April 1865); they resumed in May 1865. Taxpayers enumerated at that time are reflected in the Comprehensive Index; but, not explored further here, since it is beyond the scope of this wartime study period.

3

Civil War Era
Taxpayers' Advertisements

This chapter contains citations for Jackson County taxpayers' advertisements appearing in city directories and Kansas City newspapers.

Copies of these and other advertisements with complete citations are in an introductory folder in James A. Tharp's collection *Civil War Era Federal Income Taxpayers of Jackson County, Missouri,* archived at the Kansas City Public Library Missouri Valley Special Collections.

Adkins, John C. (Adkins & Lowell), 1865 directory, p. 27

Auer, John A. (Ditsch & Aeuer), 1 Jan 1861, p. 3. col. 5

Auer, John A. (Ditsch & Aeuer), *Kansas City* (Mo.) *Western Journal of Commerce,* 1 Jan 1861, p. 3, c. 5

Auer, John A., *Kansas City* (Mo.) *Daily Journal of Commerce*, 27 Dec 1863, p. 1, col. 2

Babbitt, Joseph P. (Babbitt & Fristoe), *Kansas City* (Mo.) *Western Journal of Commerce*, 3 Jan 1861, p. 3, col. 4

Balis, John R. (Balis & Hicks), *Kansas City* (Mo.) *Western Journal of Commerce*, 01 Jan 1861, p. 4, col. 4

Bernard, William R., *Kansas City* (Mo.) *Daily Journal of Commerce*, 27 Dec 1863, p. 1, col. 5

Beyga, Adolph, *Kansas City* (Mo.) *Daily Journal of Commerce*, 04 Oct 1863, p. 1, col. 1

Boggs, Joseph O. *Westport* (Mo.) *Border Star,* 28 Jan 1859, p. 3, c. 7

Bouton, Henry B., *Kansas City* (Mo.) *Daily Journal of Commerce*, 08 Sep 1863, p. 1, col. 1

Brown, Phillip Shelley, 1860 directory, p. 12

Brown, Phillip Shelley, *Kansas City* (Mo.) *Daily Journal of Commerce,* 4 Jan 1861, p. 1, c. 1

Brown, Phillip Shelley, *Kansas City* (Mo.) *Daily Journal of Commerce*, 08 Sep 1863, p. 1, col. 1

Cassidy, Edward, *Kansas City* (Mo.) *Daily Journal of Commerce*, 03 Jul 1863, p. 2, col. 6

Cassidy, Patrick, *Kansas City* (Mo.) *Daily Journal of Commerce*, 03 Jul 1863, p. 2, col. 6

Chadwick, E. B., *Kansas City* (Mo.) *Daily Journal of Commerce*, 01 Jul 1863, p. 1, col. 3; 08 Sep 1863, p. 3, col. 3

Chew, Joseph, *Kansas City* (Mo.) *Western Journal of Commerce* 04 Jan 1861, p. 1, col. 1

Chick, Joseph Smith, *Kansas City* (Mo.) *Daily Journal of Commerce*, 15 May 1861, p. 1, c. 4

Chick, Washington Henry, *Kansas City* (Mo.) *Western Journal of Commerce*, 04 Jan 1861, p. 1, col. 7

Cockrell, William B., 1860 directory, p. 86

Cockrell, William B., *Kansas City* (Mo.) *Daily Journal of Commerce*, 3 Jan 1861, p. 1, c. 5

Conwell, Henry B., 1860 directory, p. 88

Conwell, Henry B. (Drinkard & Conwell), *Kansas City* (Mo.) *Daily Journal of Commerce*, 02 Jul 1863, p. 3, col. 5

Cooper, Hiram W., 1865 directory, p. 63

Cooper, Hiram W., *Kansas City* (Mo.) *Daily Journal of Commerce*, 08 Sep 1863, p. 3, col. 1

Cottrill & Vickroy, *Kansas City* (Mo.) *Daily Journal of Commerce*, 01 Jul 1863, p. 1, col. 4

Crandall, G. G., 1865 directory, p. 65

Ditsch, Peter W. (Ditsch & Aeuer), *Kansas City* (Mo.) *Western Journal of Commerce*, 1 Jan 1861, p. 3, col. 5

Diveley, Michael, 1860 directory, p. 86

Diveley, Michael, *Kansas City* (Mo.) *Western Journal of Commerce*, 04 Jan 1861, p. 1, col. 7

Drinkard, J. B. (Drinkard & Conwell), *Kansas City* (Mo.) *Daily Journal of Commerce*, 02 Jul 1863, p. 3, col. 5

Dunbar, R. R., *Kansas City* (Mo.) *Daily Journal of Commerce*, 27 Dec 1863, p. 1, col. 1 (dissolution)

Eby, Solomon Madison, *Kansas City* (Mo.) *Daily Journal of Commerce*, 01 Jul 1863, p. 2, col. 3

Esslinger, Frederick William, *Kansas City* (Mo.) *Daily Journal of Commerce*, 23 Jan 1864, p. 3, col. 2

Fairman, Chauncey Wilmont (Pollard & Fairman), 1859 directory, p. 14

Civil War Era Federal Income Taxpayers

Flagler, Frederick P. (F. P. & E. Flagler), *Kansas City* (Mo.) *Western Journal of Commerce*, 03 Jan 1861, p. 3, c. 4
Flagler, Frederick P. (F. P. & E. Flagler), 1865 directory, p. 21
Foglesong, George D., *Westport* (Mo.) *Border Star*, 8 Apr 1859, p. 4, c. 4-5
Ford, William W., 1859 directory, p. 2
Foster, Matthew, 1865 directory, p. 27
Frank, Charles J., *Kansas City* (Mo.) *Daily Journal of Commerce,* 04 Oct 1863, p. 1, c. 1
Frank, Charles J., 1865 directory, p. 35
Frank, Henry, *Kansas City* (Mo.) *Daily Journal of Commerce*, 27 Dec 1863, p. 1, c. 1 (dissolution)
Frazier, John, *Westport* (Mo.) *Border Star,* 6 Oct 1860, p. 1, c. 2
Friedsam, Morris J., 1859 directory, p. 99
Gage, John Cutter, *Kansas City* (Mo.) *Western Journal of Commerce*, 4 jan 1861, p. 1, c. 1
Ganz, Herman, *Westport* (Mo.) *Border Star*, 28 Apr 1860, p. 2, c. 7
Ganz, Herman, *Kansas City* (Mo.) *Daily Journal of Commerce*, 14 Jul 1863, p. 2, c. 4
Gerhart, Jacob R., *Kansas City* (Mo.) *Daily Journal of Commerce*, 27 Dec 1863, p. 1, c. 1
Giles, James S., *Kansas City* (Mo.) *Daily Journal of Commerce*, 01 Jul 1863, p. 4, c. 7
Goforth, Thomas Jefferson (Goforth & Dewitt), *Westport* (Mo.) *Border Star,* 28 Jan 1859, p. 1. c. 1
Gregg, W. H. (Cooper & Gregg), *Kansas City* (Mo.) *Daily Journal of Commerce*, 08 Sep 1863, p. 3, c. 1
Gregg, W. H. (Coopy & Gregg), 1865 directory, p. 63
Grigsby, W. F. B., *Kansas City* (Mo.) *Daily Journal of Commerce*, 27 Dec 1863, p. 3, c. 4; 23 Jan 1864, p. 3, c. 3
Hale, Robert Stockton, 1859 directory, p. 12
Hammerslough, Louis (Hammerslough Brothers), *Kansas City* (Mo.) *Western Journal of Commerce*, 01 Mar 1861,
    p. 2, c. 5
Hammeslough, Louis (Hammerslough Brothers), 1859 directory, p. v., 1865 directory, p. 3
Hartel, Jacob, *Kansas City* (Mo.) *Daily Journal of Commerce*, 04 Oct 1863, p. 1, c. 5
Helmreich, Henry William, *Kansas City* (Mo.) *Daily Journal of Commerce*, 14 Jul 1863, p. 2, c. 4
Hereford, Henry F., *Westport* (Mo.) *Border Star,* 8 Apr 1859, p. 1, c. 1
Hicks, John M. (Balis & Hicks), *Kansas City* (Mo.) *Western Journal of Commerce*, 01 Jan 1861, p. 4, c. 4
Holmes, William C., *Kansas City* (Mo.) *Daily Journal of Commerce*, 01 Jul 1863, p. 2, c. 3
Hopkins, Charles Grandison (Hopkins & Valentine), *Kansas City* (Mo.) *Daily Journal of Commerce,* 15 May 1861,
    p. 2, col. 3; 02 Aug 1861, p. 2, col. 7; 01 Jul 1863, p. 1, col. 5 (W. A. Hopkins, proprietor)
Hopkins, Charles Grandison (president, Mechanics' Bank), 1865 directory, p. 21
Jewett, Albert, *Kansas City* (Mo.) *Daily Journal of Commerce*, 8 Sep 1863, p. 3, c. 1 (dissolution to Cooper & Gregg)
Kevill, James. C., 1859 directory, p. xvii
Kevill, James C., *Kansas City* (Mo.) *Daily Journal of Commerce*, 04 Oct 1863, p. 1, col. 4; 06 Oct 1863, p. 2, col. 2
    (dissolution)
Kevill, James C. (Kevill & Turner), 1865 city directory, p. 35
Kalber, Frederick, *Westport* (Mo.) *Border Star*, 28 Jan 1859, p. 2, c. 7; 5 Aug 1859, p. 4, c. 7
Kline, Charles W. (McDonald & Kline), 1859 directory, p. 4; 1860 directory, p. 88
Kline, Charles W. (McDonald & Kline), *Kansas City* (Mo.) *Western Journal of Commerce*, 05 Jan 1861, p. 3, col. 7
Kline, Charles W., *Kansas City* (Mo.) *Daily Journal of Commerce*, 01 Jul 1863, p. 1, c. 4; 28 Aug 1863, p. 2, c. 7
Kump, Franklin H., 1859 directory, p. 36; 1860 directory, p. 84
Langsenkamp, Frank, 1860 directory, p. 66
Langsenkamp, Frank, *Kansas City* (Mo.) *Western Journal of Commerce,* 03 Jan 1861, p. 2, col. 5
Langsenkamp, Frank, *Kansas City* (Mo.) *Daily Journal of Commerce,* 04 Jun 1861, p. 3, c. 4; 27 Dec 1863, p. 1, c. 6
Lester, Thomas Bryan, 1859 directory, p. 38; *Kansas City* (Mo.) *Western Journal of Commerce*, 4 Jan 1861, p. 1 c. 1
Linderman, Sarah A., *Kansas City* (Mo.) *Western Journal of Commerce*, 05 Jan 1861, p. 1, c. 3
Linderman, Sarah A., *Kansas City* (Mo.) *Daily Journal of Commerce*, 02 Jul 1865, p. 1, c. 6
Long, William M., *Kansas City* (Mo.) *Daily Journal of Commerce*, 28 Aug 1863, p. 2, col. 7 (dissolution)
McDonald, Isaac W. (McDonald & Kline), 1859 directory, p. 4; 1860 directory, p. 88
McDonald, Isaac W. (McDonald & Kline), *Kansas City* (Mo.) *Western Journal of Commerce*, 05 Jan 1861, p. 3, c. 7
McDonald, Isaac W., *Kansas City* (Mo.) *Daily Journal of Commerce*, 01 Jul 1863, p. 1, col. 4
Messerschmidt, George G., *Kansas City* (Mo.) *Daily Journal of Commerce*, 02 Aug 1861, p. 3, c. 1; 14 Jul 1863, p. 2, c. 4
Miner, Charles E., *Kansas City* (Mo.) *Daily Journal of Commerce*, 08 Sep 1863, p. 1, col. 1
Moore, Clinton H., 1859 directory, p. 32; 1865 directory, p. 31
Morris, Joel T., 1859 directory, p. 34
Morris, Joel T., *Kansas City* (Mo.) *Western Journal of Commerce*, 4 Jan 1861, p. 1, c.1

Morrison, William P., 1860 directory, p. 66; 1865 directory, p. 25
Nicholson, George, 1860 directory, p. 38
Nicholson, George G., *Kansas City* (Mo.) *Western Journal of Commerce*, 2 Aug 1861, p. 3, c. 1
Northrup, Hiram Milton, 1859 directory (Northrup & Co.), p. iv; 1859 direcotry (J. S. Chick & Co.), p. 68
Northrup, Hiram Milton, *Kansas City* (Mo.) *Western Journal of Commerce*, 03 Jan 1861, p. 3, col. 4;
    15 May 1861, p. 1, col. 4; 15 May 1861, p. 2, c. 3
Parker, James W., *Westport* (Mo.) *Border Star*, 28 Jan 1859, p. 1, c. 1
Pollard, Philip D., 1859 directory, p. 14
Ralph, Erasmus Darwin, *Kansas City* (Mo.) *Western Journal of Commerce*, 4 Jan 1861, p. 1, c. 1
Ramage, Lewis (Ramage & Withers), *Kansas City* (Mo.) *Western Journal of Commerce*, 04 Jan 1861, p. 1, col. 1
Reis, Emil, *Westport* (Mo.) *Border Star*, 28 Apr 1860, p. 2, c. 7
Reis, Emil, *Kansas City* (Mo.) *Daily Journal of Commerce*, 14 Jul 1863, p. 2, col. 4
Sager, Henry Carl, Reis, *Westport* (Mo.) *Border Star*, 28 Jan 1859, p. 2, col. 6
Sauer, Anton, *Kansas City* (Mo.) *Daily Journal of Commerce*, 04 Jun 1861, p. 3, col. 1
Schaerff, Julius, 1867 directory, p. 102
Schoepf, Henry, *Westport* (Mo.) *Border Star*, 28 Jan 1859, p. 2, c.6
Schwitzgebel, Peter, *Kansas City* (Mo.) *Daily Journal of Commerce,* 09 Jul 1865, p. 4, col. 6
Seeger, Henry R., 1859 directory, p. 26; 1860 directory, p. 48;
Seeger, Henry R., *Kansas City* (Mo.) *Western Journal of Commerce*, 01 Mar 1861, p. 1, col. 4
Setzler, Philip (Setzlery & Wolf), *Kansas City* (Mo.) *Daily Journal of Commerce*, 01 Jul 1863, p. 2, c. 3;
    08 Sep 1863, p. 3, c. 3 (dissolution)
Setzler, Philip (Setzler Brothers), 1865 directory, p. 7
Shannon, John (J & P Shannon), 1859 directory, p. xviii
Smith, Peter H., *Westport* (Mo.) *Border Star*, 28 Jan 1859, p. 3, c.4
Smith, Peter H., *Kansas City* (Mo.) *Daily Journal of Commerce*, 01 Jul 1863, p. 2, col. 3
Smith, Salathiel S., *Westport* (Mo.) *Border Star*, 28 Jan 1859, p. 3, c.5-6
Sprink, Joseph, 1859 directory, p. 4
Street, Alexander, *Westport* (Mo.) *Border Star*, 28 Jan 1859, p. 3, c.5-6
Thompson, John W., *Westport* (Mo.) *Border Star*, 28 Jan 1859, p. 3, c. 7; 1860 directory, p. 90
Thompson, John W. (Stark & Thompson), *Kansas City* (Mo.) *Western Journal of Commerce*, Jan 1861, p. 1, col. 5
Thompson, John W., 1865 directory, p. 7
Tindall, George W., 1859 directory, p. 38, *Westport* (Mo.) *Border Star*, 11 Feb 1859, p. 4, c. 6; 1860 directory, p. 84
Tindall, George W. *Kansas City* (Mo.) *Western Journal of Commerce*, 04 Jan 1861, p. 1, col. 1
Trefren, Marston David, 1869 direcory, p. xiv; *Kansas City* (Mo.) *Western Journal of Commerce*, 4 Jan 1861, p. 1, c. 1
Turner, James P., 1859 directory, p. xvii; *Kansas City* (Mo.) *Daily Journal of Commerce*, 04 Oct 1863, p. 1, col. 4;
06 Oct 1863, p. 2, col. 2 (dissolution)
Turner, James P. (Kevill & Turner), 1865 directory, p. 35
Vaughan, Samuel D., 1859 direcotry, p. xv; 1860 directory, p. 12; *Kansas City* (Mo.) *Western Journal of Commerce*,
    4 Jan 1861, p. 1, c. 1
Wagner, G. A. Henry, *Kansas City* (Mo.) *Daily Journal of Commerce*, 28 Aug 1863, p. 2, col. 7 (dissolution);
    04 Oct 1863, p. 1, col. 1
Walker, Isaiah, *Kansas City* (Mo.) *Daily Journal of Commerce*, 01 Jul 1863, p. 1, col. 3
Ward, Henry Sylvester, 1859 directory, p. xiv
Whiting, David V., *Kansas City* (Mo.) *Daily Journal of Commerce*, 27 Dec 1863, p. 1, c. 1; 27 Dec 1863, p. 1, c. 7
Wiley, James M., 1860 directory, p. 44; *Kansas City* (Mo.) *Western Journal of Commerce*, 04 Jan 1861, p. 1, col. 1
Wilhite, Presley G., 1860 directory, p. 70
Wilson, Robert T., 1859 direcotyr, p. 16
Wolf, Gustavus A., *Kansas City* (Mo.) *Daily Journal of Commerce*, 01 Jul 1863, p. 2, c. 3; 04 Oct 1863, p. 1, c.1;
    08 Sep 1863, p. 3, c. 3 (dissolution)

4

Index of 271 Civil War Taxpayers, 1862-1863

This chapter lists merchants abstracted from the Internal Revenue Act rolls for Jackson Countians taxed *during the Civil War*; that is, 1862-1863. The tax rolls for the remainder of the Civil War (1864-April 1865) do not appear to have survived.

These 271 people are separated by profession/s in Chapter 1. Those with "[no further data]" indicate few, if any, local resources were located.

James A. Tharp identified 66 of the 271 taxpayers who were *Jackson County Early Germans*. Data files for those individulas will be archived by in a separate collection at the Missouri Valley Special Collections, Kansas City Public Library, Kansas City, Missouri.

Early German Immigrant Civil War Era Taxpayers

Aeuer, John A.
Becker, Johannes Phillip/Philipp
Beyga, Adolph
Bittel/Beitel, Joseph Johann
Borgstede, Henry/Heinrich
Daenzer, Louis
Ditsch, Peter William
Eckert, Christian August Frederick/Friedrich
Eckhart, Charles B.
Erkel, Jacob Robert
Esslinger, Frederick William
Fischell, John
Frank, Charles/Karl Jacob
Frank, Henry Karl
Frey, Reinhold
Fritz, Joseph Anton
Gabel, William
Ganghofer, Joseph
Gerhart, Jacob R.
Hammerslough, Louis
Hartel/Haertel, Jacob
Heinzelmann, Andrew Christian
Hinters/Hinterschitt, Peter
Hollingshausen, Frederick "Fred/Fritz"
Huer/Hugher, Henry L.
Jacob, Philip
Jaiser (Augusta Keck), Mrs. C. Jacob
Keller, Jacob
Kevill, James C.
Klaber, Frederick "Fred/Fritz
Knapp, Bernard/Bernhardt
Kramer, Johannes Louis/Ludwig "Lud"
Kump, Franklin Hubbard "Frank"

Langsenkamp, Frank/Franz
Loesch, Wendel/Wendelin
Long, Adam
Long, John/Johannes
Long, William/Wilhelm M.
Messerschmidt, George G.
Mohr, Caspar/Kaspar H.
Raffaletti, Gaudenzio/Gaudenzie Soldani
Rahlf, Christian
Rieke, Henry
Saalborn, Leopold C. "Leo"
Sager, Henry Carl
Sampson, Moses
Sauer, Anthony/Anton Philip
Schaerff, William Julius
Scherzer, John/Johann Michael
Schoen, Dr. Nicolas Joseph
Schoepf, Henry
Seeger, Henry/Heinrich Reinhard
Setzler, Philip
Sitzler, William R.
Sprink, Joseph
Stegmiller, Joseph
Thoes, John Joseph
Thomas, Charles
Turner, James P.
Wagner, G. A. Henry
Welland, Frederick/Friedrich Christian "Fritz"
Werry, Theobald
Wiedenmann, Christian "Christ"
Wolf, Gustavus Adolphus
Wyland, Robert
Zentner, George

Civil War Era Federal Income Taxpayers

The following lists group taxpayers by the town/s in which they operated during the Civil War: Kansas City, Independence & Blue Township, Westport, & Other Areas of Jackson County.

Kansas City Civil War Era Taxpayers

Ackerman, Henry—Butcher & Ackermann
Adkins, John C.
Aeuer, John A.—Ditsch & Aeuer
Agnew, John C.
Anderson, Joseph [no further data]
Arnoldia, Peter A.
Babbitt, Joseph P.
Balis, John Reed—Balis & Hicks
Bartleson, John P.
Bartlett, James—Bartlett & Frank; Bartlett & Wyland
    (also Westport)
Beddle, [—?—]—Frank and Beddle [no further data]
Bernard, William R. (also Westport)
Beyga, Adolph
Bittel/Beitel, Joseph Johann
Blair, David G.
Boggs, Joseph Oliver (also Independence)
Booher, Asa
Borgstede, Henry
Bouton, Henry B.
Brock, Perry G.
Brown, Phillip Shelley
Bryant, James M. (also Indep.)
Buchanan, George Washington (also Indep.)
Butcher, Joseph—Butcher & Ackermann
Camp, Henry Harrison
Campbell, John Snoddy—Campbell, Nelson & Co.
Carroll, William
Cassidy, Edward—Cassady, E. & P. (also Westport)
Cassidy, Patrick—Cassady, E. & P. (also Westport)
Chadwick, Emery B.
Chalfant, David Y.
Chew, Joseph
Chick, Joseph Smith, and Co.
Chick, Washington Henry & Co.
Chick, William Sidney & Company
Coates, J. S., Giles & Coates [no further data]
Cockrell, William B.—Cockrell & Ward
Conwell, Henry B.—Drinkard & Conwell
Cook, James W.
Cooper, Hiram W.—Cooper & Gregg
Cottrill, Mahlon—Cottrill, Vickroy & Co.
Crandall, Gilbert G.—Diveley, Crandall and
    Company
Crenshaw, Aaron Lane Hardage
Cross, Asa Beebe
Daenzer, Louis
Denison/Dennison, James
Denizen/Dennison, Edward Richard
Ditsch, Peter William—Ditsch & Aeuer

Diveley, Michael
Dougherty, George **[no further data]**
Drinkard, John Bragg—Drinkard & Conwell
Dunbar, Robert Roland—Frank & Dunbar
Duncan, John S.
Dwyer, Charles
Eby, Solomon Madison
Eckert, Christian August Frederick
Eckhart, Charles B. **[no further data; also Indep.]**
Ensign, Daniel
Erkel, Jacob Robert
Esslinger, Frederick William (also Westport)
Evans, John W.
Fairman, Chauncey Wilmont
Flagler, Frederick Peet & Co.
Forb[e]s, Thomas
Ford, William Weber
Foster, Matthew
Frank, Charles Jacob
Frank, Henry Karl—Bartlett & Frank
Frazier, John Thornton
Frey, Reinhold/Reynold
Friedsam, Morris J.
Gabel, William—Gabel & Rahlf
Gage, John Cutter
Ganghofer, Joseph
Ganz, Hermann—Ganz & Reis
Gerhart, Jacob R.
Giles, James S.
Green, Thomas H.—Green & Long
Gregg, William Henry—Cooper & Gregg
Griffith, James
Grigsby, William French Bayliss
Hale, Robert Stockton
Ham, James R.
Hammerslough, Louis—Hammerslough & Brother
Harris, Alexander Lancaster
Hartel, Jacob
Hedges, Meredith B.
Heinzelmann, Andrew Christian
Helfrich, Henry—Helfrich & Milschuster
Helmreich, Henry/Heinrich William/Wilhelm—
    Helmreich & Messerschmidt
Henry, John Ward—Hovey & Henry (also Indep.)
Hereford, Henry Foote (also Indep.)
Hicks, John M.—Balis & Hicks
Hinters/Hinterschitt, Peter
Hollinghausen, Frederick "Fred/Fritz"
Hopkins, Charles Grandison
Huer/Hugher, Henry L. **[no further data]**

Irwin, Joseph Chambers—Irwin, Gloom & Co
    (also Indep.)
Jacob, Phillip
Jaiser, Mrs. C. Jacob (Augusta Keck)
    [female taxpayer]
Jewett, Albert (?-?) **[no further data]**
Jewett, Benjamin Marlin (1810-1879)
Johnson, James (?-?) **[no further data]**
Kearney, Charles Esmond (also Westport)
Kelso, Harrison Ray
Kennedy, Daniel/David (?-?) **[no further data]**
Kerr, Benjamin "Ben" **[no further data]**
Kevill, James C.—Kevill & Turner
Kline, Charles W.—McDonald & Klein
Knapp, Bernard
Kump, Franklin Hubbard "Frank" & Co.
Langsenkamp, Frank & Co.
Lester, Thomas Bryan
Linderman, Mrs. James P. (Sarah A. Yelton)
    [female taxpayer]
Loesch, Wendall
Long, Adam—Green & Long
Long, John
Long, William/Wilhelm M.—Long & Wagoner
Lykins, Johnston
Maddox, Asa
McClanahan, William D.
McDonald, Isaac W.—McDonald & Klein
McDonald, John
McKenzie, J[edediah] E.—White & McKinzie
Messerschmidt, George G.—Helmreich &
    Messerschmidt
Mettee, Leonard (also Westport)
Miner, Charles Edward
Mohr, Caspar/Kaspar
Moore, Clinton II. & Co.
Morris, Joel T.
Morrison, William P.
Muehlschuster, Michael—Helfrich & Milschuster
Nall, Carey H. & Co.
Nelson, Richard Henry—Campbell, Nelson & Co.
Neville, George Washington
Nicholson, George C./G.
Northrup, Hiram Milton & Co.
Oldham, William D.
Payne, [—?—]—Payne & Toler **[no further data]**
Pendleton, Micajah G.
Pierce, Andrew J.
Pollard, Lucian Whitman—Pollard & Fairman
Quarles, John T.
Quarles, Robert William
Raffaletti, Gaudenzio Soldani & Co.
Rahlf, Christian—Gabel & Rahlf
Ralph, Erasmus Darwin
Ramage, Lewis Albert

Reardon, Bartholomew
Reed, William S.
Reis, Emil—Ganz & Reis
Rieke, Henry
Riggins, Benjamin L.—Riggins & Ham
Rooney, John
Ross, [—?—]—Ross & Hough **[no further data]**
Russell, Egbert Freeland
Saalborn, Leopold C.
Sauer, Anthony/Anton Philip
Schaerff, William Julius
Scherzer, John Michael
Schoen, Nicolaus Joseph (also Westport)
Schoen, Louis A.
Schwitzgebel, Peter & Co.
Scully, William
Seeger, Henry Reinhard
Shannon, John—Shannon, J. and P.
Shannon, Philip—Shannon, J. and P.
Shoenbrun, Isaac **[no further data]**
Sitzler, William
Smith, Richard D.
Smith, Salathiel S.
Snell, Addison (also Westport)
Souneso, James W. **[no further data]**
Sprink, Joseph
Stevens, William
Stine, Edward
Street, [—?—] & Co. [no further data]
Sweeney, George
Thoes, John Joseph (also Westport)
Thomas, Charles
Thompson, John Wesley
Tindall, George William
Toler, George W.—Payne & Toler
Trefren, Marston David
Turner, James P.—Kevill & Turner
Vickroy, George Harlan—Cottrill, Vickroy & Co.
Vaughan, Samuel D.
Wagner, G. A. Henry—Long & Wagoner
Walker, Isaiah & Co.
Walker, James A.
Ward, [Henry Sylvester?]—Cockrell & Ward
    [no further data]
Ward, James M.
Welland, Christian Frederick "Fritz"
White, Robert Covington—White & McKinzie
Whiting, David Virdin
Wiedenmann, Christian (also Westport)
Wiley, James Newton
Wilhite, Presley Gray
Wilson, Robert Turner
Wolter, Augustus
Wood, Joseph Madison
Zentner, George

Civil War Era Federal Income Taxpayers

Independence and Blue Township Civil War Era Taxpayers

Armstrong, John J.
Beatty, Albert L.
Beckham, James C.
Boggs, Joseph Oliver (also Westport)
Bone, William Leonidas "Lee"
Brown, James Terrell
Bryant, James M. (also K.C.)
Bryant, John W.
Buchanan, George Washington (also K.C.)
Buchanan, John O.
Carmichael, Columbus G. (Blue Township)
Chrisman, William
Cogswell, Oscar H.
Comingo, Abram
Cramer, Lewis/Louis **[no further data]**
Eckhart, Charles B. **[no further data; also K.C.]**
Farrar, Asa
Farrow, John W.
Fischell, John
Gloom, [-?-]—Irwin, Gloom& Co. **[no further data]**
Head, Hadley A.
Henry, John Ward—Hovey & Henry (also K.C.)

Hereford, Henry Foote (also K.C.)
Hockensmith, William H. H.
Hough, [—?—]—Ross and Hough **[no further data]**
Hovey, Jacob Brown "John"—Hovey & Henry
Irwin, Joseph Chambers—Irwin, Gloom & Co (also K.C.)
Keller, Jacob (1785/86-1867)
McCoy, John—McCoy, John & William
McCoy, William—McCoy, John & William
McGargill, James
Meador, James H.
Modie, John W.
Pendleton, John Tinsley—Wilson & Pendleton
Perry, John W.
Pollard, Phillip D.
Roberts, Preston & Co.
Rumberg, J. H. **[no further data]**
Sampson, Moses
Taylor, John H.
Twyman, Leo
Wallace, Reuben
Weston, Robert T.
Wilson, John W.—Wilson & Pendleton

Westport Civil War Era Taxpayers

Becker, Philip
Bartlett, James—Bartlett & Wyland (also Westport)
Bernard, Joab
Bernard, William R. (also K.C.)
Boggs, Joseph Oliver (also Independence)
Cassidy, Edward—Cassady, E. & P. (also K.C.)
Cassidy, Patrick—Cassady, E. & P. (also Westport)
Conboy, Phillip **[no further data]**
Earley/Early, Jacob H.
Esslinger, Frederick William (also K.C.)
Foglesong, George Davis
Fritz, Joseph A.
Glunz, Christian
Goforth, Thomas Jefferson
Holmes/Holms, William C.
Kearney, Charles Esmond (also K.C.)
Klaber, Frederick "Fritz"
McKee, Mrs. David (nee Jane K. Hutchison) [female taxpayer]
Mettee, Leonard (also K.C.)

Morris, John Calvin
Parker, James Wilson "John," Dr.
Ross, [--?--] [no further data]
Sager, Henry Carl
Schoen, Nicolaus Joseph (also K.C.)
Schoepf, Henry
Setzler, Philip—Setzler & Wolf
Smith, Peter H.—Smith & Holms [sic.]
Snell, Addison (also K.C.)
Squires, John
Squires, Mary J., Administratrix [female taxpayer]
Stegmiller, Joseph
Street, Alexander "Alex"
Thoes, John Joseph (also K.C.)
Wedelich, Frederick/Ferdinand
Werry, Theobald
Wiedenmann, Christian (also K.C.)
Wolf, Gustavus A.—Setzler & Wolf
Wyland, Robert—Bartlett & Wyland

Civil War Era Taxpayers in Other Areas of Jackson County

Axline, Jacob (Hickman's Mill)
Brown, James T. (Sibley)
Bryant, David A. (Hickman's Mill)
Farrow/Farrar, John
Goodson, John E.

Hassett, James Blake (Sibley)
Hockensmith, William Henry Harrison
Kramer, Johannes Louis/Ludwig "Lud"
Langsenkamp & Co.
Smith, Nathan M. (Sibley)

5

Taxpayers, Later Civil War
Union Veteran Pensioners

Ten Jackson County Civil War era taxpayers (or their widows) were found to have later received pensions for their Civil War service to the Union. In some cases (shaded below) there were two different applications and/or certificates.

Applicant Last	First	Invalid / Widow	Service	Date Filed	App / Cert	# Pgs
Chalfant	David Y.	Invalid	C 25 Mo Inf & C Van Horn Battn Mo Inf C 13 Mo Inf	1890 Aug 14	459598 / 300639	47
Hollinghausen	Fritz	Invalid	B 77 En Mo Mil	1903 May 22	1300220	21
Hollinghausen	Fritz	Invalid	B 77 En Mo Mil	1906 Jan 17	841282	
Loesch	Wendell	Invalid	A 25 Mo Inf; A Van Horn's Battn Mo Inf	1889 Apr 16	393294 / 261043	30
Loesch	Wendell	Invalid	A 25 Mo Inf; A Van Horn's Battn Mo Inf	1889 Aug 23	402829	
Mohr	Caspar	Metta	A Van Horn's Battn US R C Co Mil Cav	1892 Aug 01	1124566 / 854944	31
Mohr	Caspar	Metta	A Van Horn's Battn US R C Co Mil Cav	1898 Nov 10	686136	
Reardon	Bartholomew	Margaret	B 1 Ks Inf	1897 Nov 30	664815 / 485749	58
Rieke	Henry	Lizzie	A 13 Mo Inf; A Van Horn's Battn Mo Inf	1888 Apr 27	701357	76
Rieke	Henry	Lizzie	A 13 Mo Inf; A Van Horn's Battn Mo Inf	1888 May 25	895637	

Applicant Last	First	Invalid / Widow	Service	Date Filed	App / Cert	# Pgs
Scherzer	John Michael	Josephine	A Van Horn's Battn Mo Inf; A1 US R C Mo. H G; A 25 and A 13 Mo Inf	1890 Jul 22	860789 / 695494; filed in Kansas	103
Scherzer	John Michael	Josephine	A Van Horn's Battn Mo Inf; A1 US R C Mo. H G; A 25 and A 13 Mo Inf	1902 Apr 09	760812 / 572441	
Sweeney	George	Rosanna	C 77 E Mo Mil	1895 Mar 25	611402	27
Werry	Theobald	Elizabeth	M 6 Ks Cav	1888 Nov 19	384159 Filed in Kansas	207
Zentner	George	Mattie M. Guardian-Minor	H 1 Mo Inf; H and A 1 Mo L A	1890 Aug 12	881499 / 988740	239
Zentner	George	Mattie M. Guardian-Minor	H 1 Mo Inf; H and A 1 Mo L A	1904 08 05	803470 / 598994	

There were 16 Jackson County taxpayers who were known to have served in Robert Thompson Van Horn's Battalion:

1. Arnoldia, Peter A.
2. Chalfant, David Y.
3. Erkel, Jacob Robert
4. Frank, Henry
5. Frey, Reinhold/Reynold
6. Loesch, Wendell
7. Long, John
8. Long, William
9. Mohr, Caspar/Kasper
10. Quarles, William
11. Rieke, Henry
12. Rooney, John
13. Scherzer, John Michael
14. Smith, Richard D.
15. Taylor, John H.
16. Thomas, Charles

6

Civil War Taxpayers'
Family Group Sheets

This chapter compiles Family Group Sheets for Civil War taxpayers involved in the 1862-1863 assessment/collection period.

This volume contains Family Group Sheets for surnames beginning A-G.

For surnames H-Z, consult Volume 2.

Family Group Sheets inclue taxpayers and their immediate family to reveal a variety of available, local research sources. Additional charts and copies of other vital, historical records for each taxpayer provide ample data for interested parties to create full biographical sketches of any Civil War-era Jackson Countian.

Further, printed data files for all Civil War taxpayers—complete with copies of supporting documents, Family Group Sheets for second- and sometimes third-generation descendants (and in some cases, sheets for taxpayers' ancestors)—will be donated to the Missouri Valley Special Collections, Kansas City Public Library, Kansas City, Missouri.

ALL Civil War era taxpayers from 1862-1863 <u>and</u> May 1865-1866 are included in the comprehensive index at the end of Volume 2 of this work.

Nov. 25, 1861.

SANTA FE MAIL

FOR NEW MEXICO
AND COLORADO.

 — 

U. S. MAIL

AND

EXPRESS LINE

TO THE

Gold Mines & Santa Fe, N. M

KANSAS, SANTA FE AND

DENVER CITY

EXPRESS.

WE are running a line of first class Coaches from INDEPENDENCE AND KANSAS CITY, Mo., By way of Council Grove, Fort Larnard, Fort Wise, Bent's Old Fort, Hayne's Ranch and Majors' Ranch.

This line runs up the Arkansas river, on the best natural road in the United States. It also runs in connection with the Independence and Santa Fe Mail.

We have gone to Great Expense to make it equal to any Stage Line that ever crossed the Plains, and are prepared to carry any amount of Treasure, or Express Goods, or any number of Passengers, with despatch and at low rates. Connection made at Santa Fe with a line of first class coaches for

ALBUQUERQUE,

PERALTO AND FORT CRAIG.

Every Saturday.

COACHES LEAVE KANSAS CITY EVERY FRIDAY AT 12 M.

M. COTTRILL & CO.

Father Henry ACKERMAN

Birth	1830	Pennsylvania, United States
Census	1840	
Census	1850	Page 116, Madison Township, Richland, Ohio, United States
Census	1860	Page 7, Kansas City, Jackson, Missouri, United States
Tax Lists	bet Apr 1863 and Dec 1863	Animals Slaughtered for Sale; "Butcher & Ackerman", Kansas City, Jackson, Missouri, United States
Military	Oct 1863	Civil War Draft Registration; Kaw Township, Jackson, Missouri, United States
Death	1865	
Burial		Union Cemetery, Kansas City, Jackson, Missouri, United States
Occupation		Moulder (1850), Butcher (1860)
Business		Butcher & Ackerman (Meat)
Marriage		
Father		
Mother		

Mother Sabina MEILY

Birth	Sep 1831	Pennsylvania, United States
Census	1840	
Census	1850	Page 108, Madison Township, Richland, Ohio, United States
Census	1860	Page 7, Kansas City, Jackson, Missouri, United States
Religion	4 Apr 1867	Founding Member, First English Lutheran Church; Kansas City, Jackson, Missouri, United States
Census	1870	Page 602, Kansas City, Jackson, Missouri, United States
Census	1880	ED 11, Page 330, Kansas City, Jackson, Missouri, United States
Census	1900	ED 34, Page 120, Kansas City, Jackson, Missouri, United States
Death	28 Sep 1902	Kansas City, Jackson, Missouri, United States
Misc		Funeral Notice, Kansas City (Mo.) Times, 29 Sep 1902, Page 2, Column 3
Burial	30 Sep 1902	Union Cemetery, Kansas City, Jackson, Missouri, United States
Father	Samuel MEILY (1804-1861)	
Mother	Mary [--?--] (1802-1886)	

Children

M Charles H. ACKERMAN

Birth	Aug 1858	Missouri, United States
Census	1860	Page 7, Kansas City, Jackson, Missouri, United States
Census	1870	Page 602, Kansas City, Jackson, Missouri, United States
Census	1880	ED 11, Page 330, Kansas City, Jackson, Missouri, United States
Census	1900	ED 34, Page 121, Kansas City, Jackson, Missouri, United States
Census	1905	Page 3, Family 17, Mission Township, Johnson, Kansas, United States
Death	1922	
Burial		Corinth Cemetery, Prairie Village, Johnson, Kansas, United States
Occupation		Apprentice Machinist (1880); Dry Goods (1900), Gardener (1905)
Spouse	Ida Bell JAMES (1862-1949)	
Marriage	22 Nov 1887	(1887K0090082), Jackson, Missouri, United States

M Samuel M. ACKERMAN

Birth	9 Apr 1862	Missouri, United States
Census	1870	Page 602, Kansas City, Jackson, Missouri, United States
Baptism	16 Jun 1871	First English Lutheran Church, Kansas City, Jackson, Missouri, United States
Census	1880	ED 11, Page 330, Kansas City, Jackson, Missouri, United States
Census	1900	ED 34, Page 120, Kansas City, Jackson, Missouri, United States
Census	1905	Page 3, Family 17, Mission Township, Johnson, Kansas, United States
Death	1926	
Burial		Corinth Cemetery, Prairie Village, Johnson, Kansas, United States
Occupation		Worker in Butcher Shop (1880); Grocer (1900)
Marriage		

M Henry ACKERMAN

Birth	20 Feb 1866	
Baptism	20 Jun 1868	First English Lutheran Church, Kansas City, Jackson, Missouri, United States
Death	24 Jun 1868	

Father Henry ACKERMAN	
Mother Sabina MEILY	
Children	
Henry ACKERMAN (continued)	
Burial	Union Cemetery, Kansas City, Jackson, Missouri, United States
Marriage	

Father John C. ADKINS

Birth	19 Mar 1836	Clay, Missouri, United States
Census	1840	(Robert Adkins Family), Page 7, Line 29, Clay, Missouri, United States
Census	1850	Page 306, Liberty Township, Clay, Missouri, United States
Census	1860	Page 69, Kansas City, Jackson, Missouri, United States
Tax Lists	Sep 1862	Apothecary and Retail Liquor Dealer Licenses; Kansas City, Jackson, Missouri, United States
Military		Civil War Draft Registration; Kaw Township, Jackson, Missouri, United States
Death	14 Feb 1866	Dropsy; Kansas City, Jackson, Missouri, United States
Misc		Death Notice, Kansas City (Mo.) Daily Journal of Commerce, 15 Feb 1866, Page 3, Column 1
Misc		Death Notice, Liberty (Mo.) Tribune, 16 Feb 1866
Probate	5 Mar 1866	(Letters of Administration), Volume M, Page 50, Independence, Jackson, Missouri, United States
Burial	26 Jan 1921	Elmwood Cemetery (Original Burial Place Unidentified), Kansas City, Jackson, Missouri, United States
Occupation		Druggist (1860), Apothecary, Retail Liquor
Marriage	26 Nov 1857	Clay, Missouri, United States
Father	Judge Robert ADKINS (1793-1858)	
Mother	Sarah SNELL (1796-)	

Mother Frances "Fannie" FISHER

Birth	19 Jan 1838	Liberty, Clay, Missouri, United States
Census	1840	(Merit Fisher Family), Page 10, Line 18, Clay, Missouri, United States
Census	1850	Page 343, Liberty, Clay, Missouri, United States
Residence	bet 1857 and 1921	Kansas City, Jackson, Missouri, United States
Census	1860	Page 69, Kansas City, Jackson, Missouri, United States
Census	1870	Page 585, Kansas City, Jackson, Missouri, United States
Census	1880	ED 18, Page 482, Kansas City, Jackson, Missouri, United States
Census	1900	ED 92, Page 59, Kansas City, Jackson, Missouri, United States
Census	1910	ED 166, Page 101, Kansas City, Jackson, Missouri, United States
Census	1920	ED 191, Page 175, Kansas City, Jackson, Missouri, United States
Death	24 Jan 1921	La Grippe, Acute Bronchitis, Senility; Kansas City, Jackson, Missouri, United States
Misc		Obituary, Kansas City (Mo.) Times, 25 Jan 1921, Page 4, Column 2
Misc		Obituary, Kansas City (Mo.) Daily Journal, 25 Jan 1921, Page 2, Column 3
Burial	26 Jan 1921	Elmwood Cemetery, Kansas City, Jackson, Missouri, United States
Father	Merritt R. FISHER (1807-1897)	
Mother	Martha Jane DUVALL (1817-1884)	
Other spouse	Merrit Dallas DUVALL (1844-)	
Marriage	17 Nov 1868	(1868I0060020), Kansas City, Jackson, Missouri, United States

Children

F Emma V. ADKINS

Birth	29 Jul 1859	Missouri, United States
Census	1860	Page 69, Kansas City, Jackson, Missouri, United States
Census	1870	Page 585, Kansas City, Jackson, Missouri, United States
Census	1880	ED 18, Page 482, Kansas City, Jackson, Missouri, United States
Census	1900	ED 92, Page 59, Kansas City, Jackson, Missouri, United States
Census	1910	ED 166, Page 101, Kansas City, Jackson, Missouri, United States
Census	1920	ED 191, Page 175, Kansas City, Jackson, Missouri, United States
Residence	1921	Kansas City, Jackson, Missouri, United States
Death	29 Jul 1925	
Burial	31 Jul 1925	Elmwood Cemetery, Kansas City, Jackson, Missouri, United States
Spouse	Samuel Merrick STONE (1853-1918)	
Marriage	12 May 1880	(1880I0080101), Kansas City, Jackson, Missouri, United States

F Mary J. "Mollie" ADKINS

Birth	21 Sep 1863	Missouri, United States
Census	1870	Page 585, Kansas City, Jackson, Missouri, United States
Census	1880	ED 18, Page 482, Kansas City, Jackson, Missouri, United States
Death	15 Aug 1894	Consumption; Kansas City, Jackson, Missouri, United States

Father	John C. ADKINS	
Mother	Frances "Fannie" FISHER	

Children

Mary J. "Mollie" ADKINS (continued)

Misc		Funeral Notice, Kansas City (Mo.) Star, 15 Aug 1894, Page 2, Column 2
Burial	16 Aug 1894	Elmwood Cemetery, Kansas City, Jackson, Missouri, United States
Spouse	Joel Frederick COOPER (1855-1931)	
Marriage	20 Jun 1889	(1889K0002116), Jackson, Missouri, United States

Name: John A. AEUER
Sex: Male
Father: [--?--] AEUER (-   )
Mother:

Individual Facts

Birth	1827/8	Prussia, Germany
Census	1860 (about age 32)	
Misc		Advertisement, Kansas City (Mo.) Western Journal of Commerce, 01 Jan 1861, Page 3, Column 5
Tax Lists	Sep 1862 (about age 34)	Rectifier and Retail and Wholesale Liquor Dealer Licenses; "Dietch & Auer", Kansas City, Jackson, Missouri, United States
Military		Private, Company B, 77th Regiment Enrolled Missouri Militia
Military		Civil War Draft Registration; Kaw Township, Jackson, Missouri, United States
Tax Lists	May 1866 (about age 38)	Rectifier and Wholesale Liquor Dealer Licenses; Kansas City, Jackson, Missouri, United States
Tax Lists	Aug 1866 (about age 38)	Wholesale Liquor Dealer License; Kansas City, Jackson, Missouri, United States
Census	1870 (about age 42)	Page 676, Kansas City, Jackson, Missouri, United States
Census	1880 (about age 52)	ED 5, Page 143, Kansas City, Jackson, Missouri, United States
Death	23 Mar 1882 (about age 54)	Kansas City, Jackson, Missouri, United States
Misc		Death Notice, Kansas City (Mo.) Star, 24 Mar 1882, Page 4, Column 1
Misc		Obituary, Kansas City (Mo.) Times, 24 Mar 1882, Page 8, Column 3
Misc		Death Notice, Kansas City (Mo.) Daily Journal, 24 Mar 1882, Page 8, Column 4
Burial	26 Mar 1882 (about age 54)	
Misc		Funeral Notice, Kansas City (Mo.) Star, 27 Mar 1882, Page 4, Column 1
Misc		Funeral Notice, Kansas City (Mo.) Daily Journal, 27 Mar 1882, Page 4, Column 6
Occupation		Wholesale Liquor Dealer (1870), Hotel Clerk (1880)
Business		Ditsch & Aeuer (Liquor)

Notes

Father John C. AGNEW

	Birth	1825/6	Pennsylvania, United States
	Census	1830	
	Residence	bet 1834 and 1883	Jackson, Missouri, United States
	Census	1840	
	Census	1850	Page 274, Blue Township, Jackson, Missouri, United States
	Census	1860	Page 249, Independence, Jackson, Missouri, United States
	Census		Slave Schedules, Page 363, Independence, Jackson, Missouri, United States
	Misc	19 Apr 1862	Union Provost Marshals' File of Papers Relating to Two or More Civilians, M416, Roll 5, No. 1075
	Tax Lists	Sep 1862	Apothecary License; Independence, Jackson, Missouri, United States
	Misc	abt 1863	Union Provost Marshals' File of Papers . . . Two or More Civilians, M416, Roll 82, No. 22,611
	Military		Civil War Draft Registration; Blue Township, Jackson, Missouri, United States
	Census	1870	Page 584, Kansas City, Jackson, Missouri, United States
	Misc	bet 1872 and 1874	Deputy Marshal; Jackson, Missouri, United States
	Census	1880	ED 5, Page 140, Kansas City, Jackson, Missouri, United States
	Death	abt 1883	Kansas City, Jackson, Missouri, United States
	Burial		Woodlawn Cemetery, Independence, Jackson, Missouri, United States
	Occupation		Merchant (1850), Druggist (1860); Transfer Business (1870); Bookkeeper (1880), Apothecary
	Marriage	19 Sep 1848	Cass, Missouri, United States
	Father		
	Mother		

Mother Sarah D. "Sallie" MAXWELL

	Birth	30 Apr 1833	Jessamine, Kentucky, United States
	Census	1840	(Joseph L. Maxwell Family), Page 233, Line 2, Jessamine, Kentucky, United States
	Census	1850	Page 274, Blue Township, Jackson, Missouri, United States
	Census	1860	Page 249, Independence, Jackson, Missouri, United States
	Census	1870	Page 584, Kansas City, Jackson, Missouri, United States
	Census	1880	ED 5, Page 140, Kansas City, Jackson, Missouri, United States
	Census	1900	ED 127, Page 291, Kansas City, Jackson, Missouri, United States
	Census	1910	
	Death	17 Nov 1913	Pulmonary Oedema, Epitheloma of Face; Kansas City, Jackson, Missouri, United States
	Burial	19 Nov 1913	Woodlawn Cemetery, Independence, Jackson, Missouri, United States
	Misc		Obituary, Kansas City (Mo.) Times, 19 Nov 1913, Page 3, Column 2
	Father		Dr. Joseph L. MAXWELL (-)
	Mother		Sinai ROMAN (1802-1891)

Children

M Joseph Oliver AGNEW

	Birth	abt 1850	Missouri, United States
	Census	1860	Page 249, Independence, Jackson, Missouri, United States
	Census	1870	Page 584, Kansas City, Jackson, Missouri, United States
	Census	1880	ED 5, Page 140, Kansas City, Jackson, Missouri, United States
	Census	1900	
	Census	1910	
	Census	1920	ED 168, Page 228, Kansas City, Wyandotte, Kansas, United States
	Death		
	Burial		
	Marriage		

F Isabella "Belle" AGNEW

	Birth	1853/4	Missouri, United States
	Census	1860	Page 249, Independence, Jackson, Missouri, United States
	Census	1870	Page 584, Kansas City, Jackson, Missouri, United States
	Census	1880	ED 5, Page 140, Kansas City, Jackson, Missouri, United States
	Burial		Woodlawn Cemetery, Independence, Jackson, Missouri, United States
	Death		
	Spouse		David M. KIRKPATRICK (1852-)

Father	John C. AGNEW		
Mother	**Sarah D. "Sallie" MAXWELL**		
Children			
	Isabella "Belle" AGNEW (continued)		
	Marriage	18 May 1893	(1893K0008341), Kansas City, Jackson, Missouri, United States
M	**Henry O. AGNEW**		
	Birth	1858/9	Missouri, United States
	Census	1860	Page 249, Independence, Jackson, Missouri, United States
	Death		
	Burial		
	Marriage		

Individual Summary

| Name: | Joseph ANDERSON |
| Sex: | Male |

Individual Facts

Census	1860	
Tax Lists	Sep 1862	Confectioner License; Kansas City, Jackson, Missouri, United States
Tax Lists	May 1866	Manufacturer License; Kansas City, Jackson, Missouri, United States
Census	1870	

Notes

Father Dr. John J. ARMSTRONG

Birth	15 Jun 1795	Ireland
Census	1830	
Census	1840	Page 196, Wooster Township, Wayne, Ohio, United States
Census	1850	Page 287, Blue Township, Jackson, Missouri, United States
Census	1860	Page 239, Independence, Jackson, Missouri, United States
Misc	19 Apr 1862	Union Provost Marshals' File of Papers Relating to Two or More Civilians, M416, Roll 5, No. 1075
Tax Lists	Sep 1862	Physician License; Independence, Jackson, Missouri, United States
Tax Lists	May 1866	Physician License; Independence, Jackson, Missouri, United States
Death	9 Aug 1869	
Burial		Woodlawn Cemetery, Independence, Jackson, Missouri, United States
Occupation		Physician (1850, 1860)
Marriage		
Father		
Mother		

Mother Mary [--?--]

Birth	3 Dec 1799	Pennsylvania, United States
Census	1830	
Census	1840	Page 196, Wooster Township, Wayne, Ohio, United States
Census	1850	Page 287, Blue Township, Jackson, Missouri, United States
Census	1860	Page 239, Independence, Jackson, Missouri, United States
Death	4 Jun 1866	
Burial		Woodlawn Cemetery, Independence, Jackson, Missouri, United States
Father		
Mother		

Children

M James F. ARMSTRONG

Birth	1827/8	Ohio, United States
Census	1830	
Census	1840	Page 196, Wooster Township, Wayne, Ohio, United States
Census	1850	Page 287, Blue Township, Jackson, Missouri, United States
Census	1860	Independence, Jackson, Missouri, United States
Census	1870	Page 268, Independence, Jackson, Missouri, United States
Census	1880	Independence, Jackson, Missouri, United States
Occupation		Tailor (1850, 1870, 1880)
Death		
Burial		
Spouse	Martha Ann RUBEY (1825-1880)	
Marriage	3 Aug 1851	(1851I0030053), Jackson, Missouri, United States

F Elizabeth F. ARMSTRONG

Birth	1829/30	Ohio, United States
Census	1830	
Census	1840	Page 196, Wooster Township, Wayne, Ohio, United States
Census	1850	Page 287, Blue Township, Jackson, Missouri, United States
Census	1860	
Census	1870	
Census	1880	
Death		
Burial		
Marriage		

F Euphrasia D. ARMSTRONG

Birth	1835/6	Ohio, United States
Census	1840	Page 196, Wooster Township, Wayne, Ohio, United States
Census	1850	Page 287, Blue Township, Jackson, Missouri, United States
Census	1860	Page 570, Washington Township, Yolo, California, United States
Census	1870	Page 537, Washington Township, Yolo, California, United States
Census	1880	Washington Precinct, Yolo, California, United States

Father Dr. John J. ARMSTRONG		
Mother Mary [--?--]		
Children		

Euphrasia D. ARMSTRONG (continued)

Death		
Burial		
Spouse	David MCGOWAN (1825-)	
Marriage	26 Apr 1854	(1854I0030158), Jackson, Missouri, United States

F Mary A. ARMSTRONG

Birth	1837/8	Ohio, United States
Census	1840	Page 196, Wooster Township, Wayne, Ohio, United States
Census	1850	Page 287, Blue Township, Jackson, Missouri, United States
Census	1860	Page 570, Washington Township, Yolo, California, United States
Census	1870	
Census	1880	
Death		
Burial		
Spouse	Thomas W. WHITNEY (1827-1862)	
Marriage	26 Apr 1854	(1854I0030159), Jackson, Missouri, United States

Father Dr. Peter ARNOLDIA

Birth	15 Feb 1818	Oswego, Oswego, New York, United States
Census	1820	
Census	1830	
Census	1840	
Census	1850	Page 185, Elizabeth Village, Jo Daviess, Illinois, United States
Census	1860	Page 22, Kansas City, Jackson, Missouri, United States
Tax Lists	Sep 1862	Physician License; "Peter A. Arnolde", Kansas City, Jackson, Missouri, United States
Military		Surgeon, 13th Missouri Infantry (???)
Military		Private, Company C, 25th Missouri Infantry
Military		Private, Hospital Steward, Company C, Van Horn's Battalion Cavalry Volunteers
Tax Lists	May 1866	Physician License, Income, and Gold Watch; Kansas City, Jackson, Missouri, United States
Census	1870	Page 499, Kansas City, Jackson, Missouri, United States
Will	11 Dec 1876	(Will Written), [--?--]
Death	12 Dec 1876	Kansas City, Jackson, Missouri, United States
Misc		Death Notice, Kansas City (Mo.) Daily Journal of Commerce, 13 Dec 1876, Page 1, Column 6
Burial	14 Dec 1876	Elmwood Cemetery, Kansas City, Jackson, Missouri, United States
Misc		Funeral Notice, Kansas City (Mo.) Daily Journal of Commerce, 15 Dec 1876, Page 4, Column 4
Probate	21 Dec 1876	(Will Proved), Volume A, Page 179, and Volume UK, Page 13, Kansas City, Jackson, Missouri, United States
Occupation		Physician (1850, 1860, 1870)
Marriage	10 Jul 1855	Jo Daviess, Illinois, United States
Father		
Mother		
Other spouse		Eliza KINSLEY/KINGSLEY (1827-)
Marriage	14 Sep 1851	Jo Daviess, Illinois, United States

Mother Virginia Adelia SMITH

Birth	3 May 1831	Williamstown, Oswego, New York, United States
Census	1840	(Eli B. Smith Family), Page 250, Chateaugay, Franklin, New York, United States
Census	1850	Page 144, Chateaugay, Franklin, New York, United States
Census	1860	Page 22, Kansas City, Jackson, Missouri, United States
Religion	16 Jul 1865	Charter Member, Second Presbyterian Church; Kansas City, Jackson, Missouri, United States
Census	1870	Page 499, Kansas City, Jackson, Missouri, United States
Census	1880	ED 23, Page 13, Kaw Township, Jackson, Missouri, United States
Census	1900	ED 78, Page 176, Kansas City, Jackson, Missouri, United States
Will	22 Aug 1906	(Will Written), Volume 12, Page 478, Kansas City, Jackson, Missouri, United States
Death	11 Aug 1907	Lawrence, Douglas, Kansas, United States
Misc		Death Notice, Kansas City (Mo.) Times, 13 Aug 1907, Page 9, Column 6
Burial	16 Aug 1907	Elmwood Cemetery, Kansas City, Jackson, Missouri, United States
Probate	23 Sep 1907	(Will Proved), Volume 12, Page 478, Kansas City, Jackson, Missouri, United States
Father		Eli Boardman SMITH (1806-1890)
Mother		Laura HAWKS (1806-1849)

Children

F Adeline Eliza "Ada, Addie" ARNOLDIA

Birth	8 Apr 1855	(or 08 Apr 1856), Illinois, United States
Census	1860	Page 22, Kansas City, Jackson, Missouri, United States
Census	1870	Page 499, Kansas City, Jackson, Missouri, United States
Census	1880	ED 23, Page 13, Kaw Township, Jackson, Missouri, United States
Census	1900	ED 115, Page 99, Kansas City, Jackson, Missouri, United States
Death	29 Mar 1937	
Burial		Memorial Park Cemetery, Lawrence, Douglas, Kansas, United States
Spouse		Millard F. DYER (1855-)
Marriage	7 Oct 1879	(1879I0080027), Jackson, Missouri, United States
Spouse		Francis BROWNE (1864-1960)
Marriage		

Father	Dr. Peter ARNOLDIA		
Mother	**Virginia Adelia SMITH**		
Children			
F	**Laura Ella ARNOLDIA**		
	Birth	1857/8	Iowa, United States
	Census	1860	Page 22, Kansas City, Jackson, Missouri, United States
	Census	1870	Page 499, Kansas City, Jackson, Missouri, United States
	Will	31 May 1880	(Will Written), Volume 3, Page 1, Kansas City, Jackson, Missouri, United States
	Census	1880	ED 23, Page 13, Kaw Township, Jackson, Missouri, United States
	Death	13 Aug 1888	Kansas City, Jackson, Missouri, United States
	Burial	15 Aug 1888	Elmwood Cemetery, Kansas City, Jackson, Missouri, United States
	Probate	29 Aug 1888	(Will Proved), Volume 3, Page 1, Kansas City, Jackson, Missouri, United States
	Spouse	Edward Napoleon LAVEINE (1849-1917)	
	Marriage	8 Nov 1877	(1877I0070505), Kansas City, Jackson, Missouri, United States
	Divorce	1896	
M	**Eli Smith ARNOLDIA**		
	Birth	2 Mar 1861	Kansas City, Jackson, Missouri, United States
	Census	1870	Page 499, Kansas City, Jackson, Missouri, United States
	Census	1880	ED 23, Page 13, Kaw Township, Jackson, Missouri, United States
	Census	1900	ED 78, Page 175, Kansas City, Jackson, Missouri, United States
	Census	1910	Kansas City, Jackson, Missouri, United States
	Death	3 Sep 1944	Chronic Miocarditis, Chronic Interstitial Nephritis; Kansas City, Jackson, Missouri, United States
	Burial	5 Sep 1944	Elmwood Cemetery, Kansas City, Jackson, Missouri, United States
	Occupation		Apprentice (1880); Machinist (1900, 1910)
	Spouse	Helena SCHURLEIN (1862-1947)	
	Marriage	31 Jul 1885	(1885K0050235), Jackson, Missouri, United States
F	**Mary Sophronia "Minnie" ARNOLDIA**		
	Birth	1862/3	Missouri, United States
	Census	1870	Page 499, Kansas City, Jackson, Missouri, United States
	Census	1880	ED 23, Page 13, Kaw Township, Jackson, Missouri, United States
	Residence	1907	Columbia, Boone, Missouri, United States
	Census	1910	ED 624, Page 105, Manhattan, New York, New York, United States
	Death	27 Dec 1932	(Manakin-Sabot), Manakin, Goochland, Virginia, United States
	Burial		
	Spouse	Raymond Leslie WEEKS (1863-1954)	
	Marriage	4 Mar 1885	(1885K0050043), Jackson, Missouri, United States

Father Jacob AXLINE

Birth	12 May 1813	Loudoun, Virginia, United States
Census	1820	(Jacob Axline Family), Page 139, Loudoun, Virginia, United States
Census	1830	
Census	1840	
Census	1850	Page 253, Fayette, Kentucky, United States
Property	8 Apr 1854	First Known US Land Purchase (Military Land Warrant); (Part Section 29, Township 47, Range 32), Jackson, Missouri, United States
Residence	bet 1855 and 1864	Near Hickman Mills, Jackson, Missouri, United States
Census	1860	Page 193, Jackson, Missouri, United States
Census		Agricultural Schedules, Page 15, Division 35, Jackson, Missouri, United States
Military		1st Lieutenant, 5th Battalion Missouri State Militia Cavalry
Military		1st Lieutenant, Lt. Jacob Axline's Independent Company, Enrolled Missouri Militia
Military		1st Lieutenant, Independent Company, 77th Regiment Enrolled Missouri Militia
Military		Captain, Company B, 2nd Battalion Missouri State Militia Cavalry
Tax Lists	Dec 1863	Cattle Broker License; Hickman Mills, Jackson, Missouri, United States
Death	1 Jun 1864	Murdered by Bushwhackers; Jackson, Missouri, United States
Misc		Death Notice, Kansas City (Mo.) Daily Journal of Commerce, 03 Jun 1864, Page 3, Column 1
Probate	16 May 1865	(Letters of Administration), Volume L, Page 102, Independence, Jackson, Missouri, United States
Religion		Member, Bethlehem Christian Church; Hickman Mills, Jackson. Missouri, United States
Occupation		Blacksmith (1850), Farmer (1860), Cattle Broker
Misc		Edith Wilson Thoesen, Genealogy of the Exline and Axline Family (1952), Page 198-200
Burial		
Marriage	31 Aug 1835	Kentucky, United States
Father		Jacob AXLINE (1782-1833)
Mother		Catherine MOUL (1784-1834)

Mother Mary Catherine EDMONDS

Birth	11 Sep 1820	Loudoun, Virginia, United States
Census	1830	
Census	1840	
Census	1850	Page 253, Fayette, Kentucky, United States
Property	8 Apr 1854	First Known US Land Purchase; (Sections 30, 31, and 32, Township 47, Range 32), Jackson, Missouri, United States
Census	1860	Page 193, Jackson, Missouri, United States
Residence	bet 1865 and 1886	Fairfield, Jefferson, Iowa, United States
Census	1870	Page 87, Fairfield, Jefferson, Iowa, United States
Census	1880	ED 81, Page 410, Fairfield, Jefferson, Iowa, United States
Census	1885	Page 296, Fairfield, Jefferson, Iowa, United States
Death	4 Apr 1887	Fairfield, Jefferson, Iowa, United States
Burial		Evergreen Cemetery, Fairfield, Jefferson, Iowa, United States
Religion		Member, Bethlehem Christian Church; Hickman Mills, Jackson. Missouri, United States
Misc		Edith Wilson Thoesen, Genealogy of the Exline and Axline Family (1952), Page 198-200
Father		
Mother		

Children

M John Todhunter AXLINE

Birth	4 Sep 1846	(or 06 Sep 1846), Jessamine, Kentucky, United States
Census	1850	Page 253, Fayette, Kentucky, United States
Census	1860	Page 193, Jackson, Missouri, United States
Military		Company B, 2nd Battalion Missouri State Militia Cavalry
Military		Sergeant, Lt. Jacob Axline's Independent Company, Enrolled Missouri Militia
Military		Sergeant, Independent Company, 77th Regiment Enrolled Missouri Militia
Census	1870	Page 87, Fairfield, Jefferson, Iowa, United States
Census	1880	ED 81, Page 410, Fairfield, Jefferson, Iowa, United States
Census	1885	Page 296, Fairfield, Jefferson, Iowa, United States
Census	1900	ED 47, Page 77, Fairfield, Jefferson, Iowa, United States
Death	12 Aug 1922	Fairfield, Jefferson, Iowa, United States

Father Jacob AXLINE		
Mother Mary Catherine EDMONDS		
Children		

John Todhunter AXLINE (continued)

Burial		Evergreen Cemetery, Jefferson, Iowa, United States
Occupation		School Teacher (1870); Clerk in Store (1880), Insurance Agent (1885), Carpenter (1900)
Spouse	Laura J. WHITSON (1858-1881)	
Marriage	16 Aug 1877	Jefferson, Iowa, United States
Spouse	Sarah I. LEWIS (1852-1927)	
Marriage	2 Jan 1887	Jefferson, Iowa, United States

M George M. AXLINE

Birth	18 Aug 1849	Kentucky, United States
Census	1850	Page 253, Fayette, Kentucky, United States
Death	26 Jun 1857	Accidentally Shot by John Todhunter Axline; Jackson, Missouri, United States
Death		Accidentally Killed; Jackson, Missouri, United States
Burial		
Marriage		

M Henry Morehead AXLINE

Birth	8 Oct 1850	
Death	20 Oct 1850	
Burial		
Marriage		

M William Daniel AXLINE

Birth	21 Jun 1851	Kentucky, United States
Census	1860	Page 193, Jackson, Missouri, United States
Census	1870	Page 87, Fairfield, Jefferson, Iowa, United States
Census	1880	
Census	1900	ED 101, Page 133, Tiffin, Seneca, Ohio, United States
Death	27 Mar 1913	Drowned in a Flood; Tiffin, Seneca, Ohio, United States
Burial		Greenlawn Cemetery, Tiffin, Seneca, Ohio, United States
Occupation		Printer (1870, 1900)
Spouse	Addline J. ALEXANDER (1862-1913)	
Marriage	1887/8	

M Charles Andrew AXLINE

Birth	6 Sep 1853	Kentucky, United States
Census	1860	Page 193, Jackson, Missouri, United States
Census	1870	Page 87, Fairfield, Jefferson, Iowa, United States
Census	1880	ED 243, Page 350, Allerton, Wayne, Iowa, United States
Census	1900	ED 94, Page [--?--], Bethany, Harrison, Missouri, United States
Misc		Biography & Photo, History of Harrison Co., Mo. (1921), Pages 376-377
Death	1927	
Burial		Miriam Cemetery, Bethany, Harrison, Missouri, United States
Occupation		Stone Cutter (1870); Marble Cutter (1880, 1900)
Spouse	Malinda J. CHANCE (1863-1933)	
Marriage	15 Feb 1879	Cainsville, Harrison, Missouri, United States

M Jacob Sanford AXLINE

Birth	10 Feb 1857	Missouri, United States
Death	27 Jan 1860	
Burial		
Marriage		

M Squire Thomas AXLINE

Birth	29 Aug 1860	(or 1861), Missouri, United States
Census	1870	Page 87, Fairfield, Jefferson, Iowa, United States
Death	11 Jan 1880	
Burial		Evergreen Cemetery, Fairfield, Jefferson, Iowa, United States
Marriage		

Father Joseph P. BABBITT

Birth	ca 1831	Ohio, United States
Census	1850	
Census	1860	
Misc		Advertisement, Western Journal of Commerce, 03 Jan 1861, Page 3, Column 4
Tax Lists	Sep 1862	Photographer License; "Jas. P. Babbett", Kansas City, Jackson, Missouri, United States
Misc	30 Jan 1863	Union Provost Marshals' File of Papers Relating to Two or More Civilians, M416, Roll 13, No. 3513
Residence	1865	Cabinet Card verso advertisement; Fort Scott, Bourbon, Kansas, United States
Census	1865	Page 11, Leavenworth, Leavenworth, Kansas, United States
Residence	1868	City Directory; 104 1/2 3rd St, Kansas City, Jackson, Missouri, United States
Residence	1869	City Directory; East Side Main at Junction - Babbitt & Gause, Kansas City, Jackson, Missouri, United States
Census	1870	Pages 325 and 658, Kansas City, Jackson, Missouri, United States
Residence	1871	City Directory; 807 E 10th St - Babbitt & Gause, Kansas City, Jackson, Missouri, United States
Residence	1872	City Directory; ns 13th bet McGee and Laurel - Babbitt & Shannon, 518 & 921 Main, Kansas City, Jackson, Missouri, United States
Residence	1873	City Directory; 1015 Cherry, Babbitt & Shannon, 516 & 518 Main, Kansas City, Jackson, Missouri, United States
Residence	1874	City Directory; 516 Main, west side Campbell between 11th and 12th Sts, Kansas City, Jackson, Missouri, United States
Residence	7 Oct 1875	"J P Babbitt, the well known photographer late of Kansas City, has bought the Photograph Rooms over C. W. Hill's Drug Store on Douglas Avenue..."; Wichita City Eagle, Wichita, Sedgwick, Kansas, United States
Residence	1877	City Directory; cor. Douglas & Emporia Ave, Wichita, Sedgwick, Kansas, United States
Residence	1878	City Directory; Market bet. 1st and 2nd, Wichita, Sedgwick, Kansas, United States
Census	1880	ED 66, Page 385, Abilene, Dickinson, Kansas, United States
Residence	1885	City Directory; 455 Washington St, Kansas City, Jackson, Missouri, United States
Census	1885	Page 2, Wyandotte, Wyandotte, Kansas, United States
Residence	1886	City Directory; 337 Everett, Kansas City, Wyandotte, Kansas, United States
Residence	12 Feb 1886	Virginia E. Morris to Joseph P. Babbitt, Lot 26, Block 92, Wyandotte City; Recorder of Deeds, Kansas City, Wyandotte, Kansas, United States
Residence	17 Feb 1887	J. P. Babbitt and wife to L. M. Culver, Lot 3, Block 23, Wyandotte City; Recorder of Deeds, Kansas City, Wyandotte, Kansas, United States
Residence	1888	City Directory; 2304 N 3rd St, Kansas City, Jackson, Missouri, United States
Illness	25 Mar 1888	"Frank Babbitt, a 14-year-old lad, having charge of his father's store on 3rd Street during the sickness of the parent, yesterday caused the arrest of Joe Davidson and Frank Washington, two tough colored boys...."; Kansas City Times, Kansas City, Jackson, Missouri, United States
Residence	17 Apr 1888	Joseph P. Babbitt to Edwin L. Loomis, Lot 26, Block 92, Wyandotte City; Recorder of Deeds, Kansas City, Wyandotte, Kansas, United States
Census	1888–1900	DECEADED BY 1900: Mrs. Bettie Babbitt, 65, listed with her daughter and son-in-law, Edward and Oraelle (Babbitt) Loomis, Lafayette, Missouri, United States
Occupation		Artist (1865), Photographer (1870 Census; 1873 Directory), Pho. Artist (1880), Artist (1885 Census); Photo (1885 Directory)
Business		J. P. Babbitt, R. J. Fristoe (Groceries)
Death		
Burial		
Marriage		
Father		
Mother		

Mother Elizabeth Rebecca "Bettie" HANSBROUGH

Birth	1835	Virginia, United States
Census	1850	
Census	1860	
Census	1865	Page 11, Leavenworth, Leavenworth, Kansas, United States
Census	1870	Page 658, Kansas City, Jackson, Missouri, United States
Census	1880	ED 66, Page 385, Abilene, Dickinson, Kansas, United States
Census	1885	Page 3, Wyandotte, Wyandotte, Kansas, United States

Father	Joseph P. BABBITT
Mother	Elizabeth Rebecca "Bettie" HANSBROUGH
Children	

Elizabeth Rebecca "Bettie" HANSBROUGH (continued)

Residence	6 Mar 1891	Inheritance: "Mr. Jaques Will Get a Slice: A Kansas City, Kan., Man's Interest in the French Spoliation Claims."; Kansas City (Mo.) Times, Topeka, Shawnee, Kansas, United States
Census	1900	ED 159, Page 235, Lexington, Fayette, Kentucky, United States
Census	1910	ED 26, Page 130, San Francisco, San Francisco, California, United States
Death	1912	Colma, San Mateo, California, United States
Burial	1912	Cypress Lawn Memorial Park Cemetery, Colma, San Mateo, California, United States
Father		Peter A HANSBROUGH (-)
Mother		Fannie P. MILLER (-)

Children

M   Leonard BABBITT

Birth	1858/9	Missouri, United States
Census	1860	
Census	1865	Page 11, Leavenworth, Leavenworth, Kansas, United States
Census	1870	Page 658, Kansas City, Jackson, Missouri, United States
Census	1880	ED 120, Page 430, Parsons, Labette, Kansas, United States
Occupation		Hotel Clerk (1880)
Death		
Burial		
Marriage		

F   Orielle E. "Ora" BABBITT

Birth	5 Oct 1861	(or 05 Oct 1860), Kansas City, Jackson, Missouri, United States
Census	1865	Page 11, Leavenworth, Leavenworth, Kansas, United States
Census	1870	Page 658, Kansas City, Jackson, Missouri, United States
Census	1880	ED 66, Page 385, Abilene, Dickinson, Kansas, United States
Census	1900	ED 159, Page 235, Lexington, Fayette, Kentucky, United States
Census	1910	ED 102, Page [--?--], Lexington, Fayette, Kentucky, United States
Census	1920	ED 118, Page 227, Lexington, Fayette, Kentucky, United States
Death	26 May 1927	Burned to Death, Accidental, Clothes Caught Fire from Gas Stove; Lexington, Fayette, Kentucky, United States
Burial	28 May 1927	Machpelah Cemetery, Lexington, Lafayette, Missouri, United States
Spouse		Edward George LOOMIS (1856-1926)
Marriage		

F   Louisa A. "Lulu" BABBITT

Birth	1862/3	Missouri, United States
Census	1865	Page 11, Leavenworth, Leavenworth, Kansas, United States
Census	1870	Page 658, Kansas City, Jackson, Missouri, United States
Census	1880	ED 66, Page 385, Abilene, Dickinson, Kansas, United States
Census	1885	Page 3, Wyandotte, Wyandotte, Kansas, United States
Census	1895	Pages 723-724, Topeka, Shawnee, Kansas, United States
Census	1900	ED 101, Page [--?--], San Francisco, San Francisco, California, United States
Census	1910	ED 26, Page 130, San Francisco, San Francisco, California, United States
Death	28 Mar 1932	San Mateo, California, United States
Burial		
Spouse		George M. RATHBUN (1856-1930)
Marriage	5 Oct 1887	(Recorded (1887K0080436) Jackson, Missouri, United States), Wyandotte, Kansas, United States

M   Frank P. BABBITT

Birth	1871/2	Missouri, United States
Census	1880	ED 66, Page 385, Abilene, Dickinson, Kansas, United States
Census	1885	Page 3, Wyandotte, Wyandotte, Kansas, United States
Military		Private, 11th Regiment Missouri Infantry, Spanish-American War
Census	1900	
Census	1910	ED 161, Page 224, Turlock Township, Stanislaus, California, United States
Residence	5 May 1922	U. S. National Home for Disabled Soldiers; Sawtelle, Los Angeles, California, United States

<table>
<tr><td colspan="3">Father Joseph P. BABBITT</td></tr>
<tr><td colspan="3">Mother Elizabeth Rebecca "Bettie" HANSBROUGH</td></tr>
<tr><td colspan="3">Children</td></tr>
<tr><td colspan="3">Frank P. BABBITT (continued)</td></tr>
<tr><td>Death</td><td>18 Mar 1923</td><td></td></tr>
<tr><td>Occupation</td><td></td><td>Painter House (1910)</td></tr>
<tr><td>Burial</td><td></td><td></td></tr>
<tr><td>Marriage</td><td></td><td></td></tr>
</table>

FATHER NOTES: Joseph P. BABBITT

Census (1870): There were two entries for Joseph Babbitt in the 1870 Census: Babbit J. P., white, male, 40 years old, born Ohio, photographer, personal estate $500, can read and write, head of family, ward 4, post office Kansas City Mo. (1870 United States census, Kansas City, Jackson County, Missouri, page 658, dwelling 354, family 352, line 1, National Archives microfilm M593, roll 782.) Another entry: 1870 Babbitt Joseph, white, male, 40 years old, born Ohio, photographer, personal estate $1000, can read and write, head of family, ward 1, post office Kansas City Mo. (1870 United States census, Kansas City, Jackson County, Missouri, page 325, dwelling 384, family 390, line 20, National Archives microfilm M593, roll 782.)

Residence (1871): P. Shannon was in a partnership with S. W. Kissell in 1871: Kissel & Shannon, 214 Main

Residence (1874): Neither Babbitt nor Shannon were in business in Kansas City after 1874.
Occupation: Joseph P. Babbitt's brother-in-law, was also a well-known Kansas City photographer, John A. Hansbrough, listed in city directories as such:

1898 Hansbrough J. A. 1810 e 18th
1899 Hansbrough J. A. 1803 Troost
1900 Hansbrough J A 1803 Troost
1900   Hansbrough John, white, male, 59 years old, born October 1840 Missouri (Virginia-Virginia), married for 27 years, photographer, can read and write, head of family, house rented, ward 9, 1803 Troost Avenue.
(1900 United States census, Kansas City, Jackson County, Missouri, enumeration district 102, page 197, dwelling 147, family 197, line 49, National Archives microfilm T623, roll 863.)
1901 Hansbrough J F [sic] 1803 Troost
1902 Hansbrough J A 1803 Troost
1903-
1904-Hansbrough & Son 2317 e 18th
        [Charles A.; he partnered with Wilburn E. Cowen to form DeLuxe Studio, listed in at least the 1905 and 1906 city directories]
1905 Hansbrough J A 2317 e 18th
1906 Hansbrough J A 2317 e 18th
1907 Hansbrough J A 2317 e 18th
1908 Hansbrough John A 2317 E 18th

MOTHER NOTES: Elizabeth Rebecca HANSBROUGH

Census (1900): With daughter and son-in-law, Oraelle and Edward Loomis
Death (1912): https://www.findagrave.com/memorial/243281386/elizabeth-babbitt

Father **John Reed BALIS**		
Birth	11 Jul 1834	Cairo, Greene, New York, United States
Census	1840	(Edmund Balis Family), Page 239, Greene, New York, United States
Census	1850	Page 99, Westmoreland, Oneida, New York, United States
Religion	1859	Communicant, St. Mary's (Episcopal) Church; Kansas City, Jackson, Missouri, United States
Census	1860	Page 79, Kansas City, Jackson, Missouri, United States
Misc		Advertisement, Western Journal of Commerce, 01 Jan 1861, Page 4, Column 4
Misc	19 Jun 1861	Union Provost Marshals' File of Papers Relating to Individual Civilians, M345, Roll 2
Misc	8 Jul 1862	Union Provost Marshals' File of Papers . . . Two or More Civilians, M416, Roll 81, No. 22,374
Tax Lists	Sep 1862	Retail Dealer License; "Bailey's & Hicks", Kansas City, Jackson, Missouri, United States
Military		1st Lieutenant & Battalion Adjutant, 2nd Battalion Cavalry Missouri State Militia
Military		Civil War Draft Registration; Kaw Township, Jackson, Missouri, United States
Misc		"City Assessment," Kansas City (Mo.) Daily Journal of Commerce, 01 Oct 1865, Page 2, Column 1
Tax Lists	May 1866	Carriage; Kansas City, Jackson, Missouri, United States
Tax Lists	Dec 1866	Real Estate Agent License; "Case & Balis", Kansas City, Jackson, Missouri, United States
Occupation	1866/7	City Councilman; Kansas City, Jackson, Missouri, United States
Census	1870	Page 664, Kansas City, Jackson, Missouri, United States
Census	1880	
Census	1890	ED 194, Number 48, Kansas City, Jackson, Missouri, United States
Census	1900	ED 84, Page 241, Bradenton, Manatee, Florida, United States
Census	1910	ED 94, Page 208, Bradenton, Manatee, Florida, United States
Death	5 Dec 1914	
Burial		Fogartyville Cemetery, Bradenton, Manatee, Florida, United States
Occupation		Clerk (1850); Merchant (1860); Real Estate Broker (1870); Gardener (1900); Fruit Farmer (1910)
Business		Balis & Hicks (Books, Stationery, Insurance)
Marriage	8 Oct 1872	Catskill, Greene, New York, United States
Father	Edmund BALIS (1800-)	
Mother	Harriet [--?--] (1802-1880)	
Other spouse	Caroline A. COLEMAN (1842-)	
Marriage	29 Oct 1860	(1860I0050004), Jackson, Missouri, United States
Mother **Helen Augusta "Mellie" MATTOON**		
Birth	18 Aug 1853	Cairo, Greene, New York, United States
Census	1860	
Census	1870	
Census	1880	
Census	1900	ED 84, Page 241, Bradenton, Manatee, Florida, United States
Census	1910	ED 94, Page 208, Bradenton, Manatee, Florida, United States
Census	1920	
Census	1930	
Death	1 Nov 1939	
Burial		
Father	Peleg Cornwall MATTOON (1817-1865)	
Mother	Julia PORTER (1819-)	
Children		
M **Ermine Cassius BALIS**		
Birth	27 Oct 1874	(or 27 Oct 1873), Missouri, United States
Census	1880	
Census	1900	ED 84, Page 241, Bradenton, Manatee, Florida, United States
Census	1910	ED 94, Page 208, Bradenton, Manatee, Florida, United States
Death	16 Feb 1953	Manatee, Florida, United States
Occupation		Assistant Postmaster (1900); Manager of Abstract Office (1910)
Burial		
Marriage		

Father	**John Reed BALIS**	
Mother	**Helen Augusta "Mellie" MATTOON**	
Children		

F	**May BALIS**	
	Birth	
	Chr	
	Death	(in Infancy), [--?--]
	Burial	
	Marriage	

M	**Webster BALIS**	
	Birth	
	Chr	
	Death	(in Infancy), [--?--]
	Burial	
	Marriage	

M	**George Elston BALIS**	
	Birth	7 Aug 1882	Missouri, United States
	Census	1900	ED 84, Page 241, Bradenton, Manatee, Florida, United States
	Census	1910	ED 94, Page 208, Bradenton, Manatee, Florida, United States
	Census	1920	ED 121, Page 138, Bradenton, Manatee, Florida, United States
	Death	9 Feb 1962	
	Burial		Fogartyville Cemetery, Bradenton, Manatee, Florida, United States
	Occupation		Day Laborer (1900); Drug Store Clerk (1910); Druggist (1920)
	Spouse	Pauline B. [--?--] (1892-1991)	
	Marriage		

M	**Raymond Banks BALIS**	
	Birth	13 Feb 1885	Missouri, United States
	Census	1900	ED 84, Page 241, Bradenton, Manatee, Florida, United States
	Census	1910	ED 94, Page 208, Bradenton, Manatee, Florida, United States
	Death	17 Sep 1969	Bradenton, Manatee, Florida, United States
	Burial		Manasota Memorial Park, Bradenton, Manatee, Florida, United States
	Occupation		Bank Teller (1910)
	Spouse	Anna Green SANDERS (1901-1994)	
	Marriage	8 Oct 1925	Beaufort, Beaufort, South Carolina, United States

Father John T. BARTLESON

Birth	1834	Missouri, United States
Census	1840	(John Bartleson Family), Page 62, Line 1, Jackson, Missouri, United States
Census	1850	
Census	1860	Post Office New Santa Fe, Page 204, Jackson, Missouri, United States
Census		Slave Schedules, Page 373, Jackson, Missouri, United States
Census		Agricultural Schedules, Page 17, Division 35, Jackson, Missouri, United States
Misc	10 Aug 1862	Union Provost Marshals' File of Papers Relating to Two or More Civilians, M416, Roll 8, No. 2129
Tax Lists	Sep 1862	Retail Dealer License; "John P. Bartleson", Kansas City, Jackson, Missouri, United States
Misc	27 Jan 1863	Union Provost Marshals' File of Papers Relating to Two or More Civilians, M416, Roll 13, No. 3512
Census	1870	(Township 47, Range 33), Page 114, Jackson, Missouri, United States
Census		Agricultural Schedules, Township 47, Range 33, Post Office Lee's Summit, Page 19, Jackson, Missouri, United States
Census	1880	ED 75, Page 6, Belton, Cass, Missouri, United States
Death	1896	
Burial		Adamsville Cemetery, Florence, Pinal, Arizona, United States
Occupation		Farmer (1860, 1870); Miner (1880), Retail Dealer
Marriage		
Father		John BARTLESON Sr. (1786-1848)
Mother		Frances BOGIE (1793-1848)

Mother Susan M. YOUNG

Birth	7 Jan 1839	Kentucky, United States
Residence	1842-?	Jackson, Missouri, United States
Census	1850	
Census	1860	Post Office New Santa Fe, Page 204, Jackson, Missouri, United States
Census	1870	(Township 47, Range 33), Page 114, Jackson, Missouri, United States
Census	1880	ED 75, Page 6, Belton, Cass, Missouri, United States
Census	1900	ED 55, Page 211, Township 4, Pinal, Arizona, United States
Census	1910	ED 109, Page 17, Pinal, Arizona, United States
Census	1920	ED 265, Page 174, Kansas City, Jackson, Missouri, United States
Death	26 Apr 1925	Lobar Pneumonia; Kansas City, Jackson, Missouri, United States
Misc		Obituary, Kansas City (Mo.) Times, 27 Apr 1925, Page 12, Column 2
Burial	28 Apr 1925	Forest Hill Cemetery, Kansas City, Jackson, Missouri, United States
Occupation		Farmer (1900)
Father		Solomon YOUNG (1815-1892)
Mother		Harriet Louise GREGG (1815-1909)

Children

F Emma P. BARTLESON

Birth	25 Jul 1861	Jackson, Missouri, United States
Census	1870	(Township 47, Range 33), Page 114, Jackson, Missouri, United States
Census	1880	ED 75, Page 6, Belton, Cass, Missouri, United States
Census	1900	ED 123, Page 234, Kansas City, Jackson, Missouri, United States
Census	1910	
Census	1920	ED 265, Page 174, Kansas City, Jackson, Missouri, United States
Death	5 Nov 1932	Acute Myocarditis, Chronic Myocarditis; Kansas City, Jackson, Missouri, United States
Burial	8 Nov 1932	Mount Moriah Cemetery, Kansas City, Jackson, Missouri, United States
Occupation		Nurse Private Family (1920)
Spouse		Dr. George Lewis LOVE (1849-1927)
Marriage	7 Sep 1881	Belton, Cass, Missouri, United States

F Fanny L. BARTLESON

Birth	Aug 1866	Missouri, United States
Census	1870	(Township 47, Range 33), Page 114, Jackson, Missouri, United States
Census	1880	ED 75, Page 6, Belton, Cass, Missouri, United States
Census	1900	ED 55, Page 211, Township 4, Pinal, Arizona, United States
Death		
Burial		

Father John T. BARTLESON

Mother Susan M. YOUNG

Children

Fanny L. BARTLESON (continued)

Marriage		

M Sidney A. BARTLESON

Birth	9 Dec 1868	Missouri, United States
Census	1870	(Township 47, Range 33), Page 114, Jackson, Missouri, United States
Census	1880	ED 75, Page 6, Belton, Cass, Missouri, United States
Census	1900	ED 55, Page 211, Township 4, Pinal, Arizona, United States
Census	1910	ED 109, Page 17, Pinal, Arizona, United States
Death	20 Jan 1911	
Burial		Adamsville Cemetery, Florence, Pinal, Arizona, United States
Occupation		Farm Laborer (1900), Farmer (1910)
Marriage		

F Nellie Ney BARTLESON

Birth	24 Jun 1871	Missouri, United States
Census	1880	ED 75, Page 6, Belton, Cass, Missouri, United States
Census	1900	ED 55, Page 211, Township 4, Pinal, Arizona, United States
Census	1910	ED 109, Page 7, Florence, Pinal, Arizona, United States
Census	1920	ED 109, Page 114, Florence, Pinal, Arizona, United States
Residence	1925	Florence, Pinal, Arizona, United States
Death	14 Nov 1938	
Burial		Angelus Rosedale Cemetery, Los Angeles, Los Angeles, California, United States
Occupation		Teacher (1900), Deputy Recorder Pinal Co. (1910)
Spouse	Thomas Charles WELLS (1871-)	
Marriage	30 Apr 1906	Florence, Pinal, Arizona Territory, United States

F Eugenia Bogie BARTLESON

Birth	Apr 1874	Missouri, United States
Census	1880	ED 75, Page 6, Belton, Cass, Missouri, United States
Census	1900	ED 55, Page 211, Township 4, Pinal, Arizona, United States
Death	1902	
Burial		Adamsville Cemetery, Florence, Pinal, Arizona, United States
Marriage		

F Mary BARTLESON

Birth	6 Mar 1882	Arizona, United States
Census	1900	ED 55, Page 211, Township 4, Pinal, Arizona, United States
Census	1910	
Census	1920	ED 68, Page 118, Auberry, Fresno, California, United States
Death	28 Dec 1974	Orange, California, United States
Burial		
Spouse	Robert Hiram BLOOMER (1876-1955)	
Marriage	12 Dec 1905	Florence, Pinal, Arizona Territory, United States

Father James H. BARTLETT

Birth	Jan 1835	England
Immigration	1860	
Tax Lists	Apr 1863	Retail Dealer License; "Bartlett & Frank", Independence, Jackson, Missouri, United States
Tax Lists	bet May 1863 and Jul 1863	Animals Slaughtered for Sale; "Bartlett & Frank", Kansas City, Jackson, Missouri, United States
Military		Private, Company A, 77th Regiment Enrolled Missouri Militia
Tax Lists	bet Aug 1863 and Dec 1863	Animals Slaughtered for Sale; "Bartlett & Wyland", Kansas City, Jackson, Missouri, United States
Military		Civil War Draft Registration; Kaw Township, Jackson, Missouri, United States
Tax Lists	bet Jun 1865 and May 1866	Animals Slaughtered for Sale; Kansas City, Jackson, Missouri, United States
Tax Lists	bet Jun 1866 and Jul 1866	Animals Slaughtered for Sale; "Schibley/Schibli & Bartlett", Kansas City, Jackson, Missouri, United States
Census	1870	Page 453, Kansas City, Jackson, Missouri, United States
Census	1875	Page 14, Aubry Township, Johnson, Kansas, United States
Census	1880	ED 93, Page 5, Aubry Township, Johnson, Kansas, United States
Census	1885	
Census	1895	Page 108, Kansas City, Wyandotte, Kansas, United States
Census	1900	ED 110, Page 168, Omaha, Douglas, Nebraska, United States
Census	1910	
Census	1920	
Death	1926	
Burial		Forest Lawn Memorial Park, Omaha, Douglas, Nebraska, United States
Occupation		Butcher (1870, 1895, 1900); Farmer (1875, 1880)
Religion		Roman Catholic
Business		Bartlett & Frank (Meat), Bartlett & Wyland (Meat)
Marriage	1 Jan 1881	(1881I0080243), Jackson, Missouri, United States
Father		
Mother		
Other spouse	Bridget MCCANN (1844-)	
Marriage	23 Feb 1862	(1862I0050069), Jackson, Missouri, United States

Mother Maggie [--?--]

Birth	May 1857	New York, United States
Census	1860	
Census	1870	
Census	1880	
Census	1895	Page 108, Kansas City, Wyandotte, Kansas, United States
Census	1900	ED 110, Page 168, Omaha, Douglas, Nebraska, United States
Census	1910	
Census	1920	
Census	1930	
Death		
Burial		
Father		
Mother		
Other spouse	[--?--] MARTIN (-)	
Marriage		

Children

Father Albert L. BEATTY

Birth	1812	Philadelphia, Philadelphia, Pennsylvania, United States
Census	1820	
Census	1830	
Census	1840	
Business	bet 1844 and 1886	Beatty Jewelry Store; Independence, Jackson, Missouri, United States
Census	1850	Page 264, Blue Township, Jackson, Missouri, United States
Census		Slave Schedules, Frame 106, Blue Township, Jackson, Missouri, United States
Census	1860	Page 261, Independence, Jackson, Missouri, United States
Census		Slave Schedules, Page 364, Independence, Jackson, Missouri, United States
Misc	19 Apr 1862	Union Provost Marshals' File of Papers Relating to Two or More Civilians, M416, Roll 5, No. 1075
Tax Lists	Sep 1862	Retail Dealer License; "Albert Beattey", Independence, Jackson, Missouri, United States
Military		Private, Capt. Peter Hinter's Independence Home Guards
Tax Lists	May 1866	Retail Dealer License and Pianoforte; Independence, Jackson, Missouri, United States
Will	18 Jan 1870	(Will Written), Volume O, Page 381, Independence, Jackson, Missouri, United States
Census	1870	Page 285, Independence, Jackson, Missouri, United States
Census	1880	ED 24, Page 36, Independence, Jackson, Missouri, United States
Death	1886	
Burial		Woodlawn Cemetery, Independence, Jackson, Missouri, United States
Probate	13 Apr 1891	(Will Proved), Volume O, Page 381, Independence, Jackson, Missouri, United States
Misc		"Beatty Shop Changes Hands," Kansas City (Mo.) Star, 18 Dec 1921, Want Ad Sect., P. 5, Col. 4
Misc		"A. L. Beatty Jewelry Store," Jackson County Pioneers (1975), Page 380
Occupation		Jeweler (1850, 1860), Jewelry Store (1870), Jeweler & Watch Man (1880), Retail Dealer
Marriage	28 Nov 1842	Bloomington, Muscatine, Iowa Territory, United States
Father		
Mother		

Mother Jane Harvey SUMMERS

Birth	15 Nov 1826	Frueham, Somersetshire, England
Immigration	1828	
Census	1830	
Census	1840	
Census	1850	Page 264, Blue Township, Jackson, Missouri, United States
Census	1860	Page 261, Independence, Jackson, Missouri, United States
Census	1870	Page 285, Independence, Jackson, Missouri, United States
Census	1880	ED 24, Page 36, Independence, Jackson, Missouri, United States
Census	1900	ED 6, Page 84, Independence, Jackson, Missouri, United States
Census	1910	ED 9, Page 131, Independence, Jackson, Missouri, United States
Death	1 Aug 1913	Bronchitis Acute, Senility; Independence, Jackson, Missouri, United States
Misc		Obituary, Independence (Mo.) Examiner, 02 Aug 1913, Page 1, Column 7
Burial	3 Aug 1913	Woodlawn Cemetery, Independence, Jackson, Missouri, United States
Religion		Charter Member, Christian Church; Independence, Jackson, Missouri, United States
Father		Henry SUMMERS (1782-1867)
Mother		Rachel HARVEY (1786-)

Children

M Louis A. BEATTY

Birth	1843	
Death	1844	
Burial		Woodlawn Cemetery, Independence, Jackson, Missouri, United States
Marriage		

M Albert H. C. BEATTY

Birth	18 Nov 1845	Independence, Jackson, Missouri, United States
Census	1850	Page 264, Blue Township, Jackson, Missouri, United States
Census	1860	Page 261, Independence, Jackson, Missouri, United States
Military		Home Guard Service
Census	1870	Page 285, Independence, Jackson, Missouri, United States
Census	1880	ED 24, Page 36, Independence, Jackson, Missouri, United States

Father	Albert L. BEATTY	
Mother	**Jane Harvey SUMMERS**	
Children		

Albert H. C. BEATTY (continued)

Business	bet 1886 and 1921	Beatty Jewelry Store; Independence, Jackson, Missouri, United States
Census	1900	ED 6, Page 84, Independence, Jackson, Missouri, United States
Census	1910	ED 9, Page 131, Independence, Jackson, Missouri, United States
Residence	1913	Independence, Jackson, Missouri, United States
Death	7 Dec 1921	Laryngitis, Dilatation of Heart; Independence, Jackson, Missouri, United States
Misc		Obituary, Independence (Mo.) Examiner, 08 Dec 1921, Page 1, Column 2
Burial	9 Dec 1921	Woodlawn Cemetery, Independence, Jackson, Missouri, United States
Misc		"Beatty Shop Changes Hands," Kansas City (Mo.) Star, 18 Dec 1921, Want Ad Sect., P. 5, Col. 4
Occupation		Bookkeeper (1870); Jeweler (1900, 1910), Merchant
Marriage		

F   Jane Emma/Emily BEATTY

Birth	26 Oct 1848	Independence, Jackson, Missouri, United States
Census	1850	Page 264, Blue Township, Jackson, Missouri, United States
Census	1860	Page 261, Independence, Jackson, Missouri, United States
Census	1870	
Census	1880	ED 24, Page 36, Independence, Jackson, Missouri, United States
Census	1900	ED 6, Page 84, Independence, Jackson, Missouri, United States
Census	1910	ED 9, Page 131, Independence, Jackson, Missouri, United States
Residence	1913	Independence, Jackson, Missouri, United States
Residence	1936	Independence, Jackson, Missouri, United States
Death	2 Mar 1946	Chronic Myocarditis, Senility; Kansas City, Jackson, Missouri, United States
Burial	5 Mar 1946	Woodlawn Cemetery, Independence, Jackson, Missouri, United States
Spouse	Thomas MOORE (-)	
Marriage	17 Dec 1868	(1868I0060030), Jackson, Missouri, United States
Divorce		(Before 1880)

M   Charlton Edwin "Charles" BEATTY

Birth	11 Jun 1851	Independence, Jackson, Missouri, United States
Census	1860	Page 261, Independence, Jackson, Missouri, United States
Census	1870	Page 285, Independence, Jackson, Missouri, United States
Census	1880	ED 24, Page 36, Independence, Jackson, Missouri, United States
Census	1900	ED 68, Page 44, Kansas City, Jackson, Missouri, United States
Residence	1913	Kansas City, Jackson, Missouri, United States
Residence	1921	Kansas City, Jackson, Missouri, United States
Death	14 Nov 1935	Chronic Myocarditis, Died Suddenly . . .; Kansas City, Jackson, Missouri, United States
Burial	16 Nov 1935	Woodlawn Cemetery, Independence, Jackson, Missouri, United States
Occupation		Printer (1870), Fire Reporter (1900), Advertising
Spouse	Catharine Cordelia Frances ATKINSON (1858-1907)	
Marriage	23 Dec 1874	(1874I0070216), Jackson, Missouri, United States

F   Julia/Juliette Ann BEATTY

Birth	2 Nov 1854	(or 1855), Missouri, United States
Census	1860	Page 261, Independence, Jackson, Missouri, United States
Census	1870	Page 285, Independence, Jackson, Missouri, United States
Census	1880	ED 24, Page 36, Independence, Jackson, Missouri, United States
Census	1900	ED 6, Page 84, Independence, Jackson, Missouri, United States
Census	1910	ED 9, Page 131, Independence, Jackson, Missouri, United States
Residence	1913	Independence, Jackson, Missouri, United States
Residence	bet 1921 and 1936	Kansas City, Jackson, Missouri, United States
Death	19 May 1936	Hypostatic Pneumonia . . .; Kansas City, Jackson, Missouri, United States
Misc		Obituary, Independence (Mo.) Examiner, 21 May 1936, Page 1, Column 3
Burial	22 May 1936	Woodlawn Cemetery, Independence, Jackson, Missouri, United States
Spouse	William C. ATKINSON (1853-1910)	
Marriage	12 Jun 1882	(1882K0020037), Jackson, Missouri, United States

Father Johannes Phillip/Philipp BECKER

Birth	27 Feb 1832	Brensbach, Hessen-Darmstadt, Germany
Immigration	1855	(or 1845 or 1852/53), [--?--]
Census	1860	Page 119, Westport, Jackson, Missouri, United States
Census	1860	(Industrial Schedules), Page 3, Kansas City, Jackson, Missouri, United States
Misc	10 Aug 1862	Union Provost Marshals' File of Papers Relating to Two or More Civilians, M416, Roll 8, No. 2129
Tax Lists	Sep 1862	Manufacturer License; Westport, Jackson, Missouri, United States
Tax Lists	bet SepDec 1862 and Dec 1863	Boots and Shoes Manufactured; Westport, Jackson, Missouri, United States
Military		Private, Company E, 77th Regiment Enrolled Missouri Militia
Military		Civil War Draft Registration; Kaw Township, Jackson, Missouri, United States
Tax Lists	bet May 1865 and Dec 1866	Boots and Shoes Manufactured; Westport, Jackson, Missouri, United States
Tax Lists	May 1866	Retail Dealer and Manufacturer Licenses; Westport, Jackson, Missouri, United States
Misc	1869/70	City Councilor; Westport, Jackson Co., MO
Census	1870	Pages 58 and 73, Westport, Jackson, Missouri, United States
Census	1870	(Industrial Schedules), Ward 3, Page 56, Westport, Jackson, Missouri, United States
Census	1880	ED 40, Page 255, Westport, Jackson, Missouri, United States
Misc	bet 1893 and 1894	City Treasurer; Westport, Jackson, Missouri, United States
Census	1900	ED 124, Page 247, Kansas City, Jackson, Missouri, United States
Misc		"Half a Century of Happiness," Kansas City (Mo.) Star, 30 Jul 1905, Page 2, Column 4
Misc		"In One Shoe Shop 32 Years," Kansas City (Mo.) Times, 14 Feb 1910, Page 4, Column 1
Census	1910	ED 60, Page 33, Kansas City, Jackson, Missouri, United States
Death	27 Nov 1913	Heart Trouble; Kansas City, Jackson, Missouri, United States
Misc		Obituary, Kansas City (Mo.) Times, 28 Nov 1913, Page 16, Column 1
Burial	30 Nov 1913	Forest Hill Cemetery, Kansas City, Jackson, Missouri, United States
Misc		Biography, Westport Historical Quarterly, Volume 1 (Feb 1966): Pages 19-21
Occupation		Master Shoemaker (1860, 1870), Boot & Shoemaker (1880), Shoe Merchant (1900)
Occupation		Shoe Salesman in Shoe House (1910)
Marriage	29 Jul 1855	(1855I0030218), Jackson, Missouri, United States
Father		
Mother		

Mother Louise/Louisa KNAUBER

Birth	14 Jul 1829	(Pfalz), Steinweiler, Bavaria, Germany
Immigration	1853	
Census	1860	Westport, Jackson Co., MO, Page 119
Census	1870	Westport, Jackson Co., MO, Pages 58 & 73
Census	1880	Westport, Jackson Co., MO, ED 40, Page 255
Census	1900	ED 124, Page 247, Kansas City, Jackson, Missouri, United States
Census	1910	ED 60, Page 33, Kansas City, Jackson, Missouri, United States
Death	26 Jan 1911	Arteriosclerosis, Old Age; Kansas City, Jackson, Missouri, United States
Misc		Obituary, Kansas City (Mo.) Times, 27 Jan 1911, Page 10, Column 6
Misc		Funeral Notice, Kansas City (Mo.) Times, 28 Jan 1911, Page 2, Column 2
Burial	29 Jan 1911	Forest Hill Cemetery, Kansas City, Jackson, Missouri, United States
Father		John KNAUBER (-)
Mother		Maria Anna SATTLER (1798-1884)

Children

F   Rosina "Rose/Rosa/Rosie" BECKER

Birth	1 Feb 1859	MO (or Feb 1860)
Census	1860	Westport, Jackson Co., MO, Page 119
Census	1870	Westport, Jackson Co., MO, Pages 58 & 73
Confirmation	1873	St. Peter's German Evangelical Church, Kansas City, Jackson Co., MO
Census	1880	Westport, Jackson Co., MO, ED 40, Page 255
Misc		Marriage Notice, Westport (Mo.) Sentinel-Examiner, 21 Nov 1896, Page 1, Column 3
Census	1900	ED 123, Page 242, Kansas City, Jackson, Missouri, United States
Census	1910	ED 62, Page 63, Kansas City, Jackson, Missouri, United States
Residence	1913	Kansas City, Jackson, Missouri, United States

Father	Johannes Phillip/Philipp BECKER	
Mother	**Louise/Louisa KNAUBER**	

Children

Rosina "Rose/Rosa/Rosie" BECKER (continued)

Census	1920	ED 60, Page 36, Kansas City, Jackson, Missouri, United States
Census	1930	ED 105, Page 56, Kansas City, Jackson, Missouri, United States
Death	29 Jan 1940	Peritonitis, Cancer of Colon; Kansas City, Jackson, Missouri, United States
Misc		Obituary, Kansas City (Mo.) Times, 30 Jan 1940, Page 6, Columns 3-4
Burial	1 Feb 1940	Forest Hill Cemetery, Kansas City, Jackson, Missouri, United States
Spouse	August HAHN (1845-1925)	
Marriage	19 Nov 1896	(1896K0013774) (Saint Peter's German Evangelical Church, Volume 2, Page 218), Kansas City, Jackson, Missouri, United States

M William Henry "Willy" BECKER

Birth	Apr 1863	Missouri, United States
Census	1870	Westport, Jackson Co., MO, Pages 58 & 73
Census	1880	Westport, Jackson Co., MO, ED 40, Page 255
Misc		"Married," Westport (Mo.) Sentinel-Examiner, 15 Dec 1894, Page 4, Column 4
Census	1900	ED 89, Page 200, Walla Walla, Walla Walla, Washington, United States
Census	1910	ED 107, Page 198, Odessa, Lincoln, Washington, United States
Residence	1911	(also 1913), Odessa, Lincoln, Washington, United States
Census	1920	La Crosse, Whitman Co., WA, ED 146, Page 107
Census	1930	ED 14, Page 42, Lacrosse, Whitman, Washington, United States
Residence	1940	Lacrosse, Whitman, Washington, United States
Occupation		Apprentice to Harness Maker (1880), Retail Merchant Harness Store (1910), Harness Maker (1900, 1920), Leather Mechanic (1930)
Death		
Burial		
Spouse	Rosa Ethel YORK (1874-)	
Marriage	6 Dec 1894	Walla Walla, Walla Walla, Washington, United States

M George/Georg Michael BECKER

Birth	9 Sep 1865	Kansas City, Jackson, Missouri, United States
Baptism	23 Nov 1865	Saint Peter's German Evangelical Church, Volume 1, Page 110, Kansas City, Jackson, Missouri, United States
Census	1870	Pages 58 and 73, Westport, Jackson, Missouri, United States
Census	1880	ED 40, Page 255, Westport, Jackson, Missouri, United States
Misc		Church Marriage Record, Volume 2, Page 216; Saint Peter's German Evangelical Church, Kansas City, Jackson, Missouri, United States
Census	1900	ED 100, Page 163, Kansas City, Jackson, Missouri, United States
Census	1910	ED 141, Page 12, Kansas City, Jackson, Missouri, United States
Census	1920	ED 77, Page 264, Kansas City, Jackson, Missouri, United States
Census	1930	ED 105, Page 56, Kansas City, Jackson, Missouri, United States
Death	7 Oct 1950	Pneumonia Bilateral, Cerebral Hemorrhage [illegible] Left Side of Body; Kansas City, Jackson, Missouri, United States
Burial	10 Oct 1950	Forest Hill Cemetery, Kansas City, Jackson, Missouri, United States
Occupation		Apprentice to Mechanist (1880), Moulder (Iron) (1900), Molder General Foundry (1910), Tenant Farmer Home Farm (1920)
Spouse	Elizabeth SITZLER (1866-1909)	
Marriage	23 Apr 1896	(1896K0012861), Kansas City, Jackson, Missouri, United States
Spouse	[--?--] (-)	
Marriage		

M Robert Phillip BECKER

Birth	1 Jun 1868	MO (or 7 Jun 1868)
Baptism	3 Oct 1868	St. Peter's German Evangelical Church, Kansas City, Jackson Co., MO (or 8 Oct 1868)
Census	1870	Westport, Jackson Co., MO, Pages 58 & 73
Census	1880	Westport, Jackson Co., MO, ED 40, Page 255
Misc		Marriage Notice, Westport (Mo.) Sentinel-Examiner, 07 Apr 1894, Page 3, Column 1
Census	1900	ED 124, Page 246, Kansas City, Jackson, Missouri, United States
Census	1910	ED 65, Page 122, Kansas City, Jackson, Missouri, United States
Residence	1913	Colorado Springs, El Paso, Colorado, United States

Father	Johannes Phillip/Philipp BECKER	
Mother	Louise/Louisa KNAUBER	
Children		

Robert Phillip BECKER (continued)

Census	1920	ED 80, Page 172, Seattle, King, Washington, United States
Census	1930	ED 55, Page 250, Seattle, King, Washington, United States
Residence	1940	Seattle, King, Washington, United States
Occupation		Bookkeeper (1900), Credit Man [illegible] (1910), Buyer Creamery [illegible] (1920)
Occupation		Salesman Dairy (1930)
Death		
Burial		
Spouse	Elizabeth E. ZIEGLER (1872-)	
Marriage	4 Apr 1894	(1894K0009590), Jackson, Missouri, United States

M John/Johannes Philipp BECKER

Birth	7 Nov 1875	Missouri, United States
Baptism	27 Apr 1876	St. Peter's Ger. Evang. Church, Volume 1, Page 29
Census	1880	Westport, Jackson Co., MO, ED 40, Page 255
Census	1900	ED 124, Page 247, Kansas City, Jackson, Missouri, United States
Census	1910	ED 60, Page 33, Kansas City, Jackson, Missouri, United States
Residence	1913	Kansas City, Jackson, Missouri, United States
Death	31 Jan 1920	Perforation of Ileum . . .; Kansas City, Jackson, Missouri, United States
Burial	4 Feb 1920	Forest Hill Cemetery, Kansas City, Jackson, Missouri, United States
Census	1920	ED 61, Page 49, Kansas City, Jackson, Missouri, United States
Occupation		Cashier Hotel (1900), Bookkeeper for Park Board (1910), Bookkeeper Retail Jeweler (1920)
Marriage		

M Claude Guy BECKER

Birth	15 Feb 1887	Missouri, United States
Census	1900	ED 124, Page 247, Kansas City, Jackson, Missouri, United States
Census	1910	ED 60, Page 33, Kansas City, Jackson, Missouri, United States
Military		WWI Draft Registration Cards, Draft Board 8; Kansas City, Jackson, Missouri, United States
Census	1920	
Census	1930	
Death	26 Oct 1957	
Burial		Forest Hill Cemetery, Kansas City, Jackson, Missouri, United States
Occupation		City Fireman
Marriage		

M Chester LeRoy BECKER

Birth	16 Feb 1887	Missouri, United States
Census	1900	ED 124, Page 247, Kansas City, Jackson, Missouri, United States
Census	1910	ED 141, Page 12, Kansas City, Jackson, Missouri, United States
Military		WWI Draft Registration Cards, Draft Board 4; Kansas City, Jackson, Missouri, United States
Census	1920	ED 60, Page 36, Kansas City, Jackson, Missouri, United States
Census	1930	ED 105, Page 56, Kansas City, Jackson, Missouri, United States
Occupation		Collector Carpet [illegible] (1910), Credit Man Clothing Company (1920), Clerk Railway (1930)
Death		
Burial		
Spouse	Beulah F./J. [--?--] (1888-)	
Marriage	1909/10	

Father James C. BECKHAM

Birth		1808	Kentucky, United States
Census		1810	
Census		1820	
Census		1830	
Census		1840	(James Beacham Family), Page 66, Line 21, Jackson, Missouri, United States
Property		22 Jan 1846	First Known Purchase, Part Lot 18, Old Town, Indep.; Volume L, Page 254, Independence, Jackson, Missouri, United States
Census		1850	Page 286, Blue Township, Jackson, Missouri, United States
Census		1860	Independence, Jackson, Missouri, United States
Misc		25 Jul 1862	Union Provost Marshals' File of Papers Relating to Individual Civilians, M345, Roll 22
Tax Lists		Sep 1862	Apothecary License; Independence, Jackson, Missouri, United States
Misc		abt 1863	Union Provost Marshals' File of Papers . . . Two or More Civilians, M416, Roll 82, No. 22,611
Tax Lists		Aug 1865	Retai Liquor Dealer License; Independence, Jackson, Missouri, United States
Tax Lists		May 1866	Income; Independence, Jackson, Missouri, United States
Tax Lists		Aug 1866	Retail Liquor Dealer License; Independence, Jackson, Missouri, United States
Census		1870	Township 48, Range 31, Jackson, Missouri, United States
Census			Agricultural Schedules, Township 48, Range 31, Post Office Lee's Summit, Page 67, Jackson, Missouri, United States
Census		1880	
Death		18 Dec 1892	Canon City, Fremont, Colorado, United States
Burial		21 Dec 1892	Woodlawn Cemetery, Independence, Jackson, Missouri, United States
Occupation			Cabinet Maker (1850), Druggist (1860); Farmer (1870), Apothecary, Retail Liquor Dealer
Marriage			
Father			
Mother			
Other spouse	Mary Emily SMART (1830-)		
Marriage		29 Jul 1866	(1866I0050202), Jackson, Missouri, United States

Mother Eliza Louise HERNDON

Birth		1807	Kentucky, United States
Census		1810	
Census		1810	
Census		1830	
Census		1840	(James Beacham Family), Page 66, Line 21, Jackson, Missouri, United States
Census		1850	Page 286, Blue Township, Jackson, Missouri, United States
Census		1860	Independence, Jackson, Missouri, United States
Death		1865	
Burial			Woodlawn Cemetery, Independence, Jackson, Missouri, United States
Father			
Mother			

Children

F Ann E. BECKHAM

Birth		13 Sep 1832	Kentucky, United States
Census		1840	(James Beacham Family), Page 66, Line 21, Jackson, Missouri, United States
Census		1850	Page 286, Blue Township, Jackson, Missouri, United States
Census		1860	Page 267, Independence, Jackson, Missouri, United States
Census		1870	
Census		1880	ED 157, Page 295, Woodland, Yolo, California, United States
Census		1900	ED 45, Page 37, Township 3, Lake, California, United States
Death	9 Jul 1929		
Burial			Ukiah Cemetery, Ukiah, Mendocino, California, United States
Spouse	James Irren EATON (1832-1909)		
Marriage		14 Nov 1851	(1851I0030076), Jackson, Missouri, United States

F Mary Ellen BECKHAM

Birth		1834/5	Kentucky, United States
Census		1840	(James Beacham Family), Page 66, Line 21, Jackson, Missouri, United States
Census		1850	Page 286, Blue Township, Jackson, Missouri, United States

Father James C. BECKHAM

Mother Eliza Louise HERNDON

Children

Mary Ellen BECKHAM (continued)

Burial	Woodlawn Cemetery, Independence, Jackson, Missouri, United States
Death	
Spouse	Dr. Minor T. SMITH (1827-1914)
Marriage	31 Aug 1851 (1851I0030046), Jackson, Missouri, United States

F Louisa BECKHAM

Birth	1836/7	Kentucky, United States
Census	1840	(James Beacham Family), Page 66, Line 21, Jackson, Missouri, United States
Census	1850	Page 286, Blue Township, Jackson, Missouri, United States
Census	1870	
Census	1880	
Death		
Burial		
Marriage		

F Catherine "Kate" BECKHAM

Birth	1838/9	(or 1840), Missouri, United States
Census	1840	(James Beacham Family), Page 66, Line 21, Jackson, Missouri, United States
Census	1850	Page 286, Blue Township, Jackson, Missouri, United States
Census	1860	Page 364, Blue Township, Jackson, Missouri, United States
Census	1870	(Township 48, Range 32), Page 169, Jackson, Missouri, United States
Census	1880	ED 37, Page 223, Brooking Township, Jackson, Missouri, United States
Death	1882	
Burial		Woodlawn Cemetery, Independence, Jackson, Missouri, United States
Spouse	Dr. Minor T. SMITH (1827-1914)	
Marriage	9 May 1858 (1858I0040066), Jackson, Missouri, United States	

F Tabitha Caroline BECKHAM

Birth	1841/2	(or 1840), Missouri, United States
Census	1850	Page 286, Blue Township, Jackson, Missouri, United States
Census	1860	Independence, Jackson, Missouri, United States
Death	1862	
Burial		Woodlawn Cemetery, Independence, Jackson, Missouri, United States
Spouse	Monroe MCCLANAHAN (1833-)	
Marriage	16 Jul 1861 (1861I0050035), Jackson, Missouri, United States	

M James Herndon BECKHAM

Birth	2 Apr 1843	Missouri, United States
Census	1850	Page 286, Blue Township, Jackson, Missouri, United States
Census	1860	Independence, Jackson, Missouri, United States
Military		Private, Company A, Independence Home Guard
Census	1870	Page 284, Independence, Jackson, Missouri, United States
Census	1880	
Census	1900	ED 70, Page 62, Kansas City, Jackson, Missouri, United States
Death	24 Mar 1919	Pomona, Los Angeles, California, United States
Misc		Obituary, Kansas City (Mo.) Star, 25 Mar 1919, Page 2, Column 3
Burial	1 Apr 1919	Elmwood Cemetery, Kansas City, Jackson, Missouri, United States
Occupation		Clerk (1860), Druggist (1870), Wholesale Grocer (1900)
Spouse	Margaret May America WHITE (1848-1904)	
Marriage	1 Nov 1870 (1870I0060220), Jackson, Missouri, United States	

M Henry Clay BECKHAM

Birth	8 Jun 1845	Independence, Jackson, Missouri, United States
Census	1850	Page 286, Blue Township, Jackson, Missouri, United States
Census	1860	Independence, Jackson, Missouri, United States
Census	1870	
Census	1880	
Census	1900	
Census	1910	

Father James C. BECKHAM		
Mother Eliza Louise HERNDON		
Children		

Henry Clay BECKHAM (continued)

Residence	1919	Canon City, Fremont, Colorado, United States
Census	1920	ED 54, Page 14, Canon City, Fremont, Colorado, United States
Death	4 Aug 1926	Canon City, Fremont, Colorado, United States
Burial		Lakeside Cemetery, Canon City, Fremont, Colorado, United States
Occupation		Retired (1920)
Spouse	Alice B. [--?--] (1874-)	
Marriage		

F Laura B. BECKHAM

Birth	19 Dec 1847	Independence, Jackson, Missouri, United States
Census	1850	Page 286, Blue Township, Jackson, Missouri, United States
Census	1860	Independence, Jackson, Missouri, United States
Census	1870	Township 48, Range 31, Jackson, Missouri, United States
Census	1880	ED 34, Page 191, Prairie Township, Jackson, Missouri, United States
Census	1900	
Census	1910	
Residence	1919	Lee's Summit, Jackson, Missouri, United States
Census	1920	ED 276, Page 62, Lee's Summit, Jackson, Missouri, United States
Census	1930	ED 269, Page 9, Lee's Summit, Jackson, Missouri, United States
Death	10 Mar 1932	Senility, Chronic Arthritis; Lee's Summit, Jackson, Missouri, United States
Burial	12 Mar 1932	Lee's Summit Historical Cemetery, Lee's Summit, Jackson, Missouri, United States
Spouse	William A. POWELL (1841-1897)	
Marriage	2 Mar 1873	(1873I0070103), Jackson, Missouri, United States

Father James C. BECKHAM

Birth	1808	Kentucky, United States
Census	1810	
Census	1820	
Census	1830	
Census	1840	(James Beacham Family), Page 66, Line 21, Jackson, Missouri, United States
Property	22 Jan 1846	First Known Purchase, Part Lot 18, Old Town, Indep.; Volume L, Page 254, Independence, Jackson, Missouri, United States
Census	1850	Page 286, Blue Township, Jackson, Missouri, United States
Census	1860	Independence, Jackson, Missouri, United States
Misc	25 Jul 1862	Union Provost Marshals' File of Papers Relating to Individual Civilians, M345, Roll 22
Tax Lists	Sep 1862	Apothecary License; Independence, Jackson, Missouri, United States
Misc	abt 1863	Union Provost Marshals' File of Papers . . . Two or More Civilians, M416, Roll 82, No. 22,611
Tax Lists	Aug 1865	Retai Liquor Dealer License; Independence, Jackson, Missouri, United States
Tax Lists	May 1866	Income; Independence, Jackson, Missouri, United States
Tax Lists	Aug 1866	Retail Liquor Dealer License; Independence, Jackson, Missouri, United States
Census	1870	Township 48, Range 31, Jackson, Missouri, United States
Census		Agricultural Schedules, Township 48, Range 31, Post Office Lee's Summit, Page 67, Jackson, Missouri, United States
Census	1880	
Death	18 Dec 1892	Canon City, Fremont, Colorado, United States
Burial	21 Dec 1892	Woodlawn Cemetery, Independence, Jackson, Missouri, United States
Occupation		Cabinet Maker (1850), Druggist (1860); Farmer (1870), Apothecary, Retail Liquor Dealer
Marriage	29 Jul 1866	(1866I0050202), Jackson, Missouri, United States
Father		
Mother		
Other spouse	Eliza Louise HERNDON (1807-1865)	
Marriage		

Mother Mary Emily SMART

Birth	1830/1	Missouri, United States
Census	1840	
Census	1850	Page 276, Blue Township, Jackson, Missouri, United States
Census	1860	
Census	1870	Township 48, Range 31, Jackson, Missouri, United States
Census	1880	
Census	1900	
Census	1910	
Death		
Burial		
Father	James SMART (1801-1859)	
Mother	Lucia [--?--] (1808-1851)	
Other spouse	Charles H. HARBAUGH (1826-1861)	
Marriage	19 Feb 1851	(1851I0030038), Jackson, Missouri, United States

Children

M Charles F. BECKHAM

Birth	Jun 1867	Missouri, United States
Census	1870	Township 48, Range 31, Jackson, Missouri, United States
Census	1880	
Census	1900	ED 188, Page 197, Freshwater, Park, Colorado, United States
Death	1955	
Burial		Lakeside Cemetery, Canon City, Fremont, Colorado, United States
Occupation		Stock Raiser (1900)
Spouse	Frances W. [--?--] (1874-1956)	
Marriage	1893/4	

Father Rev. Joab Mitchell BERNARD

Birth	12 Jul 1800	Virginia, United States
Census	1810	
Census	1820	
Census	1830	
Census	1840	
Residence	1842	Saint Louis, Saint Louis, Missouri, United States
Property	Dec 1842	First Known Purchase, Lot 1, Block 2, Sibley; Volume K, Page 319, Jackson, Missouri, United States
Census	1850	District 1, Page 220, Baltimore, Maryland, United States
Census	1860	Page 110, Westport, Jackson, Missouri, United States
Census		Slave Schedules, Page 368, Westport, Jackson, Missouri, United States
Tax Lists	Sep 1862	Retail Dealer License; "Joel Bernard", Westport, Jackson, Missouri, United States
Census	1870	Page 60, Westport, Jackson, Missouri, United States
Death	30 Apr 1879	Westport, Jackson, Missouri, United States
Burial	1 May 1879	Union Cemetery, Kansas City, Jackson, Missouri, United States
Misc		Funeral Notice, Kansas City (Mo.) Times, 01 May 1879, Page 4, Column 2
Occupation		Farmer (1850), Merchant (1860), Retired Merchant (1870), Retail Dealer
Marriage	1839	Baltimore, Maryland, United States
Father	Allan BERNARD (1763-1851)	
Mother		
Other spouse	Elizabeth BALL (1796-)	
Marriage	29 Mar 1836	Baltimore, Maryland, United States

Mother Arabella Mather BIER

Birth	18 Dec 1816	Baltimore, Maryland, United States
Census	1820	
Census	1830	
Census	1840	
Census	1850	District 1, Page 220, Baltimore, Maryland, United States
Census	1860	Page 110, Westport, Jackson, Missouri, United States
Census	1870	Page 60, Westport, Jackson, Missouri, United States
Census	1880	ED 40, Page 254, Westport, Jackson, Missouri, United States
Death	12 Nov 1899	Tucson, Pima, Arizona Territory, United States
Misc		Obituary, Kansas City (Mo.) Star, 16 Nov 1899, Page 3, Column 5
Burial	17 Nov 1899	Union Cemetery, Kansas City, Jackson, Missouri, United States
Father	George BIER (-)	
Mother	Jane CUNNINGHAM (-)	

Children

F   Margaret Jane BERNARD

Birth	14 Nov 1840	Missouri, United States
Census	1850	District 1, Page 220, Baltimore, Maryland, United States
Census	1860	Page 110, Westport, Jackson, Missouri, United States
Census	1870	Page 597, Kansas City, Jackson, Missouri, United States
Census	1880	ED 101, Page 149, Shawnee Township, Johnson, Kansas, United States
Census	1900	ED 87, Page 129, Thayer Township, Oregon, Missouri, United States
Census	1910	ED 1401, Page 177, Chicago, Cook, Illinois, United States
Census	1920	ED 52, Page 16, Pass Christian, Harrison, Mississippi, United States
Death	30 Mar 1920	New Orleans, Orleans, Louisiana, United States
Burial		Live Oak Cemetery, Pass Christian, Harrison, Mississippi, United States
Misc		Funeral Notice, Kansas City (Mo.) Star, 10 Apr 1920, Page 2, Column 4
Spouse	Andrew Monroe JOHNSON (1841-1902)	
Marriage	16 Mar 1864	(1864I0050110), Jackson, Missouri, United States

F   Catherine Comfort "Kate" BERNARD

Birth	1842	Maryland, United States
Census	1850	District 1, Page 220, Baltimore, Maryland, United States
Census	1860	Page 110, Westport, Jackson, Missouri, United States
Death	28 Sep 1863	Maryland, United States
Burial		Green Street Cemetery, Baltimore, Baltimore, Maryland, United States

Father Rev. Joab Mitchell BERNARD

Mother Arabella Mather BIER

Children

Catherine Comfort "Kate" BERNARD (continued)

Spouse	Rezin H. WORTHINGTON (1840-)	
Marriage	9 Feb 1863	Baltimore, Baltimore, Maryland, United States

F Mary Bier "Mamie" BERNARD

Birth	22 Jun 1844	(or 23 Jun 1844), Missouri, United States
Census	1850	District 1, Page 220, Baltimore, Maryland, United States
Census	1860	Page 110, Westport, Jackson, Missouri, United States
Residence	1863-?	Las Cruces, Dona Ana, New Mexico, United States
Residence	?-1906	Tucson, Pima, Arizona, United States
Census	1870	
Census	1880	
Census	1900	ED 47, Page 51, Pima, Pima, Arizona Territory, United States
Death	24 May 1906	San Jose, Santa Clara, California, United States
Burial	28 May 1906	Evergreen Memorial Park Cemetery, Tucson, Pima, Arizona Territory, United States
Misc		Biography, Annette Gray, Journey of the Heart: A True Story of Mamie Aguirre (1844-1906), A Southern Belle in the Wild West
Occupation		Teacher University (1900)
Spouse	Epifanio AGUIRRE (1834-1870)	
Marriage	21 Aug 1862	(1862I0050062), Jackson, Missouri, United States

F Anna Marcella "Annie/Nan/Nannie" BERNARD

Birth	17 Jun 1848	Maryland, United States
Census	1850	District 1, Page 220, Baltimore, Maryland, United States
Census	1860	Page 110, Westport, Jackson, Missouri, United States
Census	1870	Page 60, Westport, Jackson, Missouri, United States
Census	1880	ED 46, Page 501, Fremont, Colorado, United States
Census	1885	Page 11, Mesa, Colorado, United States
Census	1900	ED 74, Page 118, Grand Junction, Mesa, Colorado, United States
Death	26 Dec 1931	
Burial		Orchard Mesa Cemetery, Grand Junction, Mesa, Colorado, United States
Spouse	Phidelah A. RICE (1845-1932)	
Marriage	17 Oct 1870	(1870I0060210), Westport, Jackson, Missouri, United States

F Jessie Glencairn BERNARD

Birth	5 Jun 1850	Maryland, United States
Census	1850	District 1, Page 220, Baltimore, Maryland, United States
Census	1860	Page 110, Westport, Jackson, Missouri, United States
Census	1870	Page 60, Westport, Jackson, Missouri, United States
Census	1880	ED 40, Page 254, Westport, Jackson, Missouri, United States
Census	1900	ED 47, Page 58, Tucson, Pima, Arizona Territory, United States
Death	29 Jul 1902	Tucson, Pima, Arizona Territory, United States
Burial		Tucson, Pima, Arizona Territory, United States
Occupation		Teacher (1900)
Spouse	Thaddeus D. BYRNE (1848-1942)	
Marriage	30 Jun 1882	(1882K0020093), Jackson, Missouri, United States
Divorce		

F Arabella Wilson "Belle" BERNARD

Birth	17 Dec 1851	Maryland, United States
Census	1860	Page 110, Westport, Jackson, Missouri, United States
Death	27 Jan 1868	Accidental Gunshot Wound; Westport, Jackson, Missouri, United States
Burial		Union Cemetery, Kansas City, Jackson, Missouri, United States
Marriage		

M Noah Worthington BERNARD

Birth	4 Jan 1854	Maryland, United States
Census	1860	Page 110, Westport, Jackson, Missouri, United States
Census	1870	Page 60, Westport, Jackson, Missouri, United States
Census	1880	

Father Rev. Joab Mitchell BERNARD		
Mother Arabella Mather BIER		
Children		

	Noah Worthington BERNARD (continued)	
Census	1900	ED 47, Page 58, Tucson, Pima, Arizona Territory, United States
Death	23 Mar 1907	Peritonitis; Tucson, Pima, Arizona Territory, United States
Burial		Evergreen Memorial Park Cemetery, Tucson, Pima, Arizona, United States
Occupation		Clerk in Drug Store (1870), Cattle Raiser (1900)
Spouse	Amy C. PRICE (1855-1900)	
Marriage		

M	**Allen Cunningham "Al" BERNARD**	
Birth	11 Feb 1859	Missouri, United States
Census	1860	Page 110, Westport, Jackson, Missouri, United States
Census	1870	Page 60, Westport, Jackson, Missouri, United States
Census	1880	
Census	1900	ED 48, Page 47, Tucson, Pima, Arizona Territory, United States
Death	4 Jul 1930	Heart Attack; Phoenix, Maricopa, Arizona, United States
Burial		Evergreen Memorial Park Cemetery, Tucson, Pima, Arizona, United States
Spouse	Minnie CHOUTEAU (1862-1914)	
Marriage	7 Oct 1881	(1881K0010180), Jackson, Missouri, United States

Father William Rodney BERNARD

Birth	8 Dec 1823	Augusta, Virginia, United States
Census	1830	
Residence	bet 1839 and 1844	Callaway, Missouri, United States
Census	1840	(Thomas Bernard Family), Page 217, Line 30, Callaway, Missouri, United States
Residence	bet 1847 and 1906	Westport, Jackson, Missouri, United States
Census	1850	Page 241, Kaw Township, Jackson, Missouri, United States
Property	31 Aug 1850	First Known Purchase, Part Sect. 19, T49, R33; Volume P, Page 520, Independence, Jackson, Missouri, United States
Census	1860	Post Office Westport, Page 254, Jackson, Missouri, United States
Census		Slave Schedules, Page 376, Jackson, Missouri, United States
Tax Lists	Apr 1863	Banker and Wholesale Dealer Licenses; Westport, Jackson, Missouri, United States
Tax Lists	Dec 1865	Banker License; "Bernard & Mastin", Kansas City, Jackson, Missouri, United States
Tax Lists	May 1866	Gold Watch; Kansas City, Jackson, Missouri, United States
Tax Lists	May 1866	Banker License; "Bernard & Mastin", Kansas City, Jackson, Missouri, United States
Tax Lists	bet Jul 1866 and Dec 1866	Bank Capital and Deposits; "Bernard & Mastin", Kansas City, Jackson, Missouri, United States
Misc	1868	Mayor; (or 1869), Westport, Jackson, Missouri, United States
Census	1870	Page 62, Westport, Jackson, Missouri, United States
Misc	1873	Judge, County Court; Jackson, Missouri, United States
Census	1880	ED 40, Page 258, Westport, Jackson, Missouri, United States
Misc		Biography, History of Jackson County, Missouri (1881), Pages 739-740
Misc		Biography, Memorial & Biographical Record of Kansas City . . . (1896). Pages 435-439
Census	1900	ED 123, Page 233, Kansas City, Jackson, Missouri, United States
Death	25 Nov 1906	Kansas City, Jackson, Missouri, United States
Burial	26 Nov 1906	Union Cemetery, Kansas City, Jackson, Missouri, United States
Misc		Obituary, Kansas City (Mo.) Times, 26 Nov 1906, Page 3, Columns 1-2
Occupation		Merchant (1850, 1860), Freighter (1870), Abstract Business (1880), Landlord (1900)
Religion		Dr. Madeira's church (Presbyterian); Kansas City, Jackson, Missouri, United States
Occupation		Banker, Real Estate Dealer
Business		Bernard & Mastin (Bank)
Marriage	2 Feb 1853	(1853I0030121), Jackson, Missouri, United States
Father		Maj. Thomas BERNARD (1792-1866)
Mother		Catherine DETTOR (1796-1872)
Other spouse		Margaret Elizabeth BUCKNER (1830-1851)
Marriage	28 Jul 1850	Callaway, Missouri, United States

Mother Susan HARRIS

Birth	27 Jun 1834	Westport, Jackson, Missouri, United States
Census	1840	(John Harris Family), Page 74, Line 5, Jackson, Missouri, United States
Census	1850	Page 237, Kaw Township, Jackson, Missouri, United States
Census	1860	Post Office Westport, Page 254, Jackson, Missouri, United States
Census	1870	Page 62, Westport, Jackson, Missouri, United States
Census	1880	ED 40, Page 258, Westport, Jackson, Missouri, United States
Death	9 Apr 1895	Bright's Disease
Burial	11 Apr 1895	Union Cemetery, Kansas City, Jackson, Missouri, United States
Misc		Funeral Notice, Kansas City (Mo.) Star, 11 Apr 1895, Page 2, Column 4
Father		John HARRIS (1795-1873)
Mother		Henrietta SIMPSON (1804-1881)

Children

F Henrietta "Nettie" BERNARD

Birth	15 May 1861	Missouri, United States
Census	1870	Page 62, Westport, Jackson, Missouri, United States
Census	1880	ED 40, Page 258, Westport, Jackson, Missouri, United States
Census	1900	ED 123, Page 233, Kansas City, Jackson, Missouri, United States
Census	1910	ED 62, Page 63, Kansas City, Jackson, Missouri, United States
Will	10 Apr 1912	(Will Written), Volume 18, Page 65, Kansas City, Jackson, Missouri, United States

Father	William Rodney BERNARD	
Mother	**Susan HARRIS**	
Children		

Henrietta "Nettie" BERNARD (continued)

Death	28 Jul 1913	Acute Dilatation of Heart, Mammary Carcinoma; Kansas City, Jackson, Missouri, United States
Burial	29 Jul 1913	Union Cemetery, Kansas City, Jackson, Missouri, United States
Misc		Obituary, Kansas City (Mo.) Star, 28 Jul 1913, Page 3, Column 2
Probate	13 Aug 1913	(Will Proved), Volume 18, Page 65, Kansas City, Jackson, Missouri, United States
Spouse	Frank HENDERSON (1861-1911)	
Marriage	16 Oct 1889	(1889K0002706), Jackson, Missouri, United States

M   William R. BERNARD Jr.

Birth	6 Apr 1867	
Death	30 Aug 1867	
Burial		Union Cemetery, Kansas City, Jackson, Missouri, United States
Marriage		

F   Anna E. "Annie" BERNARD

Birth	7 Jun 1868	Missouri, United States
Census	1870	Page 62, Westport, Jackson, Missouri, United States
Census	1880	ED 40, Page 258, Westport, Jackson, Missouri, United States
Death	25 Jan 1902	
Burial	27 Jan 1902	Union Cemetery, Kansas City, Jackson, Missouri, United States
Marriage		

Father Adolph BEYGA

Birth	1830/1	Germany
Census	1860	Page 474, Shawnee, Johnson, Kansas, United States
Tax Lists	Sep 1862	Confectioner License; "Adolph Begga", Kansas City, Jackson, Missouri, United States
Military		Private, Company A, 77th Regiment Enrolled Missouri Militia
Military		Civil War Draft Registration; Kaw Township, Jackson, Missouri, United States
Misc		"Bakery, Confectionery . . .," Kansas City (Mo.) Daily Journal of Commerce, 23 Jan 1864, Page 3, Column 3
Census	1870	
Census	1880	
Census	1900	
Census	1910	
Occupation		Baker (1860), Confectioner
Death		
Burial		
Marriage	17 Aug 1858	(1858I0040074), Jackson, Missouri, United States
Father		
Mother		

Mother Louisa ENDRES

Birth	1842/3	Germany
Census	1860	Page 474, Shawnee, Johnson, Kansas, United States
Census	1870	
Census	1880	
Census	1900	
Census	1910	
Death		
Burial		
Father		
Mother		

Children

M R. BEYGA

Birth	1860	Kansas, United States
Census	1860	Page 474, Shawnee, Johnson, Kansas, United States
Census	1870	
Census	1880	
Census	1900	
Census	1910	
Census	1920	
Death		
Burial		
Marriage		

Father	**Joseph Johann BITTEL/BEITEL**	
Birth	1831/2	Germany
Census	1850	
Census	1860	
Military		Missouri State Militia
Tax Lists	Aug 1863	Animals Slaughtered for Sale; "Frank & Beddle", Kansas City, Jackson, Missouri, United States
Military	Oct 1863	Civil War Draft Registration; Kaw Township, Jackson, Missouri, United States
Death	Apr 1867	
Probate	4 May 1867	Letters of Administration, Jackson Co. (Independence), MO, Volume M, Page 200
Burial		
Marriage	12 Nov 1863	(1863I0050096), Jackson, Missouri, United States
Father		
Mother		

Mother	**Anna Catharine/Katharina "Kate" PARDONNER/PARTENNER**	
Birth	17 Jun 1840	(or 1842 or Jun 1843), Hessen-Darmstadt, Germany
Immigration	1857	
Census	1860	(Post Office Kansas City), Page 155, Jackson, Missouri, United States
Census	1870	Page 501, Kansas City, Jackson, Missouri, United States
Census	1880	ED 7, Page 213, Kansas City, Jackson, Missouri, United States
Census	1900	ED 79, Page 193, Kansas City, Jackson, Missouri, United States
Census	1910	ED 97, Page 288, Kansas City, Jackson, Missouri, United States
Will	17 Dec 1910	Will Written, Jackson Co. (Kansas City), MO, Volume 13, Page 117
Death	18 Dec 1910	Obstruction of Bowel; Kansas City, Jackson, Missouri, United States
Misc		Obituary, Kansas City (Mo.) Times, 19 Dec 1910, Page 18, Column 2
Burial	20 Dec 1910	Elmwood Cemetery, Kansas City, Jackson, Missouri, United States
Probate	21 Dec 1910	(Will Proved, Kansas City Courthouse, Volume 13, Page 117), Jackson, Missouri, United States
Occupation		Grocerywoman (1900), Proprietor Grocery (1910)
Father	George PARDONNER/PARTENNER (1804-1869)	
Mother	Elizabeth/Elisabetha VOLLRATH (1817-1896)	
Other spouse	Henry/Heinrich Franz SEPPLER (1833-1901)	
Marriage	17 Dec 1867	(1867I0060082), Jackson, Missouri, United States

Children

M	**George/Georg BITTEL/BEITEL**	
Birth	11 Aug 1864	
Baptism	29 Oct 1865	St. Peter's Ger. Evang. Church, Volume 1, Page 2
Census	1870	Page 501, Kansas City, Jackson, Missouri, United States
Census	1880	
Death	Sep 1899	
Burial	23 Sep 1899	Elmwood Cemetery, Kansas City, Jackson, Missouri, United States
Alt. Name		George Seppler
Marriage		

M	**William BITTEL/BEITEL**	
Birth		
Chr		
Death		
Burial		
Marriage		

Father David Gilbert BLAIR

Birth	Mar 1821	Waynesborough, Franklin, Pennsylvania, United States
Census	1830	
Census	1840	
Census	1850	Page 218, Cumberland, Allegeny, Pennsylvania, United States
Census	1860	Page 62, Kansas City, Jackson, Missouri, United States
Census		Industrial Schedules, Page 2, Kansas City, Jackson, Missouri, United States
Misc	Dec 1861	Union Provost Marshals' File of Papers Relating to Two or More Civilians, M416, Roll 3, No. 449.5
Tax Lists	Sep 1862	Retail Dealer License; "D. D. Blane", Kansas City, Jackson, Missouri, United States
Tax Lists	May 1865	Retail Dealer and Manufacturer Licenses; Kansas City, Jackson, Missouri, United States
Tax Lists	bet Jun 1865 and Dec 1866	Tin Ware Manufactured; Kansas City, Jackson, Missouri, United States
Census	1870	Page 325, Kansas City, Jackson, Missouri, United States
Census		Industrial Schedules, Ward 1, Page 17, Kansas City, Jackson, Missouri, United States
Census		Industrial Schedules, Ward 4, Page 72, Kansas City, Jackson, Missouri, United States
Census	1880	ED 5, Page 142, Kansas City, Jackson, Missouri, United States
Census	1900	ED 34, Page 101, Cedar Township, Carroll, Arkansas, United States
Census	1910	ED 54, Page 57, Eureka Springs, Carroll, Arkansas, United States
Death	21 Feb 1911	Eureka Springs, Carroll, Arkansas, United States
Burial	22 Feb 1911	Union Cemetery, Kansas City, Jackson, Missouri, United States
Misc		Obituary, Kansas City (Mo.) Star, 22 Feb 1911, Section 2, Page 3, Column 1
Burial		Union Cemetery, Kansas City, Jackson, Missouri, United States
Occupation		Tinner (1850, 1860), Stoves and Tinware (1870), Tinsmith (1880), Farmer (1900), Retail Dealer
Marriage	9 Jun 1846	
Father		Hugh BLAIR (1792-1824)
Mother		Anna Maria GILBERT (1789-1871)

Mother Mary Jane PIERPOINT

Birth	23 Mar 1828	Baltimore, Baltimore, Maryland, United States
Census	1830	
Census	1840	
Census	1850	Page 218, Cumberland, Allegeny, Pennsylvania, United States
Census	1860	Page 62, Kansas City, Jackson, Missouri, United States
Census	1870	Page 325, Kansas City, Jackson, Missouri, United States
Census	1880	ED 5, Page 142, Kansas City, Jackson, Missouri, United States
Census	1900	ED 989, Page 281, Watertown, Middlesex, Massachusetts, United States
Death	23 Apr 1907	Saint Louis (city), Missouri, United States
Misc		Funeral Notice, Kansas City (Mo.) Times, 26 Apr 1907, Page 9, Column 6
Burial	27 Apr 1907	Union Cemetery, Kansas City, Jackson, Missouri, United States
Father		Samuel PIERPOINT (-)
Mother		Rachel WHITE (-)

Children

M George D. BLAIR

Birth	1847	
Census	1850	Page 218, Cumberland, Allegeny, Pennsylvania, United States
Death	13 Sep 1857	
Burial		Union Cemetery, Kansas City, Jackson, Missouri, United States
Marriage		

M Lafayette Gilbert BLAIR

Birth	8 May 1849	Cumberland, Allegany, Maryland, United States
Census	1850	Page 218, Cumberland, Allegeny, Pennsylvania, United States
Census	1860	Page 62, Kansas City, Jackson, Missouri, United States
Census	1870	Page 515, Center Township, Vernon, Missouri, United States
Census	1880	ED 5, Page 142, Kansas City, Jackson, Missouri, United States
Census	1900	ED 989, Page 281, Watertown, Middlesex, Massachusetts, United States
Census	1910	ED 1056, Page 30, Watertown, Middlesex, Massachusetts, United States
Death	7 Dec 1912	Watertown, Middlesex, Massachusetts, United States

Father	David Gilbert BLAIR	
Mother	Mary Jane PIERPOINT	
Children		

Lafayette Gilbert BLAIR (continued)

Occupation		Tinner (1870), Lawyer (1880, 1887, 1900), Lawyer General Practice (1910)
Burial		
Spouse	Emma A. COON (1860-)	
Marriage	30 Jun 1887	Cambridge, [--?--], Massachusetts, United States

M Charles W. BLAIR

Birth	1856/7	Illinois, United States
Census	1860	Page 62, Kansas City, Jackson, Missouri, United States
Census	1870	Page 325, Kansas City, Jackson, Missouri, United States
Census	1880	ED 5, Page 142, Kansas City, Jackson, Missouri, United States
Census	1900	ED 36, Page 135, Eureka Springs, Carroll, Arkansas, United States
Residence	1911	Eureka Springs, Carroll, Arkansas, United States
Occupation		Tinsmith (1880), Hardware Retail (1900)
Death		
Burial		
Marriage		

F Mary P. BLAIR

Birth	1859	Missouri, United States
Census	1860	Page 62, Kansas City, Jackson, Missouri, United States
Census	1870	Page 325, Kansas City, Jackson, Missouri, United States
Census	1880	ED 5, Page 142, Kansas City, Jackson, Missouri, United States
Census	1900	
Census	1910	ED 772, Page 172, Cambridge, Middlesex, Massachusetts, United States
Census	1920	
Census	1930	
Census	1940	ED 15-365, Page 4661, Boston, Suffolk, Massachusetts, United States
Death	1946	Westborough, Worcester, Massachusetts, United States
Burial		Union Cemetery (Buried as Mary P. Blair in the David G. Blair lot), Kansas City, Jackson, Missouri, United States
Occupation		Teacher High School (1910)
Spouse	Charles E. RINER (1857-)	
Marriage	25 Jun 1883	(1883K0030223), Jackson, Missouri, United States

M Wesley Simpson BLAIR

Birth	8 Oct 1861	Kansas City, Jackson, Missouri, United States
Census	1870	Page 325, Kansas City, Jackson, Missouri, United States
Census	1880	ED 5, Page 142, Kansas City, Jackson, Missouri, United States
Death	29 Jun 1931	Cirrhosis of Liver; Kansas City, Jackson, Missouri, United States
Burial	30 Jun 1931	Union Cemetery, Kansas City, Jackson, Missouri, United States
Occupation		Baker (1880), Baker and Pastry Worker (1931)
Marriage		

M Frank Mudge BLAIR

Birth	3 Aug 1864	Kansas City, Jackson, Missouri, United States
Census	1870	Page 325, Kansas City, Jackson, Missouri, United States
Census	1880	ED 5, Page 142, Kansas City, Jackson, Missouri, United States
Census	1900	ED 111, Page 30, Kansas City, Jackson, Missouri, United States
Residence	1907	Kansas City, Jackson, Missouri, United States
Death	12 Dec 1949	Questionable Hodgkins Disease of Lung with Metastases to Liver; Kansas City, Jackson, Missouri, United States
Burial	15 Dec 1949	Union Cemetery, Kansas City, Jackson, Missouri, United States
Occupation		Letter Carrier (1900), Retired Letter Carrier 9th & Grand Post Office (1949)
Spouse	Mary Margaret CARROTHERS (1867-1949)	
Marriage	19 Sep 1888	(1888K0000772), Kansas City, Jackson, Missouri, United States

M David R. BLAIR

Birth	1867	Missouri, United States
Census	1870	Page 325, Kansas City, Jackson, Missouri, United States

Father David Gilbert BLAIR

Mother Mary Jane PIERPOINT

Children

David R. BLAIR (continued)

Census	1880	ED 5, Page 142, Kansas City, Jackson, Missouri, United States
Death	1934	
Burial		Union Cemetery, Kansas City, Jackson, Missouri, United States
Marriage		

Father Dr. Joseph Oliver BOGGS

Birth	Jan 1808	(or Feb 1808), Kentucky, United States
Census	1810	
Census	1820	
Census	1830	(Joseph O. Boggs Family), Page 161, Greene, Indiana, United States
Residence	1838-?	Jackson, Missouri, United States
Census	1840	(J. O. Boggs Family), Page 66, Jackson, Missouri, United States
Property	28 Oct 1840	First Known Purchase, Lots 4, 5, 7 & 69, Independence; Volume G, Page 189, Jackson, Missouri, United States
Property	28 Oct 1840	First Known Purchase, Part Sects. 8 & 9, T49, R33 . . .; Volume G, Page 189, Jackson, Missouri, United States
Property	29 Oct 1840	First Known US Land Purchase; (Part Section 9, Township 48, Range 33), Jackson, Missouri, United States
Misc	21 Nov 1841	Founding Member, First Presbyterian Church; Independence, Jackson, Missouri, United States
Census	1850	Page 239, Kaw Township, Jackson, Missouri, United States
Census		Slave Schedules, Frame 100, Kaw Township, Jackson, Missouri, United States
Census	1860	Page 123, Westport, Jackson, Missouri, United States
Misc	1860	Mayor; (also 1863), Westport, Jackson, Missouri, United States
Tax Lists	Dec 1863	Physician License; Westport, Jackson, Missouri, United States
Tax Lists	May 1866	Apothecary and Physician Licenses; Westport, Jackson, Missouri, United States
Census	1870	Page 52, Napa, Napa, California, United States
Census	1880	ED 127, Page 175, Cloverdale Township, Sonoma, California, United States
Death	28 Oct 1889	
Burial		Riverside Cemetery, Cloverdale, Sonoma, California, United States
Misc		Biography, Kansas City, Mo. (1908), Volume 1, Page 472
Occupation		Physician (1850, 1870, 1880) , Druggist (1860), Apothecary
Marriage		
Father	John McKinley BOGGS (1758-1847)	
Mother	Martha OLIVER (1770-1847)	
Other spouse	Deborah A. BROOKINS (1826-1889)	
Marriage		

Mother Phebe WICKLIFFE

Birth	1811/2	Vermont, United States
Census	1820	
Census	1830	
Census	1840	
Census	1840	(J. O. Boggs Family), Page 66, Jackson, Missouri, United States
Misc	21 Nov 1841	Founding Member, First Presbyterian Church; Independence, Jackson, Missouri, United States
Census	1850	Page 239, Kaw Township, Jackson, Missouri, United States
Death	abt 1852	
Burial		
Father	Charles Anderson WICKLIFFE (1788-1869)	
Mother		

Children

F Martha R. BOGGS

Birth	abt 1832	Indiana, United States
Census	1840	(J. O. Boggs Family), Page 66, Jackson, Missouri, United States
Census	1850	Page 239, Kaw Township, Jackson, Missouri, United States
Census	1860	Page 110, Westport, Jackson, Missouri, United States
Census	1870	Page 51, Napa, Napa, California, United States
Census	1880	ED 51, Page 40, Lakeport Township, Lake, California, United States
Death		
Burial		
Spouse	T. J./K./R. MCCUTCHEN (1822-)	
Marriage	15 Dec 1858	(1858I0040103), Jackson, Missouri, United States

Father Dr. Joseph Oliver BOGGS		
Mother Phebe WICKLIFFE		
Children		

F   Mary E. BOGGS

Birth	abt 1835	Kentucky, United States
Census	1840	(J. O. Boggs Family), Page 66, Jackson, Missouri, United States
Census	1850	Page 239, Kaw Township, Jackson, Missouri, United States
Census	1860	
Census	1870	
Census	1880	
Death		
Burial		
Marriage		

M   Lilburn Wickliff BOGGS

Birth	Feb 1841	Missouri, United States
Census	1850	Page 239, Kaw Township, Jackson, Missouri, United States
Census	1860	Page 123, Westport, Jackson, Missouri, United States
Census	1870	
Census	1880	ED 43, Page 456, Powellville, Humboldt, California, United States
Census	1900	ED 157, Page 54, Bodega Township, Sonoma, California, United States
Death	4 Jul 1928	Napa, California, United States
Occupation		Druggist (1860), Bookkeeper (1880), Servant Day Laborer (1900)
Burial		
Marriage		

F   Josephine BOGGS

Birth	Jan 1844	Missouri, United States
Census	1850	Page 239, Kaw Township, Jackson, Missouri, United States
Census	1860	Page 123, Westport, Jackson, Missouri, United States
Census	1870	
Census	1880	ED 51, Page 40, Lakeport Township, Lake, California, United States
Census	1900	ED 46, Page 45, Lakeport, Lake, California, United States
Death	5 May 1928	Lake, California, United States
Burial		Hartley Cemetery, Lakeport, Lake, California, United States
Spouse	James W. BOGGS (1843-1920)	
Marriage	19 Jul 1870	Napa, California, United States

F   Laura E. BOGGS

Birth	3 May 1846	Missouri, United States
Census	1850	Page 239, Kaw Township, Jackson, Missouri, United States
Census	1860	Page 123, Westport, Jackson, Missouri, United States
Census	1870	Page 661, Shawnee Township, Johnson, Kansas, United States
Census	1880	ED 102, Page 155, Shawnee Township, Johnson, Kansas, United States
Census	1900	ED 105, Page 164, Shawnee Township, Johnson, Kansas, United States
Death	21 May 1940	Kansas, United States
Burial		Lenexa Cemetery, Lenexa, Johnson, Kansas, United States
Spouse	Thomas H. MOODY (1840-1915)	
Marriage	24 Sep 1868	(1868I0060013), Jackson, Missouri, United States

F   Cara L. BOGGS

Birth	Jul 1849	Missouri, United States
Census	1850	Page 239, Kaw Township, Jackson, Missouri, United States
Census	1860	Page 123, Westport, Jackson, Missouri, United States
Census	1870	
Census	1880	
Census	1900	ED 47, Page 64, Kelseyville, Lake, California, United States
Death	7 Jul 1931	Santa Clara, California, United States
Burial		Kelseyville Cemetery, Kelseyville, Lake, California, United States
Spouse	John H. HUSTON (1841-1918)	
Marriage	1871/2	

Father Dr. Joseph Oliver BOGGS			
Mother Phebe WICKLIFFE			
Children			
F	**Fannie J. BOGGS**		
	Birth	1851/2	Missouri, United States
	Census	1860	Page 123, Westport, Jackson, Missouri, United States
	Census	1870	
	Census	1880	
	Death		
	Burial		
	Marriage		

Father Dr. Joseph Oliver BOGGS

Birth	Jan 1808	(or Feb 1808), Kentucky, United States
Census	1810	
Census	1820	
Census	1830	(Joseph O. Boggs Family), Page 161, Greene, Indiana, United States
Residence	1838-?	Jackson, Missouri, United States
Census	1840	(J. O. Boggs Family), Page 66, Jackson, Missouri, United States
Property	28 Oct 1840	First Known Purchase, Lots 4, 5, 7 & 69, Independence; Volume G, Page 189, Jackson, Missouri, United States
Property	28 Oct 1840	First Known Purchase, Part Sects. 8 & 9, T49, R33 . . .; Volume G, Page 189, Jackson, Missouri, United States
Property	29 Oct 1840	First Known US Land Purchase; (Part Section 9, Township 48, Range 33), Jackson, Missouri, United States
Misc	21 Nov 1841	Founding Member, First Presbyterian Church; Independence, Jackson, Missouri, United States
Census	1850	Page 239, Kaw Township, Jackson, Missouri, United States
Census		Slave Schedules, Frame 100, Kaw Township, Jackson, Missouri, United States
Census	1860	Page 123, Westport, Jackson, Missouri, United States
Misc	1860	Mayor; (also 1863), Westport, Jackson, Missouri, United States
Tax Lists	Dec 1863	Physician License; Westport, Jackson, Missouri, United States
Tax Lists	May 1866	Apothecary and Physician Licenses; Westport, Jackson, Missouri, United States
Census	1870	Page 52, Napa, Napa, California, United States
Census	1880	ED 127, Page 175, Cloverdale Township, Sonoma, California, United States
Death	28 Oct 1889	
Burial		Riverside Cemetery, Cloverdale, Sonoma, California, United States
Misc		Biography, Kansas City, Mo. (1908), Volume 1, Page 472
Occupation		Physician (1850, 1870, 1880) , Druggist (1860), Apothecary
Marriage		
Father	John McKinley BOGGS (1758-1847)	
Mother	Martha OLIVER (1770-1847)	
Other spouse	Phebe WICKLIFFE (1811-1852)	
Marriage		

Mother Deborah A. BROOKINS

Birth	abt 1826	Maryland, United States
Census	1830	
Census	1840	
Census	1850	Page 20, Cambridge, Wayne, Indiana, United States
Census	1860	Page 123, Westport, Jackson, Missouri, United States
Census	1870	Page 52, Napa, Napa, California, United States
Census	1880	ED 127, Page 175, Cloverdale Township, Sonoma, California, United States
Death	11 Mar 1889	
Burial		Riverside Cemetery, Cloverdale, Sonoma, California, United States
Father	Kason BROOKINS (1791-)	
Mother		

Children

Father	William Leonidas "Lee" BONE		
Birth	2 Nov 1820	Wilson, Tennessee, United States	
Census	1830		
Census	1840		
Census	1850		
Occupation	1857	School Commissioner; Jackson, Missouri, United States	
Occupation	1858	Mayor; Independence, Jackson, Missouri, United States	
Census	1860	Page 265, Independence, Jackson, Missouri, United States	
Census		Slave Schedules, Page 364, Independence, Jackson, Missouri, United States	
Occupation	1860	Chairman of City Council; Independence, Jackson, Missouri, United States	
Misc	19 Apr 1862	Union Provost Marshals' File of Papers Relating to Two or More Civilians, M416, Roll 5, No. 1075	
Tax Lists	Sep 1862	Lawyer License; Independence, Jackson, Missouri, United States	
Misc	15 Sep 1862	Union Provost Marshals' File of Papers Relating to Individual Civilians, M345, Roll 30	
Military	Sep 1863	Civil War Draft Registration; Blue Township, Jackson, Missouri, United States	
Tax Lists	May 1866	Lawyer License, Income, and Gold Watch, Independence, Jackson, Missouri, United States	
Census	1870	Page 259, Independence, Jackson, Missouri, United States	
Census	1880	ED 24, Page 57, Independence, Jackson, Missouri, United States	
Death	24 Feb 1885	Independence, Jackson, Missouri, United States	
Burial		Woodlawn Cemetery, Independence, Jackson, Missouri, United States	
Occupation		Lawyer (1860, 1870, 1880)	
Marriage	18 Jun 1854	Sumner, Tennessee, United States	
Father	Robert BONE (-1829)		
Mother	Mary S. GUNN (1799-1830)		

Mother	Jane Fulton "Jennie" CLARK		
Birth	20 Mar 1832	(or Oct 1832), Gallatin, Sumner, Tennessee, United States	
Census	1840		
Census	1850	Page 249, District 7, Sumner, Tennessee, United States	
Census	1860	Page 265, Independence, Jackson, Missouri, United States	
Census	1870	Page 259, Independence, Jackson, Missouri, United States	
Census	1880	ED 24, Page 57, Independence, Jackson, Missouri, United States	
Census	1900	ED 22, Page 299, Kansas City, Jackson, Missouri, United States	
Death	20 Dec 1904	Sumner, Tennessee, United States	
Burial		Douglas-Pardue Cemetery, Gallatin, Sumner, Tennessee, United States	
Father	William Fulton Sanders CLARK (1806-1847)		
Mother	Emma DOUGLASS (1810-1881)		

Children

M	William Clark BONE		
Birth	28 Mar 1855	Independence, Jackson, Missouri, United States	
Census	1860	Page 265, Independence, Jackson, Missouri, United States	
Census	1870	Page 259, Independence, Jackson, Missouri, United States	
Death	27 Oct 1879	Chronic Dysentery; Morrisville, Polk, Missouri, United States	
Burial		(But was to have been removed to Independence, Jackson, Missouri, United States), Morrisville, Polk, Missouri, United States	
Misc		"Independence, Mo.," Kansas City (Mo.) Daily Journal, 01 Nov 1879, Page 8, Column 3	
Marriage			

F	Camilla BONE		
Birth	20 May 1857		
Death	2 Aug 1858		
Burial			
Marriage			

M	Robert Lee BONE		
Birth	2 Mar 1859	Independence, Jackson, Missouri, United States	
Census	1860	Page 265, Independence, Jackson, Missouri, United States	
Census	1870	Page 259, Independence, Jackson, Missouri, United States	
Census	1880	ED 24, Page 57, Independence, Jackson, Missouri, United States	
Census	1900	ED 22, Page 299, Kansas City, Jackson, Missouri, United States	
Census	1910	ED 113, Page 215, Kansas City, Jackson, Missouri, United States	
Death	28 Jul 1936	Hypertrophy & Dilitation of Heart, Chronic Glandular Nephritis . . .; Kansas City, Jackson,	

			Missouri, United States
	Misc		Obituary, Independence (Mo.) Examiner, 28 Jul 1936, Page 2, Column 3
	Burial		Woodlawn Cemetery, Independence, Jackson, Missouri, United States
	Occupation		Abstractor (1900), Abstractor City (1910), Laborer, Church Choir Director
	Spouse	Flora C. [--?--] (1881-)	
	Marriage	28 Sep 1900	Wyandotte, Kansas, United States
	Spouse	Sadie N. RUSSELL (1864-)	
	Marriage	14 Feb 1884	(1884I0010524), Jackson, Missouri, United States

F Corinne BONE

Birth	10 Oct 1861	Independence, Jackson, Missouri, United States
Census	1870	Page 259, Independence, Jackson, Missouri, United States
Census	1880	ED 24, Page 57, Independence, Jackson, Missouri, United States
Census	1900	ED 22, Page 299, Kansas City, Jackson, Missouri, United States
Residence	1936	Nashville, Davidson, Tennessee, United States
Death	27 Mar 1946	Gallatin, Sumner, Tennessee, United States
Burial	28 Mar 1946	Douglas-Pardue Cemetery, Gallatin, Sumner, Tennessee, United States
Occupation		Public School Teacher
Marriage		

F Emma Douglass BONE

Birth	25 Oct 1863	Independence, Jackson, Missouri, United States
Census	1870	Page 259, Independence, Jackson, Missouri, United States
Death	3 Oct 1879	
Burial		
Marriage		

F Mary/Marie Franklin BONE

Birth	26 Oct 1866	Independence, Jackson, Missouri, United States
Census	1870	Page 259, Independence, Jackson, Missouri, United States
Census	1880	ED 24, Page 57, Independence, Jackson, Missouri, United States
Census	1900	ED 68, Page 25, Denver, Arapahoe, Colorado, United States
Residence	1936	Independence, Jackson, Missouri, United States
Death	14 Jun 1943	Coronary Occlusion, Chronic Myocarditis, Hip Fractured; Prairie Township, Jackson, Missouri, United States
Burial	17 Jun 1943	Woodlawn Cemetery, Independence, Jackson, Missouri, United States
Spouse	William W. PHELPS (1859-1922)	
Marriage	16 Nov 1887	(1887K0090046), Jackson, Missouri, United States

M Edward Payson "Eddie" BONE

Birth	11 Jun 1869	Independence, Jackson, Missouri, United States
Census	1870	Page 259, Independence, Jackson, Missouri, United States
Census	1880	ED 24, Page 57, Independence, Jackson, Missouri, United States
Census	1900	ED 22, Page 299, Kansas City, Jackson, Missouri, United States
Death	11 Oct 1927	Gastric Carcinoma; Kansas City, Jackson, Missouri, United States
Burial	13 Oct 1927	Woodlawn Cemetery, Independence, Jackson, Missouri, United States
Occupation		Abstractor (1900), Salesman Richards & Conover Hardware
Marriage		

M Charles Clark BONE

Birth	20 Jul 1873	Independence, Jackson, Missouri, United States
Census	1880	ED 24, Page 57, Independence, Jackson, Missouri, United States
Census	1900	ED 117, Page 129, Civil District 9, Sumner, Tennessee, United States
Census	1910	ED 139, Page 111, Civil Distsrict 9, Sumner, Tennessee, United States
Death	23 Jan 1933	Gallatin, Sumner, Tennessee, United States
Burial		Gallatin City Cemetery, Gallatin, Sumner, Tennessee, United States
Occupation		Farmer (1900), Farmer General Farm (1910)
Spouse	Minnie Louise BAKER (1874-1954)	
Marriage	17 Feb 1897	Sumner, Tennessee, United States

Father Asa BOOHER

Birth	15 Jan 1810	Guernsey, Ohio, United States
Census	1820	
Census	1830	
Census	1840	(Asa Booker Family), Page 440, Cumberland, Guernsey, Ohio, United States
Property	26 Apr 1850	First Known Purchase, Part Sects. 34 & 35, T50, R30; Volume P, Page 310, Independence, Jackson, Missouri, United States
Census	1850	Page 327, Fort Osage Township, Jackson, Missouri, United States
Census	1850	Agricultural Schedules, Page 571, Jackson, Missouri, United States
Property	15 Feb 1851	First Known US Land Purchase; (Part Section 34, Township 50, Range 30), Jackson, Missouri, United States
Census	1860	Page 447, Fort Osage Township, Jackson, Missouri, United States
Census	1860	Agricultural Schedules, Page Page 35, Fort Osage Township, Jackson, Missouri, United States
Tax Lists	Dec 1863	Retail Liquor Dealer License; "Asa Booker", Kansas City, Jackson, Missouri, United States
Tax Lists	May 1866	Eating House License; Kansas City, Jackson, Missouri, United States
Death	5 Sep 1866	Kansas City, Jackson, Missouri, United States
Burial		Union Cemetery, Kansas City, Jackson, Missouri, United States
Probate	5 Oct 1866	(Letters of Administration), Volume M, Page 120, Independence, Jackson, Missouri, United States
Occupation		Farmer (1850, 1860), Retail Liquor Dealer, Eating House Keeper
Marriage	5 Mar 1835	Guernsey, Ohio, United States
Father	George BOOHER (1784-1848)	
Mother	Elizabeth SLATER (1789-)	
Other spouse	Mariah SANDERS (1820-1895)	
Marriage	1 Feb 1843	Muskingum, Ohio, United States

Mother Juliann HUGGINS

Birth	26 Jun 1813	Virginia, United States
Census	1820	
Census	1830	
Census	1840	
Death	3 Apr 1842	Morrow, Ohio, United States
Burial		
Father	John HUGGINS (-)	
Mother	Rebecca PACKER (-)	

Children

F   Rebecca E. BOOHER

Birth	11 Feb 1836	Ohio, United States
Census	1840	(Asa Booker Family), Page 440, Cumberland, Guernsey, Ohio, United States
Census	1850	Page 327, Fort Osage Township, Jackson, Missouri, United States
Census	1860	ED 179, Page 577, Rock Creek Township, Cowley, Kansas, United States
Residence	1866	Platte, Missouri, United States
Census	1870	
Census	1875	Page 138, Family 95, Rock Creek Township, Cowley, Kansas, United States
Census	1880	
Death	10 Sep 1898	Dyer, Crawford, Arkansas, United States
Burial		Star Valley Cemetery, Udall, Cowley, Kansas, United States
Occupation		Farmer (1875)
Spouse	John Watts MEADOR (1834-1908)	
Marriage	20 Jul 1855	(1855I0030217), Jackson, Missouri, United States

Father Asa BOOHER

Birth	15 Jan 1810	Guernsey, Ohio, United States
Census	1820	
Census	1830	
Census	1840	(Asa Booker Family), Page 440, Cumberland, Guernsey, Ohio, United States
Property	26 Apr 1850	First Known Purchase, Part Sects. 34 & 35, T50, R30; Volume P, Page 310, Independence, Jackson, Missouri, United States
Census	1850	Page 327, Fort Osage Township, Jackson, Missouri, United States
Census	1850	Agricultural Schedules, Page 571, Jackson, Missouri, United States
Property	15 Feb 1851	First Known US Land Purchase; (Part Section 34, Township 50, Range 30), Jackson, Missouri, United States
Census	1860	Page 447, Fort Osage Township, Jackson, Missouri, United States
Census	1860	Agricultural Schedules, Page Page 35, Fort Osage Township, Jackson, Missouri, United States
Tax Lists	Dec 1863	Retail Liquor Dealer License; "Asa Booker", Kansas City, Jackson, Missouri, United States
Tax Lists	May 1866	Eating House License; Kansas City, Jackson, Missouri, United States
Death	5 Sep 1866	Kansas City, Jackson, Missouri, United States
Burial		Union Cemetery, Kansas City, Jackson, Missouri, United States
Probate	5 Oct 1866	(Letters of Administration), Volume M, Page 120, Independence, Jackson, Missouri, United States
Occupation		Farmer (1850, 1860), Retail Liquor Dealer, Eating House Keeper
Marriage	1 Feb 1843	Muskingum, Ohio, United States
Father	George BOOHER (1784-1848)	
Mother	Elizabeth SLATER (1789-)	
Other spouse	Juliann HUGGINS (1813-1842)	
Marriage	5 Mar 1835	Guernsey, Ohio, United States

Mother Mariah SANDERS

Birth	27 May 1820	Virginia, United States
Census	1850	Page 327, Fort Osage Township, Jackson, Missouri, United States
Census	1860	Page 447, Fort Osage Township, Jackson, Missouri, United States
Residence	17 Feb 1868	Non-Resident of Missouri
Census	1870	
Census	1880	ED 12, Page 356, Kansas City, Jackson, Missouri, United States
Death	1895	
Burial		
Father	Dennis SANDERS (1797-1867)	
Mother	Julia Ann [--?--] (-)	

Children

F Florence E. "Flora" BOOHER

Birth	Oct 1846	Ohio, United States
Census	1850	Page 327, Fort Osage Township, Jackson, Missouri, United States
Census	1860	Page 447, Fort Osage Township, Jackson, Missouri, United States
Residence	1866	Jackson, Missouri, United States
Census	1870	
Census	1880	ED 14, Page 401, Kansas City, Jackson, Missouri, United States
Census	1900	ED 164, Page 181, Ojai Township, Ventura, California, United States
Death		
Burial		
Spouse	Jacob SNIDER (1832-)	
Marriage	24 Feb 1871	

M William Oscar BOOHER

Birth	1847/8	Ohio, United States
Census	1850	Page 327, Fort Osage Township, Jackson, Missouri, United States
Census	1860	Page 447, Fort Osage Township, Jackson, Missouri, United States
Residence	1866	Jackson, Missouri, United States
Census	1870	
Census	1880	
Death		

Father Asa BOOHER			
Mother Mariah SANDERS			
Children			

William Oscar BOOHER (continued)

Burial		
Spouse	Isabell CLARK (1847-)	
Marriage	24 Feb 1870	

F Charlotte "Lottie" BOOHER

Birth	1849/50	Kentucky, United States
Census	1850	Page 327, Fort Osage Township, Jackson, Missouri, United States
Census	1860	Page 447, Fort Osage Township, Jackson, Missouri, United States
Residence	1866	Jackson, Missouri, United States
Census	1870	
Death	2 Jun 1876	
Religion		First Baptist Church, Kansas City, Jackson, Missouri, United States
Burial		
Spouse	Thomas L. HAFER (-)	
Marriage	4 Oct 1869	(1869I0060125), Jackson, Missouri, United States

M Doral BOOHER

Birth	16 Aug 1851	Independence, Jackson, Missouri, United States
Census	1860	Page 447, Fort Osage Township, Jackson, Missouri, United States
Residence	1866	Jackson, Missouri, United States
Census	1870	
Census	1880	
Census	1900	ED 73, Page 266, Willow Springs Township, Douglas, Kansas, United States
Death	10 Oct 1930	Elma, Grays Harbor, Washington, United States
Burial		Sutton Cemetery, Baldwin City, Douglas, Kansas, United States
Occupation		Farmer (1900)
Spouse	Francis L. INGLE (1857-1885)	
Marriage	15 Mar 1874	Ohio, United States
Spouse	Mary M. WEBSTER/ICABOD (1856-1939)	
Marriage	16 Feb 1887	

M Charles Asa BOOHER

Birth	1 Dec 1856	Independence, Jackson, Missouri, United States
Census	1860	Page 447, Fort Osage Township, Jackson, Missouri, United States
Residence	1866	Jackson, Missouri, United States
Census	1870	
Census	1880	
Death	19 May 1886	Railroad Accident; Argentine, Wyandotte, Kansas, United States
Burial		
Spouse	Mollie SKAGGS (1856-)	
Marriage	1 Jan 1880	

Father Henry/Heinrich BORGSTEDE

Birth	11 May 1835	Hannover, Prussia, Germany
Census	1860	Page 111, Westport, Jackson, Missouri, United States
Tax Lists	bet Jul 1863 and Dec 1866	Boots and Shoes Manufactured; "Henry Borgstada/Borgstede", Kansas City, Jackson, Missouri, United States
Military		Private & Corporal, Company B, 77th Regiment Enrolled Missouri Militia
Tax Lists	May 1866	Manufacturer License; "Henry Borgstada", Kansas City, Jackson, Missouri, United States
Tax Lists	Jul 1866	Retail Dealer License; "Henry Borgstada", Kansas City, Jackson, Missouri, United States
Census	1870	Page 665, Kansas City, Jackson, Missouri, United States
Census	1870	(Industrial Schedules), Ward 4, Page 71, Kansas City, Jackson, Missouri, United States
Census	1880	
Census	1885	Page 349, Argentine, Wyandotte, Kansas, United States
Will	23 Mar 1888	Will Written, Jackson Co. (Kansas City), MO, Volume 1, Page 263
Death	26 Mar 1888	
Burial		Union Cemetery, Kansas City, Jackson, Missouri, United States
Probate	7 Apr 1888	(Will Proved, Kansas City Courthouse, Volume 1, Page 263), Jackson, Missouri, United States
Occupation		Shoemaker (1860, 1870)
Marriage	26 Jun 1860	Westport, Jackson Co., MO (1860I0040197)
Father		
Mother		

Mother Catharine/Katharina KLAMM/LAMM

Birth	1838/9	Baden, Germany
Census	1870	Page 665, Kansas City, Jackson, Missouri, United States
Census	1880	
Census	1885	Page 349, Argentine, Wyandotte, Kansas, United States
Census	1900	
Census	1910	
Death		
Burial		
Father		
Mother		

Children

M George BORGSTEDE

Birth	9 Feb 1857	
Death	9 Jul 1857	
Burial		Union Cemetery, Kansas City, Jackson, Missouri, United States
Marriage		

M Henry BORGSTEDE Jr.

Birth	2 Dec 1860	
Death	20 Dec 1860	
Burial		Union Cemetery, Kansas City, Jackson, Missouri, United States
Marriage		

M Henry BORGSTEDE Jr.

Birth	4 Nov 1862	
Death	23 May 1864	
Burial		Union Cemetery, Kansas City, Jackson, Missouri, United States
Marriage		

F Theresa BORGSTEDE

Birth	16 Nov 1864	
Death	2 Feb 1866	
Burial		Union Cemetery, Kansas City, Jackson, Missouri, United States
Marriage		

F Eva Carolina BORGSTEDE

Birth	17 Jul 1868	
Baptism	3 Aug 1868	St. Peter's Ger. Evang. Church, Volume 1, Page 4
Death	23 Aug 1868	
Burial		Union Cemetery, Kansas City, Jackson, Missouri, United States

Father	Henry/Heinrich BORGSTEDE	
Mother	**Catharine/Katharina KLAMM/LAMM**	
Children		

Eva Carolina BORGSTEDE (continued)

Marriage		

F — Emma BORGSTEDE

Birth	12 Jan 1870	MO (or Dec 1869)
Baptism	1 May 1870	St. Peter's Ger. Evang. Church, Volume 1, Page 7
Census	1870	Page 665, Kansas City, Jackson, Missouri, United States
Death	24 Jul 1870	
Burial		Union Cemetery, Kansas City, Jackson, Missouri, United States
Marriage		

M — William/Wilhelm Gustav Eduard BORGSTEDE

Birth	2 Aug 1871	
Baptism	19 Mar 1872	St. Peter's Ger. Evang. Church, Volume 1, Page 11
Death	21 Mar 1872	
Burial		Union Cemetery, Kansas City, Jackson, Missouri, United States
Marriage		

F — Margaret/Margaretha BORGSTEDE

Birth	14 Jan 1874	
Baptism	27 Mar 1874	St. Peter's Ger. Evang. Church, Volume 1, Page 16
Death	17 Jan 1875	Kansas City, Jackson, Missouri, United States
Burial		Union Cemetery, Kansas City, Jackson, Missouri, United States
Marriage		

F — Augusta Maria Louise BORGSTEDE

Birth	21 Mar 1877	
Death	31 Aug 1877	Summer Complaint; St. Peter's Ger. Evang. Church, Volume 1, Page 370
Burial		Union Cemetery, Kansas City, Jackson, Missouri, United States
Marriage		

Father Henry Butler BOUTON

Event	Date	Place/Detail
Birth	22 Feb 1815	Cold Spring, Cattaraugus, New York, United States
Census	1820	
Census	1830	
Census	1840	
Census	1850	
Residence	bet 1851 and 1868	Kansas City, Jackson, Missouri, United States
Census	1860	Post Office Kansas City, Page 144, Jackson, Missouri, United States
Tax Lists	Sep 1862	Lawyer License; Kansas City, Jackson, Missouri, United States
Tax Lists	May 1866	Lawyer License; Kansas City, Jackson, Missouri, United States
Death	12 Sep 1868	Kansas City, Jackson, Missouri, United States
Burial	14 Sep 1868	Union Cemetery, Kansas City, Jackson, Missouri, United States
Misc		Death Notice, Kansas City (Mo.) Daily Journal of Commerce, 15 Sep 1868, Page 4, Column 4
Probate	12 Oct 1868	(Letters of Administration), Volume B, Page 11, Independence, Jackson, Missouri, United States
Misc		Biography, History of Kansas City, Mo. (1888), Page 344-345
Residence		Trumbull Co., OH; KY or TN; Springfield, Greene Co., MO; Harrisonville, Cass Co., MO
Misc		Henry and Mary Jane had three other children who did not survive
Occupation		Lawyer (1860)
Marriage	2 Sep 1852	(1852I0030119), Jackson, Missouri, United States
Father	Sands BOUTON (1791-)	
Mother	Janette [--?--] (1796-)	

Mother Mary Jane PEERY

Event	Date	Place/Detail
Birth	15 Feb 1836	Kansas Territory, United States
Census	1840	
Census	1850	Page 233, Kaw Township, Jackson, Missouri, United States
Census	1860	Post Office Kansas City, Page 144, Jackson, Missouri, United States
Tax Lists	Nov 1866	Succession [Inheritance]; Kansas City, Jackson, Missouri, United States
Census	1870	Page 11, Kaw Township, Jackson, Missouri, United States
Census	1870	Agricultural Schedules, Page 3, Kaw Township, Jackson, Missouri, United States
Census	1880	ED 6, Page 173, Kansas City, Jackson, Missouri, United States
Census	1900	ED 62, Page 258, Kansas City, Jackson, Missouri, United States
Census	1910	
Death	15 Mar 1918	Baltimore, Baltimore, Maryland, United States
Misc		Obituary, Kansas City (Mo.) Star, 16 Mar 1918, Page 2, Column 1
Burial		West View Cemetery, Sweetwater, Monroe, Tennessee, United States
Father	Rev. Edward Thompson PEERY (1800-1864)	
Mother	Mary Sanders PEERY (1814-1890)	

Children

F Julia E. BOUTON

Event	Date	Place/Detail
Birth	1 Sep 1854	Kansas City, Jackson, Missouri, United States
Census	1860	Post Office Kansas City, Page 144, Jackson, Missouri, United States
Census	1870	Page 11, Kaw Township, Jackson, Missouri, United States
Census	1880	ED 163, Page 244, Bloomington, McLean, Illinois, United States
Census	1900	
Census	1910	ED 142, Page 22, Sweetwater, Monroe, Tennessee, United States
Residence	1918	Sweetwater, Monroe, Tennessee, United States
Death	5 Sep 1941	Sweetwater, Monroe, Tennessee, United States
Burial		West View Cemetery, Sweetwater, Monroe, Tennessee, United States
Spouse	William Douglas GILMAN (1849-1919)	
Marriage	13 Nov 1878	(1878I0080090), Jackson, Missouri, United States

M Edward A./H. BOUTON

Event	Date	Place/Detail
Birth	1858/9	Missouri, United States
Census	1860	Post Office Kansas City, Page 144, Jackson, Missouri, United States
Census	1870	Page 11, Kaw Township, Jackson, Missouri, United States
Census	1880	ED 6, Page 173, Kansas City, Jackson, Missouri, United States
Census	1900	ED 41, Page 166, Baltimore (City), Maryland, United States

Father	Henry Butler BOUTON	
Mother Mary Jane PEERY		

Children

Edward A./H. BOUTON (continued)

Residence	1910	Baltimore, Baltimore, Maryland, United States
Residence	1918	Baltimore, Baltimore, Maryland, United States
Occupation		Grocer (1880), President & Superintendent Roland Park Company (1900)
Death		
Burial		
Spouse	Luella SIMS (1859-)	
Marriage	1888/9	

F Jessie L. BOUTON

Birth	4 Mar 1865	Missouri, United States
Census	1870	Page 11, Kaw Township, Jackson, Missouri, United States
Census	1880	ED 6, Page 173, Kansas City, Jackson, Missouri, United States
Census	1900	ED 62, Page 258, Kansas City, Jackson, Missouri, United States
Residence	1918	Baltimore, Baltimore, Maryland, United States
Death	27 Oct 1943	
Burial		Saint John's Episcopal Church Cemetery, Reistertown, Baltimore, Maryland, United States
Spouse	Augustus Pierce MARTY (1861-1941)	
Marriage	20 Oct 1886	(1886K0060435), Kansas City, Jackson, Missouri, United States

Father Perry G. BROCK

Birth	Mar 1831	Jackson, Missouri, United States
Census	1840	
Census	1850	Page 375, Jackson Township, Jasper, Missouri, United States
Census	1860	Page 291, Independence, Jackson, Missouri, United States
Census		Industrial Schedules, Page 3, Independence, Jackson, Missouri, United States
Military		Company G, 7th Regiment Provisional Enrolled Missouri Militia
Military	Oct 1863	Civil War Draft Registration; Blue Township, Jackson, Missouri, United States
Tax Lists	Dec 1863	Retail Dealer License; Independence, Jackson, Missouri, United States
Tax Lists	Sep 1866	Retail Dealer License; "Brock & Ruffner", Independence, Jackson, Missouri, United States
Census	1870	Page 291, Independence, Jackson, Missouri, United States
Census		Industrial Schedules, Ward 1, Page 54, Independence, Jackson, Missouri, United States
Census	1880	ED 20, Page 542, Kansas City, Jackson, Missouri, United States
Census	1900	
Will	10 Aug 1900	(Will Written), Volume 6, Page 68, Kansas City, Jackson, Missouri, United States
Death	9 Sep 1900	Kansas City, Jackson, Missouri, United States
Burial	11 Sep 1900	Pitcher Cemetery, Blue Township, Jackson, Missouri, United States
Misc		Obituary, Independence (Mo.) Jackson Examiner, 14 Sep 1900, Page 1, Column 3
Probate	15 Sep 1900	(Will Proved), Volume 6, Page 68, Kansas City, Jackson, Missouri, United States
Misc		Biography, Jackson County Pioneers (1975), Page 153
Occupation		Machinist (1860), Miller (1870), Engineer (1880), Retail Dealer
Business		Brock & Ruffner (Retail Dealer)
Marriage	6 Jul 1851	(1851I0030051), Jackson, Missouri, United States
Father		
Mother	L. Dicey A. [--?--] (1798-)	
Other spouse	Lavinia Adeline HALL (1842-)	
Marriage	26 May 1859	(1859I0040119), Jackson, Missouri, United States

Mother Nancy Narcissa "Ann" HALE

Birth	28 Oct 1832	Missouri, United States
Census	1840	(Bennet Hale Family), Page 76, Jackson, Missouri, United States
Census	1850	Page 293, Blue Township, Jackson, Missouri, United States
Death		
Burial		
Father	Bennet HALE (1809-)	
Mother	Elie [--?--] (1809-1859)	

Children

M   John W. BROCK

Birth	1852/3	Missouri, United States
Census	1860	Page 291, Independence, Jackson, Missouri, United States
Census	1870	Page 291, Independence, Jackson, Missouri, United States
Census	1880	
Burial		Pitcher Cemetery, Blue Township, Jackson, Missouri, United States
Death		
Marriage		

M   James W./M. BROCK

Birth	1854	Missouri, United States
Census	1860	Page 291, Independence, Jackson, Missouri, United States
Census	1870	Page 291, Independence, Jackson, Missouri, United States
Census	1880	
Death	26 Feb 1922	
Burial		Mount Calvary Cemetery, Leavenworth, Leavenworth, Kansas, United States
Spouse	Alma STINE (-)	
Marriage	2 Jan 1878	(1878I0070413), Jackson, Missouri, United States

M   Thomas Gilbert BROCK

Birth	4 Jul 1858	Missouri, United States
Census	1860	Page 291, Independence, Jackson, Missouri, United States
Census	1870	Page 291, Independence, Jackson, Missouri, United States
Census	1880	ED 20, Page 542, Kansas City, Jackson, Missouri, United States

Father Perry G. BROCK		
Mother Nancy Narcissa "Ann" HALE		
Children		
Thomas Gilbert BROCK (continued)		
Census	1900	ED 45, Page 282, Kansas City, Jackson, Missouri, United States
Census	1910	ED 47, Page 120, Kansas City, Jackson, Missouri, United States
Census	1920	ED 54, Page 32, Kansas City, Jackson, Missouri, United States
Death	1 Oct 1924	Carcinoma Liver; Kansas City, Jackson, Missouri, United States
Burial	3 Oct 1924	Mount Saint Mary's Cemetery, Kansas City, Jackson, Missouri, United States
Occupation		Stationary Engineer (1900), Engineer Stationary (1910), Stationary Engineer Railroad (1920)
Spouse	Ellen GAFFNEY (1862-1945)	

Father Perry G. BROCK

Event	Date	Place/Detail
Birth	Mar 1831	Jackson, Missouri, United States
Census	1840	
Census	1850	Page 375, Jackson Township, Jasper, Missouri, United States
Census	1860	Page 291, Independence, Jackson, Missouri, United States
Census		Industrial Schedules, Page 3, Independence, Jackson, Missouri, United States
Military		Company G, 7th Regiment Provisional Enrolled Missouri Militia
Military	Oct 1863	Civil War Draft Registration; Blue Township, Jackson, Missouri, United States
Tax Lists	Dec 1863	Retail Dealer License; Independence, Jackson, Missouri, United States
Tax Lists	Sep 1866	Retail Dealer License; "Brock & Ruffner", Independence, Jackson, Missouri, United States
Census	1870	Page 291, Independence, Jackson, Missouri, United States
Census		Industrial Schedules, Ward 1, Page 54, Independence, Jackson, Missouri, United States
Census	1880	ED 20, Page 542, Kansas City, Jackson, Missouri, United States
Census	1900	
Will	10 Aug 1900	(Will Written), Volume 6, Page 68, Kansas City, Jackson, Missouri, United States
Death	9 Sep 1900	Kansas City, Jackson, Missouri, United States
Burial	11 Sep 1900	Pitcher Cemetery, Blue Township, Jackson, Missouri, United States
Misc		Obituary, Independence (Mo.) Jackson Examiner, 14 Sep 1900, Page 1, Column 3
Probate	15 Sep 1900	(Will Proved), Volume 6, Page 68, Kansas City, Jackson, Missouri, United States
Misc		Biography, Jackson County Pioneers (1975), Page 153
Occupation		Machinist (1860), Miller (1870), Engineer (1880), Retail Dealer
Business		Brock & Ruffner (Retail Dealer)
Marriage	26 May 1859	(1859I0040119), Jackson, Missouri, United States
Father		
Mother	L. Dicey A. [--?--] (1798-)	
Other spouse	Nancy Narcissa HALE (1832-)	
Marriage	6 Jul 1851	(1851I0030051), Jackson, Missouri, United States

Mother Lavinia Adeline HALL

Event	Date	Place/Detail
Birth	1842/3	Missouri, United States
Census	1850	
Census	1860	Page 291, Independence, Jackson, Missouri, United States
Census	1870	Page 291, Independence, Jackson, Missouri, United States
Census	1880	ED 20, Page 542, Kansas City, Jackson, Missouri, United States
Census	1900	
Census	1910	
Census	1920	
Death		
Burial		
Father		
Mother		

Children

F   Anna BROCK

Event	Date	Place/Detail
Birth	1861/2	Missouri, United States
Census	1870	Page 291, Independence, Jackson, Missouri, United States
Census	1880	
Death		
Burial		
Marriage		

M   Benjamin G. BROCK

Event	Date	Place/Detail
Birth	1863/4	Missouri, United States
Census	1870	Page 291, Independence, Jackson, Missouri, United States
Census	1880	ED 20, Page 542, Kansas City, Jackson, Missouri, United States
Death		
Burial		
Marriage		

Father Dr. James Terrell BROWN

Birth	29 Jun 1827	Meade, Kentucky, United States
Census	1830	
Census	1840	
Census	1850	Page 215, Lafayette, Missouri, United States
Property	4 Nov 1854	First Known Purchase, Part Lots 4,5 & 8, Block 46, Sibley; Volume W, Page 173, Independence, Jackson, Missouri, United States
Census	1860	Page 456, Fort Osage Township, Jackson, Missouri, United States
Tax Lists	Sep 1862	Physician License; Sibley, Jackson, Missouri, United States
Military	bet Oct 1863 and Nov 1863	Civil War Draft Registration; Fort Osage Township, Jackson, Missouri, United States
Tax Lists	May 1866	Physician License, Income, Gold Watch, and Carriage; Independence, Jackson, Missouri, United States
Census	1870	Page 295, Independence, Jackson, Missouri, United States
Census	1880	ED 24, Page 40, Independence, Jackson, Missouri, United States
Death	2 Jun 1887	
Burial		Woodlawn Cemetery, Independence, Jackson, Missouri, United States
Occupation		Physician (1850, 1860, 1870), Doctor & Druggist (1880)
Marriage	3 Oct 1854	1854I0030180), Jackson, Missouri, United States
Father	William Bailey Clark BROWN (1798-)	
Mother	Matilda Jane Prather FONTAINE (1804-1876)	

Mother Susan Hannah BIGGERSTAFF

Birth	14 Sep 1840	Madison, Kentucky, United States
Census	1850	Page 327, Fort Osage Township, Jackson, Missouri, United States
Census	1860	Page 456, Fort Osage Township, Jackson, Missouri, United States
Census	1870	Page 295, Independence, Jackson, Missouri, United States
Census	1880	ED 24, Page 40, Independence, Jackson, Missouri, United States
Death	6 Jul 1897	
Burial		Woodlawn Cemetery, Independence, Jackson, Missouri, United States
Father	John BIGGERSTAFF (-)	
Mother	Hannah OLDHAM (1799-)	

Children

F Mabelle BROWN

Birth	12 Jun 1859	Sibley, Jackson, Missouri, United States
Census	1860	Page 456, Fort Osage Township, Jackson, Missouri, United States
Census	1870	Page 295, Independence, Jackson, Missouri, United States
Census	1880	ED 24, Page 40, Independence, Jackson, Missouri, United States
Census	1900	ED 6, Page 82, Independence, Jackson, Missouri, United States
Residence	1920	Independence, Jackson, Missouri, United States
Residence	1933	Independence, Jackson, Missouri, United States
Death	20 Apr 1939	Uremia, Cardio-Renal Disease, Arteriosclerosis, . . .; Independence, Jackson, Missouri, United States
Misc		Obituary, Independence (Mo.) Examiner, 21 Apr 1939, Page 1, Column 6
Burial	23 Apr 1939	Woodlawn Cemetery, Independence, Jackson, Missouri, United States
Spouse	William Larkin WEBB (1856-1931)	
Marriage	15 Mar 1894	(1894I0001515), Jackson, Missouri, United States

M Judge William Bailey Clark BROWN

Birth	11 Apr 1862	Sibley, Jackson, Missouri, United States
Census	1870	Page 295, Independence, Jackson, Missouri, United States
Census	1880	ED 24, Page 40, Independence, Jackson, Missouri, United States
Graduation	abt 1887	Law School, Harvard University, Cambridge, Middlesex, Massachusetts, United States
Census	1900	ED 126, Page 281, Kansas City, Jackson, Missouri, United States
Misc	1902	Biography, Political History of Jackson County, Missouri, Pages 84-85
Death	1 May 1920	Kansas City, Jackson, Missouri, United States
Misc		Obituary, Independence (Mo.) Examiner, 03 May 1920, Page 1, Column 5
Burial	4 May 1920	Woodlawn Cemetery, Independence, Jackson, Missouri, United States
Misc		Obituary, Independence (Mo.) Examiner, 05 May 1920, Page 1, Column 6

Father	Dr. James Terrell BROWN	
Mother	Susan Hannah BIGGERSTAFF	
Children		

Judge William Bailey Clark BROWN (continued)

Occupation		Student at Westminster College (1880), Lawyer (1900), Referee of Bankruptcy in Federal Court in Kansas City
Spouse	Anna Belle JONES (1869-1918)	
Marriage	1888/9	

F   Maude Benson BROWN

Birth	10 Apr 1866	Independence, Jackson, Missouri, United States
Census	1870	Page 295, Independence, Jackson, Missouri, United States
Census	1880	ED 24, Page 40, Independence, Jackson, Missouri, United States
Census	1900	ED 6, Page 82, Independence, Jackson, Missouri, United States
Residence	1920	Independence, Jackson, Missouri, United States
Death	8 Sep 1933	Pneumonia Bronchial Bilateral, Chronic Interstitial Nephritis; Independence, Jackson, Missouri, United States
Misc		Obituary, Independence (Mo.) Examiner, 08 Sep 1933, Page 1, Column 5
Misc		Funeral Notice, Independence (Mo.) Examiner, 09 Sep 1933, Page 1, Column 5
Burial	10 Sep 1933	Woodlawn Cemetery, Independence, Jackson, Missouri, United States
Misc		"Maude Brown Ott," Independence (Mo.) Examiner, 01 Dec 1933, Page 6, Columns 2-3
Spouse	Christian OTT Jr. (1858-1924)	
Marriage	1887	

F   Jessie BROWN

Birth	1868/9	(or 1870 or May 1872), Missouri, United States
Census	1870	Page 295, Independence, Jackson, Missouri, United States
Census	1880	ED 24, Page 40, Independence, Jackson, Missouri, United States
Census	1900	ED 213, Page 304, San Francisco, San Francisco, California, United States
Census	1910	ED 110, Page 200, Sacramento, Sacramento, California, United States
Residence	1920	Sacramento, Sacramento, California, United States
Death	12 Sep 1928	Sacramento, Sacramento, California, United States
Burial		Sacramento City Cemetery, Sacramento, Sacramento, California, United States
Spouse	John Q. BROWN Jr. (1857-1929)	
Marriage	27 Nov 1888	(1888K0001181), Jackson, Missouri, United States

Father Philip Shelley BROWN

Birth	14 Oct 1833	New Enterprise, Bedford, Pennsylvania, United States
Residence	bet 1834 and 1849	Huntington, Pennsylvania, United States
Census	1840	
Residence	bet 1849 and 1855	Hollidaysburg, Blair, Pennsylvania, United States
Census	1850	Page 8, Woodbury Township, Blair, Pennsylvania, United States
Residence	bet 1855 and 1857	Davenport, Scott, Iowa, United States
Residence	bet 1857 and 1921	Kansas City, Jackson, Missouri, United States
Misc	15 Sep 1858	Admitted to the Bar, Court of Common Pleas of Jackson Co.; Jackson, Missouri, United States
Census	1860	Page 44, Kansas City, Jackson, Missouri, United States
Tax Lists	Sep 1862	Claim Agent and Lawyer Licenses; Kansas City, Jackson, Missouri, United States
Military	Sep 1863	Civil War Draft Registration; Kaw Township, Jackson, Missouri, United States
Military		Civil War Service under Col. R. T. Van Horn
Misc	bet 1864 and 1866	City Councilman; Kansas City, Jackson, Missouri, United States
Tax Lists	May 1866	Lawyer License; Kansas City, Jackson, Missouri, United States
Census	1870	Page 533, Kansas City, Jackson, Missouri, United States
Census	1880	ED 7, Page 205, Kansas City, Jackson, Missouri, United States
Misc		Biography, History of Jackson County, Missouri (1881), Page 745.
Misc		Biography, History of Kansas City, Missouri (1888), Pages 339-340
Misc		Biography, National Cyclopaedia of American Biography (1898)
Census	1900	ED 82, Page 230, Kansas City, Jackson, Missouri, United States
Misc		Biography, Encyclopedia of the History of Missouri (1901)
Misc		Biography, Whitney, Kansas City, Missouri, Volume 3 (1908), Pages 136-140
Census	1910	ED 101, Page 32, Kansas City, Jackson, Missouri, United States
Census	1920	ED 124, Page 214, Kansas City, Jackson, Missouri, United States
Misc		"Observes 88th Birthday . . ." Kansas City (Mo.) Daily Journal, 17 Oct 1921, Page 2, Column 6
Death	10 Dec 1921	Arteriosclerosis and Apoplexy, Cerebral Hemorrhage; Kansas City, Jackson, Missouri, United States
Misc		Obituary, Kansas City (Mo.) Star, 11 Dec 1921, Page 15A, Columns 3-4
Misc		Obituary, Kansas City (Mo.) Daily Journal, 11 Dec 1921, Page 6A, Columns 2-3
Burial	13 Dec 1921	Elmwood Cemetery, Kansas City, Jackson, Missouri, United States
Misc		"Tribute to Philip S. Brown, Sr.," Annals of Kansas City ___ (December 1922), 203-206
Occupation		Laborer (1850), Lawyer (1860, 1870, 1880, 1900), Claim Agent
Religion		First Presbyterian Church and Central Presbyterian Church; Kansas City, Jackson, Missouri, United States
Marriage	3 Nov 1858	Pittsburgh, Allegheny, Pennsylvania, United States
Father		Henry BROWN (-1834)
Mother		Salome SHELLEY (-)

Mother Julia Ann SHAFFER

Birth	10 May 1835	(or Canoe Valley, Huntingdon, Pennsylvania, United States), Shaffersville, Blair, Pennsylvania, United States
Census	1840	
Census	1850	Page 8, Woodbury Township, Blair, Pennsylvania, United States
Religion	bet 1859 and 1903	Member; First Presbyterian Church, Kansas City, Jackson, Missouri, United States
Census	1860	Page 44, Kansas City, Jackson, Missouri, United States
Census	1870	Page 533, Kansas City, Jackson, Missouri, United States
Census	1880	ED 7, Page 205, Kansas City, Jackson, Missouri, United States
Census	1900	ED 82, Page 230, Kansas City, Jackson, Missouri, United States
Death	6 Jan 1908	Pneumonia; Kansas City, Jackson, Missouri, United States
Misc		Obituary, Kansas City (Mo.) Times, 07 Jan 1908, Page 2, Column 1
Burial	8 Jan 1908	Elmwood Cemetery (or 08 Jan 1908), Kansas City, Jackson, Missouri, United States
Misc		Funeral Notice, Kansas City (Mo.) Times, 08 Jan 1908, Page 9, Column 6
Misc		Biography & Photo, Whitney, Kansas City, Missouri, Volume 3 (1908), Pages 140-144
Father		William SHAFFER (1800-1880)
Mother		Catherine HILEMAN (1811-1864)

Children

Father Philip Shelley BROWN

Mother Julia Ann SHAFFER

Children

F   Julia A. BROWN

Birth	3 Nov 1859	Missouri, United States
Census	1860	Page 44, Kansas City, Jackson, Missouri, United States
Census	1870	Page 533, Kansas City, Jackson, Missouri, United States
Census	1880	ED 7, Page 205, Kansas City, Jackson, Missouri, United States
Census	1900	ED 82, Page 230, Kansas City, Jackson, Missouri, United States
Census	1910	ED 101, Page 32, Kansas City, Jackson, Missouri, United States
Census	1920	ED 124, Page 214, Kansas City, Jackson, Missouri, United States
Residence	1921	Kansas City, Jackson, Missouri, United States
Death	9 Jan 1950	Carcinoma of Pancreas, Jaundice, Senility; Kansas City, Jackson, Missouri, United States
Burial	11 Jan 1950	Elmwood Cemetery, Kansas City, Jackson, Missouri, United States
Spouse	Edward Bessom SHILLITO (1845-1912)	
Marriage	9 Feb 1881	Kansas City, Jackson, Missouri, United States

M   J. Wilkinson BROWN

Birth	1860/1	
Death	Jan 1866	
Burial		Elmwood Cemetery, Kansas City, Jackson, Missouri, United States
Marriage		

F   Lulu Kate "Lula" BROWN

Birth	Aug 1862	Missouri, United States
Census	1870	Page 533, Kansas City, Jackson, Missouri, United States
Census	1880	ED 7, Page 205, Kansas City, Jackson, Missouri, United States
Census	1900	ED 82, Page 230, Kansas City, Jackson, Missouri, United States
Census	1910	ED 101, Page 32, Kansas City, Jackson, Missouri, United States
Census	1920	ED 124, Page 214, Kansas City, Jackson, Missouri, United States
Residence	1921	Kansas City, Jackson, Missouri, United States
Death		
Burial	4 Dec 1934	Elmwood Cemetery, Kansas City, Jackson, Missouri, United States
Spouse	Joseph B. CURD (1842-1924)	
Marriage	17 Jun 1885	(1885K0050225), Kansas City, Jackson, Missouri, United States

M   William Harrison "Harry" BROWN

Birth	26 Feb 1864	Missouri, United States
Census	1870	Page 533, Kansas City, Jackson, Missouri, United States
Census	1880	ED 7, Page 205, Kansas City, Jackson, Missouri, United States
Graduation	1883	University of Missouri, Columbia, Boone, Missouri, United States
Census	1900	ED 74, Page 129, Kansas City, Jackson, Missouri, United States
Will	2 Mar 1901	(Will Written), Volume 20, Page 139, Kansas City, Jackson, Missouri, United States
Census	1910	ED 92, Page 211, Kansas City, Jackson, Missouri, United States
Death	6 Apr 1916	Hypostatic Pneumonia, Locomotor Ataxia, Paresis; Kansas City, Jackson, Missouri, United States
Burial	9 Apr 1916	Elmwood Cemetery, Kansas City, Jackson, Missouri, United States
Probate	29 Apr 1916	(Will Proved), Volume 20, Page 139, Kansas City, Jackson, Missouri, United States
Occupation		Lawyer (1900), Attorney Law (1910)
Spouse	Caroline M. SANFORD (1869-)	
Marriage	11 Jun 1896	(1896K0013079), Kansas City, Jackson, Missouri, United States

M   Sydney BROWN

Birth	1864/5	
Death	1866	
Burial		Elmwood Cemetery, Kansas City, Jackson, Missouri, United States
Marriage		

M   Phillip Sheridan "Sherry" BROWN

Birth	25 Dec 1867	(or 25 Dec 1866), Missouri, United States
Census	1870	Page 533, Kansas City, Jackson, Missouri, United States
Census	1880	ED 7, Page 205, Kansas City, Jackson, Missouri, United States
Occupation	1894/5	City Councilman; Kansas City, Jackson, Missouri, United States

Father	Philip Shelley BROWN	
Mother	**Julia Ann SHAFFER**	

Children

Phillip Sheridan "Sherry" BROWN (continued)

Occupation	bet 1896 and 1899	City Alderman; Kansas City, Jackson, Missouri, United States
Census	1900	ED 82, Page 230, Kansas City, Jackson, Missouri, United States
Census	1910	ED 92, Page 208, Kansas City, Jackson, Missouri, United States
Census	1920	ED 197, Page 253, Kansas City, Jackson, Missouri, United States
Residence	1921	Kansas City, Jackson, Missouri, United States
Death	17 Aug 1937	Uremia, Bilateral Pyo-Nephritis (Chronic), Paralytic Bladder; Kansas City, Jackson, Missouri, United States
Burial	20 Aug 1937	Elmwood Cemetery, Kansas City, Jackson, Missouri, United States
Occupation		Fire Insurance Agent (1900), Agent Insurance (1910), Agent Real Estate Insurance (1920)
Spouse	Edith A. WOLF (1885-1948)	
Marriage	13 Aug 1908	(1908K0041392), Kansas City, Jackson, Missouri, United States

M Robert Irwin BROWN

Birth	1870	
Death	Feb 1873	
Burial		Elmwood Cemetery, Kansas City, Jackson, Missouri, United States
Marriage		

M Dr. Ralph J. BROWN

Birth	8 Mar 1874	Missouri, United States
Census	1880	ED 7, Page 205, Kansas City, Jackson, Missouri, United States
Graduation	1896	University Medical College, Kansas City, Jackson, Missouri, United States
Census	1900	ED 82, Page 230, Kansas City, Jackson, Missouri, United States
Census	1910	ED 101, Page 32, Kansas City, Jackson, Missouri, United States
Census	1920	ED 124, Page 214, Kansas City, Jackson, Missouri, United States
Residence	1921	Kansas City, Jackson, Missouri, United States
Death	9 Feb 1933	Gunshot Wounds of Chest and Abdomen; Kansas City, Jackson, Missouri, United States
Burial	11 Feb 1933	Elmwood Cemetery, Kansas City, Jackson, Missouri, United States
Occupation		Doctor (1900, 1910), Physician (1920)
Marriage		

F Sara Lelie "Sadie" BROWN

Birth	8 Mar 1874	Missouri, United States
Census	1880	ED 7, Page 205, Kansas City, Jackson, Missouri, United States
Census	1900	ED 84, Page 263, Kansas City, Jackson, Missouri, United States
Census	1910	ED 101, Page 32, Kansas City, Jackson, Missouri, United States
Census	1920	ED 124, Page 214, Kansas City, Jackson, Missouri, United States
Residence	1921	Kansas City, Jackson, Missouri, United States
Death	26 May 1949	Respiratory Paralysis, Cerebral Edema, Cerebral Arteriosclerosis, Parkinson's Disease; Kansas City, Jackson, Missouri, United States
Burial	28 May 1949	Elmwood Cemetery, Kansas City, Jackson, Missouri, United States
Spouse	Allen James EPPERSON (1868-1931)	
Divorce		

Father Dr. David A. "Dave" BRYANT

Birth	18 Oct 1828	Jessamine, Kentucky, United States
Residence	bet 1828 and 1849	Jessamine, Kentucky, United States
Census	1830	
Census	1840	
Census	1850	Page 292, Blue Township, Jackson, Missouri, United States
Graduation	1850	Kentucky School of Medicine, Louisville, Jefferson, Kentucky, United States
Residence	bet 1850 and 1855	Independence, Jackson, Missouri, United States
Residence	bet 1855 and 1858	Prairie Township, Jackson, Missouri, United States
Residence	bet 1858 and 1864	Hickman Mills, Jackson. Missouri, United States
Census	1860	Post Office Independence, Page 176, Jackson, Missouri, United States
Census		Slave Schedules, Page 372, Jackson, Missouri, United States
Tax Lists	Sep 1862	Physician License; Jackson, Missouri, United States
Military	Sep 1863	Civil War Draft Registration; Washington Township, Jackson, Missouri, United States
Tax Lists	Dec 1863	Physician License; Hickman Mills, Jackson, Missouri, United States
Residence	bet 1864 and 1866	Carson City, Lyon, Nevada, United States
Tax Lists	May 1866	Physician License; Hickman Mills, Jackson, Missouri, United States
Religion	1866	Bethlehem Christian Church; Hickman Mills, Jackson. Missouri, United States
Residence	bet 1866 and 1914	Hickman Mills, Jackson. Missouri, United States
Tax Lists	Dec 1866	Physician License; Jackson, Missouri, United States
Census	1870	(Township 47, Range 32), Page 101, Jackson, Missouri, United States
Census		Agricultural Schedules, Township 48, Ranges 32 & 33, Post Office Lee's Summit, Page 53, Jackson, Missouri, United States
Misc		Biography, Illustrated Historical Atlas Map of Jackson Co., Mo. (1877), Page 30
Census	1880	ED 38, Page 237, Washington Township, Jackson, Missouri, United States
Misc		Biography, History of Jackson County, Missouri (1881), Page 978
Census	1900	ED 128, Page 18, Kansas City, Jackson, Missouri, United States
Census	1910	ED 216, Page 246, Washington Township, Jackson, Missouri, United States
Death	23 Jun 1914	Old Age, Arteriosclerosis; Kansas City, Jackson, Missouri, United States
Misc		Obituary, Independence (Mo.) Examiner, 23 Jun 1914, Page 1, Column 6
Misc		Obituary, Kansas City (Mo.) Star, 23 Jun 1914, Page 2, Column 1
Burial	25 Jun 1914	Woodlawn Cemetery, Independence, Jackson, Missouri, United States
Occupation		Physician (1860, 1870, 1880, 1900)
Marriage	13 Jun 1851	(1851I0030076), Jackson, Missouri, United States
Father	George Smith BRYANT (1790-1850)	
Mother	Keziah ARNOLD (1790-1858)	
Other spouse	Sarah C. SMART (1834-1857)	
Marriage	31 May 1853	(1853I0030130), Jackson, Missouri, United States
Other spouse	Caroline M. EATON (1835-1922)	
Marriage	28 Oct 1858	(1858I0040077), Jackson, Missouri, United States

Mother Sarah E. NEET

Birth	1832/3	Kentucky, United States
Census	1850	Page 277, Blue Township, Jackson, Missouri, United States
Death	22 May 1852	
Burial		Woodlawn Cemetery, Independence, Jackson, Missouri, United States
Father	George NEAT (1804-1872)	
Mother	Melinda [--?--] (1810-)	

Children

Father Dr. David A. "Dave" BRYANT

Birth	18 Oct 1828	Jessamine, Kentucky, United States
Residence	bet 1828 and 1849	Jessamine, Kentucky, United States
Census	1830	
Census	1840	
Census	1850	Page 292, Blue Township, Jackson, Missouri, United States
Graduation	1850	Kentucky School of Medicine, Louisville, Jefferson, Kentucky, United States
Residence	bet 1850 and 1855	Independence, Jackson, Missouri, United States
Residence	bet 1855 and 1858	Prairie Township, Jackson, Missouri, United States
Residence	bet 1858 and 1864	Hickman Mills, Jackson. Missouri, United States
Census	1860	Post Office Independence, Page 176, Jackson, Missouri, United States
Census		Slave Schedules, Page 372, Jackson, Missouri, United States
Tax Lists	Sep 1862	Physician License; Jackson, Missouri, United States
Military	Sep 1863	Civil War Draft Registration; Washington Township, Jackson, Missouri, United States
Tax Lists	Dec 1863	Physician License; Hickman Mills, Jackson, Missouri, United States
Residence	bet 1864 and 1866	Carson City, Lyon, Nevada, United States
Tax Lists	May 1866	Physician License; Hickman Mills, Jackson, Missouri, United States
Religion	1866	Bethlehem Christian Church; Hickman Mills, Jackson. Missouri, United States
Residence	bet 1866 and 1914	Hickman Mills, Jackson. Missouri, United States
Tax Lists	Dec 1866	Physician License; Jackson, Missouri, United States
Census	1870	(Township 47, Range 32), Page 101, Jackson, Missouri, United States
Census		Agricultural Schedules, Township 48, Ranges 32 & 33, Post Office Lee's Summit, Page 53, Jackson, Missouri, United States
Misc		Biography, Illustrated Historical Atlas Map of Jackson Co., Mo. (1877), Page 30
Census	1880	ED 38, Page 237, Washington Township, Jackson, Missouri, United States
Misc		Biography, History of Jackson County, Missouri (1881), Page 978
Census	1900	ED 128, Page 18, Kansas City, Jackson, Missouri, United States
Census	1910	ED 216, Page 246, Washington Township, Jackson, Missouri, United States
Death	23 Jun 1914	Old Age, Arteriosclerosis; Kansas City, Jackson, Missouri, United States
Misc		Obituary, Independence (Mo.) Examiner, 23 Jun 1914, Page 1, Column 6
Misc		Obituary, Kansas City (Mo.) Star, 23 Jun 1914, Page 2, Column 1
Burial	25 Jun 1914	Woodlawn Cemetery, Independence, Jackson, Missouri, United States
Occupation		Physician (1860, 1870, 1880, 1900)
Marriage	31 May 1853	(1853I0030130), Jackson, Missouri, United States
Father	George Smith BRYANT (1790-1850)	
Mother	Keziah ARNOLD (1790-1858)	
Other spouse	Sarah E. NEET (1832-1852)	
Marriage	13 Jun 1851	(1851I0030076), Jackson, Missouri, United States
Other spouse	Caroline M. EATON (1835-1922)	
Marriage	28 Oct 1858	(1858I0040077), Jackson, Missouri, United States

Mother Sarah C. SMART

Birth	23 Jan 1834	Kentucky, United States
Census	1850	Page 276, Blue Township, Jackson, Missouri, United States
Death	24 May 1857	
Burial		Woodlawn Cemetery, Independence, Jackson, Missouri, United States
Father	James SMART (1801-1859)	
Mother	Lucia [--?--] (1808-1851)	

Children

M James A. BRYANT

Birth	1855/6	Missouri, United States
Census	1860	Post Office Independence, Page 176, Jackson, Missouri, United States
Census	1870	(Township 47, Range 32), Page 101, Jackson, Missouri, United States
Census	1880	ED 38, Page 237, Washington Township, Jackson, Missouri, United States
Will	24 Jul 1883	(Will Written), Volume A, Page 450, Kansas City, Jackson, Missouri, United States
Death	25 Jul 1883	Kansas City, Jackson, Missouri, United States
Probate	28 Jul 1883	(Will Proved), Volume A, Page 450, Kansas City, Jackson, Missouri, United States
Occupation		Farmer (1880)
Burial		

Father Dr. David A. "Dave" BRYANT

Mother Sarah C. SMART

Children

James A. BRYANT (continued)

Spouse	Almina E. SMITH (1861-)
Marriage	20 Dec 1882 (1882K0020460), Jackson, Missouri, United States

Father Dr. David A. "Dave" BRYANT

Birth	18 Oct 1828	Jessamine, Kentucky, United States
Residence	bet 1828 and 1849	Jessamine, Kentucky, United States
Census	1830	
Census	1840	
Census	1850	Page 292, Blue Township, Jackson, Missouri, United States
Graduation	1850	Kentucky School of Medicine, Louisville, Jefferson, Kentucky, United States
Residence	bet 1850 and 1855	Independence, Jackson, Missouri, United States
Residence	bet 1855 and 1858	Prairie Township, Jackson, Missouri, United States
Residence	bet 1858 and 1864	Hickman Mills, Jackson. Missouri, United States
Census	1860	Post Office Independence, Page 176, Jackson, Missouri, United States
Census		Slave Schedules, Page 372, Jackson, Missouri, United States
Tax Lists	Sep 1862	Physician License; Jackson, Missouri, United States
Military	Sep 1863	Civil War Draft Registration; Washington Township, Jackson, Missouri, United States
Tax Lists	Dec 1863	Physician License; Hickman Mills, Jackson, Missouri, United States
Residence	bet 1864 and 1866	Carson City, Lyon, Nevada, United States
Tax Lists	May 1866	Physician License; Hickman Mills, Jackson, Missouri, United States
Religion	1866	Bethlehem Christian Church; Hickman Mills, Jackson. Missouri, United States
Residence	bet 1866 and 1914	Hickman Mills, Jackson. Missouri, United States
Tax Lists	Dec 1866	Physician License; Jackson, Missouri, United States
Census	1870	(Township 47, Range 32), Page 101, Jackson, Missouri, United States
Census		Agricultural Schedules, Township 48, Ranges 32 & 33, Post Office Lee's Summit, Page 53, Jackson, Missouri, United States
Misc		Biography, Illustrated Historical Atlas Map of Jackson Co., Mo. (1877), Page 30
Census	1880	ED 38, Page 237, Washington Township, Jackson, Missouri, United States
Misc		Biography, History of Jackson County, Missouri (1881), Page 978
Census	1900	ED 128, Page 18, Kansas City, Jackson, Missouri, United States
Census	1910	ED 216, Page 246, Washington Township, Jackson, Missouri, United States
Death	23 Jun 1914	Old Age, Arteriosclerosis; Kansas City, Jackson, Missouri, United States
Misc		Obituary, Independence (Mo.) Examiner, 23 Jun 1914, Page 1, Column 6
Misc		Obituary, Kansas City (Mo.) Star, 23 Jun 1914, Page 2, Column 1
Burial	25 Jun 1914	Woodlawn Cemetery, Independence, Jackson, Missouri, United States
Occupation		Physician (1860, 1870, 1880, 1900)
Marriage	28 Oct 1858	(1858I0040077), Jackson, Missouri, United States
Father	George Smith BRYANT (1790-1850)	
Mother	Keziah ARNOLD (1790-1858)	
Other spouse	Sarah E. NEET (1832-1852)	
Marriage	13 Jun 1851	(1851I0030076), Jackson, Missouri, United States
Other spouse	Sarah C. SMART (1834-1857)	
Marriage	31 May 1853	(1853I0030130), Jackson, Missouri, United States

Mother Caroline M. "Callie" EATON

Birth	5 Nov 1835	Illinois, United States
Census	1840	
Census	1850	Page 263, Blue Township, Jackson, Missouri, United States
Census	1860	Post Office Independence, Page 176, Jackson, Missouri, United States
Census	1870	(Township 47, Range 32), Page 101, Jackson, Missouri, United States
Census	1880	ED 38, Page 237, Washington Township, Jackson, Missouri, United States
Census	1900	ED 128, Page 18, Kansas City, Jackson, Missouri, United States
Census	1910	ED 216, Page 246, Washington Township, Jackson, Missouri, United States
Residence	1914	Independence, Jackson, Missouri, United States
Census	1920	ED 221, Page 37, Kansas City, Jackson, Missouri, United States
Death	16 Jan 1922	
Burial		Woodlawn Cemetery, Independence, Jackson, Missouri, United States
Father	John H. EATON (1807-)	
Mother	Rebecca [--?--] (1809-)	

Children

F Anna S. BRYANT

Birth	18 Jul 1862	(or Jun 1864), Hickman Mills, Jackson. Missouri, United States

Father	Dr. David A. "Dave" BRYANT	
Mother	**Caroline M. "Callie" EATON**	
Children		

Anna S. BRYANT (continued)

Census	1870	(Township 47, Range 32), Page 101, Jackson, Missouri, United States
Census	1880	ED 38, Page 237, Washington Township, Jackson, Missouri, United States
Census	1900	ED 144, Page 253, Washington Township, Jackson, Missouri, United States
Census	1910	ED 216, Page 246, Washington Township, Jackson, Missouri, United States
Residence	1914	Kansas City, Jackson, Missouri, United States
Census	1920	ED 221, Page 37, Kansas City, Jackson, Missouri, United States
Death	22 Nov 1952	Hypostatic Pneumonia, Cerebral Hemorrhage, Hypertension; Washington Township, Jackson, Missouri, United States
Burial	24 Nov 1952	Woodlawn Cemetery, Independence, Jackson, Missouri, United States
Spouse	Curtis S. CAMPBELL (1854-1924)	
Marriage	2 Sep 1883	(1883K0030441), Jackson, Missouri, United States

M Frank L. BRYANT

Birth	Jul 1867	Missouri, United States
Census	1870	(Township 47, Range 32), Page 101, Jackson, Missouri, United States
Census	1880	ED 38, Page 237, Washington Township, Jackson, Missouri, United States
Census	1900	ED 128, Page 18, Kansas City, Jackson, Missouri, United States
Census	1910	ED 5, Page 134, Tonopah, Nye, Nevada, United States
Residence	1914	(or Arizona, United States), Nevada, United States
Occupation		Deputy (1900), Bookkeeper Mining Company (1910)
Death		
Burial		
Spouse	Frances E. SMITH (1870-)	
Marriage	15 Jun 1892	(1892K0006892), Jackson, Missouri, United States

Father James M. BRYANT

	Birth	30 Oct 1826	Kentucky, United States
	Census	1830	
	Census	1840	
	Census	1850	Page 292, Blue Township, Jackson, Missouri, United States
	Property	15 Nov 1850	First Known US Land Purchase; (Part Section 35, Township 48, Range 33), Jackson, Missouri, United States
	Census	1860	Post Office Independence, Page 176, Jackson, Missouri, United States
	Census		Slave Schedules, Page 372, Jackson, Missouri, United States
	Census		Agricultural Schedules, Page 11, Post Office Westport, Jackson, Missouri, United States
	Tax Lists	bet Sep 1862 and Dec 1865	Animals Slaughtered for Sale; Independence, Jackson, Missouri, United States
	Tax Lists	Sep 1862	Retail Dealer License; Independence, Jackson, Missouri, United States
	Military	Sep 1863	Civil War Draft Registration; Blue Township, Jackson, Missouri, United States
	Tax Lists	bet Jan 1866 and Jul 1866	Animals Slaughtered for Sale; Independence, Jackson, Missouri, United States
	Religion	21 Oct 1866	Bethlehem Christian Church; Hickman Mills, Jackson. Missouri, United States
	Census	1870	Page 293, Independence, Jackson, Missouri, United States
	Census	1880	ED 6, Page 170, Kansas City, Jackson, Missouri, United States
	Census	1900	ED 70, Page 69, Kansas City, Jackson, Missouri, United States
	Death	5 Apr 1905	
	Misc		"Old Slave Patrol . . . " Kansas City (Mo.) Star, 12 Jan 1908, Sect. 2, P. 5, Cols. 1-2
	Burial		Woodlawn Cemetery, Independence, Jackson, Missouri, United States
	Occupation		Farmer (1850, 1860), Butcher (1870), Live Stock Dealer (1880), Retail Dealer
	Marriage	1852/3	
	Father	George Smith BRYANT (1790-1850)	
	Mother	Keziah ARNOLD (1790-1858)	

Mother Mary Jane VAUGHN

	Birth	28 Feb 1830	Kentucky, United States
	Census	1840	
	Census	1850	
	Census	1860	Post Office Independence, Page 176, Jackson, Missouri, United States
	Census	1870	Page 293, Independence, Jackson, Missouri, United States
	Residence	bet 1876 and 1901	Kansas City, Jackson, Missouri, United States
	Census	1880	ED 6, Page 170, Kansas City, Jackson, Missouri, United States
	Census	1900	ED 70, Page 69, Kansas City, Jackson, Missouri, United States
	Death	13 Jun 1901	Kansas City, Jackson, Missouri, United States
	Burial	14 Jun 1901	Woodlawn Cemetery, Independence, Jackson, Missouri, United States
	Misc		Obituary, Independence (Mo.) Sentinel, 14 Jun 1901, Page 8, Column 4
	Misc		Funeral Notice, Kansas City (Mo.) Star, 14 Jun 1901, Page 11, Column 1
	Father		
	Mother		

Children

M Thomas Edwin BRYANT

	Birth	5 Jun 1853	Independence, Jackson, Missouri, United States
	Census	1860	Post Office Independence, Page 176, Jackson, Missouri, United States
	Census	1870	Page 293, Independence, Jackson, Missouri, United States
	Census	1880	ED 6, Page 170, Kansas City, Jackson, Missouri, United States
	Census	1900	ED 128, Page 22, Kansas City, Jackson, Missouri, United States
	Residence	1901	Kansas City, Jackson, Missouri, United States
	Census	1910	ED 144, Page 45, Kansas City, Jackson, Missouri, United States
	Death	3 Oct 1934	Carcinoma of the Liver; Kansas City, Jackson, Missouri, United States
	Misc		Obituary, Independence (Mo.) Examiner, 04 Oct 1934, Page 1, Column 6
	Burial	5 Oct 1934	Forest Hill Cemetery, Kansas City, Jackson, Missouri, United States
	Occupation		Clerk in Store (1880), Merchant (1900), Book & Stationery Merchant (1910), Proprietor of Book Store
	Religion		Linwood Boulevard Christian Church; Kansas City, Jackson, Missouri, United States
	Spouse	Lucy B. TRICE (1859-1940)	
	Marriage	12 Dec 1883	Saint Joseph, Buchanan, Missouri, United States

Father	**James M. BRYANT**		
Mother	**Mary Jane VAUGHN**		
Children			
M	**John A. BRYANT**		
	Birth	29 Apr 1854	Missouri, United States
	Census	1860	Post Office Independence, Page 176, Jackson, Missouri, United States
	Census	1870	Page 293, Independence, Jackson, Missouri, United States
	Census	1880	ED 6, Page 170, Kansas City, Jackson, Missouri, United States
	Census	1900	ED 126, Page 285, Kansas City, Jackson, Missouri, United States
	Residence	1901	Kansas City, Jackson, Missouri, United States
	Census	1910	ED 166, Page 102, Kansas City, Jackson, Missouri, United States
	Residence	1934	Kansas City, Jackson, Missouri, United States
	Death	19 Dec 1942	Broncho-Pneumonia, Fracture Left Femur (Hip), Senility, Cerebral ARteriosclerosis; State Hospital No. 2, Saint Joseph, Buchanan, Missouri, United States
	Burial		Forest Hill Cemetery, Kansas City, Jackson, Missouri, United States
	Occupation		Bookkeeper (1880), Insurance Agent (1900), Owner Insurance Company (1910)
	Spouse	Elizabeth COCKRILL (1867-1924)	
	Marriage	23 Nov 1887	Tracy, Platte, Missouri, United States
F	**Bessie BRYANT**		
	Birth	10 May 1858	Hickman Mills, Jackson. Missouri, United States
	Census	1860	Post Office Independence, Page 176, Jackson, Missouri, United States
	Census	1870	Page 293, Independence, Jackson, Missouri, United States
	Census	1880	ED 6, Page 170, Kansas City, Jackson, Missouri, United States
	Census	1900	ED 70, Page 69, Kansas City, Jackson, Missouri, United States
	Residence	1901	Kansas City, Jackson, Missouri, United States
	Census	1910	ED 166, Page 101, Kansas City, Jackson, Missouri, United States
	Residence	1934	Kansas City, Jackson, Missouri, United States
	Death	8 Nov 1948	Cardiac Failure (Dilatation of Heart), Senility; Kansas City, Jackson, Missouri, United States
	Misc		Obituary, Independence (Mo.) Examiner, 09 Nov 1948, Page 2, Column 3
	Burial	10 Nov 1948	Woodlawn Cemetery, Independence, Jackson, Missouri, United States
	Marriage		
F	**Olive G. "Ollie" BRYANT**		
	Birth	15 Sep 1860	Jackson, Missouri, United States
	Census	1870	Page 293, Independence, Jackson, Missouri, United States
	Census	1880	ED 6, Page 170, Kansas City, Jackson, Missouri, United States
	Census	1900	ED 27, Page 259, Salem, Columbiana, Ohio, United States
	Residence	1901	Salem, Marion, Illinois, United States
	Census	1910	ED 67, Page 237, Racine, Racine, Wisconsin, United States
	Death	27 Jun 1929	
	Burial		
	Spouse	William Clark HARE (1857-)	
	Marriage	11 Jan 1882	(1882K0010373), Jackson, Missouri, United States
M	**Charles Percival J. "Charlie" BRYANT**		
	Birth	26 Feb 1867	Independence, Jackson, Missouri, United States
	Census	1870	Page 293, Independence, Jackson, Missouri, United States
	Census	1880	ED 6, Page 170, Kansas City, Jackson, Missouri, United States
	Census	1900	ED 70, Page 69, Kansas City, Jackson, Missouri, United States
	Residence	1901	Kansas City, Jackson, Missouri, United States
	Census	1910	ED 166, Page 101, Kansas City, Jackson, Missouri, United States
	Residence	1934	Kansas City, Jackson, Missouri, United States
	Burial		Forest Hill Cemetery, Kansas City, Jackson, Missouri, United States
	Death	31 Dec 1948	
	Occupation		Auditor (Smelter) (1900), President General Supply Company (1910)
	Spouse	Frances LeMoine SLOAN (1873-1932)	
	Marriage	1900/1	

Father Dr. John W. BRYANT

Birth	30 Nov 1816	Near Lancaster, Garrard, Kentucky, United States
Residence	?-1850	Nicholasville, Jessamine, Kentucky, United States
Graduation	1837	MD, Transylvania University
Residence	bet 1839 and 1850	Jessamine, Kentucky, United States
Census	1840	
Census	1850	Division 1, Page 32, Jessamine, Kentucky, United States
Residence	bet 1850 and 1902	Independence, Jackson, Missouri, United States
Property	25 Nov 1850	First Known US Land Purchase; Part Section 7, Township 47, Range 32), Jackson, Missouri, United States
Census	1860	Page 255, Independence, Jackson, Missouri, United States
Census		Slave Schedules, Page 364, Independence, Jackson, Missouri, United States
Census		Agricultural Schedules, Page 1, Blue Township, Jackson, Missouri, United States
Misc	19 Apr 1862	Union Provost Marshals' File of Papers Relating to Two or More Civilians, M416, Roll 5, No. 1075
Tax Lists	Sep 1862	Physician License; Kansas City, Jackson, Missouri, United States
Misc	abt 1863	Union Provost Marshals' File of Papers . . . Two or More Civilians, M416, Roll 81, No. 22,106
Tax Lists	May 1866	Physician License, Carriage, Gold Watch, and Pianoforte; Independence, Jackson, Missouri, United States
Census	1870	Page 294, Independence, Jackson, Missouri, United States
Misc		Biography and Portrait, US Biographical Dictionary and Portrait Gallery . . . Missouri Volume (1878), Pages 810-811
Census	1880	ED 24, Page 40, Independence, Jackson, Missouri, United States
Census	1900	ED 7, Page 100, Independence, Jackson, Missouri, United States
Death	16 Aug 1902	Independence, Jackson, Missouri, United States
Misc		Obituary, Kansas City (Mo.) Star, 16 Aug 1907, Page 2, Column 3
Burial	17 Aug 1902	Woodlawn Cemetery, Independence, Jackson, Missouri, United States
Misc		Obituary, Independence (Mo.) Jackson Examiner, 22 Aug 1902, Page 2, Columns 3-4
Misc		Obituary, Independence (Mo.) Sentinel, 23 Aug 1902, Page 1, Column 4
Misc		"George S. Bryant's School Days," Jackson County Pioneers (1975), Pages 409-411
Occupation		Physician (1850, 1860, 1870), Doctor (1880)
Religion		Christian Church; Independence, Jackson, Missouri, United States
Degree		Medical Degree; Transylvania University, Lexington, Fayette, Kentucky, United States
Marriage	20 Nov 1838	Kentucky, United States
Father	George Smith BRYANT (1790-1850)	
Mother	Keziah ARNOLD (1790-1858)	

Mother Martha Ann VAUGHN

Birth	3 Jan 1815	Richmond, Madison, Kentucky, United States
Census	1840	
Residence	1841–1892	Independence, Jackson, Missouri, United States
Census	1850	Division 1, Page 32, Jessamine, Kentucky, United States
Census	1860	Page 255, Independence, Jackson, Missouri, United States
Census	1870	Page 294, Independence, Jackson, Missouri, United States
Census	1880	ED 24, Page 40, Independence, Jackson, Missouri, United States
Death	5 Sep 1892	Independence, Jackson, Missouri, United States
Misc		Obituary, Kansas City (Mo.) Star, 05 Sep 1892, Page 2, Column 4
Burial		Woodlawn Cemetery, Independence, Jackson, Missouri, United States
Father		
Mother		

Children

M Thomas Vaughn BRYANT

Birth	16 Jul 1839	Jessamine, Kentucky, United States
Census	1840	
Census	1850	Division 1, Page 32, Jessamine, Kentucky, United States
Census	1860	Page 255, Independence, Jackson, Missouri, United States
Census	1870	Page 305, Kansas City, Jackson, Missouri, United States
Census	1880	ED 16, Page 430, Kansas City, Jackson, Missouri, United States
Census	1900	ED 7, Page 100, Independence, Jackson, Missouri, United States

Father Dr. John W. BRYANT

Mother Martha Ann VAUGHN

Children

Thomas Vaughn BRYANT (continued)

Residence	1902	Independence, Jackson, Missouri, United States
Death	24 Jul 1906	Independence, Jackson, Missouri, United States
Misc		Obituary, Independence (Mo.) Examiner, 25 Jul 1906, Page 1, Column 1
Burial		Woodlawn Cemetery, Independence, Jackson, Missouri, United States
Probate	17 Aug 1906	(Administrator's Bond), Volume C, Page 253, Independence, Jackson, Missouri, United States
Occupation		Lawyer (1870), Attorney at Law (1880), State Senator
Spouse	Livia Stuart HATCH (1850-)	
Marriage	27 Apr 1886	New Orleans, Orleans, Louisiana, United States

M Prof. George S. BRYANT

Birth	2 Apr 1841	Nicholasville, Jessamine, Kentucky, United States
Census	1850	Division 1, Page 32, Jessamine, Kentucky, United States
Census	1860	Page 255, Independence, Jackson, Missouri, United States
Military		Private, Company H, 77th Regiment Enrolled Missouri Militia
Census	1870	Page 294, Independence, Jackson, Missouri, United States
Residence	bet 1871 and 1883	President of Christian College; Columbia, Boone, Missouri, United States
Census	1880	ED 16, Page 163, Columbia, Boone, Missouri, United States
Residence	bet 1883 and 1901	President of Woodland College; Independence, Jackson, Missouri, United States
Census	1900	ED 5, Page 69, Independence, Jackson, Missouri, United States
Occupation	bet 1901 and 1915	Principal of Independence High School; Independence, Jackson, Missouri, United States
Residence	1902	Independence, Jackson, Missouri, United States
Death	2 Dec 1916	Arteriosclerosis with High Blood Pressure; Independence, Jackson, Missouri, United States
Misc		Obituary, Kansas City (Mo.) Star, 3 Dec 1916, Page 2, Column 4
Burial	4 Dec 1916	Mount Washington Cemetery, Independence, Jackson, Missouri, United States
Misc		"George S. Bryant's School Days," Jackson County Pioneers (1975), Pages 409-411
Misc		Photo, Jackson County Pioneers (1975), Page 414
Occupation		Teacher (1870), School Teacher (1880), Teacher (1900), Principal of Independence, MO, High School (1901-1915)
Graduation		Bethany College, Bethany, Brooke, West Virginia, United States
Religion		Christian Church; Independence, Jackson, Missouri, United States
Occupation		Principal of Woodlawn College; Independence, Jackson, Missouri, United States
Occupation		President; Christian Female College, Columbia, Boone, Missouri, United States
Spouse	Margaret FERGUSON (1852-1919)	
Marriage	Jul 1871	Columbia, Boone, Missouri, United States

M Dr. John W. BRYANT Jr.

Birth	19 Mar 1843	Jessamine, Kentucky, United States
Census	1850	Division 1, Page 32, Jessamine, Kentucky, United States
Census	1860	Page 255, Independence, Jackson, Missouri, United States
Graduation	1864	Saint Louis Medical College, Saint Louis, Saint Louis, Missouri, United States
Graduation	1866	Jefferson Medical College, Philadelphia, Philadelphia, Pennsylvania, United States
Census	1870	Page 294, Independence, Jackson, Missouri, United States
Census	1880	ED 24, Page 39, Independence, Jackson, Missouri, United States
Census	1900	ED 7, Page 110, Independence, Jackson, Missouri, United States
Residence	1902	Independence, Jackson, Missouri, United States
Death	16 Jul 1921	Berkeley, Alameda, California, United States
Misc		Obituary, Independence (Mo.) Examiner, 16 Jul 1921, Page 1, Column 1
Burial		Woodlawn Cemetery, Independence, Jackson, Missouri, United States
Misc		Biography, Jackson County Pioneers (1975), Pages 478-479
Religion		Christian Church; Independence, Jackson, Missouri, United States
Occupation		Physician (1870), Doctor (1880), Doctor Medicine (1900)
Spouse	Harriet Matilda SMART (1849-1920)	
Marriage	11 Oct 1866	(1866I0050219), Kansas City, Jackson, Missouri, United States

M William Lawrence BRYANT

Birth	3 Apr 1845	Nicholasville, Jessamine, Kentucky, United States

Father	Dr. John W. BRYANT
Mother	Martha Ann VAUGHN
Children	

William Lawrence BRYANT (continued)

Census	1850	Division 1, Page 32, Jessamine, Kentucky, United States
Census	1860	Page 255, Independence, Jackson, Missouri, United States
Census	1870	Page 294, Independence, Jackson, Missouri, United States
Census	1880	ED 24, Page 40, Independence, Jackson, Missouri, United States
Census	1900	ED 7, Page 100, Independence, Jackson, Missouri, United States
Residence	1902	Independence, Jackson, Missouri, United States
Death	22 Jan 1918	Angina Pectoris; Independence, Jackson, Missouri, United States
Misc		Obituary, Independence (Mo.) Examiner, 23 Jan 1918, Page 1, Column 3
Misc		Obituary, Kansas City (Mo.) Times, 23 Jan 1918, Page 8, Column 4
Burial	24 Jan 1918	Woodlawn Cemetery, Independence, Jackson, Missouri, United States
Occupation		Farmer (1870), Druggist (1880), Capitalist (1900), Grocer, Deputy Sheriff, Civil Engineer
Religion		First Christian Church; Independence, Jackson, Missouri, United States
Spouse		Amanda Ella HUGHES (1846-1916)
Marriage	9 May 1871	(1871I0060284), Jackson, Missouri, United States

M Oliver P. V. BRYANT

Birth	23 Nov 1848	Jessamine, Kentucky, United States
Census	1850	Division 1, Page 32, Jessamine, Kentucky, United States
Census	1860	Page 255, Independence, Jackson, Missouri, United States
Census	1870	Page 294, Independence, Jackson, Missouri, United States
Census	1880	ED 24, Page 40, Independence, Jackson, Missouri, United States
Census	1900	ED 7, Page 100, Independence, Jackson, Missouri, United States
Residence	1902	Independence, Jackson, Missouri, United States
Census	1910	ED 11, Page 158, Independence, Jackson, Missouri, United States
Death	2 May 1914	Chronic Interstitial Myocarditis with Sudden Failure, Obstruction of the Sigmoid; Independence, Jackson, Missouri, United States
Misc		Obituary, Kansas City (Mo.) Star, 03 May 1914, Page 5, Column 3
Burial	4 May 1914	Woodlawn Cemetery, Independence, Jackson, Missouri, United States
Misc		Obituary, Independence (Mo.) Examiner, 04 May 1914, Page 1, Column 1
Occupation		Lawyer (1900), Attorney Law (1910)
Spouse		Lydia G. [--?--] (1866-)
Marriage	1894/5	
Spouse		Mollie ROBERTS (1867-)
Marriage		

F Martha A. "Mattie" BRYANT

Birth	4 Sep 1855	Missouri, United States
Census	1860	Page 255, Independence, Jackson, Missouri, United States
Census	1870	Page 294, Independence, Jackson, Missouri, United States
Census	1880	ED 24, Page 40, Independence, Jackson, Missouri, United States
Death	16 May 1888	Blue Township, Jackson, Missouri, United States
Burial		Woodlawn Cemetery, Independence, Jackson, Missouri, United States
Spouse		William Lyman STOCKING (1855-1931)
Marriage	21 Oct 1880	(1880I0080168), Jackson, Missouri, United States

Father George Washington BUCHANAN

Birth	23 Apr 1814	Smyth, Virginia, United States
Census	1820	
Census	1830	
Graduation	1835	Greenville, Davidson, Tennessee, United States
Residence	bet 1838 and 1862	Independence, Jackson, Missouri, United States
Census	1840	
Misc	bet 1844 and 1848	County Surveyor; Jackson, Missouri, United States
Occupation	1846/7	Postmaster; Independence, Jackson, Missouri, United States
Property	3 Feb 1846	First Known Purchase, Part Sects. 2 & 24, T50, R31; Volume L, Page 195, Independence, Jackson, Missouri, United States
Property	3 Feb 1846	First Known Purchase, Part Sect. 25, T50, R22; Volume L, Page 195, Independence, Jackson, Missouri, United States
Occupation	bet 1848 and 1852	Sheriff; Jackson, Missouri, United States
Census	1850	Page 261, Blue Township, Jackson, Missouri, United States
Census		Slave Schedules, Frame 105, Blue Township, Jackson, Missouri, United States
Census	1860	Page 289, Independence, Jackson, Missouri, United States
Census		Slave Schedules, Page 366, Independence, Jackson, Missouri, United States
Census		Agricultural Schedules, Page 1, Blue Township, Jackson, Missouri, United States
Misc	19 Apr 1862	Union Provost Marshals' File of Papers Relating to Two or More Civilians, M416, Roll 5, No. 1075
Tax Lists	Sep 1862	Lawyer License; Independence, Jackson, Missouri, United States
Residence	bet 1863 and 1865	Saint Louis, Saint Louis, Missouri, United States
Residence	bet 1865 and 1901	Independence, Jackson, Missouri, United States
Census	1870	Page 289, Independence, Jackson, Missouri, United States
Misc	1871	Trustee, Original Board of Trustees, Independence Female College; Independence, Jackson, Missouri, United States
Census	1880	ED 24, Page 39, Independence, Jackson, Missouri, United States
Census	1900	ED 8, Page 114, Independence, Jackson, Missouri, United States
Misc		Biography, Encyclopedia of the History of Missouri (1901)
Death	25 Sep 1901	Independence, Jackson, Missouri, United States
Misc		Obituary, Kansas City (Mo.) Star, 25 Sep 1901, Page 2, Column 4
Misc		Obituary, Independence (Mo.) Jackson Examiner, 27 Sep 1901, Page 3, Columns 1-2
Burial	28 Sep 1901	Woodlawn Cemetery, Independence, Jackson, Missouri, United States
Misc		Photograph, Jackson County Historical Society Journal, Winter 1981, Page 6
Occupation		Sheriff (1850), Lawyer (1860, 1880, 1900), Attorney at Law (1870)
Religion		First Presbyterian Church; Independence, Jackson, Missouri, United States
Marriage	20 Nov 1838	Smyth, Virginia, United States
Father	George BUCHANAN (1774-1842)	
Mother	Nancy Agnes LAMIE (1774-1861)	
Other spouse	Eliza Jane GALBRAITH (1823-1914)	
Marriage	23 Nov 1849	(1849I0020213), Jackson, Missouri, United States

Mother Louise Eliza Jane BUCHANAN

Birth	abt Dec 1817	
Death	23 Jun 1839	Virginia, United States
Burial		Rural Retreat, Wythe, Virginia, United States
Father		
Mother		

Children

Father George Washington BUCHANAN

Birth	23 Apr 1814	Smyth, Virginia, United States
Census	1820	
Census	1830	
Graduation	1835	Greenville, Davidson, Tennessee, United States
Residence	bet 1838 and 1862	Independence, Jackson, Missouri, United States
Census	1840	
Misc	bet 1844 and 1848	County Surveyor; Jackson, Missouri, United States
Occupation	1846/7	Postmaster; Independence, Jackson, Missouri, United States
Property	3 Feb 1846	First Known Purchase, Part Sects. 2 & 24, T50, R31; Volume L, Page 195, Independence, Jackson, Missouri, United States
Property	3 Feb 1846	First Known Purchase, Part Sect. 25, T50, R22; Volume L, Page 195, Independence, Jackson, Missouri, United States
Occupation	bet 1848 and 1852	Sheriff; Jackson, Missouri, United States
Census	1850	Page 261, Blue Township, Jackson, Missouri, United States
Census		Slave Schedules, Frame 105, Blue Township, Jackson, Missouri, United States
Census	1860	Page 289, Independence, Jackson, Missouri, United States
Census		Slave Schedules, Page 366, Independence, Jackson, Missouri, United States
Census		Agricultural Schedules, Page 1, Blue Township, Jackson, Missouri, United States
Misc	19 Apr 1862	Union Provost Marshals' File of Papers Relating to Two or More Civilians, M416, Roll 5, No. 1075
Tax Lists	Sep 1862	Lawyer License; Independence, Jackson, Missouri, United States
Residence	bet 1863 and 1865	Saint Louis, Saint Louis, Missouri, United States
Residence	bet 1865 and 1901	Independence, Jackson, Missouri, United States
Census	1870	Page 289, Independence, Jackson, Missouri, United States
Misc	1871	Trustee, Original Board of Trustees, Independence Female College; Independence, Jackson, Missouri, United States
Census	1880	ED 24, Page 39, Independence, Jackson, Missouri, United States
Census	1900	ED 8, Page 114, Independence, Jackson, Missouri, United States
Misc		Biography, Encyclopedia of the History of Missouri (1901)
Death	25 Sep 1901	Independence, Jackson, Missouri, United States
Misc		Obituary, Kansas City (Mo.) Star, 25 Sep 1901, Page 2, Column 4
Misc		Obituary, Independence (Mo.) Jackson Examiner, 27 Sep 1901, Page 3, Columns 1-2
Burial	28 Sep 1901	Woodlawn Cemetery, Independence, Jackson, Missouri, United States
Misc		Photograph, Jackson County Historical Society Journal, Winter 1981, Page 6
Occupation		Sheriff (1850), Lawyer (1860, 1880, 1900), Attorney at Law (1870)
Religion		First Presbyterian Church; Independence, Jackson, Missouri, United States
Marriage	23 Nov 1849	(1849I0020213), Jackson, Missouri, United States
Father		George BUCHANAN (1774-1842)
Mother		Nancy Agnes LAMIE (1774-1861)
Other spouse		Louise Eliza Jane BUCHANAN (1817-1839)
Marriage	20 Nov 1838	Smyth, Virginia, United States

Mother Eliza Jane GALBRAITH

Birth	20 Apr 1823	Rockbridge, Virginia, United States
Census	1850	Page 261, Blue Township, Jackson, Missouri, United States
Census	1860	Page 289, Independence, Jackson, Missouri, United States
Census	1870	Page 289, Independence, Jackson, Missouri, United States
Census	1880	ED 24, Page 39, Independence, Jackson, Missouri, United States
Census	1900	ED 8, Page 114, Independence, Jackson, Missouri, United States
Census	1910	ED 12, Page 168, Independence, Jackson, Missouri, United States
Misc		"Her Ninetieth Birthday," Independence (Mo.) Examiner, 01 May 1913, Page 1, Columns 5-6
Death	22 Oct 1914	Broncho-Pneumonia, Senility; Independence, Jackson, Missouri, United States
Misc		Obituary, Independence (Mo.) Examiner, 23 Oct 1914, Page 1, Column 1
Burial	25 Oct 1914	Woodlawn Cemetery, Independence, Jackson, Missouri, United States
Religion		First Presbyterian Church; Independence, Jackson, Missouri, United States
Occupation		Own Income (1910)
Father		John GALBRAITH (-)
Mother		Katharine PEERS (-)

Children

Father	**George Washington BUCHANAN**	
Mother	**Eliza Jane GALBRAITH**	
Children		

F	**Katherine Agnes "Kate" BUCHANAN**	
Birth	10 Oct 1850	Missouri, United States
Census	1860	Page 289, Independence, Jackson, Missouri, United States
Census	1870	Page 290, Independence, Jackson, Missouri, United States
Census	1880	ED 24, Page 39, Independence, Jackson, Missouri, United States
Census	1900	ED 8, Page 114, Independence, Jackson, Missouri, United States
Residence	1901	Independence, Jackson, Missouri, United States
Census	1910	ED 12, Page 168, Independence, Jackson, Missouri, United States
Residence	1912	Independence, Jackson, Missouri, United States
Residence	1914	Independence, Jackson, Missouri, United States
Census	1920	
Residence	1924	Independence, Jackson, Missouri, United States
Death	28 Feb 1929	Chronic Myocarditis, Senility, and Psychosis; State Hospital No. 2, Saint Joseph, Buchanan, Missouri, United States
Misc		Obituary, Independence (Mo.) Examiner, 01 Mar 1929, Page 1, Column 5
Burial	2 Mar 1929	Woodlawn Cemetery, Independence, Jackson, Missouri, United States
Religion		First Presbyterian Church; Independence, Jackson, Missouri, United States
Occupation		Own Income (1910), Public School Teacher
Marriage		

M	**James Fulton BUCHANAN**	
Birth	3 Sep 1851	(or 3 Sep 1852), Independence, Jackson, Missouri, United States
Census	1860	Page 289, Independence, Jackson, Missouri, United States
Census	1870	Page 290, Independence, Jackson, Missouri, United States
Census	1880	ED 26, Page 75, Blue Township, Jackson, Missouri, United States
Census	1900	ED 6, Page 86, Independence, Jackson, Missouri, United States
Residence	1901	Independence, Jackson, Missouri, United States
Census	1910	ED 9, Page 129, Independence, Jackson, Missouri, United States
Residence	1912	Independence, Jackson, Missouri, United States
Residence	1914	Independence, Jackson, Missouri, United States
Census	1920	ED 9, Page 196, Independence, Jackson, Missouri, United States
Death	19 Jan 1924	Streptococcus Laryngitis, Septic Pericarditis; Independence, Jackson, Missouri, United States
Misc		Obituary, Independence (Mo.) Examiner, 19 Jan 1924, Page 1, Column 7
Burial	21 Jan 1924	Woodlawn Cemetery, Independence, Jackson, Missouri, United States
Occupation		Judge of Independence Police Court, Justice of the Peace of Blue Twp.
Occupation		Farmer (1880), Real Estate Agent (1900), Abstractor of Deeds (1910), Abstractor Real Estate (1920), Proprietor of Buchanan Abstract Company
Spouse		Ella Shanks WILMOTT (1860-1942)
Marriage	25 Oct 1881	Cass, Missouri, United States

F	**Margaretta W. BUCHANAN**	
Birth	abt 24 Oct 1854	
Death	11 Feb 1857	
Burial		Woodlawn Cemetery, Independence, Jackson, Missouri, United States
Marriage		

F	**Mary Scott "Scottie" BUCHANAN**	
Birth	25 Dec 1856	Independence, Jackson, Missouri, United States
Census	1860	Page 289, Independence, Jackson, Missouri, United States
Census	1870	Page 290, Independence, Jackson, Missouri, United States
Census	1880	ED 24, Page 39, Independence, Jackson, Missouri, United States
Residence	1901	Independence, Jackson, Missouri, United States
Residence	1912	Independence, Jackson, Missouri, United States
Residence	1924	Independence, Jackson, Missouri, United States
Death	17 Feb 1927	Mitral Regurgitation with Failing Compensation and Auricular Fibrilation . . .; Independence, Jackson, Missouri, United States
Burial	18 Feb 1927	Woodlawn Cemetery, Independence, Jackson, Missouri, United States

Father George Washington BUCHANAN		
Mother Eliza Jane GALBRAITH		
Children		
Mary Scott "Scottie" BUCHANAN (continued)		
Misc		Obituary, Independence (Mo.) Examiner, 18 Feb 1927, Page 1, Column 7
Spouse	Allen L. MCCOY (1854-1914)	
Marriage	14 Sep 1882	(1882I0010221), Jackson, Missouri, United States
M George V. BUCHANAN		
Birth	1859/60	Missouri, United States
Census	1860	Page 289, Independence, Jackson, Missouri, United States
Census	1870	Page 290, Independence, Jackson, Missouri, United States
Census	1880	ED 26, Page 75, Blue Township, Jackson, Missouri, United States
Census	1900	
Residence	1901	California, United States
Census	1910	ED 27, Page 126, Monrovia, Los Angeles, California, United States
Residence	1912	San Diego, San Diego, California, United States
Residence	1914	San Diego, San Diego, California, United States
Residence	1924	Near Los Angeles, Los Angeles, California, United States
Occupation		Teamster Street Work (1910)
Death		
Burial		
Spouse	Frederica COMBS (1866-1959)	
Marriage	7 Oct 1885	(1885I0020111), Jackson, Missouri, United States

Father John O. BUCHANAN

Birth	3 Nov 1811	Niagara, New York, United States
Census	1820	
Census	1830	(Samuel Buchannon Family), Page 393, Lockport, Niagara, New York, United States
Census	1840	(Samuel Buchannan Family), Page 63, Lockport, Niagara, New York, United States
Census	1840	
Property	1 Apr 1842	First Known Purchase, 175 Acres in Sects. 16, 17 & 21, T49, R30; Volume H, Page 499, Jackson, Missouri, United States
Census	1850	Page 288, Blue Township, Jackson, Missouri, United States
Census		Slave Schedules, Frame 116, Blue Township, Jackson, Missouri, United States
Census	1860	Page 335, Blue Township, Jackson, Missouri, United States
Census		Slave Schedules, Page 355, Blue Township, Jackson, Missouri, United States
Misc	19 Apr 1862	Union Provost Marshals' File of Papers Relating to Two or More Civilians, M416, Roll 5, No. 1075
Military		Private, District of the Border Six Months Militia
Tax Lists	Dec 1863	Retail Dealer License; Independence, Jackson, Missouri, United States
Census	1870	Page 618, Oxford Township, Johnson, Kansas, United States
Census	1875	Page 38, Family 264, Oxford Township, Johnson, Kansas, United States
Death	17 Aug 1875	Johnson, Kansas, United States
Burial		Tomahawk Cemetery, Johnson, Kansas, United States
Misc		"George S. Bryant's School Days," Jackson County Pioneers (1975), Pages 409-411
Occupation		Principal of Independence Academy (1850), Real Estate Dealer (1860), Farmer (1870), Retail Dealer
Marriage		
Father	Samuel BUCHANAN (1777-1857)	
Mother	Margaret TROTTER (1782-1862)	

Mother Ann A. "Annie" [--?--]

Birth	1824/5	Kentucky, United States
Census	1850	Page 288, Blue Township, Jackson, Missouri, United States
Census	1860	Page 335, Blue Township, Jackson, Missouri, United States
Census	1870	Page 618, Oxford Township, Johnson, Kansas, United States
Census	1875	Page 38, Family 264, Oxford Township, Johnson, Kansas, United States
Census	1880	ED 100, Page 135, Oxford Township, Johnson, Kansas, United States
Census	1885	Page 10, Family 5, Crawford Township, Crawford, Kansas, United States
Census	1895	Page 1, Family 1, Lincoln Township, Crawford, Kansas, United States
Census	1900	
Burial		Tomahawk Cemetery, Johnson, Kansas, United States
Death		
Father		
Mother		

Children

F Martha M. "Mattie" BUCHANAN

Birth	May 1847	(or 1846), Jackson, Missouri, United States
Census	1850	Page 288, Blue Township, Jackson, Missouri, United States
Census	1860	Page 335, Blue Township, Jackson, Missouri, United States
Census	1875	Page 38, Family 264, Oxford Township, Johnson, Kansas, United States
Census	1880	ED 100, Page 135, Oxford Township, Johnson, Kansas, United States
Census	1885	Page 10, Family 5, Crawford Township, Crawford, Kansas, United States
Census	1895	Page 1, Family 1, Lincoln Township, Crawford, Kansas, United States
Census	1900	ED 30, Page 14, Drywood Township, Bourbon, Kansas, United States
Census	1905	Page 39, Family 32, Drywood Township, Bourbon, Kansas, United States
Census	1910	ED 36, Page 9, Drywood Township, Bourbon, Kansas, United States
Death	1919	
Burial		Pleasant Valley Cemetery, Arcadia, Crawford, Kansas, United States
Occupation		Farmer (1905), Farmer General Farm (1910)
Spouse	George W. RIDGE (1842-1897)	
Marriage	1 Oct 1868	Volume B, Page 107, Johnson, Kansas, United States

Father Joseph BUTCHER

Birth	1819/20	England
Census	1850	
Census	1860	
Tax Lists	Sep 1862	Retail Dealer License; Kansas City, Jackson, Missouri, United States
Tax Lists	bet SepDec 1862 and Apr 1863	Animals Slaughtered for Sale; Kansas City, Jackson, Missouri, United States
Tax Lists	bet May 1863 and Dec 1863	Animals Slaughtered for Sale; "Butcher & Ackerman", Kansas City, Jackson, Missouri, United States
Tax Lists	bet May 1865 and Jul 1865	Animals Slaughtered for Sale; "Butcher & Raub", Kansas City, Jackson, Missouri, United States
Tax Lists	bet Jul 1865 and Aug 1865	Animals Slaughtered for Sale; "Butcher & Bartlett", Kansas City, Jackson, Missouri, United States
Tax Lists	bet Sep 1865 and Jan 1866	Animals Slaughtered for Sale; "Butcher & Raub", Kansas City, Jackson, Missouri, United States
Tax Lists	bet Feb 1866 and Apr 1866	Animals Slaughtered for Sale; Kansas City, Jackson, Missouri, United States
Tax Lists	bet May 1866 and Jul 1866	Animals Slaughtered for Sale; "Butcher, Brooks & Company", Kansas City, Jackson, Missouri, United States
Census	1870	(Township 47, Range 33), Page 113, Jackson, Missouri, United States
Occupation		Farmer (1870), Butcher
Death		
Burial		
Marriage	24 Oct 1869	(1869I0060128), Jackson, Missouri, United States
Father		
Mother		

Mother Rhoda Jane DAVIS

Birth	11 Feb 1842	Indiana, United States
Census	1850	Page 405, Henry Township, Fulton, Indiana, United States
Census	1860	Page 687, Meredosia Township, Morgan, Illinois, United States
Census	1870	(Township 47, Range 33), Page 113, Jackson, Missouri, United States
Census	1880	ED 38, Page 241, Washington Township, Jackson, Missouri, United States
Census	1900	ED 144, Page 243, Washington Township, Jackson, Missouri, United States
Census	1910	ED 216, Page 245, Washington Township, Jackson, Missouri, United States
Census	1920	ED 470, Page 167, Saint Louis (city), Missouri, United States
Death	8 Jul 1924	Chronic Myocarditis; Saint Louis (city), Missouri, United States
Burial	10 Jul 1924	Saint Matthew Cemetery, Saint Louis (city), Missouri, United States
Occupation		Farmer (1900)
Father	James R. DAVIS (1810-)	
Mother	Isabel CLIFTON (1819-1909)	
Other spouse	Christopher Columbus Lum BRYANT (1835-1867)	
Marriage		

Children

M Nathaniel Joseph BUTCHER

Birth	14 Sep 1871	(or 14 Sep 1870), Missouri, United States
Census	1880	ED 38, Page 241, Washington Township, Jackson, Missouri, United States
Census	1900	ED 144, Page 243, Washington Township, Jackson, Missouri, United States
Census	1910	ED 216, Page 245, Washington Township, Jackson, Missouri, United States
Census	1920	ED 284, Page 172, Washington Township, Jackson, Missouri, United States
Death	9 Feb 1924	Lobar Pneumonia; Washington Township, Jackson, Missouri, United States
Burial	12 Feb 1924	Lee's Summit Historical Cemetery, Lee's Summit, Jackson, Missouri, United States
Occupation		Farm Laborer (1900), Farmer General (1910), Farmer General Farm (1920)
Spouse	Ivy Scott GREENE (1882-1967)	
Marriage	10 Oct 1914	Cass, Missouri, United States

F Eva Lena BUTCHER

Birth	2 Oct 1872	(or Oct 1869), Jackson, Missouri, United States
Census	1880	ED 38, Page 241, Washington Township, Jackson, Missouri, United States
Census	1900	ED 144, Page 243, Washington Township, Jackson, Missouri, United States
Census	1910	ED 209, Page 138, Saint Louis (city), Missouri, United States

Father Joseph BUTCHER

Mother Rhoda Jane DAVIS

Children

Eva Lena BUTCHER (continued)

Census	1920	ED 470, Page 167, Saint Louis (city), Missouri, United States
Census	1930	ED 7, Page 182, Lebanon, Laclede, Missouri, United States
Death	8 May 1958	Acute Myocarditis, Far Advanced Arteriosclerosis, Cystitis; Belleview, Iron, Missouri, United States
Burial	11 May 1958	Arcadia Valley Memorial Park, Ironton, Iron, Missouri, United States
Spouse	Charles E. WILSON (1865-1933)	
Marriage		

Father Henry Harrison CAMP

Birth	9 Oct 1838	Beaver, Pennsylvania, United States
Census	1840	(Michal Camp Family), Page 110, Beaver, Beaver, Pennsylvania, United States
Census	1850	Page 53, Beaver, Beaver, Pennsylvania, United States
Census	1860	Page 81, Kansas City, Jackson, Missouri, United States
Tax Lists	Sep 1862	Retail Liquor Dealer License; Kansas City, Jackson, Missouri, United States
Military		Corporal, Company A, 77th Regiment Enrolled Missouri Militia
Misc	22 Nov 1863	Union Provost Marshals' File of Papers Relating to Individual Civilians, M345, Roll 44
Census	1870	Page 163, Ohio Township, Beaver, Pennsylvania, United States
Census	1880	ED 185, Page 180, Glasgow, Beaver, Pennsylvania, United States
Census	1900	ED 32, Page 54, Glasgow, Beaver, Pennsylvania, United States
Census	1910	ED 27, Page 74, Glasgow, Beaver, Pennsylvania, United States
Death	1 Jun 1914	Hemorrhage of Brain, Neurasthenia; Glasgow, Beaver, Pennsylvania, United States
Burial	3 Jun 1914	Georgetown Cemetery, Georgetown, Beaver, Pennsylvania, United States
Occupation		Shoemaker (1860, 1870, 1880), Merchant (1900), Retired Merchant Grocery Store (1910)
Occupation		Retail Liquor Dealer
Marriage	11 Feb 1861	(1861I0050032), Independence, Jackson, Missouri, United States
Father	Johann Georg Michael CAMP/KAEMPF (1803-1879)	
Mother	Anna Barbara SCHLESSMANN (1804-1871)	

Mother Helen R. GILCHRIST

Birth	Aug 1842	Ireland
Census	1850	Page 279, Independence, Jackson, Missouri, United States
Census	1860	Page 276, Independence, Jackson, Missouri, United States
Census	1870	Page 163, Ohio Township, Beaver, Pennsylvania, United States
Census	1880	ED 185, Page 180, Glasgow, Beaver, Pennsylvania, United States
Census	1900	ED 32, Page 54, Glasgow, Beaver, Pennsylvania, United States
Census	1910	ED 27, Page 74, Glasgow, Beaver, Pennsylvania, United States
Death	1918	
Burial		Georgetown Cemetery, Georgetown, Beaver, Pennsylvania, United States
Father	Owen GILCHRIST (1814-1870)	
Mother	Ellen [--?--] (1814-1884)	

Children

M James P. CAMP

Birth	1863	Nebraska, United States
Census	1870	Page 163, Ohio Township, Beaver, Pennsylvania, United States
Census	1880	ED 185, Page 180, Glasgow, Beaver, Pennsylvania, United States
Death	1884	
Burial		Georgetown Cemetery, Georgetown, Beaver, Pennsylvania, United States
Marriage		

F Anna M. "Annie" CAMP

Birth	Aug 1867	Pennsylvania, United States
Census	1870	Page 163, Ohio Township, Beaver, Pennsylvania, United States
Census	1880	ED 185, Page 180, Glasgow, Beaver, Pennsylvania, United States
Census	1900	ED 20, Page 124, East Liverpool, Columbiana, Ohio, United States
Census	1910	ED 17, Page 8, Liverpool Township, Columbiana, Ohio, United States
Census	1920	ED 100, Page 51, Dixonville, Columbiana, Ohio, United States
Death	7 Jul 1922	Columbiana, Ohio, United States
Burial		Riverview Cemetery, East Liverpool, Columbiana, Ohio, United States
Spouse	Samuel D. TORRENCE (1858-)	
Marriage	29 Dec 1886	Beaver, Pennsylvania, United States
Spouse	Willis W. CHAMBERLAIN (1864-1938)	
Marriage	1895/6	

F Ella R. CAMP

Birth	1868/9	Pennsylvania, United States
Census	1870	Page 163, Ohio Township, Beaver, Pennsylvania, United States
Census	1880	ED 185, Page 180, Glasgow, Beaver, Pennsylvania, United States
Death		
Burial		

Father Henry Harrison CAMP		
Mother Helen R. GILCHRIST		
Children		

Ella R. CAMP (continued)

Marriage		

F Elizabeth CAMP

Birth	1870/1	Pennsylvania, United States
Census	1880	ED 185, Page 180, Glasgow, Beaver, Pennsylvania, United States
Death		
Burial		
Marriage		

M Charles Owen CAMP

Birth	15 May 1873	Pennsylvania, United States
Census	1880	ED 185, Page 180, Glasgow, Beaver, Pennsylvania, United States
Census	1900	ED 32, Page 54, Glasgow, Beaver, Pennsylvania, United States
Census	1910	ED 27, Page 74, Glasgow, Beaver, Pennsylvania, United States
Census	1920	ED 42, Page 87, Glasgow, Beaver, Pennsylvania, United States
Death	10 Jun 1958	
Burial		Georgetown Cemetery, Georgetown, Beaver, Pennsylvania, United States
Occupation		Electrician (1900), Electrician Power House (1910), Electrician Electrical Company (1920)
Spouse	Anna M. THORNBY (1873-1916)	
Marriage	1898/9	

F Myrtilla W. CAMP

Birth	1875	Pennsylvania, United States
Census	1880	ED 185, Page 180, Glasgow, Beaver, Pennsylvania, United States
Census	1900	
Census	1910	ED 27, Page 74, Glasgow, Beaver, Pennsylvania, United States
Death	1966	
Burial		Georgetown Cemetery, Georgetown, Beaver, Pennsylvania, United States
Occupation		Clerk Dry Goods (1910)
Marriage		

F Leavenia H. CAMP

Birth	Aug 1883	Pennsylvania, United States
Census	1900	ED 32, Page 54, Glasgow, Beaver, Pennsylvania, United States
Death		
Burial		
Marriage		

Father John Snoddy CAMPBELL

Birth	31 May 1814	(or 17 Nov 1814), Madison, Kentucky, United States
Residence	bet 1814 and 1825	Madison, Kentucky, United States
Residence	bet 1825 and 1833	Clay, Missouri, United States
Census	1830	
Residence	bet 1833 and 1865	Jackson, Missouri, United States
Census	1840	
Census	1850	Page 356, Platte Township, Clay, Missouri, United States
Occupation	bet 1855 and 1857	City Councilman; Kansas City, Jackson, Missouri, United States
Census	1860	Page 103, Kansas City, Jackson, Missouri, United States
Census		Slave Schedules, Pages 267-268, Kansas City, Jackson, Missouri, United States
Occupation	1860/1	City Councilman; Kansas City, Jackson, Missouri, United States
Misc	10 Aug 1862	Union Provost Marshals' File of Papers Relating to Two or More Civilians, M416, Roll 8, No. 2129
Tax Lists	bet SepDec 1862 and Nov 1863	Gross Receipts of Ferry; "Nelson, Campbell & Company / Campbell, Nelson & Company"", Kansas City, Jackson, Missouri, United States
Misc	27 Jan 1863	Union Provost Marshals' File of Papers Relating to Two or More Civilians, M416, Roll 13, No. 3512
Misc	abt 1863	Union Provost Marshals' File of Papers . . . Two or More Civilians, M416, Roll 81, No. 22,106
Tax Lists	bet May 1865 and Dec 1865	Gross Receipts of Ferry; "Campbell, Nelson & Company", Kansas City, Jackson, Missouri, United States
Death	11 Jul 1865	Cholera
Burial	15 Jul 1865	Campbell Family Cemetery, Clay, Missouri, United States
Misc		Obituary, Kansas City (Mo.) Daily Journal of Commerce, 15 Jul 1865, Page 2, Column 1
Probate	29 Jul 1865	(Letters of Administration), Volume L, Page 120, Independence, Jackson, Missouri, United States
Burial	maybe 1889	Elmwood Cemetery, Kansas City, Jackson, Missouri, United States
Misc		"Fashionable Pearl Street," Annals of Kansas City, Volume 1 (3 Oct 1921), Page 112-113
Occupation		Farmer (1850), Ferry
Marriage	10 Aug 1843	(1843I0020062), Jackson, Missouri, United States
Father		Col. William CAMPBELL (1788-1859)
Mother		Elizabeth SNODDY (1790-1857)

Mother Eleanor R. "Ellen" MCGEE

Birth	11 Nov 1825	Shelby, Kentucky, United States
Residence	bet 1828 and 1889	Jackson, Missouri, United States
Census	1830	
Residence	bet 1836 and 1889	Jackson, Missouri, United States
Census	1840	
Census	1850	Page 356, Platte Township, Clay, Missouri, United States
Census	1860	Page 103, Kansas City, Jackson, Missouri, United States
Census	1870	Page 374, Kansas City, Jackson, Missouri, United States
Census	1880	
Will	23 Jul 1888	(Will Written), Volume 1, Page 388, Kansas City, Jackson, Missouri, United States
Death	3 Dec 1889	Kansas City, Jackson, Missouri, United States
Misc		Obituary, Kansas City (Mo.) Star, 04 Dec 1889, Page 2, Column 2
Burial	5 Dec 1889	Elmwood Cemetery, Kansas City, Jackson, Missouri, United States
Probate	10 Dec 1889	(Will Proved), Volume 1, Page 388, Kansas City, Jackson, Missouri, United States
Occupation		Boards (1870)
Misc		Genealogy, The Johnsons and McGees: Pioneer Settlers of Kansas City (Tompkins, 2004), Part 2, Page 42
Religion		Charter Member (1858); First Christian Church, Kansas City, Jackson, Missouri, United States
Father		Col. James H. MCGEE (1786-1840)
Mother		Eleanor A. FRYE (1798-1880)

Children

Father John Snoddy CAMPBELL

Mother Eleanor R. "Ellen" MCGEE

Children

M   James H. M. CAMPBELL

Birth	31 May 1844	
Death	6 May 1849	
Burial		Elmwood Cemetery, Kansas City, Jackson, Missouri, United States
Marriage		

F   Elizabeth "Lizzie" CAMPBELL

Birth	14 Jan 1848	Clay, Missouri, United States
Census	1850	Page 356, Platte Township, Clay, Missouri, United States
Census	1860	
Census	1870	Page 374, Kansas City, Jackson, Missouri, United States
Census	1880	ED 4, Page 118, Kansas City, Jackson, Missouri, United States
Death	16 Nov 1905	Excelsior Springs, Clay, Missouri, United States
Misc		Obituary, Kansas City (Mo.) Star, 17 Nov 1905, Page 1, Column 2
Burial	19 Nov 1905	Elmwood Cemetery, Kansas City, Jackson, Missouri, United States
Spouse	Turner Anderson GILL (1841-1919)	
Marriage	9 Mar 1871	(1871I0060252), Jackson, Missouri, United States

F   Emma M. CAMPBELL

Birth		
Chr		
Death		(Before 1865)
Burial		Elmwood Cemetery, Kansas City, Jackson, Missouri, United States
Marriage		

M   J. William CAMPBELL

Birth	9 May 1855	Kansas City, Jackson, Missouri, United States
Residence	bet 1855 and 1875	Kansas City, Jackson, Missouri, United States
Census	1860	Page 103, Kansas City, Jackson, Missouri, United States
Census	1870	Page 375, Kansas City, Jackson, Missouri, United States
Census	1880	ED 35, Page 203, Prairie Township, Jackson, Missouri, United States
Misc		Biography, History of Jackson County, Missouri (1881), Page 959
Residence	1889	Kansas City, Jackson, Missouri, United States
Census	1900	ED 25, Page 121, Colorado Springs, El Paso, Colorado, United States
Occupation		Farmer (1880)
Death		
Burial		
Spouse	Mary E. MURRAY (1853-)	
Marriage	1 Oct 1874	Clay, Missouri, United States

Father Columbus G. CARMICHAEL

Birth	5 Jul 1832	Washington, Tennessee, United States
Census	1850	Page 357, Van Buren Township, Jackson, Missouri, United States
Census	1860	Page 362, Blue Township, Jackson, Missouri, United States
Misc	31 Jul 1862	Union Provost Marshals' File of Papers Relating to Two or More Civilians, M416, Roll 7, No. 1691
Tax Lists	Apr 1863	Cattle Broker License; Blue Township, Jackson, Missouri, United States
Military	1863	Civil War Draft Registration; Blue Township, Jackson, Missouri, United States
Census	1870	Page 208, Blue Township, Jackson, Missouri, United States
Census	1870	Agricultural Schedules, Page 9, Blue Township, Jackson, Missouri, United States
Census	1880	
Death	3 Feb 1881	Leadville, Lake, Colorado, United States
Occupation		Farmer (1860, 1870), Cattle Broker, Trader
Burial		
Marriage	16 Nov 1865	(1865I0050168), Jackson, Missouri, United States
Father	William M. CARMICHAEL (-)	
Mother	Martha BLAIR (1796-)	

Mother Mary E. COMPTON

Birth	1842/3	Kentucky, United States
Census	1850	
Census	1860	
Census	1870	Page 208, Blue Township, Jackson, Missouri, United States
Census	1880	
Census	1900	
Census	1910	
Census	1920	
Death		
Burial		
Father		
Mother		

Children

Father William CARROLL

Birth	28 Jun 1813	Ireland
Census	1850	Page 278, Loudoun, Virginia, United States
Census	1860	Page 54, Kansas City, Jackson, Missouri, United States
Will	30 Apr 1861	(Will Written), Volume A, Page 107, Kansas City, Jackson, Missouri, United States
Misc	10 Aug 1862	Union Provost Marshals' File of Papers Relating to Two or More Civilians, M416, Roll 8, No. 2129
Tax Lists	Sep 1862	Retail Dealer License; Kansas City, Jackson, Missouri, United States
Misc	abt 1863	Union Provost Marshals' File of Papers . . . Two or More Civilians, M416, Roll 81, No. 22,106
Census	1870	Page 309, Kansas City, Jackson, Missouri, United States
Death	24 Oct 1874	
Burial		Burkittsville Union Cemetery, Burkittsville, Frederick, Maryland, United States
Probate	19 Nov 1874	(Will Proved), Volume A, Page 107, Kansas City, Jackson, Missouri, United States
Occupation		Merchant (1850, 1860), Retail Dealer
Marriage	2 Feb 1850	Frederick, Maryland, United States
Father	William CARROLL (1775-1825)	
Mother	Mary BOLAND (1782-1872)	
Other spouse		
Marriage		

Mother Emily Augusta BISER

Birth	3 Jan 1830	Frederick, Frederick, Maryland, United States
Census	1850	Page 278, Loudoun, Virginia, United States
Census	1860	Page 54, Kansas City, Jackson, Missouri, United States
Census	1870	Page 309, Kansas City, Jackson, Missouri, United States
Census	1880	ED 2, Page 19, Aiken, Aiken, South Carolina, United States
Census	1900	ED 70, Page 39, District 2, Knox, Tennessee, United States
Death	1903	Frederick, Frederick, Maryland, United States
Burial		
Father	Dr. Tilghman BISER (1805-1874)	
Mother	Mary Ann LAMAR (1803-1880)	

Children

Father Patrick CASSIDY

Birth	1827	Ireland
Census	1850	
Residence	bet 1856 and 1870	Kansas City, Jackson, Missouri, United States
Census	1860	Page 102, Kansas City, Jackson, Missouri, United States
Tax Lists	Sep 1862	Livery Stable License, 2 Hacks, 2 Buggies, and 1 Omnibus; "E. & P. Cassady", Westport, Jackson, Missouri, United States
Military		Private, Companies C & H, 77th Regiment Enrolled Missouri Militia
Misc		Advertisement, Kansas City (Mo.) Daily Journal of Commerce, 03 Jul 1863, Page 2, Column 6
Tax Lists	Aug 1865	Gross Recipts of Hacks; "Pat Casseday & Company", Kansas City, Jackson, Missouri, United States
Tax Lists	Aug 1865	Gross Receipts of Hacks; "Casseday & Wyland", Kansas City, Jackson, Missouri, United States
Tax Lists	May 1866	Livery Stable License; "E. & P. Cassady", Westport, Jackson, Missouri, United States
Tax Lists	May 1866	5 Carriages; "E. & P. Casady", Kansas City, Jackson, Missouri, United States
Census	1870	Page 639, Kansas City, Jackson, Missouri, United States
Will	5 Oct 1870	(Will Written), Volume N, Page 43, Independence, Jackson, Missouri, United States
Death	Oct 1870	
Burial	7 Oct 1870	Mount Saint Mary's Cemetery, Kansas City, Jackson, Missouri, United States
Misc		Funeral Notice, Kansas City (Mo.) Daily Journal of Commerce, 07 Oct 1870, Page 4, Column 1
Probate	21 Oct 1870	(Will Proved), Volume N, Pge 43, Independence, Jackson, Missouri, United States
Occupation		Laborer (1860), Proprietor of Omnibus (1870), Livery Stable Keeper
Business		E. & P. Cassidy (Livery Stable)
Marriage		New York, New York, New York, United States
Father		
Mother		

Mother Alice REILLY

Birth	1 Aug 1831	Dublin, Ireland
Immigration	1859	(or 1850), United States
Census	1860	Page 102, Kansas City, Jackson, Missouri, United States
Census	1870	Page 639, Kansas City, Jackson, Missouri, United States
Census	1880	ED 40, Page 254, Westport, Jackson, Missouri, United States
Census	1900	ED 112, Page 45, Kansas City, Jackson, Missouri, United States
Census	1910	ED 152, Page 183, Kansas City, Jackson, Missouri, United States
Death	14 Aug 1911	Peritonitis Probably In____ by Acute Indigestive Senility & Bad Heart; Kansas City, Jackson, Missouri, United States
Misc		Obituary, Kansas City (Mo.) Times, 15 Aug 1911, Page 11, Column 4
Burial	16 Aug 1911	Mount Saint Mary's Cemetery, Kansas City, Jackson, Missouri, United States
Misc		Obituary, Kansas City (Mo.) Times, 16 Aug 1911, Page 9, Column 7
Father	George REILLY (-)	
Mother		

Children

F Mary CASSIDY

Birth	9 May 1858	Missouri, United States
Baptism	16 May 1858	Roman Catholic Parish, Kansas City, Jackson, Missouri, United States
Census	1860	Page 102, Kansas City, Jackson, Missouri, United States
Census	1870	Page 639, Kansas City, Jackson, Missouri, United States
Census	1880	ED 6, Page 162, Kansas City, Jackson, Missouri, United States
Census	1900	ED 112, Page 43, Kansas City, Jackson, Missouri, United States
Death	5 Mar 1928	Cerebral Embolism, Hypertension; Kansas City, Jackson, Missouri, United States
Burial	8 Mar 1928	Mount Saint Mary's Cemetery, Kansas City, Jackson, Missouri, United States
Spouse	John MARTIN (1847-1892)	
Marriage	28 Jul 1877	(1877I0070452), Jackson, Missouri, United States

M George E. CASSIDY

Birth	1860	Missouri, United States
Census	1860	Page 102, Kansas City, Jackson, Missouri, United States
Census	1870	Page 639, Kansas City, Jackson, Missouri, United States

Father	Patrick CASSIDY	
Mother	**Alice REILLY**	
Children		

George E. CASSIDY (continued)

Census	1880	ED 19, Page 512, Kansas City, Jackson, Missouri, United States
Death	20 Nov 1887	Kansas City, Jackson, Missouri, United States
Misc		Funeral Notice, Kansas City (Mo.) Star, 21 Nov 1887, Page 3, Column 3
Burial	22 Nov 1887	Mount Saint Mary's Cemetery, Kansas City, Jackson, Missouri, United States
Occupation		Teamster (1880), "Formerly of No. 2 hook and ladder company" (1887)
Marriage		

F Annie CASSIDY

Birth	Mar 1865	(or 1863/4, Missouri, United States
Census	1870	Page 639, Kansas City, Jackson, Missouri, United States
Census	1880	
Census	1885	Page 22, Family 137, Ridgeway Township, Osage, Kansas, United States
Census	1900	ED 159, Page 213, Kansas City, Wyandotte, Kansas, United States
Census	1905	Page 324, Family 156, Kansas City, Wyandotte, Kansas, United States
Census	1910	ED 181, Page 103, Kansas City, Wyandotte, Kansas, United States
Death		
Burial		
Spouse	Forest Jay PHILBRICK (1861-)	
Marriage	30 Oct 1881	(1881K0010210), Kansas City, Jackson, Missouri, United States

F Alice CASSIDY

Birth	1867/8	Missouri, United States
Census	1870	Page 639, Kansas City, Jackson, Missouri, United States
Census	1880	ED 40, Page 254, Westport, Jackson, Missouri, United States
Death		
Burial		
Marriage		

F Elizabeth P. "Lizzie" CASSIDY

Birth	12 Sep 1870	Kansas City, Jackson, Missouri, United States
Census	1880	ED 40, Page 254, Westport, Jackson, Missouri, United States
Census	1900	ED 112, Page 45, Kansas City, Jackson, Missouri, United States
Census	1910	ED 152, Page 183, Kansas City, Jackson, Missouri, United States
Death	20 Mar 1963	Broncho-Pneumonia (Hypostatic), Arteriosclerosis; Kansas City, Jackson, Missouri, United States
Burial	23 Mar 1963	Mount Saint Mary's Cemetery, Kansas City, Jackson, Missouri, United States
Spouse	James F. CLINTON (1861-1934)	
Marriage	12 Feb 1896	(1896K0012574), Kansas City, Jackson, Missouri, United States

Father Edward CASSIDY

Birth	12 Oct 1824	Westmeath, Ireland
Residence	bet 1847 and 1852	Philadelphia, Philadelphia, Pennsylvania, United States
Immigration	1847/8	Philadelphia, Philadelphia, Pennsylvania, United States
Census	1850	
Residence	bet 1852 and 1906	(1858I0040084), Westport, Jackson, Missouri, United States
Census	1860	Page 130, Westport, Jackson, Missouri, United States
Tax Lists	Sep 1862	Livery Stable License, 2 Hacks, 2 Buggies, and 1 Omnibus; "E. & P. Cassaday", Westport, Jackson, Missouri, United States
Misc		Advertisement, Kansas City (Mo.) Daily Journal of Commerce, 03 Jul 1863, Page 2, Column 6
Military	Sep 1863	Civil War Draft Registration; Kaw Township, Jackson, Missouri, United States
Tax Lists	Aug 1865	Gross Receipts of Hacks; "Pat Casseday & Company", Kansas City, Jackson, Missouri, United States
Tax Lists	May 1866	Livery Stable License; "E. & P. Cassady", Westport, Jackson, Missouri, United States
Tax Lists	May 1866	5 Carriages; "E. & P. Casady", Kansas City, Jackson, Missouri, United States
Census	1870	Page 58, Westport, Jackson, Missouri, United States
Census	1880	ED 40, Page 254, Westport, Jackson, Missouri, United States
Census	1900	ED 124, Page 248, Kansas City, Jackson, Missouri, United States
Death	27 Mar 1906	Asthma; Kansas City, Jackson, Missouri, United States
Misc		Obituary, Kansas City (Mo.) Star, 27 Mar 1906, Page 10, Column 4
Burial	29 Mar 1906	Mount Saint Mary's Cemetery, Kansas City, Jackson, Missouri, United States
Occupation		Laborer (1860, 1870, 1880), Teamster (1900), Livery Stable Keeper
Business		E. & P. Cassidy (Livery Stable)
Marriage	6 Sep 1858	(1858I0040084), Jackson, Missouri, United States
Father		
Mother		

Mother Catherine REILLY

Birth	1830/1	(or Feb 1838), Ireland
Census	1850	
Census	1860	Page 130, Westport, Jackson, Missouri, United States
Census	1870	Page 58, Westport, Jackson, Missouri, United States
Census	1880	ED 40, Page 254, Westport, Jackson, Missouri, United States
Census	1900	ED 124, Page 248, Kansas City, Jackson, Missouri, United States
Death	15 Jul 1904	Kansas City, Jackson, Missouri, United States
Misc		Obituary, Kansas City (Mo.) Star, 15 Jul 1904, Page 5, Column 4
Burial		
Father		
Mother		

Children

M Christopher C. CASSIDY

Birth	18 Aug 1859	(or 06 Aug 1859), Kansas City, Jackson, Missouri, United States
Baptism	11 Sep 1859	Roman Catholic Parish, Kansas City, Jackson, Missouri, United States
Census	1860	Page 130, Westport, Jackson, Missouri, United States
Census	1870	Page 58, Westport, Jackson, Missouri, United States
Census	1880	ED 40, Page 254, Westport, Jackson, Missouri, United States
Census	1900	ED 123, Page 239, Kansas City, Jackson, Missouri, United States
Misc		"Tried to Cut His Throat," Kansas City (Mo.) Star, 03 Nov 1904, Page 1, Column 4
Death	17 Feb 1936	Valvular Heart Disease, Arteriosclerosis, Chronic Nephritis; Kansas City, Jackson, Missouri, United States
Burial	19 Feb 1936	Mount Saint Mary's Cemetery, Kansas City, Jackson, Missouri, United States
Occupation		Laborer (1860), Janitor Public School (1900)
Spouse	Catherine F. KENNEDY (1870-1903)	
Marriage	28 Aug 1889	(1889K0002416), Kansas City, Jackson, Missouri, United States

F Mary Agnes "Mollie" CASSIDY

Birth	Apr 1862	Missouri, United States
Census	1870	Page 58, Westport, Jackson, Missouri, United States
Census	1880	

Father Edward CASSIDY

Mother Catherine REILLY

Children

Mary Agnes "Mollie" CASSIDY (continued)

Census	1900	ED 16, Page 225, Rich Hill, Bates, Missouri, United States
Census	1910	ED 65, Page 122, Kansas City, Jackson, Missouri, United States
Death	1 Mar 1911	Mitral Regurgitation; Kansas City, Jackson, Missouri, United States
Misc		Funeral Notice, Kansas City (Mo.) Star, 02 Mar 1911, Page 3, Column 4
Burial	3 Mar 1911	Mount Saint Mary's Cemetery, Kansas City, Jackson, Missouri, United States
Spouse		Dr. William F. HUDELSON (1854-)
Marriage	5 Apr 1883	Bates, Missouri, United States
Divorce		

F Katherine "Kate, Katy" CASSIDY

Birth	26 Apr 1865	Kansas City, Jackson, Missouri, United States
Census	1870	Page 58, Westport, Jackson, Missouri, United States
Census	1880	ED 40, Page 254, Westport, Jackson, Missouri, United States
Census	1900	ED 33, Page 228, Muncie, Delaware, Indiana, United States
Death	1 Jul 1919	Acute Dilatation of Heart . . .; Kansas City, Jackson, Missouri, United States
Misc		Obituary, Kansas City (Mo.) Times, 02 Jul 1919, Page 9, Column 2
Burial	3 Jul 1919	Forest Hill Cemetery, Kansas City, Jackson, Missouri, United States
Spouse		William D. KILANDER (1853-1927)

F Julia Agnes CASSIDY

Birth	31 Oct 1868	Kansas City, Jackson, Missouri, United States
Census	1870	Page 58, Westport, Jackson, Missouri, United States
Census	1880	ED 40, Page 254, Westport, Jackson, Missouri, United States
Census	1900	ED 16, Page 225, Rich Hill, Bates, Missouri, United States
Census	1910	ED 16, Page 180, Rich Hill, Bates, Missouri, United States
Residence	1919	Kansas City, Jackson, Missouri, United States
Death	5 Oct 1956	Bronchopneumonia (Hypostatic), Chronic Interstitial Nephritis, Arteriosclerosis; Little Sisters of the Poor, Kansas City, Jackson, Missouri, United States
Burial	8 Oct 1956	Mount Saint Mary's Cemetery, Kansas City, Jackson, Missouri, United States
Spouse		Edward C. MCCARTY (1869-1942)
Marriage	1 Oct 1890	Bates, Missouri, United States

F Alice CASSIDY

Birth	13 Jan 1871	Missouri, United States
Census	1880	ED 40, Page 254, Westport, Jackson, Missouri, United States
Census	1900	ED 124, Page 248, Kansas City, Jackson, Missouri, United States
Residence	1919	Kansas City, Jackson, Missouri, United States
Death	10 Jun 1931	Pulmonary Tuberculosis, Tuberculosis of Intestines; Leeds, Jackson, Missouri, United States
Burial	12 Jun 1931	Mount Saint Mary's Cemetery, Kansas City, Jackson, Missouri, United States
Marriage		

M Henry Patrick CASSIDY

Birth	13 Feb 1873	Westport, Jackson, Missouri, United States
Census	1880	ED 40, Page 254, Westport, Jackson, Missouri, United States
Death	6 Dec 1897	Bright's Disease; Westport, Jackson, Missouri, United States
Misc		Death Notice, Kansas City (Mo.) Times, 07 Dec 1897, Page 7, Column 5
Burial	9 Dec 1897	Mount Saint Mary's Cemetery, Kansas City, Jackson, Missouri, United States
Misc		Funeral Notice, Westport (Mo.) Sentinel-Examiner, 11 Dec 1897, Page 1, Column 1
Marriage		

Father Emery B. CHADWICK		
Birth	1823/4	Massachusetts, United States
Census	1830	
Census	1840	
Census	1850	Page 29, Hanover, Grafton, New Hampshire, United States
Census	1860	Page 468, Chicago, Cook, Illinois, United States
Tax Lists	Sep 1862	5th Class Hotel Keeper License; Kansas City, Jackson, Missouri, United States
Misc		"Pacific House," Kansas City (Mo.) Daily Journal of Commerce, 01 Jul 1863, Page 1, Column 3
Misc		Advertisement, Western Journal of Commerce, 01 Jul 1863, Page 1, Column 3
Misc		"Pacific House Saloon," Kansas City (Mo.) Daily Journal of Commerce, 08 Sep 1863, Page 3, Column 3
Military	Sep 1863	Civil War Draft Registration; Kaw Township, Jackson, Missouri, United States
Census	1865	Page 14, Lawrence, Douglas, Kansas, United States
Census	1865	Page 119, Family 794, Eudora Township, Douglas, Kansas, United States
Census	1870	Page 351, Lawrence, Douglas, Kansas, United States
Census	1875	Page 20, Family 105, Eudora Township, Douglas, Kansas, United States
Census	1880	
Residence	1888	Lawrence, Douglas, Kansas, United States
Census	1890	ED 114, Pages 2 and 4, Kansas City, Jackson, Missouri, United States
Death	19 Feb 1893	Softening of the Brain; Kansas City, Jackson, Missouri, United States
Burial	20 Feb 1893	Union Cemetery, Kansas City, Jackson, Missouri, United States
Misc		Death Notice, Kansas City (Mo.) Star, 20 Feb 1893, Pgae 2, Column 7
Occupation		Saddler (1850), Hotel Keeper (1860), Trader (1865, 1875),Stock Trader (1865), Auctioneer & Com. Mercht. (1870)
Marriage	1 Jul 1849	New London, Merrimack, New Hampshire, United States
Father		
Mother		

Mother Mary C. HUTCHINS		
Birth	20 Nov 1826	New London, Merrimack, New Hampshire, United States
Census	1830	
Census	1840	
Census	1850	Page 29, Hanover, Grafton, New Hampshire, United States
Census	1860	Page 468, Chicago, Cook, Illinois, United States
Census	1865	Page 14, Lawrence, Douglas, Kansas, United States
Census	1865	Page 119, Family 794, Eudora Township, Douglas, Kansas, United States
Census	1870	Page 351, Lawrence, Douglas, Kansas, United States
Census	1880	ED 68, Page 104, Lawrence, Douglas, Kansas, United States
Census	1900	
Death		
Burial		
Father		
Mother		

Children		

M	**Frank T. CHADWICK**	
Birth	6 Sep 1852	Hanover, Grafton, New Hampshire, United States
Census	1860	Page 468, Chicago, Cook, Illinois, United States
Census	1865	Page 14, Lawrence, Douglas, Kansas, United States
Census	1865	Page 119, Family 794, Eudora Township, Douglas, Kansas, United States
Census	1870	Page 351, Lawrence, Douglas, Kansas, United States
Census	1875	Page 20, Family 105, Eudora Township, Douglas, Kansas, United States
Census	1880	ED 64, Page 23, Eudora Township, Douglas, Kansas, United States
Census	1900	
Census	1910	ED 35, Page 211, Washington Township, Benton, Arkansas, United States
Death	1912	
Burial		Stony Point Cemetery, Pleasant Ridge, Benton, Arkansas, United States
Occupation		Clerk in Store (1870), Farmer (1875, 1880), Farmer Fruit Farm (1910)
Spouse	Harriet EMMETT (1857-1908)	

Father	Emery B. CHADWICK		
Mother Mary C. HUTCHINS			
Children			
	Frank T. CHADWICK (continued)		
	Marriage		
M	**John/James Edwin/Edward CHADWICK**		
	Birth	1851/2	New Hampshire, United States
	Census	1860	Page 468, Chicago, Cook, Illinois, United States
	Census	1865	Page 14, Lawrence, Douglas, Kansas, United States
	Census	1865	Page 119, Family 794, Eudora Township, Douglas, Kansas, United States
	Census	1870	Page 351, Lawrence, Douglas, Kansas, United States
	Census	1880	
	Occupation		Civil Engineer (1870)
	Death		
	Burial		
	Marriage		

Father Dr. David Young CHALFANT

	Birth	1830/1	Ohio, United States
	Census	1840	(John Chalfont Family), Page 352, Line 27, Washington Township, Cochocton, Ohio, United States
	Census	1850	Page 62, Washington Township, Cochocton, Ohio, United States
	Residence	bet 1855 and 1883	Jackson, Missouri, United States
	Census	1860	Page 16, Kansas City, Jackson, Missouri, United States
	Tax Lists	Sep 1862	Physician License; Kansas City, Jackson, Missouri, United States
	Military		Private, Company C, Van Horn's Battalion Cavalry Volunteers
	Military		Company C, 25th Missouri Infantry
	Military		Surgeon, Companies F & S, 77th Regiment Enrolled Missouri Militia
	Military		Company C, 13th Missouri Infantry
	Military		Private, Company C, 1st Missouri Infantry
	Military	Oct 1863	Civil War Draft Registration; Kaw Township, Jackson, Missouri, United States
	Tax Lists	May 1866	Physician License; Kansas City, Jackson, Missouri, United States
	Census	1870	Page 483, Kansas City, Jackson, Missouri, United States
	Census	1880	ED 8, Page 247, Kansas City, Jackson, Missouri, United States
	Death	11 Jan 1883	Softening of the Brain; Kansas City, Jackson, Missouri, United States
	Misc		Obituary, Kansas City (Mo.) Times, 13 Jan 1883, Page 8, Column 4
	Misc		Obituary, Kansas City (Mo.) Daily Journal, 13 Jan 1883, Page 3, Column 4
	Burial	14 Jan 1883	Union Cemetery, Kansas City, Jackson, Missouri, United States
	Misc		Funeral Notice, Kansas City (Mo.) Daily Journal, 15 Jan 1883, Page 3, Column 3
	Occupation		Laborer (1850), Physician (1860, 1870, 1880)
	Misc		Member, Grand Army of the Republic
	Marriage	4 Dec 1855	Delaware, Delaware, United States
	Father		John Reed CHALFANT (1809-1887)
	Mother		Delila HAYES (1812-1881)

Mother Sarah Elizabeth BEEDLE

	Birth	Feb 1836	Ohio, United States
	Census	1850	
	Census	1860	Page 16, Kansas City, Jackson, Missouri, United States
	Census	1870	Page 483, Kansas City, Jackson, Missouri, United States
	Census	1880	ED 8, Page 247, Kansas City, Jackson, Missouri, United States
	Census	1890	ED 138, Page 1, Kansas City, Jackson, Missouri, United States
	Census	1900	ED 65, Page 299, Kansas City, Jackson, Missouri, United States
	Census	1910	ED 201, Page 145, Shawnee Township, Wyandotte, Kansas, United States
	Census	1920	ED 62, Page 67, Kansas City, Jackson, Missouri, United States
	Census	1925	Page 26, Family 194, Shawnee Township, Wyandotte, Kansas, United States
	Census	1930	ED 73, Page 118, Shawnee Township, Wyandotte, Kansas, United States
	Death	23 May 1932	(or 23 Apr 1932), Wyandotte, Kansas, United States
	Burial	25 May 1932	(or 25 Apr 1932) Union Cemetery, Kansas City, Jackson, Missouri, United States
	Father		
	Mother		

Children

F   Millie J. CHALFANT

	Birth	1856	
	Death	1857	
	Burial		Union Cemetery, Kansas City, Jackson, Missouri, United States
	Marriage		

M   Frank L. CHALFANT

	Birth	28 May 1859	Kansas City, Jackson, Missouri, United States
	Census	1860	Page 16, Kansas City, Jackson, Missouri, United States
	Census	1870	Page 483, Kansas City, Jackson, Missouri, United States
	Census	1880	ED 8, Page 247, Kansas City, Jackson, Missouri, United States
	Census	1900	ED 65, Page 299, Kansas City, Jackson, Missouri, United States
	Census	1910	ED 87, Page 136, Kansas City, Jackson, Missouri, United States

Father Dr. David Young CHALFANT

Mother Sarah Elizabeth BEEDLE

Children

Frank L. CHALFANT (continued)

Death	6 Mar 1917	Heart Lesion with Lost Compensation Complicated with La Grippe; Kansas City, Jackson, Missouri, United States
Burial	8 Mar 1917	Elmwood Cemetery, Kansas City, Jackson, Missouri, United States
Occupation		Printer (1880), Mail Carrier (1900), Letter Carrier Post Office Department (1910)
Spouse	Winona R. WILLIAMSON (1879-)	
Marriage	18 Jul 1901	(1901K0022543), Jackson, Missouri, United States

F Harriet D. CHALFANT

Birth	1860	
Death	1861	
Burial		Union Cemetery, Kansas City, Jackson, Missouri, United States
Marriage		

F Maggie Ellen CHALFANT

Birth	Mar 1864	Missouri, United States
Census	1870	Page 483, Kansas City, Jackson, Missouri, United States
Census	1880	ED 8, Page 247, Kansas City, Jackson, Missouri, United States
Census	1900	ED 49, Page 41, Kansas City, Jackson, Missouri, United States
Census	1910	ED 201, Page 145, Shawnee Township, Wyandotte, Kansas, United States
Census	1920	
Census	1925	Page 26, Family 194, Shawnee Township, Wyandotte, Kansas, United States
Census	1930	ED 73, Page 118, Shawnee Township, Wyandotte, Kansas, United States
Death	30 Jul 1944	Kansas City, Wyandotte, Kansas, United States
Burial	1 Aug 1944	Union Cemetery, Kansas City, Jackson, Missouri, United States
Occupation		Artist Studio Kansas City, Missouri (1925), Artist Novelty Company (1930)
Spouse	Charles M. PIERCE (1862-1954)	
Marriage	20 Sep 1888	(1888K0000783), Kansas City, Jackson, Missouri, United States

F Nettie Esther CHALFANT

Birth	14 Dec 1879	Kansas City, Jackson, Missouri, United States
Census	1880	ED 8, Page 247, Kansas City, Jackson, Missouri, United States
Baptism	1 Feb 1885	Grand Avenue Methodist Episcopal Church, Kansas City, Jackson, Missouri, United States
Census	1900	ED 119, Page 162, Kansas City, Jackson, Missouri, United States
Census	1910	ED 178, Page 19, Kansas City, Jackson, Missouri, United States
Death	16 Jun 1957	Cerebral Hemorhage; State Hospital No. 2, Saint Joseph, Buchanan, Missouri, United States
Burial	18 Jun 1957	Union Cemetery, Kansas City, Jackson, Missouri, United States
Spouse	William H. TOOHEY (1878-)	
Marriage	7 Feb 1900	(1900K0019524), Kansas City, Jackson, Missouri, United States

Father Dr. Joseph William CHEW

Birth	16 Oct 1812	Fredericksburg (Independent City), Virginia, United States
Residence	bet 1812 and 1830	Fredericksburg (Independent City), Virginia, United States
Residence	bet 1830 and 1842	Lexington, Fayette, Kentucky, United States
Census	1840	
Degree	1842	Medical Degree; Transylvania University, Lexington, Fayette, Kentucky, United States
Residence	bet 1843 and 1860	Richmond, Ray, Missouri, United States
Census	1850	Page 284, Ray, Missouri, United States
Residence	bet 1860 and 1883	Kansas City, Jackson, Missouri, United States
Census	1860	Page 71, Kansas City, Jackson, Missouri, United States
Census		Slave Schedules, Page 367, Kansas City, Jackson, Missouri, United States
Misc		Advertisement, Western Journal of Commerce, 04 Jan 1861, Page 1, Column 1
Tax Lists	Sep 1862	Physician License; Kansas City, Jackson, Missouri, United States
Misc	27 Jan 1863	Union Provost Marshals' File of Papers Relating to Two or More Civilians, M416, Roll 13, No. 3512
Misc	1863	General Order 11 forced Dr. Chew to spend the Civil War years in St. Louis, MO
Misc	abt 1863	Union Provost Marshals' File of Papers . . . Two or More Civilians, M416, Roll 81, No. 22,106
Tax Lists	May 1866	Physician License and Pianoforte; Kansas City, Jackson, Missouri, United States
Census	1870	Page 471, Kansas City, Jackson, Missouri, United States
Census	1880	ED 6, Page 172, Kansas City, Jackson, Missouri, United States
Misc		Biography, History of Jackson County, Mo. (1881), Pages 753-754
Death	9 Apr 1883	Heart Disease, Apoplexy; Kansas City, Jackson, Missouri, United States
Burial	10 Apr 1883	Union Cemetery, Kansas City, Jackson, Missouri, United States
Misc		Obituary, Kansas City (Mo.) Times, 10 Apr 1883, Page 8, Column 1
Misc		Funeral Notice, Kansas City (Mo.) Times, 11 Apr 1883, Page 8, Columns 3-4
Occupation		Physician (1850, 1860, 1870), Aleopathic Physician (1880)
Marriage	23 Dec 1833	(or 23 Dec 1834)
Father		
Mother		
Other spouse	Mary A. MOORE (1825-1894)	
Marriage	1 Feb 1844	Ray, Missouri, United States

Mother Mary Jane LAMME

Birth	abt 1815	Fayette, Kentucky, United States
Residence	23 Dec 1833	Fayette, Kentucky, United States
Census	1840	
Death	11 Jun 1843	Fayette, Kentucky, United States
Burial		
Father	Jesse LAMME (1772-1845)	
Mother	Jane TILFORD (1771-1847)	

Children

M Dr. Vernon Tilford CHEW

Birth	8 Dec 1836	Kentucky, United States
Census	1840	
Census	1850	Page 284, Ray, Missouri, United States
Census	1860	
Military		Surgeon, 1st Missouri Infantry (CSA)
Military		Officer, Company S, Medical Staff Infantry Regiment (CSA)
Census	1870	
Census	1880	Justice Precinct 6, Collin, Texas, United States
Census	1900	ED 9, Page 82, Justice Precinct 1, Fort Bend, Texas, United States
Death	26 Mar 1911	Fort Bend, Texas, United States
Burial		Rosenberg Cemetery, Rosenberg, Fort Bend, Texas, United States
Residence		Collin, Texas, United States
Occupation		Doctor (1880), Physician (1900)
Spouse	Temperance Ann WILLIAMS (1845-1926)	
Marriage	26 Apr 1864	Greene, Alabama, United States

Father Dr. Joseph William CHEW

Mother Mary Jane LAMME

Children

	M	**Samuel CHEW**		
		Birth	1837	
		Death		(In Infancy)
		Burial		
		Marriage		

	F	**Maria Helen CHEW**		
		Birth	25 Oct 1839	(or 1837/38), Kentucky, United States
		Census	1840	
		Census	1850	Page 284, Ray, Missouri, United States
		Census	1860	Page 55, Kansas City, Jackson, Missouri, United States
		Census	1870	
		Census	1880	ED 356, Page 325, Saint Louis (city), Missouri, United States
		Death	20 Oct 1911	Carcinoma of Peritoneum; Kansas City, Jackson, Missouri, United States
		Misc		Obituary, Kansas City (Mo.) Star, 20 Oct 1911, Page 3, Column 3
		Burial	22 Oct 1911	Bellefontaine Cemetery, Saint Louis (city), Missouri, United States
		Residence		Saint Louis (city), Missouri, United States
		Spouse	Ewing McGready SLOAN (1831-1906)	
		Marriage	9 Nov 1855	Ray, Missouri, United States

	M	**Joseph William CHEW**		
		Birth	Nov 1841	Kentucky, United States
		Census	1850	Page 284, Ray, Missouri, United States
		Census	1860	
		Death	May 1864	California, United States
		Burial		
		Marriage		

Father Joseph Smith CHICK

Birth	3 Aug 1828	Howard, Missouri, United States
Residence	bet 1828 and 1836	Howard, Missouri, United States
Residence	bet 1836 and 1862	Kansas City, Jackson, Missouri, United States
Census	1840	(Wm. M. Chick Family), Page 69, Jackson, Missouri, United States
Census	1850	Page 233, Kaw Township, Jackson, Missouri, United States
Census	1860	Page 65, Kansas City, Jackson, Missouri, United States
Census		Slave Schedules, Page 367, Kansas City, Jackson, Missouri, United States
Occupation	1860	President, Kansas City and New Mexico Insurance Company; Kansas City, Jackson, Missouri, United States
Misc		Advertisement, Western Journal of Commerce, 15 May 1861, Page 1, Column 4
Residence	bet 1862 and 1874	Brooklyn, Kings, New York, United States
Tax Lists	Sep 1862	Wholesale Dealer License; "A. S. Chick & Company", Kansas City, Jackson, Missouri, United States
Misc	27 Jan 1863	Union Provost Marshals' File of Papers Relating to Two or More Civilians, M416, Roll 13, No. 3512
Misc	30 Jan 1863	Union Provost Marshals' File of Papers Relating to Two or More Civilians, M416, Roll 13, No. 3513
Tax Lists	Aug 1863	408 Pounds Tobacco; "J. S. Chick & Company", Kansas City, Jackson, Missouri, United States
Military	Sep 1863	Civil War Draft Registration; Kaw Township, Jackson, Missouri, United States
Census	1870	Page 269, Roll 946, Brooklyn, Kings, New York, United States
Residence	bet 1874 and 1908	Kansas City, Jackson, Missouri, United States
Misc		Biography, US Biographical Dictionary and Portrait Gallery . . . Missouri Volume (1878), Pages 215-217
Census	1880	ED 22, Page 8, Kaw Township, Jackson, Missouri, United States
Misc		Biography, Kansas City (Mo.) Star, 29 Nov 1880, Page 1, Column 2
Misc		Biography, History of Kansas City, Mo. (1888), Pages 449-451
Misc		Portrait, Kansas City, Its Resources and Their Development (1890), Page 18
Census	1900	ED 71, Page 87, Kansas City, Jackson, Missouri, United States
Misc		Biography, Encyclopedia of the History of Missouri (1901)
Misc		Biography & Photo, Men Who Are Making Kansas City (1902), Page 27
Death	7 Dec 1908	Kansas City, Jackson, Missouri, United States
Misc		Obituary, Kansas City (Mo.) Times, 08 Dec 1908, Page 2, Column 4
Burial	9 Dec 1908	Mount Washington Cemetery, Independence, Jackson, Missouri, United States
Misc		Funeral Notice, Kansas City (Mo.) Times, 10 Dec 1908, Page 12, Column 2
Misc		"William Miles Chick," Jackson County Pioneers (1975), 259-260
Occupation		Clerk (1850), Merchant (1860), Bank Broker (1870), Banker (1880), Real Estate (1900)
Business		J. S. Chick & Company (Tobacco)
Occupation		Wholesale Dealer, Tobacco
Business		H. M. Northrup, J. S. Chick (Banking House)
Tax Lists		
Marriage	31 Aug 1858	
Father	Col. William Miles CHICK (1794-1847)	
Mother	Ann Elizabeth SMITH (1796-1876)	

Mother Julia SEXTON

Birth	7 Feb 1840	Howard, Missouri, United States
Residence	bet 1840 and 1858	Howard, Missouri, United States
Census	1850	Page 462, Boone, Missouri, United States
Census	1860	Page 65, Kansas City, Jackson, Missouri, United States
Census	1870	Page 269, Roll 946, Brooklyn, Kings, New York, United States
Census	1880	ED 22, Page 8, Kaw Township, Jackson, Missouri, United States
Will	1 Aug 1898	(Will Written), Volume 16, Page 456, Kansas City, Jackson, Missouri, United States
Census	1900	ED 71, Page 87, Kansas City, Jackson, Missouri, United States
Census	1910	ED 104, Page 80, Kansas City, Jackson, Missouri, United States
Death	27 Aug 1911	Bronchopneumonia, Cerebral Hemorrhage, Arteriosclerosis; Kansas City, Jackson, Missouri, United States
Misc		Obituary, Kansas City (Mo.) Times, 28 Aug 1911, Page 2, Column 4
Burial	29 Aug 1911	Mount Washington Cemetery, Independence, Jackson, Missouri, United States

Father Joseph Smith CHICK

Mother Julia SEXTON

Children

Julia SEXTON (continued)

Probate	7 Sep 1911	(Will Proved), Volume 16, Page 456, Kansas City, Jackson, Missouri, United States
Father	James M. SEXTON (1808-1878)	
Mother	Ann B. FORD (1813-1867)	

Children

M Frank N. CHICK

Birth	3 Dec 1860	Kansas City, Jackson, Missouri, United States
Census	1870	Page 269, Roll 946, Brooklyn, Kings, New York, United States
Census	1880	ED 22, Page 8, Kansas City, Jackson, Missouri, United States
Will	17 Nov 1888	(Will Written), Volume 2, Page 132, Kansas City, Jackson, Missouri, United States
Death	27 Jan 1893	Kansas City, Jackson, Missouri, United States
Burial		Union Cemetery, Kansas City, Jackson, Missouri, United States
Probate	4 Mar 1893	(Will Proved), Volume 2, Page 132, Kansas City, Jackson, Missouri, United States
Burial	15 Nov 1905	Removed from United Cemetery, Kansas City, Jackson, Missouri, United States
Burial	1905	Mount Washington Cemetery, Independence, Jackson, Missouri, United States
Occupation		Banker (1880)
Spouse	Mamie CHOUTEAU (1864-1899)	
Marriage	2 May 1882	(1882K0020051), Jackson, Missouri, United States

F Lavina CHICK

Birth	7 Mar 1863	
Death	17 Mar 1863	
Burial		Mount Washington Cemetery, Independence, Jackson, Missouri, United States
Marriage		

F Anna V. CHICK

Birth	25 Mar 1864	New York, United States
Census	1870	Page 269, Roll 946, Brooklyn, Kings, New York, United States
Death	17 Oct 1876	Jackson, Missouri, United States
Burial		Union Cemetery, Kansas City, Jackson, Missouri, United States
Burial	15 Nov 1905	Removed from United Cemetery, Kansas City, Jackson, Missouri, United States
Marriage		

F Helen/Ellen M. CHICK

Birth	18 May 1866	(or New York, United States), Missouri, United States
Census	1870	Page 269, Roll 946, Brooklyn, Kings, New York, United States
Census	1880	ED 22, Page 8, Kansas City, Jackson, Missouri, United States
Death	27 Jul 1884	Brain Fever; Kansas City, Jackson, Missouri, United States
Burial	29 Jul 1884	Union Cemetery, Kansas City, Jackson, Missouri, United States
Burial	15 Nov 1905	Removed from United Cemetery, Kansas City, Jackson, Missouri, United States
Marriage		

F Julia Lucy CHICK

Birth	28 Feb 1870	Brooklyn, Kings, New York, United States
Census	1870	Page 269, Roll 946, Brooklyn, Kings, New York, United States
Census	1880	ED 22, Page 8, Kansas City, Jackson, Missouri, United States
Census	1900	ED 71, Page 87, Kansas City, Jackson, Missouri, United States
Census	1910	ED 104, Page 80, Kansas City, Jackson, Missouri, United States
Census	1920	ED 74, Page 214, Kansas City, Jackson, Missouri, United States
Death	30 Oct 1955	Severe Coronary Arteriosclerosis, . . . Pulmonary Edema . . .; Kansas City, Jackson, Missouri, United States
Burial	1 Nov 1955	Mount Washington Cemetery, Independence, Jackson, Missouri, United States
Spouse	Edward Everett PORTERFIELD (1861-1933)	
Marriage	8 Oct 1889	(1889K0002652), Kansas City, Jackson, Missouri, United States

M Joseph Sexton CHICK Jr.

Birth	19 Jun 1877	Missouri, United States
Census	1880	ED 22, Page 8, Kansas City, Jackson, Missouri, United States
Census	1900	ED 71, Page 87, Kansas City, Jackson, Missouri, United States
Census	1910	ED 157, Page 267, Kansas City, Jackson, Missouri, United States

Father Joseph Smith CHICK		
Mother Julia SEXTON		
Children		
Joseph Sexton CHICK Jr. (continued)		
Census	1920	ED 74, Page 214, Kansas City, Jackson, Missouri, United States
Death	6 Dec 1954	Myocardial Infarction, Coronary Arteriosclerosis, Generalized Arteriosclerosis; Kansas City, Jackson, Missouri, United States
Burial	8 Dec 1954	Mount Washington Cemetery, Independence, Jackson, Missouri, United States
Occupation		Real Estate (1900), Agent Real Estate (1910), Automobile Salesman (1920), Clerk of Probate Court
Spouse	Anna LYLE (1877-1967)	
Marriage	28 Oct 1903	(1903K0028050), Kansas City, Jackson, Missouri, United States

Father Washington Henry CHICK		
Birth	9 Feb 1826	Saline, Missouri, United States
Residence	bet 1826 and 1836	Saline, Missouri, United States
Census	1830	
Residence	bet 1836 and 1849	Jackson, Missouri, United States
Census	1840	(Wm. M. Chick Family), Page 69, Jackson, Missouri, United States
Residence	bet 1849 and 1851	California, United States
Census	1850	Page 269, Placerville, El Dorado, California, United States
Residence	1851/2	Indian Territory, United States
Residence	1852/3	Boone, Missouri, United States
Residence	bet 1854 and 1865	Kansas City, Jackson, Missouri, United States
Census	1860	Page 71, Kansas City, Jackson, Missouri, United States
Misc		Advertisement, Western Journal of Commerce, 04 Jan 1861, Page 1, Column 7
Misc	31 Jul 1862	Union Provost Marshals' File of Papers Relating to Two or More Civilians, M416, Roll 28, No. 2054
Misc	10 Aug 1862	Union Provost Marshals' File of Papers Relating to Two or More Civilians, M416, Roll 8, No. 2129
Misc	23 Aug 1862	Union Provost Marshals' File of Papers Relating to Individual Civilians, M345, Roll 50
Tax Lists	Sep 1862	Commercial Broker License; "W. H. Chick & Company", Kansas City, Jackson, Missouri, United States
Misc		U. S. Internal Revenue Tax Lists for Jackson Co., MO--Sep 1862 to Nov 1866
Misc	27 Jan 1863	Union Provost Marshals' File of Papers Relating to Two or More Civilians, M416, Roll 13, No. 3512
Misc	30 Jan 1863	Union Provost Marshals' File of Papers Relating to Two or More Civilians, M416, Roll 13, No. 3513
Military		Private, Company C, 77th Regiment Enrolled Missouri Militia
Military	Sep 1863	Civil War Draft Registration; Kaw Township, Jackson, Missouri, United States
Tax Lists	Jun 1865	Broker Sales; "W. H. Chick & Company", Kansas City, Jackson, Missouri, United States
Residence	bet 1865 and 1884	Saint Louis, Saint Louis, Missouri, United States
Tax Lists	Aug 1865	Wholesale Liquor Dealer License; "W. H. Chick & Company", Kansas City, Jackson, Missouri, United States
Tax Lists	Sep 1865	Broker Sales; "W. H. Chick & Company", Kansas City, Jackson, Missouri, United States
Tax Lists	Apr 1866	Wholesale Liquor Dealer License; "W. H. Chick & Company", Kansas City, Jackson, Missouri, United States
Tax Lists	May 1866	Wholesale Liquor Dealer and Commercial Broker Licenses; "W. H. Chick & Company", Kansas City, Jackson, Missouri, United States
Tax Lists	Oct 1866	Gross Sales; "W. H. Chick & Company", Kansas City, Jackson, Missouri, United States
Tax Lists	Nov 1866	Gross Sales; "W. H. Chick & Company", Kansas City, Jackson, Missouri, United States
Census	1870	Page 479, Saint Louis Township, Saint Louis, Missouri, United States
Census	1880	ED 371, Page 454, Saint Louis (city), Missouri, United States
Residence	bet 1884 and 1918	Kansas City, Jackson, Missouri, United States
Misc		Biography, History of Kansas City, Mo. (1888), Pages 516-517
Census	1900	ED 84, Page 256, Kansas City, Jackson, Missouri, United States
Census	1910	ED 104, Page 82, Kansas City, Jackson, Missouri, United States
Misc		"The Oldest Inhabitant," Kansas City (Mo.) Star, 24 May 1914, Page 2D, Columns 3-6
Death	18 Dec 1918	Chronic Nephritis, Age; Kansas City, Jackson, Missouri, United States
Misc		Obituary, Kansas City (Mo.) Star, 18 Dec 1918, Page 3, Columns 1-2
Burial	19 Dec 1918	Mount Washington Cemetery, Independence, Jackson, Missouri, United States
Misc		Funeral Notice, Kansas City (Mo.) Times, 19 Dec 1918, Page 3, Column 5
Misc		"William Miles Chick," Jackson County Pioneers (1975), 259-260
Occupation		Miner for Gold (1850), Merchant (1860), Wholesale Grocer (1870), Commission Merchant (1880)
Occupation		Commission Broker, Wholesale Liquor Dealer
Business		W. H. Chick & Company (Commission Broker)
Misc		"Fashionable Pearl Street," Annals of Kansas City, Volume 1 (3 Oct 1921), Page 110
Marriage	1853	
Father	Col. William Miles CHICK (1794-1847)	
Mother	Ann Elizabeth SMITH (1796-1876)	

Father Washington Henry CHICK			
Mother Eugenia Pauline "Eugenie" OLIVER			
Children			

Mother Eugenia Pauline "Eugenie" OLIVER		
Birth	23 Mar 1835	(or 19 Mar 1835), McDonald, Missouri, United States
Census	1840	(Alfred Oliver Family), Page 252, Elk Over (Elk Mills), Newton, Missouri, United States
Census	1850	Page 117, McDonald, Missouri, United States
Census	1860	Page 71, Kansas City, Jackson, Missouri, United States
Census	1870	Page 479, Saint Louis Township, Saint Louis, Missouri, United States
Census	1880	ED 371, Page 454, Saint Louis (city), Missouri, United States
Census	1900	ED 84, Page 256, Kansas City, Jackson, Missouri, United States
Death	23 Sep 1905	Kansas City, Jackson, Missouri, United States
Misc		Obituary, Kansas City (Mo.) Star, 23 Sep 1905, Page 2, Column 5
Burial	25 Sep 1905	Mount Washington Cemetery, Independence, Jackson, Missouri, United States
Father	Alfred OLIVER (1805-1854)	
Mother	Eugenie [--?--] (1814-)	

Children

M	**Leonidus "Lee" CHICK**	
Birth	9 Apr 1854	Kansas City, Jackson, Missouri, United States
Census	1860	Page 71, Kansas City, Jackson, Missouri, United States
Census	1870	Page 479, Saint Louis Township, Saint Louis, Missouri, United States
Census	1880	ED 371, Page 454, Saint Louis (city), Missouri, United States
Residence	1905	Pittsburg, Crawford, Kansas, United States
Death	31 Jan 1935	Chronic Endarteritis, Chronic Arteriosclerosis; Kansas City, Jackson, Missouri, United States
Burial	2 Feb 1935	Mount Washington Cemetery, Independence, Jackson, Missouri, United States
Occupation		Clerk (1880), Secretary/Treasurer of Pittsburgh Coal & Mining Company
Marriage		

F	**Ida May CHICK**	
Birth	1855/6	Missouri, United States
Census	1860	Page 71, Kansas City, Jackson, Missouri, United States
Census	1870	Page 479, Saint Louis Township, Saint Louis, Missouri, United States
Census	1880	ED 371, Page 454, Saint Louis (city), Missouri, United States
Death		
Burial		
Marriage		

M	**Henry CHICK**	
Birth	7 Nov 1856	Kansas City, Jackson, Missouri, United States
Census	1860	Page 71, Kansas City, Jackson, Missouri, United States
Census	1870	Page 479, Saint Louis Township, Saint Louis, Missouri, United States
Census	1880	ED 371, Page 454, Saint Louis (city), Missouri, United States
Census	1900	ED 84, Page 256, Kansas City, Jackson, Missouri, United States
Census	1910	ED 104, Page 82, Kansas City, Jackson, Missouri, United States
Death	30 Aug 1925	Chronic Interstitial Nephritis, Chronic Myocarditis; Kansas City, Jackson, Missouri, United States
Burial	1 Sep 1925	Mount Washington Cemetery, Independence, Jackson, Missouri, United States
Occupation		Commission Merchant (1880), Clerk d[ry] g[oods] (1900), Agent Real Estate (1910)
Spouse	Dixie WINSHIP (1862-1951)	
Marriage	7 Jun 1887	(1887K0070505), Jackson, Missouri, United States

F	**Nellie M. CHICK**	
Birth	7 Jul 1858	Kansas City, Jackson, Missouri, United States
Census	1870	Page 479, Saint Louis Township, Saint Louis, Missouri, United States
Census	1880	ED 90, Page 49, Fort Worth, Tarrant, Texas, United States
Census	1900	ED 84, Page 256, Kansas City, Jackson, Missouri, United States
Census	1910	ED 104, Page 82, Kansas City, Jackson, Missouri, United States
Death	18 Feb 1911	Paresis; Kansas City, Jackson, Missouri, United States
Burial	19 Feb 1911	Mount Washington Cemetery, Independence, Jackson, Missouri, United States
Residence		Death Certificate: 20 Years Former Residence Fort Worth, [--?--] Co., TX

Father	Washington Henry CHICK	
Mother	Eugenia Pauline "Eugenie" OLIVER	
Children		

Nellie M. CHICK (continued)

Spouse		Joseph H. BROWN (-1890)
Marriage	26 Nov 1879	Saint Louis (city), Missouri, United States

M Charles Peery CHICK

Birth	1860	Missouri, United States
Census	1860	Page 71, Kansas City, Jackson, Missouri, United States
Census	1870	Page 479, Saint Louis Township, Saint Louis, Missouri, United States
Census	1880	ED 371, Page 454, Saint Louis (city), Missouri, United States
Occupation		Clerk (1880)
Death		
Burial		
Marriage		

M Oliver Alfred CHICK

Birth	15 Sep 1861	Missouri, United States
Census	1870	Page 479, Saint Louis Township, Saint Louis, Missouri, United States
Census	1880	ED 371, Page 454, Saint Louis (city), Missouri, United States
Census	1900	ED 84, Page 256, Kansas City, Jackson, Missouri, United States
Census	1910	ED 104, Page 82, Kansas City, Jackson, Missouri, United States
Death	22 Oct 1919	Paresis, Arteriosclerositic Brain; Kansas City, Jackson, Missouri, United States
Burial	24 Oct 1919	Mount Washington Cemetery, Independence, Jackson, Missouri, United States
Occupation		Clerk (1880), Salesman
Marriage		

M Thomas M. CHICK

Birth	1863/4	Missouri, United States
Census	1870	Page 479, Saint Louis Township, Saint Louis, Missouri, United States
Census	1880	ED 371, Page 454, Saint Louis (city), Missouri, United States
Residence	1905	Chicago, Cook, Illinois, United States
Death		
Burial		
Marriage		

M Allen Smith CHICK

Birth	15 Aug 1868	(or Aug 1869), Saint Louis, St. Louis, Missouri, United States
Census	1870	Page 479, Saint Louis Township, Saint Louis, Missouri, United States
Census	1880	ED 371, Page 454, Saint Louis (city), Missouri, United States
Census	1900	ED 14, Page 9, Fishing River Township, Clay, Missouri, United States
Residence	1905	Kansas City, Jackson, Missouri, United States
Death	19 Sep 1950	Coronary Occlusion, Cerebral & Coronary Arteriosclerosis; Kansas City, Jackson, Missouri, United States
Burial	22 Sep 1950	Mount Washington Cemetery, Independence, Jackson, Missouri, United States
Occupation		Farmer (1900), Manager of Gillis Building
Spouse		Florence Ella BOOTH (1871-1953)
Marriage	14 Nov 1894	(1894K0010535), Jackson, Missouri, United States

F Jane CHICK

Birth	1868/9	Missouri, United States
Census	1870	Page 479, Saint Louis Township, Saint Louis, Missouri, United States
Census	1880	
Death		
Burial		
Marriage		

M Howard Eugene CHICK

Birth	4 Aug 1870	Saint Louis, Saint Louis, Missouri, United States
Census	1880	ED 371, Page 454, Saint Louis (city), Missouri, United States
Census	1900	ED 84, Page 256, Kansas City, Jackson, Missouri, United States
Census	1910	ED 200, Page 69, Kansas City, Jackson, Missouri, United States
Census	1920	ED 283, Page 152, Washington Township, Jackson, Missouri, United States

Father	Washington Henry CHICK	
Mother	Eugenia Pauline "Eugenie" OLIVER	

Children

Howard Eugene CHICK (continued)

Census	1930	
Census	1940	ED 48-60, Page 1005, Washington Township, Jackson, Missouri, United States
Death	3 Nov 1944	Cerebral Hemorrhage, Arteriosclerosis, Hypertension, Chronic Nephritis; Washington Township, Jackson, Missouri, United States
Burial	6 Nov 1944	Mount Washington Cemetery, Independence, Jackson, Missouri, United States
Occupation		Bank Clerk (1900), Bookkeeper Bank (1910), Retired Bookkeeper of First National Bank (1944)
Spouse	Eleanor E. ACKLEY (1869-1954)	
Marriage	16 Dec 1905	(1905K0033649), Kansas City, Jackson, Missouri, United States

Father William Sidney CHICK

Birth	1818/9	Missouri, United States
Misc		PROBABLY NOT A TAXPAYER
Census	1840	(Wm. M. Chick Family), Page 69, Jackson, Missouri, United States
Census	1850	Page 243, Kaw Township, Jackson, Missouri, United States
Census	1860	Page 50, Kansas City, Jackson, Missouri, United States
Census	1870	(Township 55, Range 20), Page 334, Chariton, Missouri, United States
Census	1880	ED 101, Page 146, Shawnee Township, Johnson, Kansas, United States
Death	10 Apr 1895	Welda, Anderson, Kansas, United States
Misc		Death Notice, Kansas City (Mo.) Daily Journal, 11 Apr 1895, Page 8.
Burial	12 Apr 1895	Union Cemetery, Kansas City, Jackson, Missouri, United States
Misc		Funeral Notice, Kansas City (Mo.) Daily Journal, 13 Apr 1895, Page 4
Occupation		Merchant (1850), Commission Merchant (1860), Farmer (1870, 1880)
Marriage	7 Dec 1842	(1842I0020047), Jackson, Missouri, United States
Father		Col. William Miles CHICK (1794-1847)
Mother		Ann Elizabeth SMITH (1796-1876)

Mother Margaret C. FINDLAY

Birth	May 1823	Missouri, United States
Census	1850	Page 243, Kaw Township, Jackson, Missouri, United States
Census	1860	Page 50, Kansas City, Jackson, Missouri, United States
Census	1870	(Township 55, Range 20), Page 334, Chariton, Missouri, United States
Census	1880	ED 101, Page 146, Shawnee Township, Johnson, Kansas, United States
Death	17 Jan 1890	Kansas City, Jackson, Missouri, United States
Burial		Union Cemetery, Kansas City, Jackson, Missouri, United States
Father		
Mother		Henrietta C. D. [--?--] (1789-)

Children

F Emma CHICK

Birth	1842/3	Missouri, United States
Census	1850	Page 243, Kaw Township, Jackson, Missouri, United States
Census	1860	Page 50, Kansas City, Jackson, Missouri, United States
Census	1870	
Census	1880	
Death		
Burial		
Marriage		

M Henry F. CHICK

Birth	18 Sep 1845	Missouri, United States
Census	1850	
Census	1860	Page 50, Kansas City, Jackson, Missouri, United States
Census	1870	
Census	1880	
Death	17 Dec 1919	Acute Nephritis, Uremia, Senility; Kansas City, Jackson, Missouri, United States
Burial	19 Dec 1919	Mount Washington Cemetery, Independence, Jackson, Missouri, United States
Spouse		Mary E. F. CUMMINGS (1849-1935)
Marriage		

M William M. CHICK

Birth	8 Jul 1848	
Census	1850	
Death	Sep 1859	
Burial		Union Cemetery, Kansas City, Jackson, Missouri, United States
Marriage		

F Mary D. CHICK

Birth	1851/2	Missouri, United States
Census	1860	Page 50, Kansas City, Jackson, Missouri, United States
Census	1870	(Township 55, Range 20), Page 334, Chariton, Missouri, United States
Census	1880	
Death		

Father	William Sidney CHICK	
Mother	**Margaret C. FINDLAY**	
Children		

Mary D. CHICK (continued)

Burial		
Marriage		

F	**Anna Julia "Ann" CHICK**	
Birth	16 Mar 1854	Missouri, United States
Census	1860	Page 50, Kansas City, Jackson, Missouri, United States
Census	1870	(Township 55, Range 20), Page 334, Chariton, Missouri, United States
Census	1880	ED 101, Page 146, Shawnee Township, Johnson, Kansas, United States
Death	6 Dec 1936	Arteriosclerosis, Senility, Infantile Paralysis Occurring when 3 Years Old; Kansas City, Jackson, Missouri, United States
Burial	8 Dec 1936	Union Cemetery, Kansas City, Jackson, Missouri, United States
Marriage		

F	**Frances V. "Fannie" CHICK**	
Birth	8 Feb 1857	Missouri, United States
Census	1860	Page 50, Kansas City, Jackson, Missouri, United States
Census	1870	(Township 55, Range 20), Page 334, Chariton, Missouri, United States
Death	30 Dec 1878	Glenwood, Johnson, Kansas, United States
Burial	1 Jan 1879	Union Cemetery, Kansas City, Jackson, Missouri, United States
Misc		Funeral Notice, Kansas City (Mo.) Daily Journal, 1 Jan 1879, Page 8, Column 4
Marriage		

M	**Wilburn CHICK**	
Birth	1860	Missouri, United States
Census	1860	Page 50, Kansas City, Jackson, Missouri, United States
Census	1870	(Township 55, Range 20), Page 334, Chariton, Missouri, United States
Census	1880	ED 101, Page 146, Shawnee Township, Johnson, Kansas, United States
Occupation		Works on Farm (1880)
Death		
Burial		
Marriage		

M	**Charles S. CHICK**	
Birth	1862/3	Missouri, United States
Census	1870	(Township 55, Range 20), Page 334, Chariton, Missouri, United States
Census	1880	ED 101, Page 146, Shawnee Township, Johnson, Kansas, United States
Death		
Burial		
Marriage		

M	**Joseph S. CHICK**	
Birth	1866/7	Missouri, United States
Census	1870	(Township 55, Range 20), Page 334, Chariton, Missouri, United States
Census	1880	ED 101, Page 146, Shawnee Township, Johnson, Kansas, United States
Death		
Burial		
Marriage		

Father William CHRISMAN

Birth	23 Nov 1822	Fayette, Kentucky, United States
Census	1840	(Joseph Chrisman Family), Eastern Division, Page 136, Fayette, Kentucky, United States
Degree	1846	AB Degree; Center College, Danville, Boyle, Kentucky, United States
Degree	1847	Admitted to the Bar
Residence	bet 1848 and 1897	Independence, Jackson, Missouri, United States
Census	1850	Page 261, Blue Township, Jackson, Missouri, United States
Census		Slave Schedules, Frame 105, Blue Township, Jackson, Missouri, United States
Property	13 Nov 1850	First Known Purchase, Lot Adj. Hansbrough's Add., Indep.; Volume R, Page 72, Independence, Jackson, Missouri, United States
Census	1860	Page 265, Independence, Jackson, Missouri, United States
Census		Slave Schedules, Page 364, Independence, Jackson, Missouri, United States
Occupation	1860	City Councilman; Independence, Jackson, Missouri, United States
Misc	19 Apr 1862	Union Provost Marshals' File of Papers Relating to Two or More Civilians, M416, Roll 5, No. 1075
Tax Lists	Sep 1862	Lawyer License; Independence, Jackson, Missouri, United States
Military	Sep 1863	Civil War Draft Registration; Blue Township, Jackson, Missouri, United States
Tax Lists	May 1866	Lawyer License; Independence, Jackson, Missouri, United States
Census	1870	Page 294, Independence, Jackson, Missouri, United States
Census		Agricultural Schedules, Ward 3, Page 1, Independence, Jackson, Missouri, United States
Misc		Biography and Portrait, Commonwealth of Missouri (1877), Pages 767-768
Misc		Sketch of Chrisman's House, Illustrated Atlas Map of Jackson Co., Mo. (1877), Page 65
Misc		Biography and Portrait, US Biographical Dictionary and Portrait Gallery . . . Missouri Volume (1878), Pages 442-444
Census	1880	ED 24, Page 33, Independence, Jackson, Missouri, United States
Misc		Biography, History of Jackson Co., Mo. (1881), Pages 869-870
Misc		"Costly Residence Burned," Kansas City (Mo.) Star, 28 Nov 1887, Page 1, Column 1
Misc		Biography, Memorial & Biographical Record of Kansas City . . . (1896), Pages 582-586
Death	28 Jan 1897	Paralytic Stroke; Near Lee's Summit, Jackson, Missouri, United States
Misc		Obituary, Kansas City (Mo.) Star, 28 Jan 1897, Page 2, Column 4
Burial	29 Jan 1897	Mount Washington Cemetery, Independence, Jackson, Missouri, United States
Misc		Obituary, Kansas City (Mo.) Times, 29 Jan 1897, Page 8, Column 4
Misc		Funeral Notice, Kansas City (Mo.) Star, 29 Jan 1897, Page 2, Column 3
Probate	1 Feb 1897	(Administrator's Bond), Volume C, Page 133, Independence, Jackson, Missouri, United States
Misc		Biography, Encyclopedia of the History of Missouri (1901)
Misc		Mary Gentry Shaw, "William Chrisman, a Leader, Educator, Banker and Statesman," Jackson County Historical Society quarterly 15 (Dec. 1973): 6-7
Misc		Photo, Jackson County Pioneers (1975), Page 468
Occupation		Lawyer (1850, 1860, 1870), Banker (1880)
Religion		First Presbyterian Church; Independence, Jackson, Missouri, United States
Marriage	10 May 1848	Boyle, Kentucky, United States
Father	Joseph S. CHRISMAN (1800-1875)	
Mother	Elenor H. SOPER (1803-1879)	

Mother Lucy Ann LEE

Birth	12 Jul 1828	Kentucky, United States
Census	1850	Page 261, Blue Township, Jackson, Missouri, United States
Census	1860	Page 265, Independence, Jackson, Missouri, United States
Census	1870	Page 294, Independence, Jackson, Missouri, United States
Census	1880	ED 24, Page 33, Independence, Jackson, Missouri, United States
Death	16 Feb 1889	(or Feb 1885); El Paso, El Paso, Texas, United States
Burial		Mount Washington Cemetery, Independence, Jackson, Missouri, United States
Father	George LEE (1792-1879)	
Mother	Lucy Ann THOMPSON (1792-1842)	

Children

Father	William CHRISMAN		
Mother	Lucy Ann LEE		
Children			

M	George Lee CHRISMAN		
Birth	2 Aug 1851	(or 08 Aug 1851), Jackson, Missouri, United States	
Census	1860	Page 265, Independence, Jackson, Missouri, United States	
Census	1870	Page 294, Independence, Jackson, Missouri, United States	
Graduation	1870	Forest Hill Academy, Anchorage, [--?--], Kentucky, United States	
Census	1880	Page 76, Blue Township, Jackson, Missouri, United States	
Death	21 May 1916	Cancer of Left Kidney; Independence, Jackson, Missouri, United States	
Misc		Obituary, Independence (Mo.) Examiner, 22 May 1916, Page 1, Column 1	
Burial	24 May 1916	Mount Washington Cemetery, Independence, Jackson, Missouri, United States	
Occupation		Farmer (1880)	
Spouse	Lutie Lucy DUKE (1866-1933)		
Marriage	8 Aug 1900	(1900K0020461), Jackson, Missouri, United States	

M	James Lee CHRISMAN		
Birth	1853	Missouri, United States	
Census	1860	Page 265, Independence, Jackson, Missouri, United States	
Census	1870	Page 294, Independence, Jackson, Missouri, United States	
Death	29 Oct 1872	(While a Student at Westminster College), Fulton, Callaway, Missouri, United States	
Burial		Mount Washington Cemetery, Independence, Jackson, Missouri, United States	
Marriage			

F	Margaret W. "Maggie" CHRISMAN		
Birth	12 Jun 1855	Independence, Jackson, Missouri, United States	
Census	1860	Page 265, Independence, Jackson, Missouri, United States	
Census	1870	Page 294, Independence, Jackson, Missouri, United States	
Census	1880	ED 24, Page 33, Independence, Jackson, Missouri, United States	
Census	1900	ED 8, Page 131, Independence, Jackson, Missouri, United States	
Census	1910		
Residence	1920	New York, United States	
Death	21 Jan 1942	Cerebral Hemorrhage, Arteriosclerosis . . .; Independence, Jackson, Missouri, United States	
Misc		Obituary, Independence (Mo.) Examiner, 22 Jan 1942, Page 2, Column 3	
Burial	23 Jan 1942	Mount Washington Cemetery, Independence, Jackson, Missouri, United States	
Occupation		Capitalist (1900)	
Spouse	Logan Oliver SWOPE (1847-1900)		
Marriage	10 May 1877	(1877I0070367), Jackson, Missouri, United States	

Father William B. COCKRELL

Birth	1833/4	Virginia, United States
Census	1850	
Census	1860	Page 26, Kansas City, Jackson, Missouri, United States
Tax Lists	Sep 1862	Wholesale Dealer License; "Cockrell & Ward", Kansas City, Jackson, Missouri, United States
Military		Enrolled Missouri Militia
Military	Dec 1863	Civil War Draft Registration; Kaw Township, Jackson, Missouri, United States
Tax Lists	May 1865	Wholesale Liquor Dealer License; Kansas City, Jackson, Missouri, United States
Tax Lists	May 1866	Wholesale Liquor Dealer License; Kansas City, Jackson, Missouri, United States
Tax Lists	Aug 1866	Wholesale Liquor Dealer License; Kansas City, Jackson, Missouri, United States
Census	1870	Page 429, Kansas City, Jackson, Missouri, United States
Death	May 1871	
Burial	19 May 1871	Liberty, Clay, Missouri, United States
Misc		Funeral Notice, Kansas City (Mo.) Daily Journal of Commerce, 19 May 1871, Page 4, Column 1
Misc		Funeral Notice, Kansas City (Mo.) Daily Journal of Commerce, 20 May 1871, Page 4, Column 2
Probate	22 May 1871	(Administrator's Bond), Volume BB, Page 7, Independence, Jackson, Missouri, United States
Occupation		Merchant (1860, 1870), Wholesale Dealer, Wholesale Liquor Dealer
Business		Cockrell & Ward (Wholesale Dealer)
Marriage	29 Dec 1857	Clay, Missouri, United States
Father		
Mother		

Mother Louisa Anna TURNER

Birth	1 Feb 1841	(or May 1842), Clay, Missouri, United States
Census	1850	Page 342, Liberty, Clay, Missouri, United States
Census	1860	Page 26, Kansas City, Jackson, Missouri, United States
Census	1870	Page 429, Kansas City, Jackson, Missouri, United States
Census	1875	Page 146, Wyandotte, Wyandotte, Kansas, United States
Census	1880	ED 127, Page 245, Sedalia, Pettis, Missouri, United States
Census	1900	ED 112, Page 238, Sedalia, Pettis, Missouri, United States
Census	1910	ED 204, Page 9, Oklahoma City, Oklahoma, Oklahoma, United States
Death	7 Nov 1910	
Burial		Crown Hill Cemetery, Sedalia, Pettis, Missouri, United States
Father		
Mother		
Other spouse		Gilbert Shaw LANDER (1827-1901)
Marriage	21 Oct 1873	(1873I0070129), Jackson, Missouri, United States

Children

M William B. COCKRELL

Birth	1859	Missouri, United States
Census	1860	Page 27, Kansas City, Jackson, Missouri, United States
Death		
Burial		
Marriage		

F Flora COCKRELL

Birth	1860	Missouri, United States
Census	1870	Page 429, Kansas City, Jackson, Missouri, United States
Census	1875	Page 146, Wyandotte, Wyandotte, Kansas, United States
Census	1880	ED 127, Page 245, Sedalia, Pettis, Missouri, United States
Occupation		Pupil (1875), Typesetter (1880)
Death		
Burial		
Marriage		

Father	William B. COCKRELL		
Mother	Louisa Anna TURNER		
Children			
M	**James Ward COCKRELL**		
	Birth	Jun 1863	Missouri, United States
	Census	1870	Page 429, Kansas City, Jackson, Missouri, United States
	Census	1875	Page 146, Wyandotte, Wyandotte, Kansas, United States
	Census	1880	
	Census	1900	ED 112, Page 253, Sedalia, Pettis, Missouri, United States
	Occupation		Pupil (1875), Machinist (1900)
	Death		
	Burial		
	Spouse	Mary M. YOPST (1863-)	
	Marriage	17 Jun 1886	Sedalia, Pettis, Missouri, United States
F	**Mary K. COCKRELL**		
	Birth	6 Aug 1872	Missouri, United States
	Census	1875	Page 146, Wyandotte, Wyandotte, Kansas, United States
	Census	1880	ED 127, Page 245, Sedalia, Pettis, Missouri, United States
	Census	1900	ED 171, Page 259, Oklahoma City, Oklahoma, Oklahoma Territory, United States
	Census	1910	ED 204, Page 9, Oklahoma City, Oklahoma, Oklahoma, United States
	Census	1920	ED 101, Page 129, Crutcho Township, Oklahoma, Oklahoma, United States
	Residence	May 1971	Rexford, Saratoga, New York, United States
	Death		May 1971
	Burial		
	Spouse	Kenner Rice COBINE (1870-1929)	
	Marriage	28 Nov 1895	(1895K0012240), Kansas City, Jackson, Missouri, United States
	Spouse	George W. LONGAN (1870-)	
	Marriage	24 Nov 1913	(Book 21, Page 391), Oklahoma, Oklahoma, United States

Father Oscar H. COGSWELL

Birth	6 Jun 1820	Randolph, Orange, Vermont, United States
Residence		Saint Louis, Saint Louis, Missouri, United States
Property	16 Sep 1848	First Known Purchase, Part Lot 115, Indep.; Volume N, Page 332, Independence, Jackson, Missouri, United States
Census	1850	Page 292, Blue Township, Jackson, Missouri, United States
Census	1860	Page 245, Independence, Jackson, Missouri, United States
Census		Slave Schedules, Page 363, Independence, Jackson, Missouri, United States
Misc	19 Apr 1862	Union Provost Marshals' File of Papers Relating to Two or More Civilians, M416, Roll 5, No. 1075
Occupation	1862	Judge, County Court; Jackson, Missouri, United States
Tax Lists	Sep 1862	Retail Dealer License; "A. H. Cogswell", Independence, Jackson, Missouri, United States
Tax Lists	Apr 1863	Livery Stable License, 2 One-Horse Carriages, and 2 Two-Horse Carriages; Independence, Jackson, Missouri, United States
Military	Sep 1863–Oct 1863	Civil War Draft Registration; Blue Township, Jackson, Missouri, United States
Census	1870	Page 283, Independence, Jackson, Missouri, United States
Census	1880	ED 24, Page 39, Independence, Jackson, Missouri, United States
Death	16 Jun 1881	
Burial		Woodlawn Cemetery, Independence, Jackson, Missouri, United States
Misc		"Cogswell Store Raided," Jackson County Pioneers (1975), Pages 379-380
Occupation		Leather Dealer (1850), Merchant (1860), Retail Grocer (1870), Retail Dealer, Livery Stable Keeper
Marriage		
Father		Harvey COGSWELL (1790-1862)
Mother		Emily MORGAN (1789-1831)
Other spouse		Elenora E. SHAFTNER (1815-)
Marriage		

Mother Nancy B. "Nannie" ROGERS

Birth	25 Aug 1830	Pittsylvania, Virginia, United States
Residence	bet 1830 and 1846	Pittsylvania, Virginia, United States
Residence	bet 1846 and 1919	(Except for 1-2 Years in Salt Lake City, UT); Independence, Jackson, Missouri, United States
Census	1850	Page 266, Blue Township, Jackson, Missouri, United States
Census	1860	Page 245, Independence, Jackson, Missouri, United States
Census	1870	Page 283, Independence, Jackson, Missouri, United States
Census	1880	ED 24, Page 39, Independence, Jackson, Missouri, United States
Census	1900	ED 7, Page 101, Independence, Jackson, Missouri, United States
Census	1910	ED 10, Page 142, Independence, Jackson, Missouri, United States
Residence	1912	Independence, Jackson, Missouri, United States
Death	16 Jul 1919	Senility Complicated with Fractured Thigh (Accidental Fall); Independence, Jackson, Missouri, United States
Misc		Obituary, Independence (Mo.) Examiner, 17 Jul 1919, Page 1, Column 5
Burial	18 Jul 1919	Woodlawn Cemetery, Independence, Jackson, Missouri, United States
Misc		Funeral Notice, Kansas City (Mo.) Times, 19 Jul 1919, Page 3, Column 1
Occupation		Dressmaker (1900), Own Income (1910)
Religion		Charter Member, First Christian Church; Independence, Jackson, Missouri, United States
Father		William B. ROGERS (1804-1863)
Mother		Sarah STONE (1809-1871)

Children

F   Emma COGSWELL

Birth	23 Mar 1854	Salt Lake City, Salt Lake, Utah Territory, United States
Census	1860	Page 245, Independence, Jackson, Missouri, United States
Census	1870	Page 283, Independence, Jackson, Missouri, United States
Census	1880	ED 24, Page 39, Independence, Jackson, Missouri, United States
Census	1900	ED 7, Page 101, Independence, Jackson, Missouri, United States
Census	1910	ED 10, Page 142, Independence, Jackson, Missouri, United States
Residence	1919	Independence, Jackson, Missouri, United States
Residence	1931	Independence, Jackson, Missouri, United States
Death	26 Mar 1936	Influenza, Bronchopneumonia; Kansas City, Jackson, Missouri, United States

Father	Oscar H. COGSWELL	
Mother	Nancy B. "Nannie" ROGERS	
Children		

Emma COGSWELL (continued)

Misc		Obituary, Independence (Mo.) Examiner, 27 Mar 1936, Page 1, Column 7
Burial	28 Mar 1936	Woodlawn Cemetery, Independence, Jackson, Missouri, United States
Occupation		Dressmaker (1900)
Marriage		

M Oscar W. COGSWELL

Birth	2 Sep 1856	(or Sep 1857), Independence, Jackson, Missouri, United States
Census	1860	Page 245, Independence, Jackson, Missouri, United States
Census	1870	Page 284, Independence, Jackson, Missouri, United States
Census	1880	ED 24, Page 39, Independence, Jackson, Missouri, United States
Census	1900	ED 5, Page 70, Independence, Jackson, Missouri, United States
Census	1910	ED 7, Page 118, Independence, Jackson, Missouri, United States
Residence	1912	Independence, Jackson, Missouri, United States
Residence	1919	Independence, Jackson, Missouri, United States
Census	1920	ED 12, Page 245, Independence, Jackson, Missouri, United States
Death	17 Dec 1931	Cerebral Edema, Hypostatic Pneumonia Bronchial; Independence, Jackson, Missouri, United States
Misc		Obituary, Independence (Mo.) Examiner, 18 Dec 1931, Page 1, Column 4
Burial	19 Dec 1931	Woodlawn Cemetery, Independence, Jackson, Missouri, United States
Occupation		Clerk in Store (1880), Clerk of Probate Court (1900, 1910, 1920)
Spouse	Myra Lee SHAW (1870-1945)	
Marriage	19 Sep 1893	(1893K0008855), Jackson, Missouri, United States

M John Rogers COGSWELL

Birth	14 Dec 1866	(or Dec 1865), Independence, Jackson, Missouri, United States
Census	1870	Page 284, Independence, Jackson, Missouri, United States
Census	1880	ED 24, Page 39, Independence, Jackson, Missouri, United States
Census	1900	ED 7, Page 99, Independence, Jackson, Missouri, United States
Census	1910	ED 13, Page 195, Independence, Jackson, Missouri, United States
Death	22 Aug 1912	Streptococcic Meningitis (Metastatic) . . .; Kansas City, Jackson, Missouri, United States
Misc		Obituary, Independence (Mo.) Examiner, 22 Aug 1912, Page 1, Column 3
Burial	24 Aug 1912	Mount Washington Cemetery, Independence, Jackson, Missouri, United States
Occupation		Clerk in Store (1880), Assistant Cashier (1900), Banker President (1910)
Occupation		President of Chrisman-Sawyer Bank (1912); Independence, Jackson, Missouri, United States
Spouse	Etta BURDETTE (1866-1942)	
Marriage	8 Feb 1893	(1893I0001281), Independence, Jackson, Missouri, United States

Father Abram COMINGO

Birth	9 Jan 1820	Near Harrodsburg,, Mercer, Kentucky, United States
Graduation		Centre College, Danville, Boyle, Kentucky, United States
Residence	1847	Danville, Boyle, Kentucky, United States
Residence	bet 1848 and 1881	Independence, Jackson, Missouri, United States
Census	1850	Page 262, Blue Township, Jackson, Missouri, United States
Census		Slave Schedules, Frame 105, Blue Township, Jackson, Missouri, United States
Census	1860	Page 266, Independence, Jackson, Missouri, United States
Census		Slave Schedules, Page 364, Independence, Jackson, Missouri, United States
Tax Lists	Sep 1862	Lawyer License; "Abraham Comingo", Kansas City, Jackson, Missouri, United States
Occupation	May 1863	Appointed Provost Marshal of the Sixth District of Missouri
Military	1863	Civil War Draft Registration; Blue Township, Jackson, Missouri, United States
Tax Lists	May 1866	Lawyer License, Income, Carriage, Gold Watch, and Pianoforte; Independence, Jackson, Missouri, United States
Tax Lists	Dec 1866	Real Estate Agent License; "Comingo, Hickman & Company", Independence, Jackson, Missouri, United States
Occupation	1868	Elected Recorder of Deeds; Jackson, Missouri, United States
Census	1870	Page 297, Independence, Jackson, Missouri, United States
Occupation	bet 1871 and 1875	United States Representative; Washington, District of Columbia, United States
Misc		Biography, Biographical Annals of the Civil Government of the U. S. During Its First Century (1876)
Misc		Sketch of Comingo's House, Illustrated Atlas Map of Jackson Co., Mo. (1877), Page 60
Census	1880	ED 24, Page 48, Independence, Jackson, Missouri, United States
Residence	bet 1881 and 1889	Kansas City, Jackson, Missouri, United States
Will	7 Mar 1885	(Will Written), Volume 3, Page 32, Kansas City, Jackson, Missouri, United States
Misc		Biography, History of Kansas City, Mo. (1888), Page 331
Death	10 Nov 1889	Cancer; Kansas City, Jackson, Missouri, United States
Misc		Obituary, Kansas City (Mo.) Times, 11 Nov 1889, Page 2, Columns 5-6
Misc		Obituary and Portrait, Kansas City (Mo.) Daily Journal, 11 Nov 1889, Page 4, COlumns 6-7
Burial	12 Nov 1889	Elmwood Cemetery, Kansas City, Jackson, Missouri, United States
Misc		Funeral Notice, Kansas City (Mo.) Star, 12 Nov 1889, Page 1, Column 2
Probate	18 Nov 1889	(Will Proved), Volume 3, Page 32, Kansas City, Jackson, Missouri, United States
Misc		Biography, Encyclopedia of the History of Missouri (1901)
Misc		Biography, Herringshaw's National Library of American Biography (1909-14)
Misc		Biography, Biographical Directory of the United States Congress, 1774-2005 . . . (2005), Page ___
Occupation		Lawyer (1850, 1860, 1880), Attorney at Law (1870)
Marriage	8 May 1848	(Book 2, Page 1), Boyle, Kentucky, United States
Father	John COMINGO (1785-1841)	
Mother	Sally COZINE (1787-1839)	

Mother Lucy J. MORTON

Birth	1821/2	Kentucky, United States
Census	1850	Page 262, Blue Township, Jackson, Missouri, United States
Census	1860	Page 266, Independence, Jackson, Missouri, United States
Census	1870	Page 297, Independence, Jackson, Missouri, United States
Census	1880	ED 24, Page 48, Independence, Jackson, Missouri, United States
Death	24 Aug 1890	Quogue, Suffolk, New York, United States
Misc		Obituary, Kansas City (Mo.) Star, 27 Aug 1890, Page 1, Column 3
Burial	28 Aug 1890	Elmwood Cemetery, Kansas City, Jackson, Missouri, United States
Father		
Mother		

Children

F Sallie A. COMINGO

Birth	25 Sep 1853	(or Sep 1854), Missouri, United States
Census	1860	Page 266, Independence, Jackson, Missouri, United States
Census	1870	Page 297, Independence, Jackson, Missouri, United States
Census	1880	ED 18, Page 474, Kansas City, Jackson, Missouri, United States
Census	1900	ED 121, Page 203, Kansas City, Jackson, Missouri, United States
Death	8 Mar 1916	Arteriosclerosis, Coronary Embolism; Kansas City, Jackson, Missouri, United States

Father Abram COMINGO			
Mother Lucy J. MORTON			
Children			
	Sallie A. COMINGO (continued)		
	Burial	10 Mar 1916	Elmwood Cemetery, Kansas City, Jackson, Missouri, United States
	Spouse	Dr. Jefferson Davis GRIFFITH (1850-1924)	
	Marriage	28 Jan 1880	(1880I0080047), Jackson, Missouri, United States
M	**John COMINGO**		
	Birth	1852	Independence, Jackson, Missouri, United States
	Death	Jun 1853	Independence, Jackson, Missouri, United States
	Burial		Elmwood Cemetery, Kansas City, Jackson, Missouri, United States
	Marriage		

Father Henry Beatty CONWELL

Birth	1831/2	Xenia, Greene, Ohio, United States
Census	1850	Page 16, Xenia Township, Greene, Ohio, United States
Census	1860	Post Office Kansas City, Page 142, Jackson, Missouri, United States
Misc	abt 1862	Union Provost Marshals' File of Papers . . . Two or More Civilians, M416, Roll 80, No. 21,974
Tax Lists	Sep 1862	Wholesale Dealer License; "Dinker [Drinkard] & Conwell", Kansas City, Jackson, Missouri, United States
Military		Chaplain, U. S. Army
Misc		"Drinkard & Conwell," Kansas City (Mo.) Daily Journal of Commerce, 02 Jul 1863, Page 3, Column 5
Misc		Advertisement, Kansas City (Mo.) Western Journal of Commerce, 02 Jul 1863, Page 3, Column 5
Military	bet Sep 1863 and Oct 1863	Civil War Draft Registration; Kaw Township, Jackson, Missouri, United States
Tax Lists	May 1866	Retail Dealer License; Kansas City, Jackson, Missouri, United States
Census	1870	Page 379, Kansas City, Jackson, Missouri, United States
Census	1880	ED 9, Page 272, Kansas City, Jackson, Missouri, United States
Census	1890	
Death	14 Oct 1890	Duodenitis; Kansas City, Jackson, Missouri, United States
Burial	16 Oct 1890	Union Cemetery, Kansas City, Jackson, Missouri, United States
Misc		Obituary, Kansas City (Mo.) Times, 16 Oct 1890, Page 2, Column 2
Misc		Biography, Soldiers of Various Wars Interred at Union Cemetery (1989), Page 26
Occupation		Tanner (1850), Trader (1860), Gunpowder Agent (1870), Powder Dealer (1880)
Business		Drinkard & Conwell (Wholesale Dealer, Groceries & Provisions)
Occupation		Merchant, Wholesale Dealer
Religion		Episcopal Church
Marriage	18 Jun 1861	Lafayette, Missouri, United States
Father		Richard CONWELL (1787-1845)
Mother		Eliza BEATTY (1799-1887)

Mother Jennie L. SMITH

Birth	1843/4	Virginia, United States
Census	1860	
Religion	1869	Confirmed; Saint Mary's Episcopal Church, Kansas City, Jackson, Missouri, United States
Census	1870	Page 379, Kansas City, Jackson, Missouri, United States
Census	1880	ED 9, Page 272, Kansas City, Jackson, Missouri, United States
Census	1900	
Census	1910	ED 77, Page 49, Los Angeles Township, Los Angeles, California, United States
Death	10 Feb 1916	Los Angeles, California, United States
Burial		
Father		
Mother		

Children

M Herbert CONWELL

Birth	1861/2	Missouri, United States
Census	1870	
Census	1880	ED 9, Page 272, Kansas City, Jackson, Missouri, United States
Occupation		Apprentice to Bricklayer (1880)
Death		
Burial		
Marriage		

M Henry Leftwich CONWELL

Birth	22 Aug 1862	
Death	11 Jun 1863	
Burial		Union Cemetery, Kansas City, Jackson, Missouri, United States
Marriage		

Father	Henry Beatty CONWELL	
Mother	Jennie L. SMITH	
Children		

F	**Sallie E. CONWELL**	
Birth	4 Feb 1864	Missouri, United States
Census	1870	Page 379, Kansas City, Jackson, Missouri, United States
Census	1880	ED 9, Page 272, Kansas City, Jackson, Missouri, United States
Death	28 Apr 1939	Hypostatic Carcinoma, Apoplexy; Kansas City, Jackson, Missouri, United States
Burial	1 May 1939	Union Cemetery, Kansas City, Jackson, Missouri, United States
Spouse	James Richard BRYAN (1858-1935)	
Marriage		

M	**John W. CONWELL**	
Birth	1865/6	Missouri, United States
Census	1870	Page 379, Kansas City, Jackson, Missouri, United States
Census	1880	ED 9, Page 272, Kansas City, Jackson, Missouri, United States
Death		
Burial		
Marriage		

F	**Rose Mary CONWELL**	
Birth	1866/7	Missouri, United States
Census	1870	Page 379, Kansas City, Jackson, Missouri, United States
Census	1880	ED 9, Page 272, Kansas City, Jackson, Missouri, United States
Death		
Burial		
Marriage		

F	**Susie Trella "Trell" CONWELL**	
Birth	24 Jan 1872	Missouri, United States
Census	1880	ED 9, Page 272, Kansas City, Jackson, Missouri, United States
Census	1900	
Census	1910	ED 77, Page 48, Los Angeles Township, Los Angeles, California, United States
Death	10 Jan 1955	Los Angeles, California, United States
Burial		
Spouse	Marshall S. ANDERSON (1870-)	
Marriage	24 May 1899	(1899K0018072), Kansas City, Jackson, Missouri, United States
Spouse	[--?--] ELLIS (-)	

M	**Harry Beatty CONWELL**	
Birth	19 Nov 1874	(or Nov 1873), Kansas City, Jackson, Missouri, United States
Census	1880	ED 9, Page 272, Kansas City, Jackson, Missouri, United States
Census	1900	ED 46, Page 302, Kansas City, Jackson, Missouri, United States
Census	1910	ED 45. {age, Kansas City, Jackson, Missouri, United States
Census	1910	ED 45, Page 106, Kansas City, Jackson, Missouri, United States
Census	1920	ED 66, Page 118, Kansas City, Jackson, Missouri, United States
Death	14 Jul 1938	Myocardive Failure, Hypertension, Coronary Occlusion, Chronic Interstitial Nephritis; Kansas City, Jackson, Missouri, United States
Cremation	16 Jul 1938	
Burial		Union Cemetery, Kansas City, Jackson, Missouri, United States
Occupation		Shipping Clerk Packing House (1900), Foreman Packing House (1910), Superintendent Oil Refinery (1920)
Spouse	Margaret Jiletti PAYNE (1878-)	
Marriage	1894/5	(or 1891/2)

Father James W. COOK

Birth	31 Mar 1821	Lexington, Fayette, Kentucky, United States
Census	1830	
Census	1840	
Census	1850	Page 207, Fayette, Kentucky, United States
Residence	1856-?	Kansas City, Jackson, Missouri, United States
Property	9 Dec 1856	First Known Purchase, Lot on Delaware St., City of Kansas; Volume Z, Page 367, Jackson, Missouri, United States
Census	1860	Page 6, Kansas City, Jackson, Missouri, United States
Census	1860	Agricultural Schedules, Page 1, Jackson, Missouri, United States
Tax Lists	Sep 1862	Auctioneer License; Kansas City, Jackson, Missouri, United States
Tax Lists	SepDec 1862	Auction Sales; Kansas City, Jackson, Missouri, United States
Military		Private, Company C, 77th Regiment Enrolled Missouri Militia
Military	Sep 1863	Civil War Draft Registration; Kaw Township, Jackson, Missouri, United States
Tax Lists	Sep 1865	Auctioneer License; Kansas City, Jackson, Missouri, United States
Tax Lists	May 1866	Income; Kansas City, Jackson, Missouri, United States
Occupation	bet 1868 and 1870	City Councilman; Kansas City, Jackson, Missouri, United States
Census	1870	Page 604, Kansas City, Jackson, Missouri, United States
Census	1880	ED 12, Page 354, Kansas City, Jackson, Missouri, United States
Misc		Biography, History of Jackson Co., Mo. (1881), Pages 756-757
Death	Jun 1886	
Burial	8 Jun 1886	Lexington Cemetery, Lexington, Fayette, Kentucky, United States
Misc		Funeral Notice, Kansas City (Mo.) Daily Journal, 14 Jun 1886, Page 3, Column 4
Occupation		Auctioneer (1850, 1860), Real Estate Agent (1870), Merchant
Marriage	30 Jan 1846	Fayette, Kentucky, United States
Father	Thomas Booth COOK (1786-1835)	
Mother	Jennie CHURCH (1790-1836)	
Other spouse	Fannie A. BAIRD (-)	
Marriage	Apr 1881	Lexington, Fayette, Kentucky, United States

Mother Elizabeth Arnett "Eliza" PICKETT

Birth	8 May 1825	Kentucky, United States
Census	1830	
Census	1840	
Residence	1846	Lexington, Fayette, Kentucky, United States
Census	1850	Page 207, Fayette, Kentucky, United States
Census	1860	Page 6, Kansas City, Jackson, Missouri, United States
Census	1870	Page 604, Kansas City, Jackson, Missouri, United States
Death	15 Mar 1880	Kansas City, Jackson, Missouri, United States
Burial	16 Mar 1880	Union Cemetery, Kansas City, Jackson, Missouri, United States
Misc		Funeral Notice, Kansas City (Mo.) Times, 16 Mar 1880, Page 8, Columns 1 & 4
Father	Jeremiah PICKETT (1793-1871)	
Mother	Frances ARNETT (1797-1827)	

Children

M William Pickett COOK

Birth	May 1847	Kentucky, United States
Census	1850	Page 207, Fayette, Kentucky, United States
Census	1860	Page 6, Kansas City, Jackson, Missouri, United States
Census	1870	Page 84, Arapahoe, Colorado Territory, United States
Census	1880	ED 95, Page 183, Alma, Park, Colorado, United States
Census	1900	ED 57, Page 243, Nogales, Santa Cruz, Arizona Territory, United States
Death	1908	Nogales, Santa Cruz, Arizona Territory, United States
Occupation		Cattle Dealer (1870), Druggist (1880), Miner Quartz (1900)
Burial		
Spouse	Mary Jane MANKER (1849-)	
Marriage	4 Jan 1870	(1870I0060197), Jackson, Missouri, United States

M George W. COOK

Birth	1850	Fayette, Kentucky, United States
Census	1850	Page 207, Fayette, Kentucky, United States

Father James W. COOK			
Mother Elizabeth Arnett "Eliza" PICKETT			
Children			

	George W. COOK (continued)		
Census		1860	Page 6, Kansas City, Jackson, Missouri, United States
Census		1870	Page 604, Kansas City, Jackson, Missouri, United States
Census		1880	ED 12, Page 354, Kansas City, Jackson, Missouri, United States
Death			
Burial			
Marriage			

M	**Thomas J./H. COOK**		
Birth		1851/2	Kentucky, United States
Census		1860	Page 6, Kansas City, Jackson, Missouri, United States
Census		1870	
Census		1880	ED 12, Page 354, Kansas City, Jackson, Missouri, United States
Census		1900	
Census		1910	ED 197, Page 108, Denver, Denver, Colorado, United States
Death			
Burial			
Marriage			

M	**James T. COOK**		
Birth		1858/9	Missouri, United States
Census		1860	Page 6, Kansas City, Jackson, Missouri, United States
Census		1870	
Census		1880	
Death			
Burial			
Marriage			

F	**Jennie C. COOK**		
Birth		May 1861	Missouri, United States
Census		1870	Page 604, Kansas City, Jackson, Missouri, United States
Census		1880	ED 95, Page 183, Alma, Park, Colorado, United States
Census		1880	ED 12, Page 354, Kansas City, Jackson, Missouri, United States
Census		1885	Page 75, Arapahoe, Colorado, United States
Census		1885	Page 72, Arapahoe, Colorado, United States
Census		1900	ED 124, Page 300, Arapahoe, Colorado, United States
Census		1910	ED 197, Page 108, Denver, Denver, Colorado, United States
Death		1912	Colorado, United States
Burial			
Spouse	John Baylor ARMOR (1854-)		
Marriage		11 Apr 1882	Arapahoe, Colorado, United States

M	**John R. COOK**		
Birth		1863/4	Missouri, United States
Census		1870	Page 604, Kansas City, Jackson, Missouri, United States
Census		1880	ED 12, Page 354, Kansas City, Jackson, Missouri, United States
Death			
Burial			
Marriage			

M	**Dr. Henry Churchill COOK**		
Birth		18 Dec 1868	Kansas City, Jackson, Missouri, United States
Census		1870	Page 604, Kansas City, Jackson, Missouri, United States
Census		1880	ED 12, Page 354, Kansas City, Jackson, Missouri, United States
Residence		1915	Kansas City, Jackson, Missouri, United States
Death			
Burial			
Marriage			

Father Hiram W. COOPER

Birth	6 Oct 1834	Ohio, United States
Census	1850	Page 307, Adrian Township, Lenawee, Michigan, United States
Census	1860	
Military		1st Sergeant, Company A, 77th Regiment Enrolled Missouri Militia
Tax Lists	Nov 1863	Retail Dealer License; "Cooper & Gregg", Kansas City, Jackson, Missouri, United States
Tax Lists	May 1866	Wholesale Dealer License; "Bidwell & Cooper", Kansas City, Jackson, Missouri, United States
Tax Lists	May 1866	Income; Kansas City, Jackson, Missouri, United States
Tax Lists	bet Oct 1866 and Dec 1866	Gross Sales; "Bidwell & Cooper", Kansas City, Jackson, Missouri, United States
Occupation	bet 1867 and 1869	City Councilman; Kansas City, Jackson, Missouri, United States
Census	1870	Page 584, Kansas City, Jackson, Missouri, United States
Census	1880	ED 127, Page 54, La Cygne, Linn, Kansas, United States
Census	1885	Page 20, Family 148, La Cygne, Linn, Kansas, United States
Residence	1899/1900	La Cygne, Linn, Kansas, United States
Death	8 Apr 1900	La Cygne, Linn, Kansas, United States
Misc		Obituary, Kansas City (Mo.) Star, 09 Apr 1900, Page 12, Column 4
Burial	10 Apr 1900	Union Cemetery, Kansas City, Jackson, Missouri, United States
Misc		"One of Those Who Helped," Kansas City (Mo.) Star, 27 May 1900, Page 14, Columns 1-2
Occupation		Hardware Merchant (1860, 1870), Hardware Dealer (1880), Mercantile (1885), Retail Dealer, Wholesale Dealer
Marriage		
Father		Nathaniel COOPER (1810-1859)
Mother		Permilla [--?--] (1814-1889)

Mother Julia E. GREGG

Birth	3 Feb 1829	New York, United States
Census	1850	Page 48, Palmyra, Wayne, New York, United States
Census	1860	
Census	1870	Page 584, Kansas City, Jackson, Missouri, United States
Census	1880	ED 127, Page 54, La Cygne, Linn, Kansas, United States
Census	1885	Page 20, Family 148, La Cygne, Linn, Kansas, United States
Death	13 May 1897	Cirrhosis; Kansas City, Jackson, Missouri, United States
Misc		Funeral Notice, Kansas City (Mo.) Star, 13 May 1897, Page 10, Column 2
Burial	14 May 1897	Union Cemetery, Kansas City, Jackson, Missouri, United States
Father		John GREGG (1798-)
Mother		Anne WILCOX (1806-1895)

Children

F Orie A. COOPER

Birth	21 Apr 1858	Walton, Grand Traverse, Michigan, United States
Census	1860	
Census	1870	Page 584, Kansas City, Jackson, Missouri, United States
Census	1880	ED 127, Page 54, La Cygne, Linn, Kansas, United States
Census	1885	Page 20, Family 148, La Cygne, Linn, Kansas, United States
Census	1900	
Census	1910	ED 250, Page 163, Mount Vernon, Skagit, Washington, United States
Census	1920	ED 167, Page 130, Billings, Yellowstone, Montana, United States
Census	1930	ED 9, Page 117, Billings, Yellowstone, Montana, United States
Death	30 Oct 1936	(Tombstone: 29 Oct 1936); Yellowstone, Montana, United States
Burial		Mountview Cemetery, Billings, Yellowstone, Montana, United States
Occupation		Boarding House (1910)
Marriage		

F Annie Gregg COOPER

Birth	9 Jul 1863	
Death	7 Aug 1864	
Burial		Union Cemetery, Kansas City, Jackson, Missouri, United States
Marriage		

Father	Hiram W. COOPER	
Mother	**Julia E. GREGG**	
Children		
F	**Emily/Emaline J. COOPER**	

Birth	Sep 1871	Missouri, United States
Census	1880	ED 127, Page 54, La Cygne, Linn, Kansas, United States
Census	1885	Page 20, Family 148, La Cygne, Linn, Kansas, United States
Census	1900	ED 185, Page 162, Manhattan, Gallatin, Montana, United States
Census	1910	ED 131, Page 7, Logan, Gallatin, Montana, United States
Census	1920	ED 167, Page 130, Billings, Yellowstone, Montana, United States
Census	1930	ED 9, Page 117, Billings, Yellowstone, Montana, United States
Death	4 Apr 1942	Yellowstone, Montana, United States
Burial	7 Apr 1942	Mountview Cemetery, Billings, Yellowstone, Montana, United States
Occupation		Teacher High School (1920)
Spouse	Charles M. SMITH (1869-1958)	
Marriage	14 Jun 1899	(1899K0018181), Kansas City, Jackson, Missouri, United States

Father Mahlon COTTRILL

Birth	1797	New Jersey, United States
Census	1820	
Occupation	bet 1826 and 1856	Proprietor; Pavilion Hotel, Montpelier, Washington, Vermont, United States
Census	1830	Page 377, Montpelier, Washington, Vermont, United States
Census	1840	Page 327, Montpelier, Washington, Vermont, United States
Census	1850	Page 181, Montpelier, Washington, Vermont, United States
Census	1860	Page 86, Montpelier, Washington, Vermont, United States
Tax Lists	1863	2 Two-Horse Seated Hacks; (Residence Pueblo and Kansas City) "Cottrill M. & Company", Pueblo, Pueblo, Colorado Territory, United States
Tax Lists	Apr 1863	8 Two-Horse Carriages; "Cottull Vickroy & Company", Kansas City, Jackson, Missouri, United States
Tax Lists	Aug 1863	Gross Express Receipts; "Catrell M. & Company", Kansas City, Jackson, Missouri, United States
Tax Lists	Oct 1863	Gross Express Receipts; "[Co]ttull M. & Company", Kansas City, Jackson, Missouri, United States
Death	20 Oct 1864	Kansas City, Jackson, Missouri, United States
Burial	21 Oct 1864	(Funeral) Methodist Church, Kansas City, Jackson, Missouri, United States
Occupation		Innkeeper (1850), Retired (1860)
Misc		Biography, First Mail West (Taylor, 1971), Pages 88-105
Marriage	8 Sep 1822	Montpelier, Washington, Vermont, United States
Father		
Mother		

Mother Catherine Smith COUCH

Birth	1 Apr 1792	Landaff, Grafton, New Hampshire, United States
Census	1830	(Mahlon Cottrill Family), Page 377, Montpelier, Washington, Vermont, United States
Census	1840	(Mahlon Cottrill Family), Page 327, Montpelier, Washington, Vermont, United States
Census	1850	Page 181, Montpelier, Washington, Vermont, United States
Census	1860	Page 86, Montpelier, Washington, Vermont, United States
Death	28 Apr 1861	Montpelier, Washington, Vermont, United States
Burial		
Father		Stephen COUCH (1763-1813)
Mother		Ann EDMOND (1764-1813)

Children

M William Hutchins COTTRILL

Birth	6 Jun 1823	Montpelier, Washington, Vermont, United States
Census	1830	(Mahlon Cottrill Family), Page 377, Montpelier, Washington, Vermont, United States
Census	1840	(Mahlon Cottrill Family), Page 327, Montpelier, Washington, Vermont, United States
Census	1850	Page 181, Montpelier, Washington, Vermont, United States
Census	1860	Page 767, Augusta, Richmond, Georgia, United States
Census	1870	
Census	1880	ED 114, Page 28, Appleton, Outagamie, Wisconsin, United States
Death	1897	
Burial		Forest Home Cemetery, Milwaukee, Milwaukee, Wisconsin, United States
Occupation		Clerk (1850), Messenger Adams Express (1860), Hotel Keeper (1880)
Spouse		Frances Ella HALL (1826-1901)
Marriage	14 Jun 1848	(Recorded in Montpelier, Washington, Vermont, United States), Burlington, Chittenden, Vermont, United States

M Lyman Hawley COTTRILL

Birth	16 May 1825	Montpelier, Washington, Vermont, United States
Census	1830	(Mahlon Cottrill Family), Page 377, Montpelier, Washington, Vermont, United States
Census	1840	(Mahlon Cottrill Family), Page 327, Montpelier, Washington, Vermont, United States
Census	1850	Page 512, Winnebago, Winnebago, Wisconsin, United States
Census	1860	Page 679, Oshkosh, Winnebago, Wisconsin, United States
Military	Sep 1863	Civil War Draft Registration; Kaw Township, Jackson, Missouri, United States
Census	1870	
Misc	1 Oct 1875	Voter Registration,, Lakeport, Lake, California, United States
Death	Nov 1877	Oregon, United States
Occupation		Merchant (1850, 1860)

Father	Mahlon COTTRILL	
Mother	**Catherine Smith COUCH**	
Children		

Lyman Hawley COTTRILL (continued)

Burial		
Spouse		Sarah A. [--?--] (1826-)

M Charles Edward Huntington COTTRILL

Birth	11 Jul 1826	(or 21 Jul 1826), Montpelier, Washington, Vermont, United States
Census	1830	(Mahlon Cottrill Family), Page 377, Montpelier, Washington, Vermont, United States
Death	3 Feb 1833	
Burial		
Marriage		

M George Washington COTTRILL

Birth	18 May 1828	Montpelier, Washington, Vermont, United States
Census	1830	(Mahlon Cottrill Family), Page 377, Montpelier, Washington, Vermont, United States
Census	1840	(Mahlon Cottrill Family), Page 327, Montpelier, Washington, Vermont, United States
Graduation	1847	University of Vermont, Vermont, United States
Census	1850	Page 181, Montpelier, Washington, Vermont, United States
Census	1860	
Census	1870	Page 764, Microfilm Roll 1041, New York, New York, New York, United States
Census	1880	ED 191, Page 332, New York, New York, New York, United States
Residence	1883	New York, New York, New York, United States
Occupation		Lawyer (1850, 1860, 1880)
Death		
Burial		
Marriage		

M Henry Clay COTTRILL

Birth	26 Jun 1830	
Death	12 Feb 1833	
Burial		
Marriage		

M Jedediah Philo Clarke "Jedd" COTTRILL

Birth	15 Apr 1832	Vermont, United States
Census	1840	(Mahlon Cottrill Family), Page 327, Montpelier, Washington, Vermont, United States
Census	1850	Page 181, Montpelier, Washington, Vermont, United States
Graduation	1852	University of Vermont, Vermont, United States
Residence	1856	Milwaukee, Milwaukee, Wisconsin, United States
Census	1860	
Military	Jun 1863	Civil War Draft Registration; Milwaukee, Milwaukee, Wisconsin, United States
Census	1870	
Census	1880	ED 97, Page 274, Milwaukee, Milwaukee, Wisconsin, United States
Residence	1883	Milwaukee, Milwaukee, Wisconsin, United States
Death	5 Feb 1889	Milwaukee, Wisconsin, United States
Burial		Forest Home Cemetery, Milwaukee, Milwaukee, Wisconsin, United States
Occupation		Student (1850), Attorney at Law (1856), Lawyer (1880)
Spouse		Ellen M. CAMP (1835-1915)
Marriage	14 Oct 1856	Montpelier, Washington, Vermont, United States

M Charles Mahlon COTTRILL

Birth	20 Oct 1834	Vermont, United States
Census	1840	(Mahlon Cottrill Family), Page 327, Montpelier, Washington, Vermont, United States
Residence	bet 1849 and 1859	Oshkosh, Winnebago, Wisconsin, United States
Census	1850	Page 181, Montpelier, Washington, Vermont, United States
Residence	bet 1859 and 1883	Steamboat Business; Milwaukee, Milwaukee, Wisconsin, United States
Census	1860	Page 251, Milwaukee, Milwaukee, Wisconsin, United States
Census	1870	Page 482, Milwaukee, Milwaukee, Wisconsin, United States
Census	1880	ED 110, Page 150, Milwaukee, Milwaukee, Wisconsin, United States
Death	1899	
Burial		Forest Home Cemetery, Milwaukee, Milwaukee, Wisconsin, United States

Father	Mahlon COTTRILL	
Mother	**Catherine Smith COUCH**	
Children		

Charles Mahlon COTTRILL (continued)

Occupation	Clerk (1860), Steamboat Agent (1870), Trans. Agent (1880)
Spouse	Lillie E. [--?--] (1838-1923)
Marriage	

Father	**Gilbert G. CRANDALL**	
Birth	1834/5	New York, United States
Census	1840	(Amas Crandall Family), Page 44, Nichols, Tioga, New York, United States
Census	1850	Page 58, Nichols, Tioga, New York, United States
Census	1860	Page 82, Kansas City, Jackson, Missouri, United States
Military		Private, Company A, 77th Regiment Enrolled Missouri Militia
Military		2nd Lieutenant, Company C, 77th Regiment Enrolled Missouri Militia
Military	Oct 1863	Civil War Draft Registration; Kaw Township, Jackson, Missouri, United States
Tax Lists	Dec 1863	Animals Slaughtered for Sale; "Diveley, Crandall & Company", Kansas City, Jackson, Missouri, United States
Tax Lists	May 1866	Retail Dealer License; Kansas City, Jackson, Missouri, United States
Census	1870	Page 217, Kinderhook, Branch, Michigan, United States
Census	1875	Page 41, Olathe, Johnson, Kansas, United States
Census	1880	ED 99, Page 114, Olathe, Johnson, Kansas, United States
Census	1885	Page 35, Olathe, Johnson, Kansas, United States
Census	1895	Page 42, Lexington Township, Johnson, Kansas, United States
Census	1900	ED 96, Page 30, Lexington Township, Johnson, Kansas, United States
Census	1910	ED 1, Page 10, Bettina Township, Beckham, Oklahoma, United States
Business		Diveley, Crandall & Company (Meat)
Occupation		Laborer (1850), Clerk (1860), Farmer (1870), Gardener (1875, 1885), Broom Maker (1880, 1900), Farmer (1895), Farm Laborer Home Farm (1910), Wholesale & Retail Grocer
Death		
Burial		
Divorce	ca 1890	
Marriage		
Father	Amos CRANDALL (1804-)	
Mother	Mercy CARY (1813-)	

Mother	**Sophia Chapline BARKLEY**	
Birth	8 Oct 1846	Kentucky, United States
Census	1850	Page 422, Trimble, Kentucky, United States
Census	1860	Page 40, Kansas City, Jackson, Missouri, United States
Census	1870	Page 217, Kinderhook, Branch, Michigan, United States
Census	1875	Page 41, Olathe, Johnson, Kansas, United States
Census	1880	ED 99, Page 114, Olathe, Johnson, Kansas, United States
Census	1885	Page 35, Olathe, Johnson, Kansas, United States
Census	1895	Page 42, Olathe, Johnson, Kansas, United States
Census	1900	ED 101, Page 96, Olathe, Johnson, Kansas, United States
Census	1910	
Census	1920	ED 5, Page 51, Blue Township, Jackson, Missouri, United States
Death	10 Oct 1926	Independence, Jackson, Missouri, United States
Burial	11 Oct 1926	Olathe Memorial Cemetery, Olathe, Johnson, Kansas, United States
Occupation		Washwoman and Keeping House (1880), Washing and Ironing (1900)
Father	Napoleon B. BARKLEY (1812-1853)	
Mother	Julia BARCLAY (1818-1883)	

Children

M	**Amos Barclay CRANDALL**	
Birth	26 Jul 1868	Missouri, United States
Census	1870	Page 217, Kinderhook, Branch, Michigan, United States
Census	1875	Page 41, Olathe, Johnson, Kansas, United States
Census	1880	ED 99, Page 114, Olathe, Johnson, Kansas, United States
Census	1885	Page 35, Olathe, Johnson, Kansas, United States
Census	1900	
Census	1910	ED 1, Page 47, Juneau, Alaska District, United States
Census	1920	ED 231, Page 189, Butte, Silver Bow, Montana, United States
Census	1930	ED 181, Page 175, Kansas City, Jackson, Missouri, United States
Death	18 Apr 1945	Chronic Bronchitis, Kansas City, Jackson, Missouri, United States
Burial	20 Apr 1945	Mount Moriah Cemetery, Kansas City, Jackson, Missouri, United States

Father Gilbert G. CRANDALL

Mother Sophia Chapline BARKLEY

Children

Amos Barclay CRANDALL (continued)

Occupation		[illegible] (1910), Engineer Stationary (1920), Engineer Steel Mill (1930), Engineer Sheffield Steel Works
Spouse	Flora THAYER (1876-1944)	
Marriage	29 Jul 1915	Shoshone, Idaho, United States
Spouse	Florence TASKER (1879-)	
Marriage	5 Dec 1900	Helena, Lewis and Clark, Montana, United States
Divorce		

M   Frank T. CRANDALL

Birth	1870/1	(or 1868), Missouri, United States
Census	1875	Page 41, Olathe, Johnson, Kansas, United States
Census	1880	ED 99, Page 114, Olathe, Johnson, Kansas, United States
Census	1885	Page 35, Olathe, Johnson, Kansas, United States
Death	1889	
Burial		Olathe Memorial Cemetery, Olathe, Johnson, Kansas, United States
Marriage		

M   Henry Ruel "Harry" CRANDALL

Birth	1873	Kansas, United States
Census	1875	Page 41, Olathe, Johnson, Kansas, United States
Census	1880	ED 99, Page 114, Olathe, Johnson, Kansas, United States
Census	1885	Page 35, Olathe, Johnson, Kansas, United States
Death	1899	
Burial	2 Sep 1899	Olathe Memorial Cemetery, Olathe, Johnson, Kansas, United States
Marriage		

M   George Parker CRANDALL

Birth	1877	(or Nov 1876), Kansas, United States
Census	1880	ED 99, Page 114, Olathe, Johnson, Kansas, United States
Census	1885	Page 35, Olathe, Johnson, Kansas, United States
Death	1926	
Burial	10 Jun 1926	Olathe Memorial Cemetery, Olathe, Johnson, Kansas, United States
Marriage		

F   Maude D. CRANDALL

Birth	Jan 1882	Kansas, United States
Census	1885	Page 35, Olathe, Johnson, Kansas, United States
Census	1895	Page 42, Olathe, Johnson, Kansas, United States
Census	1900	ED 101, Page 96, Olathe, Johnson, Kansas, United States
Census	1910	
Census	1920	ED 5, Page 51, Blue Township, Jackson, Missouri, United States
Residence	1926	Independence, Jackson, Missouri, United States
Census	1930	ED 257, Page 149, Englewood, Blue Township, Jackson, Missouri, United States
Death		
Burial		
Spouse	Warren H. CROZIER (1870-1935)	
Marriage		
Spouse	William F. RAWN (1889-)	
Marriage		

M   Weller Rollin CRANDALL

Birth	15 May 1886	Olathe, Johnson, Kansas, United States
Census	1895	Page 42, Olathe, Johnson, Kansas, United States
Census	1900	ED 101, Page 96, Olathe, Johnson, Kansas, United States
Census	1910	
Census	1920	ED 98, Page 113, Leavenworth, Leavenworth, Kansas, United States
Census	1930	ED 19, Page 13, Leavenworth, Leavenworth, Kansas, United States
Death	13 Oct 1957	Heart Ailment; Salt Lake City, Salt Lake, Utah, United States
Burial		Salt Lake City Cemetery, Salt Lake City, Salt Lake, Utah, United States
Occupation		Printer Publishing Company (1920), Commercial Salesman Novelty Company (1930),

		Employee of Salt Lake City Deseret News and of Lancaster (Calif.) Gazette
Residence		Lancaster, Los Angeles, California, United States
Spouse	Lillie DEROSIA (1883-1969)	
Marriage	1 Feb 1940	Las Vegas, Clark, Nevada, United States
Spouse	Gertrude Amelia BEAL (1886-1981)	
Marriage	4 Oct 1911	Leavenworth, Kansas, United States

Father Aaron Lane Hardage CRENSHAW

Birth	18 Apr 1805	Culpepper, Virginia, United States
Census	1840	Page 70, Jackson, Missouri, United States
Census	1850	Page 266, Blue Township, Jackson, Missouri, United States
Census	1860	Page 442, Sniabar Township, Jackson, Missouri, United States
Census		Slave Schedules, Page 379, Sniabar Township, Jackson, Missouri, United States
Tax Lists	Sep 1862	Cattle Broker License; Sniabar Township, Jackson, Missouri, United States
Census	1870	Page 27, Sniabar Township, Jackson, Missouri, United States
Census	1880	ED 31, Page 156, Blue Springs, Jackson, Missouri, United States
Death	23 Mar 1890	
Burial		Lobb Cemetery, Sniabar Township, Jackson, Missouri, United States
Probate	7 Apr 1890	(Administrator's Bond), Volume C, Page 66, Independence, Jackson, Missouri, United States
Occupation		Farmer (1850, 1860, 1870, 1880), Cattle Broker
Marriage	5 Jul 1836	Marion, MIssouri, United States
Father	Nicholas CRENSHAW (1784-1853)	
Mother	Eleanor LANE (1785-)	

Mother Eliza Ellen GARNER

Birth	abt 28 Oct 1817	Bourbon, Kentucky, United States
Census	1840	Page 70, Jackson, Missouri, United States
Census	1850	Page 266, Blue Township, Jackson, Missouri, United States
Census	1860	Page 442, Sniabar Township, Jackson, Missouri, United States
Census	1870	Page 27, Sniabar Township, Jackson, Missouri, United States
Death	9 Jul 1872	
Burial		Lobb Cemetery, Sniabar Township, Jackson, Missouri, United States
Father		
Mother		

Children

M   William Nicholas CRENSHAW

Birth	23 May 1837	Missouri, United States
Census	1840	Page 70, Jackson, Missouri, United States
Census	1850	Page 266, Blue Township, Jackson, Missouri, United States
Census	1860	Page 442, Sniabar Township, Jackson, Missouri, United States
Census	1870	Page 27, Sniabar Township, Jackson, Missouri, United States
Census	1880	ED 31, Page 156, Blue Springs, Jackson, Missouri, United States
Death	3 Sep 1910	Mexico City, Distrito Federal, Mexico
Burial		American Cemetery, Mexico City, Distrito Federal, Mexico
Occupation		Farmer (1860, 1870, 1880)
Spouse	Mary W. POMEROY (1850-1932)	
Marriage	31 Dec 1868	(1868I0060034), Jackson, Missouri, United States

M   Henry Clay CRENSHAW

Birth	Mar 1841	Missouri, United States
Census	1850	Page 266, Blue Township, Jackson, Missouri, United States
Census	1860	Page 442, Sniabar Township, Jackson, Missouri, United States
Military		Private, Quantrill Raiders, CSA
Census	1870	
Census	1880	ED 4, Page 108, Kansas City, Jackson, Missouri, United States
Death	15 Jul 1915	Senility, Dementia, Chronic Bronchitis; Kansas City, Jackson, Missouri, United States
Burial	17 Jul 1915	Elmwood Cemetery, Kansas City, Jackson, Missouri, United States
Occupation		Farm Hand (1860), Stock Dealer (1880), Horse & Mule Trader
Spouse	Anna C. [--?--] (1855-1894)	
Marriage		

M   Thomas Lane CRENSHAW

Birth	15 Nov 1843	Jackson, Missouri, United States
Census	1850	Page 266, Blue Township, Jackson, Missouri, United States
Census	1860	Page 442, Sniabar Township, Jackson, Missouri, United States
Census	1870	Page 27, Sniabar Township, Jackson, Missouri, United States
Census	1880	ED 31, Page 157, Blue Springs, Jackson, Missouri, United States
Census	1900	ED 139, Page 188, Sniabar Township, Jackson, Missouri, United States
Death	10 May 1922	Cancer of the Prostate Obstructive, Sugical Shock; Independence, Jackson, Missouri,

			United States
	Burial	12 May 1922	Lobb Cemetery, Sniabar Township, Jackson, Missouri, United States
	Occupation		Farm Hand (1860), Farmer (1870, 1880, 1900)
	Spouse	Nancy J. PURCELL (1849-1916)	
	Marriage	21 Jan 1869	(1869I0060104), Jackson, Missouri, United States

M	**Coleman Hardage CRENSHAW**		
	Birth	14 May 1845	Jackson, Missouri, United States
	Census	1850	Page 266, Blue Township, Jackson, Missouri, United States
	Census	1860	Page 442, Sniabar Township, Jackson, Missouri, United States
	Census	1870	
	Census	1880	
	Census	1900	ED 24, Page 78, Sundance Precinct Outside, Crook, Wyoming, United States
	Death	3 May 1920	Sundance, Crook, Wyoming, United States
	Burial		Mount Moriah Cemetery, Sundance, Crook, Wyoming, United States
	Occupation		Farmer (1900)
	Spouse	Virginia C. TRIMBLE (-)	
	Marriage	30 Dec 1868	(1868I0060104), Jackson, Missouri, United States

M	**John Zachariah Taylor "Zack" CRENSHAW**		
	Birth	5 Jul 1848	(or 1847), Independence, Jackson, Missouri, United States
	Census	1850	Page 266, Blue Township, Jackson, Missouri, United States
	Census	1860	Page 442, Sniabar Township, Jackson, Missouri, United States
	Census	1870	Page 27, Sniabar Township, Jackson, Missouri, United States
	Census	1880	ED 31, Page 156, Blue Springs, Jackson, Missouri, United States
	Census	1900	ED 139, Page 186, Sniabar Township, Jackson, Missouri, United States
	Death	30 Dec 1931	Atrophic Cirrhosis of the Liver; Independence, Jackson, Missouri, United States
	Burial		Woodlawn Cemetery, Independence, Jackson, Missouri, United States
	Occupation		Farm Labor (1870), Farmer (1880, 1900)
	Spouse	Sallie Adaline WATKINS (1847-1927)	
	Marriage	30 Jan 1872	(1872I0060340), Jackson, Missouri, United States

F	**Eliza Eleanor CRENSHAW**		
	Birth	1851/2	Missouri, United States
	Census	1860	Page 442, Sniabar Township, Jackson, Missouri, United States
	Census	1870	
	Census	1880	
	Death		
	Burial		
	Marriage		

M	**George Washington CRENSHAW**		
	Birth	28 Jul 1855	(or Jul 1856), Jackson, Missouri, United States
	Census	1860	Page 442, Sniabar Township, Jackson, Missouri, United States
	Census	1870	Page 27, Sniabar Township, Jackson, Missouri, United States
	Census	1880	ED 31, Page 156, Blue Springs, Jackson, Missouri, United States
	Census	1900	ED 7, Page 107, Independence, Jackson, Missouri, United States
	Death	14 Feb 1912	Myocarditis; Independence, Jackson, Missouri, United States
	Burial	16 Feb 1912	Lobb Cemetery, Sniabar Township, Jackson, Missouri, United States
	Occupation		Farm Laborer (1870), Farmer (1880), Day Laborer (1900)
	Spouse	Martha J. MAYS (1863-1936)	
	Marriage	12 Mar 1879	(1879I0070503), Jackson, Missouri, United States

Father Asa Beebe CROSS

Birth	9 Dec 1826	Camden, Gloucester, New Jersey, United States
Residence	bet 1826 and 1847	Tuckahoe, Cape May, New Jersey, United States
Census	1840	(Thomas Cross Family), Page 64, Weymouth Township, Atlantic, New Jersey, United States
Residence	bet 1847 and 1849	New York, New York, New York, United States
Residence	bet 1849 and 1856	Saint Louis, Saint Louis, Missouri, United States
Census	1850	Page 98, Weymouth Township, Atlantic, New Jersey, United States
Residence	bet 1856 and 1858	Saint Paul, Ramsey, Minnesota, United States
Residence	bet 1858 and 1894	Kansas City, Jackson, Missouri, United States
Census	1860	Page 61, Kansas City, Jackson, Missouri, United States
Tax Lists	Sep 1862	Retail Dealer License; Kansas City, Jackson, Missouri, United States
Military		Corporal, Company A, 77th Regiment Enrolled Missouri Militia
Military	Sep 1863	Civil War Draft Registration; Kaw Township, Jackson, Missouri, United States
Occupation	1863/4	City Treasurer; Kansas City, Jackson, Missouri, United States
Tax Lists	May 1866	Retail Dealer License, Income, and Gold Watch; "A. B. Cross & Company", Kansas City, Jackson, Missouri, United States
Census	1870	Page 657, Kansas City, Jackson, Missouri, United States
Misc		"Architectural Changes," Kansas City (Mo.) Times, 04 Jun 1876, Page 4, Column 4
Census	1880	ED 17, Page 458, Kansas City, Jackson, Missouri, United States
Misc		Biography, History of Jackson Co., Mo. (1881), Page 758
Misc		Biography and Ad, Kansas City, Its Resources and Their Development (1890), Pages 28 and 75
Census	1890	ED 178, Page 3, Kansas City, Jackson, Missouri, United States
Death	18 Aug 1894	Kansas City, Jackson, Missouri, United States
Misc		Obituary, Kansas City (Mo.) Star, 18 Aug 1894, Page 1, Column 1
Misc		Obituary, Kansas City (Mo.) Times, 19 Aug 1894, Page 5, Columns 3-4
Burial	21 Aug 1894	Mount Saint Mary's Cemetery, Kansas City, Jackson, Missouri, United States
Misc		Biography, Biographical Dictionary of American Architects (Deceased) (1956)
Misc		Biography, Here Lies Kansas City (1984), Page 45
Occupation		House Carpenter (1850), Lumberman (1860), Architect (1870, 1880), Retail Dealer, Merchant
Marriage	Apr 1858	Saint Louis, Saint Louis, Missouri, United States
Father	Thomas B. CROSS (1799-)	
Mother	Millicent BEEBE (1804-)	

Mother Rachel Genevieve HUGHES

Birth	1834/5	(or 18 Mar 1838) (or Pennsylvania, United States), Maryland, United States
Census	1850	
Census	1860	
Census	1870	Page 657, Kansas City, Jackson, Missouri, United States
Census	1880	ED 17, Page 458, Kansas City, Jackson, Missouri, United States
Death	24 Jul 1890	Kansas City, Jackson, Missouri, United States
Misc		Obituary, Kansas City (Mo.) Star, 24 Jul 1890, Page 1, Column 1
Misc		Obituary, Kansas City (Mo.) Daily Journal, 25 Jul 1890, Page 3, Column 6
Burial	26 Jul 1890	Mount Saint Mary's Cemetery, Kansas City, Jackson, Missouri, United States
Father		
Mother		
Other spouse	William E. TAYLOR (-)	
Marriage	25 Dec 1851	(Volume 5, Page 421), Saint Louis, Missouri, United States

Children

F Elizabeth G. "Lizzie" CROSS

Birth	1859/60	(or 1863/64), Missouri, United States
Census	1860	
Census	1870	Page 657, Kansas City, Jackson, Missouri, United States
Census	1880	ED 17, Page 458, Kansas City, Jackson, Missouri, United States
Residence	1890	Cincinnati, Hamilton, Ohio, United States
Residence	1890	Cincinnati, Hamilton, Ohio, United States
Residence	18 Aug 1894	Pittsburgh, Allegheny, Pennsylvania, United States
Death		

Father	Asa Beebe CROSS	
Mother	**Rachel Genevieve HUGHES**	
Children		

		Elizabeth G. "Lizzie" CROSS (continued)	
		Burial	
		Spouse	Walter L. RAY (1855-)
		Marriage	29 Nov 1883 (1883K0040036), Kansas City, Jackson, Missouri, United States

F	**Mary Emma CROSS**		
	Birth	8 Feb 1862	Missouri, United States
	Census	1870	Page 658, Kansas City, Jackson, Missouri, United States
	Census	1880	ED 17, Page 458, Kansas City, Jackson, Missouri, United States
	Residence	1890	Kansas City, Jackson, Missouri, United States
	Death	28 Feb 1934	Pulmonary Edema, Deibetes, Chronic Myocardial Degeneration; Kansas City, Jackson, Missouri, United States
	Burial	2 Mar 1934	Mount Saint Mary's Cemetery, Kansas City, Jackson, Missouri, United States
	Marriage		

F	**Catherine Beebe "Kate" CROSS**		
	Birth	19 Dec 1866	Kansas City, Jackson, Missouri, United States
	Census	1870	Page 658, Kansas City, Jackson, Missouri, United States
	Census	1880	ED 17, Page 458, Kansas City, Jackson, Missouri, United States
	Residence	1890	Kansas City, Jackson, Missouri, United States
	Census	1900	ED 118, Page 151, Kansas City, Jackson, Missouri, United States
	Death	29 Mar 1924	Chronic Interstitial Nephritis, Diabetes Melitus; Kansas City, Jackson, Missouri, United States
	Burial	31 Mar 1924	Mount Washington Cemetery, Independence, Jackson, Missouri, United States
	Spouse		Alfred Edward BARNES (1869-1928)
	Marriage	3 Jun 1891	(1891K0005377), Kansas City, Jackson, Missouri, United States

M	**Frank CROSS**		
	Birth	1866/7	Missouri, United States
	Census	1870	Page 658, Kansas City, Jackson, Missouri, United States
	Death		(in Infancy)
	Burial		
	Marriage		

M	**Louis CROSS**		
	Birth		
	Chr		
	Death		(in Infancy)
	Burial		
	Marriage		

Father Louis DAENZER

Birth	8 Mar 1828	Rheinland, Prussia, Germany
Residence	bet 1842 and 1845	Giessen, [--?--], Germany
Residence	abt 1848	Heidelberg, [--?--], Germany
Residence	abt 1851	(and Manchester, Lancashire, England, United Kingdom), London, Middlesex, England
Immigration	Apr 1854	New York, NY
Residence	1854/5	New York, NY
Residence	bet 1855 and 1857	Chicago, Cook, Illinois, United States
Residence	bet 1857 and 1874	Kansas City, Jackson, Missouri, United States
Census	1860	Page 87, Kansas City, Jackson, Missouri, United States
Misc	10 Aug 1862	Union Provost Marshals' File of Papers Relating to Two or More Civilians, M416, Roll 8, No. 2129
Tax Lists	Sep 1862	Confectioner License; "Lewis Denzer", Kansas City, Jackson, Missouri, United States
Military		Private & Corporal, Company A, 77th Regiment Enrolled Missouri Militia
Military	Sep 1863	Civil War Draft Registration; Kaw Township, Jackson, Missouri, United States
Tax Lists	May 1865	Income and Gold Watch; "Lewis Denzer", Kansas City, Jackson, Missouri, United States
Tax Lists	May 1866	Income; Kansas City, Jackson, Missouri, United States
Census	1870	Page 305, Kansas City, Jackson, Missouri, United States
Residence	bet 1874 and 1910	Wyandotte, Kansas, United States
Census	1880	ED 195, Page 398, Wyandotte Township, Wyandotte, Kansas, United States
Misc		Biography, History of Jackson Co., Mo. (1881), Pages 758-579
Census	1900	ED 71, Page 78, Kansas City, Jackson, Missouri, United States
Census	1910	ED 50, Page 174, Kansas City, Jackson, Missouri, United States
Misc	1910	Inmate, Home for the Aged, Locust Street; Kansas City, Jackson, Missouri, United States
Death	21 Apr 1910	Cerebral Hemorrhage, Arteriosclerosis; Kansas City, Jackson, Missouri, United States
Misc		Obituary, Kansas City (Mo.) Star, 21 Apr 1910, Page 12, Column 3
Misc		Funeral Notice, Kansas City (Mo.) Times, 22 Apr 1910, Page 16, Column 2
Burial	24 Apr 1910	Elmwood Cemetery, Kansas City, Jackson, Missouri, United States
Occupation		Fruit Store (1860, 1870), Farmer (1880), Confectioner
Marriage	Nov 1856	Chicago, Cook, Illinois, United States
Father		Louis DAENZER (-)
Mother		

Mother Amelia/Amalia "Mollie" STEIGER

Birth	abt 1833	Baden, Germany
Census	1860	Page 87, Kansas City, Jackson, Missouri, United States
Census	1870	Page 305, Kansas City, Jackson, Missouri, United States
Death	14 Sep 1877	Cardiac Disease; (Saint Peter's German Evangelical Church, Kansas City, Jackson, Missouri, United States, Volume 1, Page 370, Kansas, United States
Misc		Death Notice, "Wyandott," Kansas City (Mo.) Daily Journal of Commerce, 16 Sep 1877, Page 4, Coumn. 5
Burial		Elmwood Cemetery, Kansas City, Jackson, Missouri, United States
Father		
Mother		

Children

M   George/Georg DAENZER

Birth	23 Dec 1857	MO (or 23 Dec 1856)
Census	1860	Page 87, Kansas City, Jackson, Missouri, United States
Baptism	23 May 1869	St. Peter's Ger. Evang. Church, Volume 1, Page 5
Census	1870	Page 305, Kansas City, Jackson, Missouri, United States
Confirmation	1871	St. Peter's German Evangelical Church, Kansas City, Jackson Co., MO
Census	1880	ED 15, Page 411, Kansas City, Jackson, Missouri, United States
Census	1900	
Census	1910	
Census	1920	
Census	1930	
Occupation		Show Case Maker (1880)
Death		
Burial		

Father	Louis DAENZER	
Mother	**Amelia/Amalia "Mollie" STEIGER**	
Children		

George/Georg DAENZER (continued)

Spouse		Rosina Caecilia TESETOR/TEXTOR (1857-)
Marriage	21 Jan 1880	(1880I0080035), Kansas City, Jackson, Missouri, United States

M Louis DAENZER

Birth	4 Oct 1859	Missouri, United States
Census	1860	Page 87, Kansas City, Jackson, Missouri, United States
Baptism	23 May 1869	St. Peter's Ger. Evang. Church, Volume 1, Page 5
Census	1870	Page 305, Kansas City, Jackson, Missouri, United States
Confirmation	1874	St. Peter's German Evangelical Church, Kansas City, Jackson Co., MO
Census	1880	ED 195, Page 398, Wyandotte Township, Wyandotte, Kansas, United States
Death	2 Sep 1884	Accident; Kansas City, Jackson, Missouri, United States
Misc		Death Record, St. Peter's Ger. Evang. Church, Volume 3, Page 56
Misc		Obituary, Kansas City (Mo.) Star, 03 Sept 1884, Page 1, Column 5
Misc		Death Notice, Kansas City (Mo.) Daily Journal, 03 Sep 1884, page 3, columns 1-2
Burial	4 Sep 1884	Elmwood Cemetery; Saint Peter's German Evangelical Church, Volume 3, Page 56, Kansas City, Jackson, Missouri, United States
Occupation		Farmer (1880)
Spouse		Jessie [--?--] (1859-)
Marriage	abt 1879	

M Emil DAENZER

Birth	15 May 1861	Missouri, United States
Baptism	23 May 1869	St. Peter's Ger. Evang. Church, Volume 1, Page 5
Census	1870	Page 305, Kansas City, Jackson, Missouri, United States
Census	1880	ED 15, Page 419, Kansas City, Jackson, Missouri, United States
Census	1880	ED 2, Page 46, Kansas City, Jackson, Missouri, United States
Census	1900	
Death	1906	
Burial	23 Dec 1906	Elmwood Cemetery, Kansas City, Jackson, Missouri, United States
Occupation		Apprentice (1880), Cabinet Maker (1880)
Spouse		Jessie [--?--] (1859-)
Marriage	10 Sep 1885	(1885K0050354), Jackson, Missouri, United States

M Frederick/Friedrich "Fred" DAENZER

Birth	30 Sep 1863	Missouri, United States
Baptism	23 May 1869	St. Peter's Ger. Evang. Church, Volume 1, Page 5
Census	1870	Page 305, Kansas City, Jackson, Missouri, United States
Census	1880	ED 195, Page 398, Wyandotte Township, Wyandotte, Kansas, United States
Census	1900	
Death	1905	
Burial	27 Sep 1905	Elmwood Cemetery, Kansas City, Jackson, Missouri, United States
Occupation		Laborer on Farm (1880)
Marriage		

M John Carl "Johnny" DAENZER

Birth	2 Dec 1865	Missouri, United States
Baptism	23 May 1869	St. Peter's Ger. Evang. Church, Volume 1, Page 5
Census	1870	Page 305, Kansas City, Jackson, Missouri, United States
Death	Aug 1872	
Burial	31 Aug 1872	Elmwood Cemetery, Kansas City, Jackson, Missouri, United States
Marriage		

F Amalia "Mollie" DAENZER

Birth	2 Dec 1865	Kansas City, Jackson, Missouri, United States
Baptism	23 May 1869	St. Peter's Ger. Evang. Church, Volume 1, Page 5
Census	1870	Page 305, Kansas City, Jackson, Missouri, United States
Census	1880	ED 195, Page 398, Wyandotte Township, Wyandotte, Kansas, United States
Census	1900	ED 71, Page 78, Kansas City, Jackson, Missouri, United States
Census	1910	

Father Louis DAENZER

Mother Amelia/Amalia "Mollie" STEIGER

Children

Amalia "Mollie" DAENZER (continued)

Census	1920	
Census	1930	
Death	7 Sep 1959	Ruptured Myocardium, Acute Myocardial Infarction; Kansas City, Jackson, Missouri, United States
Burial	8 Sep 1959	Forest Hill Cemetery, Kansas City, Jackson, Missouri, United States
Spouse	Dr. Owen William KRUEGER (1865-1949)	
Marriage	1885/6	

Father James DENISON		
Birth	10 Oct 1818	Greenfield, Fairfield, Ohio, United States
Census	1850	Page 237, Salt Creek Township, Pickaway, Ohio, United States
Census	1860	
Tax Lists	May 1863	Animals Slaughtered for Sale; James [Denn]ison, Kansas City, Jackson, Missouri, United States
Tax Lists	May 1866	Retail Dealer License, Income, and Gold Watch; "James Dennison", Kansas City, Jackson, Missouri, United States
Census	1870	Page 507, Kansas City, Jackson, Missouri, United States
Census	1880	ED 11, Page 320, Kansas City, Jackson, Missouri, United States
Death	1899	
Occupation		Farmer (1850), Hides & Leather Merchant (1870), Retired Merchant (1880), Butcher, Retail Dealer
Burial		Evergreen Cemetery, Los Angeles, Los Angeles, California, United States
Marriage		
Father		
Mother		

Mother Maria Louise SLAUGHTER		
Birth	Feb 1818	Ohio, United States
Census	1850	Page 237, Salt Creek Township, Pickaway, Ohio, United States
Census	1860	
Census	1870	Page 507, Kansas City, Jackson, Missouri, United States
Census	1880	ED 11, Page 320, Kansas City, Jackson, Missouri, United States
Census	1900	ED 109, Page 155, Long Beach, Los Angeles, California, United States
Death	1901	
Burial		Evergreen Cemetery, Los Angeles, Los Angeles, California, United States
Father	Robert Field SLAUGHTER (1769-)	
Mother	Sarah BOND (1789-)	

Children

F	**Mary Ellen DENISON/DENNISON**		
	Birth	10 Oct 1852	Ohio, United States
	Census	1860	
	Census	1870	Page 507, Kansas City, Jackson, Missouri, United States
	Census	1880	ED 23, Page 196, Los Angeles, Los Angeles, California, United States
	Census	1900	ED 38, Page 223, Los Angeles, Los Angeles, California, United States
	Death	20 May 1936	Los Angeles, Los Angeles, California, United States
	Burial		
	Spouse	William Andrew SPALDING (1852-1941)	
	Marriage	14 Oct 1875	Saint Louis (city), Missouri, United States

M	**James Richard DENISON/DENNISON**		
	Birth	1 May 1853	(or May 1852), Ohio, United States
	Census	1860	
	Census	1870	Page 507, Kansas City, Jackson, Missouri, United States
	Census	1880	
	Census	1900	ED 33, Page 108, Kansas City, Jackson, Missouri, United States
	Death	26 Oct 1933	Los Angeles, California, United States
	Burial		Evergreen Cemetery, Los Angeles, Los Angeles, California, United States
	Burial		
	Occupation		Farmer (1900)
	Spouse	Matilda L. RIGGERT (1864-1947)	
	Marriage	15 Apr 1896	(1896K0012801), Kansas City, Jackson, Missouri, United States

M	**Thomas Slaughter DENISON/DENNISON**		
	Birth	Apr 1859	Ohio, United States
	Census	1860	
	Census	1870	Page 507, Kansas City, Jackson, Missouri, United States
	Census	1880	ED 11, Page 320, Kansas City, Jackson, Missouri, United States
	Census	1900	ED 109, Page 155, Long Beach, Los Angeles, California, United States
	Death	1902	

Father James DENISON

Mother Maria Louise SLAUGHTER

Children

Thomas Slaughter DENISON/DENNISON (continued)

Occupation	Law Student (1880), Attorney (1900)
Burial	Evergreen Cemetery, Los Angeles, Los Angeles, California, United States
Spouse	Louise [--?--] (-)
Marriage	

Father Edward Richard DENNISON

Birth	6 Mar 1841	Milford, Clermont, Ohio, United States
Census	1850	Page 117, Miami Township, Clermont, Ohio, United States
Census	1860	Page 110, Miami Township, Clermont, Ohio, United States
Tax Lists	Sep 1862	Wholesale Dealer License; "Rich. Denizen", Kansas City, Jackson, Missouri, United States
Census	1870	Page 659, Kansas City, Jackson, Missouri, United States
Census	1880	ED 213, Page 252, Wichita, Sedgwick, Kansas, United States
Death	20 Feb 1884	
Burial		Highland Cemetery, Wichita, Sedgwick, Kansas, United States
Occupation		Auctioneer, Wholesale Dealer; Kansas City, Jackson, Missouri, United States
Occupation		Salesman (1860), Boarding House (1870), Auctioneer (1880)
Marriage	11 Feb 1864	Saint Charles, Missouri, United States
Father	James DENNISON (1799-)	
Mother	Caroline Sophia BARWISE (1807-)	

Mother Agnes Lydia COWGUILL

Birth	14 Nov 1844	Louisiana, United States
Census	1850	"Right Hand Miss. River", Jefferson, Louisiana, United States
Census	1860	Page 754, Saint Charles, Saint Charles, Missouri, United States
Census	1870	Page 659, Kansas City, Jackson, Missouri, United States
Census	1875	Page 5, Wichita, Sedgwick, Kansas, United States
Census	1880	ED 213, Page 252, Wichita, Sedgwick, Kansas, United States
Census	1885	Page 80, Family 123, Wichita, Sedgwick, Kansas, United States
Census	1900	ED 145, Page 68, Axial, Routt, Colorado, United States
Death	14 Nov 1908	Delta, Colorado, United States
Occupation		Boarding House (1885)
Burial		
Father	Samuel COWGUILL (1802-1868)	
Mother	Mary Elizabeth ALEXANDER (1824-1895)	

Children

F Jennie DENNISON

Birth	1865/6	Missouri, United States
Census	1870	Page 659, Kansas City, Jackson, Missouri, United States
Census	1880	
Death		
Burial		
Marriage		

M Henry Arthur "Harry" DENNISON

Birth	6 Apr 1868	(or 6 Apr 1869), Kansas City, Jackson, Missouri, United States
Census	1870	Page 659, Kansas City, Jackson, Missouri, United States
Census	1875	Page 5, Wichita, Sedgwick, Kansas, United States
Census	1880	ED 213, Page 252, Wichita, Sedgwick, Kansas, United States
Census	1885	Page 80, Family 123, Wichita, Sedgwick, Kansas, United States
Census	1900	ED 145, Page 68, Axial, Routt, Colorado, United States
Residence	1918	Pinole, Contra Costa, California, United States
Death	11 Mar 1935	Hunt, Texas, United States
Occupation		Farmer (1900)
Burial		
Spouse	Josie ALEXANDER (1863-1921)	
Marriage	4 Aug 1888	Wichita, Sedgwick, Kansas, United States
Spouse	Elizabeth Melissa BROWND (-)	
Marriage		

M Bennett Searcy DENNISON

Birth	1 Aug 1875	Topeka, Shawnee, Kansas, United States
Census	1880	ED 213, Page 252, Wichita, Sedgwick, Kansas, United States
Census	1885	Page 80, Family 123, Wichita, Sedgwick, Kansas, United States
Census	1900	ED 14, Page 277, Delta, Delta, Colorado, United States
Military		World War I Draft Registration Cards; Seattle, King, Washington, United States

Father	**Edward Richard DENNISON**	
Mother	**Agnes Lydia COWGUILL**	
Children		
	Bennett Searcy DENNISON (continued)	
Misc	7 Oct 1925	Convicted of Using United States Mails to Defraud; Portland, Multnomah, Oregon, United States
Residence	bet Apr 1927 and Jan 1928	McNeil Island Penitentiary, McNeil Island, Pierce, Washington, United States
Death	25 Oct 1958	Redondo Beach, Los Angeles, California, United States
Burial		San Gabriel Cemetery, San Gabriel, Los Angeles, California, United States
Occupation		Salesman (1918)
Illness		Hunchback (1918)
Spouse	May R. [--?--] (1873-)	
Marriage	1896/7	
Spouse	Patti F. [--?--] (1898-1977)	
Marriage		
F	**Mabel/Mabelle DENNISON**	
Birth	3 Sep 1879	Kansas City, Wyandotte, Kansas, United States
Census	1880	ED 213, Page 252, Wichita, Sedgwick, Kansas, United States
Census	1885	Page 80, Family 123, Wichita, Sedgwick, Kansas, United States
Census	1900	ED 125, Page 37, Gillett, Teller, Colorado, United States
Death	26 Mar 1949	Los Angeles, Los Angeles, California, United States
Burial		
Spouse	Edward Austin ELLIOTT (1871-1961)	
Marriage	1899/1900	
M	**Edward O. "Eddy" DENNISON**	
Birth	25 Nov 1882	Kansas, United States
Census	1885	Page 80, Family 123, Wichita, Sedgwick, Kansas, United States
Census	1900	ED 145, Page 68, Axial, Routt, Colorado, United States
Census	1910	ED 99, Page 104, Denver, Denver, Colorado, United States
Census	1920	ED 580, Page 263, Alhambra, Los Angeles, California, United States
Death	25 Feb 1941	Los Angeles, California, United States
Burial		Pierce Brothers Valhalla Memorial Park, North Hollywood, Los Angeles, California, United States
Occupation		Office Manager Tunnel Machine Company (1910), Broker Stocks (1920)
Spouse	Sarah Jo B. FERGUSON (1887-)	
Marriage	1907/8	

Father Peter William DITSCH

Birth	9 Apr 1821	Trier, Rheinland, Prussia, Germany
Census	1850	Page 496, Burlington, Des Moines, Iowa, United States
Census	1854	(P. W. Dietch Family), Page 15, Muscatine, Muscatine, Iowa, United States
Census	1856	Page 95, Bloomington Township, Muscatine, Iowa, United States
Residence	1849/60-1891	Kansas City, Jackson, Missouri, United States
Census	1860	Page 784, Muscatine, Muscatine, Iowa, United States
Misc		Advertisement, Kansas City (Mo.) Western Journal of Commerce, 01 Jan 1861, Page 3, Column 5
Misc	30 Jul 1862	Union Provost Marshals' File of Papers Relating to Individual Civilians, M345, Roll 74
Tax Lists	Sep 1862	Wholesale Liquor Dealer, Retail Liquor Dealer, Rectifier, and Tobacconist Licenses; "Dietch & Auer", Kansas City, Jackson, Missouri, United States
Military		Civil War Service
Tax Lists	May 1866	Income and Gold Watch; "B. W. Deitsch", Kansas City, Jackson, Missouri, United States
Tax Lists	Nov 1866	Whisky Produced; "P. W. Ditsch", Kansas City, Jackson, Missouri, United States
Tax Lists	Dec 1866	Wholesale Liquor Dealer and Rectifier Licenses; "P. W. Ditsch", Kansas City, Jackson, Missouri, United States
Census	1870	Page 441, Kansas City, Jackson, Missouri, United States
Census	1880	ED 15, Page 413, Kansas City, Jackson, Missouri, United States
Misc		Biography, History of Jackson Co., MO (1881), Pages 760-761
Census	1890	ED 108, Page 2, Kansas City, Jackson, Missouri, United States
Will	17 Oct 1890	Will Written, Jackson Co. (Kansas City), MO, Volume 1, Page 611
Death	23 Oct 1891	Old Age; Kansas City, Jackson, Missouri, United States
Misc		Obituary, Kansas City (Mo.) Times, 24 Oct 1891, Page 5, Column 4
Misc		Obituary, Kansas City (Mo.) Daily Journal, 24 Oct 1891, Page 3, Column 2
Burial	26 Oct 1891	Saint Louis (city), Missouri, United States
Probate	23 Nov 1891	(Will Proved, Kansas City Courthouse, Volume 1, Page 611), Jackson, Missouri, United States
Occupation		Brewer (1850), Cooper (1856), Rectifier (1860), Landlord (1880)
Marriage		
Father		Peter DITSCH (-)
Mother		

Mother Julia GEISS

Birth	1823/4	(or Prussia, Germany), Bavaria, Germany
Census	1850	
Census	1854	(P. W. Dietch Family), Page 15, Muscatine, Muscatine, Iowa, United States
Census	1856	Page 95, Bloomington Township, Muscatine, Iowa, United States
Census	1860	Page 784, Muscatine, Muscatine, Iowa, United States
Census	1870	Page 441, Kansas City, Jackson, Missouri, United States
Death	3 Sep 1871	Kansas City, Jackson, Missouri, United States
Burial	4 Sep 1871	Union Cemetery, Kansas City, Jackson, Missouri, United States
Misc		Funeral Notice, Kansas City (Mo.) Daily Journal of Commerce, 05 Sep 1871, Page 4, Column 1
Burial	19 Nov 1914	Removed from Union Cemetery, Kansas City, Jackson, Missouri, United States
Father		
Mother		

Children

M Charles L. DITSCH

Birth	20 Nov 1850	Burlington, Des Moines, Iowa, United States
Census	1854	(P. W. Dietch Family), Page 15, Muscatine, Muscatine, Iowa, United States
Census	1856	Page 95, Bloomington Township, Muscatine, Iowa, United States
Census	1860	Page 784, Muscatine, Muscatine, Iowa, United States
Residence	bet 1863 and 1888	Kansas City, Jackson, Missouri, United States
Census	1870	Page 441, Kansas City, Jackson, Missouri, United States
Misc		"Hymenial," Kansas City (Mo.) Times, 27 Nov 1872, Page 4, Column 1
Census	1880	ED 15, Page 413, Kansas City, Jackson, Missouri, United States
Death	22 Dec 1888	Suicide by Gunshot; Kansas City, Jackson, Missouri, United States
Misc		Obituary, Kansas City (Mo.) Star, 24 Dec 1888, Page 1, Column 3
Misc		Obituary, Kansas City (Mo.) Daily Journal, 24 Dec 1888, Page 3, Columns 1-4

Father	Peter William DITSCH
Mother	Julia GEISS

Children

Charles L. DITSCH (continued)

Burial	26 Dec 1888	Union Cemetery, Kansas City, Jackson, Missouri, United States
Misc		"The Inquest Finished," Kansas City (Mo.) Star, 26 Dec 1888, Page 1, Column 3
Burial	19 Nov 1914	Removed from Union Cemetery, Kansas City, Jackson, Missouri, United States
Occupation		Printer (1870), Policeman (1880), Captain of Police
Spouse	Helene HELMREICH (1854-1937)	
Marriage	25 Nov 1872	(1872I0070089), Kansas City, Jackson, Missouri, United States

M Peter William DITSCH

Birth	4 Mar 1852	(or 04 May 1852), Burlington, Des Moines, Iowa, United States
Census	1854	(P. W. Dietch Family), Page 15, Muscatine, Muscatine, Iowa, United States
Census	1856	Page 95, Bloomington Township, Muscatine, Iowa, United States
Census	1856	Page 95, Bloomington Township, Muscatine, Iowa, United States
Census	1860	Page 784, Muscatine, Muscatine, Iowa, United States
Census	1870	Page 441, Kansas City, Jackson, Missouri, United States
Census	1880	
Census	1900	ED 16, Page 233, Kansas City, Jackson, Missouri, United States
Census	1910	
Census	1920	
Death	12 Jan 1926	Cardiac Hypertrophy and Decompensation, Nephritis Chronic; Kansas City, Jackson, Missouri, United States
Burial	15 Jan 1926	Mount Saint Mary's Cemetery, Kansas City, Jackson, Missouri, United States
Occupation		Printer (1870), Sign Painter (1900), Night Watchman for William Volker Company
Spouse	Catherine M. GAHLEY (1847-1921)	
Marriage		

M Henry DITSCH

Birth	abt 1857	Iowa, United States
Census	1860	Page 784, Muscatine, Muscatine, Iowa, United States
Census	1870	Page 441, Kansas City, Jackson, Missouri, United States
Census	1880	ED 15, Page 411, Kansas City, Jackson, Missouri, United States
Census	1900	
Will	30 Mar 1903	Will Written, Jackson Co. (Kansas City), MO, Volume 15, Page 102
Death	Jun 1909	
Burial	16 Jun 1909	Union Cemetery, Kansas City, Jackson, Missouri, United States
Probate	17 Jun 1909	(Will Proved, Kansas City Courthouse, Volume 15, Page 102), Jackson, Missouri, United States
Burial	21 Nov 1914	Removed from Union Cemetery, Kansas City, Jackson, Missouri, United States
Occupation		Druggist (1880)
Marriage		

M Oscar William DITSCH

Birth	10 Oct 1859	Iowa, United States
Census	1860	Page 784, Muscatine, Muscatine, Iowa, United States
Census	1870	Page 441, Kansas City, Jackson, Missouri, United States
Census	1880	ED 15, Page 424, Kansas City, Jackson, Missouri, United States
Census	1900	ED 16, Page 233, Kansas City, Jackson, Missouri, United States
Will	22 May 1907	Will Written, Jackson Co. (Kansas City), MO, Volume 19, Page 638
Census	1910	
Death	18 Dec 1915	Concussion of Brain and Probable Fracture of Base of Skull (Traffic Accident); Kansas City, Jackson, Missouri, United States
Burial	21 Dec 1915	Elmwood Cemetery, Kansas City, Jackson, Missouri, United States
Probate	5 Jan 1916	(Will Proved, Kansas City Courthouse, Volume 19, Page 638), Jackson, Missouri, United States
Occupation		Machinist (1880), Electrician (1900)
Spouse	Anna R. KESSLER (1863-1941)	
Marriage	10 Oct 1906	(1906K0035963), Kansas City, Jackson, Missouri, United States

Father Michael DIVELEY

Birth	8 Dec 1828	Somerset, Pennsylvania, United States
Census	1850	Page 288, Elk Lick Township, Somerset, Pennsylvania, United States
Residence	bet 1855 and 1858	Iowa City, Johnson, Iowa, United States
Residence	bet 1858 and 1901	Kansas City, Jackson, Missouri, United States
Census	1860	Page 77, Kansas City, Jackson, Missouri, United States
Misc		Advertisement, Western Journal of Commerce, 04 Jan 1861, Page 1, Column 7
Misc	31 Jul 1862	Union Provost Marshals' File of Papers Relating to Individual Civilians, M345, Roll 74
Tax Lists	Sep 1862	Wholesale Dealer, Wholesale Liquor Dealer, and Retail Liquor Dealer Licenses; "Mike Dively", Kansas City, Jackson, Missouri, United States
Occupation	1862/3	City Councilman; Kansas City, Jackson, Missouri, United States
Military	Sep 1863	Civil War Draft Registration; Kaw Township, Jackson, Missouri, United States
Tax Lists	Dec 1863	Animals Slaughtered for Sale; "Diveley, Crandall & Company", Kansas City, Jackson, Missouri, United States
Misc		"City Assessment," Kansas City (Mo.) Daily Journal of Commerce, 01 Oct 1865, Page 2, Column 1
Tax Lists	Apr 1866	Wholesale Liquor Dealer License; Kansas City, Jackson, Missouri, United States
Tax Lists	May 1866	Wholesale Liquor Dealer License; Kansas City, Jackson, Missouri, United States
Tax Lists	Aug 1866	Wholesale Liquor Dealer License; "Michel Diveley", Kansas City, Jackson, Missouri, United States
Tax Lists	bet Oct 1866 and Dec 1866	Gross Sales; Kansas City, Jackson, Missouri, United States
Census	1870	Page 690, Kansas City, Jackson, Missouri, United States
Occupation	1872	City Councilman; Kansas City, Jackson, Missouri, United States
Misc	14 Apr 1873	United States Passport Application; Jackson, Missouri, United States
Misc		Biography, US Biographical Dictionary and Portrait Gallery . . . Missouri Volume (1878), Pages 632-633
Census	1880	ED 21, Page 566, Kansas City, Jackson, Missouri, United States
Misc		Biography, History of Jackson Co., MO (1881), Page 761
Will	5 Aug 1891	(Will Written), Volume 6, Page 103, Kansas City, Jackson, Missouri, United States
Census	1900	ED 24, Page 4, Kansas City, Jackson, Missouri, United States
Death	19 Nov 1901	Senility; Kansas City, Jackson, Missouri, United States
Burial	21 Nov 1901	Union Cemetery, Kansas City, Jackson, Missouri, United States
Misc		Funeral Notice, Kansas City (Mo.) Star, 21 Nov 1901, Page 1, Column 4
Probate	2 Dec 1901	(Will Proved), Volume 6, Page 103, Kansas City, Jackson, Missouri, United States
Misc		"An Early Day Merchant Prince," Kansas City (Mo.) Star, 03 Sep 1922, Page 1 Ad Section, Column 7
Occupation		Clerk (1850), Merchant (1860), Real Estate Dealer (1870), Retired Merchant (1880), Capitalist (1900)
Religion		Communicant (1866); Saint Mary's Episcopal Church, Kansas City, Jackson, Missouri, United States
Occupation		Wholesale Dealer, Wholesale & Retail Liquor Dealer
Business		Diveley, Crandall & Company (Meat)
Misc		Brother of William M. Diveley, Kansas City Merchant
Occupation		President and Director of Mechanics' Bank of Kansas City and of First National Bank of Kansas City; Kansas City, Jackson, Missouri, United States
Marriage	13 Sep 1860	Pennsylvania, United States
Father		Michael DIVELEY (1787-1840)
Mother		Juliana SCHWARTZ (1793-1853)
Other spouse		Cornelia L. MCINTOSH (1844-1920)
Marriage	15 Jan 1885	Will, Illinois, United States

Mother Harriet E. "Hattie" SHERMAN

Birth	1834/5	(or 1839/40), New York, United States
Census	1850	
Census	1860	
Census	1870	Page 690, Kansas City, Jackson, Missouri, United States
Death	17 Mar 1880	Paralysis of the Brain; Kansas City, Jackson, Missouri, United States
Misc		Funeral Notice, Kansas City (Mo.) Daily Journal, 19 Mar 1880, Page 8, Columns 3-4
Burial	21 Mar 1880	Union Cemetery, Kansas City, Jackson, Missouri, United States

Father Michael DIVELEY	
Mother Harriet E. "Hattie" SHERMAN	

Children

Harriet E. "Hattie" SHERMAN (continued)

Religion	Received by Experience (November 1867); First Baptist Church, Kansas City, Jackson, Missouri, United States
Father	
Mother	

Children

M	**George Sherman DIVELEY**	
Birth	4 Jul 1861	Kansas City, Jackson, Missouri, United States
Census	1870	Page 690, Kansas City, Jackson, Missouri, United States
Census	1880	ED 21, Page 566, Kansas City, Jackson, Missouri, United States
Census	1900	ED 75, Page 239, Medford, Grant, Oklahoma Territory, United States
Death	8 Feb 1928	Acute Suppurative Peritonitis Following Operation for Removal of Adenocarcinoma of Rectum; Kansas City, Jackson, Missouri, United States
Burial	13 Feb 1928	Forest Hill Cemetery, Kansas City, Jackson, Missouri, United States
Occupation		Merchant Dry Goods (1900), Real Estate (1928)
Spouse	Nellie E. WILLIAMS (1868-1944)	
Marriage	1891/2	

Father	**John Bragg DRINKARD**	
Birth	17 Nov 1831	Petersburg, Dinwiddie, Virginia, United States
Census	1840	(Beverly Drinkard Family), Page 41, Petersburg, Dinwiddie, Virginia, United States
Census	1850	Page 426, Petersburg, Dinwiddie, Virginia, United States
Residence	bet 1855 and 1859	Hartford, North Carolina, United States
Census	1859	Page 3, Leavenworth, Kansas Territory, United States
Residence	bet 1859 and 1869	Kansas City, Jackson, Missouri, United States
Census	1860	Page 724, Leavenworth, Leavenworth, Kansas Territory, United States
Misc	abt 1862	Union Provost Marshals' File of Papers . . . Two or More Civilians, M416, Roll 80, No. 21,974
Tax Lists	Sep 1862	Wholesale Dealer License; "Dinker & Conwell", Kansas City, Jackson, Missouri, United States
Misc	27 Jan 1863	Union Provost Marshals' File of Papers Relating to Two or More Civilians, M416, Roll 13, No. 3512
Misc		Advertisement, Kansas City (Mo.) Western Journal of Commerce, 02 Jul 1863, Page 3, Column 5
Misc		U. S. Internal Revenue Tax Lists for Leavenworth Co., KS--Oct-Dec 1864 to Dec 1865
Tax Lists	Nov 1864	Real Estate Agent License; Leavenworth, Leavenworth, Kansas, United States
Census	1865	Page 64, Family 496, Leavenworth, Leavenworth, Kansas, United States
Tax Lists	May 1865	Carriage, Gold Watch; Leavenworth, Leavenworth, Kansas, United States
Tax Lists	Dec 1865	Common Carrier License; Leavenworth, Leavenworth, Kansas, United States
Occupation	1868/9	City Assessor; Kansas City, Jackson, Missouri, United States
Death	12 Aug 1869	Kansas City, Jackson, Missouri, United States
Misc		Obituary, Kansas City (Mo.) Daily Journal of Commerce, 13 Aug 1869, Page 4, Column 3
Burial	13 Aug 1869	Funeral, Kansas City, Jackson, Missouri, United States
Occupation		Bookkeeper for Alexander Majors; Kansas City, Jackson, Missouri, United States
Occupation		Printer (1850), Clerk (1859, 1860), Bookkeeper (1865)
Occupation		Printer and News Forman, Richmond (Va.) Examiner; Richmond, Richmond, Virginia, United States
Religion		Presbyterian
Marriage	19 Jun 1855	
Father	Beverly DRINKARD (1793-1875)	
Mother	Elizabeth Ann FIRTH (1809-1864)	

Mother	**Louisa "Lou" WINSTON**	
Birth	1840	Goochland, Virginia, United States
Census	1850	
Census	1860	Page 724, Leavenworth, Leavenworth, Kansas Territory, United States
Census	1865	Page 64, Family 496, Leavenworth, Leavenworth, Kansas, United States
Census	1870	
Census	1880	ED 18, Page 490, Kansas City, Jackson, Missouri, United States
Death	1 Apr 1892	Marasmus; Kansas City, Jackson, Missouri, United States
Misc		Funeral Notice, Kansas City (Mo.) Daily Journal, 03 Apr 1892, Page 2, Column 7
Burial	3 Apr 1892	Union Cemetery, Kansas City, Jackson, Missouri, United States
Father		
Mother		

Children

M	**Beverly Winston DRINKARD**	
Birth	17 Mar 1857	Hartford, North Carolina, United States
Census	1860	Page 724, Leavenworth, Leavenworth, Kansas Territory, United States
Census	1865	Page 64, Family 496, Leavenworth, Leavenworth, Kansas, United States
Census	1870	
Census	1880	
Census	1900	ED 109, Page 311, Kansas City, Jackson, Missouri, United States
Census	1910	
Death	22 Feb 1912	Lobar Pneumonia, Delirium Tremens; Kansas City, Jackson, Missouri, United States
Burial	24 Feb 1912	Union Cemetery, Kansas City, Jackson, Missouri, United States
Occupation		Civil Engineer (1900)
Marriage		

Father	John Bragg DRINKARD	
Mother	Louisa "Lou" WINSTON	
Children		

F	**Mary Elizabeth DRINKARD**	
	Birth	10 Jan 1860
	Census	1860	Page 724, Leavenworth, Leavenworth, Kansas Territory, United States
	Census	1865	"Alexander Drinkard," Page 64, Family 496, Leavenworth, Leavenworth, Kansas, United States
	Census	1870	
	Census	1880	
	Death		
	Burial		
	Marriage		

M	**Alexander Street DRINKARD**	
	Birth	15 Aug 1863	Kansas City, Jackson, Missouri, United States
	Census	1870	
	Residence	bet 1872 and 1882	Petersburg, Dinwiddie, Virginia, United States
	Census	1880	
	Census	1900	ED 86, Page 286, Kansas City, Jackson, Missouri, United States
	Death	29 Apr 1936	Chronic Valvular Heart Disease, Fracture of Hip; Kansas City, Jackson, Missouri, United States
	Burial	2 May 1936	Mount Moriah Cemetery, Kansas City, Jackson, Missouri, United States
	Occupation		Shipping Clerk Furniture (1900), Montgomery Ward
	Spouse	Anne Augusta CAMPBELL (1874-1953)	
	Marriage	26 Apr 1893	(1893K0006265), Kansas City, Jackson, Missouri, United States

F	**Lillie Lee DRINKARD**	
	Birth	Nov 1866	Leavenworth, Leavenworth, Kansas, United States
	Census	1870	
	Census	1880	ED 18, Page 490, Kansas City, Jackson, Missouri, United States
	Census	1900	ED 108, Page 279, Kansas City, Jackson, Missouri, United States
	Death	21 May 1903	Heart Disease; Kansas City, Jackson, Missouri, United States
	Burial	22 May 1903	Union Cemetery, Kansas City, Jackson, Missouri, United States
	Spouse	Robert BOTELER (1866-1902)	
	Marriage	1 Jun 1895	(1895K0011409), Jackson, Missouri, United States

Father Robert Roland DUNBAR

Birth	17 Aug 1824	Breckinridge, Kentucky, United States
Census	1850	Page 290, Bureau, Illinois, United States
Census	1860	Page 58, Princeton, Bureau, Illinois, United States
Residence	bet 1861 and 1907	Kansas City, Jackson, Missouri, United States
Tax Lists	Oct 1863	Animals Slaughtered for Sale; "Frank & Dunbar", Kansas City, Jackson, Missouri, United States
Tax Lists	Nov 1863	Butcher License; Kansas City, Jackson, Missouri, United States
Tax Lists	Dec 1863	Animals Slaughtered for Sale; Kansas City, Jackson, Missouri, United States
Census	1870	Page 467, Wakarusa Township, Douglas, Kansas, United States
Census	1880	ED 39, Page 195, Ridgeway Township, Osage, Kansas, United States
Misc		Biography, History of the State of Kansas (Cutler, 1883), Page [--?--]
Census	1885	Page 19, Carbondale, Osage, Kansas, United States
Census	1900	ED 141, Page 45, Argentine, Wyandotte, Kansas, United States
Death	12 Oct 1907	Kansas City, Jackson, Missouri, United States
Burial	14 Oct 1907	Union Cemetery, Kansas City, Jackson, Missouri, United States
Misc		Obituary, Kansas City (Mo.) Times, 14 Oct 1907, Page 1, Column 1
Misc		Funeral Notice, Kansas City (Mo.) Times, 14 Oct 1907, Page 10, Column 6
Occupation		Butcher; Kansas City, Jackson, Missouri, United States
Occupation		Farmer (1850, 1860, 1870, 1880), Clerk (1885), Lawyer (1900)
Marriage	27 Aug 1860	Princeton, Bureau, Illinois, United States
Father		
Mother	Sarah PRATHER (1792-1859)	
Other spouse	Emily TUCKER (1829-1861)	
Marriage	15 Aug 1850	Bureau, Illinois, United States

Mother Elizabeth Sarah YOUNG

Birth	Jul 1838	Vermont, United States
Census	1850	
Census	1860	
Census	1870	Page 467, Wakarusa Township, Douglas, Kansas, United States
Census	1880	ED 39, Page 195, Ridgeway Township, Osage, Kansas, United States
Census	1885	Page 19, Carbondale, Osage, Kansas, United States
Census	1900	ED 141, Page 45, Argentine, Wyandotte, Kansas, United States
Death	31 Oct 1906	Kansas City, Jackson, Missouri, United States
Burial	2 Nov 1906	Union Cemetery, Kansas City, Jackson, Missouri, United States
Misc		Funeral Notice, Kansas City (Mo.) Times, 02 Nov 1906, Page 11, Column 7
Occupation		Grain Dealer (1885)
Father		
Mother		

Children

F Edith DUNBAR

Birth	1860/1	Kansas, United States
Census	1870	Page 467, Wakarusa Township, Douglas, Kansas, United States
Death		
Burial		
Marriage		

M George T. C. DUNBAR

Birth	Apr 1865	Vermont, United States
Census	1870	Page 467, Wakarusa Township, Douglas, Kansas, United States
Census	1880	ED 39, Page 195, Ridgeway Township, Osage, Kansas, United States
Census	1885	Page 19, Carbondale, Osage, Kansas, United States
Census	1900	ED 141, Page 45, Argentine, Wyandotte, Kansas, United States
Residence	1907	Kansas City, Jackson, Missouri, United States
Census	1910	ED 59, Page 181, Denver, Denver, Colorado, United States
Occupation		Works on Farm (1880), Painter (1900), Proprietor Restaurant (1910)
Death		
Burial		
Spouse	Dollie E. [--?--] (1877-)	

Father	Robert Roland DUNBAR		
Mother	**Elizabeth Sarah YOUNG**		

Children

George T. C. DUNBAR (continued)

Marriage	1896/7	

M Sanford DUNBAR

Census	1870	Page 467, Wakarusa Township, Douglas, Kansas, United States
Birth	Jan 1870	Kansas, United States
Death		
Burial		
Marriage		

F Elizabeth A. "Lizzie" DUNBAR

Birth	Apr 1871	Kansas, United States
Census	1880	ED 39, Page 195, Ridgeway Township, Osage, Kansas, United States
Census	1885	Page 20, Carbondale, Osage, Kansas, United States
Census	1900	ED 140, Page 13, Argentine, Wyandotte, Kansas, United States
Residence	1907	Pueblo, Pueblo, Colorado, United States
Census	1910	ED 176, Page 80, Pueblo, Pueblo, Colorado, United States
Death		
Burial		
Spouse	Ora J. MEYERS (1869-)	
Marriage	1885/6	

F Daisy Pearl DUNBAR

Birth	1870/1	Kansas, United States
Census	1880	ED 39, Page 195, Ridgeway Township, Osage, Kansas, United States
Death		
Burial		
Marriage		

F Claudia May DUNBAR

Birth	21 Feb 1873	Kansas, United States
Census	1880	ED 39, Page 195, Ridgeway Township, Osage, Kansas, United States
Census	1885	Carbondale, Osage, Kansas, United States
Census	1900	ED 165, Page 87, Kansas City, Wyandotte, Kansas, United States
Residence	1907	Kansas City, Jackson, Missouri, United States
Census	1910	ED 202, Page 104, Kansas City, Jackson, Missouri, United States
Census	1920	ED 220, Page 24, Kansas City, Jackson, Missouri, United States
Death	3 Jul 1940	Los Angeles, California, United States
Burial		Pierce Brothers Valhalla Memorial Park, North Hollywood, Los Angeles, California, United States
Spouse	Floyd H. PYBURN (1867-1938)	
Marriage	1898/9	
Spouse	Charles Murray CAMPBELL (1869-1894)	
Marriage		

Father John S. DUNCAN

Birth	1834	Ohio, United States
Census	1850	
Residence	bet 1856 and 1859	Near Keokuk, Lee, Iowa, United States
Residence	1859	Memphis, Shelby, Tennessee, United States
Residence	bet 1860 and 1867	Kansas City, Jackson, Missouri, United States
Census	1860	Page 105, Kansas City, Jackson, Missouri, United States
Census		Industrial Schedules, Page 2, Kansas City, Jackson, Missouri, United States
Tax Lists	Sep 1862	Retail Dealer License; Kansas City, Jackson, Missouri, United States
Military		Private, Company A, 77th Regiment Enrolled Missouri Militia
Military		Quarter Master Sergeant, Company A, 77th Regiment Enrolled Missouri Militia
Military	Dec 1863	Civil War Draft Registration; Kaw Township, Jackson, Missouri, United States
Residence	bet 1867 and 1873	Linwood, Leavenworth, Kansas, United States
Census	1870	Page 510, Sherman Township, Leavenworth, Kansas, United States
Death	1873	Grand Tower, Jackson, Illinois, United States
Burial		Mount Sidney Cemetery, Linwood, Leavenworth, Kansas, United States
Misc		Biography of Son Francis M. Duncan, History of the State of Kansas (1883), Pages 470
Occupation		Miller (1860), Farmer (1870), Retail Dealer, Lumber Dealer
Marriage		
Father		
Mother		

Mother Anna "Ann, Annie" WICKELL

Birth	May 1836	(or 1833/34), Pickaway, Ohio, United States
Census	1850	
Census	1860	Page 105, Kansas City, Jackson, Missouri, United States
Census	1870	Page 510, Sherman Township, Leavenworth, Kansas, United States
Census	1880	ED 152, Page 185, Sherman Township, Leavenworth, Kansas, United States
Census	1885	Pages 131-133, Sherman Township, Leavenworth, Kansas, United States
Census	1895	Page 3, Linwood, Leavenworth, Kansas, United States
Census	1900	ED 104, Page 104, Sherman Township, Leavenworth, Kansas, United States
Census	1910	ED 107, Page 184, Linwood, Leavenworth, Kansas, United States
Death	1911	
Burial		Mount Sidney Cemetery, Linwood, Leavenworth, Kansas, United States
Father	Daniel WICKELL (1781-1841)	
Mother	Christianna HOLT (1793-)	

Children

M Francis M. "Frank" DUNCAN

Birth	17 Nov 1857	Missouri, United States
Census	1860	Page 105, Kansas City, Jackson, Missouri, United States
Residence	bet 1860 and 1867	Kansas City, Jackson, Missouri, United States
Residence	1867-?	Linwood, Leavenworth, Kansas, United States
Census	1870	Page 510, Sherman Township, Leavenworth, Kansas, United States
Census	1880	ED 152, Page 185, Sherman Township, Leavenworth, Kansas, United States
Misc		Biography, History of the State of Kansas (1883), Page 470
Census	1900	ED 56, Page 237, Denver, Arapahoe, Colorado, United States
Death	1939	
Burial		Fairmount Cemetery, Denver, Denver, Colorado, United States
Occupation		Telegraph Operator (1880), Chief Clerk Railroad (1900)
Spouse	Viola TUDHOPE (1856-1880)	
Marriage	15 Sep 1880	Linwood, Leavenworth, Kansas, United States
Spouse	Cosby J. [--?--] (1864-1922)	
Marriage	1884/5	

F Anna May/Millie DUNCAN

Birth	1866/7	Kansas, United States
Census	1870	Page 510, Sherman Township, Leavenworth, Kansas, United States
Census	1880	ED 152, Page 185, Sherman Township, Leavenworth, Kansas, United States
Census	1885	Pages 131-133, Sherman Township, Leavenworth, Kansas, United States
Census	1895	Page 3, Linwood, Leavenworth, Kansas, United States

Father John S. DUNCAN

Mother Anna "Ann, Annie" WICKELL

Children

Anna May/Millie DUNCAN (continued)

Census	1900	ED 104, Page 104, Sherman Township, Leavenworth, Kansas, United States
Census	1910	ED 107, Page 184, Linwood, Leavenworth, Kansas, United States
Death		
Burial		
Spouse	John William Henry HARBAUGH (1867-1914)	
Marriage	27 Apr 1893	

Father Charles DWYER

Birth	1826/7	Quea, Tyrone, Ireland
Immigration	1840	Pennsylvania, United States
Residence	bet 1840 and 1844	Pennsylvania, United States
Residence	bet 1844 and 1853	Lexington, Fayette, Kentucky, United States
Census	1850	
Residence	bet 1853 and 1890	Kansas City, Jackson, Missouri, United States
Census	1860	Page 100, Kansas City, Jackson, Missouri, United States
Misc	1860	Member of Shamrock Benevolent Society; Kansas City, Jackson, Missouri, United States
Tax Lists	Sep 1862	Retail Dealer and Retail Liquor Dealer Licenses; Kansas City, Jackson, Missouri, United States
Occupation	bet 1863 and 1865	City Councilman; Kansas City, Jackson, Missouri, United States
Occupation	1866/7	City Councilman; Kansas City, Jackson, Missouri, United States
Census	1870	Page 601, Kansas, United States
Census	1880	ED 13, Page 376, Kansas City, Jackson, Missouri, United States
Death	10 Jan 1890	Kansas City, Jackson, Missouri, United States
Misc		Obituary, Kansas City (Mo.) Daily Journal, 11 Jan 1890, Page 4, COlumn 6
Burial	12 Jan 1890	Mount Saint Mary's Cemetery, Kansas City, Jackson, Missouri, United States
Misc		Funeral Notice, Kansas City (Mo.) Daily Journal, 13 Jan 1890, Page 3, Column 2
Occupation		Boarding House (1860), Street Contractor (1870), Saloon (1880), Retail Dealer, Retail Liquor Dealer
Religion		Church of the Sacred Heart (Roman Catholic); Kansas City, Jackson, Missouri, United States
Marriage		
Father		
Mother		

Mother Winifred "Unay" CARR

Birth	1834/5	Ireland
Census	1850	
Census	1860	Page 100, Kansas City, Jackson, Missouri, United States
Census	1870	Page 601, Kansas City, Jackson, Missouri, United States
Census	1880	ED 13, Page 376, Kansas City, Jackson, Missouri, United States
Death	1 May 1890	Heart Disease; Kansas City, Jackson, Missouri, United States
Misc		Obituary, Kansas City (Mo.) Star, 1 May 1890, Page 2, Column 3
Burial		
Father		
Mother		

Children

M Francis Patrick Thomas DWYER

Birth	3 Sep 1857	Missouri, United States
Census	1860	Page 100, Kansas City, Jackson, Missouri, United States
Census	1870	Page 601, Kansas City, Jackson, Missouri, United States
Census	1880	ED 13, Page 376, Kansas City, Jackson, Missouri, United States
Census	1900	ED 45, Page 276, Kansas City, Jackson, Missouri, United States
Residence	1918	Kansas City, Jackson, Missouri, United States
Death	28 Jul 1927	Cerebral Hemorrhage, Chronic Interstitial Nephritis, Arterio-Hypertension; Kansas City, Jackson, Missouri, United States
Burial	30 Jul 1927	Mount Saint Mary's Cemetery, Kansas City, Jackson, Missouri, United States
Occupation		Laborer (1870, 1880), Postal Clerk (1900)
Spouse	Anna E. DOCKWEILER (1865-1895)	
Marriage	30 Jul 1883	(1883K0030292), Kansas City, Jackson, Missouri, United States

F Mary Ann DWYER

Birth	1860	(or Dec 1865), Missouri, United States
Census	1860	Page 100, Kansas City, Jackson, Missouri, United States
Census	1870	Page 601, Kansas City, Jackson, Missouri, United States
Census	1880	ED 13, Page 376, Kansas City, Jackson, Missouri, United States
Census	1900	ED 154, Page 69, Kansas City, Wyandotte, Kansas, United States
Census	1910	ED 164, Page 116, Kansas City, Wyandotte, Kansas, United States

Father	Charles DWYER	
Mother	Winifred "Unay" CARR	
Children		

Mary Ann DWYER (continued)

Death	17 Apr 1918	Sepsis and Gangrene of Both Legs . . .; Kansas City, Jackson, Missouri, United States
Misc		Obituary, Kansas City (Mo.) Star, 17 Apr 1918, Page 4, Columns 4-5
Burial	19 Apr 1918	Mount Saint Mary's Cemetery, Kansas City, Jackson, Missouri, United States
Occupation		Clerk in Store (1880)
Spouse	Frank N. TSCHUDI (1859-1921)	
Marriage	6 Dec 1887	(1887K0090186), Jackson, Missouri, United States

M John E. DWYER

Birth	abt 1863	Missouri, United States
Census	1870	Page 601, Kansas City, Jackson, Missouri, United States
Census	1880	ED 13, Page 376, Kansas City, Jackson, Missouri, United States
Census	1900	ED 101, Page 186, Kansas City, Jackson, Missouri, United States
Occupation		Brakeman (1880), Police Detective (1900)
Death		
Burial		
Marriage		

F Margaret "Maggie" DWYER

Birth	abt 1864	Missouri, United States
Census	1870	Page 601, Kansas City, Jackson, Missouri, United States
Census	1880	ED 13, Page 376, Kansas City, Jackson, Missouri, United States
Census	1900	
Census	1910	
Residence	1918	Lincoln, Lancaster, Nebraska, United States
Census	1920	ED 67, Page 22, Lincoln, Lancaster, Nebraska, United States
Census	1930	ED 27, Page 151, Lincoln, Lancaster, Nebraska, United States
Death		
Burial		
Spouse	W. S. TURNER (1854-)	
Marriage	25 Aug 1886	(1886K0060307), Jackson, Missouri, United States
Spouse	John M. MULVIHILL (-)	
Marriage		

M Charles M. DWYER

Birth	Oct 1870	Missouri, United States
Census	1880	ED 13, Page 376, Kansas City, Jackson, Missouri, United States
Census	1900	ED 45, Page 276, Kansas City, Jackson, Missouri, United States
Death	31 Jan 1901	Kansas City, Jackson, Missouri, United States
Misc		Funeral Notice, Kansas City (Mo.) Star, 1 Feb 1901, Page 2, Column 3
Burial	2 Feb 1901	
Occupation		Day Laborer (1900)
Marriage		

Father Jacob H. EARLY

Birth	25 Feb 1816	Washington, Tennessee, United States
Military		3rd Missouri Regiment Volunteer Cavalry, War with Mexico
Census	1850	Page 238, Kaw Township, Jackson, Missouri, United States
Census	1860	Page 122, Westport, Jackson, Missouri, United States
Tax Lists	Sep 1862	Retail Liquor Dealer License; "J. H. Early", Westport, Jackson, Missouri, United States
Misc		U. S. Internal Revenue Tax Lists for Jackson Co., MO--Sep 1862
Census	1870	Page 167, Atchison, Kansas, United States
Census	1875	Page 111, Atchison, Atchison, Kansas, United States
Census	1880	ED 1, Page 252, Atchison, Kansas, United States
Census	1885	Page 61, Rich Township, Anderson, Kansas, United States
Death	1885	Atchison, Atchison, Kansas, United States
Burial		Mount Vernon Cemetery, Atchison, Atchison, Kansas, United States
Occupation		Gunsmith (1850, 1860, 1870, 1875, 1880, 1885), Retail Liquor
Marriage	29 Jul 1849	(1849I0020209), Jackson, Missouri, United States
Father		
Mother		

Mother Elizabeth H. "Lizzie" ADKINS

Birth	26 Oct 1827	Harlan, Kentucky, United States
Census	1850	Page 238, Kaw Township, Jackson, Missouri, United States
Census	1860	Page 122, Westport, Jackson, Missouri, United States
Census	1870	Page 167, Atchison, Kansas, United States
Census	1875	Page 111, Atchison, Atchison, Kansas, United States
Census	1880	ED 1, Page 252, Atchison, Kansas, United States
Census	1885	Page 61, Rich Township, Anderson, Kansas, United States
Census	1895	Page 28, Atchison, Atchison, Kansas, United States
Census	1900	ED 1, Page 10, Atchison, Kansas, United States
Census	1910	ED 1, Page 10, Atchison, Kansas, United States
Death	28 Dec 1912	Atchison, Atchison, Kansas, United States
Burial	30 Dec 1912	Mount Vernon Cemetery, Atchison, Atchison, Kansas, United States
Occupation		Own Income (1910)
Father		
Mother		

Children

M Benjamin R. EARLY

Birth	Jun 1850	Missouri, United States
Census	1850	Page 238, Kaw Township, Jackson, Missouri, United States
Census	1860	Page 122, Westport, Jackson, Missouri, United States
Census	1870	Page 167, Atchison, Kansas, United States
Census	1880	ED 1, Page 252, Atchison, Kansas, United States
Census	1885	Page 61, Rich Township, Anderson, Kansas, United States
Census	1895	Page 27, Atchison, Atchison, Kansas, United States
Census	1900	ED 1, Page 10, Atchison, Kansas, United States
Census	1910	ED 1, Page 10, Atchison, Kansas, United States
Census	1920	ED 1, Page 8, Atchison, Kansas, United States
Death	16 Nov 1927	
Burial		Mount Vernon Cemetery, Atchison, Atchison, Kansas, United States
Occupation		Teamster (1880, 1895), Farmer (1885), Express Driver (1900, 1910), Express Man Baggage Wagon (1910)
Spouse	Kate RINGO (1862-1926)	
Marriage	11 Jul 1872	Atchison, Kansas, United States
Divorce		
Spouse	Laura B. [--?--] (1861-1901)	
Marriage	1883/4	
Spouse	Alice Jane CHESLEY (1857-1925)	
Marriage	1909/10	

Father Solomon Madison EBY

Birth	1810/1	Pennsylvania, United States
Residence	1844	Mansfield, Wright, Missouri, United States
Residence	bet 1844 and 1848	Brookfield, Linn, Missouri, United States
Census	1850	Page 34, Saline, Missouri, United States
Census	1860	Page 70, Kansas City, Jackson, Missouri, United States
Tax Lists	Sep 1862	Photographer License; "Sol M. Ebby", Kansas City, Jackson, Missouri, United States
Census	1870	Page 603, Kansas City, Jackson, Missouri, United States
Census	1880	ED 191, Page 293, Quindaro Township, Wyandotte, Kansas, United States
Census	1885	Page 56, Quindaro Township, Wyandotte, Kansas, United States
Death	22 Nov 1886	Suicide by Poisoning; Quindaro, Wyandotte, Kansas, United States
Burial	23 Nov 1886	Quindaro Cemetery, Quindaro, Wyandotte, Kansas, United States
Occupation		Miller (1850), Artist (1860), Portrait Painter (1870, 1880), Fruit Grower (1885), Photographer
Marriage		
Father		
Mother		

Mother Elizabeth J. [--?--]

Birth	abt 1819	Ohio, United States
Census	1850	Page 34, Saline, Missouri, United States
Census	1860	Page 70, Kansas City, Jackson, Missouri, United States
Census	1870	Page 603, Kansas City, Jackson, Missouri, United States
Census	1880	ED 191, Page 293, Quindaro Township, Wyandotte, Kansas, United States
Death	3 Jun 1884	Quindaro Township, Wyandotte, Kansas, United States
Burial	4 Jun 1884	
Misc		Funeral Notice, Kansas City (Mo.) Daily Journal, 04 Jun 1884, Page 3, Column 3
Father		
Mother		

Children

F Antonette EBY

Birth	1840/1	Missouri, United States
Census	1850	Page 34, Saline, Missouri, United States
Census	1860	
Census	1870	
Census	1880	
Death		
Burial		
Marrlage		

M Upton EBY

Birth	4 May 1844	Mansfield, Wright, Missouri, United States
Census	1850	Page 34, Saline, Missouri, United States
Census	1860	Page 70, Kansas City, Jackson, Missouri, United States
Military		Company C, Van Horn's Battallion Missouri Cavalry
Military		Company C, 13th Missouri Infantry
Military		Company B, 2nd Battallion Missouri State Militia Cavalry
Misc		U. S. Internal Revenue Tax Lists for Jackson Co., MO--May 1866
Census	1870	
Census	1880	ED 11, Page 333, Kansas City, Jackson, Missouri, United States
Death	4 Jun 1904	Stomach Trouble, Heart Disease; Kansas City, Jackson, Missouri, United States
Misc		Obituary, Kansas City (Mo.) Star, 05 Jun 1904, Page 4, Column 4
Burial	6 Jun 1904	Elmwood Cemetery, Kansas City, Jackson, Missouri, United States
Occupation		Wholesale Grocer (1880), Photographer
Spouse		Elizabeth A. WATSON (1844-1922)
Marriage	5 Apr 1865	(186510050146), Jackson, Missouri, United States

Father Christian August Frederick/Friedrich ECKERT

Birth	26 Jul 1833	Ronneburg, Sachsen-Altenburg, Germany
Immigration	1859	
Census	1860	Page 1, Kansas City, Jackson, Missouri, United States
Military		Private, Company A, 77th Regiment Enrolled Missouri Militia
Military		Private, Companies A and D, 50th Missouri Infantry
Military		Company A, 43rd Missouri Infantry
Tax Lists	Aug 1863	Cigars Manufactured; "Chas. B. Eckhart", Kansas City, Jackson, Missouri, United States
Tax Lists	bet Sep 1863 and Dec 1863	Cigars Manufactured; "F./Fr./Frederick Eckert", Kansas City, Jackson, Missouri, United States
Tax Lists	May 1865	Cigars Manufactured; "Fred. Eckert", Kansas City, Jackson, Missouri, United States
Census	1870	Page 454, Kansas City, Jackson, Missouri, United States
Census	1870	(Industrial Schedules), Page 26, Kansas City, Jackson, Missouri, United States
Census	1870	(Industrial Schedules), Ward 2, Page 27, Kansas City, Jackson, Missouri, United States
Census	1880	ED 19, Page 501, Kansas City, Jackson, Missouri, United States
Census	1890	ED 190, Page 5, Kansas City, Jackson, Missouri, United States
Census	1900	ED 124, Page 252, Kansas City, Jackson, Missouri, United States
Death	15 Jan 1910	
Burial		East Mount Pleasant Cemetery, Blaine, Oklahoma, United States
Occupation		Tobacconist (1850), Cigar Manufacturer (1870), Grocer (1880), Retired (1900)
Marriage		
Father	Frederick ECKERT (-)	
Mother	Augusta MENELE (-)	

Mother Emilie/Amalia Johanna SACHSE

Birth	18 Feb 1837	Ronneburg, Sachsen-Altenburg, Germany
Immigration	29 Jun 1857	From Bremen Aboard Bark "Edmund", Baltimore, Baltimore City, Maryland, United States
Census	1860	Page 1, Kansas City, Jackson, Missouri, United States
Census	1870	Page 454, Kansas City, Jackson, Missouri, United States
Census	1880	ED 19, Page 501, Kansas City, Jackson, Missouri, United States
Census	1900	ED 14, Page 149, Lincoln Township, Blaine, Oklahoma Territory, United States
Census	1910	ED 41, Page 83, Lincoln Township, Blaine, Oklahoma, United States
Census	1920	ED 18, Page 103, Lincoln Township, Blaine, Oklahoma, United States
Census	1930	ED 27, Page 274, Watonga, Blaine, Oklahoma, United States
Death	28 Oct 1932	Watonga, Blaine, Oklahoma, United States
Burial		
Father		
Mother		

Children

F Mary/Maria ECKERT

Birth	4 Jul 1859	Pennsylvania, United States
Census	1860	Page 1, Kansas City, Jackson, Missouri, United States
Baptism	8 Feb 1870	St. Peter's Ger. Evang. Church, Volume 1, Page 7
Census	1870	Page 454, Kansas City, Jackson, Missouri, United States
Confirmation	1873	St. Peter's German Evangelical Church, Kansas City, Jackson Co., MO
Census	1880	
Census	1900	
Census	1910	ED 41, Page 81, Lincoln Township, Blaine, Oklahoma, United States
Census	1920	ED 18, Page 103, Lincoln Township, Blaine, Oklahoma, United States
Death	1926	Watonga, Blaine, Oklahoma, United States
Burial		East Mount Pleasant Cemetery, Blaine, Oklahoma, United States
Spouse	Oliver MERRILL (-)	
Marriage	19 Sep 1877	(1877I0070386), Jackson, Missouri, United States
Spouse	Bernard KRELL (1849-1896)	
Marriage	23 Oct 1884	(1884K0040502), Kansas City, Jackson, Missouri, United States
Spouse	Albert UHRIG (1855-)	
Marriage	17 Nov 1897	Westport, Jackson, Missouri, United States

Father	Christian August Frederick/Friedrich ECKERT	
Mother	Emilie/Amalia Johanna SACHSE	
Children		

F   Lena/Lina Emilie ECKERT

Birth	21 Dec 1866	Fort Scott, Bourbon, Kansas, United States
Baptism	8 Feb 1870	St. Peter's Ger. Evang. Church, Volume 1, Page 7
Census	1870	Page 454, Kansas City, Jackson, Missouri, United States
Census	1880	ED 19, Page 501, Kansas City, Jackson, Missouri, United States
Census	1900	ED 124, Page 252, Kansas City, Jackson, Missouri, United States
Census	1910	ED 191, Page 222, Kansas City, Jackson, Missouri, United States
Census	1920	ED 266, Page 197, Kansas City, Jackson, Missouri, United States
Census	1930	ED 150, Page 60, Kansas City, Jackson, Missouri, United States
Death	4 Oct 1940	Bronchial Pneumonia, Chronic Bronchitis; Kansas City, Jackson, Missouri, United States
Burial	7 Oct 1940	Forest Hill Cemetery, Kansas City, Jackson, Missouri, United States
Spouse	Charles Edward SMALLFIELD (1858-1928)	
Marriage	1891/2	

M   Lidia ECKERT

Birth	6 Nov 1869	
Baptism	8 Feb 1870	St. Peter's Ger. Evang. Church, Volume 1, Page 7
Census	1870	
Census	1880	
Census	1900	
Census	1910	
Census	1920	
Census	1930	
Death		
Burial		
Marriage		

M   Louis Frederick/Friedrich Karl ECKERT

Census	1870	Page 454, Kansas City, Jackson, Missouri, United States
Birth	18 May 1871	Missouri, United States
Baptism	25 Oct 1871	St. Peter's Ger. Evang. Church, Volume 1, Page 10
Census	1880	
Census	1900	
Census	1910	
Census	1920	
Census	1930	
Death		
Burial		
Marriage		

F   Emma ECKERT

Birth	18 Dec 1874	
Baptism	5 Jul 1875	St. Peter's Ger. Evang. Church, Volume 1, Page 23
Death	5 Jul 1875	"Gehirnentzuendung"; St. Peter's Ger. Evang. Church, Volume 1, Page 369
Burial	6 Jul 1875	St. Peter's Ger. Evang. Church, Volume 1, Page 369
Marriage		

M   Johann Philipp William/Wilhelm ECKERT

Birth	25 May 1876	Missouri, United States
Baptism	19 Aug 1877	St. Peter's Ger. Evang. Church, Volume 1, Page 40
Census	1880	ED 19, Page 501, Kansas City, Jackson, Missouri, United States
Census	1900	ED 14, Page 149, Lincoln Township, Blaine, Oklahoma Territory, United States
Census	1910	ED 41, Page 83, Lincoln Township, Blaine, Oklahoma, United States
Census	1920	ED 18, Page 103, Lincoln Township, Blaine, Oklahoma, United States
Census	1930	
Occupation		Farmer (1900), Farmer General Farm (1910, 1920)
Death		
Burial		
Spouse	Dora [--?--] (1899-)	

Father	Christian August Frederick/Friedrich ECKERT	
Mother	**Emilie/Amalia Johanna SACHSE**	
Children		
	Johann Philipp William/Wilhelm ECKERT (continued)	
	Marriage	
F	**Amelia ECKERT**	
	Birth	May 1880	Missouri, United States
	Census	1880	ED 19, Page 501, Kansas City, Jackson, Missouri, United States
	Census	1900	ED 14, Page 150, Lincoln Township, Blaine, Oklahoma Territory, United States
	Census	1910	ED 69, Page 264, Mound Valley Township, Caddo, Oklahoma, United States
	Census	1920	ED 26, Page 166, Watonga, Blaine, Oklahoma, United States
	Census	1930	ED 27, Page 274, Watonga, Blaine, Oklahoma, United States
	Death	1967	
	Burial		Watonga IOOF Cemetery, Watonga, Blaine, Oklahoma, United States
	Spouse	Frederick Ross ARNOLD (1874-1953)	
	Marriage	13 Aug 1898	

Father Daniel ENSIGN

Birth	1826/7	New York, United States
Census	1850	
Census	1860	Page 82, Kansas City, Jackson, Missouri, United States
Misc	1 Aug 1862	Union Provost Marshals' File of Papers Relating to Individual Civilians, M345, Roll 85
Tax Lists	Apr 1863	Retail Dealer License; Kansas City, Jackson, Missouri, United States
Military	Oct 1863	Civil War Draft Registration; Kaw Township, Jackson, Missouri, United States
Tax Lists	May 1866	Income and Gold Watch; Kansas City, Jackson, Missouri, United States
Census	1870	Page 437, Kansas City, Jackson, Missouri, United States
Census	1880	Page 129, Oxford Township, Johnson, Kansas, United States
Will	9 Aug 1897	(Will Written), Volume 5, Page 172, Kansas City, Jackson, Missouri, United States
Death	3 Feb 1898	Old Age; Johnson, Kansas, United States
Burial	5 Feb 1898	Forest Hill Cemetery, Kansas City, Jackson, Missouri, United States
Misc		Obituary, Kansas City (Mo.) Daily Journal, 05 Feb 1898, Page 7, Column 4
Probate	12 Feb 1898	(Will Proved), Volume 5, Page 172, Kansas City, Jackson, Missouri, United States
Occupation		Merchant (1860), Retail Grocer (1870), Farmer (1880), Retail Dealer, Retail Liquor Dealer
Marriage	26 Jul 1873	(1873I0070111), Westport, Jackson, Missouri, United States
Father		
Mother		

Mother Caroline "Carrie" THARP`

Birth	1 Mar 1845	(or Mar 1844 or 03 Sep 1839), Illinois, United States
Census	1850	
Census	1860	
Census	1870	Page 437, Kansas City, Jackson, Missouri, United States
Census	1880	Page 129, Oxford Township, Johnson, Kansas, United States
Census	1900	ED 84, Page 285, Seattle, King, Washington, United States
Census	1910	
Census	1920	
Occupation		Dressmaker (1900)
Death		
Burial		
Father	John C. THARP` (1792-1871)	
Mother	Mariah MOZURE (1815-1856)	

Children

M   Dewey ENSIGN

Birth	25 Jan 1871	Kansas, United States
Census	1880	Page 129, Oxford Township, Johnson, Kansas, United States
Census	1900	ED 134, Page 115, Kansas City, Jackson, Missouri, United States
Census	1910	ED 169, Page 184, Seattle, King, Washington, United States
Death	26 Aug 1945	San Diego, California, United States
Burial		Greenwood Memorial Park, San Diego, San Diego, California, United States
Occupation		Carpenter (1900), Carpenter House (1910)
Spouse	Della WILLIAMS (1875-)	
Marriage	16 Nov 1899	(Recorded in Clay, Missouri, United States), Kansas City, Jackson, Missouri, United States
Spouse	Lizzie BENTLEY (1865-1950)	
Marriage	1904/5	

Father Jacob Robert ERKEL

Birth	1830/1	Germany
Immigration	3 Jul 1849	New York, from Ghent, Belgium, aboard "Mary T. Rundlett"
Census	1850	Page 234, Saint Louis, Saint Louis, Missouri, United States
Census	1860	Page 100, Kansas City, Jackson, Missouri, United States
Tax Lists	Sep 1862	Manufacturer License; Kansas City, Jackson, Missouri, United States
Tax Lists	SepDec 1862	Tin Ware Manufactured; Kansas City, Jackson, Missouri, United States
Military		Private, Company C, Van Horn's Battalion Missouri Cavalry Volunteers
Military		13th Missouri Volunteers
Military	Oct 1863	Civil War Draft Registration; Kaw Township, Jackson, Missouri, United States
Misc		"A Frame Dwelling Destroyed," Kansas City (Mo.) Daily Journal . . . , 05 Jan 1870, Page 4, Col. 2
Misc		"Correction," Kansas City (Mo.) Daily Journal of Commerce, 07 Jan 1870, Page 4, Column 1
Census	1870	
Misc		A Sad Affair," Kansas City (Mo.) Daily Journal of Commerce, 23 Aug 1870, Page 4, Column 2
Misc		"Localizings," Kansas City (Mo.) Daily Journal of Commerce, 26 Aug 1870, Page 4, Column 1
Misc		"John Glasheen," Kansas City (Mo.) Daily Journal of Commerce, 1 Sep 1870, Page 4, Column 1
Death	1870/1	
Occupation		Ropemaker (1850), Tinner (1860)
Burial		
Marriage	24 Nov 1854	Boyle, Kentucky, United States
Father		
Mother	Barbara [--?--] (1802-)	

Mother Susan CUADLISS

Birth	1831/2	England
Census	1850	
Census	1860	Page 100, Kansas City, Jackson, Missouri, United States
Census	1870	
Census	1880	ED 188, Page 237, Edwardsville, Wyandotte, Kansas, United States
Death	2 Oct 1895	Kansas City, Jackson, Missouri, United States
Occupation		Milliner (1880)
Burial		
Father		
Mother		

Children

F Mary ERKEL

Birth	Sep 1858	Kentucky, United States
Census	1860	Page 100, Kansas City, Jackson, Missouri, United States
Census	1870	
Census	1880	ED 188, Page 237, Edwardsville, Wyandotte, Kansas, United States
Census	1900	ED 143, Page 70, Delaware Township, Wyandotte, Kansas, United States
Census	1910	ED 174, Page 83, Kansas City, Wyandotte, Kansas, United States
Census	1920	
Census	1930	
Death		
Burial		
Spouse	Herman B. HUNT (1847-)	
Marriage	18 Dec 1878	(1878I0080090), Jackson, Missouri, United States

M Francis ERKEL

Birth	1863/4	Missouri, United States
Census	1870	
Census	1880	ED 188, Page 237, Edwardsville, Wyandotte, Kansas, United States
Census	1900	
Census	1910	
Census	1920	

Father Jacob Robert ERKEL		
Mother Susan CUADLISS		
Children		
Francis ERKEL (continued)		
Census	1930	
Occupation		Help in Store (1880)
Death		
Burial		
Marriage		

Father Frederick William ESSLINGER

Birth	13 Apr 1818	Sutz (Black Forest), Wuerttemberg, Germany
Immigration	1849	St. Louis via New York City
Residence	bet 1849 and 1851	Saint Louis, Saint Louis, Missouri, United States
Census	1850	
Residence	1850/1	Saint Louis, Saint Louis, Missouri, United States
Residence	bet 1851 and 1861	Westport, Jackson, Missouri, United States
Property	10 Jan 1855	First Known Purchase, Lot 22, Westport; Volume W, Page 416, Independence, Jackson, Missouri, United States
Census	1860	Page 110, Westport, Jackson, Missouri, United States
Residence	bet 1861 and 1865	Kansas City, Jackson, Missouri, United States
Tax Lists	Sep 1862	Retail Dealer License; "Fred Eslinger", Kansas City, Jackson, Missouri, United States
Military		Missouri Home Guards, Civil War
Tax Lists	Dec 1863	Retail Dealer License; Kansas City, Jackson, Missouri, United States
Residence	bet 1865 and 1898	Westport, Jackson, Missouri, United States
Tax Lists	May 1866	Retail Dealer License and Income; Kansas City, Jackson, Missouri, United States
Census	1870	Page 62, Westport, Jackson, Missouri, United States
Census	1880	ED 40, Page 262, Westport, Jackson, Missouri, United States
Misc	1881	Biography, History of Jackson Co., Mo. (1881), Page 996
Census	1890	
Misc	1896	Biography & Photo, Memorial & Biographical Record of Kansas City . . . (1896), Pages 866-868
Will	11 Dec 1897	(Will Written) (Kansas City) Volume 3, Page 183, Jackson, Missouri, United States
Death	13 Dec 1898	Pneumonia; Kansas City, Jackson, Missouri, United States
Misc		Obituary, Kansas City (Mo.) Star, 14 Dec 1898, Page 1, Column 2
Misc		Obituary, Kansas City (Mo.) Times, 14 Dec 1898, Page 6, Column 5
Burial	16 Dec 1898	Forest Hill Cemetery, Kansas City, Jackson, Missouri, United States
Misc		Obituary, Westport (Mo.) Sentinel-Examiner, 17 Dec 1898, Page 4, Column 3
Probate	19 Dec 1898	(Will Proved) (Kansas City) Volume 3, Page 183, Jackson, Missouri, United States
Occupation		Jeweler (1860), Laborer (1870), Wine Grower (1880), Organ Builder
Religion		Lutheran
Occupation		Proprietor of Esslinger Wine Garden; Westport, Jackson Co., MO
Occupation		Pipe Organ Builder; Sutz (Black Forest), Wuerttemberg, Germany
Marriage	16 Feb 1853	(1853I0030110), Jackson, Missouri, United States
Father		
Mother		
Other spouse	Anna Louise/Louisa HAUK (1827-1872)	
Marriage	Aug 1856	Cincinnati, Hamilton, Ohio, United States
Other spouse	Marie/Maria Theresa ANDRE (1838-1925)	
Marriage	31 Oct 1871	(1871I0060301), Westport, Jackson, Missouri, United States

Mother Christina/Christiana S. MATNEY

Birth	2 Dec 1831	Missouri, United States
Census	1850	Page 250, Kaw Township, Jackson, Missouri, United States
Death	May 1855	Cholera; Jackson, Missouri, United States
Burial		
Father	William MATNEY (1782-1854)	
Mother	Sarah [--?--] (1782-1858)	

Children

F Amelia/Amalia Wilhelmina Mary "Mollie" ESSLINGER

Birth	Nov 1853	Missouri, United States
Census	1860	Westport, Jackson Co., MO, Page 110
Census	1870	Westport, Jackson Co., MO, Page 62
Census	1880	ED 40, Page 261, Westport, Jackson, Missouri, United States
Census	1900	ED 123, Page 238, Kansas City, Jackson, Missouri, United States
Will	25 Sep 1909	(Will Executed, Kansas City Courthouse, Volume 15, Page 329), Jackson, Missouri, United States
Death	1909	
Burial		Forest Hill Cemetery, Kansas City, Jackson, Missouri, United States

Father Frederick William ESSLINGER

Mother Christina/Christiana S. MATNEY

Children

Amelia/Amalia Wilhelmina Mary "Mollie" ESSLINGER (continued)

Probate	22 Dec 1909	(Will Proved, Kansas City Courthouse, Volume 15, Page 329), Jackson, Missouri, United States
Spouse	Christian Boly VOGEL (1849-1917)	
Marriage	29 Oct 1872	(1872I0070066), Jackson, Missouri, United States

Father William Brassfield "Cash" EVANS

Birth	abt 31 Dec 1806	
Residence	bet 1818 and 1829	Howard, Missouri Territory, United States
Residence	bet 1829 and 1830	Clinton, Missouri, United States
Residence	bet 1830 and 1855	Jackson, Missouri, United States
Misc	1846	Stockholder, Reorganized Town Company; Kansas City, Jackson, Missouri, United States
Census	1850	Page 247, Kaw Township, Jackson, Missouri, United States
Death	27 Jan 1855	
Burial		McGee Cemetery, Kaw Township, Jackson, Missouri, United States
Burial	1881	Elmwood Cemetery, Kansas City, Jackson, Missouri, United States
Misc		Builder & Owner of First Missouri River Ferry at Kansas City (1830)
Occupation		Farmer (1850)
Marriage	26 Aug 1830	(1830I0010020), Jackson, Missouri, United States
Father		
Mother		

Mother Amelia L. MCGEE

Birth	17 Jun 1813	Nelson, Kentucky, United States
Census	1850	Page 247, Kaw Township, Jackson, Missouri, United States
Census	1860	Page 142, Jackson, Missouri, United States
Census		Slave Schedules, Page 370, Jackson, Missouri, United States
Census	1870	
Census	1880	
Will	21 Nov 1883	(Will Written), Volume 4, Page 405, Kansas City, Jackson, Missouri, United States
Burial		McGee Cemetery, Kaw Township, Jackson, Missouri, United States
Will	7 Jul 1888	(Last Codicil Added), Volume 4, Page 405, Kansas City, Jackson, Missouri, United States
Death	28 Jul 1895	Kansas City, Jackson, Missouri, United States
Burial	29 Jul 1895	Elmwood Cemetery, Kansas City, Jackson, Missouri, United States
Probate	16 Sep 1895	(Will Proved), Volume 4, Page 405, Kansas City, Jackson, Missouri, United States
Misc		Genealogy, The Johnsons and McGees: Pioneer Settlers of Kansas City (Tompkins, 2004), Part 2, Pages 22-23
Father		Col. James H. MCGEE (1786-1840)
Mother		Eleanor A. FRYE (1798-1880)
Other spouse		Enoch STEEN (-)
Marriage	30 Sep 1890	Jackson, Missouri, United States

Children

F Amanda EVANS

Birth	28 Jan 1832	Missouri, United States
Census	1840	
Census	1850	Page 247, Kaw Township, Jackson, Missouri, United States
Census	1860	
Census	1870	
Census	1880	
Census	1900	
Death	1 Mar 1906	
Burial	3 Mar 1906	Elmwood Cemetery, Kansas City, Jackson, Missouri, United States
Spouse		William C. CAMPBELL (1820-1897)
Marriage		

M James Calvin EVANS

Birth	25 Apr 1833	Missouri, United States
Census	1840	
Census	1850	Page 247, Kaw Township, Jackson, Missouri, United States
Census	1860	
Census	1870	
Census	1880	
Census	1900	
Census	1910	
Death		
Burial		

Father	William Brassfield "Cash" EVANS	
Mother	Amelia L. MCGEE	
Children		

James Calvin EVANS (continued)

Spouse		Elizabeth CAMPBELL (-1882)
Marriage	15 Nov 1860	Clay, Missouri, United States

F   Ellen E. EVANS

Birth	18 Jan 1835	
Death	8 Aug 1847	
Burial		McGee Cemetery, Kaw Township, Jackson, Missouri, United States
Burial	1881	Elmwood Cemetery, Kansas City, Jackson, Missouri, United States
Marriage		

F   Elizabeth E. EVANS

Birth	5 Jul 1836	Missouri, United States
Census	1840	
Census	1850	Page 247, Kaw Township, Jackson, Missouri, United States
Death	19 May 1851	
Burial		McGee Cemetery, Kaw Township, Jackson, Missouri, United States
Burial	1881	Elmwood Cemetery, Kansas City, Jackson, Missouri, United States
Marriage		

F   Emily "Emma" EVANS

Birth	1838	Missouri, United States
Census	1840	
Census	1850	Page 247, Kaw Township, Jackson, Missouri, United States
Census	1860	
Census	1870	
Census	1880	
Census	1900	
Census	1910	
Death	1920	
Census	1920	
Burial	10 May 1920	Elmwood Cemetery, Kansas City, Jackson, Missouri, United States
Spouse		William VINEYARD (1835-1914)
Marriage		

M   John W. EVANS

Birth	abt 1842	Missouri, United States
Census	1850	Page 247, Kaw Township, Jackson, Missouri, United States
Census	1860	Page 143, Jackson, Missouri, United States
Census		Slave Schedules, Page 370, Jackson, Missouri, United States
Tax Lists	Sep 1862	Dentist License; Kansas City, Jackson, Missouri, United States
Misc	1863	Deputy Sheriff of Jackson County
Military	Oct 1863	Civil War Draft Registration; Kaw Township, Jackson, Missouri, United States
Death	25 Dec 1863	Gunshot Wound; Jackson, Missouri, United States
Burial	30 Dec 1863	McGee Cemetery, Kaw Township, Jackson, Missouri, United States
Misc		Obituary, Kansas City (Mo.) Daily Journal of Commerce, 30 Dec 1863, Page 3, Column 1
Probate	13 Jan 1864	(Administrator's Bond), Volume L, Page 268, Independence, Jackson, Missouri, United States
Burial	1881	Elmwood Cemetery, Kansas City, Jackson, Missouri, United States
Occupation		Dentist
Marriage		

F   Harriet "Hattie" EVANS

Birth	19 Feb 1843	Missouri, United States
Census	1850	
Census	1860	Page 143, Jackson, Missouri, United States
Census	1870	
Census	1880	
Death	4 Jul 1887	
Burial	8 Jul 1887	Elmwood Cemetery, Kansas City, Jackson, Missouri, United States

Father William Brassfield "Cash" EVANS			
Mother Amelia L. MCGEE			
Children			
	Harriet "Hattie" EVANS (continued)		
	Spouse	William BALES (-)	
	Marriage	4 Nov 1861	Jackson, Missouri, United States
M	**Menard EVANS**		
	Birth	1844/5	Missouri, United States
	Census	1850	
	Census	1860	Page 143, Jackson, Missouri, United States
	Census	1870	
	Census	1880	
	Census	1900	
	Census	1910	
	Census	1920	
	Death		
	Burial		
	Spouse	Ola [--?--] (-)	
	Marriage		
M	**Benjamin K. EVANS**		
	Birth	1846/7	Missouri, United States
	Census	1850	
	Census	1860	Page 143, Jackson, Missouri, United States
	Census	1870	
	Census	1880	
	Census	1900	
	Census	1910	
	Census	1920	
	Death		
	Burial		
	Marriage		
F	**Anna EVANS**		
	Birth	10 Nov 1852	
	Death	27 May 1857	
	Burial		
	Marriage		

Father Chauncey Wilmont FAIRMAN

Birth	11 May 1832	Hastings, Ontario/Nova Scotia, Canada
Immigration	abt 1849	United States
Census	1850	Page 216, Quincy, Adams, Illinois, United States
Residence	bet 1854 and 1856	Quincy, Adams, Illinois, United States
Residence	bet 1856 and 1858	Independence, Jackson, Missouri, United States
Residence	bet 1858 and 1892	Kansas City, Jackson, Missouri, United States
Census	1860	Page 50, Kansas City, Jackson, Missouri, United States
Census		Industrial Schedules, Page 1, Kansas City, Jackson, Missouri, United States
Tax Lists	Sep 1862	Retail Dealer and Manufacturer Licenses; "Pollard & Farmer", Kansas City, Jackson, Missouri, United States
Tax Lists	bet SepDec 1862 and Dec 1863	Tin Ware Manufactured; "Pollard & Farman/Farmer/Fairman", Kansas City, Jackson, Missouri, United States
Military		Private & Sergeant, Company A, 77th Regiment Enrolled Missouri Militia
Military	Oct 1863	Civil War Draft Registration; Kaw Township, Jackson, Missouri, United States
Occupation	1863/4	City Councilman; Kansas City, Jackson, Missouri, United States
Tax Lists	bet May 1865 and Dec 1866	Tin Ware Manufactured; "Pollard & Fairman", Kansas City, Jackson, Missouri, United States
Tax Lists	May 1866	Retail Dealer and Manufacturer Licenses; "Pollard & Fairman", Kansas City, Jackson, Missouri, United States
Tax Lists	May 1866	Income; "C. W. Fairman", Kansas City, Jackson, Missouri, United States
Census	1870	Page 442, Kansas City, Jackson, Missouri, United States
Census		Industrial Schedules, Ward 1, Page 14, Kansas City, Jackson, Missouri, United States
Misc		Biography, US Biographical Dictionary and Portrait Gallery . . . Missouri Volume (1878), Pages 485-486
Census	1880	ED 2, Page 50, Kansas City, Jackson, Missouri, United States
Death	21 Mar 1892	Heart Failure; Kansas City, Jackson, Missouri, United States
Misc		Death Notice, Kansas City (Mo.) Star, 22 Mar 1892, Page 1, Column 1
Burial	23 Mar 1892	Union Cemetery, Kansas City, Jackson, Missouri, United States
Occupation		Tinner (1850, 1860, 1870), Stoves & Tinware (1880)
Business		Pollard & Fairman (Retail Dealer, Tinware)
Marriage	12 Aug 1858	Quincy, Adams, Illinois, United States
Father		Hugh FAIRMAN (1780-)
Mother		

Mother Jane Ann "Jennie" PARMALEY

Birth	abt 1835	Ohio, United States
Census	1850	
Census	1860	Page 50, Kansas City, Jackson, Missouri, United States
Census	1870	Page 442, Kansas City, Jackson, Missouri, United States
Death	24 Apr 1875	Kansas City, Jackson, Missouri, United States
Misc		Funeral Notice, Kansas City (Mo.) Times, 25 Apr 1875, Page 4, Column 6
Burial	26 Apr 1875	Union Cemetery, Kansas City, Jackson, Missouri, United States
Father		
Mother		

Children

M James W. FAIRMAN

Birth	1859	Missouri, United States
Census	1860	Page 51, Kansas City, Jackson, Missouri, United States
Census	1870	Page 442, Kansas City, Jackson, Missouri, United States
Census	1880	ED 2, Page 50, Kansas City, Jackson, Missouri, United States
Residence	23 Mar 1892	Quincy, Adams, Illinois, United States
Death	13 Jun 1906	Kansas City, Jackson, Missouri, United States
Misc		Funeral Notice, Kansas City (Mo.) Star, 14 Jun 1906, Page 1, Column 6
Burial	15 Jun 1906	Forest Hill Cemetery, Kansas City, Jackson, Missouri, United States
Occupation		Clerk (1880)
Marriage		

Father Chauncey Wilmont FAIRMAN			
Mother Jane Ann "Jennie" PARMALEY			
Children			
F	**Susie FAIRMAN**		
	Birth	28 Dec 1862	
	Burial		Union Cemetery, Kansas City, Jackson, Missouri, United States
	Death		
	Marriage		
M	**Chauncey Parmaley FAIRMAN**		
	Birth	25 Jun 1865	Kansas City, Jackson, Missouri, United States
	Census	1870	Page 442, Kansas City, Jackson, Missouri, United States
	Census	1880	ED 2, Page 50, Kansas City, Jackson, Missouri, United States
	Census	1900	ED 77, Page 161, Kansas City, Jackson, Missouri, United States
	Misc		Biography, The Book of Missourians (1906), Page 228
	Misc	14 May 1923	Passport Issued; Colón, Panama
	Death	10 May 1951	Gorgas Hospital, Cristobal, Canal Zone, Panama
	Cremation	14 May 1951	Cristobal, Canal Zone, Panama
	Occupation		Lawyer (1900, 1951)
	Burial		
	Spouse	Eleanor Josephine HARBAUGH (1871-1952)	
	Marriage	8 Jan 1890	(1890K0003153), Kansas City, Jackson, Missouri, United States

Father Dr. Asa FARRAR

Birth	1809/10	Kentucky, United States
Census	1840	(Asa Farer Family), Page 207, Fulton, Callaway, Missouri, United States
Census	1840	Owned 3 Slaves
Census	1844	(Asa Farar Family), Page 126, Fulton, Callaway, Missouri, United States
Census	1850	Page 271, Blue Township, Jackson, Missouri, United States
Census		Slave Schedules, Frame 109, Blue Township, Jackson, Missouri, United States
Property	15 Sep 1852	First Known Purchase, Lot 42, Annexed Part, Indep.; Volume U, Page 52, Independence, Jackson, Missouri, United States
Census	1860	Page 247, Independence, Jackson, Missouri, United States
Census		Slave Schedules, Page 363, Independence, Jackson, Missouri, United States
Misc	19 Apr 1862	Union Provost Marshals' File of Papers Relating to Two or More Civilians, M416, Roll 5, No. 1075
Tax Lists	Sep 1862	Physician License; "Assa Farrer", Independence, Jackson, Missouri, United States
Military		Sergeant, Civil War
Tax Lists	May 1866	Physician License, Carriage, Gold Watch, and Pianoforte; Independence, Jackson, Missouri, United States
Census	1870	Page 266, Independence, Jackson, Missouri, United States
Census	1880	ED 24, Page 27, Independence, Jackson, Missouri, United States
Will	11 Jul 1888	(Will Written), Volume O, Page 361, Independence, Jackson, Missouri, United States
Will	28 Jan 1890	(Last Addendum Added), Volume O, Page 361, Independence, Jackson, Missouri, United States
Census	1890	ED 82, Page 2, Independence, Jackson, Missouri, United States
Death	1890	
Probate	23 Aug 1890	(Will Proved), Volume O, Page 361, Independence, Jackson, Missouri, United States
Occupation		Physician (1850, 1860, 1870), Doctor (1880)
Burial		
Marriage		
Father		
Mother		

Mother Amanda PARKER

Birth	3 Jul 1817	Kentucky, United States
Census	1840	(Asa Farer Family), Page 207, Fulton, Callaway, Missouri, United States
Census	1844	(Asa Farar Family), Page 126, Fulton, Callaway, Missouri, United States
Census	1850	Page 271, Blue Township, Jackson, Missouri, United States
Census	1860	Page 247, Independence, Jackson, Missouri, United States
Census	1870	Page 266, Independence, Jackson, Missouri, United States
Census	1880	ED 24, Page 27, Independence, Jackson, Missouri, United States
Death	13 Sep 1886	
Burial		Woodlawn Cemetery, Independence, Jackson, Missouri, United States
Father		
Mother		

Children

M Edwin H. "Ed" FARRAR

Birth	Apr 1837	Kentucky, United States
Census	1840	(Asa Farer Family), Page 207, Fulton, Callaway, Missouri, United States
Census	1844	(Asa Farar Family), Page 126, Fulton, Callaway, Missouri, United States
Census	1850	Page 271, Blue Township, Jackson, Missouri, United States
Census	1860	
Census	1870	
Census	1880	ED 17, Page 170, Centralia, Boone, Missouri, United States
Census	1900	ED 19, Page 113, Centralia, Boone, Missouri, United States
Death	1913	
Burial		Columbia Cemetery, Columbia, Boone, Missouri, United States
Occupation		Druggist (1880, 1900)
Spouse		Sarah KENNAN/KENNON (1846-1928)
Marriage	30 Mar 1876	Boone, Missouri, United States

Father Dr. Asa FARRAR		
Mother Amanda PARKER		
Children		
M	**William Hugh FARRAR**	
	Birth	1843/4	Missouri, United States
	Census	1844	(Asa Farar Family), Page 126, Fulton, Callaway, Missouri, United States
	Census	1850	Page 271, Blue Township, Jackson, Missouri, United States
	Census	1860	Page 247, Independence, Jackson, Missouri, United States
	Census	1870	
	Census	1880	ED 60, Page 315, Salt Lake. Utah, United States
	Census	1900	
	Census	1910	
	Census	1920	ED 114, Page 145, Cornwall, Latah, Idaho, United States
	Occupation		Assayer (1880), None (1920)
	Death		
	Burial		
	Spouse		Martha [--?--] (1850-)
	Marriage		
F	**Mary Ella FARRAR**	
	Birth	10 Oct 1844	Fulton, Callaway, Missouri, United States
	Census	1850	Page 271, Blue Township, Jackson, Missouri, United States
	Census	1860	Page 247, Independence, Jackson, Missouri, United States
	Census	1870	Page 266, Independence, Jackson, Missouri, United States
	Census	1880	ED 24, Page 27, Independence, Jackson, Missouri, United States
	Death	21 Jan 1921	Intestinal Stasis with Auto-Infection, Hypostatic Pneumonia; Independence, Jackson, Missouri, United States
	Misc		Obituary, Independence (Mo.) Examiner, 22 Jan 1921, Page 1, Column 6
	Burial	23 Jan 1921	Woodlawn Cemetery, Independence, Jackson, Missouri, United States
	Marriage		
F	**Jessica A. "Jessie" FARRAR**	
	Birth	1850	Missouri, United States
	Census	1850	Page 271, Blue Township, Jackson, Missouri, United States
	Census	1860	Page 247, Independence, Jackson, Missouri, United States
	Census	1870	Page 266, Independence, Jackson, Missouri, United States
	Census	1880	ED 24, Page 27, Independence, Jackson, Missouri, United States
	Residence	1921	Independence, Jackson, Missouri, United States
	Death	27 Dec 1930	Pedestrian Struck by Automobile; Saint Paul, Ramsey, Minnesota, United States
	Burial		Roselawn Cemetery, Roseville, Ramsey, Minnesota, United States
	Misc		Obituary, Independence (Mo.) Examiner, 09 Jan 1931, Page 1, Column 5
	Occupation		Elementary Teacher
	Religion		First Presbyterian Church; Independence, Jackson, Missouri, United States
	Marriage		
F	**Emilia "Emma" FARRAR**	
	Birth	Nov 1853	Missouri, United States
	Census	1860	Page 247, Independence, Jackson, Missouri, United States
	Census	1870	Page 266, Independence, Jackson, Missouri, United States
	Census	1880	ED 24, Page 27, Independence, Jackson, Missouri, United States
	Census	1900	ED 117, Page 188, Saint Paul, Ramsey, Minnesota, United States
	Residence	1921	Saint Paul, Ramsey, Minnesota, United States
	Residence	1931	Saint Paul, Ramsey, Minnesota, United States
	Death	14 Aug 1939	Ramsey, Minnesota, United States
	Burial		Roselawn Cemetery, Roseville, Ramsey, Minnesota, United States
	Spouse		Howard L. PARSONS (1844-1906)
	Marriage	30 Nov 1876	(1876I0070329), Jackson, Missouri, United States
F	**Idalette Preston "Ida" FARRAR**	
	Birth	1856/7	Missouri, United States
	Census	1860	Page 247, Independence, Jackson, Missouri, United States
	Census	1870	Page 266, Independence, Jackson, Missouri, United States

Father Dr. Asa FARRAR

Mother Amanda PARKER

Children

Idalette Preston "Ida" FARRAR (continued)

Census	1880	ED 24, Page 27, Independence, Jackson, Missouri, United States
Census	1900	ED 1019, Page 151, Brookline, Suffolk, Massachusetts, United States
Census	1910	
Census	1920	ED 583, Page 14, Boston, Suffolk, Massachusetts, United States
Residence	1921	Boston, Suffolk, Massachusetts, United States
Death	4 May 1928	Injuries from a Fall Downstairs; Boston, Suffolk, Massachusetts, United States
Burial		Boston, Suffolk, Massachusetts, United States
Misc		Obituary, Independence (Mo.) Examiner, 16 May 1928, Page 1, Column 2
Occupation		Public School Teacher
Spouse		George KENDALL (1861-)
Marriage		

M David Coulter FARRAR

Birth	12 Jul 1859	Missouri, United States
Census	1860	Page 247, Independence, Jackson, Missouri, United States
Death	1 Dec 1861	
Burial		Woodlawn Cemetery, Independence, Jackson, Missouri, United States
Marriage		

Father John W. FARROW

Birth	1825/6	(or Kentucky, United States), Virginia, United States
Census	1850	Page 306, Newtown, Yuba, California, United States
Census	1860	Page 279, Independence, Jackson, Missouri, United States
Census		Slave Schedules, Page 364, Independence, Jackson, Missouri, United States
Tax Lists	Apr 1863	Cattle Broker License; Jackson, Missouri, United States
Census	1870	Page 292, Independence, Jackson, Missouri, United States
Census	1880	ED 8, Page 236, Kansas City, Jackson, Missouri, United States
Census	1900	
Occupation		Miner (1850), None (1870), Retired (1880), Cattle Broker
Death		
Burial		
Marriage		
Father		
Mother		

Mother Elizabeth [--?--]

Birth	1829/30	Missouri, United States
Census	1850	
Census	1860	Page 279, Independence, Jackson, Missouri, United States
Census	1870	Page 292, Independence, Jackson, Missouri, United States
Census	1880	ED 8, Page 236, Kansas City, Jackson, Missouri, United States
Census	1900	
Census	1910	
Census	1920	
Death		
Burial		
Father		
Mother		

Children

M William Frank FARROW

Birth	20 Jan 1854	(or 1852/53), Missouri, United States
Census	1860	Page 279, Independence, Jackson, Missouri, United States
Census	1870	Page 292, Independence, Jackson, Missouri, United States
Census	1880	
Death	1 Mar 1885	Raton, Colfax, New Mexico Territory, United States
Misc		Death Notice, Kansas City (Mo.) Times, 04 Mar 1885, Page 8, Columns 3-4
Burial	4 Mar 1885	Union Cemetery, Kansas City, Jackson, Missouri, United States
Misc		"Deceased leaves a wife and several children."
Misc		Funeral Notice, Kansas City (Mo.) Times, 05 Mar 1885, Page 8, Column 3
Marriage		

F Madora "Dora" FARROW

Birth	1854/5	Missouri, United States
Census	1860	Page 279, Independence, Jackson, Missouri, United States
Census	1870	Page 292, Independence, Jackson, Missouri, United States
Census	1880	ED 8, Page 236, Kansas City, Jackson, Missouri, United States
Death		
Burial		
Marriage		

Father John FISCHELL

Birth	1824/5	Prussia, Germany
Census	1850	
Census	1860	Page 261, Independence, Jackson, Missouri, United States
Tax Lists	Sep 1862	Retail Dealer License; Independence, Jackson, Missouri, United States
Military	Sep 1863	Civil War Draft Registration; Blue Township, Jackson, Missouri, United States
Death	Dec 1865	Independence, Jackson, Missouri, United States
Probate	21 Dec 1865	(Administrators' Bond), Volume M, Page 398, Independence, Jackson, Missouri, United States
Occupation		Jeweler (1860)
Religion		Roman Catholic
Burial		
Marriage		
Father		
Mother		

Mother Caroline [--?--]

Birth	1829/30	Prussia, Germany
Census	1850	
Census	1860	Page 261, Independence, Jackson, Missouri, United States
Tax Lists	May 1866	Retail Dealer License; "Caroline Fishell", Independence, Jackson, Missouri, United States
Census	1870	Page 284, Independence, Jackson, Missouri, United States
Death	1872	
Probate	Nov 1872	(Order of Publication), Independence Courthouse, Volume OP, Page 95, Jackson, Missouri, United States
Burial		
Father		
Mother		
Other spouse		Frederick GLASER (-)
Marriage	15 Dec 1867	(1867I0060068), Jackson, Missouri, United States

Children

F Hortense FISCHELL

Birth	Nov 1865	Missouri, United States
Census	1870	Page 284, Independence, Jackson, Missouri, United States
Census	1880	ED 24, Page 53, Independence, Jackson, Missouri, United States
Occupation	Apr 1883	Teacher; Reed School (west of Independence), Blue Township, Jackson, Missouri, United States
Misc		"Independence," Kansas City (Mo.) Daily Journal, 10 Apr 1883, Page 5, Column 2
Misc		"Independence," Kansas City (Mo.) Daily Journal, 03 Jul 1883, Page 5, Column 3
Census	1900	ED 5, Page 68, Independence, Jackson, Missouri, United States
Census	1910	ED 81, Page 53, Kansas City, Jackson, Missouri, United States
Census	1920	ED 29, Page 174, Dallas, Dallas, Texas, United States
Census	1930	
Occupation		Boarder in Boarding School (1880), Teacher (1883)
Death		
Burial		
Spouse		William F. SWALWELL (1859-)
Marriage	12 Jan 1887	(Date of Unused License), Jackson, Missouri, United States

Father Frederick Peet FLAGLER

Birth	24 Jan 1832	Brooklyn, Kings, New York, United States
Census	1840	(Phillip Flagler Family), Page 160, Cortlandt, Westchester, New York, United States
Census	1850	Page 178, Cortlandt, Westchester, New York, United States
Census	1860	Page 227, Cortlandt, Westchester, New York, United States
Misc		Advertisement, Western Journal of Commerce, 03 Jan 1861, Page 3, Column 4
Tax Lists	Sep 1862	Retail Liquor Dealer License; "F. P. Flaler & Company", Kansas City, Jackson, Missouri, United States
Military		Private, Company A, 77th Regiment Enrolled Missouri Militia
Military	Oct 1863	Civil War Draft Registration; Kaw Township, Jackson, Missouri, United States
Occupation	1863/4	City Councilman; Kansas City, Jackson, Missouri, United States
Tax Lists	May 1866	Retail Dealer License; "F. P. & E. Flagler", Kansas City, Jackson, Missouri, United States
Tax Lists	May 1866	Income; "F. P. Flagler", Kansas City, Jackson, Missouri, United States
Tax Lists	Oct 1866	Wholesale Dealer License; "E. P. & F. Flagler", Kansas City, Jackson, Missouri, United States
Census	1870	Page 312, Kansas City, Jackson, Missouri, United States
Census	1880	ED 6, Page 179, Kansas City, Jackson, Missouri, United States
Census	1900	ED 63, Page 268, Kansas City, Jackson, Missouri, United States
Death	25 Oct 1906	Kansas City, Jackson, Missouri, United States
Burial	27 Oct 1906	Union Cemetery, Kansas City, Jackson, Missouri, United States
Misc		Funeral Notice, Kansas City (Mo.) Times, 27 Oct 1906, Page 11, Column 7
Occupation		Clerk (1850), Hardware Merchant (1860), No Business (1870), Bookkeeper (1880), Hardware (1900)
Marriage	29 Apr 1866	(1866I0050192), Kansas City, Jackson, Missouri, United States
Father		Philip FLAGLER (1802-1874)
Mother		Frances Harriet HAMLIN (1805-1867)

Mother Lucy Ann WAKEFIELD

Birth	30 Jun 1842	Summerfield, Saint Clair, Illinois, United States
Census	1850	Page 290, Saint Clair, Illinois, United States
Census	1860	(Township 2N, Range 6W), Page 874, Saint Clair, Illinois, United States
Census	1870	Page 312, Kansas City, Jackson, Missouri, United States
Census	1880	ED 6, Page 179, Kansas City, Jackson, Missouri, United States
Census	1900	ED 63, Page 268, Kansas City, Jackson, Missouri, United States
Census	1910	ED 145, Page 59, Kansas City, Jackson, Missouri, United States
Census	1920	ED 163, Page 257, Kansas City, Jackson, Missouri, United States
Death	25 Feb 1922	Epilepsy, Arterioslcerosis; Kansas City, Jackson, Missouri, United States
Misc		Obituary, Kansas City (Mo.) Star, 26 Feb 1922, Page 9A, Column 2
Burial	27 Feb 1922	Union Cemetery, Kansas City, Jackson, Missouri, United States
Father		John WAKEFIELD (1796-1871)
Mother		Harriet STILSTON (1812-1904)

Children

M George Hamlin FLAGLER

Birth	26 Oct 1867	
Death	12 Aug 1869	
Burial		Union Cemetery, Kansas City, Jackson, Missouri, United States
Marriage		

F Harriet J. "Hattie" FLAGLER

Birth	18 Apr 1870	Kansas City, Jackson, Missouri, United States
Census	1870	Page 312, Kansas City, Jackson, Missouri, United States
Census	1880	ED 6, Page 179, Kansas City, Jackson, Missouri, United States
Census	1900	ED 63, Page 268, Kansas City, Jackson, Missouri, United States
Census	1910	ED 145, Page 59, Kansas City, Jackson, Missouri, United States
Census	1920	ED 163, Page 257, Kansas City, Jackson, Missouri, United States
Residence	1922	Kansas City, Jackson, Missouri, United States
Death	1 Oct 1959	Hypostatic Pneumonia, Myocardial Degeneration, Chronic Bronchitis; Kansas City, Jackson, Missouri, United States
Burial	5 Oct 1959	Union Cemetery, Kansas City, Jackson, Missouri, United States
Spouse		George Cory FULTZ (1878-1962)

Father Frederick Peet FLAGLER		
Mother Lucy Ann WAKEFIELD		
Children		
Harriet J. "Hattie" FLAGLER (continued)		
Marriage	14 Sep 1899	(18899K0018616), Jackson, Missouri, United States
M	**Edward Albert "Eddie" FLAGLER**	
Birth	10 Nov 1872	Kansas City, Jackson, Missouri, United States
Census	1880	ED 6, Page 179, Kansas City, Jackson, Missouri, United States
Census	1895	Page 6, Spring Hill Township, Johnson, Kansas, United States
Census	1910	ED 202, Page 110, Kansas City, Jackson, Missouri, United States
Residence	1922	Kansas City, Jackson, Missouri, United States
Death	3 Sep 1926	Intestinal Obstruction, General Peritonitis, Chronic Appendicitis; Kansas City, Jackson, Missouri, United States
Burial	6 Sep 1926	Mount Moriah Cemetery, Kansas City, Jackson, Missouri, United States
Occupation		Farmer (1895), Carpenter House (1910)
Spouse	Alma Eliza ENSLOW (1872-1926)	
Marriage	17 Feb 1895	Edna, Labette, Kansas, United States

Father George Davis FOGLESONG Sr.

Birth	abt 24 Jul 1823	(now Lewisburg, Greenbrier, West Virginia, United States), Lewisburg, Greenbrier, Virginia, United States
Property	5 Oct 1841	First Known Purchase, Part Lot 12, Old Town, Indep.; Volume R, Page 588, Independence, Jackson, Missouri, United States
Census	1850	Page 268, Greenbrier, Virginia, United States
Census	1860	Page 109, Westport, Jackson, Missouri, United States
Census		Slave Schedules, Page 368, Westport, Jackson, Missouri, United States
Misc	10 Aug 1862	Union Provost Marshals' File of Papers Relating to Two or More Civilians, M416, Roll 8, No. 2129
Tax Lists	Sep 1862	Retail Dealer License; "George B. Foglesong", Westport, Jackson, Missouri, United States
Census	1870	Page 418, Cheyenne, Laramie, Wyoming Territory, United States
Residence	bet 1880 and 1891	Lawrence, Dakota Territory, United States
Census	1880	ED 126, Page 333, False Bottom, Lawrence, Dakota Territory, United States
Death	13 Dec 1891	Heart Failure, Pneumonia; Terraville, Lawrence, South Dakota, United States
Burial	15 Dec 1891	South Lead Cemetery, Lead, Lawrence, South Dakota, United States
Misc		Obituary, Black Hills Daily Times, 15 Dec 1891
Misc		Biography of Son (George D. Foglesong), History of South Dakota (D. Robinson, 1904)
Occupation		Tailor (1850), Merchant (1860), Dry Goods Merchant Retail (1870), Farmer (1880)
Occupation		Retail Liquor Dealer
Marriage	25 Nov 1842	Greenbrier, Virginia, United States
Father	Christopher FOGLESONG (1777-1846)	
Mother	Julia WHITMAN (1781-1845)	

Mother Martha "Mattie" WETZEL

Birth	abt 11 Jul 1824	(now Lewisburg, Greenbrier, West Virginia, United States), Lewisburg, Greenbrier, Virginia, United States
Census	1850	Page 268, Greenbrier, Virginia, United States
Census	1860	Page 109, Westport, Jackson, Missouri, United States
Census	1870	Page 418, Cheyenne, Laramie, Wyoming Territory, United States
Census	1880	ED 25, Page 165, Cheyenne, Laramie, Wyoming Territory, United States
Death	19 Mar 1898	Bronchitis; Lead, Lawrence, South Dakota, United States
Misc		Obituary, Evening Call, 20 Mar 1898
Burial	21 Mar 1898	South Lead Cemetery, Lead, Lawrence, South Dakota, United States
Father	George WETZEL (1776-)	
Mother	Elizabeth [--?--] (1786-)	

Children

M Henry Woodson FOGLESONG

Birth	22 Apr 1846	Lewisburg, Greenbrier, Virginia, United States
Census	1850	Page 268, Greenbrier, Virginia, United States
Census	1860	Page 109, Westport, Jackson, Missouri, United States
Census	1870	Page 418, Cheyenne, Laramie, Wyoming Territory, United States
Census	1880	ED 126, Page 333, False Bottom, Lawrence, Dakota Territory, United States
Death	29 Sep 1896	
Burial		South Lead Cemetery, Lead, Lawrence, South Dakota, United States
Occupation		Clerk in Store (1870), Farmer (1880)
Spouse	Kate [--?--] (1848-1920)	
Marriage		

M Wilburn L. FOGLESONG

Birth	25 May 1854	Westport, Jackson, Missouri, United States
Census	1860	Page 109, Westport, Jackson, Missouri, United States
Census	1870	Page 418, Cheyenne, Laramie, Wyoming Territory, United States
Census	1880	ED 126, Page 333, False Bottom, Lawrence, Dakota Territory, United States
Residence	1898	Lead, Lawrence, South Dakota, United States
Death	17 Dec 1905	Pneumonia; Lead, Lawrence, South Dakota, United States
Misc		Obituary, Lead Daily Call, 18 Dec 1905
Burial	19 Dec 1905	South Lead Cemetery, Lead, Lawrence, South Dakota, United States
Occupation		Clerk in Store (1870), Laborer (1880)
Occupation		Manager Bobtail Store; Terraville, Lawrence, South Dakota, United States

Father	George Davis FOGLESONG Sr.	
Mother	Martha "Mattie" WETZEL	
Children		

	Wilburn L. FOGLESONG (continued)	
	Residence	Chadron, Dawes, Nebraska, United States
	Marriage	

F	**Etta Belle "Ettie" FOGLESONG**	
	Birth	7 Aug 1860	Westport, Jackson, Missouri, United States
	Census	1870	Page 418, Cheyenne, Laramie, Wyoming Territory, United States
	Census	1880	ED 25, Page 165, Cheyenne, Laramie, Wyoming Territory, United States
	Residence	1898	Lead, Lawrence, South Dakota, United States
	Death	5 Jan 1953	Pneumonia; Lawrence, South Dakota, United States
	Burial	8 Jan 1953	South Lead Cemetery, Lead, Lawrence, South Dakota, United States
	Spouse	Homer P. MULLEN (1855-1923)	
	Marriage	1885	

M	**George Davis FOGLESONG**	
	Birth	5 Dec 1862	Westport, Jackson, Missouri, United States
	Census	1870	Page 418, Cheyenne, Laramie, Wyoming Territory, United States
	Census	1880	ED 25, Page 165, Cheyenne, Laramie, Wyoming Territory, United States
	Residence	1898	Lead, Lawrence, South Dakota, United States
	Census	1900	ED 27, Page 220, Lead, Lawrence, South Dakota, United States
	Misc		Biography, History of South Dakota (D. Robinson, 1904)
	Death	21 Oct 1945	Congestive Heart Failure, Arteriosclerosis; Lead, Lawrence, South Dakota, United States
	Burial	23 Oct 1945	South Lead Cemetery, Lead, Lawrence, South Dakota, United States
	Occupation		Telegraph Operator (1880), Bookkeeper Gold Mine (1900), Secretary of Homestake Mining Company; Lead, Lawrence, South Dakota, United States
	Religion		Protestant Episcopal
	Spouse	Olivia Amey HOKINS (1866-1921)	
	Marriage	30 Jun 1892	

M	**Walter Stonewall Jackson "Wallie" FOGLESONG**	
	Birth	29 Apr 1865	(or 29 Apr 1866), Nebraska, United States
	Census	1870	Page 418, Cheyenne, Laramie, Wyoming Territory, United States
	Census	1880	ED 25, Page 165, Cheyenne, Laramie, Wyoming Territory, United States
	Residence	1898	Lead, Lawrence, South Dakota, United States
	Census	1900	ED 27, Page 220, Lead, Lawrence, South Dakota, United States
	Residence	1905	Saint Onge, Lawrence, South Dakota, United States
	Census	1910	ED 36, Page 15, Lawrence, South Dakota, United States
	Census	1920	ED 117, Page 221, Lead, Lawrence, South Dakota, United States
	Death	24 Feb 1934	Saint Onge, Lawrence, South Dakota, United States
	Burial		Gate of Heaven Cemetery, Saint Onge, Lawrence, South Dakota, United States
	Occupation		Messenger (1880), Amalgamator (1900), Farmer General Farm (1910), Coal Retailer Office (1920)
	Spouse	Olida E. SANFORD (1869-1950)	
	Marriage	12 Aug 1897	Lead, Lawrence, South Dakota, United States

Father Thomas FORBES

Birth	1822/3	Ireland
Census	1850	Page 332, Salisbury, LaSalle, Illinois, United States
Census	1860	Page 33, Kansas City, Jackson, Missouri, United States
Census		Industrial Schedules, Page 1, Kansas City, Jackson, Missouri, United States
Tax Lists	Apr 1863	Peddler License; "Thomas Forbs", Kansas City, Jackson, Missouri, United States
Tax Lists	Dec 1865	Manufacturer License and Lime Manufactured; Kansas City, Jackson, Missouri, United States
Tax Lists	May 1866	Manufacturer License; Kansas City, Jackson, Missouri, United States
Tax Lists	bet Jun 1866 and Jul 1866	Brick Manufactured; Kansas City, Jackson, Missouri, United States
Census	1870	Page 374, Kansas City, Jackson, Missouri, United States
Census		Industrial Schedules, Ward 1, Page 13, Kansas City, Jackson, Missouri, United States
Census	1880	
Census	1900	
Occupation		Brickmaker (1850, 1860), Brick Manufacturer (1870), Peddler
Death		
Burial		
Marriage	16 Mar 1848	Peoria, Illinois, United States
Father		
Mother		

Mother Sarah SHAY

Birth	1828/9	Ohio, United States
Census	1850	Page 332, Salisbury, LaSalle, Illinois, United States
Census	1860	Page 33, Kansas City, Jackson, Missouri, United States
Census	1870	
Census	1880	
Census	1900	
Census	1910	
Death		
Burial		
Father		
Mother		

Children

F Mary A. FORBES

Birth	1848/9	Illinois, United States
Census	1850	Page 332, Salisbury, LaSalle, Illinois, United States
Census	1860	Page 33, Kansas City, Jackson, Missouri, United States
Census	1870	
Census	1880	
Death		
Burial		
Marriage		

M Isaac E. FORBES

Birth	1849/50	Illinois, United States
Census	1850	
Census	1860	Page 33, Kansas City, Jackson, Missouri, United States
Census	1870	Page 374, Kansas City, Jackson, Missouri, United States
Census	1880	ED 139, Page 115, Washington Township, Washington, Iowa, United States
Occupation		Laborer (1870), Laborer (1880)
Death		
Burial		
Marriage		

M John W. "Johnny" FORBES

Birth	1853/4	Illinois, United States
Census	1860	Page 33, Kansas City, Jackson, Missouri, United States
Census	1870	Page 374, Kansas City, Jackson, Missouri, United States
Census	1880	ED 139, Page 115, Washington Township, Washington, Iowa, United States

Father Thomas FORBES		
Mother Sarah SHAY		
Children		

John W. "Johnny" FORBES (continued)

Death	21 May 1889	Kansas City, Jackson, Missouri, United States
Misc		"Drowned in a Pond," Kansas City (Mo.) Star, 22 May 1889, Page 1, Column 4
Occupation		Laborer (1870, 1880)
Misc		
Burial		
Marriage		

M Thomas Longworth FORBES

Birth	1860	Missouri, United States
Census	1860	Page 33, Kansas City, Jackson, Missouri, United States
Census	1870	Page 374, Kansas City, Jackson, Missouri, United States
Census	1880	ED 140, Page 156, Washington, Washington, Iowa, United States
Census	1880	ED 139, Page 115, Washington Township, Washington, Iowa, United States
Census	1920	ED 22, Page 204, Kansas City, Jackson, Missouri, United States
Death	1926	
Burial		Forest Hill Cemetery, Kansas City, Jackson, Missouri, United States
Occupation		Laborer (1880), Brickmaking (1880), Brick Setter Building (1920)
Spouse	Rhoda Ann DAWSON (1860-1923)	
Marriage	20 Mar 1879	Washington, Iowa, United States
Divorce		

Father William Webber FORD

Birth	6 Apr 1824	Garrard, Kentucky, United States
Residence	bet 1824 and 1855	Garrard, Kentucky, United States
Census	1830	(Reuben Ford Family), Page 202, Garrard, Kentucky, United States
Census	1840	(Rheubin Ford Family), Page 54), Garrard, Kentucky, United States
Census	1850	District 2, Page 39, Jessamine, Kentucky, United States
Residence	bet 1856 and 1890	Kansas City, Jackson, Missouri, United States
Census	1860	Page 15, Kansas City, Jackson, Missouri, United States
Occupation	1860/1	City Councilman; Kansas City, Jackson, Missouri, United States
Tax Lists	Sep 1862	Apothecary License; Kansas City, Jackson, Missouri, United States
Military		Private, Company A, 77th Regiment Enrolled Missouri Militia
Military	Sep 1863	Civil War Draft Registration; Kaw Township, Jackson, Missouri, United States
Tax Lists	May 1866	Manufacturer and Builder Licenses, Sash and Blinds Manufactured; Kansas City, Jackson, Missouri, United States
Tax Lists	Jun 1866	Sash and Blinds Manufactured; Kansas City, Jackson, Missouri, United States
Census	1870	Page 49, Westport Township, Jackson, Missouri, United States
Census	1870	Agricultural Schedules, Page 1, Westport Township, Jackson, Missouri, United States
Census	1880	ED 6, Page 180, Kansas City, Jackson, Missouri, United States
Death	18 Feb 1890	Carbuncle, Pyaemia; Kansas City, Jackson, Missouri, United States
Burial	19 Feb 1890	Union Cemetery, Kansas City, Jackson, Missouri, United States
Misc		Obituary, Kansas City (Mo.) Star, 19 Feb 1890, Page 2, Column 1
Occupation		Apothecary, Manufacturer, Builder, Sash & Blinds; Kansas City, Jackson, Missouri, United States
Occupation		Carpenter (1850, 1870, 1880), Master Carpenter (1860), Building Contractor
Marriage	13 Feb 1845	Jessamine, Kentucky, United States
Father	Reuben FORD (1794-1859)	
Mother	Keturah ENGLAND (1797-1877)	

Mother Mary Ann QUEST

Birth	18 Oct 1825	Jessamine, Kentucky, United States
Census	1830	
Census	1840	(George Quest Family), Page 240, Jessamine, Kentucky, United States
Census	1850	District 2, Page 39, Jessamine, Kentucky, United States
Census	1860	Page 15, Kansas City, Jackson, Missouri, United States
Census	1870	Page 49, Westport Township, Jackson, Missouri, United States
Census	1880	ED 6, Page 180, Kansas City, Jackson, Missouri, United States
Census	1900	ED 94, Page 88, Kansas City, Jackson, Missouri, United States
Census	1910	ED 4, Page 44, Blue Township, Jackson, Missouri, United States
Death	6 Sep 1911	Endocarditis, Arteriosclerosis; Blue Township, Jackson, Missouri, United States
Misc		Obituary, Kansas City (Mo.) Star, 07 Sep 1911, Page 2, Column 2
Burial	8 Sep 1911	Union Cemetery, Kansas City, Jackson, Missouri, United States
Father	George QUEST (1786-1877)	
Mother	Malinda UTLEY (1804-1884)	

Children

F   Elizabeth Frances FORD

Birth	15 Feb 1846	Jessamine, Kentucky, United States
Death	18 Mar 1847	
Burial		
Marriage		

M   Winfield Scott FORD

Birth	14 May 1848	Jessamine, Kentucky, United States
Census	1850	District 2, Page 39, Jessamine, Kentucky, United States
Census	1860	Page 15, Kansas City, Jackson, Missouri, United States
Census	1870	Page 48, Westport Township, Jackson, Missouri, United States
Census	1880	ED 7, Page 206, Kansas City, Jackson, Missouri, United States
Census	1880	ED 6, Page 180, Kansas City, Jackson, Missouri, United States
Census	1900	ED 52, Page 51, Portland, Multnomah, Oregon, United States
Residence	1911	Portland, Multnomah, Oregon, United States
Occupation		Attorney at Law (1870), Painter (1880), Reporter (1880), Journalist Newspaper (1900)

Father William Webber FORD		
Mother Mary Ann QUEST		
Children		

Winfield Scott FORD (continued)		
Death		
Burial		
Spouse	Josephine H./M. BRAMLETTE (1849-)	
Marriage	21 Nov 1869	(1869I0060135), Jackson, Missouri, United States

M	**William Thomas FORD**	
Birth	26 May 1850	(or 26 May 1851), Jessamine, Kentucky, United States
Census	1860	Page 15, Kansas City, Jackson, Missouri, United States
Census	1870	Page 49, Westport Township, Jackson, Missouri, United States
Census	1880	ED 6, Page 180, Kansas City, Jackson, Missouri, United States
Census	1900	ED 94, Page 86, Kansas City, Jackson, Missouri, United States
Residence	1911	Kansas City, Jackson, Missouri, United States
Death	31 Jul 1921	General Paralysis of the Insane; Kansas City, Jackson, Missouri, United States
Burial	2 Aug 1921	Union Cemetery, Kansas City, Jackson, Missouri, United States
Occupation		Druggist (1880), Commercial Traveler (1900), Salesman
Spouse	Cornelia GREGG (1852-1942)	
Marriage	28 May 1873	(1873I0070105), Kansas City, Jackson, Missouri, United States

M	**Charles Clemmon FORD**	
Birth	25 Dec 1853	(or Jan 1853), Jessamine, Kentucky, United States
Census	1860	Page 15, Kansas City, Jackson, Missouri, United States
Census	1870	Page 49, Westport Township, Jackson, Missouri, United States
Census	1880	ED 5, Page 105, Denver, Arapahoe, Colorado, United States
Census	1900	ED 11, Page 93, Denver, Arapahoe, Colorado, United States
Census	1910	ED 204, Page 151, Kansas City, Jackson, Missouri, United States
Residence	1911	Fort Scott, Bourbon, Kansas, United States
Census	1920	ED 80, Page 274, Minneapolis, Hennepin, Minnesota, United States
Census	1930	ED 250, Page 211, San Francisco, San Francisco, California, United States
Death	1931	
Occupation		Book Binder (1880, 1900), Paper Cutter Printing Company (1920)
Burial		
Spouse	Eliza C. LINTON (1853-)	
Marriage	9 Feb 1879	Arapahoe, Colorado, United States

F	**Sarah Jessamine "Sallie" FORD**	
Birth	15 Apr 1856	(or Apr 1855), Jessamine, Kentucky, United States
Census	1860	Page 15, Kansas City, Jackson, Missouri, United States
Census	1870	
Census	1880	ED 98, Page 85, Olathe, Johnson, Kansas, United States
Census	1900	ED 105, Page 164, Shawnee Township, Johnson, Kansas, United States
Residence	1911	Lenexa, Johnson, Kansas, United States
Death	1 Jan 1932	Lenexa, Johnson, Kansas, United States
Burial		Lenexa Cemetery, Lenexa, Johnson, Kansas, United States
Spouse	Edgar Campbell WOOD (1855-1949)	
Marriage	1876/7	

M	**George Reuben FORD**	
Birth	28 Sep 1858	Kansas City, Jackson, Missouri, United States
Census	1860	Page 15, Kansas City, Jackson, Missouri, United States
Census	1870	Page 49, Westport Township, Jackson, Missouri, United States
Census	1880	ED 6, Page 182, Kansas City, Jackson, Missouri, United States
Census	1900	ED 98, Page 89, San Antonio, Bexar, Texas, United States
Residence	1911	Kansas City, Jackson, Missouri, United States
Occupation		Furniture (1880), Druggist (1900)
Death		
Burial		
Spouse	A. Mary KENDALL (1860-)	
Marriage	28 Sep 1881	(1881K0010434), Jackson, Missouri, United States

Father	**William Webber FORD**
Mother	**Mary Ann QUEST**
Children	

M	**Edmund Albert Dorrell "Ed" FORD**	
	Birth	11 Jan 1861	Kansas City, Jackson, Missouri, United States
	Census	1870	Page 49, Westport Township, Jackson, Missouri, United States
	Census	1880	ED 6, Page 182, Kansas City, Jackson, Missouri, United States
	Death	24 Mar 1909	Jackson, Missouri, United States
	Misc		Funeral Notice, Kansas City (Mo.) Times, 25 Mar 1909, Page 5, Column 3
	Burial	25 Mar 1909	(or 26 Mar 1909) Elmwood Cemetery, Kansas City, Jackson, Missouri, United States
	Occupation		Carpenter (1880)
	Spouse	Mayme Garth ROUNDS (1869-)
	Marriage	10 Jul 1907	(1907K0038231), Jackson, Missouri, United States

M	**James Walter FORD**	
	Birth	Apr 1863	Kansas City, Jackson, Missouri, United States
	Census	1870	Page 49, Westport Township, Jackson, Missouri, United States
	Census	1880	ED 6, Page 182, Kansas City, Jackson, Missouri, United States
	Death	30 Apr 1896	Chloral Hydrate Poisoning (Accidental); Saint Louis (city), Missouri, United States
	Burial		Bellefontaine Cemetery, Saint Louis (city), Missouri, United States
	Occupation		Clerk in Mer [illegible] (1880), Member Missouri Board fo Commissioners of Pharmacy (1896), Bookkeeper (1896)
	Spouse	Anna Mercy EVERLY (1864-)
	Marriage	14 May 1883	(1883K0030527), Kansas City, Jackson, Missouri, United States

F	**Lillie May FORD**	
	Birth	16 Jan 1866	Kansas City, Jackson, Missouri, United States
	Census	1870	Page 49, Westport Township, Jackson, Missouri, United States
	Census	1880	ED 6, Page 182, Kansas City, Jackson, Missouri, United States
	Census	1900	ED 94, Page 88, Kansas City, Jackson, Missouri, United States
	Census	1910	ED 4, Page 44, Blue Township, Jackson, Missouri, United States
	Residence	1911	Jackson, Missouri, United States
	Death	25 Oct 1952	Uremia-[illegible], Generalized Arteriosclerosis, Hypertensive Cardiovascular Disease; Kansas City, Jackson, Missouri, United States
	Burial	28 Oct 1952	Mount Washington Cemetery, Independence, Jackson, Missouri, United States
	Spouse	Nova DOUTHITT (1860-1930)
	Marriage	18 Oct 1887	(1887K0080498), Jackson, Missouri, United States

Father Matthew "Matt" FOSTER

Birth	28 May 1832	Tempo, Farmanagh, Ireland
Immigration	9 Oct 1850	(Aboard "Shannon" from Liverpool, England), New York, New York, New York, United States
Residence	bet 1854 and 1857	Lansing, Ingham, Michigan, United States
Residence	bet 1857 and 1893	Kansas City, Jackson, Missouri, United States
Census	1860	Page 86, Kansas City, Jackson, Missouri, United States
Naturalization	2 Jul 1860	Court of Common Pleas of Jackson County, Kansas City, Jackson, Missouri, United States
Tax Lists	Sep 1862	Retail Dealer License; "Mathew Foster", Kansas City, Jackson, Missouri, United States
Military		Private, Company A, 77th Regiment Enrolled Missouri Militia
Military	Sep 1863	Civil War Draft Registration; Kaw Township, Jackson, Missouri, United States
Tax Lists	Aug 1865	Retail Dealer License; "Matt Foster", Kansas City, Jackson, Missouri, United States
Tax Lists	May 1866	Retail Dealer License and Income; Kansas City, Jackson, Missouri, United States
Census	1870	Page 333, Kansas City, Jackson, Missouri, United States
Misc		Biography, US Biographical Dictionary and Portrait Gallery . . . Missouri Volume (1878), Pages 636-637
Census	1880	ED 18, Page 481, Kansas City, Jackson, Missouri, United States
Misc	14 Mar 1889	U. S. Passport Issued to Matt Foster and Wife Minnie W. Foster
Will	21 Aug 1890	(Will Written), Volume 4, Page 67, Kansas City, Jackson, Missouri, United States
Death	27 Mar 1893	Pneumonia with Sympathetic Heart Trouble; Kansas City, Jackson, Missouri, United States
Misc		Obituary, Kansas City (Mo.) Star, 27 Mar 1893, Page 1, Column 7
Burial	29 Mar 1893	Elmwood Cemetery, Kansas City, Jackson, Missouri, United States
Probate	3 Apr 1893	(Will Proved), Volume 4, Page 67, Kansas City, Jackson, Missouri, United States
Occupation		Clerk in Post Office (1860), Stationer (1870), Wholesale Stationer (1880), Retail Dealer
Religion		Methodist Episcopal Church
Marriage	24 Sep 1873	Seneca, Ohio, United States
Father	William FOSTER (1774-1852)	
Mother	Jane GRAHAM (1794-1870)	

Mother Minnie/Mina E. WEIRICK

Birth	19 May 1852	Tiffin, Seneca, Ohio, United States
Census	1860	Page 336, Tiffin, Seneca, Ohio, United States
Census	1870	Page 309, Tiffin, Seneca, Ohio, United States
Census	1880	ED 18, Page 481, Kansas City, Jackson, Missouri, United States
Census	1900	
Census	1910	
Census	1920	
Census	1930	
Death		
Burial		
Father	Jesse WEIRICH (1814-1871)	
Mother	Elizabeth FLENNER (1822-1896)	

Children

Father Charles/Karl Jacob FRANK

Birth	7 Jul 1835	Hessen-Darmstadt, Germany
Immigration	1854	
Census	1860	Page 92, Kansas City, Jackson, Missouri, United States
Misc	5 Aug 1862	Union Provost Marshals' File of Papers Relating to Individual Civilians, M345, Roll 96
Tax Lists	Sep 1862	Retail Dealer and Retail Liquor Dealer Licenses; "Chas. J. Frank", Kansas City, Jackson, Missouri, United States
Military		Private, Company B, 77th Regiment Enrolled Missouri Militia
Misc		Advertisement, Kansas City (Mo.) Daily Journal of Commerce, 04 Oct 1863, Page 1, Column 1
Military	Oct 1863	Civil War Draft Registration; Kaw Township, Jackson, Missouri, United States
Tax Lists	Dec 1863	Animals Slaughtered for Sale; "C. J. Frank", Kansas City, Jackson, Missouri, United States
Tax Lists	Mar 1866	Retail Liquor Dealer License; "Hollinghausen & Frank", Kansas City, Jackson, Missouri, United States
Tax Lists	May 1866	Wholesale Liquor Dealer License; "Chas. J. Frank", Kansas City, Jackson, Missouri, United States
Tax Lists	May 1866	Retail Liquor Dealer License; "Hollinghausen & Frank", Kansas City, Jackson, Missouri, United States
Misc	15 Mar 1869	U. S. Passport Application; Circuit Court, Jackson, Missouri, United States
Census	1870	Page 662, Kansas City, Jackson, Missouri, United States
Census	1880	Page 321, Shawnee Township, Wyandotte, Kansas, United States
Census	1900	ED 139, Page 11, Argentine, Wyandotte, Kansas, United States
Census	1910	ED 192, Page 173, Kansas City, Wyandotte, Kansas, United States
Occupation		Grocery Merchant (1860), Retired Merchant (1870), Farmer (1880)
Occupation		Dairy Man (1900), Own Income (1910)
Death		
Burial		
Marriage	1859/60	
Divorce	31 Jul 1874	San Francisco, San Francisco, California, United States
Father		
Mother		

Mother Emily/Emmaline "Emma" ECKERT

Birth	Jul 1842	New York, United States
Census	1850	
Census	1860	Page 92, Kansas City, Jackson, Missouri, United States
Census	1870	Page 662, Kansas City, Jackson, Missouri, United States
Census	1880	Page 321, Shawnee Township, Wyandotte, Kansas, United States
Census	1900	ED 139, Page 11, Argentine, Wyandotte, Kansas, United States
Census	1910	ED 192, Page 173, Kansas City, Wyandotte, Kansas, United States
Census	1920	ED 169, Page 211, Los Angeles, Los Angeles, California, United States
Death		
Burial		
Father		
Mother		

Children

M   Georg Johann FRANK

Birth	23 Jul 1875	
Baptism	27 Sep 1879	St. Peter's Ger. Evang. Church, Volume 1, Page 54
Census	1880	
Census	1900	
Census	1910	
Census	1920	
Census	1930	
Death		
Burial		
Marriage		

Father Charles/Karl Jacob FRANK

Mother Emily/Emmaline "Emma" ECKERT

Children

M	**Charles J. FRANK Jr.**		
	Birth	Aug 1876	California, United States
	Census	1880	Page 321, Shawnee Township, Wyandotte, Kansas, United States
	Census	1900	ED 139, Page 11, Argentine, Wyandotte, Kansas, United States
	Census	1910	ED 192, Page 173, Kansas City, Wyandotte, Kansas, United States
	Census	1920	ED 169, Page 211, Los Angeles, Los Angeles, California, United States
	Census	1930	
	Occupation		Day Laborer (1900), Driver Automobile (1920)
	Death		
	Burial		
	Marriage		

Father Henry FRANK

Birth	abt 1827	(or 1832/33), Hessen-Darmstadt, Germany
Census	1860	Page 18, Kansas City, Jackson, Missouri, United States
Tax Lists	Apr 1863	Retail Dealer License; "Bartlett & Frank", Independence, Jackson, Missouri, United States
Tax Lists	bet May 1863 and Jul 1863	Animals Slaughtered for Sale; "Bartlett & Frank", Kansas City, Jackson, Missouri, United States
Military		Private, Company A, Van Horn's Battalion Missouri Cavalry Volunteers
Military		Private, Company B, 77th Regiment Enrolled Missouri Militia
Military		Companies A and B, 25th Missouri Regiment
Tax Lists	Aug 1863	Animals Slaughtered for Sale; "Frank & Beddle", Kansas City, Jackson, Missouri, United States
Tax Lists	Sep 1863	Animals Slaughtered for Sale; "Henry Frank & Company", Kansas City, Jackson, Missouri, United States
Tax Lists	Oct 1863	Animals Slaughtered for Sale; "Frank & Dunbar", Kansas City, Jackson, Missouri, United States
Census	1870	Page 640, Kansas City, Jackson, Missouri, United States
Census	1870	(Industrial Schedules), Ward 4, Page 74, Kansas City, Jackson, Missouri, United States
Census	1880	ED 20, Page 533, Kansas City, Jackson, Missouri, United States
Census	1890	ED 127, Page 2, Kansas City, Jackson, Missouri, United States
Census	1900	
Census	1910	
Occupation		Butcher (1860, 1870, 1880)
Business		Bartlett & Frank, Frank & Beddle, Henry Frank & Company, Frank & Dunbar (Meat)
Death		
Burial		
Marriage		
Father		
Mother		

Mother Mary [--?--]

Birth	1827/8	Ireland
Census	1860	Page 18, Kansas City, Jackson, Missouri, United States
Census	1870	Page 640, Kansas City, Jackson, Missouri, United States
Census	1880	ED 20, Page 533, Kansas City, Jackson, Missouri, United States
Census	1900	
Census	1910	
Death	1 Nov 1910	Senility with Accompanying Heart Failure, Acute Indigestion; Kansas City, Jackson, Missouri, United States
Burial	3 Nov 1910	Mount Saint Mary's Cemetery, Kansas City, Jackson, Missouri, United States
Misc		Funeral Notice, Kansas City (Mo.) Times, 03 Nov 1910, Page 2, Column 2
Father		
Mother		

Children

M Henry F. FRANK

Birth	1859	Missouri, United States
Census	1860	Page 18, Kansas City, Jackson, Missouri, United States
Census	1870	
Census	1880	
Census	1900	
Census	1920	
Census	1930	
Death		
Burial		
Marriage		

M Edward FRANK

Birth	1861/2	Missouri, United States
Census	1870	Page 640, Kansas City, Jackson, Missouri, United States
Census	1880	ED 20, Page 533, Kansas City, Jackson, Missouri, United States
Census	1900	
Census	1910	

Father Henry FRANK			
Mother Mary [--?--]			
Children			

Edward FRANK (continued)

Census	1920	
Census	1930	
Occupation		Butcher (1880)
Death		
Burial		
Marriage		

M John FRANK

Birth	1863/4	Missouri, United States
Census	1870	Page 640, Kansas City, Jackson, Missouri, United States
Census	1880	ED 20, Page 533, Kansas City, Jackson, Missouri, United States
Census	1900	
Census	1910	
Census	1920	
Census	1930	
Death		
Burial		
Marriage		

M Frederick FRANK

Birth	1865/6	Missouri, United States
Census	1870	Page 640, Kansas City, Jackson, Missouri, United States
Census	1880	ED 20, Page 533, Kansas City, Jackson, Missouri, United States
Census	1900	
Census	1910	
Census	1920	
Census	1930	
Death		
Burial		
Marriage		

M Henry FRANK

Birth	1868/9	Missouri, United States
Census	1870	Page 640, Kansas City, Jackson, Missouri, United States
Census	1880	
Census	1900	
Census	1910	
Census	1920	
Census	1930	
Death		
Burial		
Marriage		

Father John Thornton FRAZIER

Birth	26 Jul 1819	Saint Charles, Saint Charles, Missouri, United States
Residence	bet 1848 and 1854	Independence, Jackson, Missouri, United States
Census	1850	Page 277, Blue Township, Jackson, Missouri, United States
Residence	bet 1854 and 1900	Westport, Jackson, Missouri, United States
Census	1860	Page 112, Westport, Jackson, Missouri, United States
Tax Lists	Sep 1862	Retail Liquor Dealer and Billiard Table Licenses; Westport, Jackson, Missouri, United States
Misc	3 Oct 1862	Union Provost Marshals' File of Papers Relating to Individual Civilians, M345, Roll 97
Military	bet Sep 1864 and Nov 1864	Sergeant, Company B, 34th Missouri Infantry
Tax Lists	May 1865	Auctioneer License; Westport, Jackson, Missouri, United States
Census	1870	Page 72, Westport, Jackson, Missouri, United States
Census	1880	ED 40, Page 256, Westport, Jackson, Missouri, United States
Census	1890	ED 190, Page 5, Kansas City, Jackson, Missouri, United States
Death	17 Apr 1900	Cavity in Lower Lobe of Left Lung; Kansas City, Jackson, Missouri, United States
Misc		Obituary, Kansas City (Mo.) Star, 18 Apr 1900, Page 1, Column 1
Burial	19 Apr 1900	Union Cemetery, Kansas City, Jackson, Missouri, United States
Occupation		Daguerian (1850), Artist (1860), Takes Pictures (1870), Painter (1880)
Occupation		Billiard Table, Retail Liquor Dealer, Auctioneer
Marriage	22 May 1850	Callaway, Missouri, United States
Father	Thomas FRAZIER (1780-)	
Mother		

Mother Elizabeth HARRISON

Birth	15 Jan 1830	Columbia, Boone, Missouri, United States
Census	1850	Page 277, Blue Township, Jackson, Missouri, United States
Census	1860	Page 112, Westport, Jackson, Missouri, United States
Census	1870	Page 72, Westport, Jackson, Missouri, United States
Death	7 Mar 1879	
Burial	8 Mar 1879	Union Cemetery, Kansas City, Jackson, Missouri, United States
Misc		Funeral Notice, Kansas City (Mo.) Daily Journal, 08 March 1879, Page 8, Column 5
Father	George Washington HARRISON (1800-1859)	
Mother	Malinda LYNES (1803-1892)	

Children

F   Mary Kezia FRAZIER

Birth	May 1848	Jefferson City, Cole, Missouri, United States
Census	1850	
Census	1860	Page 112, Westport, Jackson, Missouri, United States
Census	1870	
Census	1880	ED 389, Page 42, Saint Louis (city), Missouri, United States
Census	1880	ED 148, Page 331, Saint Louis (city), Missouri, United States
Census	1900	ED 419, Page 168, Saint Louis (city), Missouri, United States
Death		
Burial		
Spouse	Warren Abbott SOUTHER (1837-1887)	
Marriage		

F   Martha Luella "Ella" FRAZIER

Birth	4 Jun 1855	Westport, Jackson, Missouri, United States
Census	1860	Page 112, Westport, Jackson, Missouri, United States
Census	1870	Page 72, Westport, Jackson, Missouri, United States
Census	1880	ED 40, Page 256, Westport, Jackson, Missouri, United States
Residence	1900	Westport, Jackson, Missouri, United States
Death	9 Nov 1945	Evanston, Cook, Illinois, United States
Burial	12 Nov 1945	Rosehill Cemetery and Mausoleum, Chicago, Cook, Illinois, United States
Marriage		

F   Ida Julia FRAZIER

Birth	17 Jun 1857	Jackson, Missouri, United States
Census	1860	Page 112, Westport, Jackson, Missouri, United States

Father John Thornton FRAZIER		
Mother Elizabeth HARRISON		
Children		

Ida Julia FRAZIER (continued)

Census	1870	Page 72, Westport, Jackson, Missouri, United States
Census	1880	ED 40, Page 256, Westport, Jackson, Missouri, United States
Death	31 Jan 1945	Chicago, Cook, Illinois, United States
Burial	3 Feb 1945	Rosehill Cemetery and Mausoleum, Chicago, Cook, Illinois, United States
Spouse	Tasso Jay WRIGHT (1859-1945)	
Marriage	20 Feb 1884	Jackson, Missouri, United States

F Susan O. FRAZIER

Birth	1860	Missouri, United States
Census	1860	Page 112, Westport, Jackson, Missouri, United States
Census	1870	Page 72, Westport, Jackson, Missouri, United States
Census	1880	ED 40, Page 256, Westport, Jackson, Missouri, United States
Death		
Burial		
Marriage		

M John Thornton FRAZIER

Birth	3 Apr 1863	Westport, Jackson, Missouri, United States
Census	1870	Page 72, Westport, Jackson, Missouri, United States
Census	1880	ED 40, Page 257, Westport, Jackson, Missouri, United States
Residence	17 Apr 1900	Saint Louis (city), Missouri, United States
Residence	1900	Saint Louis (city), Missouri, United States
Death	2 Jan 1948	Cardiac Decompensation, Myocardial Infarction; Saint Louis (city), Missouri, United States
Burial	5 Jan 1948	Valhalla Cemetery, Saint Louis (city), Missouri, United States
Occupation		Carpenter Railroad Terminal
Spouse	Sarah Jane MUDGE (1869-1950)	
Marriage		

Father Reinhold FREY

Birth	Mar 1831	(or Bavaria), Hessen-Darmstadt, Germany
Census	1850	
Census	1860	
Tax Lists	Jul 1863	Barrels Manufactured; "Reynold Fry", Kansas City, Jackson, Missouri, United States
Military		Private, Company A, Van Horn's Battalion Missouri Cavalry Volunteers
Military		Sergeant & 2nd Sergeant, Company B, 77th Regiment Enrolled Missouri Militia
Tax Lists	Oct 1863	Barrels Manufactured; "Fry & Reynold", Kansas City, Jackson, Missouri, United States
Tax Lists	Dec 1863	Cooperage Manufactured; "Reynold Fry", Kansas City, Jackson, Missouri, United States
Tax Lists	Nov 1865	Manufacturer License; "Reynold Fry", Kansas City, Jackson, Missouri, United States
Tax Lists	bet Jan 1866 and Mar 1866	Cooperage Manufactured; "Reynold Fry", Kansas City, Jackson, Missouri, United States
Tax Lists	May 1866	Manufacturer License and Cooperage Manufactured; "Reynold Fry", Kansas City, Jackson, Missouri, United States
Tax Lists	Jun 1866	Cooperage Manufactured; Reinhold Fry, Kansas City, Jackson, Missouri, United States
Tax Lists	bet Nov 1866 and Dec 1866	Cooperage Manufactured; "Reinhold Frey, Kansas City, Jackson, Missouri, United States
Census	1870	Page 454, Kansas City, Jackson, Missouri, United States
Census	1870	(Industrial Schedules), Ward 2, Page 27, Kansas City, Jackson, Missouri, United States
Census	1880	ED 223, Page 387, San Francisco, San Francisco, California, United States
Census	1900	ED 95, Page 360, San Francisco, San Francisco, California, United States
Death	9 Dec 1904	
Occupation		Cooper (1870, 1880, 1900)
Burial		San Francisco National Cemetery, San Francisco, San Francisco, California, United States
Marriage	23 Aug 1863	(1863I0050096), Jackson, Missouri, United States
Father		
Mother		

Mother Caroline BRETTHAUER

Birth	1844/5	Braunschweig, Germany
Census	1860	
Census	1870	Page 454, Kansas City, Jackson, Missouri, United States
Census	1880	
Census	1900	
Census	1910	
Census	1920	
Death		
Burial		
Father		
Mother		

Children

F Caroline FREY

Birth	1863/4	(or Missouri, United States), Kansas, United States
Census	1870	Page 454, Kansas City, Jackson, Missouri, United States
Census	1880	ED 223, Page 387, San Francisco, San Francisco, California, United States
Census	1900	
Census	1910	
Census	1920	
Census	1930	
Death		
Burial		
Marriage		

F Julia FREY

Birth	1866/7	(or Nov 1869), Missouri, United States
Census	1870	Page 454, Kansas City, Jackson, Missouri, United States
Census	1880	ED 223, Page 387, San Francisco, San Francisco, California, United States
Census	1900	ED 95, Page 360, San Francisco, San Francisco, California, United States
Census	1910	
Census	1920	

Father	Reinhold FREY		
Mother	**Caroline BRETTHAUER**		
Children			

Julia FREY (continued)

Census	1930	
Death		
Burial		
Spouse	[--?--] HANLON (-)	
Marriage	1889/90	

M   Gustave/Gustavus FREY

Birth	1867/8	Missouri, United States
Census	1870	Page 454, Kansas City, Jackson, Missouri, United States
Census	1880	ED 223, Page 387, San Francisco, San Francisco, California, United States
Census	1900	
Census	1910	
Census	1920	
Census	1930	
Death		
Burial		
Marriage		

M   Herman FREY

Birth	1870/1	Missouri, United States
Census	1880	ED 223, Page 387, San Francisco, San Francisco, California, United States
Census	1900	
Census	1910	
Census	1920	
Census	1930	
Death		
Burial		
Marriage		

M   Henry FREY

Birth	Apr 1874	Missouri, United States
Census	1880	ED 223, Page 387, San Francisco, San Francisco, California, United States
Census	1900	
Census	1910	
Census	1920	
Census	1930	
Occupation		Cooper (1900)
Death		
Burial		
Marriage		

Father Morris J. FRIEDSAM

Birth	abt 1841	New York, United States
Census	1850	
Census	1860	
Tax Lists	Sep 1862	Retail Liquor Dealer License; Kansas City, Jackson, Missouri, United States
Military		Private, Company C, 77th Regiment Enrolled Missouri Militia
Military	Oct 1863	Civil War Draft Registration; Kaw Township, Jackson, Missouri, United States
Tax Lists	Jan 1866	Retail Dealer License; Kansas City, Jackson, Missouri, United States
Tax Lists	May 1866	Retail Dealer License; Kansas City, Jackson, Missouri, United States
Tax Lists	Dec 1866	Retail Dealer License; (Supplemental List), Kansas City, Jackson, Missouri, United States
Census	1870	Page 686, Kansas City, Jackson, Missouri, United States
Census	1880	ED 15, Page 420, Kansas City, Jackson, Missouri, United States
Census	1900	ED 47, Page 20, Canton, Lewis, Missouri, United States
Census	1910	ED 53, Page 158, Canton, Lewis, Missouri, United States
Misc		"Renewed a River Acquaintance," Kansas City (Mo.) Star, 24 Jun 1911, Page 9, Column 6
Census	1920	
Death	2 Nov 1923	Acute Bronchitis, Chronic Myocarditis; Kansas City, Jackson, Missouri, United States
Burial	5 Nov 1923	Mount Washington Cemetery, Independence, Jackson, Missouri, United States
Misc		Funeral Notice, Kansas City (Mo.) Times, 05 Nov 1923, Page 11, Column 3
Occupation		Assistant Cashier (1870), Merchant (1880), Button Manufacturer (1900), Own Income (1910)
Occupation		Retail Dealer, Retail Liquor Dealer
Marriage	28 Jan 1896	La Grange, Lewis, Missouri, United States
Father		
Mother		

Mother Margaret C./K. "Maggie" CASHMAN

Birth	7 Apr 1860	La Grange, Lewis, Missouri, United States
Census	1870	Page 683, LaGrange, Lewis, Missouri, United States
Census	1880	ED 25, Page 30, LaGrange, Lewis, Missouri, United States
Census	1900	ED 47, Page 20, Canton, Lewis, Missouri, United States
Census	1910	ED 53, Page 158, Canton, Lewis, Missouri, United States
Census	1920	
Death	16 May 1928	Chronic Myocarditis, Arteriosclerosis; Kansas City, Jackson, Missouri, United States
Burial	19 May 1928	Mount Washington Cemetery, Independence, Jackson, Missouri, United States
Misc		Funeral Notice, Kansas City (Mo.) Times, 19 May 1928, Page 21, Column 6
Occupation		Dressmaker (1880)
Father	John M. CASHMAN (1823-1871)	
Mother	Susan KARR (1833-1904)	

Children

Father Joseph Anton FRITZ

Birth	1828/9	Wuerttemberg, Germany
Census	1850	
Property	17 Apr 1854	First Known Purchase, Lot 13, Vogel's Add., Westport; Volume W, Page 95, Independence, Jackson, Missouri, United States
Census	1860	
Tax Lists	Sep 1862	Manufacturer License; Westport, Jackson, Missouri, United States
Tax Lists	bet SepDec 1862 and Apr 1863	Boots and Shoes Manufactured; Westport, Jackson, Missouri, United States
Tax Lists	May 1866	Retail Liquor Dealer License; "Enders & Fritz", Westport Landing, Jackson, Missouri, United States
Census	1870	Page 72, Westport, Jackson, Missouri, United States
Census	1880	ED 40, Page 255, Westport, Jackson, Missouri, United States
Death	13 Jun 1881	(or 13 Jun 1886)
Burial		Union Cemetery, Kansas City, Jackson, Missouri, United States
Occupation		Grocer (1870), Saloon Keeper (1880)
Marriage		
Father		
Mother		

Mother Catherine/Katharina [--?--]

Birth		Prussia, Germany
Census	1850	
Census	1860	
Census	1870	Page 72, Westport, Jackson, Missouri, United States
Census	1880	ED 40, Page 255, Westport, Jackson, Missouri, United States
Death		
Burial		
Father		
Mother		

Children

Father William G. GABEL

Birth	22 Jan 1835	Hessen-Darmstadt, Germany
Misc		U. S. Internal Revenue Tax Lists for Jackson Co., MO--Sep 1862 to Dec 1866
Death	13 Mar 1919	Kansas City, Jackson, Missouri, United States
Burial	15 Mar 1919	Kansas City, Jackson, Missouri, United States
Marriage	19 Feb 1866	(1866I00______) (Saint Peter's German Evangelical Church, Volume 1, Page [--?--]), Kansas City, Jackson, Missouri, United States
Father		
Mother		

Mother Josephine SCHMITZ

Birth	Jan 1843	Prussia, Germany
Death	12 Feb 1927	Kansas City, Jackson, Missouri, United States
Burial	14 Feb 1927	Kansas City, Jackson, Missouri, United States
Father		
Mother		

Children

M   Henry Joseph GABEL

Birth	28 Feb 1875	Kansas, United States
Census	1880	ED 4, Page 104, Kansas City, Jackson, Missouri, United States
Census	1900	ED 4, Page 104, Kansas City, Jackson, Missouri, United States
Census	1910	ED 122, Page 42, Kansas City, Jackson, Missouri, United States
Residence	1919	Kansas City, Jackson, Missouri, United States
Census	1920	ED 190, Page 159, Kansas City, Jackson, Missouri, United States
Residence	1927	Kansas City, Jackson, Missouri, United States
Census	1930	ED 98, Page 187, Kansas City, Jackson, Missouri, United States
Death	13 Jul 1957	Pneumonia Bronchial, Exposure & Hot Weather, Cerebral Hemorrhage; Kansas City, Jackson, Missouri, United States
Burial	15 Jul 1957	Elmwood Cemetery, Kansas City, Jackson, Missouri, United States
Occupation		Produce Com. (1900), Broker (1910), Broker Merchandise (1920, 1930)
Spouse	Helen Freeland TSCHUDI (1892-1950)	
Marriage	30 Oct 1915	(1915K0067840), Kansas City, Jackson, Missouri, United States

Father John Cutter GAGE

Birth	20 Apr 1835	Pelham, Hillsborough, New Hampshire, United States
Census	1840	(Frye Gage Family), Page 180, Pelham, Hillsborough, New Hampshire, United States
Census	1850	Page 99, Pelham, Hillsborough, New Hampshire, United States
Graduation	1856	Harvard University, Cambridge, Middlesex, Massachusetts, United States
Misc	1 Mar 1858	Admitted to the Bar, Court of Common Pleas of Jackson Co.; Jackson, Missouri, United States
Residence	bet 1859 and 1915	Kansas City, Jackson, Missouri, United States
Census	1860	Page 79, Kansas City, Jackson, Missouri, United States
Misc	10 Aug 1862	Union Provost Marshals' File of Papers Relating to Two or More Civilians, M416, Roll 8, No. 2129
Tax Lists	Sep 1862	Lawyer and Claim Agent Licenses; "John C. Gague", Kansas City, Jackson, Missouri, United States
Military		Private, Enrolled Missouri Militia
Military	Nov 1863	Civil War Draft Registration; Kaw Township, Jackson, Missouri, United States
Tax Lists	May 1866	Lawyer License and Income; Kansas City, Jackson, Missouri, United States
Occupation	1867/8	State Senator; Jackson, Missouri, United States
Census	1870	Page 671, Kansas City, Jackson, Missouri, United States
Occupation	1875/6	City Counselor; Kansas City, Jackson, Missouri, United States
Census	1880	
Occupation	1882/3	State Senator; Jackson, Missouri, United States
Misc		Biography, The History of Kansas City (1888), Pages 340
Misc		Biography, Kansas City, Its Resources and Their Development (1890), Page 106
Occupation	1894/5	City Board of Public Works; Kansas City, Jackson, Missouri, United States
Misc		Biography, Universities and Their Sons (1899-1900)
Census	1900	ED 66, Page 16, Kansas City, Jackson, Missouri, United States
Misc		Biography, Encyclopedia of the History of Missouri (1901)
Misc		Biography & Photo, Creel & Slavens, Men Who Are Making Kansas City, (1902) Page 46
Misc		Biography, The Book of Missourians (1906), Pages 368-369
Misc		Biography, Whitney, Kansas City, Missouri, Volume 2 (1908), Pages 197-198
Misc		"Fifty Years at the Bar," Kansas City (Mo.) Star, 07 Mar 1909, Page 12A, Column 4
Census	1910	ED 88, Page 152, Kansas City, Jackson, Missouri, United States
Will	13 Jun 1914	(Will Written), Volume 20, Page 26, Kansas City, Jackson, Missouri, United States
Death	27 Feb 1915	Pneumonia Lobar; Kansas City, Jackson, Missouri, United States
Misc		Obituary, Kansas City (Mo.) Star, 27 Feb 1915, Page 2, Column 1
Burial	28 Feb 1915	Mount Washington Cemetery, Independence, Jackson, Missouri, United States
Probate	3 Mar 1915	(Will Proved), Volume 20, Page 26, Kansas City, Jackson, Missouri, United States
Misc		"John Cutter Gage," a Memorial Booklet (1915)
Occupation		Lawyer (1860, 1870, 1900), Attorney General Practice (1910)
Marriage	26 Apr 1886	(1886K0060102), Kansas City, Jackson, Missouri, United States
Father	Frye GAGE (1782-1868)	
Mother	Keziah CUTTER (1794-1880)	

Mother Ida Marie BAILEY

Birth	11 Nov 1860	Missouri, United States
Census	1870	Page 674, Monroe City, Monroe, Missouri, United States
Census	1880	ED 51, Page 578, Monroe City, Monroe, Missouri, United States
Census	1900	ED 66, Page 16, Kansas City, Jackson, Missouri, United States
Census	1910	ED 88, Page 152, Kansas City, Jackson, Missouri, United States
Census	1920	ED 194, Page 205, Kansas City, Jackson, Missouri, United States
Census	1930	ED 87, Page 207, Kansas City, Jackson, Missouri, United States
Death	10 Dec 1948	Myocardial Insufficiency, Arteriosclerotic Heart Disease . . .; Kansas City, Jackson, Missouri, United States
Burial	11 Dec 1948	Mount Washington Cemetery, Independence, Jackson, Missouri, United States
Misc		Funeral Notice, Kansas City (Mo.) Times, 11 Dec 1948, Page 23, Column 8
Father	Dr. Elijah Iles BAILEY (1817-1890)	
Mother	Elizabeth Ara PEPPER (1824-)	

Children

Father	John Cutter GAGE	
Mother	**Ida Marie BAILEY**	

Children

M	**John Bailey "Jack" GAGE**	
Birth	24 Feb 1887	Jackson, Missouri, United States
Census	1900	ED 66, Page 16, Kansas City, Jackson, Missouri, United States
Graduation	1907	University of Kansas, Lawrence, Douglas, Kansas, United States
Graduation	1909	Kansas City School of Law, Kansas City, Jackson, Missouri, United States
Census	1910	ED 88, Page 152, Kansas City, Jackson, Missouri, United States
Misc	bet 1940 and 1948	Mayor; Kansas City, Jackson, Missouri, United States
Death	15 Jan 1970	Struck by a car while crossing the street
Burial		Mount Washington Cemetery, Independence, Jackson, Missouri, United States
Misc		Biography, Dictionary of Missouri Biography (1999), Pages 327-328
Occupation		Attorney General Practice (1910)
Spouse	Marjorie P. HIRES (1895-1993)	
Marriage	12 Sep 1922	(1922A0003797), Kansas City, Jackson, Missouri, United States
Spouse	Constant Ruggles LANE (1894-1920)	
Marriage	1916	

F	**Marion Mansur GAGE**	
Birth	14 Mar 1889	Kansas City, Jackson, Missouri, United States
Census	1900	ED 66, Page 16, Kansas City, Jackson, Missouri, United States
Census	1910	ED 199, Page 55, Kansas City, Jackson, Missouri, United States
Census	1920	ED 194, Page 205, Kansas City, Jackson, Missouri, United States
Census	1930	ED 87, Page 207, Kansas City, Jackson, Missouri, United States
Death	22 Jan 1957	Cerebral Thrombosis, Cerebral Arteriosclerosis, Multiple Sclerosis Advanced (30 Years), Chronic Pyelonephritis (2 Years); Kansas City, Jackson, Missouri, United States
Burial	26 Jan 1957	Mount Washington Cemetery, Independence, Jackson, Missouri, United States
Occupation		Manufacturer Clothing (1930)
Spouse	Frank Simpson GROVES (1886-1950)	
Marriage	6 Jan 1909	(1909K0042732), Kansas City, Jackson, Missouri, United States
Divorce		
Spouse	Henry Clayton FRASER (1887-1939)	
Marriage	5 Apr 1923	(1923A0006913), Kansas City, Jackson, Missouri, United States

Father Dr. Joseph GANGHOFER

Birth	abt 1817	Bavaria, Germany
Census	1860	Page 62, Kansas City, Jackson, Missouri, United States
Tax Lists	Sep 1862	Physician License; "Jos. Ganghafer", Kansas City, Jackson, Missouri, United States
Military		Surgeon, 77th Provision Enrolled Missouri Militia
Tax Lists	May 1866	Physician and Retail Liquor Dealer Licenses, Kansas City, Jackson, Missouri, United States
Census	1870	Page 376, Kansas City, Jackson, Missouri, United States
Naturalization	Nov 1875	("Missouri District"), [--?--]
Misc		"The Missing Boy," Kansas City (Mo.) Times, 27 Sep 1879, Page 7, Column 1
Misc	29 Jun 1880	Military Pension Application 398,015
Census	1880	ED 153, Page 207, Leavenworth, Leavenworth, Kansas, United States
Misc	26 Feb 1884	Registered to Vote; Los Angeles, Los Angeles, California, United States
Occupation		Physician (1860, 1870), Physician & Surgeon (1880)
Death		
Burial		
Marriage		
Father		
Mother		

Mother Anna M. "Annie" [--?--]

Birth	abt 1827	Bavaria, Germany
Census	1860	Page 62, Kansas City, Jackson, Missouri, United States
Census	1870	Page 376, Kansas City, Jackson, Missouri, United States
Death	13 Aug 1875	Kansas City, Jackson, Missouri, United States
Misc		Death Notice, Kansas City (Mo.) Times, 15 Aug 1875, Page 4, Column 1
Burial		
Father		
Mother		

Children

M Henry GANGHOFER

Birth	1864/5	Missouri, United States
Adoption	ca 1865	(Adopted When a Few Weeks Old; Birth Father a Rich Man Living in New Mexico in 1879)
Census	1870	Page 375, Kansas City, Jackson, Missouri, United States
Misc		"The Missing Boy," Kansas City (Mo.) Times, 27 Sep 1879, Page 7, Column 1
Census	1880	ED 153, Page 207, Leavenworth, Leavenworth, Kansas, United States
Census	1900	
Census	1910	
Census	1920	
Census	1930	
Misc		"Adopted Son" (1880)
Death		
Burial		
Marriage		

Father Herman/Hermann GANZ

Birth	2 Jul 1833	Sachsen-Meiningen, Saxony, Germany
Immigration	1856	(or 1860)
Residence	?-1856	Louisvile, Jefferson, Kentucky, United States
Residence	bet 1856 and 1920	Kansas City, Jackson, Missouri, United States
Census	1860	Page 109, Westport, Jackson, Missouri, United States
Tax Lists	Sep 1862	Retail Dealer License; "Ganz & Reis", Kansas City, Jackson, Missouri, United States
Military		Col. Frank Foster's Westport Home Guard, Civil War
Military	Oct 1863	Civil War Draft Registration; Kaw Township, Jackson, Missouri, United States
Tax Lists	May 1866	Retail Dealer License; "H. Ganz & Bro.", Kansas City, Jackson, Missouri, United States
Tax Lists	May 1866	Income and Gold Watch; "H. Ganz", Kansas City, Jackson, Missouri, United States
Census	1870	Page 585, Kansas City, Jackson, Missouri, United States
Religion	1872	Charter Member, Congregation B'Nai Jehudah; Kansas City, Jackson, Missouri, United States
Census	1880	ED 17, Page 454, Kansas City, Jackson, Missouri, United States
Census	1900	ED 42, Page 231, Kansas City, Jackson, Missouri, United States
Misc		"Married Forty Years," Kansas City (Mo.) Star, 22 Feb 1903, Page 5, Column 4
Census	1910	ED 39, Page 22, Kansas City, Jackson, Missouri, United States
Misc		"He Came Here 63 Years Ago," Kansas City (Mo.) Star, 07 May 1919, Page 2, Column 4
Death	20 Jan 1920	Pulmonary Oedema, Senility; Kansas City, Jackson, Missouri, United States
Burial	23 Jan 1920	Elmwood Cemetery, Kansas City, Jackson, Missouri, United States
Occupation		Merchant (1860), Clothing Merchant (1870). Merchant (1880), Insurance Agent (1900), Solicitor Insurance (1910)
Business		Ganz & Reis (Retail Dealer)
Marriage	24 Mar 1862	Congregation Rodeph Shalom, Philadelphia, Philadelphia, Pennsylvania, United States
Father		
Mother		

Mother Hannah "Hanche" FRIEDMAN

Birth	27 Jun 1838	Sachsen-Meiningen, Saxony, Germany
Immigration	1860	
Census	1860	
Census	1870	Page 585, Kansas City, Jackson, Missouri, United States
Census	1880	ED 17, Page 454, Kansas City, Jackson, Missouri, United States
Census	1900	ED 42, Page 231, Kansas City, Jackson, Missouri, United States
Will	4 Mar 1907	(Will Executed, Kansas City Courthouse, Volume 15, Page 500), Jackson, Missouri, United States
Census	1910	ED 39, Page 22, Kansas City, Jackson, Missouri, United States
Death	5 Jun 1910	Uremia Resulting from Chronic Interstitial Nephritis; Kansas City, Jackson, Missouri, United States
Misc		Obituary, Kansas City (Mo.) Times, 06 Jun 1910, Page 2, Column 1
Burial	7 Jun 1910	Elmwood Cemetery, Kansas City, Jackson, Missouri, United States
Misc		Obituary, Kansas City (Mo.) Times, 7 Jun 1910, Page 10, Column 2
Probate	11 Jun 1910	(Will Proved, Kansas City Courthouse, Volume 15, Page 486), Jackson, Missouri, United States
Father	Jacob FRIEDMAN (-)	
Mother	Jetta [--?--] (-)	

Children

F Pauline GANZ

Birth	27 Oct 1866	Missouri, United States
Census	1870	Page 585, Kansas City, Jackson, Missouri, United States
Census	1880	ED 17, Page 454, Kansas City, Jackson, Missouri, United States
Census	1900	ED 42, Page 231, Kansas City, Jackson, Missouri, United States
Census	1910	ED 39, Page 22, Kansas City, Jackson, Missouri, United States
Census	1920	ED 35, Page 63, Kansas City, Jackson, Missouri, United States
Census	1930	ED 113, Page 45, Kansas City, Jackson, Missouri, United States
Death	28 May 1930	Chronic Myocarditis, Acute Delatation; Kansas City, Jackson, Missouri, United States
Burial	3 Jun 1930	Elmwood Cemetery, Kansas City, Jackson, Missouri, United States
Occupation		Clerk Insurance Company (1910), Saleslady Insurance (1930)
Marriage		

Father Herman/Hermann GANZ

Mother Hannah "Hanche" FRIEDMAN

Children

F	**Louise/Louisa G. GANZ**		
	Birth	24 Oct 1867	Missouri, United States
	Census	1870	Page 585, Kansas City, Jackson, Missouri, United States
	Census	1880	ED 17, Page 454, Kansas City, Jackson, Missouri, United States
	Census	1900	ED 42, Page 231, Kansas City, Jackson, Missouri, United States
	Census	1910	ED 39, Page 22, Kansas City, Jackson, Missouri, United States
	Census	1920	ED 35, Page 63, Kansas City, Jackson, Missouri, United States
	Census	1930	ED 113, Page 45, Kansas City, Jackson, Missouri, United States
	Death	28 Feb 1939	
	Burial	1 Mar 1939	Elmwood Cemetery, Kansas City, Jackson, Missouri, United States
	Spouse	Joseph H. GUTMANN (1868-1939)	
	Marriage	24 Feb 1908	(1908K0040082), Kansas City, Jackson, Missouri, United States

M	**Henry GANZ**		
	Birth	Nov 1869	Missouri, United States
	Census	1870	Page 585, Kansas City, Jackson, Missouri, United States
	Census	1880	ED 17, Page 454, Kansas City, Jackson, Missouri, United States
	Census	1900	ED 334, Page 214, Chicago, Cook, Illinois, United States
	Census	1910	ED 158, Page 286, Kansas City, Jackson, Missouri, United States
	Census	1920	
	Census	1930	ED 168, Page 124, Chicago, Cook, Illinois, United States
	Death	20 Jan 1940	Chicago, Cook, Illinois, United States
	Occupation		Bookkeeper (1900), Traveling Salesman Liquor Company (1910), Salesman Medicine Company (1930)
	Burial		
	Spouse	Mary C. HILL (1866-1938)	
	Marriage	1892/3	

Father Jacob R. GERHART

Birth	Jan 1840	Bavaria, Germany
Immigration	1843	Saint Louis, Saint Louis, Missouri, United States
Residence	bet 1843 and 1857	Saint Louis, Saint Louis, Missouri, United States
Census	1850	
Residence	bet 1857 and 1866	Kansas City, Jackson, Missouri, United States
Census	1860	Page 118, Westport, Jackson, Missouri, United States
Tax Lists	Sep 1862	Manufacturer License; "J. R. Gerhard", Westport, Jackson, Missouri, United States
Tax Lists	bet SepDec 1862 and Jan 1863	Harness Manufactured; Westport, Jackson, Missouri, United States
Tax Lists	bet Apr 1863 and Dec 1863	Saddlery Manufactured; "Jacob R. Garhard/Gerhart", Westport, Jackson, Missouri, United States
Military		Corporal, Company E, 77th Regiment Enrolled Missouri Militia
Tax Lists	bet May 1865 and Jun 1865	Saddlery Manufactured; "J. R. Gerhart", Kansas City, Jackson, Missouri, United States
Tax Lists	Jul 1865	Saddlery Manufactured; "J. R. Gerhart & Co.", Kansas City, Jackson, Missouri, United States
Tax Lists	Aug 1865	Manufacturer License and Saddlery Manufactured; "J. R. Gerhart & Bro.", Kansas City, Jackson, Missouri, United States
Tax Lists	bet Sep 1865 and Sep 1866	Saddlery Manufactured; "J. R. Gerhart & Bro.", Kansas City, Jackson, Missouri, United States
Tax Lists	May 1866	Manufacturer and Retail Dealer Licenses; "J. R. Gerhart & Bro.", Kansas City, Jackson, Missouri, United States
Residence	bet 1866 and 1879	Saint Louis, Saint Louis, Missouri, United States
Tax Lists	Nov 1866	Saddlery Manufactured; "J. R. Gerhart & Bro.", Westport, Jackson, Missouri, United States
Tax Lists	Dec 1866	Saddlery Manufactured; "J. R. Gerhart & Bro.", Kansas City, Jackson, Missouri, United States
Census	1870	Page 426, Saint Louis, Saint Louis, Missouri, United States
Census	1870	Page 426, Saint Louis, Saint Louis, Missouri, United States
Residence	bet 1879 and 1903	Kansas City, Jackson, Missouri, United States
Census	1880	ED 9, Page 270, Kansas City, Jackson, Missouri, United States
Census	1900	ED 96, Page 106, Kansas City, Jackson, Missouri, United States
Death	1 Apr 1903	Heart Failure; Kansas City, Jackson, Missouri, United States
Misc		Obituary, Kansas City (Mo.) Times, 02 Apr 1903, Page 2, Column 4
Burial	5 Apr 1903	Elmwood Cemetery, Kansas City, Jackson, Missouri, United States
Occupation		Saddler (1860, 1870, 1880), Harness Maker (1900)
Misc		Brother of Francis E. Gerhart, also brother of P. G. Gerhart of St. Louis
Marriage	20 Sep 1860	(1860I0050002), Jackson, Missouri, United States
Father		
Mother		

Mother Susan M. CARTER

Birth	1837/8	(or Jul 1843), Kansas Territory, United States
Census	1850	Page 240, Kaw Township, Jackson, Missouri, United States
Census	1860	Page 135, Westport, Jackson, Missouri, United States
Census	1870	Page 426, Saint Louis, Saint Louis, Missouri, United States
Census	1880	ED 9, Page 270, Kansas City, Jackson, Missouri, United States
Census	1900	ED 96, Page 106, Kansas City, Jackson, Missouri, United States
Census	1910	ED 111, Page 183, Kansas City, Jackson, Missouri, United States
Death	21 Jun 1914	Lincoln, Lancaster, Nebraska, United States
Misc		Obituary, Kansas City (Mo.) Times, 22 Jun 1914, Page 5, Column 3
Burial	24 Jun 1914	Elmwood Cemetery, Kansas City, Jackson, Missouri, United States
Misc		Susan Carter Gerhart, "Reminiscences of Old Westport," Westport Historical Quarterly 1 (May 1965): 6-7
Father		Rev. Luther M. CARTER (1808-)
Mother		Susan H. [--?--] (1805-)

Children

M William George "Willie" GERHART

Birth	Jun 1861	Missouri, United States
Census	1870	Page 426, Saint Louis, Saint Louis, Missouri, United States

Father Jacob R. GERHART

Mother Susan M. CARTER

Children

William George "Willie" GERHART (continued)

Census	1880	ED 9, Page 270, Kansas City, Jackson, Missouri, United States
Census	1900	ED 202, Page 186, Miles City, Custer, Montana, United States
Residence	1903	Miles City, Custer, Montana, United States
Census	1910	ED 40, Page 118, Long Beach, Los Angeles, California, United States
Residence	1914	Covina, Los Angeles, California, United States
Census	1920	ED 45, Page 104, Covina, Los Angeles, California, United States
Burial	30 Mar 1925	Elmwood Cemetery, Kansas City, Jackson, Missouri, United States
Occupation		Saddler (1880), Dray Man (1900), Own Income (1910), Manager and Part Owner Transfer Company (1920)
Death		
Spouse	Cora [--?--] (1867-)	
Marriage	1884/5	
Spouse		

F   Nellie M. GERHART

Birth	1865/6	MO (or Feb 1870)
Census	1870	Page 426, Saint Louis, Saint Louis, Missouri, United States
Census	1880	ED 9, Page 270, Kansas City, Jackson, Missouri, United States
Census	1900	ED 96, Page 106, Kansas City, Jackson, Missouri, United States
Census	1910	ED 111, Page 183, Kansas City, Jackson, Missouri, United States
Residence	1914	Kansas City, Jackson, Missouri, United States
Census	1920	
Death	27 Mar 1925	
Burial	30 Mar 1925	Elmwood Cemetery, Kansas City, Jackson, Missouri, United States
Occupation		Saleswoman (1900), Clerk Store (1910)
Marriage		

M   Edward Charles GERHART

Birth	26 Jan 1874	Missouri, United States
Census	1880	ED 9, Page 270, Kansas City, Jackson, Missouri, United States
Census	1900	ED 729, Page 52, Chicago, Cook, Illinois, United States
Residence	1903	Colorado City, Pueblo, Colorado, United States
Census	1910	ED 111, Page 183, Kansas City, Jackson, Missouri, United States
Residence	1914	Kansas City, Jackson, Missouri, United States
Military	12 Sep 1918	World War I Draft Registration; Kansas City, Jackson, Missouri, United States
Census	1920	
Census	1930	ED 8, Page 209, Los Angeles, Los Angeles, California, United States
Census	1940	ED 331, Page 6683, Los Angeles, Los Angeles, California, United States
Death	23 Mar 1946	Los Angeles, California, United States
Occupation		Tobacco Worker (1900), Steam Fitter (1910), Stationary Engineer Oil Company (1930), Pipe Fitter Building Contractor (1940)
Burial		
Spouse	Mabel L. [--?--] (1889-)	
Marriage		

F   Emma Estelle GERHART

Birth	10 Apr 1876	Missouri, United States
Census	1880	ED 9, Page 270, Kansas City, Jackson, Missouri, United States
Census	1900	
Census	1905	Page 8, Beloit, Mitchell, Kansas, United States
Census	1910	ED 92, Page 25, Beloit, Mitchell, Kansas, United States
Residence	1914	Lincoln, Lancaster, Nebraska, United States
Census	1920	ED 410, Page 7, Los Angeles, Los Angeles, California, United States
Census	1930	ED 8, Page 209, Los Angeles, Los Angeles, California, United States
Death	13 Jun 1940	Los Angeles, California, United States
Burial	19 Jun 1940	Elmwood Cemetery, Kansas City, Jackson, Missouri, United States
Spouse	Joseph F. ALDERS (1868-)	

Father Jacob R. GERHART		
Mother Susan M. CARTER		
Children		

	Emma Estelle GERHART (continued)		
	Marriage		
	Spouse	Martin L. GREGORY (1876-)	
	Marriage		
F	**Daisy E. GERHART**		
	Birth	May 1880	Missouri, United States
	Census	1880	
	Census	1900	ED 96, Page 106, Kansas City, Jackson, Missouri, United States
	Residence	1903	Kansas City, Jackson, Missouri, United States
	Census	1910	
	Census	1920	
	Census	1930	
	Death		
	Burial		
	Spouse	Henry R. SMITH (1864-)	
	Marriage	12 Mar 1901	(1901K0021787), Kansas City, Jackson, Missouri, United States

Father Thomas B. GILES

Birth	29 Jan 1807	Somerset, Maryland, United States
Death	1840	Sussex, Delaware, United States
Burial		
Marriage	abt 1835	
Father		
Mother		

Mother Hattie WAPLES

Birth	29 Jan 1807	Somerset, Maryland, United States
Census	1860	Page 455, Little Creek Hundred, Sussex, Delaware, United States
Death		
Burial		
Father		
Mother		
Other spouse	Nathaniel LAWLESS (1815-)	
Marriage	abt 1840	

Children

M James S. GILES

Birth	1834/5	Delaware, United States
Census	1850	Page 282, Sussex, Delaware, United States
Census	1860	Page 455, Little Creek Hundred, Sussex, Delaware, United States
Tax Lists	Sep 1862	Retail Liquor Dealer License; "James Giles", Kansas City, Jackson, Missouri, United States
Tax Lists	Sep 1862	Wholesale Dealer License; "Giles & Coats", Kansas City, Jackson, Missouri, United States
Misc		Advertisement, Kansas City (Mo.) Western Journal of Commerce, 01 Jul 1863, Page 4, Column 7
Military	Sep 1863–Oct 1863	Civil War Draft Registration; Kaw Township, Jackson, Missouri, United States
Census	1864	Page 191, Arizona Territory, United States
Tax Lists	Nov 1866	Retail Dealer License; "J. W. Giles & Company", Blue Springs, Jackson, Missouri, United States
Census	1870	Page 33, Sniabar Township, Jackson, Missouri, United States
Census	1880	
Census	1900	
Census	1910	
Business		Giles & Coates (Wholesale Dealer)
Occupation		Merchant (1870)
Business		J. S. Giles & Company (Groceries & Provisions)
Death		
Burial		
Marriage		

Father Christian "Chris" GLUNZ

	Birth	1833/4	Germany
	Census	1860	Page 539, Shawnee Township, Johnson, Kansas, United States
	Tax Lists	Oct 1863	Wagons Manufactured; "Christ. Gleinz", Westport, Jackson, Missouri, United States
	Tax Lists	Dec 1863	Wagons Manufactured; "Christian Gluntz", Westport, Jackson, Missouri, United States
	Tax Lists	Jun 1865	Wagons Manufactured; Westport, Jackson, Missouri, United States
	Tax Lists	bet Dec 1865 and Jan 1866	Wagons Manufactured; Westport, Jackson, Missouri, United States
	Tax Lists	bet Apr 1866 and Jun 1866	Wagons Manufactured; Westport, Jackson, Missouri, United States
	Tax Lists	May 1866	Wagons Manufactured and Income; Westport, Jackson, Missouri, United States
	Tax Lists	May 1866	Manufacturer License and Income; Westport, Jackson, Missouri, United States
	Tax Lists	Sep 1866	Wagons Manufactured; Westport, Jackson, Missouri, United States
	Death	Oct 1866	"Killed by Indians"; Near Fort Laramie
	Misc		Death Notice, Kansas City (Mo.) Daily Journal of Commerce, 27 Oct 1866, Page 3, Column 1
	Probate	27 Oct 1866	(Administrators' Bond), Volume M, Page 481, Independence, Jackson, Missouri, United States
	Misc		"Frank Hahn, The Village Blacksmith," Westport Historical Quarterly 5 (Mar 1970): 7-9
	Occupation		Blacksmith (1860), Wagon Maker
	Burial		
	Marriage		
	Father		
	Mother		

Mother Mary [--?--]

	Birth	1833/4	Germany
	Immigration	1856	Westport, Jackson, Missouri, United States
	Census	1860	Page 539, Shawnee Township, Johnson, Kansas, United States
	Census	1870	Page 648, Shawnee Township, Johnson, Kansas, United States
	Census	1880	ED 101, Page 152, Shawnee Township, Johnson, Kansas, United States
	Death	10 Sep 1893	Cancer
	Burial	11 Sep 1893	Forest Hill Cemetery, Kansas City, Jackson, Missouri, United States
	Misc		Obituary, Westport (Mo.) Sentinel-Examiner, 16 Sep 1893, Page 3, Column 2
	Father		
	Mother		
	Other spouse	August HAHN (1845-1925)	
	Marriage	22 Sep 1868	(1868I0060009), Jackson, Missouri, United States

Children

M John GLUNZ

	Birth	9 Nov 1856	Missouri, United States
	Census	1860	Page 539, Shawnee Township, Johnson, Kansas, United States
	Census	1870	Page 683, Kansas City, Jackson, Missouri, United States
	Census	1870	Page 648, Shawnee Township, Johnson, Kansas, United States
	Census	1880	
	Census	1900	ED 107, Page 189, Mission Township, Johnson, Kansas, United States
	Census	1905	Page 31, Chetopa, Neosho, Kansas, United States
	Census	1910	ED 106, Page 67, Mission Township, Johnson, Kansas, United States
	Census	1920	
	Census	1930	ED 107, Page 100, Kansas City, Jackson, Missouri, United States
	Death	1 Jan 1932	Cancer of Stomach Primary, Secondary Cancer of Liver; Kansas City, Jackson, Missouri, United States
	Burial	4 Jan 1932	Forest Hill Cemetery, Kansas City, Jackson, Missouri, United States
	Occupation		Porter (1870), Farmer (1870), Farm Laborer (1900, 1910), Clerk Pool Hall (1930)
	Marriage		

M Lewis GLUNZ

	Birth	1857/8	Missouri, United States
	Census	1860	Page 539, Shawnee Township, Johnson, Kansas, United States
	Census	1870	
	Census	1880	

Father	Christian "Chris" GLUNZ	
Mother	**Mary [--?--]**	
Children		

Lewis GLUNZ (continued)

Census	1900	
Census	1910	
Census	1920	
Census	1930	
Death		
Burial		
Marriage		

F Anna L. "Annie" GLUNZ

Birth	Aug 1859	Kansas, United States
Census	1860	Page 539, Shawnee Township, Johnson, Kansas, United States
Census	1870	Page 648, Shawnee Township, Johnson, Kansas, United States
Census	1880	ED 101, Page 152, Shawnee Township, Johnson, Kansas, United States
Census	1900	ED 151, Page 93, Thayer, Neosho, Kansas, United States
Census	1905	Page 31, Chetopa, Neosho, Kansas, United States
Census	1910	ED 200, Page 171, Chetopa, Neosho, Kansas, United States
Census	1920	ED 212, Page 146, Chetopa, Neosho, Kansas, United States
Census	1930	
Death		
Burial		
Spouse	John B. QUINN (1851-)	
Marriage	14 Oct 1890	(1890K0004398), Kansas City, Jackson, Missouri, United States

M Christian GLUNZ

Birth	25 Dec 1860	Johnson, Kansas, United States
Census	1870	
Census	1880	ED 101, Page 152, Shawnee Township, Johnson, Kansas, United States
Census	1900	
Census	1910	
Census	1920	
Census	1930	ED 16, Page 196, Olathe, Johnson, Kansas, United States
Death	30 Jul 1944	Carcinoma of Prostate with Metastases, Hypertensive . . .; Kansas City, Jackson, Missouri, United States
Burial	1 Aug 1944	Forest Hill Cemetery, Kansas City, Jackson, Missouri, United States
Occupation		Farm Laborer (1880), Farmer (1930)
Spouse	Anna L. [--?--] (1878-)	
Marriage	1920/1	

F Clara D. "Clarrie" GLUNZ

Birth	1862/3	
Census	1870	Page 648, Shawnee Township, Johnson, Kansas, United States
Census	1880	ED 101, Page 152, Shawnee Township, Johnson, Kansas, United States
Census	1900	
Census	1910	
Census	1920	
Death		
Burial		
Spouse	James M. KELTNER (1862-)	
Marriage	20 Mar 1889	(1889K0001689), Kansas City, Jackson, Missouri, United States

F Mollie GLUNZ

Birth	12 Jan 1864	Missouri, United States
Census	1870	Page 648, Shawnee Township, Johnson, Kansas, United States
Census	1880	ED 101, Page 152, Shawnee Township, Johnson, Kansas, United States
Death	8 Aug 1892	
Burial		Corinth Cemetery, Prairie Village, Johnson, Kansas, United States
Spouse	Jefferson D. GABBERT (1861-)	
Marriage	19 Nov 1890	Westport, Jackson Co., MO (1890K0004582)

Father Thomas Jefferson GOFORTH		
Birth	18 Dec 1804	Cincinnati, Hamilton, Ohio, United States
Census	1840	(T. J. Goforth Family), Page 65, Jefferson City, Cole, Missouri, United States
Census	1850	Page 269, Blue Township, Jackson, Missouri, United States
Census		Slave Schedules, Frame 108, Blue Township, Jackson, Missouri, United States
Residence	bet 1850 and 1882	Westport, Jackson, Missouri, United States
Property	23 Aug 1850	First Known Purchase, Part Lot 1, Old Town, Indep.; Volume S, Page 46, Independence, Jackson, Missouri, United States
Occupation	bet 1854 and 1863	Justice of the Peace; Kaw Township, Jackson, Missouri, United States
Misc	1857	Mayor (also 1870, 1875, 1876, 1879); Westport, Jackson, Missouri, United States
Census	1860	Page 121, Westport, Jackson, Missouri, United States
Tax Lists	Sep 1862	Lawyer License; Westport, Jackson, Missouri, United States
Occupation	bet 1867 and 1869	Justice of the Peace; Kaw Township, Jackson, Missouri, United States
Occupation	bet 1869 and 1882	Justice of the Peace; Westport Township, Jackson, Missouri, United States
Census	1870	Page 63, Westport, Jackson, Missouri, United States
Census	1880	ED 40, Page 259, Westport, Jackson, Missouri, United States
Will	11 Feb 1881	(Will Written), Volume A, Page 387, Kansas City, Jackson, Missouri, United States
Death	11 Apr 1882	Westport, Jackson, Missouri, United States
Burial	13 Apr 1882	Union Cemetery, Kansas City, Jackson, Missouri, United States
Misc		Funeral Notice, Kansas City (Mo.) Times, 13 Apr 1882, Page 8, Column 5
Probate	14 Apr 1882	(Will Written), Volume A, Page 387, Kansas City, Jackson, Missouri, United States
Misc		"Mayor Thomas J. Goforth & His Home," William A. Goff, Old Westport (1977), Unpaginated
Occupation		Sign Painter (1850), Justice of the Peace (1860), Notary Public (1870), J. P. N. P. (1880), Lawyer
Marriage	15 Mar 1826	
Father	William GOFORTH Jr. (1766-1817)	
Mother	Elizabeth WOOD (1769-1850)	

Mother Eliza V. MATHEWS		
Birth	5 Nov 1804	(or 1805), New Brunswick, Somerset, New Jersey, United States
Census	1840	(T. J. Goforth Family), Page 65, Jefferson City, Cole, Missouri, United States
Census	1850	Page 269, Blue Township, Jackson, Missouri, United States
Census	1860	Page 121, Westport, Jackson, Missouri, United States
Census	1870	Page 63, Westport, Jackson, Missouri, United States
Death	3 Jan 1877	
Burial		Union Cemetery, Kansas City, Jackson, Missouri, United States
Religion		Westport Baptist Church (1853)
Father		
Mother		

Children

M	**Thomas Jefferson GOFORTH**		
	Birth	30 Dec 1826	Ohio, United States
	Census	1840	(T. J. Goforth Family), Page 65, Jefferson City, Cole, Missouri, United States
	Census	1850	Page 269, Blue Township, Jackson, Missouri, United States
	Death	17 Nov 1857	
	Occupation		Sign Painter (1850)
	Burial		
	Marriage		

F	**Catherine Eliza "Kate" GOFORTH**		
	Birth	23 Oct 1828	Ohio, United States
	Census	1840	(T. J. Goforth Family), Page 65, Jefferson City, Cole, Missouri, United States
	Census	1850	Page 269, Blue Township, Jackson, Missouri, United States
	Census	1860	Page 121, Westport, Jackson, Missouri, United States
	Census	1870	Page 63, Westport, Jackson, Missouri, United States
	Census	1880	ED 40, Page 259, Westport, Jackson, Missouri, United States
	Death		
	Burial		
	Marriage		

Father Thomas Jefferson GOFORTH

Mother Eliza V. MATHEWS

Children

M Edwin Marion GOFORTH

Birth	26 Apr 1831	
Death		
Burial		
Marriage		

M Dr. Edwin Gano GOFORTH

Birth	26 Sep 1832	Tazewell, Illinois, United States
Census	1840	(T. J. Goforth Family), Page 65, Jefferson City, Cole, Missouri, United States
Census	1850	Page 269, Blue Township, Jackson, Missouri, United States
Census	1860	Page 121, Westport, Jackson, Missouri, United States
Census	1870	Page 57, Westport, Jackson, Missouri, United States
Census	1880	ED 76, Page 19, Union Township, Cass, Missouri, United States
Death	3 Mar 1891	
Burial		Freeman Cemetery, Freeman, Cass, Missouri, United States
Occupation		Painter (1850, 1870), Attorney (1860), M. D. (1880)
Spouse	Eliza Ann JONES (1837-1876)	
Marriage	9 Feb 1859	(1859I0040098), Jackson, Missouri, United States
Spouse	Zylphia Emeline HARVILLE (1862-1936)	
Marriage	30 May 1882	Cass, Missouri, United States

F Malissa Amelia GOFORTH

Birth	10 Jan 1835	(or 1840/41), Missouri, United States
Census	1850	Page 269, Blue Township, Jackson, Missouri, United States
Census	1860	Page 121, Westport, Jackson, Missouri, United States
Census	1870	Page 63, Westport, Jackson, Missouri, United States
Census	1880	
Religion		Westport Baptist Church (1853)
Death		
Burial		
Spouse	[--?--] BANAY (-)	
Marriage		

F Martha Louisa "Mattie" GOFORTH

Birth	6 Apr 1837	(or 1835), Illinois, United States
Census	1840	(T. J. Goforth Family), Page 65, Jefferson City, Cole, Missouri, United States
Census	1850	Page 270, Blue Township, Jackson, Missouri, United States
Census	1860	Page 115, Westport, Jackson, Missouri, United States
Census	1870	Page 63, Westport, Jackson, Missouri, United States
Census	1880	ED 7, Page 207, Kansas City, Jackson, Missouri, United States
Census	1900	ED 38, Page, Kansas City, Jackson, Missouri, United States
Death	12 Apr 1911	Erysepilas, Senility, Debility; Kansas City, Jackson, Missouri, United States
Burial	15 Apr 1911	Forest Hill Cemetery, Kansas City, Jackson, Missouri, United States
Occupation		Dressmaker (1880), Canvasser (Dry Goods) (1900)
Spouse	Lewis L. CRAWFORD (-1858)	
Marriage		
Spouse	James A. ALLENDER (1835-)	
Marriage		

F Charlotte L. GOFORTH

Birth	4 Oct 1839	
Death	5 Jan 1840	
Burial		Woodland-Old City Cemetery, Jefferson City, Cole, Missouri, United States
Marriage		

F Caroline E. "Carrie" GOFORTH

Birth	Nov 1845	Missouri, United States
Census	1850	Page 269, Blue Township, Jackson, Missouri, United States
Census	1860	Page 121, Westport, Jackson, Missouri, United States
Census	1870	Page 337, Iuka, Tishomingo, Mississippi, United States

Father	Thomas Jefferson GOFORTH	
Mother	**Eliza V. MATHEWS**	
Children		

Caroline E. "Carrie" GOFORTH (continued)

Census	1880	
Census	1900	ED 112, Page 167, Iuka, Tishomingo, Mississippi, United States
Death		
Burial		
Spouse	Humphrey Posey MILLSAPS (1843-1921)	
Marriage	21 Oct 1869	(1869I0060128), Jackson, Missouri, United States

Father Dr. John E. GOODSON

Birth	23 Dec 1819	(or 30 Sep 1819), Cumberland, Kentucky, United States
Census	1850	
Census	1860	Page 132, Boone Township, Bates, Missouri, United States
Tax Lists	Apr 1863	Physician License; Jackson, Missouri, United States
Census	1870	Page 143, Liberty Township, Macon, Missouri, United States
Census	1880	ED 125, Page 392, Macon, Macon, Missouri, United States
Death	16 Sep 1892	Macon, Missouri, United States
Burial		Chariton Cemetery, Cash, Macon, Missouri, United States
Occupation		Physician (1860), Practicing Physician (1870). Editor Semimonthly Paper (1880)
Marriage	9 Oct 1842	Cumberland, Harlan, Kentucky, United States
Father	Samuel Robert GOODSON (1792-1872)	
Mother	Mary Elizabeth BECK (1795-1873)	

Mother Mary ELSEA

Birth	27 Jun 1822	Front Royal, Warren, Virginia, United States
Census	1850	
Census	1860	Page 132, Boone Township, Bates, Missouri, United States
Census	1870	Page 143, Liberty Township, Macon, Missouri, United States
Death	21 Feb 1878	
Burial		Chariton Cemetery, Cash, Macon, Missouri, United States
Father	Johnathan ELSEA (1780-1851)	
Mother	Sarah Ginn MATTHEWS (1791-1835)	

Children

M Dr. D. Virgil GOODSON

Birth	2 Oct 1846	Missouri, United States
Census	1850	
Census	1860	Page 132, Boone Township, Bates, Missouri, United States
Census	1870	Page 262, Russell Township, Macon, Missouri, United States
Census	1880	ED 47, Page 67, Bodie, Mono, California, United States
Death	16 Jul 1890	
Burial		Chariton Cemetery, Cash, Macon, Missouri, United States
Occupation		Practicing Physician (1870), Carpenter (1880)
Spouse	Isabell [--?--] (1850-1920)	
Marriage		

M Grandison "Gran" GOODSON

Birth	27 May 1848	Carroll, Missouri, United States
Census	1850	
Census	1860	Page 132, Boone Township, Bates, Missouri, United States
Census	1870	Page 262, Russell Township, Macon, Missouri, United States
Census	1880	ED 139, Page 572, New Cambria, Macon, Missouri, United States
Residence	1929	New Cambria, Macon, Missouri, United States
Death	21 Sep 1937	Coronary Thrombosis; New Cambria, Macon, Missouri, United States
Burial	24 Sep 1937	New Cambria Cemetery, New Cambria, Macon, Missouri, United States
Occupation		Druggist (1870, 1880), Farmer
Spouse	Missouri HAMMACK (1859-1941)	
Marriage		

M Rufus GOODSON

Birth	Aug 1850	(or 1851), Missouri, United States
Census	1860	Page 132, Boone Township, Bates, Missouri, United States
Census	1870	Page 143, Liberty Township, Macon, Missouri, United States
Census	1880	ED 133, Page 493, Independence Township, Macon, Missouri, United States
Death	20 May 1929	Dilation Heart, Flu; Atlanta, Macon, Missouri, United States
Burial	21 May 1929	Chariton Cemetery, Cash, Macon, Missouri, United States
Misc		Obituary, La Plata (Mo.) Home Press, 23 May 1929
Occupation		Farmer (1870, 1880)
Spouse	Sarah F. GROSS (1851-1933)	
Marriage	30 Dec 1870	Macon, Missouri, United States

Father	**Dr. John E. GOODSON**	
Mother	**Mary ELSEA**	
Children		

M	**John E. GOODSON Jr.**	
Birth	15 Nov 1853	Missouri, United States
Census	1860	Page 132, Boone Township, Bates, Missouri, United States
Census	1870	Page 143, Liberty Township, Macon, Missouri, United States
Census	1880	ED 125, Page 392, Macon, Macon, Missouri, United States
Death	19 Aug 1890	
Burial		Chariton Cemetery, Cash, Macon, Missouri, United States
Occupation		Publisher of Paper (1880)
Spouse	Idress E. DENNISON (1853-1939)	
Marriage		

F	**Elizabeth Rovella GOODSON**	
Birth	12 Oct 1855	Missouri, United States
Census	1860	Page 132, Boone Township, Bates, Missouri, United States
Census	1870	Page 143, Liberty Township, Macon, Missouri, United States
Census	1880	ED 141, Page 595, Drake Township, Macon, Missouri, United States
Census	1900	ED 80, Page 259, Atlanta, Macon, Missouri, United States
Residence	1929	Goldsberry, Macon, Missouri, United States
Death	12 Dec 1945	
Burial		Old Chariton Cemetery, Callao, Macon, Missouri, United States
Spouse	William A. GRIFFIN (1853-)	
Marriage		

F	**Martha B. GOODSON**	
Birth	21 Nov 1856	(or Jun 1856), Carroll, Missouri, United States
Census	1860	
Census	1870	Page 143, Liberty Township, Macon, Missouri, United States
Census	1880	ED 132, Page 481, Liberty Township, Macon, Missouri, United States
Census	1900	ED 90, Page 350, Ethel, Macon, Missouri, United States
Death	8 Apr 1945	Senility with Hypostatic Pneumonia, Compression Fracture of Right Humerous (Fall, Accident); Still-Hildreth Osteopathic Sanatorium, Macon, Missouri, United States
Burial	10 Apr 1945	Chariton Cemetery, Cash, Macon, Missouri, United States
Spouse	William R. PHIPPS (1856-1902)	
Marriage	6 Dec 1876	Macon, Missouri, United States

F	**Mary E. GOODSON**	
Birth	19 Jul 1859	Kansas, United States
Census	1860	
Census	1870	Page 143, Liberty Township, Macon, Missouri, United States
Census	1880	ED 137, Page 538, Valley Township, Macon, Missouri, United States
Census	1900	ED 88, Page 330, Valley Township, Macon, Missouri, United States
Residence	1929	Callao, Macon, Missouri, United States
Death	7 Sep 1947	Myocardial Decompensation, Senile Debility; Columbia, Boone, Missouri, United States
Burial	7 Sep 1947	Chariton Cemetery, Cash, Macon, Missouri, United States
Spouse	William J. OWINGS (1857-1940)	
Marriage	8 Aug 1878	Macon, Missouri, United States

M	**Samuel Jonathan "Sam" GOODSON**	
Birth	20 Oct 1861	Cass, Missouri, United States
Census	1870	Page 143, Liberty Township, Macon, Missouri, United States
Census	1880	ED 125, Page 392, Macon, Macon, Missouri, United States
Census	1900	ED 79, Page 233, Lingo Township, Macon, Missouri, United States
Residence	1929	New Cambria, Macon, Missouri, United States
Death	4 Nov 1956	Uremia, Advanced Arteriolar Nephrosclerosis & Purulent Cystitis, Arteriosclerosis, Hypertrophy of Prostate Gland; Lingo Township, Macon, Missouri, United States
Burial	6 Nov 1956	New Cambria Cemetery, New Cambria, Macon, Missouri, United States
Occupation		Clerk in Grocery (1880), Merchant (1900), Retired Hardware Merchant (1956)
Spouse	Frances Lucetta NICHOLS (1868-1925)	
Marriage	24 Nov 1885	New Cambria, Macon, Missouri, United States

Father Dr. John E. GOODSON

Mother Mary ELSEA

Children

M | Martin S. GOODSON

Birth		16 Jan 1865	Missouri, United States
Census		1870	Page 143, Liberty Township, Macon, Missouri, United States
Census		1880	ED 125, Page 392, Macon, Macon, Missouri, United States
Death	26 Mar 1900		
Burial			Chariton Cemetery, Cash, Macon, Missouri, United States
Occupation			Farmer (1880)
Marriage			

Father Thomas H. GREEN

Birth	27 May 1837	Cavan, Ireland
Immigration	1854	Philadelphia, Philadelphia, Pennsylvania, United States
Residence	bet 1854 and 1858	Philadelphia, Philadelphia, Pennsylvania, United States
Residence	bet 1858 and 1916	Kansas City, Jackson, Missouri, United States
Census	1860	Page 68, Kansas City, Jackson, Missouri, United States
Tax Lists	Sep 1862	Wholesale Dealer, Retail Liquor Dealer, and Wholesale Liquor Dealer Licenses; "Green & Long", Kansas City, Jackson, Missouri, United States
Military		2nd Lieutenant, Company C, 77th Regiment Enrolled Missouri Militia
Military	Sep 1863–Oct 1863	Civil War Draft Registration; Kaw Township, Jackson, Missouri, United States
Tax Lists	May 1866	Wholesale Liquor Dealer License; "Green & Long", Kansas City, Jackson, Missouri, United States
Tax Lists	May 1866	Income; "Thomas Green", Kansas City, Jackson, Missouri, United States
Tax Lists	Aug 1866	Wholesale Liquor Dealer License; "Green & Long", Kansas City, Jackson, Missouri, United States
Tax Lists	Dec 1866	Sales of Merchanidse; "Green & Long", Kansas City, Jackson, Missouri, United States
Census	1870	Page 585, Kansas City, Jackson, Missouri, United States
Census	1880	ED 18, Page 483, Kansas City, Jackson, Missouri, United States
Misc	1888	Biography, Case, History of Kansas City, Missouri, Pages 531-532
Census	1890	ED 191, Page 2, Kansas City, Jackson, Missouri, United States
Census	1900	ED 128, Page 5, Kansas City, Jackson, Missouri, United States
Will	30 Apr 1910	(Will Written), Volume 12, Page 604, Kansas City, Jackson, Missouri, United States
Census	1910	ED 162, Page 40, Kansas City, Jackson, Missouri, United States
Death	6 Dec 1916	Diabetes Milletus, Bright's Disease; Kansas City, Jackson, Missouri, United States
Misc		Obituary, Kansas City (Mo.) Times, 07 Dec 1916, Page 12, Column 1
Misc		Obituary, Kansas City (Mo.) Daily Journal, 07 Dec 1916, Page 5, Column 2
Misc		Funeral Notice, Kansas City (Mo.) Times, 08 Dec 1916, Page 11, Column 4
Burial	9 Dec 1916	Mount Saint Mary's Cemetery, Kansas City, Jackson, Missouri, United States
Probate	14 Dec 1916	(Will Proved), Volume 12, Page 604, Kansas City, Jackson, Missouri, United States
Occupation		Carpenter (1860), Wholesale Grocer (1870), Grocer (1880, 1900), Salesman Grocery (1910)
Occupation		Wholesale Dealer, Wholesale Liquor Dealer, Retail Liquor Dealer
Business		Green & Long (Wholesale Dealer, Wholesale & Retail Liquor)
Religion		Roman Catholic
Marriage	26 Nov 1862	(1862I0050098), Jackson, Missouri, United States
Father		John GREEN (-)
Mother		Ann Nancy REILLY (1811-1909)

Mother Mary Bridget A. SMITH

Birth	Feb 1843	Cavan, Ireland
Census	1860	Page 98, Kansas City, Jackson, Missouri, United States
Immigration	1860	Page 98, Kansas City, Jackson, Missouri, United States
Census	1870	Page 585, Kansas City, Jackson, Missouri, United States
Census	1880	ED 18, Page 483, Kansas City, Jackson, Missouri, United States
Census	1900	ED 128, Page 5, Kansas City, Jackson, Missouri, United States
Death	21 May 1901	Kansas City, Jackson, Missouri, United States
Misc		Obituary, Kansas City (Mo.) Star, 22 May 1901, Page 1, Column 2
Misc		Death Notice, Kansas City (Mo.) Star, 22 May 1901, Page 10, Column 3
Burial	24 May 1901	
Occupation		Housekeeper (1860)
Father		John SMITH (-)
Mother		Anne [--?--] (-)

Children

F Geraldine GREEN

Birth		
Chr		
Death		
Burial		
Marriage		

Father **Thomas H. GREEN**

Mother **Mary Bridget A. SMITH**

Children

F   Rosa Margaret "Rose" GREEN

Birth	16 Feb 1867	Kansas City, Jackson, Missouri, United States
Census	1870	Page 585, Kansas City, Jackson, Missouri, United States
Census	1880	ED 18, Page 483, Kansas City, Jackson, Missouri, United States
Residence	1916	Independence, Jackson, Missouri, United States
Death	24 Apr 1945	Generalized Arteriosclerosis; Liberty, Clay, Missouri, United States
Burial	26 Apr 1945	Woodlawn Cemetery, Independence, Jackson, Missouri, United States
Spouse	George W. CLINTON (1864-1924)	
Marriage	10 Jun 1897	(1897I0002399), Kansas City, Jackson, Missouri, United States

F   Elizabeth Agnes GREEN

Birth	25 Sep 1868	Kansas City, Jackson, Missouri, United States
Census	1870	Page 585, Kansas City, Jackson, Missouri, United States
Census	1880	ED 18, Page 483, Kansas City, Jackson, Missouri, United States
Census	1900	ED 128, Page 5, Kansas City, Jackson, Missouri, United States
Census	1910	ED 162, Page 40, Kansas City, Jackson, Missouri, United States
Residence	1916	Kansas City, Jackson, Missouri, United States
Misc	15 Jun 1922	United States Passport Application; Kansas City, Jackson, Missouri, United States
Death	3 Feb 1940	Lobar Pneumonia; Kansas City, Jackson, Missouri, United States
Burial	6 Feb 1940	Mount Saint Mary's Cemetery, Kansas City, Jackson, Missouri, United States
Occupation		Secretary Green Brothers Merc. Co.
Marriage		

F   Ellen Josephine "Birdie" GREEN

Birth	14 Mar 1872	Kansas City, Jackson, Missouri, United States
Census	1880	ED 18, Page 483, Kansas City, Jackson, Missouri, United States
Census	1900	ED 128, Page 5, Kansas City, Jackson, Missouri, United States
Census	1910	ED 162, Page 40, Kansas City, Jackson, Missouri, United States
Residence	1916	Kansas City, Jackson, Missouri, United States
Misc	19 Apr 1921	United States Passport Application; Kansas City, Jackson, Missouri, United States
Misc	28 Jan 1922	United States Passport Application (Renewal); Kansas City, Jackson, Missouri, United States
Death	16 Nov 1949	Arteriosclerotic Heart Disease; Kansas City, Jackson, Missouri, United States
Burial	18 Nov 1949	Mount Saint Mary's Cemetery, Kansas City, Jackson, Missouri, United States
Marriage		

M   Thomas Bernard GREEN

Birth	15 Sep 1874	Kansas City, Jackson, Missouri, United States
Census	1880	ED 18, Page 483, Kansas City, Jackson, Missouri, United States
Census	1900	ED 128, Page 5, Kansas City, Jackson, Missouri, United States
Residence	1916	Kansas City, Jackson, Missouri, United States
Death	20 Feb 1927	Acute Dilitation of Heart, Pulmonary Oedema, Arteriosclerosis, Chronic Dilitation of Heart; Kansas City, Jackson, Missouri, United States
Burial	23 Feb 1927	Calvary Cemetery, Kansas City, Jackson, Missouri, United States
Occupation		Salesman (1900), Wholesale Grocer
Spouse	Sarah Virginia DUVALL (1879-1948)	
Marriage		

M   James Michael GREEN

Birth	30 Nov 1876	Missouri, United States
Census	1880	ED 18, Page 483, Kansas City, Jackson, Missouri, United States
Census	1900	ED 128, Page 5, Kansas City, Jackson, Missouri, United States
Census	1910	ED 162, Page 40, Kansas City, Jackson, Missouri, United States
Residence	1916	Kansas City, Jackson, Missouri, United States
Military		World War I Draft Registration Cards; Kansas City, Jackson, Missouri, United States
Death	11 Jun 1963	Severe Pulmonary Edema, Aspirating Gastric Contents [illegible] Lung, Parital obstruction Due to Adhesions; Kansas City, Jackson, Missouri, United States
Burial	14 Jun 1963	Mount Saint Mary's Cemetery, Kansas City, Jackson, Missouri, United States
Occupation		Salesman (1900), Salesman Grocery Company (1910), Grocer Grocery Store (1963)

	Father	**Thomas H. GREEN**	
	Mother	**Mary Bridget A. SMITH**	
	Children		

James Michael GREEN (continued)

	Spouse		Sabina Mary OCTIGAN (1880-1925)
	Marriage	23 Jun 1920	Chicago, Cook, Illinois, United States

M Francis Washington GREEN

Birth	22 Sep 1879	Missouri, United States
Census	1880	ED 18, Page 483, Kansas City, Jackson, Missouri, United States
Census	1900	ED 128, Page 5, Kansas City, Jackson, Missouri, United States
Residence	1916	Kansas City, Jackson, Missouri, United States
Death	17 Oct 1951	Cardiac Failure, Auricular Fibrillation, Malnutrition, Arteriosclerosis; Kansas City, Jackson, Missouri, United States
Burial	19 Oct 1951	Mount Saint Mary's Cemetery, Kansas City, Jackson, Missouri, United States
Occupation		Clerk (1900)
Marriage		

F Christine Bernice Donnelly GREEN

Birth	12 Jan 1881	Kansas City, Jackson, Missouri, United States
Census	1900	ED 128, Page 5, Kansas City, Jackson, Missouri, United States
Census	1910	ED 162, Page 40, Kansas City, Jackson, Missouri, United States
Residence	1916	Kansas City, Jackson, Missouri, United States
Misc	19 Apr 1921	United States Passport Application; Kansas City, Jackson, Missouri, United States
Misc	28 Jan 1922	United States Passport Application (Renewal); Kansas City, Jackson, Missouri, United States
Death	19 Apr 1960	Broncho-Pneumonia, Metastatic Carcinoma Cerebral, Carcinoma Left Breast 1956, Left Lower Lung 1958, Arteriosclerosis; Kansas City, Jackson, Missouri, United States
Burial	22 Apr 1960	Mount Saint Mary's Cemetery, Kansas City, Jackson, Missouri, United States
Marriage		

Father William Henry GREGG

Birth	24 Mar 1831	Palmyra, Wayne, New York, United States
Residence	1849–1916	Saint Louis, Saint Louis, Missouri, United States
Census	1850	
Census	1860	Page 89, Saint Louis, Saint Louis, Missouri, United States
Tax Lists	Nov 1863	Retail Dealer License; "Cooper & Gregg", Kansas City, Jackson, Missouri, United States
Census	1870	Page 330, Saint Louis, Saint Louis, Missouri, United States
Census	1880	ED 135, Page 97, Saint Louis (city), Missouri, United States
Census	1880	ED 351, Page 297, Saint Louis (city), Missouri, United States
Misc	9 Jul 1885	("William H. Gregg of Saint Louis, State of Missouri"); Circuit Court, Green Lake, Wisconsin, United States
Census	1900	ED 337, Page 99, Saint Louis (city), Missouri, United States
Census	1910	ED 269, Page 113, Saint Louis (city), Missouri, United States
Death	15 Jan 1916	Myocarditis Chronic, Senile Arteriosclerosis; Saint Louis (city), Missouri, United States
Burial	16 Jan 1916	Bellefontaine Cemetery, Saint Louis (city), Missouri, United States
Occupation		Wholesale Commission Merchant (1860), President White Lead Company (1870, 1880), President of Southern White Lead Company (1880), Capitalist (1900), Own Income (1910)
Business		Cooper & Gregg (Retail Hardware Dealer); Kansas City, Jackson, Missouri, United States
Marriage	1854/5	
Father	John GREGG (1798-)	
Mother	Anne WILCOX (1806-1895)	

Mother Orian "Ora/Orie" THOMPSON

Birth	24 Oct 1836	Near, Collinsville, Madison, Illinois, United States
Census	1850	
Census	1860	Page 89, Saint Louis, Saint Louis, Missouri, United States
Census	1870	Page 330, Saint Louis, Saint Louis, Missouri, United States
Census	1880	ED 135, Page 97, Saint Louis (city), Missouri, United States
Census	1880	ED 351, Page 297, Saint Louis (city), Missouri, United States
Census	1900	ED 337, Page 99, Saint Louis (city), Missouri, United States
Census	1910	ED 269, Page 113, Saint Louis (city), Missouri, United States
Death	3 Nov 1914	Chronic Catarrhal Enteritis, Arteriosclerosis; Saint Louis (city), Missouri, United States
Burial	6 Nov 1914	Bellefontaine Cemetery, Saint Louis (city), Missouri, United States
Father	James Jennings THOMPSON (-)	
Mother	Eliza Holden LAWRENCE (-)	

Children

M Norris Bradford GREGG

Birth	8 May 1856	(or May 1857), Saint Louis, St. Louis, Missouri, United States
Census	1860	Page 89, Saint Louis, Saint Louis, Missouri, United States
Census	1870	Page 330, Saint Louis, Saint Louis, Missouri, United States
Census	1880	ED 135, Page 97, Saint Louis (city), Missouri, United States
Census	1880	ED 351, Page 297, Saint Louis (city), Missouri, United States
Census	1900	ED 376, Page 79, Saint Louis, St. Louis, Missouri, United States
Death	1927	
Occupation		Clerk in White Lead Factory (1880), Manufacturing Paints & Oils (1900)
Burial		Bellefontaine Cemetery, Saint Louis (city), Missouri, United States
Spouse	Mary HAWLEY (1860-1926)	
Marriage	1885	

F Clara Jennings GREGG

Birth	13 Oct 1859	Saint Louis, Saint Louis, Missouri, United States
Census	1860	Page 89, Saint Louis, Saint Louis, Missouri, United States
Census	1870	Page 330, Saint Louis, Saint Louis, Missouri, United States
Census	1880	ED 135, Page 97, Saint Louis (city), Missouri, United States
Census	1880	ED 351, Page 297, Saint Louis (city), Missouri, United States
Death	1 Feb 1955	Montréal, Quebec, Canada
Burial		Mount Royal Cemetery, Montréal, Quebec, Canada
Misc		Survivor of the Sinking of the RSM Titanic, 14/15 Apr 1912
Spouse	Charles Melville HAYS (1856-1912)	
Marriage	13 Oct 1881	Saint Louis, St. Louis, Missouri, United States

Father	William Henry GREGG	
Mother	**Orian "Ora/Orie" THOMPSON**	
Children		

M	**William H. "Willie" GREGG Jr.**	
Birth	5 Jan 1862	Saint Louis, Saint Louis, Missouri, United States
Census	1870	Page 330, Saint Louis, Saint Louis, Missouri, United States
Census	1880	ED 135, Page 97, Saint Louis (city), Missouri, United States
Census	1880	ED 351, Page 297, Saint Louis (city), Missouri, United States
Death	26 Mar 1938	Broncho-Pneumonia, Acute Cardiac Dilatation; Saint Louis (city), Missouri, United States
Burial	30 Mar 1938	Bellefontaine Cemetery, Saint Louis (city), Missouri, United States
Occupation		Clerk in Drug Store (1880), Paint Manufacturer
Spouse	Lilly Rietta KURTZEBORN (1871-1916)	
Marriage		

F	**Julia Frances GREGG**	
Birth	21 May 1864	Saint Louis, Saint Louis, Missouri, United States
Census	1870	Page 330, Saint Louis, Saint Louis, Missouri, United States
Census	1880	ED 135, Page 97, Saint Louis (city), Missouri, United States
Census	1880	ED 351, Page 297, Saint Louis (city), Missouri, United States
Death	4 Jul 1915	Lympho-Sarcoma; Saint Louis (city), Missouri, United States
Burial	6 Jul 1915	Bellefontaine Cemetery, Saint Louis (city), Missouri, United States
Spouse	Ezra Hunt DYER (1864-1894)	
Marriage		

F	**Ora L. "Orie" GREGG**	
Birth	17 Mar 1867	Saint Louis, St. Louis, Missouri, United States
Census	1870	Page 330, Saint Louis, Saint Louis, Missouri, United States
Census	1880	ED 135, Page 97, Saint Louis (city), Missouri, United States
Census	1880	ED 351, Page 297, Saint Louis (city), Missouri, United States
Census	1900	ED 337, Page 99, Saint Louis (city), Missouri, United States
Misc	4 Jun 1902	U. S. Passport Issued; Saint Louis (city), Missouri, United States
Death		
Burial		
Marriage		

Father Dr. James GRIFFITH

Birth	11 Dec 1801	Virginia, United States
Census	1850	Page 181, Big Grove Township, Johnson, Iowa, United States
Census	1860	Page 78, Kansas City, Jackson, Missouri, United States
Tax Lists	Sep 1862	Retail Dealer License; Kansas City, Jackson, Missouri, United States
Census	1865	Page 47, Leavenworth, Leavenworth, Kansas, United States
Census	1870	Page 608, Hannibal, Marion, Missouri, United States
Census	1880	ED 96, Page 315, Chicago, Cook, Illinois, United States
Death	27 Apr 1884	Chicago, Cook, Illinois, United States
Burial		Oak Woods Cemetery, Chicago, Cook, Illinois, United States
Occupation		Farmer (1850), Merchant (1860), Physician (1865), Horse M. D. (1870), Doctor of Medicine (1880), Retail Dealer
Marriage	11 Jan 1825	Knox, Ohio, United States
Father	Joseph GRIFFITH (1758-1845)	
Mother	Catherine CASSADAY (1765-1837)	

Mother Elizabeth Mary HALL

Birth	12 Apr 1805	Ohio, United States
Census	1850	Page 181, Big Grove Township, Johnson, Iowa, United States
Census	1860	Page 78, Kansas City, Jackson, Missouri, United States
Census	1865	Page 47, Leavenworth, Leavenworth, Kansas, United States
Census	1870	Page 608, Hannibal, Marion, Missouri, United States
Census	1880	ED 96, Page 315, Chicago, Cook, Illinois, United States
Death	23 Sep 1891	Chicago, Cook, Illinois, United States
Burial		Oak Woods Cemetery, Chicago, Cook, Illinois, United States
Father	William HALL (1762-1852)	
Mother	Jane LANE (1767-1852)	

Children

F Catharine GRIFFITH

Birth	1826/7	Bladensburg, Knox, Ohio, United States
Census	1850	Page 181, Big Grove Township, Johnson, Iowa, United States
Census	1860	Page 89, Kansas City, Jackson, Missouri, United States
Census	1870	Page 445, Quincy, Adams, Illinois, United States
Death	1879	Quincy, Adams, Illinois, United States
Burial		
Spouse	Orson C. WEST (1827-1901)	
Marriage		

F Rachel GRIFFITH

Birth	25 Mar 1832	Bladensburg, Knox, Ohio, United States
Census	1850	Page 181, Big Grove Township, Johnson, Iowa, United States
Census	1860	
Census	1870	Page 608, Hannibal, Marion, Missouri, United States
Census	1880	ED 96, Page 315, Chicago, Cook, Illinois, United States
Death	5 May 1904	Kansas City, Jackson, Missouri, United States
Burial		Union Cemetery, Kansas City, Jackson, Missouri, United States
Spouse	[--?--] MARTIN (-)	
Marriage		
Spouse	Pleasant Morris HARLAN (1823-1892)	
Marriage	28 Sep 1858	Quincy, Adams, Illinois, United States

F Ruth GRIFFITH

Birth	6 Nov 1836	
Death	16 Nov 1838	Hopewell, Muskingum, Ohio, United States
Burial		
Marriage		

M William H. GRIFFITH

Birth	1837/8	Ohio, United States
Census	1850	Page 181, Big Grove Township, Johnson, Iowa, United States
Census	1860	Page 78, Kansas City, Jackson, Missouri, United States
Military		Private, Company H, 77th Regiment Enrolled Missouri Militia

Father	Dr. James GRIFFITH	
Mother	Elizabeth Mary HALL	
Children		

William H. GRIFFITH (continued)

Census	1870	
Census	1880	
Death	7 Aug 1889	Chicago, Cook, Illinois, United States
Occupation		Merchant (1860)
Burial		
Marriage		

M James GRIFFITH

Birth	1840/1	Ohio, United States
Census	1850	Page 181, Big Grove Township, Johnson, Iowa, United States
Census	1860	Page 78, Kansas City, Jackson, Missouri, United States
Misc	27 Jan 1863	Union Provost Marshals' File of Papers Relating to Two or More Civilians, M416, Roll 13, No. 3512
Misc	30 Jan 1863	Union Provost Marshals' File of Papers Relating to Two or More Civilians, M416, Roll 13, No. 3513
Census	1870	
Census	1880	
Death		
Burial		
Marriage		

F Elizabeth GRIFFITH

Birth	1842/3	Ohio, United States
Census	1850	Page 181, Big Grove Township, Johnson, Iowa, United States
Census	1860	Page 78, Kansas City, Jackson, Missouri, United States
Census	1870	
Census	1880	
Death		
Burial		
Marriage		

M Cyrus H. GRIFFITH

Birth	1844/5	Big Grove Township, Johnson, Iowa Territory, United States
Census	1850	Page 181, Big Grove Township, Johnson, Iowa, United States
Census	1860	Page 78, Kansas City, Jackson, Missouri, United States
Census	1865	Page 47, Leavenworth, Leavenworth, Kansas, United States
Census	1870	Page 608, Hannibal, Marion, Missouri, United States
Census	1880	
Death	30 Sep 1899	Chicago, Cook, Illinois, United States
Occupation		Laborer (1870)
Illness		Insane (1865)
Burial		
Marriage		

Father William French Bayliss GRIGSBY

Birth	Oct 1834	Clark, Kentucky, United States
Census	1840	(John Grigsby Family), Page 278, Clark, Kentucky, United States
Census	1850	District 2, Page 2, Clark, Kentucky, United States
Census	1860	Page 948, Liberty, Clay, Missouri, United States
Tax Lists	Sep 1862	Retail Dealer License; "W. T. B. Gregsby", Kansas City, Jackson, Missouri, United States
Military		Private & Sergeant, Company C, 77th Regiment Enrolled Missouri Militia
Military	bet Sep 1863 and Oct 1863	Civil War Draft Registration; Kaw Township, Jackson, Missouri, United States
Tax Lists	May 1866	Retail Dealer License and Income; "W. F. B. Griggsby", Westport, Jackson, Missouri, United States
Tax Lists	Dec 1866 (Supplemental)	Retail Dealer License; "W. F. B. Griggsby", Westport, Jackson, Missouri, United States
Census	1870	Page 394, Franklin Township, Bourbon, Kansas, United States
Census	1880	ED 63, Page 473, San Bernardino, San Bernardino, California, United States
Census	1900	ED 187, Page 52, National City, San Diego, California, United States
Census	1910	ED 155, Page 5, Los Angeles, Los Angeles, California, United States
Census	1920	ED 341, Page 120, Los Angeles, Los Angeles, California, United States
Death	7 May 1922	Los Angeles, California, United States
Occupation		Merchant (1860), Merchant Ret. (1870), Store Keeper (1880), Variety Store (1900), Retail Merchant Groceries (1910), None (1920)
Burial		
Marriage	14 Dec 1857	Clay, Missouri, United States
Father	John GRIGSBY (1799-1865)	
Mother	Sarah J. DUNCAN (1793-1876)	

Mother Mary E. BRIGHT

Birth	Oct 1838	Missouri, United States
Census	1840	(Joseph Bright Family), Page 16, Clay, Missouri, United States
Census	1850	Page 307, Liberty Township, Clay, Missouri, United States
Census	1860	Page 948, Liberty, Clay, Missouri, United States
Census	1870	Page 71, Westport, Jackson, Missouri, United States
Census	1880	ED 63, Page 473, San Bernardino, San Bernardino, California, United States
Census	1900	ED 187, Page 52, National City, San Diego, California, United States
Census	1910	ED 155, Page 5, Los Angeles, Los Angeles, California, United States
Death	19 Jun 1915	Los Angeles, California, United States
Burial		
Father	Joseph BRIGHT (1802-)	
Mother	Mary [--?--] (1809-)	

Children